# CENTURY 21

## 75 YEARS

## Keyboarding
## & Information Processing

**Jerry W. Robinson, Ed.D.**
Former Keyboarding Instructor
Moeller High School
Cincinnati (OH)

**Jack P. Hoggatt, Ed.D.**
Professor, Department of Business
Communication
University of Wisconsin
Eau Claire (WI)

**Jon A. Shank, Ed.D.**
Professor of Education
Robert Morris College
Coraopolis (PA)

**Lee R. Beaumont, Ed.D.**
Professor of Business, Emeritus
Indiana University of Pennsylvania
Indiana (PA)

**T. James Crawford, Ph.D., LI.D.**
Professor of Business/Education, Emeritus
Indiana University
Bloomington (IN)

**Lawrence W. Erickson, Ed.D.**
Professor of Education, Emeritus
University of California
Los Angeles (CA)

*contributing author:*
**Pat R. Graves, Ed.D.**
Associate Professor
Eastern Illinois University
Charleston (Il)

Business Education
lost a dedicated friend
and teacher in 1997
with the passing of
Dr. Jerry W. Robinson.

VISIT US ON THE INTERNET
# www.swep.com

## South-Western Educational Publishing
*an International Thomson Publishing company* ITP®

www.thomson.com

Cincinnati • Albany, NY • Belmont, CA • Bonn • Boston • Detroit • Johannesburg • London • Madrid
Melbourne • Mexico City • New York • Paris • Singapore • Tokyo • Toronto • Washington

| | |
|---|---|
| Team Leader: | Karen Schmohe |
| Development: | Penworthy, Susan Bechtel |
| Editor: | Kimberlee Kusnerak |
| Production Coordinator: | Jane Congdon |
| Manufacturing Coordinator: | Carol Chase |
| Marketing Manager: | Tim Gleim |
| Marketing Coordinator: | Lisa Barto |
| Art/Design Coordinator: | Michelle Kunkler |
| Designer: | Lou Ann Thesing |
| Production: | Cover to Cover Publishing, Inc. |

ISBN: 0-538-69155-7

1 2 3 4 5 6 7 8 9 10 11 12 13 14 WV 09 08 07 06 05 04 03 02 01 00 99

Printed in the United States of America

## Photo Credits:

Pages: 1, A13: computer: © 1999 PhotoDisc, Inc.

Pages: 10, 11, 14, 16, 18, 20, 21, 22, 23, 25, 27, 30, 31, 33, 36, 37, 38, 39, 41, 43, 46, 47, 49, 53, 64, 66, 68, 70, 72, 85, A14:

Page A60: Courtesy of nVIEW Corporation

Phase Opener 2: Mark Twain: Library of Congress, LC-USZ 62-28844; girl reading: Greg Grosse

Phase Opener 3: Harriet Tubman: Library of Congress, LC-USZ 62-7816

Phase Opener 4: Toyota car: Jeff Greenberg, Photographer; student at PC: Greg Grosse

Phase Opener 5: Babe Ruth: Library of Congress, LC-USZ 62-31512

Phase Opener 6: Marie Curie: Library of Congress, LC-USZ 62-91224

## Reviewers

The following teachers of keyboarding and word processing reviewed manuscripts and gave valuable feedback:

**Shirley Dembo**, Port Richmond High School, Staten Island, NY

**Juliana Delafave**, Richardson High School, Dallas, TX

**Jennifer McDonald**, Princeton High School, Cincinnati, OH

**Lynn Matthews**, Moorestown (NJ) High School

**Nancy Purcell**, Mechanicsburg (PA) High School

# PREFACE

You have made a wise decision to learn keyboarding skills. These skills will be extremely important to your success. For in the new millennium, keyboarding skills, Internet skills, and basic software application skills will be needed in virtually every career.

Today it is almost impossible to find a job that does not require the use of a keyboard. Most workers, including executives, managers, and administrative employees, use a computer to create, edit, analyze, and organize data. Even people who never thought they would use a computer are now banking, placing orders, balancing their checkbooks, researching, and communicating online.

## The More Things Change . . .

However, over seventy-five years' worth of teaching and publishing experience packs the pages of *Century 21 Keyboarding & Information Processing*. Time has brought changes in equipment, teaching methods, and industry, and the 6th edition of *Century 21* embraces these changes with a synergy created from traditional keyboarding methodology, instructional technology, and powerful software. With the same confidence as before, the publisher offers you a textbook for the times.

For this new edition, South-Western surveyed 1,500 business teachers to determine the needs of today's keyboarding students. The following new features of *Century 21 Keyboarding & Information Processing*, 6th Edition, address those needs:

◆ Keyboarding is for everyone, and the cross-curricular themes throughout the text demonstrate this fact.

◆ The *Complete Course* contains 225 planned lessons and a semester's worth of optional activities. *Book 1* contains 150 lessons, plus the options.

◆ Generic word processing instructions for software features are applied in the lessons.

◆ Six "Your Perspective" sections provide opportunities for students to collaborate to resolve ethical, global awareness, and cultural diversity issues, thus heeding findings of the SCANS report (Department of Labor, 1992).

◆ Appendix material includes an entire semester's worth of extras: an overview of *Windows*; Internet basics and activities; word publishing and electronic presentations tutorials; integrated software applications; repetitive stress injury information; and an expanded Reference Guide.

◆ Software options are available for learning to key, building speed and accuracy, and checking documents.

◆ Numerous supplemental activities reinforce workplace skills, apply integrated suite applications, and increase multicultural awareness (see page iv).

## . . . the More They Stay the Same

Regardless of changes in equipment and methods, instruction in *Century 21* still centers around three critical skills: keying, formatting, and information processing. The emphasis given to each facet of learning is geared to the difficulty of the learning task and the level of skill required for effective performance.

**Basic keying skills**. Lessons 1–37 build a strong foundation in keyboarding skills.

◆ To ensure master, only two alphabet or figure keys are presented in each new-key lesson. Top-row keys are not introduced until correct technique and an essential level of skill have been developed.

◆ Timed paragraphs are *triple-controlled* for copy difficulty (from easy to average) to ensure reliable measurement of speed and accuracy.

◆ Keying technique is stressed first (without timing); then, speed of manipulation (with strategic timed writings); and accuracy last (using *restricted-speed* practice). This instructional design is in harmony with skill-learning principles and research findings.

**Formatting skills**. Formatting involves transferring facts and ideas into meaningful, useful documents of quality. Look for these features:

◆ Streamlined document formats are quick and easy to produce.

◆ Document formats are reviewed and reinforced before new formats are introduced.

◆ Language skills are reviewed early on and integrated often in formatting tasks.

**Information processing skills**. Information processing skills are taught through a learn/practice/sustain/assess plan of skill building.

◆ Common errors for students to correct occur in source copy. Proofreading tips are provided throughout.

◆ School-to-work transition is provided with simulations occurring every half-semester after Phase 1.

# FAMILY OF PRODUCTS

South-Western Educational Publishing provides everything you and your students need to have a successful keyboarding and information processing classroom.

## Technology

*A variety of key presentation, speed building, and accuracy development software. Each is available in either Windows or Macintosh.*

**MicroType Pro:** New key learning plus a word processor with timer.

**MicroType Multimedia:** New key learning on CD-ROM with enhanced graphics, 3-D viewer, and video clips.

**Century 21 Quick Check:** Checks over 180 documents and timed writings that are created in the built-in word processor.

**MicroPace Pro:** Timed writing, error diagnostics, and paced skill development software.

**KeyChamp:** Designed to build speed. For use after keys are learned.

**Skillbusters: Mystery at Wellsley Manor:** Fun, interactive skillbuilding.

**MLS Century 21 Multimedia:** Interactive, graphical presentation of new learning, including document formats, word processing features, and language skills.

**Internet Typing Challenge:** Compete against other keyboarders nationwide. Compare rates on the Internet at itc.swep.com.

## Simulations

*Seven simulations apply skills ranging from entry level keyboarding to word processing and integrated applications.*

**The Candidate:** Beginning word processing simulation. 20–25 hours.

**SBI:** Advanced word processing. 20–25 hours.

**Line Rollering:** Entry level. 15 hours.

**River Oaks Mall:** Intermediate level. 20 hours.

**Coasters, Etc.: An Integrated Office Simulation:** 25–30 hours.

**The Word Specialists: A Collaborative Simulation:** Emphasizes team building and SCANS competencies. 25–40 hours.

**Sports Connection Integrated Simulation:** 35–40 hours.

## Enrichment Materials

*Available in the Teacher's Resource Kit, the following materials are reproducible for classroom use.*

**Integrated Computer Applications:** Activities apply spreadsheets, charts, database, calendar, and desktop publishing skills.

**Workplace Enrichment:** Projects focus on topics such as entrepreneurship, personal assessment, leadership, and ethics. Activities support or extend textbook documents. Presentation disk for teachers.

**Using Technology and the Internet:** Activities apply basic Internet skills presented in the textbook appendix (pages A7–A11).

**Multicultural Projects:** Diversity activities.

## Teacher Support

**Teacher's Editions:** Three editions available.

**Teacher's Resource Kit:** Includes the following:
Certificate of Proficiency
Integrated Computer Applications
Keys; Lesson Plans
Multicultural Projects
Placement and Performance Test Packets (2)
Posters; Roll of Honor; Speed Chart
Teacher's Manual
Workplace Enrichment with presentation software
Voice Technology Basics

**Transparency Masters:** Includes word processing specific instruction. Available for most versions of software.

**South-Western, Teaching Tools:** Request these additional supplements to enrich your teaching: *Alternative Assessment, Teaching a Diverse Population and Addressing Diverse Learning Styles, Involving Parents and the Community in the Classroom, Test Preparation and Study Skills,* and *Strategies for Block Scheduling.*

# CONTENTS

**Contents vi**

# PHASE 6 SCIENCE/MATH

## ICONS

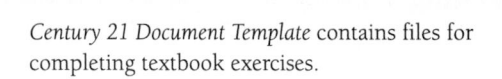
*Century 21 Document Template* contains files for completing textbook exercises.

The textbook timed writing referenced by the icon can be checked by *MicroPace Pro/MicroPace Plus.*

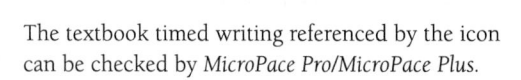
Indicates a new-learning module in *MLS™ Century 21 Multimedia.*

Proofreading guidelines.

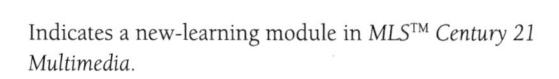
*R* stands for *reinforcement*; *E* for *enrichment*. R&E indicates material that goes "above and beyond" the fundamentals.

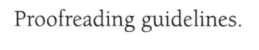
*Wp* stands for *word processing* notes.

# GLOSSARY

**Accuracy** Degree of freedom from keying errors; expressed as 1 error, 2 errors, etc.; sometimes expressed as errors a minute or percent of errors.

**Centering** Placing text so half of the text is on each side of the center point.

**Control** Power to cause hands and fingers to make correct keyboarding motions; also, the ability to slow down motion to reduce keyboarding errors.

**Cursor/Insertion Point** Point on a display screen where the next character or space is entered.

**Default** Preset condition in software and electronic typewriters for margin, line spacing, and tab settings. Default settings may be changed.

**Desktop** Screen background area on which windows and icons are displayed.

**Dialog Box** In software, small window where the user can input information needed for software to perform a function.

**Directory/Folder** Listing of files stored on a disk.

**Disk** Medium used to save and store electronic files.

**Document Window** Area on display screen where text is keyed.

**Editing** Proofreading, arranging, changing, and correcting existing text.

**Electronic Mail** Means of sending messages from one computer to another.

**Error** Any misstroke of a key or variation between source copy and displayed or printed copy; departure from acceptable document format.

**Facsimile (Fax)** Copy of information scanned and transmitted over telephone lines.

**File** Information named and stored on a disk.

**Font** Appearance of printed text; consists of the typeface name, the style, and the size.

**Format** Arrangement, placement, and spacing of a document; also, to arrange a document in proper form.

**Function Keys** Set of keys (F1, F2, etc.) used alone or with Shift, Ctrl, and Alt keys to issue software commands.

**GWAM (Gross Words a Minute)** Measure of the rate of keying speed; *GWAM* = total 5-stroke words keyed divided by the time required to key those words.

**Icon** Picture that represents a command, program, or document.

**Insert Mode** Software feature that allows text to be keyed into existing text; default software mode.

**Line Spacing** Number of blank lines between lines of text; usually single (0 blank lines), double (1 blank line), or quadruple (3 blank lines).

**Key** To strike keys for printing or displaying copy.

**Margins** Space on a page to the left, right, top, and bottom of area that displays text, usually expressed in inches, but sometimes in line or character spaces.

**Menu** List of options on a display screen from which operating features are selected.

**N-PRAM (Net Production Rate A Minute)** Measure of document productivity; *N-PRAM* = total 5-stroke words keyed less a penalty for uncorrected errors, divided by the time used to prepare the document(s).

**Prompt** Message displayed on a screen to inform user that the computer is awaiting a specific response.

**Proofreading** Comparing keyed text to the original copy and correcting errors; one of the editing steps.

**Rate** Speed of doing a task; see *gross words a minute* and *net production rate a minute*.

**Scroll** Software feature that makes room for more lines of copy by causing the first line to "disappear" off the top of the display screen.

**Software** Instructions or programs that tell a computer what to do.

**Status Bar (Line)** Bar (or line) containing menu descriptions, prompts to action or specific information about the document on the screen.

**Technique** Keyboard operator's form or keying style.

**Typeover Mode** Software feature that allows new text to be keyed over existing text.

## Formatting Abbreviations

| | | | |
|---|---|---|---|
| **CS** | columnar spacing | **QS** | quadruple spacing |
| **DS** | double spacing | **RM** | right margin |
| **LM** | left margin | **SM** | side margins |
| **LS** | line spacing | **SS** | single spacing |
| **PE** | page end | **TM** | top margin |

The diagram above illustrates the major parts of an electronic typewriter. If you have the manufacturer's booklet, use it to identify the exact location of each major part, including special parts that may be on one machine but not on another.

1. **Left platen knob:** used to turn platen manually (not on some models).

2. **Line-of-writing (margin) scale:** indicates pitch scales (10, 12, and 15); may indicate margin positions and the printing point.

3. **Paper-bail release lever:** used to pull paper bail away from platen.

4. **Paper guide:** used to position paper for insertion.

5. **Paper support:** supports paper when it is in the machine.

6. **Print carrier:** includes ribbon cassette, correction tape, carrier adjust lever, and printing mechanism.

7. **Paper bail and rollers:** used to hold paper against platen.

8. **Platen (cylinder):** provides a hard surface against which the print mechanism strikes.

9. **Paper release lever:** used to allow paper to be removed or aligned.

10. **Backspace:** used to move printing point to left one space.

11. **Paper insert:** used to feed paper to specified loading position.

12. **Relocate (RELOC)*:** used to return printing point to previous position after corrections are made.

13. **Return:** used to return printing point to left margin and to move paper up.

14. **Right shift:** used with keys controlled by the left hand to key capitals or symbols.

15. **Correction:** used to erase a character.

16. **Space bar:** used to move printing point to the right one space at a time.

17. **Code:** used simultaneously with another key to cause that key to perform a special function.

18. **Left shift:** used with keys controlled by the right hand to key capitals or symbols.

19. **Caps Lock:** used to key text in ALL CAPS (capital letters).

20. **Tab set*:** used to set tabulator stops (tabs); tab clear may be same key on some models.

21. **Repeat:** used to repeat a previously struck key or function.

22. **Bold:** used to print boldface characters.

23. **Underline (UNDLN):** used to print underlined characters.

24. **Pitch select:** used to set type size (10-, 12-, or 15-).

25. **Line-space selector:** sets printing device being used.

26. **Centering:** used to center text automatically between the left and right margins.

27. **Auto*:** set to return the printing point automatically to the left margin, next line when it reaches the right margin.

28. **Margin release*:** used to move printing point beyond the margin settings.

29. **Left margin (L MAR):** used to set left margin.

30. **Right margin (R MAR):** used to set right margin.

31. **Tabulator (Tab)*:** used to move printing point to tab locations.

\* Key that performs special functions when depressed together with the CODE key.

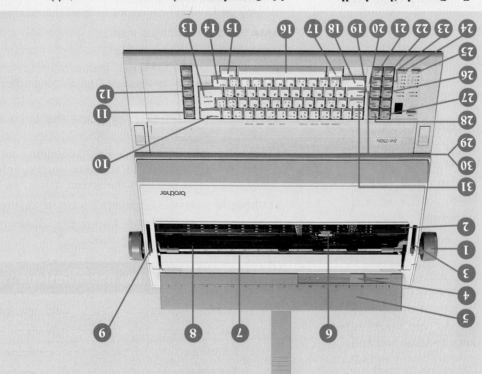

# INTRODUCTION

## Know Your Computer

The numbered parts are found on most computers, but their locations vary.

1. **CPU (Central Processing Unit):** The internal operating unit or "brain" of a computer.
2. **Disk drive:** A unit that reads and writes onto disks.

### Keyboard Arrangement

3. **Monitor:** Displays information on a screen.
4. **Mouse:** Input device.
5. **Keyboard:** An arrangement of letter, figure, symbol, control, function, and editing keys and a numeric keypad.

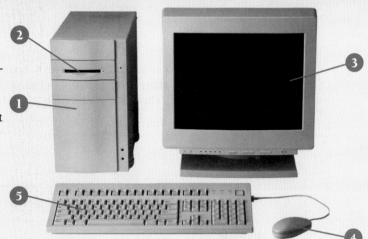

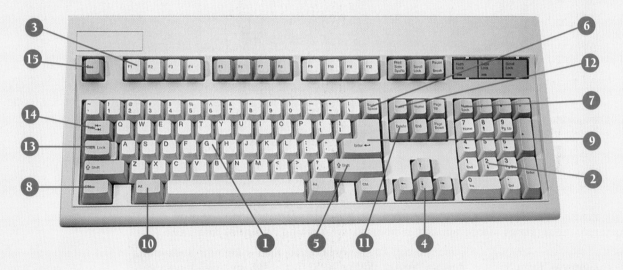

1. **Alphanumeric keys:** Center portion of the keyboard.
2. **Numeric keypad:** A calculator-type keyboard used to enter all-number copy and perform calculations.
3. **Function keys:** Perform a software function; used by themselves or with other keys.
4. **Arrow keys:** Move the insertion point.

5. **SHIFT keys:** Make capital letters and certain symbols when used with those keys.
6. **BACKSPACE:** Deletes the character to the left of the insertion point.
7. **NUM LOCK:** Switches the numeric keypad between numeric entry and editing.
8. **CTRL (Control):** Performs a software function when depressed as another key is struck.

9. **ENTER (RETURN):** Moves the cursor to the left margin and down to the next line.
10. **ALT (Alternate):** Used with another key to execute a function.
11. **DELETE:** Erases text to the right of the insertion point.
12. **INSERT:** Switches between insert mode and typeover mode.

13. **CAPS LOCK:** Capitalizes all alphabetic characters.
14. **TAB:** Moves the cursor to a preset position.
15. **ESC (Escape):** Exits a menu or dialog box in word processing software.
16. ⌘ **(Command—Mac only):** Performs a software command when depressed with another key; menu alternative.

# Know How to Operate Computer Hardware and Software

## Turning Computer System On and Off

**Turning on:**

1. Remove any disks from the disk drives.
2. Turn on the power switches on the CPU, monitor (if it has a separate switch), and printer.

**Turning off:**

1. Remove any disks from the disk drives.
2. In reverse order, turn off the power switch for each piece of equipment. Turn off the CPU last.

## Word Processing Software Basics

More detailed information is provided in the Word Processing sections within the text and in the Windows and Word Publishing appendices. The basic functions of a word processing program are creating, opening, saving, closing, and printing documents. Word processing functions may be accessed using these tools:

**Power bar/Toolbar:** Buttons on the toolbar provide access to common commands. These buttons can be rearranged. Typically the buttons for starting a document appear on the left of the toolbar.

**Menu bar:** Functions can also be accessed through pull-down menus. Click the appropriate menu name in the menu bar; then click the desired option.

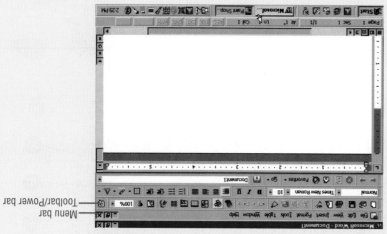

Menu bar

Toolbar/Power bar

Microsoft Word 97 Opening Screen

**Keyboard commands.** Specific keyboard commands, which may appear on a pull-down menu, are another way to perform word processing functions. Usually the ALT or CTRL key is used in combination with a letter key. For example, keying CTRL + S accesses the Save function.

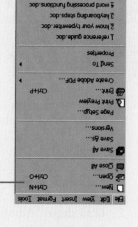

Keyboard Commands

File Pull-Down Menu

## Save a Document

When you save a document, you place a copy of it on a disk in one of the computer's disk drives, while leaving a copy of it on the screen. You should save a document whenever you make changes to it that you want to keep.

The first time you save a new document, use the **Save As** feature and give the document a filename. After you have saved a document once, you can resave it using the **Save** option. To save a new document, you must give it a filename.

1. Select *Save As* to name and save a new document or to save a document with a new name.
2. Name the document and specify the drive to which it is to be saved.
3. Select *Save* to save a document without renaming it.

## Print a Document

1. Turn on your printer, making sure it is loaded with paper.
2. Select the print option.
3. Select new print settings or use the preset (default) print settings. The default setting usually prints on 8.5" x 11" paper in vertical (portrait) orientation.

## Close a Document

Closing a document removes it from the display screen. If you have not saved the document, you will be prompted to save it before closing it.

1. Select *Close* from the File menu.
2. Elect to save or not to save the document.

## Set Line Spacing

Word processing software packages offer single spacing, one-and-a-half spacing, and double spacing, with single spacing being the default setting. You can also specify other line-spacing options (1.12, 1.75, 2.5, 4, etc.).

1. Place the insertion point at the point in the document where you want the line spacing to change.
2. Select the line spacing option and specify the desired line spacing.

## Computer and Disk Care

Follow the guidelines below to protect yourself, your computer, and your disks from harm.

◆ Place all computer components on a sturdy, flat surface out of direct sunlight, making sure ventilation openings on the equipment are unobstructed.

◆ Keep food and liquids away from your computer. If something does spill, unplug the computer and notify your teacher immediately.

 Do not expose disks to heat, cold, or moisture.

 Do not remove disks from the drive when the in-use light is on.

 Keep disks away from magnets, x-ray devices, and direct sunlight.

 Do not touch the exposed part of a disk.

 Use a felt-tip marker, not a ballpoint pen or a pencil, to write on disk labels.

# File Management in Windows

## Windows Explorer

Establishing a logical and easy-to-use file management system will help you access, modify, and organize your files quickly and efficiently. Your file management program in *Windows 95* and *Windows 98* is called Windows Explorer. In Windows Explorer you can store files in folders and subfolders much like documents stored in folders within a filing cabinet. The Explorer window is split into two sides. The left side shows how the folders, subfolders, and files are organized in a hierarchical or "tree" view. The right side displays the contents of the selected folder or file, also arranged in a hierarchy.

Document Folder     Contents

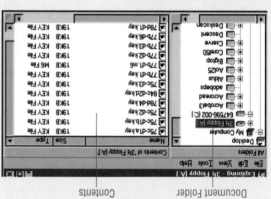

## Drill 1: Use Windows Explorer

1. Insert your data disk.
2. Click **Start.** Highlight *Programs.* Click **Windows Explorer.**
3. Maximize the Explorer window.
4. If *Desktop* is not the top object in the All Folders pane, click the up scroll arrow until it is displayed.
5. If a plus sign (+) displays beside the My Computer icon, click the + to extend its sublevels.
6. Click **3 1/2" Floppy (A:).**
7. From the View menu, click **List** to display the contents of drive A in numerical and alphabetical order.

## Create Folders and Subfolders

The top-level folder on the disk is the main folder. On the hard drive (drive C), the main folder is Desktop. On the disk, the main folder is represented by the drive icon. This folder was created when your disk was formatted. All folders branch from the main folder.

Small boxes containing plus (+) or minus (-) symbols display to the left of some folder icons. Boxes containing a plus sign indicate folders that have sublevels not currently displayed. If a box contains a minus sign, the folder is already expanded.

## Drill 2: Create a folder and subfolder

In the example below, note that the Keyboarding folder has two subfolders—Classwork and Homework.

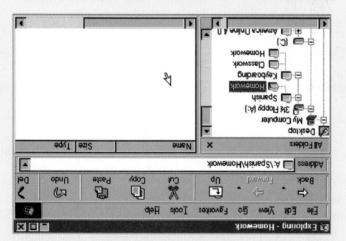

1. From the File menu, choose *New,* then *Folder.* A new folder icon labeled "New folder" displays in the Contents pane.
2. Key the folder name and press ENTER. In this drill, enter **Documents.** A new folder named *Documents* has been created on your disk.
3. To create a subfolder within the new folder, double-click the folder, then click **New,** then **Folder.** Name the new subfolder. Repeat the process for as many subfolders as you need.

## Select Folders and Files

Only one folder can be selected at a time in the left pane. Multiple files or folders can be selected in the right pane. To select multiple files or folders listed in consecutive order, click the first object to be selected, hold down the SHIFT key, and click the last object to be selected. To select files or folders that are scattered throughout the Contents pane, hold down the CTRL key while you click each of the desired objects.

## Delete or Rename Files and Folders

To delete files or entire folders within your Windows Explorer, click the folder or file, then click **File,** and then **Delete.** Respond *Yes* to the inquiry, *Are you sure you want to remove the folder. . .* (or *file . . .*).

If you want to rename the file or folder, click it, then click **File,** and then **Rename.** Key the new name.

## Move and Copy Files

As you create more files, you will probably need to create additional folders and then rearrange existing files by moving or copying them into the new folders. When a file is copied, the original file remains in place, and another copy of the file is placed at the destination. When a file is moved, the original file is removed from its original location and placed at the destination.

The file or folder that is to be copied is referred to as the **source copy**, and the location where the copy is to be moved is called the **destination**. Drag the object from the Contents pane to its destination. If you drag a folder to the same disk, it will be moved. If you drag a file to another disk (from A: to C:), it will be copied.

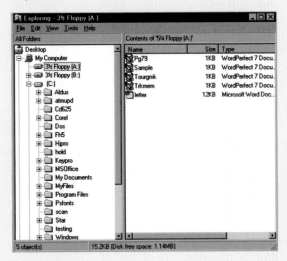

### Drill 3: Move files

You will copy and move files from drive A to the **Documents** folder.

1. In Windows Explorer, click **3 1/2" Floppy (A:)** to display the contents of your disk.

2. Point to a file in the Contents pane that was created in *Word* or *WordPerfect*. Hold down the left mouse button and drag the file to your **Documents** folder.

3. Click **3 1/2" Floppy (A:)** again to display the contents of your disk.

### Drill 4: Copy files

1. Click **3 1/2" Floppy (A:)**. The **Documents** folder displays in the All Folders pane under 3 1/2" Floppy (A:).

2. Hold down the CTRL key and point to another file in the Contents pane. Drag the file into the **Documents** folder.

## File Naming Conventions

Selecting appropriate filenames is extremely important. Files that are named in a logical, systematic manner are easier to locate than files that are named in a haphazard way. Filenames can be 255 characters long, including spaces. The following symbols cannot be used in a filename: = [ ] : ; < > ? \ / *.

A period is used to separate the filename from the extension. Each software program has its own extension. In the filename *Lesson1.wpd* the *wpd* extension indicates that the file is a *WordPerfect* document.

## Organize Files and Folders

Using a logical system of folders, subfolders, and filenames makes it easier to find files when you need them. If you need to find the first lesson that you did as classwork in your Keyboarding class, it would be logical and easy to remember to look in the Keyboarding class folder, then in the Classwork subfolder, and finally for Lesson 1. Files can be opened by clicking **File** on the menu bar, then clicking **Open**.

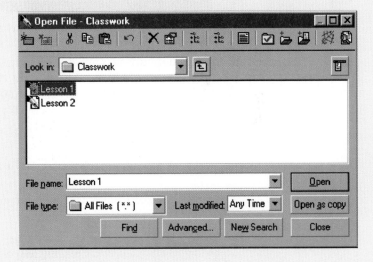

# Welcome to MicroType Pro or MicroType Multimedia

*MicroType Multimedia* is the multimedia-enhanced version of *MicroType Pro*. With the full-featured *MicroType Pro* or *MicroType Multimedia* software, you can use the power of your computer to learn alphabetic and numeric keyboarding and keypad operation. The Alphabetic Keyboarding and the Numeric Keyboarding modules of *MicroType* correspond to the new-key lessons in the *Century 21 Keyboarding* textbook. After you complete Lesson 19, you can use Skill Builder to boost your speed and accuracy.

Your computer should be turned on.

**Start MicroType Pro/ MicroType Multimedia**

**Windows Users:**

1. Open *MicroType Pro* or *MicroType Multimedia*.

*Windows 95/98:*

◆ Click the **Start** button.

◆ Point to the Programs menu; select the *South-Western Keyboarding* submenu from the program list.

◆ Click **MicroType** in the Keyboarding submenu.

*Windows 3.1:*

◆ Locate the *South-Western Keyboarding* program group, and double-click the icon to open it.

◆ Double-click the **MicroType** icon to start the program.

2. Click anywhere in the opening screen to remove it and bring up the Log In dialog box.

3. Select the appropriate name from the list that appears in the Log In dialog box. Then enter the correct password to continue. Click the **Guest** button only if instructed.

◆ When using the program for the first time, click the **New User** button and complete the New Student Registration dialog box (described on the next page).

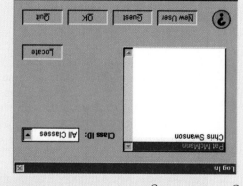

Student Log In Dialog Box

**Macintosh Users:**

1. Locate the *MicroType Pro//Multimedia* folder and open it.

2. Double-click the **MicroType** icon to start the program.

3. Select the appropriate name from the list that appears in the Log In dialog box. Then enter the correct password to continue. Click the **Guest** button only if instructed.

**Main Menu**

After you log in, the program will either display the Main menu or prompt you to continue where you left off. If the Main menu appears, choose the appropriate lesson. A check mark appears next to each lesson that you have completed unless you used the Guest option to log in. Check marks also appear on the notebook tabs to show which exercises have been completed.

## New Student Registration

The first time you use *MicroType Pro*, you must enter the following information: name, class ID, and password. You must also specify where to store the data.

1. Click the **New User** button shown in the Log In dialog box. The New Student dialog box appears.
2. Enter user name (first name, last name).
3. Enter the class ID.
4. Enter a password. Write the password on a piece of paper and store it in a safe place.
5. Specify the data location if necessary. For example, for a *Windows* user, the path may already be set to **c:\mtpro\ students** (or for a Mac user, **Hard drive:South-Western Keyboarding:Students**). If you have your own subdirectory, which was created previously, you must set the path accordingly (e.g., **c:\mtpro\students\lopez** or **South-Western Keyboarding students:Mark Lopez**). You can click the **Folder** icon to browse through the directories or folders to locate the folder.
6. If necessary, click the **Preferences** button and update the required information.
7. Click **OK** to complete the registration process.

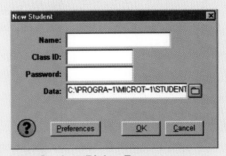

New Student Dialog Box

## Main Menu

Click one of the four modules in the center of the Main menu to proceed directly to the corresponding *MicroType* module.

**Alphabetic Keyboarding:** These 20 lessons teach the alphabetic keys, operational keys, and the basic punctuation keys.

**Numeric Keyboarding:** These 12 lessons (16 lessons in *Multimedia*) teach the top-row figure keys and the more commonly used symbols. Activities focus on building skill as well as learning the top-row and symbol keys.

**Keyboarding Skill Builder:** After you learn the alphabetic keys, use these 20 lessons to boost your keyboarding speed and control. Each lesson can focus on either speed or accuracy, so you really have 40 lessons.

**Numeric Keypad:** You will learn numeric keypad operation by completing this module.

**Games:** Each of the keyboarding modules incorporates a game into every lesson. The games offer exciting graphics and action to help you build skill while having fun. Top-ten lists provide a way for students to compare scores.

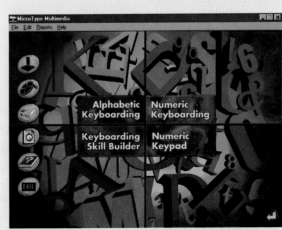

MicroType Multimedia Main Menu

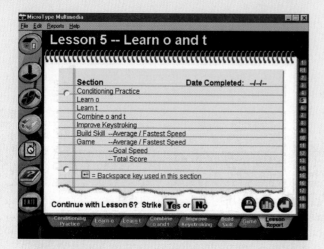

**Lesson Report:** The Lesson Report shows which lesson parts were completed and your speed scores and keying lines for *Build Skill* and the game. Performance graphs are accessed by clicking the **Graph** button on the Lesson Report.

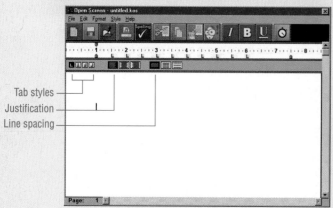

**Open Screen:** The Open Screen is a full-featured word processor that includes a spell checker and a built-in timer. You can practice your keyboarding skills, key letters and reports, or take a timed writing. These features can be accessed from the Menu bar, and many of them are available on the toolbar. When you take a timed writing in the Open Screen, click the **Timer** button and save each timing with its own name. For example, *16b-t1* (exercise 16b, timing 1).

**Diagnostic Writing Selection**

**Diagnostic Writings:** This feature checks speed and accuracy and provides simple error diagnostics. The writings are keyed from hard copy printed from the File menu in the Diagnostic Writings screen.

**Quick Review:** This feature of the Skill Builder module presents drill lines for practicing alphabetic and numeric reaches and operational keys. The Quick Review Report displays the average *gwam* for each section attempted.

## Other Student Reports

In addition to the Lesson Reports, *MicroType* software provides a Summary Report, Keypad Data Sets, Top-Ten Lists, Certificate of Completion, and Performance Graphs. All of these reports, except the Lesson Report, are accessed by using the Reports menu.

## Multimedia Features

**3-D Viewer®:** This feature demonstrates proper posture and hand positioning from all angles.

**3-D Animations:** This feature shows proper keystroking in action. Video clips emphasize how keyboarding is used in every profession.

## Keyboarding & Language Skills

Since Samuel Clemens (Mark Twain) turned in the first typed manuscript in the mid-1870s, keyboarding has become a universal writing skill.

Reporters, short story writers, poets, and novelists today compose at computer keyboards. Likewise, many musicians now use the computer keyboard to compose and arrange music. Also, artists now use the keyboard for graphic design. In fact, a high percentage of people in all walks of life employ a computer keyboard to simplify and speed up their work.

So, too, do students from elementary school through college use their keyboarding skill to prepare school assignments, papers, and reports. In fact, many former students say that, next to language, keyboarding is the most useful skill they have ever learned.

Fortunate indeed are those who have an early opportunity to develop a skill that has so many wide-ranging uses.

# ETHICS: The Right Thing to Do

Doctors, teachers, lawyers, and other professionals in the United States have developed general guides (or principles) that they are expected to follow in their relationships with each other and with the people they serve. These principles of behavior are usually written in a document called a Code of Ethics.

The listed behaviors are important so that people can relate to each other honestly and fairly. For example, a Code of Ethics for teachers may include these statements: The teacher is to help students develop knowledge and understanding of the subject(s) for which he/she is responsible; the teacher is responsible for preserving the reputations of students, teachers, and administrators; the teacher is to safeguard the exchange of confidential material. Similarly, a Code of Ethics for doctors would include the principle that doctors deal honestly and fairly with patients and colleagues.

We do not often think about an official Code of Ethics when we relate to other people. We know, from talking and watching the actions of others, that there are accepted ways in which we should relate to and treat other people. To remind us how we should treat others, society has passed laws to govern behavior. Schools, too, have rules and regulations (or a Code of Conduct) to govern student behavior so that there is a safe environment for all members of the school community.

In a society made up of people of different backgrounds and values, mutually accepted behaviors are necessary to our personal and social growth. Societal behaviors and values change over time, and mutually accepted Codes of Conduct usually change along with them.

## ACTIVITIES

1. Read at the left the material about Codes of Conduct.

2. Select a profession that you might like to enter (teacher, doctor, electrician, business owner, pro athlete, etc.).

3. Identify both acceptable and unacceptable behaviors for members of this profession. Consider:
   a. treatment of others: those above/below you/clients
   b. expected productivity
   c. best use of time, effort, and materials
   d. sharing of information
   e. sharing credit/blame

4. Compare lists and note *common threads* among them.

# CULTURAL DIVERSITY

Artists, musicians, and writers have throughout the centuries shared with others their ideas and feelings through their art, music, and literature. Art as a form of communication has a long history. Humankind has drawn and painted for at least thirteen thousand years. The animal drawings found in the Luscau Cave in France are examples of the earliest artwork done by humankind. No portion of the globe, however, has been without the artistic expression of its people. Such art expresses the beliefs, philosophy, and values of the culture that produces it.

Although our study of art often concentrates on the artwork of Europe, some opportunity is provided to learn about the artwork of other cultures. Among these works are examples of art done by earlier peoples in the Tigres Euphrates Valley, in the Indus Valley, and in the African empires of Ghana, Mali, and Songhai. The artwork of artists from these regions affected not only people in their own time but also the art, ideas, and culture of their descendents.

Art is a reflection of a people's history and culture. Museums and published books of art are testimony to the value humans place on art that depicts the history of their development as a society. And artwork in our homes often reflects the pride we have in our culture and in its ways of approaching and understanding life.

Studying the art of other cultures helps us to understand their folkways; values; history; and, to some degree, how they became what they are today.

## ACTIVITIES

1. Read at the left the comments about the function of art in a people's culture.

2. Using library facilities or the Internet, compose/key a report on the art of one of the regions mentioned in the reading.

3. Bring to class a picture, painting, drawing, sculpture, or other artifact to illustrate your report (a library photocopy will do if an actual object is not available).

4. Present your report orally, using the artifact as an example of that culture's art.

# UNIT 1

## LESSONS 1–20

## Learn Letter-Key Operation

## LESSON 1

### Home Keys (FDSA JKL;)

**Objectives:**

**1.** To learn control of home keys (**FDSA JKL;**).
**2.** To learn control of Space Bar and Return/Enter.

### 1A •
### Work Area Arrangement

1. Arrange work area as shown at right.

**Computers**

- alphanumeric (main) keyboard directly in front of chair; front edge of keyboard even with edge of table or desk
- monitor placed for easy viewing; disk drives placed for easy access
- *Alphabetic Keyboarding* software and/or your word processing disk-ettes within easy reach
- book behind or at right of keyboard; top raised for easy reading

**Electronics**

- front frame of machine even with front edge of desk
- book at right of machine, top raised for easy reading
- paper at left of machine
2. Turn on equipment (ON/OFF control of computer/monitor or electronic typewriter).
3. Boot computer program (follow teacher direction).

Properly arranged work area: computer

Properly arranged work area: electronics

# *your* PERSPECTIVE

## GLOBAL AWARENESS

The word "foreigner," although it has a legitimate dictionary definition as "someone from a foreign land," is sometimes used in the United States and in other countries in a negative (or perjorative) way. It is one of the words that suggest a *them* versus *us* attitude on the part of the user.

U.S. citizens often need reminding that they and/or their ancestors were once from "foreign" countries and were thus foreigners when they first came here. Only American Indians can lay claim to being *native* Americans, and even *their* claim is doubted by some historians.

Settlers of the original thirteen colonies came primarily from England, France, and Germany to escape the religious persecution of the day. Later, Africans were brought here under duress to work for plantation owners. Still later, Chinese were "imported" to work on, among other things, the transcontinental railway. The Irish, following a famine caused by a potato blight, settled here in substantial numbers. Before and during World War II, Jews fled here to escape mistreatment and even death at the hands of Nazi Germany. In more recent years, Cubans came in great numbers to escape the political and economic oppression of the Castro regime. Mexican citizens have for years crossed the border in an effort to improve their economic lot.

As all these people came, it took time and much effort to assimilate themselves into the society they had entered. People from different cultures tended to settle in areas that were populated mostly by people from their "home country." As descendents of the earliest settlers scattered through the states and cities, more recent arrivals were drawn to settlements of people of the same origin as themselves.

At certain periods in our history, it was common to read about the plight of the English, the French, the Germans, and so on. That is much less true today. Now, however, we are likely to see on TV and read in newspapers and magazines about the problems of African-Americans, Hispanic-Americans, and others. Many members of these groups have become assimilated into the mainstream of society; others, usually later arrivals plus many living in poor economic conditions, have not. Some social scientists offer evidence to suggest that in certain states and cities there is a movement toward the maintenance of subcultures within the main culture of these areas. The opposite forces of assimilation into the mainstream and of subculture maintenance, some say, are at least partially responsible for some of the social unrest and political strains that exist among people in our country today.

As we continue to work through our social, political, and legal problems and challenges, we all need to remember that we and/or our ancestors were all at one time "foreigners" and that "no man is an island." Only through trying to understand and to cooperate with one another in resolving the issues and attitudes that divide us can we hope to live in peace and harmony and to be able to say, as Louis (Satchmo) Armstrong sang with such feeling, "What a wonderful world!" ✳

## ACTIVITIES

1. Read at the left the story about immigrants to the United States.

2. Make a list of the countries of origin of the ancestors of all members of the class and in what years the most recent ancestral immigrants of each student came to the U.S.

3. Discuss why the various ancestors came here.

4. Compose/key a report about immigration.

Consider:
a. the value immigration can have on the country new immigrants enter
b. the problems immigration poses for the country new immigrants enter
c. whether immigration should be open to everyone or limited in some way
d. whether "foreigner" should ever be used to identify immigrants, whatever their ethnic origin

## 1B •
## Keying Position

Proper position is the same for typewriters and computers. The essential features of proper position are shown at right and listed below:

- fingers curved and upright over home keys
- wrists low, but not touching frame of machine or keyboard
- forearms parallel to slant of keyboard
- body erect, sitting back in chair
- feet on floor for balance

Proper position at computer

Proper position at electronic typewriter

## 1C •
## Home-Key Position

1. Find the home keys on the chart: **F D S A** for left hand and **J K L ;** for right hand.

2. Locate the home keys on your keyboard. Place left-hand fingers on **F D S A** and right-hand fingers on **J K L ;** *with your fingers well curved and upright (not slanting).*

3. Remove your fingers from the keyboard; then place them in home-key position again, curving and holding them *lightly* on the keys.

## 1D •
## Technique: Home Keys and Space Bar

1. Read the statements and study the illustrations at right.

2. Place your fingers in home-key position as directed in 1C, above.

3. Strike each letter key for the first group of letters in the line of type below the technique illustrations.

4. After striking **;** (semicolon), strike the **Space Bar** once.

5. Continue to key the line; strike the **Space Bar** once at the point of each arrow.

**TECHNIQUE** *hints:*

**Keystroking:** Strike each key with a light tap with the tip of the finger, snapping the fingertip toward the palm of the hand.

**Spacing:** Strike the Space Bar with the right thumb; use a quick down-and-in motion (toward the palm). Avoid pauses before or after spacing.

Space once.

```
fdsajkl;  f  d  s  a  j  k  l  ;  ff  jj  dd  kk  ss  ll  aa  ;;
```

**ACCD**

*My Notes*
- *Newsletter in 3 columns.*
- *Name: **ACCD** (spell out) **UPDATE**.*
- *Design a graphic for heading, which includes title, pub. date (**Summer ----**), and edition number (**1**); may use clip art.*
- *3 articles: Text in 2 files : TRENOVA and TCOMPUTE; more articles to come later.*
- *I decide other formatting.*
- *Proofread!!*

## ACCD's New Strategic Plan

At the March ACCD Board of Directors meeting, the board approved a strategic plan that sets forth an ambitious strategy to guide the coalition's work for the next three years.  Board and staff members began working on the plan last September.   All planning sessions were facilitated by Charles Stucker, Chair of ACCD's Planning Committee.   Charles is a resident of West Aliquippa and employed by Beaver Valley Electric Company as a quality process leader.  Mr. Stucker currently teaches strategic planning in the College of Business at Beaver College, and he has been a member of ACCD's board for five years.

The opening question for the first planning session was:  "What should ACCD focus on over the next three years in order to make Aliquippa the number one city in Western Pennsylvania relative to education, business, social services, and housing?"

Staff and board participated fully in the development of the plan.  As chair of the Planning Committee, Chuck Stucker states, "I am enthusiastic about the challenges that await ACCD in the coming years, and I look forward to this new phase of ACCD's development."

ACCD's mission is to improve the quality of life for the citizens and businesses of Aliquippa by empowering the citizens and business people to create and manage economic and social change.   To achieve this mission, ACCD is committed:

- to be a stronger partner with the community by focusing on the needs of the citizens and businesses in Aliquippa;
- to form regional partnerships that will bring additional resources to the citizens and businesses in Aliquippa;
- to be a model for community revitalization by getting the job done;
- to facilitate quality and delivery within each of our services;
- to enhance staff, board-member and volunteer participation in the organization and to make that participation a satisfying process;
- to facilitate a renewed spirit within Aliquippa that will ultimately improve Aliquippa's image.

## 1E

### Technique: Hard Return at Line Endings

To return the cursor or print point to left margin and move it down to next line, strike **Return/Enter** key (hard return).

Study illustrations at right; then return 4 times (quadruple-space) below the line you completed in 1D, p. 11.

**Hard Return**

Striking the **Enter** (computers) or **Return** (electronics) key is called a "hard return." You will use a hard return at the end of all drill lines in this lesson and those that follow in this unit. Reach the little finger of the right hand to the **Return** key or **Enter** key, tap the key, and return the finger quickly to home-key position.

## 1F

### Home-Key and Space-Bar Practice

1. Place your hands in home-key position (left-hand fingers on **F D S A** and right-hand fingers on **J K L ;**).
2. Key the lines once: single-spaced (SS) with a double space (DS) between 2-line groups. Do not key line numbers.

Fingers curved and upright

Down-and-in spacing motion

Strike Space Bar once to space.

```
1  j  jj  f  ff  k  kk  d  dd  l  ll  s  ss  ;  ;;  a  aa  jkl;  fdsa
2  j  jj  f  ff  k  kk  d  dd  l  ll  s  ss  ;  ;;  a  aa  jkl;  fdsa
```
Strike the Return/Enter key twice to double-space (DS).

```
3  a  aa  ;  ;;  s  ss  l  ll  d  dd  k  kk  f  ff  j  jj  fdsa  jkl;
4  a  aa  ;  ;;  s  ss  l  ll  d  dd  k  kk  f  ff  j  jj  fdsa  jkl;
```
DS

```
5  jf  jf  kd  kd  ls  ls  ;a  ;a  fj  fj  dk  dk  sl  sl  a;  a;  f
6  jf  jf  kd  kd  ls  ls  ;a  ;a  fj  fj  dk  dk  sl  sl  a;  a;  f
```
DS

```
7  a;fj  a;sldkfj  a;sldkfj  a;sldkfj  a;sldkfj  a;sldkfj
8  a;fj  a;sldkfj  a;sldkfj  a;sldkfj  a;sldkfj  a;sldkfj
```
Strike the Return/Enter key 4 times to quadruple-space (QS).

## 1G

### Technique: Return-Key Practice

each line twice single-spaced (SS); double-space (DS) between 2-line groups

**SPACING *cue*:**

When in SS mode, strike **Return/Enter** twice to insert a DS between 2-line groups.

Reach out with little finger; tap **Return/Enter** key quickly; return finger to home key.

```
1  a;sldkfj  a;sldkfj
```
DS
```
2  ff  jj  dd  kk  ss  ll  aa  ;;
```
DS
```
3  fj  fj  dk  dk  sl  sl  a;  a;  asdf  ;lkj
```
DS
```
4  fj  dk  sl  a;  jf  kd  ls  ;a  fdsa  jkl;  a;sldkfj
```
QS

**Job 11**

**ACCD**

**Mrs. Shaw** needs to send this agenda this afternoon. It's for the **ACCD Board of Directors Meeting** on **May 18** at **6:30 p.m.** in the **Coalition Headquarters Building**.

1.  Call to Order ............................ Edward Jessop

2.  Review of Last Year's Audit Report .......... Mark Furnley, CPA

3.  Approval of April Minutes ...................... Emma Kulis

4.  Financial Report ............................... Lori Oberst

5.  Executive Committee Report ................... Edward Jessop

6.  Planning Committee Report ....................Charles Stucker

7.  Education Committee Report          Delores Paskus

8.  Fundraising Committee Report         Angela Ghiardi

9.  Personnel Report          Anita Shaw

10. Executive Director's Report  *add leaders*  Anita Shaw

11. Other Business          Edward Jessop

12. Adjournment          Edward Jessop

**Job 12**
**Memo with Table**

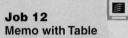

**ACCD**

Open file T222J12 and prepare the memo for **Anita Shaw** from **David Renk, Business Development Specialist**. Date it **May 12** and supply all other missing memo parts. Insert this table after the first ¶.

| Business | Address | Points | Grant Amount |
|---|---|---|---|
| Avenue Deli | 309 Franklin Ave. | 92 | $15,000 |
| Ford's News Stand | 202 Franklin Ave. | 88 | $15,000 |
| Hannon Shoes | 415 Shefield Ave. | 86 | $10,000 |
| Unger Appliances | 525 Station St. | 83 | $10,000 |
| Best Food Market | 311 Franklin Ave. | 80 | $10,000 |
| Avenue Restaurant | 376 Franklin Ave. | 76 | $ 5,000 |
| Clinton Printing | 527 Station St. | 75 | $ 5,000 |
| Aliquippa Credit Union | 418 Franklin Ave. | 74 | $ 5,000 |
| Modern Electronics | 402 Shefield Ave. | 73 | none |
| Joan's Styling Salon | 382 Franklin Ave. | 71 | none |

## 1H •
## Home-Key Mastery

1. Key the lines once (without the numbers); strike the **Return/Enter** key twice to double-space (DS).
2. Rekey the drill at a faster pace.

**TECHNIQUE** *cue:*

Keep fingers curved and upright over home keys, right thumb just barely touching the Space Bar.

**SPACING** *cue:*

Space once after ; used as punctuation.

Correct finger alignment

```
1  aa ;; ss ll dd kk ff jj a; sl dk fj jf kd ls ;a jf
                                                        DS
2  a a as as ad ad ask ask lad lad fad fad jak jak la
                                                        DS
3  all all fad fad jak jak add add ask ask ads ads as
                                                        DS
4  a lad; a jak; a lass; all ads; add all; ask a lass
                                                        DS
5  as a lad; a fall fad; ask all dads; as a fall fad;
```

## 1I •
## End-of-Lesson Routine

### Computers

1. Exit the software.
2. Remove from disk drive any floppy disk you have inserted.
3. Turn off equipment if directed to do so.
4. Store materials as teacher directs.

### Electronics

1. Press the **Paper Up** (or **Eject**) key to remove paper.
2. Turn machine off.

**R&e**

1. Key drill once as shown to improve control of home keys.
2. Key the drill again to quicken your keystrokes.

**SPACING** *cue:*

To DS when in SS mode, strike **Return/Enter** twice.

Disk removal

Paper up (or Eject)

```
1  ja js jd jf f; fl fk fj ka ks kd kf d; dl dk dj a;
                                                        DS
2  la ls ld lf s; sl sk sj ;a ;s ;d ;f a; al ak aj fj
                                                        DS
3  jj aa kk ss ll dd ;; ff fj dk sl a; jf kd ls ;a a;
                                                        DS
4  as as ask ask ad ad lad lad all all fall fall lass
                                                        DS
5  as a fad; as a dad; ask a lad; as a lass; all lads
                                                        DS
6  a sad dad; all lads fall; ask a lass; a jak salad;
                                                        DS
7  add a jak; a fall ad; all fall ads; ask a sad lass
```

**Job 9**

Format this information as a one-page flyer. Use type font, borders, clip-art, and other features that you think will make people notice and want to read it. If needed, you can rearrange the text.

## AN ACCD COMMUNITY WORKSHOP

Are you  . . .Job hunting?

. . .Considering a career change?

. . .Interested in the local job market outlook?

The Aliquippa Coalition for Community Development is offering a series of community workshops on employment-seeking skills. All workshops are free and will be offered at:

Coalition Headquarters, 392 Franklin Ave., Aliquippa

### Schedule

| Tuesday, June 5 7-8 p.m. | Tuesday, June 12 7-8 p.m. | Tuesday, June 19 7-8 p.m. |
|---|---|---|
| Ms. Carla Manko, ACCD education director, will discuss steps to begin a job search. Topics will include: | Mr. David Keaton, director of human resources for JK Communications, will present information essential to writing letters of application and preparing resumes. Topics will include: | Ms. Janet McClarin, technical training coordinator, MAPCO Chemical, will present techniques for interviewing. Topics will include: |
| ✓ Understanding the local job market | ✓ Style | ✓ Preparing and dressing for an interview |
| ✓ Using local resources | ✓ Purpose | ✓ Observing do's & don'ts at an interview |
| ✓ Understanding employer needs | ✓ Language | ✓ Handling questions |
| ✓ Developing an action plan | | ✓ Writing follow-up letters |
| ✓ Upgrading skills | | |

Please plan to attend this informational series. Seating is limited. Refreshments will be served. Call 175-2882 to register.

**Job 10**

Create a data file with these names and addresses. All are in **Aliquippa, PA  15001**. The last 4 ZIP Code digits are given. Merge this file with the form letter you created in Job 2 as soon as you can. Use **5/11** as date.

Mr. George Gunderson, Avenue Deli, 309 Franklin Ave., 1309

Ms. Susan Loya, Best Food Market, 311 Franklin Ave., 1311

Mrs. Dorothy Allen, Hospital Baby Pictures, 412 Franklin Ave., 1412

Dr. Lloyd Wesson, Family Practice Center, 428 Franklin Ave., 1428

Dr. Margaret Hunter, Family Practice Center, 428 Franklin Ave., 1428

Ms. Felicia Gomez, Home Appliance Center, 536 Franklin Ave., 1536

# Home Keys (FDSA JKL;)

**Objectives:**
1. To improve control of home keys (**FDSA JKL;**).
2. To improve control of **Space Bar** and **Return/Enter**.

## R1A • Keying Readiness

1. Arrange your work area (see p. 10).
2. Get to know your equipment (see pp. x, 1-3).
3. Use default margins and spacing (unless your teacher guides you in making format adjustments).
4. Take keying position as shown at right.

## R1B • Home-Key Position

1. Locate the home keys on the chart: **F D S A** for left hand and **J K L ;** for right hand.
2. Locate the home keys on your keyboard. Place left-hand fingers on **F D S A** and right-hand fingers on **J K L ;** with *fingers well curved and upright (not slanting).*
3. Remove fingers from the keyboard; then place them in home-key position.

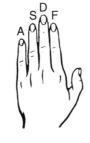  

## R1C • Technique Review

Remember to use a hard return at the end of all drill lines. To double-space (DS), use two hard returns.

### Keystroke

Curve fingers over home keys. Strike each key with a quick-snap stroke; release key quickly.

### Space

Strike the **Space Bar** with a quick down-and-in motion of the right thumb. Do not pause before or after spacing stroke.

### Hard Return

Reach the right little finger to the **Return/Enter** key; strike the key and return the finger quickly to home key.

**ACCD**

Here's copy that **Mrs. Shaw** drafted and printed out at home. Please rekey it as a news release, using a 10-pt. font. Be sure you proofread it well. Use the logo. It is for immediate release. **Ms. Manko** is the contact person. Make it fit on one page.

ALIQUIPPA, PA, MAY 11, ----. The Business Kids Program sponsored by the Aliquippa Coaliton for Community Development brought 11 young men and women together to learn the fundamentals of small business ownership last summer.

Ernest Mansell enroled in the program because he saw it as a ticket to a better life for him and his mother. 9 months later, "Quip Cookie" remains in business.

Though limited in time because of school and afterschool activities, Mansell continues his cookie making much to the delight of his Aliquippa neighbors and classmates.

His secret recipies came from his grandmother, and he absolutely refuses to mix the selected ingredients in front of anyone.

Ernest looks to use his baking skills one day too purchase a single-level house for his mother, who is confined to a wheelchair. He is determined to become a business owner and realizes that the Business Kids Program has given him a foundatin of knowledge and character to succeed.

ACCD is sponsoring the Business Kids Program agian this summer. Applications will be accepted until June 10 at ACCD's Coalition Headquarters at 392 Franklin Avenue.

**ACCD**

Here's the enclosure for the memo you prepared earlier. Prepare it and place it with the memo.

| ALIQUIPPA TEEN SKILL BANK AND JOB REFERRAL BUDGET | | |
|---|---|---|
| **May 15 to June 30, ----** | | |
| **Budget Line Item** | | **Cost** |
| **Salary:** | College student for 40 hours per week from May 15 to June 30 at $6.50/hour | $2,080 |
| **Benefits:** | Includes FICA, unemployment insurance, and workers' compensation | $400 |
| **Travel:** | 600 miles at $.25/mile for travel to prospective employers | $150 |
| **Workshop Materials:** | Booklets, paper, pens, etc. | $125 |
| **Rental of Space and Utilities** | | $600 |
| **Office Supplies/Telephone** | | $200 |
| **Total** | | $3,555 |

Key the lines once (without the numbers), single-spaced (SS) with a double space (DS) between 2-line groups.

**Technique goals**

- curved, upright fingers
- quick-snap keystrokes
- down-and-in spacing
- quick return without spacing at line ending

Strike Space Bar once to space.

```
1 f ff j jj d dd k kk s ss l ll a aa ; ;; fdsa jkl;
2 f ff j jj d dd k kk s ss l ll a aa ; ;; fdsa jkl;
```
Strike the Return/Enter key twice to double-space (DS).
```
3 j jj f ff k kk d dd l ll s ss ; ;; a aa asdf ;lkj
4 j jj f ff k kk d dd l ll s ss ; ;; a aa asdf ;lkj

5 a;a sls dkd fjf ;a; lsl kdk jfj a;sldkfj a;sldkfj
6 a;a sls dkd fjf ;a; lsl kdk jfj a;sldkfj a;sldkfj
```
Strike the Return/Enter key 4 times to quadruple-space (QS).

## R1D
### Home-Key Stroking

Key the lines once single-spaced (SS) with a double space (DS) between 2-line groups. Do not key the line numbers.

**Goal:** To improve keying and spacing techniques.

```
1 f f ff j j jj d d dd k k kk s s ss l l ll a a aa;
2 f f ff j j jj d d dd k k kk s s ss l l ll a a aa;

3 fj dk sl a; jf kd ls ;a ds kl df kj sd lk sa ;l j
4 fj dk sl a; jf kd ls ;a ds kl df kj sd lk sa ;l j

5 sa as ld dl af fa ls sl fl lf al la ja aj sk ks j
6 sa as ld dl af fa ls sl fl lf al la ja aj sk ks j
```

## R1E
### Technique: Return

each line twice single-spaced (SS); double-space (DS) between 2-line groups

**Technique goals**

- curved, upright fingers
- quick-snap keystrokes
- down-and-in spacing
- quick return without spacing at line ending

**TECHNIQUE** *cue*:

Reach out with the little finger, not the hand; tap **Return/Ente**r key quickly; return finger to home key.

```
1 a;sldkfj a;sldkfj
                    DS
2 a ad ad a as as ask ask
                          DS
3 as as jak jak ads ads all all
                                DS
4 a jak; a lass; all fall; ask all dads
                                        DS
5 as a fad; add a jak; all fall ads; a sad lass
                                                QS
```

**Job 6**

**ACCD**

Process this memo from **Carla Manko,** the **Education Director**, to **Anita Shaw**. Date it **May 10, ----.** I'll give you the budget later.

I recommend that ACCD operate a skill bank and employment referral service for Aliquippa teens from May 15 to June 30.

One college student could be hired to work with local employers to determine the types and number of jobs available and the salary scales offered. During the first week of the program, the ACCD would present a workshop to teens on employers' expectations and on how to conduct a successful job search. After that, the ACCD would maintain a job board and screen applicants so that local employers would be linked to the best possible candidates.

Many summer jobs are available at the Pittsburgh International Airport and Robinstown Center, and I will work with the community churches to see if their vans can be used to transport the teens to these two sites on a regular basis.

The entire cost of the project to the ACCD would be about $3,555, including the cost of hiring a college student at $6.50 per hour for about 230 hours. A detailed budget is enclosed.

Do you want me to prepare a more detailed proposal for the Education Committee to study and act upon at its upcoming meeting?

## R1F •
### Home-Key Mastery

each line twice single-spaced (SS); double-space (DS) between 2-line groups

**Technique goals**
- curved, upright fingers
- eyes on copy in book or on screen
- quick-snap keystrokes
- steady pace

Correct finger curvature

Correct finger alignment

Down-and-in spacing motion

1 a jak; a jak; ask dad; ask dad; as all; as all ads
Return twice to DS.

2 a fad; a fad; as a lad; as a lad; all ads; all ads
DS

3 as a fad; as a fad; a sad lass; a sad lass; a fall
DS

4 ask a lad; ask a lad; all jaks fall; all jaks fall
DS

5 a sad fall; a sad fall; all fall ads; all fall ads
DS

6 add a jak; a lad asks a lass; as a jak ad all fall

## R1G •
### End-of-Lesson Routine

**Computers**
1. Exit the software.
2. Remove from disk drive any floppy disk you have inserted.
3. Turn off equipment if directed to do so.
4. Store materials as teacher directs.

**Electronics**
1. Press the **Paper Up** (or **Eject**) key to remove paper.
2. Turn machine off.

### R&e

1. Key each line twice SS; DS between 2-line groups.
2. Key each line again to quicken your keystrokes if time permits.

**PRACTICE cue:**
Key slowly the first time you key a line to master the required motions. As you key a line a second time, try to make each motion a bit faster.

1 ff jj dd kk ss ll aa ;; fj dk sl a; jf kd ls ;a a;
DS

2 aa ;; ss ll dd kk ff jj ja js jd jf fj fk fl f; fj
DS

3 fjf dkd sls a;a jfj kdk lsl ;a;a a;sldkfj a;sldkfj
DS

4 fdsa jkl; asdf ;lkj all all ask ask jak jak ad add
DS

5 a a as as ask ask ad ad lad lad add add fall falls
DS

6 a jak ad; a sad dad; a lad asks; a lad asks a lass
DS

7 a sad fall; all fall ads; as a lass asks a sad lad
DS

8 as a fall fad; add a jak salad; as a sad lad falls

**ACCD**

Open file T222J5 and format it as an unbound report for Mrs. Shaw.

*My Notes*

✓ DS the body.

✓ Use 20-pt. font size for the main heading; 16-pt. font for the secondary and side headings; and 12-pt. font for the body.

✓ Bold all headings.

✓ Underline ¶ headings.

✓ Keep text together correctly.

✓ Replace non-profit and non-profits with **nonprofit** and **nonprofits**, respectively.

✓ Insert the header and footer that are given on the next page.

✓ Proofread after using spell and grammar checks.

✓ I decide other formatting features.

---

*Insert this text at the end of the first ¶ in the ACCD Operations section of the report.*

The long list includes the following:

◆ The Franklin Center serves approximately 1,800 to 2,500 people each month through social service outreach programs.

◆ The ACCD Learning Center, located in the Franklin Center Annex, provides educational opportunities for residents of all ages. Learning programs initially focused upon Aliquippa's at-risk youth. Though serving this group remains a high priority, the educational programs have been expanded in recent years to include adult education, skills enhancement, apprenticeship training, and job retention techniques.

◆ ACCD's Business and Technology Center offers a broad range of services for start-up enterprises and existing businesses.

◆ Youth development programs provide summer employment and youth mentoring programs to high-risk young people.

◆ The Aliquippa Business Corporation, a subsidiary of the ACCD, offers a Financial Incentive Program to property owners and merchants for investment in the rehabilitation of store fronts in a designated target area within the central business district.

---

*Insert this table after the Budget ¶—must print on one page.*

| Component | Financial Need |
|---|---|
| Business development | $69,680 |
| Educational programs | $119,908 |
| Real estate revitalization and development | $160,970 |
| Community relations and communications | $56,544 |
| Social services | $58,300 |
| General and administrative (not included in above components) | $24,788 |
| **TOTAL** | $490,190 |

*(continued on next page)*

# New Keys: H and E

**Objectives:**

**1.** To learn reach technique for **H** and **E**.

**2.** To combine smoothly **H** and **E** with home keys.

## 2A
### Get Ready to Key

At the beginning of each practice session, follow the *Standard Plan* given at the right to get ready to key the lesson.

**Standard Plan for Getting Ready to Key**

**Computers**

1. Arrange work area as shown on p. 10.
2. Check to see that the computer, monitor, and printer (if any) are plugged in.
3. Boot the computer software and select the proper program as your teacher directs.
4. Align the front of the keyboard with the front edge of the desk or table.
5. Position the monitor and the textbook for easy reading.

**Electronics**

1. Arrange work area as shown on p. 10.
2. Adjust **Paper Guide** to line up with 0 (zero) on the **Line-of-Writing** or **Format Scale**. See p. x.
3. Insert paper (long edge against the **Paper Guide**). See p. x.
4. Set the **Line-Space Selector** to single-space (SS) your practice lines. See pp. x, RG18.
5. Use default margins unless your teacher directs you to set 1.5" margins so that your copy is more nearly centered.

## 2B
### Plan for Learning New Keys

All keys except the home keys (**FDSA JKL;**) require the fingers to reach in order to strike them. Follow the *Standard Plan* given at the right in learning the proper reach for each new key.

**Standard Plan for Learning New Keys**

1. Find the new key on the keyboard chart given on the page where the new key is introduced.
2. Look at your own keyboard and find the new key on it.
3. Study the reach-technique picture at the left of the practice lines for the new key. (See p. 18 for illustrations.) Read the statement below the illustration.
4. Identify the finger to be used to strike the new key.

5. Curve your fingers; place them in home-key position (over **FDSA JKL;**).
6. Watch your finger as you reach it to the new key and back to home position a few times (keep it curved).
7. Refer to the set of 3 drill lines at the right of the reach-technique illustration. Key each line twice SS (single-spaced).
   - once slowly, to learn new reach;
   - then faster, for a quick-snap stroke. DS (double-space) between 2-line groups.

## 2C
### Home-Key Review

each line twice single-spaced (SS): once slowly; again, at a faster pace; double-space (DS) between 2-line groups

**All keystrokes learned**

1 a;sldkfj a; sl dk fj ff jj dd kk ss ll aa ;; fj a;

2 as as ad ad all all jak jak fad fad fall fall lass

3 a jak; a fad; as a lad; ask dad; a lass; a fall ad

Return 4 times to quadruple-space (QS) between lesson parts.

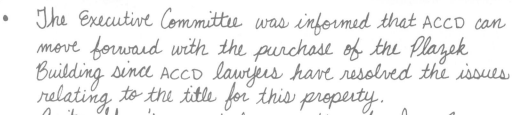

- The Executive Committee was informed that ACCD can move forward with the purchase of the Plazek Building since ACCD lawyers have resolved the issues relating to the title for this property.
- Anita Shaw's request for vacation for June 3–June 7 was approved.
- The meeting was adjourned at 6:35 p.m.

Minutes prepared by:
Emma Kulis, Secretary

**Job 4**

Mrs. Shaw wants to present this information to the Fundraising Committee at its meeting tomorrow. List the foundations in the order of the month that initial contact is to be made.

| ALIQUIPPA COALITION FOR COMMUNITY DEVELOPMENT | | | |
|---|---|---|---|
| Foundation Strategy for Next Year | | | |
| Agency | Initial Contact Month | Contact Person(s) | Request to Support |
| Alma Foundation | June | Shaw & Ghiardi | General |
| Artco Foundation | September | Shaw & Kulis | Education |
| Engineers Trust | October | Oberst & Ghiardi | Education |
| Calahan Foundation | October | Stucker | Endowment |
| Eicher Foundation | February | Foster & Paskus | General |
| Grettle Foundation | November | Samy | Arts |
| Hult Charitable Trust | December | Shaw & Paskus | Science |
| Knorr Charities | December | Tisdale & Eury | Computers |
| Laura Foundation | July | Tisdale & Foster | General |
| Laferty Trust | August | Eury & Shaw | Endowment |
| Mable Charities | August | Stucker & Shaw | Education |
| Mastey Trust | November | Shaw & Kulis | General |
| Milton Foundation | January | Paskus & Oberst | Endowment |
| MNE Charitable Trust | February | Ghiardi & Eury | Equipment |
| Smith Family Charity | March | Stucker & Shaw | Services |
| USP Foundation | March | Paskus & Samy | General |

## 2D •
### New Keys: H and E

Use the *Standard Plan for Learning New Keys* (p. 17) for each key to be learned. Study the plan now.

Relate each step of the plan to the illustrations and copy at right. Then key each line twice SS; leave a DS between 2-line groups.

**h** *Right index* finger

**e** *Left middle* finger

Do not attempt to key line numbers, the vertical lines separating word groups, or the labels (home row, h/e).

**Learn h**

1 j j hj hj ah ah ha ha had had has has ash ash hash
2 hj hj ha ha ah ah hah hah had had ash ash has hash
3 ah ha; had ash; has had; a hall; has a hall; ah ha

*Return twice to double-space (DS) after you complete the set of lines.*

**Learn e**

4 d d ed ed el el led led eel eel eke eke ed fed fed
5 ed ed el el lee lee fed fed eke eke led led ale ed
6 a lake; a leek; a jade; a desk; a jade eel; a deed

**Combine h and e**

7 he he he|she she she|shed shed|heed heed|held held
8 a lash; a shed; he held; she has jade; held a sash
9 has fled; he has ash; she had jade; she had a sale

*Return 4 times to quadruple-space (QS) between lesson parts.*

## 2E •
### New-Key Mastery

1. Key the lines once SS with a DS between 2-line groups.
2. Key the lines again with quick, sharp strokes at a faster pace.

**SPACING cue:**
Space once after ; used as punctuation.

**[wp] note:**
Once the screen is filled with keyed lines, the top line disappears when a new line is added at the bottom. This is called **scrolling**.

Fingers curved

Fingers upright

home row
1 ask ask|has has|lad lad|all all|jak jak|fall falls
2 a jak; a lad; a sash; had all; has a jak; all fall
DS

h/e
3 he he|she she|led led|held held|jell jell|she shed
4 he led; she had; she fell; a jade ad; a desk shelf
DS

all keys learned
5 elf elf|all all|ask ask|led led|jak jak|hall halls
6 ask dad; he has jell; she has jade; he sells leeks
DS

all keys learned
7 he led; she has; a jak ad; a jade eel; a sled fell
8 she asked a lad; he led all fall; she has a jak ad

## Job 1

**ACCD**

Here's a copy of the Coalition's logo. Make a macro of it that you can use for all letters, memos, minutes, and news releases.

## Job 2

**ACCD**

Open file TLNGFORM; Mrs. Shaw needs it prepared as a two-page form letter. Include the fields noted at the right. Insert the ¶ at the right as the 4th ¶. Date the letter **May 6**; find and correct all errors in the file.

## Job 3

**ACCD**

Process these executive committee meeting minutes that Emma Kulis recorded. Use the ACCD logo.

---

**A**liquippa                    392 Franklin Ave.

**C**oalition for               Aliquippa, PA 15001-2356

**C**ommunity                  Telephone: (412) 175-2882

**D**evelopment                Fax: (412) 175-2884

---

Fields include: **<Name>**, **<Company>**, **<Street>**, **<City>**, **<State>**, **<ZIP>**, and **<Salutation>**

Our goal for "Aliquippa Loves Art" is threefold:  to bring positive attention to Aliquippa, to provide residents with an opportunity to view the work of local artists, and to give artists a chance to display their art.

---

Executive Committee Meeting

May 5, ----

Attendees: Angela Ghiardi, Emma Kulis, Edward Jessop, Lori Oberst, Anita Shaw, and Elmer Stuckeman

- The meeting was called to order at 6:10 p.m. by Edward Jessop, Chairperson.
- Director Shaw recommended that ACCD submit two grant proposals-- one to the Human Development Fund for $5,000 for use in the Community Science Project; another to the Community Development Block Grant for $15,000 to be used for improvement to ACCD buildings and parking lots on Franklin Avenue. The Executive Committee approved these recommendations.
- Susan Pletcher's resignation dated April 30 was accepted. Her last day at ACCD as an administrative secretary will be May 31.

*(continued on next page)*

**New Keys: I and R**

**Objectives:**

1. To learn reach technique for **I** and **R**.
2. To combine smoothly **I** and **R** with all other learned keys.

**3A • 3**
**Keying Readiness**

Follow the steps on p. 17.

**3B • 5**
**Conditioning Practice**

each line twice SS; DS between 2-line groups

**PRACTICE cues:**

- Key each line first at a slow, steady pace, but strike and release each key quickly.

- Key each line again at a faster pace; move from key to key quickly–keep cursor or print point moving steadily.

home keys 1 `a;sldkfj a;sldkfj as jak ask fad all dad lads fall`
Return twice to DS.

h/e 2 `hj hah has had sash hash ed led fed fled sled fell`
DS

all keys learned 3 `as he fled; ask a lass; she had jade; sell all jak`
Return 4 times to quadruple-space (QS) between lesson parts.

**3C • 5**
**Speed Building**

each line once DS

**SPACING cue:**

To DS when in SS mode, strike **Enter** twice at end of line.

**SPEED cue:**

In lines 1-3, quicken the keying pace as you key each letter combination or word when it is repeated within the line.

1 `hj hj|ah ah|ha ha|had had|ash ash|has has|had hash`
2 `ed ed|el el|ed ed|led led|eke eke|lee lee|ale kale`
3 `he he|she she|led led|has has|held held|sled sleds`
4 `he fled; she led; she had jade; he had a jell sale`
5 `a jak fell; she held a leek; he has had a sad fall`
6 `he has ash; she sells jade; as he fell; has a lake`
7 `she had a fall jade sale; he leads all fall sales;`
8 `he held a fall kale sale; she sells leeks as a fad`

# Aliquippa Coalition for Community Development [A Word Processing Simulation]

## Volunteer Assignment

You have decided to do volunteer work after school so that you will have work experience that may help you gain a competitive advantage when you seek full-time employment. You have selected the Aliquippa Coalition for Community Development (ACCD) as the place you want to volunteer because it is a nonprofit organization that is striving to revitalize your community, which has lost many of its manufacturing plants. Also, working at ACCD will give you an opportunity to "give back" to your community.

The ACCD performs many important functions in your community. The coalition offers business development services for start-up and existing businesses; gives job training, career development, and computer instruction to adults and teenagers; and provides space for many social service agencies that serve the residents of Aliquippa. ACCD's operations and projects are funded by private foundations, government agencies, and income derived from real estate rentals and transactions.

You have been assigned to work with Ms. Loretta H. Lewis, the administrative assistant who works directly for Mrs. Anita D. Shaw, ACCD executive director. As a volunteer, you will serve as an administrative specialist, producing documents according to the directions given. If specific directions are not given or sufficiently detailed, you are to complete your work according to what you have learned in your document processing course. A copy of your *Century 21* textbook is at ACCD for you to use as a reference.

During the interview, you learned that you will likely prepare letters and memos, reports, board meeting agendas and minutes, articles for the ACCD newsletter, financial reports, and posters and pamphlets that explain ACCD's services. The variety of documents appealed to you because they relate directly to what you have learned and will give you a chance to do them in a real-world setting.

You are expected to produce error-free documents, so proofread carefully for spelling and other language-skill errors—do NOT rely solely on your spell checker. Proofread documents before printing so that you do not waste time and paper. The work you produce is to be neat, so safeguard your completed work from dirt, stains, wrinkles, etc.

## LESSONS 222-225

## Aliquippa Coalition for Community Development

**Objectives:**
1. To demonstrate your ability to integrate document processing knowledge and skills.
2. To demonstrate your ability to use good judgment in varied situations.

**222-225A • 5 (daily) Conditioning Practice**

each line twice; 1' writings on lines 1-3 as time permits

| | | |
|---|---|---|
| alphabet | 1 | Zed quickly explained how my job was lost over internal fighting. |
| speed | 2 | Claudia may pay them to work with us when we dismantle the docks. |
| figures | 3 | The study guides for the exam are on pages 56, 197, 280, and 304. |

| gwam | 1' | 1 | 2 | 3 | 4 | 5 | 6 | 7 | 8 | 9 | 10 | 11 | 12 | 13 |
|---|---|---|---|---|---|---|---|---|---|---|---|---|---|---|

## 3D • 18
### New Keys: I and R

each line twice SS (slowly, then faster); DS between 2-line groups; if time permits, key lines 7-9 again

**Technique goals**
- curved, upright fingers
- finger-action keystrokes
- eyes on copy

**i** *Right middle* finger

**r** *Left index* finger

Follow the *Standard Plan for Learning New Keys* outlined on p. 17.

**Learn i**

1 k k ik ik is is if if did did aid aid kid kid hail

2 ik ik if if is is kid kid his his lie lie aid aide

3 a kid; a lie; if he; he did; his aide; if a kid is

DS

**Learn r**

4 f f rf rf jar jar her her are are ark ark jar jars

5 rf rf re re fr fr jar jar red red her her far fare

6 a jar; a rake; a lark; red jar; hear her; are dark

DS

**Combine i and r**

7 fir fir|rid rid|sir sir|ire ire|fire fire|air airs

8 a fir; if her; a fire; is fair; his ire; if she is

9 he is; if her; is far; red jar; his heir; her aide

Quadruple-space (QS) between lesson parts.

## 3E • 19
### New-Key Mastery

1. Key the lines once SS with a DS between 2-line groups.
2. Key the lines again at a faster pace.

**Technique goals**
- fingers deeply curved
- wrists low, but not resting
- hands/arms steady
- eyes on copy as you key

reach review
1 hj ed ik rf hj de ik fr hj ed ik rf jh de ki fr hj
2 he he|if if|all all|fir fir|jar jar|rid rid|as ask

DS

h/e
3 she she|elf elf|her her|hah hah|eel eel|shed shelf
4 he has; had jak; her jar; had a shed; she has fled

DS

i/r
5 fir fir|rid rid|sir sir|kid kid|ire ire|fire fired
6 a fir; is rid; is red; his ire; her kid; has a fir

DS

all keys learned
7 if if|is is|he he|did did|fir fir|jak jak|all fall
8 a jak; he did; ask her; red jar; she fell; he fled

DS

all keys learned
9 if she is; he did ask; he led her; he is her aide;
10 she has had a jak sale; she said he had a red fir;

words

## ITALY TOUR ITINERARY

| | | |
|---|---|---|
| | | 4 |
| Tuesday, March 1 | Arrive in Turin by motor coach; depart at 2:15 p.m. | 18 |
| | by train for Milan; check in at Milan Hotel. | 27 |
| Wednesday, March 2 | Tour Milan during day; go to Milan opera in evening. | 42 |
| Thursday, March 3 | Depart at 7:35 a.m. by train to Venice; check in Hotel | 56 |
| | Uno; tour Venice; take overnight train to Florence at | 67 |
| | 9:30 p.m., Friday. | 71 |
| Saturday, March 5 | Check in Firenze Hotel; visit Florence art museums; | 85 |
| | take overnight train to Rome at 8:15 p.m. | 94 |
| Sunday, March 6 | Tour Rome historic ruins; depart for home via Inter- | 107 |
| | national Airways at 1 p.m. | 112 |

## 221C • 15
## Straight-Copy Skills

Key two 5' writings on the ¶s at the right. Find *gwam* and number of errors on each. Record your better score.

  all letters used

| | gwam | 3' | 5' |
|---|---|---|---|

All students should ponder the advantages of continuing their   4   2   58
education after finishing high school.  A greater number of jobs   8   5   61
than ever before require post-high school training in order to   13   8   64
meet the minimum standards of entry level.  Many jobs that were   17  10   66
previously open to individuals who had a high school diploma no   21  13   69
longer exist, or technology has changed the duties of the job to   26  15   71
such an extent that some type of training after high school is   30  18   74
now required in order to be qualified.   34  21   77

The secretarial position is an example of a job that has changed   39  23   79
a great deal by improved technology.   Years ago one of the major   43  26   82
duties for this type of work was to be able to use a manual   47  28   84
typewriter with a great deal of skill.  Today the position has   51  31   87
changed into one that requires competence in operating word pro-   55  33   89
cessing equipment and the ability to utilize the computer as well   60  36   92
as deal with customers and clients in a skillful manner.   64  38   94

These changes are examples of how the current job market has   68  41   97
made it important for people to contemplate attending college in   72  43   99
order to be considered for some of the higher paying jobs.  Advo-   76  46  102
cates of more schooling also mention having a richer and more   80  48  104
rewarding life as a reason for continuing school.  These factors   85  51  107
are just a few of the reasons why, over the years, young people   89  53  109
as well as old have enrolled in some form of advanced schooling.   93  56  112

| gwam | 3' | 1 | 2 | 3 | 4 |
|---|---|---|---|---|---|
| | 5' | 1 | 2 | 3 | |

# LESSON 4  Review

**Objectives:**

**1.** To improve reach-stroke control and keying speed.

**2.** To improve technique on **Space Bar** and **Enter**.

## 4A • 3
### Keying Readiness

1. Review the steps for arranging your work area (see p. 10).
2. Review the steps required to ready your equipment.
3. Take good keying position.

- fingers curved and upright
- wrists low, but not touching frame of machine
- forearms parallel to slant of keyboard
- body erect, sitting back in chair
- feet on floor for balance

## 4B • 5
### Conditioning Practice

each line twice SS; DS between 2-line groups

1 a;sldkfj fj dk sl a; jh de ki fr hj ed ik rf fj a;

2 a if is el he la as re led fir did she has jak jar

3 he has fir; she had a jak; a jade jar; a leek sale

QS

## 4C • 10
### Technique:  Space Bar

1. Key lines 1-6 once SS; DS between 3-line groups.  Space *immediately* after each word.
2. Key the lines again at a faster pace.

Use down-and-in motion

**Short, easy words**

1 if is ha la ah el as re id did sir fir die rid lie

2 as lad lei rah jak had ask lid her led his kid has

3 hah all ire add iris hall fire keel sell jeer fall

DS

**Short-word phrases**

4 if he|he is|if he is|if she|she is|if she is|as is

5 as he is|if he led|if she has|if she did|had a jak

6 as if|a jar lid|all her ads|as he said|a jade fish

QS

## 4D • 10
### Technique:  Enter

each line twice SS; DS between 2-line groups

**PRACTICE cue:**
Keep up your pace to the end of the line, return quickly, and begin the new line without a pause or stop.

1 if he is;

2 as if she is;

3 he had a fir desk;

4 she has a red jell jar;

5 he has had a lead all fall;

6 she asked if he reads fall ads;

7 she said she reads all ads she sees;

8 his dad has had a sales lead as he said;

QS

Reach out and tap **Enter**

## 221B • 30
## Special Document Skills

**Time Schedule**

Plan and prepare ............. 4'
Timed production .......... 20'
Proofread/compute
   *n-pram* ...................... 6'

**Document 1**

Process the news release at the right.

**Document 2**

Process the agenda at the right.

1. Format and key the special documents in the order they are given on this and the next page. Key as much as you can in 20'. If you finish before time is called, begin again with Document 1.

2. Compute *n-pram* and turn in your work arranged in the order it was completed: *n-pram* = words keyed - (15 x errors) divided by 20.

words

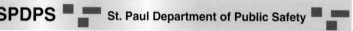

**SPDPS**    **St. Paul Department of Public Safety**

175 W. Seventh St.
St. Paul, MN 55102-2373

Telephone: 612-192-8394
Fax: 612-192-8494

News Release      For Release:   Immediately   7
              **Contact:**   Kelly T. Sloan   12

ST. PAUL, MN, May 15, ----. St. Paul police and firefighters will fly the   27
red, white, and blue to promote "Buckle-Up America" Week starting Mon-   41
day.   43

Red, white, and blue ribbons will be attached to the antennas of   55
police and fire vehicles as visible and colorful reminders for motorists to   71
use their seat belts and not to drink and drive.   81

Police Chief Sally Rost said the reminders are critical as the sum-   94
mer travel season begins. She said the campaign will "encourage motor-   108
ists to drive responsibly and safely." Fire Chief David Ungarean believes   123
the ribbons will remind high school students to drive and act safely and   139
to avoid alcohol, especially during the period of proms and graduation   152
celebrations.   155

This is the fourth annual ribbon campaign to support the "Buckle-   168
Up America" program that is designed to increase safety belt use to more   183
than 80 percent and to reduce alcohol-related fatalities by 50 percent in   197
the next two years.   201

###   202

CRESTWOOD NEIGHBORHOOD YARD SALE   7

May 15, ----, Meeting   11

Janet Duffy's Residence: 4422 Crestwood St.   20

1. Call to Order ............................... Janet Duffy   33
2. Approval of April Minutes .................. Harry McClintock   46
3. Treasurer's Report ........................ Sherri Ribnicky   59
4. Organizing Committee Report ................ Quentin Riccio   72
5. Publicity Committee Report ............. Michelle Drummond   85
6. Safety Committee Report .................... Donald Barnes   98
7. Sign Committee Report ..................... Sam Waskaskie   111
8. Unfinished Business ........................ Janet Duffy   124
9. New Business .............................. Janet Duffy   137
10. Next Meeting and Adjournment ............ Janet Duffy   150

## 4E • 10
## Speed Building: Words

1. Key each line once SS; DS below line 3.
2. Key each line again at a faster pace; QS (4 hard returns) at end of drill.

**PRACTICE cues:**
Key the first word of each pair at an easy speed: rekey it at a faster speed. Think and say each word; key it with quick-snap strokes.

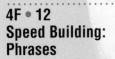
Fingers curved

**Goal: to speed up the combining of letters**

```
1 is is|if if|ah ah|he he|el el|irk irk|aid aid|aide
2 as as|ask ask|ad ad|had had|re re|ire ire|are hare
3 if if|fir fir|id id|did did|el el|eel eel|jak jaks
                                                    QS
```

## 4F • 12
## Speed Building: Phrases

1. Key each line once SS.
2. Key the lines once more to improve your speed.

**PRACTICE cues:**
Speed up the second keying of each phrase: space quickly between words and phrases.

Space with right thumb

Use down-and-in motion

**Goal: to speed up spacing between words**

```
1 ah ha|ah ha|if he|if he|as if|as if|as he|as he is
2 if a|if a|a fir|a fir|a jar|a jar|irk her|irks her
3 he did|he did|if all|if all|if she led|if she fled
4 a lad|a lad|if her|if her|as his aide|as his aides
```

**R&e**

1. Key the drill once SS at an easy pace to gain control of all your reach-stroke motions. DS between 2-line groups.
2. Key the drill again to speed up your motions and build continuity (keeping the cursor or print point moving steadily across the screen or paper).

reach review
```
1 hj ed ik rf jh de ki fr jhj ded kik frf hj ed ik ;
2 he if fir sir she jar rid ask led kid his did risk
```

h/e
```
3 he el she elf her led had held desk dash jade fled
4 her dad led; a lad fled; he has jade; she had eel;
```

i/r
```
5 is his kid ski fir rid ire die slid kids fife dike
6 a kid led; she is fair; as her aide; he is a risk;
```

all keys learned
```
7 if he is; as she fled; risk a lead; has a red sled
8 a jade fish; ask if she slid; she has asked a kid;
```

all keys learned
```
9 as if he did; he asked a lad; his aide has a sled;
10 he has a sled; if she has a jar; see if he is here
```

**Table 3**

Process the table at the right. Calculate the cycling and jogging miles for each week.

| HENRY LUCAK'S EXERCISE LOG | | | | | | |
|---|---|---|---|---|---|---|
| Week | Cycling Miles | | | Jogging Miles | | |
| | Day 1 | Day 2 | Total | Day 1 | Day 2 | Total |
| 1 | 10 | 15 | | 5 | 4 | |
| 2 | 8 | 15 | | 7 | 3 | |
| 3 | 15 | 10 | | 6 | 6 | |
| 4 | 0 | 12 | | 4 | 5 | |
| 5 | 12 | 12 | | 6 | 6 | |
| 6 | 11 | 13 | | 5 | 5 | |
| 7 | 7 | 0 | | 0 | 3 | |
| 8 | 5 | 5 | | 4 | 5 | |
| 9 | 10 | 10 | | 5 | 6 | |
| 10 | 14 | 18 | | 7 | 8 | |

**Table 4**

Process the table at the right. Calculate the average quiz scores by class in Row 6 and by quiz in Column G. Round averages to 2 decimal places.

| PHYSICS QUIZ SCORE REPORT | | | | | |
|---|---|---|---|---|---|
| Class | quiz 1 | Quiz 2 | Quiz 3 | Quiz 4 | Qiuz 5 |
| Period 2 | 9.3 | 8.5 | 8.7 | 8.5 | 27.3 |
| Period 4 | 10.5 | 9.4 | 9.6 | 18.8 | 27.9 |
| period 7 | 9.2 | 8.6 | 9.4 | 8.2 | 28.1 |

# LESSON 221 Assess Keyboarding and Special Document Skills

**Objectives:**

1. To demonstrate ability to format and key a news release, an agenda and an itinerary.
2. To demonstrate straight-copy skill.

## 221A • 5 Conditioning Practice

each line twice

alphabet 1 Zelda will judge quickly and pay them for excellent book reviews.

speed 2 The official paid the men for the handiwork they did on the dock.

fig/sym 3 A loan (3270-56) was made on 5/14/97 for $68,000 at a rate of 7%.

gwam 1' | 1 | 2 | 3 | 4 | 5 | 6 | 7 | 8 | 9 | 10 | 11 | 12 | 13 |

# LESSON 5

## New Keys: O and T

**Objectives:**

1. To learn reach technique for **O** and **T**.
2. To combine smoothly **O** and **T** with all other learned keys.

### 5A • 8
### Conditioning Practice

each line twice SS (slowly, then faster); DS between 2-line groups

In Lessons 5-10, the time for the *Conditioning Practice* is changed to 8'. During this time, you are to arrange your work area, prepare your equipment for keying, and practice the lines of the *Conditioning Practice* as directed.

Fingers curved                Fingers upright

home row 1 a sad fall; had a hall; a jak falls; as a fall ad;

3d row 2 if her aid; all he sees; he irks her; a jade fish;

all keys learned 3 as he fell; he sells fir desks; she had half a jar

### 5B • 20
### New Keys: O and T

each line twice SS (slowly, then faster); DS between 2-line groups; if time permits, key lines 7-9 again

**o** *Right ring* finger

**t** *Left index* finger

Follow the *Standard Plan for Learning New Keys* outlined on p. 17.

**Learn o**

1 l l ol ol do do of of so so lo lo old old for fore

2 ol ol of of or or for for oak oak off off sol sole

3 do so; a doe; of old; of oak; old foe; of old oak;

**Learn t**

4 f f tf tf it it at at tie tie the the fit fit lift

5 tf tf ft ft it it sit sit fit fit hit hit kit kite

6 if it; a fit; it fit; tie it; the fit; at the site

**Combine o and t**

7 to to|too too|toe toe|dot dot|lot lot|hot hot|tort

8 a lot; to jot; too hot; odd lot; a fort; for a lot

9 of the; to rot; dot it; the lot; for the; for this

## Assess Table Skills

**Objectives:**

**1.** To demonstrate ability to prepare tables.

**2.** To demonstrate ability to key from rough-draft and script copy.

### 220A • 5
### Conditioning Practice

each line twice

| | | |
|---|---|---|
| alphabet | 1 | Mary Jane quickly realized that the beautiful gown was expensive. |
| speed | 2 | When I visit the man in a wheelchair, we may go to the town mall. |
| figures | 3 | After a 45-minute delay, Tour 8374 left from Gate 26 at 1:09 p.m. |

gwam  1' | 1 | 2 | 3 | 4 | 5 | 6 | 7 | 8 | 9 | 10 | 11 | 12 | 13 |

### 220B • 45
### Table Skills

Format and key as many of the tables as you can in the time permitted. Key them in the order they are given on this and the next page. Center each table horizontally and vertically. You decide column spacing for each table.

### Table 1

Process the table at the right. Calculate the quarterly totals in Row 8.

| INVESTMENT PORTFOLIO | | | | |
|---|---|---|---|---|
| Investment | 1st Quarter | 2d Quarter | 3d Quarter | 4th Quarter |
| Galaxy Asset | $5,025 | $4,987 | $4,956 | $5,250 |
| Franklin Bonds | $10,678 | $10,890 | $11,110 | $11,335 |
| Invest Tax Free | $8,734 | $8,865 | $9,002 | $9,160 |
| Muny Bonds | $14,592 | $14,890 | $15,127 | $15,397 |
| Money Growth | $12,457 | $12,850 | $13,435 | $13,879 |
| Totals | | | | |

### Table 2

Process the table at the right. Calculate the column averages for this year and last year in Row 5 and the percent of change for Rows 3-5 in Column D. Use 2 decimal places in all calculations; express numbers in Column D as percents.

| SPECIAL EVENT ATTENDANCE REPORT | | | |
|---|---|---|---|
| Special Event | This Year | Last Year | % Change |
| Homecoming | 3,508 | 3,476 | |
| Parents' Night | 3,923 | 3,845 | |
| Average | | | |

## 5C • 22
## New-Key Mastery

1. Key the lines once SS; DS between 2-line groups.
2. Key the lines again at a faster pace.

### Technique goals
- curved, upright fingers
- wrists low, but not resting
- down-and-in spacing
- eyes on copy as you key

**PRACTICE *cue*:**

In lines of repeated words (lines 3, 5, and 7), speed up the second keying of each word.

reach review
1 hj ed ik rf ol tf jh de ki fr lo ft hj ed ol rf tf
2 is led fro hit old fit let kit rod kid dot jak sit

h/e
3 he he|she she|led led|had had|see see|has has|seek
4 he led|ask her|she held|has fled|had jade|he leads

i/t
5 it it|fit fit|tie tie|sit sit|kit kit|its its|fits
6 a kit|a fit|a tie|lit it|it fits|it sits|it is fit

o/r
7 or or|for for|ore ore|fro fro|oar oar|roe roe|rode
8 a rod|a door|a rose|or for|her or|he rode|or a rod

space bar
9 of he or it is to if do el odd off too for she the
10 it is|if it|do so|if he|to do|or the|she is|of all

all keys learned
11 if she is; ask a lad; to the lake; off the old jet
12 he or she; for a fit; if she left the; a jak salad

## R&e

1. Key the drill once SS at an easy pace to gain control of all your reach-stroke motions. DS between 2-line groups.
2. Key the drill again to speed up your motions and build continuity (keeping the cursor or print point moving steadily across the screen or paper).

reach review
1 hj ed ik rf jhj ded kik frf a;sldkfj a;sldkfj fja;
2 if led ski fir she ire sir jak has did jar kid rid

o/t
3 ol ol|old old|for for|oak oak|ode ode|doe doe|does
4 tf tf|it it|to to|kit kit|the the|fit fit|sit sits

i/r
5 ik ik|if if|it it|fir fir|ski ski|did did|kid kids
6 rf rf|or or|for for|her her|fir fir|rod rod|or for

h/e
7 hj hj|he he|ah ah|ha ha|he he|she she|ash ash|hash
8 ed ed|el el|he he|her her|elk elk|jet jet|she|shed

all keys learned
9 of hot kit old sit for jet she oak jar ore lid lot
10 a ski; old oak; too hot; odd jar; for the; old jet

all keys learned
11 she is to ski; is for the lad; ask if she has jade
12 he sold leeks to her; she sells jade at their lake

In addition to housing offices for many physicians, the Marshall Family Health Center will provide radiology, diagnostic testing, speech and language therapy, and dialysis services.

## Have a Sporting Good Time

Valley Hospital's Ninth Annual Auction will be held at the Renaissance Hotel on February 15. The theme for this year's event is "Have a sporting good time." ~~It~~ The auction is intended to be a celebration of sports in the Valley area and should raise close to $75,000 for scholarships. The legendary former

football coach, Jim Penn, will be honored.

An outstanding reception is planned for 6 p.m. A silent auction will be conducted from 6-11 p.m. Dinner will be served at 7:30 p.m., and a live auction will begin at 9:30 p.m.

Individual tickets are *spell* priced at $65; tables of (10) can be reserved for $595. Black tie or elegant attire is appropriate dress.

Donations for the auction should be given to Ms. Debbie Hershey in Public Relations. Persons submitting items before January 31 will be recognized in the auction program.

## How Much Fat to Eat

Many nutritionists *state* ~~believe~~ that a healthy diet averages no more than:

- 30% of calories from fat
- 300 mg of cholesterol daily
- 2,400 mg of sodium daily

To determine the *maximum* number of fat grams you should eat each day, use this easy formula:

$$\frac{\text{Desired calories} \times .3}{9}$$

The answer you get is the ~~maximum~~ fat grams you should consume each day. For example, if you want to consume 1,800 calories a day, your fat grams should not exceed 60:

$$\frac{1,800 \times .3}{9} = 60$$

# LESSON 6

## New Keys: N and G

**Objectives:**
1. To learn reach technique for **N** and **G**.
2. To combine smoothly **N** and **G** with all other learned keys.

### 6A • 8
### Conditioning Practice

each line twice SS (slowly, then faster); DS between 2-line groups

home row 1 `has a jak; ask a lad; a fall fad; had a jak salad;`

o/t 2 `to do it; as a tot; do a lot; it is hot; to dot it`

e/i/r 3 `is a kid; it is far; a red jar; her skis; her aide`

### 6B • 20
### New Keys: N and G

each line twice SS (slowly, then faster); DS between 2-line groups; if time permits, key lines 7-9 again

**n** *Right index* finger

**g** *Left index* finger

Follow the *Standard Plan for Learning New Keys* outlined on p. 17.

**Learn n**

1 `j j nj nj an an and and end end ant ant land lands`

2 `nj nj an an en en in in on on end end and and hand`

3 `an en; an end; an ant; no end; on land; a fine end`

**Learn g**

4 `f f gf gf go go fog fog got got fig figs jogs jogs`

5 `gf gf go go got got dig dig jog jog logs logs golf`

6 `to go; he got; to jog; to jig; the fog; is to golf`

**Combine n and g**

7 `go go|no no|nag nag|ago ago|gin gin|gone gone|long`

8 `go on; a nag; sign in; no gain; long ago; into fog`

9 `a fine gig; log in soon; a good sign; lend a hand;`

### 6C • 5
### Technique: Return

each line twice SS; DS between 2-line groups

**PRACTICE** *cue:*
Keep up your pace to end of line, return quickly, and start new line without pause.

1 `she is gone;`

2 `she got an old dog;`

3 `she jogs in a dense fog;`

4 `she and he go to golf at nine;`

5 `he is a hand on a rig in the north;`

Reach out and tap **Enter**

# Assess Report Skills

**Objectives:**
1. To demonstrate ability to prepare a report in newspaper format.
2. To demonstrate ability to decide formatting features and to use graphics.

**219A • 5**
**Conditioning Practice**

each line twice

alphabet 1 Major Quanz will get the five packs by the boxes on the new desk.

speed 2 The eight men with the problems may wish to see the tax official.

fig/sym 3 Invoice #647 for $2,958.40 was sent to J&L Trade, Inc. on May 13.

gwam 1' | 1 | 2 | 3 | 4 | 5 | 6 | 7 | 8 | 9 | 10 | 11 | 12 | 13 |

**219B • 45**
**Report Skills**

1. Key the text below and on p. 525 in 3-column newspaper format. Key as much as you can in the time permitted.

2. Use 1" margins, SS, hyphenation, and full justification.

3. Center the name of the newsletter over all three columns using 24-pt. font size.

4. Use 16-pt. font size for article headings, and shade the text boxes.

5. You decide all other formatting features.

## THE VALLEY UPDATE

### VALLEY HOSPITAL

Vol. 8, No. 4      Fall, ----

### Family Health Center For Marshall Township

The board of directors announced that it plans to construct a Family Health Center in Marshall Township within the coming year. Valley Hospital has

purchased 10 *spell* acres of land on Route 322 just north of Marshall Plaza, and construction of the three-story *Health Center* building is scheduled to begin within 6 *spell* weeks.

> **Valley Hospital comes to Marshall Township.**

Mrs. Maria Abraham, president of the board, stated, "The Marshall Township facility provides convenient access to a range

of medical services frequently needed by thousands of Marshall Township residents."

Since the Health Center is an extension of Valley Hospital, it gives customers the added benefit of hospital support systems. Test results, for instance, are automatically entered into the hospitals medical data bank to ensure that physicians have *rapid* access to *each patient's* your test history.

(continued on next page)

## 6D • 17
### New-Key Mastery

1. Key the lines once SS; DS between 2-line groups.
2. Key the lines again at a faster pace.

**Technique goals**
- curved, upright fingers
- wrists low, but not resting
- quick-snap keystrokes
- down-and-in spacing
- eyes on copy as you key

reach review

1 a;sldkfj ed ol rf hj tf nj gf lo de jh ft nj fr a;
2 he jogs; an old ski; do a log for; she left a jar;

n/g

3 an an|go go|in in|dig dig|and and|got got|end ends
4 go to; is an; log on; sign it; and golf; fine figs

space bar

5 if if|an an|go go|of of|or or|he he|it it|is is|do
6 if it is|is to go|he or she|to do this|of the sign

all keys learned

7 she had an old oak desk; a jell jar is at the side
8 he has left for the lake; she goes there at eight;

all keys learned

9 she said he did it for her; he is to take the oars
10 sign the list on the desk; go right to the old jet

---

### R&e

each line twice SS; DS between 2-line groups; QS after each grouping

**lines 1-3**
curved, upright fingers; steady, easy pace

**Reach review**

1 nj nj gf gf ol ol tf tf ik ik rf rf hj hj ed ed fj
2 go fog an and got end jog ant dog ken fig fin find
3 go an on and lag jog flag land glad lend sign hand

**Spacing**

**lines 4-7**
space immediately after each word; down-and-in motion of thumb

4 if an it go is of do or to as in so no off too gin
5 ah ha he or if an too for and she jog got hen then
6 he is to go|if it is so|is to do it|if he is to go
7 she is to ski on the lake; he is also at the lake;

**Returning**

**lines 8-12**
maintain pace to end of line; return quickly and start new line immediately

8 he is to go;
9 she is at an inn;
10 he goes to ski at one;
11 he is also to sign the log;
12 she left the log on the old desk

**Keying short words and phrases**

**lines 13-16**
speed up the second keying of each repeated word or phrase; think words

13 do do|it it|an an|is is|of of|to to|if if|or or or
14 he he|go go|in in|so so|at at|no no|as as|ha ha ha
15 to do|to do|it is|it is|of it|of it|is to|is to do
16 she is to do so; he did the sign; ski at the lake;

## Document 2
### Letter

Prepare the text at right as a modified block with ¶ indention; mixed punctuation; 14-pt. font; full justification; envelope with POSTNET bar code below address. Create an appropriately sized replica of the following letterhead to use on all letters in this lesson.

```
┌─────────────────────┐
│      Bank Mart      │
│   330 W. First St.  │
│     Dayton, OH      │
│     45402-2269      │
└─────────────────────┘
```

## Document 3
### Letter Merge

1. Use the information below to prepare a data file, using USPS address style:

| | |
|---|---|
| Name: | Mr. Luke Nanasi |
| St: | 100 Parkview Dr. |
| City: | Dayton |
| State: | OH |
| ZIP: | 45309-6592 |
| Sal: | Mr. Nanasi |

| | |
|---|---|
| Name: | Miss Donna Kardaz |
| St: | 7470 Miller Ln. |
| City: | Dayton |
| State: | OH |
| ZIP: | 45414-5571 |
| Sal: | Miss Kardaz |

| | |
|---|---|
| Name: | Ms. Joanne Teck |
| St: | 1702 Clara St. |
| City: | Columbus |
| State: | OH |
| ZIP: | 43211-1700 |
| Sal: | Ms. Teck |

2. Save file as CARDDATA.
3. Key the form file at the right in block letter format with open punctuation.
4. Save file as CARDFORM.
5. Merge CARDDATA and CARDFORM. Save the merged file as CARDDOCS.

---

(Current date)  Dr. Fouad A. Siha  212 Seventh St.  Bangor, ME 04401- 4447    Dear Dr. Siha:    13 / 17

Thank you for conducting the "Actuarial Forecasts" seminar for the administrative support staff at Bank Mart last week.    31 / 42

I have reviewed the enclosed results of the evaluation completed by the participants. Without exception, the participants ranked each of your topics as relevant to their needs. The topic pertaining to probability received the highest ranking.    55 / 70 / 85 / 91

You should also know that almost all participants rated your presentation style and materials as very good or excellent. Most of the staff involved stated they wanted you back for another seminar.    105 / 119 / 131

Sincerely,  Ms. Susan L. Delpiore  Training and Development Enclosure  c Mr. L. James Walter,  Vice President, Operations    143 / 155

---

words

(Current date)

<Name>
<Street>
<City> <State> <ZIP>

Dear <Salutation>    opening (ave.) 17

Your Instant Access electronic banking card was found in the automatic teller at Bank Mart's Harshman Road branch. Your card was not returned because it was damaged while being used.    31 / 46 / 54

Since the card will not operate an automatic teller anymore, it must be replaced. We have ordered a new card, and you will receive it in the mail within one week.    69 / 84 / 87

You will be able to use this convenient form of banking again as soon as you receive your replacement card.    102 / 109

Sincerely    111

Miss Trudi A. Pitts    115
Branch Manager    118
closing 119

# LESSON 7

## New Keys: Left Shift and Period (.)

**Objectives:**

1. To learn reach technique for **Left Shift** and . (period).
2. To combine smoothly **Left Shift** and . (period) with all other learned keys.

Finger-action
keystrokes

Down-and-in
spacing

Quick out-and-
tap return

### 7A • 8
### Conditioning Practice

each line twice SS (slowly,
then faster); DS between
2-line groups

reach review **1** ed ik rf ol gf hj tf nj de ki fr lo fg jh ft jn a;

space bar **2** or is to if an of el so it go id he do as in at on

all keys learned **3** he is; if an; or do; to go; a jak; an oak; of all;

### 7B • 20
### New Keys: Left Shift and . (Period)

each line twice SS (slowly,
then faster); DS between
2-line groups; if time
permits, rekey lines 7-9

**Left Shift** *Left little* finger

**.** (period) *Right ring* finger

**SPACING** *cue:*

Space once after . following abbreviations and initials. Do not space after . within abbreviations. Space twice after . at end of a sentence except at line endings. There, return without spacing.

**SHIFTING** *cue:*

Shift, strike key, and release both in a quick 1-2-3 count.

**Learn Left Shift key**

**1** a a Ja Ja Ka Ka La La Hal Hal Kal Kal Jae Jae Lana

**2** Kal rode; Kae did it; Hans has jade; Jan ate a fig

**3** I see that Jake is to aid Kae at the Oak Lake sale

**Learn . (period)**

**4** l l .l .l fl. fl. ed. ed. ft. ft. rd. rd. hr. hrs.

**5** .l .l fl. fl. hr. hr. e.g. e.g. i.e. i.e. in. ins.

**6** fl. ft. hr. ed. rd. rt. off. fed. ord. alt. asstd.

**Combine Left Shift and . (period)**

**7** I do.  Ian is.  Ola did.  Jan does.  Kent is gone.

**8** Hal did it.  I shall do it.  Kate left on a train.

**9** J. L. Han skis on Oak Lake; Lt. Haig also does so.

## LESSON 218

## Assess Keyboarding and Correspondence Skills

**Objectives:**

1. To demonstrate straight-copy skills.
2. To demonstrate ability to prepare letters and memos, including a letter merge.

---

**218A • 5**
**Conditioning Practice**

each line twice; take
1' writings on line 2 as
time permits

| | | |
|---|---|---|
| alphabet | 1 | Freda enjoyed checking the tax problems in the law quiz she gave. |
| speed | 2 | They may go to the social held at the giant chapel on the island. |
| figures | 3 | Out of 647 seniors and 893 juniors, 1,250 attended the last prom. |

**gwam** 1' | 1 | 2 | 3 | 4 | 5 | 6 | 7 | 8 | 9 | 10 | 11 | 12 | 13 |

---

**218B • 15**
**Straight-Copy Skills**

1. Key two 5' writings on the ¶s in 221C, p. 529.

2. Find *gwam* and number of errors in each writing.

3. Record the better score.

---

**218C • 30**
**Correspondence Skills**

**Time Schedule**

Plan and prepare .............3'
Timed production ...........20'
Proofread/compute
  *n-pram* .........................7'

**Document 1**
**Memo**

Prepare a memo in standard format. Since this memo is going to be faxed, use a 14-pt. font. Supply needed memo parts; use current date.

1. Format and key the letters and memos on this and the next page. Key as many as you can in 20'.

2. Compute *n-pram: n-pram* = words keyed - (15 x errors) divided by 20.

Turn in your work arranged in document number order.

| | words |
|---|---|
| TO: Olu T. Sangoeyhi, Physical Therapy | 8 |
| FROM: William M. Gause, Administrative Services | 18 |
| SUBJECT: PHYSICAL THERAPY PAMPHLET | 30 |

Here is the first draft of the physical therapy pamphlet that has been authorized for publication in this year's budget. Please check the copy very carefully and make sure the pictures are correct. — 44 / 58 / 70

Public relations is in the process of getting permission to use each person's picture in the pamphlet. All permission forms should be completed within the next ten days. If there are any changes in the pictures we are using, I will see that you get to review the changes. — 85 / 100 / 115 / 125

Please make the necessary changes in the copy and return the pamphlet to me by next Monday. — 139 / 143

closing 146

## 7C • 17
### New-Key Mastery

1. Key the lines once SS; DS between 2-line groups.
2. Key the lines again at a faster pace.

**Technique goals**

- curved, upright fingers
- finger-action keystrokes
- quiet hands/arms
- out-and-down shifting

**TECHNIQUE cue:**
Eyes on copy except when you lose your place.

*abbrev./initials*

1 He said ft. for feet; rd. for road; fl. for floor.
2 Lt. Hahn let L. K. take the old gong to Lake Neil.

*3d row emphasis*

3 Lars is to ask at the old store for a kite for Jo.
4 Ike said he is to take the old road to Lake Heidi.

*key words*

5 a an or he to if do it of so is go for got old led
6 go the off aid dot end jar she fit oak and had rod

*key phrases*

7 if so|it is|to do|if it|do so|to go|he is|to do it
8 to the|and do|is the|got it|if the|for the|ask for

*all letters learned*

9 Ned asked her to send the log to an old ski lodge.
10 J. L. lost one of the sleds he took off the train.

## 7D • 5
### Technique:  Space Bar and Return

1. Key each line once SS; DS at end of line 7.
2. Key the drill again at a faster pace if time permits.

**SPACING cue:**
Quickly strike **Space Bar** *immediately* after last letter in the word.

1 Jan is to sing.
2 Karl is at the lake.
3 Lena is to send the disk.
4 Lars is to jog to the old inn.
5 Hanna took the girls to a ski lake.
6 Hal is to take the old list to his desk.
7 Lana is to take the jar to the store at nine.

Return and start each new line quickly.

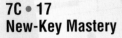

1. Key each line once SS; DS between 3-line groups.
2. Rekey the drill at a faster pace if time permits.

**PRACTICE cue:**
In lines 4-7, keep cursor or print point moving steadily—no stops or pauses within the line.

**Spacing/Shifting**

1 K. L. Jakes is to see Lt. Hahn at Oak Lake at one.
2 Janet Harkins sent the sales sheet to Joel Hansen.
3 Karla Kent is to go to London to see Laska Jolson.

**Keying easy sentences**

4 Kae is to go to the lake to fish off an old skiff.
5 Joel is to ask his good friend to go to the shore.
6 Lara and her dad took eight girls for a long hike.
7 Kent said his dad is to sell the oak and ash logs.

# Skill Builder

## Skill Check

1. Key three 1' writings on each ¶; find *gwam*. Count errors. If errors are 2 or fewer on any writing, goal is to increase speed by 1 or 2 words on next writing. If errors on any writing are more than 2, goal is control on next writing.
2. Key two 3' writings on ¶s 1-3 combined; find *gwam* and count errors.
3. Key a 5' writing on ¶s 1-3 combined; find *gwam* and count errors.

all letters used

| | gwam | 3' | 5' |
|---|---|---|---|
| You are nearing the end of your keyboarding classes. The | 4 | 2 | 53 |
| skill level you have attained is much better than that with which | 8 | 5 | 55 |
| you started when you were given keyboarding instruction for the | 13 | 8 | 58 |
| very first time. During the early phase of your training, you were | 17 | 10 | 61 |
| taught to key the letters of the alphabet and the figures by touch. | 22 | 13 | 64 |
| During the initial period of learning, the primary emphasis was | 26 | 16 | 66 |
| placed on your keying technique. | 28 | 17 | 67 |
| After learning to key the alphabet and figures, your next | 32 | 19 | 70 |
| job was to learn to format documents. The various types of | 36 | 22 | 72 |
| documents formatted included letters, tables, and manuscripts. | 40 | 24 | 75 |
| During this time of training, an emphasis also was placed on | 44 | 27 | 77 |
| increasing the rate at which you were able to key. Parts of the | 49 | 29 | 80 |
| lessons keyed at this time also were used to help you recognize the | 53 | 32 | 82 |
| value of and to improve language skills. | 56 | 34 | 84 |
| The final phase of your training dealt with increasing your | 60 | 36 | 86 |
| skill at producing documents of high quality at a rapid rate. | 64 | 38 | 89 |
| Directions were provided for keying special documents; drills | 68 | 41 | 91 |
| were given to build skill; and problems were provided to assess | 72 | 43 | 94 |
| your progress. You were also given a number of simulations to | 77 | 46 | 96 |
| allow you to apply what you had learned. Now you have a skill | 81 | 49 | 99 |
| that you will be able to use throughout your life. | 84 | 51 | 101 |

gwam  3' | 1 | 2 | 3 | 4 |
5' | 1 | 2 | 3 |

## LESSON 8 | Review

**Objectives:**
1. To improve use of **Space Bar, Left Shift key,** and **Enter**.
2. To improve keying speed on words, phrases, and sentences.

### 8A • 8
### Conditioning Practice

each line twice SS (slowly, then faster); DS between 2-line groups; if time permits, practice each line again

Space once.

reach review    1   ik rf ol ed nj gf hj tf .1 ft. i.e. e.g. rt. J. L.

spacing    2   a an go is or to if he and got the for led kit lot

left shift    3   I got it.  Hal has it.  Jan led Nan.  Kae is gone.

### 8B • 8
### Keyboard Mastery

each line once SS; DS between 2-line groups; QS at end of drill

**Technique goals**
- curved, upright fingers
- low wrists, but not resting
- quick-snap keystrokes
- finger reaches; hands and arms steady

h/e    1   hj ed jhj ded ha el he she led had eke hal ale die

2   Heidi had a good lead at the end of the first set.
                  DS

i/r    3   ik rf kik frf is or sir ire ore his risk fire ride

4   Kier is taking a high risk if he rides that horse.
                  DS

o/t    5   ol tf lol ftf so it of too oft hot toe lot the old

6   Ola has lost the list she took to that food store.
                  DS

n/g    7   nj gf jnj fgf go an got and nag gin hang gone sign

8   Lang and she are going to sing nine songs at noon.
                  DS

left shift/.    9   Oak Lake; N. J. Karis; Lt. L. J. Oates; Lara Nador

10   J. K. Larkin is going to Idaho to see Linda Jakes.
                  QS

### 8C • 4
### Technique: Return

each line once SS; DS between 2-line groups

**RETURN** *cue:*
Keep up your pace to the end of the line; return *immediately;* start the new line without pausing.

1 Nan has gone to ski;

2 she took a train at nine.

3 Janet asked for the disk;

4 she is to take it to the lake.

5 Karl said he left at the lake

6 a file that has the data she needs.

7 Nadia said she felt ill as the ski

8 lift left to take the girls to the hill.

> Keep eyes on copy as you return.

## 215C • 20
### Functional Resume: Qualifications

1. From the job qualifications (or personal attributes) given at right, select three or more attributes that describe you and that are supported by your work and/or school activities.
2. Draft a functional resume using these attributes and the supporting activities. On the model (p. 519) these three qualifications appear: Interpersonal Skills, Organizational Skills, and Computer Skills.
3. Retain your work for use in Lessons 216-217.

**Attributes:**

| | |
|---|---|
| Accurate | Honest |
| Ambitious | Logical |
| Clear-thinking | Motivated |
| Confident | Organized |
| Cooperative | Reliable |
| Creative | Resourceful |
| Efficient | Responsible |
| Flexible | Teachable |

## LESSONS 216-217

## Employment Documents

**Objectives:**

1. To prepare a functional resume for yourself.
2. To process a letter of application.
3. To complete an employment application form.
4. To compose an interview follow-up letter.

### 216-217A • 5 (daily)
### Conditioning Practice

each line twice

| | | |
|---|---|---|
| alphabet | 1 | Cody acquired six new blue jackets to give as prizes to freshmen. |
| speed | 2 | Turn down the lane by the lake to see them work in the cornfield. |
| figures | 3 | Lori served 439 hot dogs, 528 donuts, and 1,067 drinks yesterday. |

**gwam** 1' | 1 | 2 | 3 | 4 | 5 | 6 | 7 | 8 | 9 | 10 | 11 | 12 | 13 |

### 216-217B • 45 (daily)
### Processing Employment Documents

Review the document guidelines for letters of application, job application forms, and follow-up letters on pp. 517 and 518 before completing the activities at the right.

Your teacher encourages you to apply for the job at the right or one that you find advertised.

1. **Resume.** Using the draft from 215C, prepare a functional resume that you will submit with other employment documents for the position at the right or one that you find advertised.
2. **Letter of application.** Compose at the keyboard your application letter for the position for which you are applying. Proofread your letter, revise as needed, and process a final copy.
3. **Employment application form** (stationery pack or supplied by your teacher). Review the application form to identify the information you need to complete it. Complete the application form by keying (or neatly printing) the information on the form.
4. **Follow-up letter.** Assume that you have been interviewed for the position for which you are applying. Include in the letter a statement that indicates you can operate the computer software that is required for the position (at right)—or a similar detail for the job you chose.

---

### CUSTOMER SERVICE REPRESENTATIVE

Baxter's Office Depot has an opening for a service-oriented person to perform account transactions and respond to customer inquiries, complaints, and requests for refunds, exchanges, and adjustments.

Must have data-entry, keyboarding, and computer software skills.

Send application letter and resume to

Ms. Jackie Dragan
Baxter's Office Depot
2735 Sheraton Dr.
Macon, GA 31204-2481

*An Equal Opportunity Employer*

## 8D • 10
## Technique: Space Bar and Left Shift

each line twice SS; DS between 2-line groups

**Goals**

- to reduce the pause between words
- to reduce the time taken to shift/strike key/release when making capital letters

Down-and-in spacing

Out-and-down shifting

## 8E • 20
## Speed Building

each line twice SS (slowly, then faster); DS between 2-line groups

Correct finger curvature

Correct finger alignment

Upright fingers

**Space Bar (Space *immediately* after each word.)**

```
1 if is an he go is or ah to of so it do el id la ti
2 an el|go to|if he|of it|is to|do the|for it|and so
3 if she is|it is the|all of it|go to the|for an oak
```

**Left Shift key (Shift; strike key; release both quickly.)**

```
4 Lt. Ho said he left the skiff at Ord Lake for her.
5 Jane or Hal is to go to Lake Head to see Kate Orr.
6 O. J. Halak is to ask for her at Jahn Hall at one.
```

**Key words (*Think, say, and key the words.*)**

```
1 an the did oak she for off tie got and led jar all
2 go end air her dog his aid rid sit and fir ask jet
3 talk side jell gold fled sign stir fork high shall
```

**Key phrases (*Think, say, and key the phrases.*)**

```
4 to do|it is|of an|if he|is to|or do|to it|if he is
5 to aid|if she|he did|of the|to all|is for|is a tie
6 is to ask|is to aid|he or she|to rig it|if she did
```

**Key sentences (Strike keys at a brisk, steady pace.)**

```
7 Joan is to go to the lake to get her old red skis.
8 Les asked for a list of all the old gold she sold.
9 Laska said she left the old disk list on his desk.
```

# Douglas H. Ruckert
## 8503 Kirby Dr.
## Houston, TX 77054-8220
## (713) 196-0421

## SKILLS AND EXPERIENCE SUMMARY

Part-time employment and leadership positions in school activities that required me to work individually and as part of a team, manage resources, interact with and represent other people, interpret and communicate information, and use organization skills.

## EDUCATION

Will be graduated from Eisenhower Technical High School in June, ----, with a high school diploma, business technology emphasis.

| | |
|---|---|
| **INTERPERSONAL SKILLS** | ❐ Represented all business technology students as delegate to student council for two years. Worked as a member of a team on three committees to raise funds for computers, assist in preparation of student handbook, and prepare for parents' day. |
| | ❐ Served customers in culturally diverse area, oriented new part-time employees, and referred customer complaints in a restaurant. |
| **ORGANIZATION SKILLS** | ❐ Successfully managed personal schedule to attain honor-roll status for 12 grading periods, earned two varsity soccer letters, participated in school clubs, held office in one club, and worked an average of ten hours each week during the school year. |
| **COMPUTER EXPERIENCE** | ❐ Skilled in operating word processing, spreadsheet, database, and presentation software packages. Able to transfer knowledge of features from one software package to another. |

## EMPLOYMENT HISTORY

Hinton's Family Restaurant, Server (1997-present)
Tuma Lawn Service, Laborer (1995-1996)

## SCHOOL ACTIVITIES

Student Council, Business Technology Delegate (1997-present)
Business Technology Club, President (1998)

## REFERENCES (with Permission)

Ms. Anne D. Salgado, Student Council Advisor, Eisenhower Technical High School, 100 W. Cavalcade, Houston, TX 77009-2451, (713) 196-6634.

Mr. James R. Veloski, Manager, Hinton's Family Restaurant, 2204 S. Wayside Ave., Houston, TX 77023-8841, (713) 128-3482.

Mrs. Helen T. Landis, Owner, Landis Garden Supply, 10155 East Fwy., Houston, TX 77029-4419, (713) 175-3349.

**Functional Resume**

# LESSON 9

## New Keys: U and C

**Objectives:**

**1.** To learn reach technique for **U** and **C**.

**2.** To combine smoothly **U** and **C** with all other learned keys.

### 9A • 8
### Conditioning Practice

each line twice SS (slowly, then faster); DS between 2-line groups

| | |
|---|---|
| reach review | 1 nj gf ol rf ik ed .l tf hj fr ki ft jn de lo fg l. |
| space bar | 2 an do in so to go fan hen log gin tan son not sign |
| left shift | 3 Olga has the first slot; Jena is to skate for her. |

### 9B • 20
### New Keys: U and C

each line twice SS (slowly, then faster); DS between 2-line groups: if time permits, repeat lines 7-9

Follow the *Standard Plan for Learning New Keys* outlined on p. 17.

**u** *Right index* finger

**c** *Left middle* finger

**Learn u**

1 j j uj uj us us us jug jug jut jut due due fur fur

2 uj uj jug jug sue sue lug lug use use lug lug dues

3 a jug; due us; the fur; use it; a fur rug; is just

**Learn c**

4 d d cd cd cod cod cog cog tic tic cot cot can cans

5 cd cd cod cod ice ice can can code code dock docks

6 a cod; a cog; the ice; she can; the dock; the code

**Combine u and c**

7 cud cud cut cuts cur curs cue cues duck ducks clue

8 a cud; a cur; to cut; the cue; the cure; for luck;

9 use a clue; a fur coat; take the cue; cut the cake

Application Form

Follow-Up Letter

The last section (paragraph) should request an interview. Remember to provide information to make it easy for the prospective employer to contact you to arrange an interview.

For additional information about the application letter, see p. 323.

## Application Form

Many companies require an applicant to complete a standard application form even though a resume and application letter have been received. In some cases you will complete the application form at the company location. In these instances, follow the directions to print the information on the form.

In other cases you may take the form with you, complete it, and then return it. In these instances, the information should be keyed on the form, although hand printing is acceptable. Whether printed or keyed, the application form must be neat and accurate.

To lessen the chance of error on the application you submit, make a copy of the form to complete as a rough-draft copy.

For additional information about the job application form, see p. 323 and the models on p. 327.

## Follow-Up Letter

The follow-up letter should be an important part of your job search. It is a "thank you" for the time given and courtesies extended to you during your interview. This letter lets the interviewer know that you are still interested in the job, and it will remind him/her of your application. This letter should be sent soon after an interview (as early as the same or next day) to increase the likelihood that the interviewer will receive it before selecting a person for the position.

For additional information about writing follow-up letters, see p. 323 and p. 331.

# LESSON 215    Learn Functional Resume

**Objectives:**
1. To learn about the functional resume style.
2. To process a resume in functional style.

## 215A • 5
### Conditioning Practice

each line twice; then
1' writings on line 2 as time permits

| | | |
|---|---|---|
| alphabet | 1 | Vicki expects to query a dozen boys and girls for the major show. |
| speed | 2 | Pamela laid the authentic antique handiwork by the island shanty. |
| fig/sym | 3 | Ramon Jones & Company's fax number was changed to (385) 109-2647. |
| **gwam** | 1' | 1 \| 2 \| 3 \| 4 \| 5 \| 6 \| 7 \| 8 \| 9 \| 10 \| 11 \| 12 \| 13 \| |

## 215B • 25
### Functional Resume

1. Read the information on p. 517 about the functional resume and study the model on p. 519 before completing Step 2.

2. Format and key the functional resume from the model on p. 519.

## 9C • 17
### New-Key Mastery

1. Key the lines once SS; DS between 2-line groups.
2. Key the lines again at a faster pace.

*Technique goals*

- reach up without moving hands away from you
- reach down without moving hands toward your body
- use quick-snap key-strokes

3d/1st rows
1 in cut nut ran cue can cot fun hen car urn den cog
2 Nan is cute; he is curt; turn a cog; he can use it

left shift and .
3 Kae had taken a lead.  Jack then cut ahead of her.
4 I said to use Kan. for Kansas and Ore. for Oregon.

key words
5 and cue for jut end kit led old fit just golf coed
6 an due cut such fuss rich lack turn dock turf curl

key phrases
7 an urn|is due|to cut|for us|to use|cut off|such as
8 just in|code it|turn on|cure it|as such|is in luck

all keys learned
9 Nida is to get the ice; Jacki is to call for cola.
10 Ira is sure that he can go there in an hour or so.

## 9D • 5
### Technique: Space Bar and Left Shift

Key the lines once SS; DS between 3-line groups. Keep hand movement to a minimum.

space bar
1 Ken said he is to sign the list and take the disk.
2 It is right for her to take the lei if it is hers.
3 Jae has gone to see an old oaken desk at the sale.

left shift
4 He said to enter Oh. for Ohio and Kan. for Kansas.
5 It is said that Lt. Li has an old jet at Lake Ida.
6 L. N. is at the King Hotel; Harl is at the Leland.

1. Key each line once SS; DS between 2-line groups.
2. If time permits, key the lines again at a faster pace.

**PRACTICE** *cue:*
Try to reduce hand movement and the tendency of unused fingers to fly out or follow reaching finger.

u/c
1 uj cd uc juj dcd cud cut use cog cue urn curl luck
2 Huck can use the urn for the social at the church.

n/g
3 nj gf nj gin can jog nick sign nigh snug rung clog
4 Nan can jog to the large sign at the old lake gin.

all keys learned
5 nj gf uj cd ol tf ik rf hj ed an go or is to he 1.
6 Leona has gone to ski; Jack had left here at nine.

all keys learned
7 an or is to he go cue for and jak she all use curt
8 Nick sells jade rings; Jahn got one for good luck.

# Process Employment Documents

**Format Guides**

Functional Resume

Application Letter

## Employment Document Guidelines

Employment documents provide applicants an opportunity to present their best qualities to prospective employers. These qualities are represented by the content of the documents as well as by the format, neatness, and accuracy of the documents. The care with which you prepare your documents is a strong indication to a company of the highest level of performance it can expect from you; therefore, special attention should be given to preparation of employment documents.

In addition to a data sheet, or resume, common types of employment documents are an application letter; application form; and interview follow-up letter.

For additional information about employment documents, see p. 323.

## Functional Resume

Resumes, or data sheets, that present your experience and employment history in reverse chronological order were prepared in Lesson 134 (refer to pp. 323 and 324). This traditional resume should be used when your job history reflects a steady progression toward the position you are seeking.

If you are a first-time job seeker or if you can easily categorize your strengths, you should consider using a functional resume.

Functional resumes place emphasis on your experience, skills, and accomplishments rather than on the progression of

the jobs or leadership positions you have held. Functional resumes allow you to be selective—including only those skills, experiences, and accomplishments that relate to the position you are seeking.

Since the dates of school attendance and employment and school activities are important to many prospective employers, you should include this information on your functional resume without describing the responsibilities and duties of jobs or school activities.

Functional resumes also present personal information, education, and references and are formatted in the same manner as the chronological resumes prepared in Lesson 134. Review the data sheet format guides on p. 323 and the model of a functional resume on p. 519.

## Application Letter

The letter of application should include three sections. The first section (paragraph) may state something positive about the company, how you learned of the job opening, and the specific position for which you are applying.

The second section (one, two, or three paragraphs) provides evidence that you are qualified for the position. This is the place to interpret information you present in your resume and to show how your qualifications relate to the job for which you are applying and how your qualifications can benefit the employer. Be sure to focus on what you can do for the position or company and not on what the position or company can do for you.

# LESSON 10

## New Keys: W and Right Shift

**Objectives:**

**1.** To learn reach technique for **W** and **Right Shift**.

**2.** To combine smoothly **W** and **Right Shif**t with other learned keys.

---

### 10A • 8
### Conditioning Practice

each line twice SS (slowly, then faster); DS between 2-line groups

reach review — 1   a;sldkfj a;sldkfj uj cd ik rf nj ed hj tf ol gf .l

u/c — 2   us cod use cut sue cot jut cog nut cue con lug ice

all letters learned — 3   Hugh has just taken a lead in a race for a record.

---

### 10B • 20
### New Keys: W and Right Shift

each line twice SS (slowly, then faster); DS between 2-line groups; if time permits, repeat lines 7-9

**w** *Left ring* finger

**Right Shift** *Right little* finger

**SHIFTING cue:**
Shift, strike key, and release both in a quick 1-2-3 count.

Follow the *Standard Plan for Learning New Keys* outlined on p. 17.

#### Learn w

1   s s ws ws sow sow wow wow low low how how cow cows

2   sw sw ws ws ow ow now now row row own own tow tows

3   to sow; is how; so low; to own; too low; is to row

#### Learn Right Shift key

4   A; A; Al Al; Cal Cal; Ali or Flo; Di and Sol left.

5   Ali lost to Ron; Cal lost to Elsa; Di lost to Del.

6   Tina has left for Tucson; Dori can find her there.

#### Combine w and Right Shift

7   Dodi will ask if Willa went to Town Center at two.

8   Wilf left the show for which he won a Gower Award.

9   Walt will go to Rio on a golf tour with Wolf Lowe.

**Document 8**

Process the minutes at the right. You decide all formatting features.

words

SUMMARY MINUTES — 3
CURRICULUM PLANNING COUNCIL MEETING — 10
November 12, ---- — 14

Council members present:  All members were present. — 25

1.  Council Chair Michael Mariani called the meeting to order at 6:30 p.m. — 40

2.  Minutes of the October 11, ----, meeting were read and approved. — 54

3.  Council Facilitator Nancy Thayer explained the planning procedures the — 69
council would use at the meeting to identify external factors that are likely to — 85
affect the school's curriculum during the next five-year period.  She explained — 101
that the planning council members will: — 109

    A.  Spend ten minutes writing the external factors on small notepaper. — 123
       Council members will prepare their notes individually. — 135

    B.  Post their notes on the wall in the meeting room. — 146

    C.  Review all posted notes and group similar ones.  Members will — 160
       not talk to each other during this time. — 167

    D.  Discuss the groupings and attempt to name each group. — 179

    E.  Make additions, deletions, and revisions to the factors in each — 193
       group. — 194

4.  The planning council carried out the planning procedures and generated — 209
more than fifty external factors and grouped them into six categories.  The — 224
factors and categories will be processed and distributed to the council — 239
members prior to the next planning session.  At that session, revisions will be — 255
made before a final list is prepared. — 263

5.  The planning council adjourned at 8:30 p.m. — 272

# LESSON 214

# Special Documents:  Sustained Practice

**Objectives:**

**1.** To process special documents during sustained timing.

**2.** To improve ability to work under time pressure.

**214A • 5**
**Conditioning Practice**
each line twice

alphabet 1 Danny bought major equipment to vitalize work after the tax cuts.

speed 2 The busy maid bid for the ivory soap dish and antique ivory bowl.

figures 3 Call 192-7648 in 30-35 days to get the orders Sean has requested.

**gwam** 1' | 1 | 2 | 3 | 4 | 5 | 6 | 7 | 8 | 9 | 10 | 11 | 12 | 13 |

**214B • 45**
**Special Documents**

**Time Schedule**

Plan and prepare ............5'
Timed practice ...............30'
Proofread/compute
*n-pram* .......................10'

1.  Make a list of the documents to be processed:
   p. 512, 212-213B, Document 2
   p. 513, 212-213B, Document 4
   p. 514, 212-213B, Document 6
   p. 516, 212-213B, Document 8

2.  Arrange materials for easy access.  Process (in the order listed) as many of the special documents as you can.  Proofread and correct each document before beginning the next.

3.  After time is called, proofread the final document and, if needed, print all completed work.

4.  Identify uncorrected errors; compute *n-pram:*
*npram* = words keyed – (15 x errors) divided by 30.
Turn in work in order listed in Step 1.

## 10C • 17
### New-Key Mastery

1. Key the lines once SS; DS between 2-line groups.
2. Key the lines again at a faster pace.

**PRACTICE cues:**

Key at a steady pace; space quickly after each word; keep cursor or print point moving steadily.

**Goal: finger-action reaches; quiet hands and arms**

|   |   |
|---|---|
| w and right shift | 1 Dr. Rowe is in Tulsa now; Dr. Cowan will see Rolf.<br>2 Gwinn took the gown to Golda Swit on Downs Circle. |
| n/g | 3 to go\|go on\|no go\|an urn\|dug in\|and got\|and a sign<br>4 He is to sign for the urn to go on the high chest. |
| key words | 5 if ow us or go he an it of own did oak the cut jug<br>6 do all and for cog odd ant fig rug low cue row end |
| key phrases | 7 we did\|for a jar\|she is due\|cut the oak\|he owns it<br>8 all of us\|to own the\|she is to go\|when he has gone |
| all keys learned | 9 Jan and Chris are gone; Di and Nick get here soon.<br>10 Doug will work for her at the new store in Newton. |

## 10D • 5
### Technique: Spacing with Punctuation

each line once DS

**SPACING cues:**

Do not space after an internal period in an abbreviation; space once after each period following initials.

No space     Space once.

1 Use i.e. for that is; cs. for case; ck. for check.
2 Dr. Wong said to use wt. for weight; in. for inch.
3 R. D. Roth has used ed. for editor; Rt. for Route.
4 Wes said Ed Rowan got an Ed.D. degree last winter.

## R&e

1. Key each pair of lines once SS.
2. Key each even-numbered line again to increase speed.

**Technique goals**
- steady hands/arms
- finger-action keystrokes
- unused fingers curved, upright over home keys
- eyes on copy as you key

|   |   |
|---|---|
| u/c | 1 uj cd uc cut cut cue cue use use cod cod dock dock<br>2 Jud is to cut the corn near the dock for his aunt. |
| w and right shift | 3 Don and Willa\|Dot or Wilda\|R. W. Gowan\|Dr. Wilford<br>4 Dr. Wold will set the wrist of Sgt. Wills at noon. |
| left shift and . | 5 Jane or Harl\|Jae and Nan\|L. N. Hagel\|Lt. J. O. Hao<br>6 Lt. Hawser said that he will see us in New London. |
| n/g | 7 nj gf ng gun gun nag nag got got nor nor sign sign<br>8 Angie hung a huge sign in front of the union hall. |
| o/t | 9 ol tf to too dot dot not not toe toe got gild gild<br>10 Todd took the tool chest to the dock for a worker. |
| i/r | 11 ik rf or ore fir fir sir sir ire ire ice ice irons<br>12 Risa fired the fir log to heat rice for the girls. |
| h/e | 13 hj ed he the the hen hen when when then then their<br>14 He was with her when she chose her new snow shoes. |

Under unfinished business, President McClinton reported 143
that the 28th Annual Greenwood Science Fair will have more 155
than 150 exhibits from 5th through 12th graders. Awards 166
will be given to first-, second-, and third-place winners in 178
each grade level. In addition, three prizes will be awarded 191
to the top three winners in 12 different categories. 201
Engineers and scientists from Greenwood Laboratories will 213
judge all the events. Members of the Science Club will serve 225
as hosts and hostesses for the judges and then assist the 237
Greenwood High science teachers in presenting the awards. 249

The club approved the purchase of a microscope as 259
the Science Club's gift to Greenwood High School Science 270
Department. The microscope will be presented to the 281
Greenwood Board of Education at it's June meeting. 291

Under new business, Jason Gillen made a motion 301
that the club adopt a community service project. Jason's 312
motion was seconded by Millie Wilson and approved 322
by voice vote of all members present. President McClinton 334
appointed a committee to identify at least three projects. 346
The committee members are Ervin Gillespie (chair), 356
Kimberly Nehr, Lori Sehgal, and George Bafford. The 367
committee is to present its report at the June meeting. 378

The meeting ended at 3:35 p.m. 385
Minutes prepared by: 389
Chris Smedley 391

# New Keys: B and Y

**Objectives:**

1. To learn reach technique for **B** and **Y**.
2. To combine smoothly **B** and **Y** with all other learned keys.

Fingers curved

Fingers upright

---

## 11A • 7
### Conditioning Practice

each line twice SS (slowly, then faster); DS between 2-line groups

reach review  1 uj ws ik rf ol cd nj ed hj tf .1 gf sw ju de lo fr

c/n  2 an can and cut end cue hen cog torn dock then sick

all letters learned  3 A kid had a jag of fruit on his cart in New Delhi.

---

## 11B • 5
### Technique: Space Bar

each line once

**Technique goal**
Space with a down-and-in motion *immediately* after each word.

1 He will take an old urn to an art sale at the inn.

2 Ann has an old car she wants to sell at this sale.

3 Len is to work for us for a week at the lake dock.

4 Gwen is to sign for the auto we set aside for her.

5 Jan is in town for just one week to look for work.

6 Juan said he was in the auto when it hit the tree.

---

## 11C • 4
### Technique: Return

1. Key each line once SS; return and start each new line quickly.

2. On line 4, see how many words you can key in 30 seconds (30").

1 Dot is to go at two.

2 He saw that it was a good law.

3 Rilla is to take the auto into the town.

4 Wilt has an old gold jug he can enter in the show.

**gwam** 1' | 1 | 2 | 3 | 4 | 5 | 6 | 7 | 8 | 9 | 10 |

A **standard word** in keyboarding is 5 characters or any combination of 5 characters and spaces, as indicated by the number scale under line 4 above. The number of standard words keyed in 1' is called gross words a minute *(gwam)*.

**To find 1-minute (1') *gwam*:**

1. Note on the scale the figure beneath the last word you keyed. That is your 1' *gwam* if you key the line partially or only once.

2. If you completed the line once and started over, add the figure determined in Step 1 to the figure 10. The resulting figure is your 1' *gwam*.

**To find 30-second (30") *gwam*:**

1. Find 1' *gwam* (total words keyed).

2. Multiply 1' *gwam* by 2. The resulting figure is your 30" *gwam*.

## Document 6

1. Create and save a macro for the heading from the letterhead information at right.

2. Retrieve the macro (Step 1) and prepare the news release at the right. It is for **immediate release** and the contact person is **Jane Franklin**.

# Wegard College
## ●●●S P O R T S    R E L E A S E●●●

Intercollegiate Athletics ■ Patton Ave. ■ Asheville, NC 28801-1123 ■ 704-154-0900

opening 10

ASHEVILLE, NC, April 17, ----.  Wegard College's freshman pitcher    23
Martina Galosie (Burlington, NC/Burlington H. S.) has been named the    37
Midsouth Conference Softball Pitcher of the Week for April 10-16.    50

The rookie right-hander pitched 3 complete-game victories last    63
week, over MSC rivals Charlotte College, Franklin College, and Durham    77
State University, posting one shutout and allowing only 5 earned runs    91
in 22 2/3 innings, for a 1.54 earned run average.  Martina scattered 13    105
hits and struck out 22 batters over 4 games (making one relief appear-    119
ance), including a career-high 12 strikeouts in a 3-0 victory over Char-    133
lotte on April 11.  Galosie now has won each of her last 4 starts,    147
allowing only 5 earned runs and recording 2 shutouts in 30 2/3    160
innings.  Her ERA now stands at 2.87, seventh best in the Midsouth    173
Conference, and her 92 strikeouts rank third in the MSC for this sea-    187
son.  She is 9-7 for Wegard and has pitched 112 1/3 innings, allowing    201
91 hits.    203

### ###    204

## **L** ANGUAGE SKILLS

## Document 7

Process the minutes at the right and on the next page. Proofread carefully to identify any errors.

Refer: Document 1, p. 412.

GREENWOOD HIGH SCHOOL SCIENCE CLUB    7

May 15, ----, Meeting Minutes    13

All officers, committee heads, and 15 members were present.    25
Sponsor Terry L. Gronbacher was present.    34

President Dorothy McClinton called the meeting to order at    45
2:25 p.m. Secretary Chris Smedley read the minutes and they    58
were accpeted by unanimous vote. LaVerne Blatt    67
distributed the Aprie 30 balance sheet and income statement    79
and reported that the Science Club has a positive balance    91
of $1,056. Her report was approved by unanimous vote.    102
Victor Bloch, fundraising committee chair, reported that    114
$376.09 was razed from the sale of wind socks and $123.75    125
from the sell of thermometers.    132

*(continued on next page)*

## 11D • 19
### New Keys: B and Y

each line twice SS (slowly, then faster): DS between 2-line groups; QS between groupings; if time permits, rekey lines 7-9

**b** *Left index* finger

**y** *Right index* finger

Follow the *Standard Plan for Learning New Keys* outlined on p. 17.

**Learn b** ▼

1 f f bf bf fib fib rob rob but but big big fib fibs
2 bf bf rob rob lob lob orb orb bid bid bud bud ribs
3 a rib; to fib; rub it; an orb; or rob; but she bid

**Learn y** ▼

4 j j yj yj jay jay lay lay hay hay day day say says
5 yj yj jay jay eye eye dye dye yes yes yet yet jays
6 a jay; to say; an eye; he says; dye it; has an eye

**Combine b and y**

7 by by buy buy boy boy bye bye byte byte buoy buoys
8 by it; to buy; by you; a byte; the buoy; by and by
9 Jaye went by bus to the store to buy the big buoy.

## 11E • 15
### New-Key Mastery

1. Key the lines once SS; DS between 2-line groups.
2. Key the lines again at a faster pace.

**PRACTICE *cues*:**
- reach up without moving hands away from you
- reach down without moving hands toward your body
- use quick-snap keystrokes

reach review

1 a;sldkfj bf ol ed yj ws ik rf hj cd nj tf .l gf uj
2 a kit low for jut led sow fob ask sun cud jet grow

3d/1st rows

3 no in bow any tub yen cut sub coy ran bin cow deck
4 Cody wants to buy this baby cub for the young boy.

key words

5 by and for the got all did but cut now say jut ask
6 work just such hand this goal boys held furl eight

key phrases

7 to do|can go|to bow|for all|did jet|ask her|to buy
8 if she|to work|and such|the goal|for this|held the

all letters learned

9 Becky has auburn hair and wide eyes of light jade.
10 Juan left Bobby at the dog show near our ice rink.

**gwam** 1' | 1 | 2 | 3 | 4 | 5 | 6 | 7 | 8 | 9 | 10 |

## Document 4

Key the itinerary at the right in proper format. Include a confirmation number for each hotel:

*Park Hotel*

**33729-X45602**

*Chicago House*

**CV579-1279**

# L ANGUAGE SKILLS

## Document 5

1. Create and save a macro for the heading from the information at the right.
2. Play back the macro (Step 1) and prepare the news release at the right.
3. Proofread carefully to identify any errors.

Refer: Document 3, p. 413.

---

|  | words |
|---|---|
| TRAVEL AND ACCOMMODATIONS ITINERARY | 7 |
| Martha V. Huega | 10 |
| June 4-June 6 | 13 |

**June 4** — 15

9:43 a.m.   Depart Pittsburgh International Airport for Logan — 27
International (Boston) on USEast Flight 327.  Upon — 37
arrival, take courtesy van to Park Hotel, 1254 Soldiers — 55
Field Rd., Boston (617) 154-1234. — 62

**June 5** — 63

7:47 a.m.   Depart Logan International Airport for Miami Interna- — 76
tional on USEast Flight 758.  Upon arrival, take — 86
airport limousine to Mitchell's Engineering, 665 NW — 96
81 St., Miami (305) 166-3498. — 102

5:45 p.m.   Depart Miami International Airport for Chicago--O'Hare — 115
International on Midcontinent Air Flight 251.  Upon — 126
arrival, take courtesy van to Chicago House Hotel, 644 — 143
N. Lake Shore Dr., Chicago (312) 143-0909. — 152

**June 6** — 153

4:50 p.m.   Depart Chicago--O'Hare International Airport for Pitts- — 166
burgh International on USEast Flight 972. — 175

---

# █•█•█•LAKELAND AMPHITHEATER

12348 Hwy. 155 N. & I-20            Telephone:  903-177-9236
Tyler, TX 75702-5503                     Fax:  903-177-9237

News Release                 For Release:   Immediately — 7
                                    Contact:   Johnny Williams — 12

TYLER, TX, March 18, ----.  Prepare for lift off with New Space — 25

Spectacular, a new show that is destained to delight science fiction — 39

fans of all ages. — 43

The show will land at Lakeland Amphitheater in Tyler at 8:15 p.m. on — 56

June 24 feturing the world renowned Dallas Symphony in a multimedia — 70

symphonic consert using laser beams.  Music featured includes both clas- — 85

sical and movie soundtrack selections of a celestial nature. — 97

Tickets are $24.75 for gold circle seats, $18.75 for reserved seats, and — 112

$10.25 for lawn seats.  They go on sell April 1 at all Ticketpoint locations. — 127

The charge-by-phone number is 123-5349. — 135

### — 136

## Review

**Objectives:**

**1.** To improve spacing, shifting, and returning.
**2.** To increase keying control and speed.

Before you begin each practice session:

- Position your body directly in front of the keyboard; sit erect, with feet on the floor for balance.
- Curve your fingers deeply and place them in an upright position over the home keys.
- Position the textbook for easy reading (at about a 90° angle to the eyes).

Fingers properly curved

Fingers properly upright

Body properly positioned

### 12A • 7
### Conditioning Practice

each line twice SS (slowly, then faster); DS between 2-line groups; if time permits, practice each line again

reach review    1 we ok at in be on by re no us if la do ah go C. J.
b/y    2 by rub jay fib lay rob hay big say buy boy yet but
all letters learned    3 Fran knew it was her job to guide your gold truck.

### 12B • 13
### Technique: Space Bar and Shift Keys

1. Key lines once SS; DS between 2-line groups.
2. Key the lines again at a faster pace.

Down-and-in spacing

Out-and-down shifting

**Space bar (Space *immediately* after each word.)**

1 an by win buy den sly won they than flay when clay
2 in a way|on a day|buy a hen|a fine day|if they win

3 Jay can bid on the old clay urn he saw at the inn.
4 I know she is to be here soon to talk to the club.

**Shift keys (Shift; strike key; release both quickly.)**

5 Lt. Su; Nan and Dodi; Karl and Sol; Dr. O. C. Goya
6 Kara and Rod are in Italy; Jane and Bo go in June.

7 Sig and Bodie went to the lake with Cory and Lana.
8 Aida Rios and Jana Hardy work for us in Los Gatos.

**Document 2**

Process the agenda at the right. You decide all formatting features.

AGENDA — 1

QUANTITATIVE REASONING SKILLS TASK FORCE — 10

May 5, ----, Conference Room — 15

1. Call to Order . . . . . . . . . . . . . . . . . . Carlos Diego, Task Force Head — 29
2. Superintendent's Charge . . . . . . . . . . . Kate Lewis, Superintendent — 42
3. Task Force Discussion and Questions . . . . . . . . . C. Diego/K. Lewis — 55
4. Preliminary Research Plans . . . . . . . . . . . . . . . . . . C. Diego — 68
5. Available Budget . . . . . . . . . . . . . . Florence Wilson, Principal — 81
6. Consultants . . . . . . . . . . . . . . . . . . . . . . . . . . K. Lewis — 95
7. Meeting Schedule and Rules . . . . . . . . . . . . . . . . . C. Diego — 108
8. Other Business . . . . . . . . . . . . . . . . . Task Force Members — 121
9. Adjournment . . . . . . . . . . . . . . . . . . . . . . . . . . C. Diego — 134

## LANGUAGE SKILLS

**Document 3**

Process the itinerary at the right. If needed, review format guides on p. 368. Proofread carefully to identify unmarked errors.

ITINERARY — 2

Charles R. Rhodes--Prospective Biology Teacher — 11

Wednesday, May 12, ---- — 16

12:15 p.m.  Meet with Principal Reilly and Search Committee — 28
Chair Cummins--principle's office. — 35

1:07 p.m.  Observe Ms. ~~Hopkin's~~ *Haverford's* 7th-period Applied — 46
Biology/Chemisty class--Room 215. — 53

1:50 p.m  Observe Ms. ~~Haverford's~~ *Hopkins'* 8th-period Principles — 64
of Technolgy Class--Room 219. — 70

2:30 p.m.  Inteview with Science Department Head — 80
Underwood and Science Faculty--Room 217. — 88

3:10 p.m.  Interview with Superintentent Bevacqua-- — 98
superintendent's office. — 104

3:35 p.m.  Driving tour *of* district's elementary and junior high — 116
schools and ~~tour of~~ various residential areas within — 125
the district-- *school* Mr. Cummins. — 132

5:15 p.m.  Diner with School Board directors Harriett P. Jamison, — 145
Bill W. Quinonnes, and Laura L. Landa, Superintendent — 156
Bevacqua, and Vincent Cummins--Rillton's Restaurant. — 167

7:15 p.m.  Attend the science fair with Mr. Cummins--high school — 180
gymnasium. — 182

## 12C • 15
## Speed Building

1. Key the lines once SS; DS between 2-line groups.
2. Key the lines again at a faster pace.

**Technique goals**
- curved, upright fingers
- quiet hands/arms
- quick spacing—no pause between words
- finger-reach action to shift keys

 Finger-action keystrokes

 Down-and-in thumb motion

**Key words and phrases (*Think, say,* and *key* words and phrases.)**

1 by dig row off but and jet oak the cub all got rid

2 ah she own dug irk buy cog jak for yet ask led urn

3 of us|if the|all of|and do|cut it|he got|to do the

4 is to be|as it is|if we do|in all the|if we own it

**All letters learned (Strike keys at a brisk, steady pace.)**

5 Judy had gone for that big ice show at Lake Tahoe.

6 Jack said that all of you will find the right job.

7 Cindy has just left for work at the big ski lodge.

8 Rudy can take a good job at the lake if he wishes.

gwam  1' | 1 | 2 | 3 | 4 | 5 | 6 | 7 | 8 | 9 | 10 |

## 12D • 15
## Speed Check

1. Key each line once DS. To DS when in SS mode, strike **Return/Enter** twice at line ends.
2. Key a 20-second (20") timed writing on each line. Your rate in gross words a minute *(gwam)* is shown word-for-word above the lines.
3. Key another 20" writing on each line. Try to increase your keying speed.

**Goal:** At least 15 *gwam*.

**R&e**

1. Key each line twice SS (slowly, then faster); DS between 2-line groups.
2. Rekey the drill for better control of reach-strokes.

20" *gwam*

| 3 | 6 | 9 | 12 | 15 | 18 | 21 | 24 | 27 | 30 |

1 Al is to do it.

2 Di has gone to work.

3 Jan is to go to the sale.

4 Rog is to row us to your dock.

5 Harl has an old kayak and two oars.

6 She told us to set a goal and go for it.

7 It is our job to see just how high we can go.

8 Jake will go to the city to work on the big signs.

1 Rob saw the bird on the lake by the big boat dock.

2 June had left for the club just as the news ended.

3 Bro led a task force whose goal was to lower cost.

4 Lyn knew the surf was too rough for kids to enjoy.

5 Ceil hikes each day on the side roads near school.

gwam  1' | 1 | 2 | 3 | 4 | 5 | 6 | 7 | 8 | 9 | 10 |

# UNIT 45

# Process Special Documents

## LESSONS 212–213

### Agenda, Itinerary, News Release, and Minutes

**Objectives:**
1. To correctly format an agenda, itinerary, a news release, and minutes.
2. To improve proofreading and rough-draft and script keying skills.

---

**212-213A • 5 (daily)**
**Conditioning Practice**

each line twice; then 1'
writings on line 2 as time
permits

| | | |
|---|---|---|
| alphabet | 1 | Tezz quickly indexed jokes for a public performance he will give. |
| speed | 2 | The eight busy men may do the work for us if he pays for the ivy. |
| fig/sym | 3 | Sales discounts (15%) amount to $134,682, an increase of $21,790. |
| **gwam** | 1' | 1 \| 2 \| 3 \| 4 \| 5 \| 6 \| 7 \| 8 \| 9 \| 10 \| 11 \| 12 \| 13 \| |

---

## F ORMATTING

**212-213B • 45 (daily)**
**Special Documents**

[wp] **note:**
A 12-pt. variable space font
is recommended for all the
documents in this unit
(except when another size
is specified).

**Document 1**
Process the agenda at the
right. If needed, review
format guides on p. 369.

|  | words |
|---|---|
| MATHEMATICS AND SCIENCE DEPARTMENT MEETING | 9 |
| March 15, ----, 2:40 p.m. | 14 |
| John Wilson High School--Room 218 | 21 |

1. Call to order . . . . . . . . Mary Underwood, Department Head — 34
2. Approval of February minutes . . . . . . . . . M. Underwood — 47
3. Preliminary Fall Teaching Assignments . .Sam Relily, Principal — 60
4. Science teacher applicants . . . . . . . . Vincent Cummins — 73
   Search Committee Chair — 77
5. Interview dates and itinerary . . . . . . . M. Undnerwood — 90
6. Math teacher applicants . . . . . . . . . . .Susan Hughes — 103
   Search Committee Cahir — 108
   m. Underwood
7. Interview dates and itnerary . . . . . . . . M. Underwood — 120
8. Science Fair Judges . . . Janis Haverford, Biology Teacher — 134
9. Other business . . . . . . . . . . . . . . . . m. Underwood — 147
10. Retirement Party Plans . . . Becky Hopkins, Physics Teacher — 160
11. Text book orders . . . . . . . . . . . . . . M. Underwood — 173
12. Next meeting date and adjournment . . . . . M. Unerwood — 186

# LESSON 13

## New Keys: M and X

**Objectives:**

**1.** To learn reach technique for **M** and **X**.

**2.** To combine smoothly **M** and **X** with all other learned keys.

---

### 13A • 7
### Conditioning Practice

each line twice SS (slowly, then faster); DS between 2-line groups

reach review 1 bf ol rf yj ed nj ws ik tf hj cd uj gf by us if ow

b/y 2 by bye boy buy yes fib dye bit yet but try bet you

all letters learned 3 Robby can win the gold if he just keys a new high.

---

### 13B • 20
### New Keys: M and X

each line twice SS (slowly, then faster); DS between 2-line groups; if time permits, rekey lines 7-9

Follow the *Standard Plan for Learning New Keys* outlined on p. 17.

**m** *Right index* finger

**x** *Left ring* finger

**Learn m**

1 j j mj mj am am am me me ma ma jam jam ham ham yam

2 mj mj me me me may may yam yam dam dam men men jam

3 am to; if me; a man; a yam; a ham; he may; the hem

**Learn x**

4 s s xs xs ox ox ax ax six six fix fix fox fox axis

5 xs xs sx sx ox ox six six nix nix fix fix lax flax

6 a fox; an ox; fix it; by six; is lax; to fix an ax

**Combine m and x**

7 me ox am ax ma jam six ham mix fox men lax hem lox

8 to fix; am lax; mix it; may fix; six men; hex them

9 Mala can mix a ham salad for six; Max can fix tea.

# Activity 3:

1. Read the ¶s describing a mature person as given at the right.
2. Assess your own level of maturity in terms of the attitudes and behaviors depicted in the ¶s.
3. Compose/key a ¶ in which you describe a situation or two in which you thought and acted maturely.
4. Compose/key a ¶ in which you describe a situation or two in which you thought and acted immaturely.
5. Compose/key a final ¶ in which you discuss how you plan to become more mature and in what ways.

**Compose (think) as you key**

All of us have to cope with many problems as we go through life. Not the least of these problems is the art of getting along with others. Part of the solution to the problem of getting along with others is to go about all our activities in the right way. Going about things in the right way–whether working or playing–is one of the marks of a mature person.

It has been said that the mature person is one who can face reality. A mature person is one who finds more satisfaction in giving than in getting or taking. A mature person is one who can solve problems of life without "flipping his lid," who does not make the same mistakes again and again, and who will reason with another person instead of punching that person in the nose.

A mature person is one who is forgiving of others, does not hold grudges against them, and does not try to "get even" for some slight or misdeed. A mature person is one who does not resent the accomplishments, possessions, and popularity of others or try to "take them down a peg or two." A mature person lives within the reality that, while all people are created equal, all do not acquire equal levels of material things, emotional security, or spiritual happiness.

## 13C • 17
### New-Key Mastery

1. Key each line once SS; DS between 2-line groups.
2. Key the lines again at a faster pace.

**TECHNIQUE** *cue:*

- reach up without moving hands away from you
- reach down without moving hands toward your body
- use quick-snap keystrokes

**Goal: finger-action keystrokes; quiet hands and arms**

3d/1st rows
1 by am end fix men box hem but six now cut gem ribs
2 me ox buy den cub ran own form went oxen fine club

space bar
3 an of me do am if us or is by go ma so ah ox it ow
4 by man buy fan jam can any tan may rob ham fun guy

key words
5 if us me do an sow the cut big jam rub oak lax boy
6 curl work form born name flex just done many right

key phrases
7 or jam|if she|for me|is big|an end|or buy|is to be
8 to fix|and cut|for work|and such|big firm|the call

all keys learned
9 Jacki is now at the gym; Lex is due there by four.
10 Joni saw that she could fix my old bike for Gilda.

## 13D • 6
### Technique: Spacing with Punctuation

each line once DS

**SPACING** *cue:*
Do not space after an internal period in an abbreviation, such as Ed.D.

1 Mrs. Dixon may take her Ed.D. exam early in March.
2 Lex may send a box c.o.d. to Ms. Fox in St. Croix.
3 J. D. and Max will go by boat to St. Louis in May.
4 Owen keyed ect. for etc. and lost the match to me.

## R&e

1. Key each line twice SS (slowly, then faster); DS between 2-line groups.
2. Key each line once more at a faster pace.

**PRACTICE** *cue:*
Keep the cursor or print point moving steadily across each line (no pauses).

m/x
1 Max told them that he will next fix the main axle.

b/y
2 Byron said the boy went by bus to a bayou to hunt.

w/right shift
3 Wilf and Rona work in Tucson with Rowena and Drew.

u/c
4 Lucy cut a huge cake for just the four lucky boys.

. /left shift
5 Mr. and Mrs. J. L. Nance set sail for Long Island.

n/g
6 Bing may bring a young trio to sing songs at noon.

o/t
7 Lottie will tell the two little boys a good story.

i/r
8 Ria said she will first build a large fire of fir.

h/e
9 Chet was here when the eight hikers hit the trail.

## Activity 1:

1. Study the spelling/definitions of the words in the color block at the right.
2. Key the **Learn** line in the first set of sentences.
3. Key the **Apply** lines, choosing the right words to complete each sentence correctly.
4. Key the second set of lines in the same way.
5. Check your work; rekey lines containing word-choice errors.

**Choose the right word**

| | |
|---|---|
| **real** (adj/n) genuine; not artificial; actually exists | **stationary** (adj) fixed in position, course, or mode; unchanging in condition |
| **reel** (n/vb) revolving device on which to wind lines; to turn round and round | **stationery** (n) paper and envelopes used for processing personal and business documents |

Learn 1 Lori didn't believe an old reel-to-reel tape recorder was real.

Apply 2 Juan Estes found a (real/reel) buy on a new rod and (real/reel).

Apply 3 "Get (real/reel)," my partner said, as I began to (real/reel).

Learn 4 We store stationery on stationary shelves in the supply room.

Apply 5 Desks remain (stationary/stationery), but we'll shift the files.

Apply 6 Were you able to get a good discount on (stationary/stationery)?

## Activity 2:

1. Read carefully the letter at the right, noting errors in punctuation. number expression, word choice, and subject/predicate agreement.
2. Format/key the letter in modified block style with indented ¶s and mixed punctuation—all errors corrected; use the current date; address letter to:

   **Mrs. Rowanda L. Doakes**
   **1450 Chester Pk.**
   **Ridley Park, PA 19078-0358**

   Supply appropriate salutation.
3. As closing lines, use:
   **Sincerely yours**

   **John M. Conte,**
   **Research Director**
4. Include an enclosure notation and use your initials for reference.

**Proofread & correct**

Sum of the questions you razed in your recent letter is difficult to answer because of the rapid changes that are now occurring in the office. The introduction of electronic equipment, such as computers and e-mail have had a great affect on office procedures and practices.

The use of electronic equipment however has not changed vary much the work done by office assistants. Several surveys, including one we conducted last month reveal that assistants in the office spend more than 90 percent of there time processing correspondence (letters and memos) reports, forms, and tables. Correspondence accounts for almost 50 percent of all documents produced.

Despite the growing use of electronic equipment studies reveal that almost half the source documents from which office assistants work is in handwritten form. Reports are often handwritten but many are produced in final form from rough draft. Their is some indication, though that the use of dictating machines are growing in popularity.

More detailed information about office practices can be obtained from the report of hour national survey. if you would like a copy please complete and return the enclosed form.

# LESSON 14

## New Keys: P and V

**Objectives:**

1. To learn reach technique for **P** and **V**.
2. To combine smoothly **P** and **V** with all other learned keys.

Fingers curved

Fingers upright

### 14A • 7
### Conditioning Practice

each line twice SS (slowly, then faster); DS between 2-line groups

one-hand words | 1 in we no ax my be on ad on re hi at ho cad him bet

phrases | 2 is just|of work|to sign|of lace|to flex|got a form

all letters learned | 3 Jo Buck won a gold medal for her sixth show entry.

### 14B • 20
### New Keys: P and V

each line twice SS; DS between 2-line groups; if time permits, rekey lines 7-9

**p** *Right little* finger

**v** *Left index* finger

> Follow the *Standard Plan for Learning New Keys* outlined on p. 17.

**Learn p**

1 ; ; p; p; pa pa up up apt apt pen pen lap lap kept
2 p; p; pa pa pa pan pan nap nap paw paw gap gap rap
3 a pen; a cap; apt to pay; pick it up; plan to keep

**Learn v**

4 f f vf vf via via vie vie have have five five live
5 vf vf vie vie vie van van view view dive dive jive
6 go via; vie for; has vim; a view; to live; or have

**Combine p and v**

7 up cup vie pen van cap vim rap have keep live plan
8 to vie; give up; pave it; very apt; vie for a cup;
9 Vic has a plan to have the van pick us up at five.

**Table 4**

Key the table at the right. Insert four columns at the right and four rows at the bottom: Total, Average, Maximum, and Minimum. Determine the value for each column and row inserted. If needed, use a smaller font size to print table on 8.5" x 11" paper. You decide all formatting features.

| MAY CONCERT ATTENDANCE | | | | |
|---|---|---|---|---|
| Concert | May 1 | May 5 | May 11 | May 23 |
| Freebies | 9,012 | 8,765 | 7,609 | 10,003 |
| Greats | 10,134 | 9,451 | 12,098 | 6,953 |
| Handos | 13,578 | 12,934 | 17,032 | 12,569 |
| Millitt | 5,312 | 4,129 | 6,329 | 2,587 |
| Reeds | 4,312 | 6,581 | 5,736 | 4,982 |

**Table 5**

Process the table at the right. Calculate the Column D ratios by dividing Column C by Column B and rounding to 4 decimal places. You decide all formatting features.

| PENNSYLVANIA HIGH SCHOOL GRADUATES AND COLLEGE FIRST-TIME FRESHMAN ENROLLMENTS | | | |
|---|---|---|---|
| Year | High School Graduates | College First-Time Enrollments | |
| | | Enrollments | Ratio to High School Graduates |
| 1986 | 145,005 | 96,238 | |
| 1987 | 142,811 | 99,189 | |
| 1988 | 145,929 | 99,466 | |
| 1989 | 139,232 | 100,836 | |
| 1990 | 129,514 | 96,066 | |
| 1991 | 123,087 | 95,641 | |
| 1992 | 122,259 | 96,463 | |
| 1993 | 120,875 | 94,964 | |
| 1994 | 118,509 | 94,867 | |

Source: Pennsylvania Department of Education, 1995.

**211B • 45**
**Tables: Sustained Practice**

1. Make a list of the tables to be processed:
   p. 501, 206-207B, Table 1
   p. 502, 206-207B, Table 3
   p. 503, 208-209B, Table 1
   p. 504, 208-209B, Table 3
   p. 506, 210B, Table 1

2. Arrange materials for easy access. Process (in the order listed) as many of the tables as you can in the time permitted. Proofread and correct each table before beginning the next.

3. After time is called, proofread the final table and, if needed, print all completed work.

## 14C • 17
### New-Key Mastery

1. Key the lines once SS; DS between 2-line groups.
2. Key the lines again at a faster pace.

**Technique goals**
- reach up without moving hands away from you
- reach down without moving hands toward your body
- use quick-snap keystrokes

**Goal: finger-action keystrokes; quiet hands and arms**

reach review
1 vf p; xs mj ed yj ws nj rf ik tf ol cd hj gf uj bf
2 if lap jag own may she for but van cub sod six oak

3d/1st rows
3 by vie pen vim cup six but now man nor ton may pan
4 by six but now may cut sent me fine gems five reps

key words
5 with kept turn corn duty curl just have worn plans
6 name burn form when jury glad vote exit came eight

key phrases
7 if they|he kept|with us|of land|burn it|to name it
8 to plan|so sure|is glad|an exit|so much|to view it

all letters learned
9 Kevin does a top job on your flax farm with Craig.
10 Dixon flew blue jets eight times over a city park.

## 14D • 6
### Technique: Shift Keys and Return

Key each 2-line sentence once SS as "Return" is called every 30 seconds (30"). Leave a DS between sentences.

**Goal:** To reach the end of each line just as the 30" guide ("Return") is called.

The **30" gwam scale** shows your gross words a minute if you reach the end of each line as the 30" guide is called.

**R&e**

1. Key each line once at a steady, easy pace to master reach-strokes.
2. Key each line again at a faster pace.

**Technique goals**
- keep fingers upright
- keep hands/arms steady

**Eyes on copy as you shift and as you return**

| | gwam | 30" | 20" |
|---|---|---|---|
| 1 Marv is to choose a high goal | | 12 | 18 |
| 2 and to do his best to make it. | | 12 | 18 |
| 3 Vi said she had to key from a book | | 14 | 21 |
| 4 as one test she took for a top job. | | 14 | 21 |
| 5 Lexi knows it is good to keep your goal | | 16 | 24 |
| 6 in mind as you key each line of a drill. | | 16 | 24 |
| 7 Viv can do well many of the tasks she tries; | | 18 | 27 |
| 8 she sets top goals and makes them one by one. | | 18 | 27 |

m/p
1 mj p; me up am pi jam apt ham pen map ape mop palm
2 Pam may pack plums and grapes for my trip to camp.

b/x
3 bf xs be ax by xi fix box but lax buy fox bit flax
4 Bix used the box of mix to fix bread for six boys.

y/v
5 yj vf buy vow boy vie soy vim very have your every
6 Vinny may have you buy very heavy silk and velvet.

## Table 2

Process the table at the right. Insert a row and calculate the total for each appropriate column. You decide all formatting features.

| BUSINESS ADMINISTRATION ENROLLMENT REPORT | | | | | | | | |
|---|---|---|---|---|---|---|---|---|
| Major | Sex | Full-Time Students | | | Part-Time Students | | | % Change Overall |
| | | This Year | Last Year | % Chg | This Year | Last Year | % Chg | |
| Acctg | F | 453 | 442 | | 375 | 335 | | |
| | M | 412 | 418 | | 359 | 341 | | |
| Admn | F | 157 | 149 | | 163 | 140 | | |
| Mgt | M | 82 | 75 | | 62 | 54 | | |
| Fin | F | 174 | 161 | | 98 | 86 | | |
| | M | 164 | 135 | | 64 | 61 | | |
| Mgt | F | 350 | 328 | | 402 | 385 | | |
| | M | 378 | 356 | | 409 | 398 | | |
| MIS | F | 124 | 136 | | 86 | 88 | | |
| | M | 136 | 134 | | 97 | 92 | | |
| Mkt | F | 273 | 286 | | 152 | 138 | | |
| | M | 224 | 215 | | 146 | 158 | | |

## Table 3

Process the table at the right. Calculate the Column D values and if the number is negative, replace that value with a zero (0). Calculate Column F values. You decide all formatting features.

| PURCHASING PROJECTIONS TO END OF YEAR | | | | | |
|---|---|---|---|---|---|
| Product | Present Inventory | Expected Needs | Purchases Needed | Cost/Item | Total Cost |
| A-222 | 30,000 | 44,000 | | $1.05 | |
| A-222E | 55,500 | 77,600 | | $1.15 | |
| A-433 | 49,875 | 65,000 | | $1.34 | |
| A-443E | 33,200 | 88,250 | | $1.39 | |
| B-224 | 25,000 | 20,000 | | $1.67 | |
| B-224E | 55,750 | 62,000 | | $1.72 | |
| C-666 | 45,000 | 40,000 | | $1.73 | |
| C-666E | 32,900 | 59,000 | | $1.78 | |

# New Keys: Q and Comma (,)

**Objectives:**

**1.** To learn reach technique for **Q** and , (comma).

**2.** To combine smoothly **Q** and , (comma) with all other learned keys.

## 15A • 7
### Conditioning Practice

each line twice SS (slowly, then faster); DS between 2-line groups; if time permits, rekey the lines

| | |
|---|---|
| all letters learned | 1 do fix all cut via own buy for the jam cop ask dig |
| p/v | 2 a map; a van; apt to; vie for; her plan; have five |
| all letters learned | 3 Beth will pack sixty pints of guava jam for David. |

## 15B • 20
### New Keys: Q and , (Comma)

each line twice SS; DS between 2-line groups; if time permits, rekey lines 7-9

**q** *Left little* finger

**, (comma)** *Right middle* finger

**SPACING** *cue:*
Space once after , used as punctuation.

Follow the *Standard Plan for Learning New Keys* outlined on p. 17.

### Learn q

1 a qa qa aq aq quo quo qt. qt. quad quad quit quits

2 qa quo quo qt. qt. quay quay aqua aqua quite quite

3 a qt.; pro quo; a quad; to quit; the quay; a squad

### Learn , (comma)

4 k k ,k ,k kit, kit; Rick, Ike, or I will go, also.

5 a ski, a ski; a kit, a kit; a kite, a kite; a bike

6 Ike, I see, is here; Pam, I am told, will be late.

### Combine q and , (comma)

7 Enter the words quo, quote, quit, quite, and aqua.

8 I have quit the squad, Quen; Raquel has quit, too.

9 Marquis, Quent, and Quig were quite quick to quit.

**Table 9**

Process the table at the right. Calculate the percent of change from last quarter to this quarter to two decimal places. You decide all formatting features.

| INVESTMENT PORTFOLIO | | | |
|---|---|---|---|
| Investment | This Quarter | Last Quarter | % Change |
| Growth Stocks | $118,948 | $115,652 | |
| Income Stocks | $56,476 | $55,824 | |
| High-Yield Bonds | $91,795 | $90,523 | |
| Municipal Bonds | $74,256 | $73,989 | |
| Technology Stocks | $37,817 | $36,912 | |
| Savings Account | $12,861 | $12,765 | |
| Totals | $392,153 | $385,665 | |

## LESSONS 210-211

# Table Processing

**Objectives:**
1. To improve table formatting skills.
2. To process tables under time pressure.

**210-211A • 5 (daily)**
**Conditioning Practice**

each line twice

| | | |
|---|---|---|
| alphabet | 1 | Zeke opened jam jars quickly but avoided ruining the waxed floor. |
| speed | 2 | Jane may work with the girls to make the ritual for the sorority. |
| figures | 3 | I wrote checks 398-430 and 432-457 in July and 458-461 in August. |

gwam  1' | 1 | 2 | 3 | 4 | 5 | 6 | 7 | 8 | 9 | 10 | 11 | 12 | 13 |

# F ORMATTING

**210B • 45**

**Table 1**

Key the table at the right. Insert a row and calculate the column totals. Shade the empty cell (E8). You decide all formatting features.

| JAMIE YOUKON'S WEEKLY EXPENSE LOG | | | | |
|---|---|---|---|---|
| Day | Mileage | Parking/ Tolls | Meals | Notes |
| Mon | $25.51 | $6.75 | $5.50 | Travel to Evans Storage |
| Tues | $3.56 | $7.75 | $4.75 | Meeting with John Gunn |
| Wed | $13.35 | | $24.75 | Dinner meeting -- Joe Uram |
| Thu | $15.35 | $3.50 | | Travel to Robinson Company |
| Fri | $17.84 | $10.50 | $13.50 | Meeting with Beth Ford |

## 15C • 17
## New-Key Mastery

1. Key lines once SS; DS between 2-line groups.
2. Key the lines again at a faster pace.

**Technique goals**
- reach *up* without moving hands away from you
- reach *down* without moving hands toward your body
- use quick-snap keystrokes

**Goal: finger-action keystrokes; quiet hands and arms**

*reach review*
1 qa .l ws ,k ed nj rf mj tf p; xs ol cd ik vf hj bf
2 yj gf hj quo vie pay cut now buy got mix vow forms

*3d/1st rows*
3 six may sun coy cue mud jar win via pick turn bike
4 to go|to win|for me|a peck|a quay|by then|the vote

*key words*
5 pa rub sit man for own fix jam via cod oak the got
6 by quo sub lay apt mix irk pay when rope give just

*key phrases*
7 an ox|of all|is to go|if he is|it is due|to pay us
8 if we pay|is of age|up to you|so we own|she saw me

*all letters learned*
9 Jevon will fix my pool deck if the big rain quits.
10 Verna did fly quick jets to map the six big towns.

## 15D • 6
## Technique: Spacing with Punctuation

each line once DS

**SPACING *cue*:**
Space once after , and ; used as punctuation.

Space once.

1 Aqua means water, Quen; also, it is a unique blue.
2 Quince, enter qt. for quart; also, sq. for square.
3 Ship the desk c.o.d. to Dr. Quig at La Quinta Inn.
4 Q. J. took squid and squash; Monique, roast quail.

## R&e

each set of lines twice SS (once slowly; then again at a faster pace); DS between 6-line groups

**Technique goals**
**lines 1-3**
fingers upright
**lines 4-6**
hands/arms steady
**lines 7-9**
two quick taps of each doubled letter

**Adjacent keys**

1 re io as lk rt jk df op ds uy ew vc mn gf hj sa ui
2 as ore ask opt buy pew say art owe try oil gas her
3 Sandy said we ought to buy gifts at her new store.

**Long direct reaches**

4 ce un gr mu br ny rv ym rb my ice any mug orb grow
5 nice curb must brow much fume sync many dumb curve
6 Brian must bring the ice to the curb for my uncle.

**Double letters**

7 all off odd too see err boo lee add call heed good
8 door meek seen huff less will soon food leek offer
9 Lee will seek help to get all food cooked by noon.

**Table 5**

Create the table at the right. Calculate the percent of the amount pledged that each fundraiser has received. Round to a whole percent. Insert a totals row and determine the overall percent of the pledges that have been received. You decide all formatting features.

**Table 6**

Arrange Table 5 in descending order according to the amount received.

**Table 7**

Create the table at the right. Calculate the 2.5% annual raise (present salary x 2.5%), new salary, and percent the new salary has increased over the present salary. Round dollar amounts to nearest dollar and percents to two decimal places. Insert rows to calculate total and average for each column. You decide all formatting features.

**Table 8**

Revise Table 7 by making the changes given at the right.

| FUNDRAISING REPORT | | | |
|---|---|---|---|
| Fundraiser | Amount Pledged | Amount Received | Percent of Pledge Received |
| Mary Whitner | $1,600 | $1,625 | |
| Gregg Foster | $350 | $350 | |
| Orlando Martinez | $750 | $730 | |
| Donald Espinosa | $2,500 | $2,400 | |
| Michael McCoskey | $2,305 | $2,205 | |
| Nancy Schneider | $1,775 | $1,660 | |
| Alice Gomory | $750 | $701 | |
| Diane Aldridge | $1,500 | $1,258 | |
| Marcia Kelly | $1,675 | $1,342 | |

| PROPOSED SALARY INCREASES FOR RADIOLOGY STAFF | | | | | |
|---|---|---|---|---|---|
| Employee | Present Salary | 2.5% Raise | Merit Raise | New Salary | Percent Increase |
| S. Morris | $25,000 | | $1,500 | | |
| J. Raleigh | $27,250 | | $1,250 | | |
| W. Bossey | $23,750 | | $1,300 | | |
| R. Perez | $44,010 | | $1,700 | | |
| H. Huto | $32,050 | | $1,435 | | |
| H. Katski | $27,800 | | $1,100 | | |

1. Change Raleigh's salary to **$37,250** and merit raise to **$1,550**.
2. Arrange the employees' names in alphabetical order (last name).
3. Add an employee: **J. Newton** at a salary of **$33,950** with a merit raise of **$1,525**.
4. Recalculate amounts as needed.

# LESSON 16

## Review

**Objectives:**

**1.** To learn to key block paragraphs.
**2.** To improve keying technique and speed.

Fingers curved

Fingers properly aligned

### 16A • 7
### Conditioning Practice

each line twice SS (slowly, then faster); DS between 2-line groups; if time permits, practice each line again

reach review 1 Virgil plans to find that mosque by six with Jack.
shift keys 2 Pam, Van, and Quin have to be in New Hope by five.
easy 3 Vi is to aid the girl with the sign work at eight.

`gwam` 1' | 1 | 2 | 3 | 4 | 5 | 6 | 7 | 8 | 9 | 10 |

### 16B • 10
### Block Paragraphs

each paragraph (¶) once SS; DS between ¶s; then key the ¶s again at a faster pace

If your equipment has **automatic return** (word-wrap), do *not* strike **Enter** at the end of each line; the equipment will return for you with what is called a "soft return." You must, however, strike **Enter** twice ("hard returns") at the end of ¶ 1 to leave a DS between ¶s.

**Paragraph 1**                                      `gwam` 1'

When you strike the return or enter key at the end    10
of a line to space down and start a new line, this    20
process is called a hard return.                      26

**Paragraph 2**

If a machine returns at line ends for you, what is    10
known as a soft return or wordwrap is in use.  You    20
must use a hard return, though, between paragraphs.   30

`gwam` 1' | 1 | 2 | 3 | 4 | 5 | 6 | 7 | 8 | 9 | 10 |

### 16C • 10
### Speed Check

1. Key a 30-second (30") timed writing on each line. Your rate in gross words a minute *(gwam)* is shown word for word above the lines.

2. If time permits, key another 30" writing on each line. Try to increase your keying speed.

**Goal:** At least 18 *gwam*.

**30" gwam**

2 | 4 | 6 | 8 | 10 | 12 | 14 | 16 | 18 | 20

1 I am to fix the sign for them.
2 Jaye held the key to the blue auto.
3 Todd is to go to the city dock for fish.
4 Vi paid the girl to make a big bowl of salad.
5 Kal may keep the urn he just won at the quay show.

| 2| 4| 6| 8| 10| 12| 14| 16| 18| 20

If you finish a line before time is called and start over, your *gwam* is the figure at the end of the line PLUS the figure above or below the point at which you stopped.

## Table 2

Create the table at the right. Calculate the percent of change to two decimal places. Insert a totals row; sum this year's and last year's tuition and calculate the total percent of change to two decimal places. Sort table by percent of change in descending order. Add a shadow border. You decide other formatting features.

| TUITION INCOME COMPARISON | | | |
|---|---|---|---|
| Department | This Year | Last Year | % Change |
| Accounting | $96,948 | $98,543 | |
| Administrative Management | $25,548 | $24,967 | |
| Business Teacher Education | $14,750 | $15,324 | |
| Computer Information Systems | $126,455 | $123,769 | |
| English | $44,653 | $43,543 | |
| Finance | $35,980 | $33,988 | |
| Social Sciences | $112,274 | $110,934 | |
| Management | $95,613 | $97,633 | |

## Table 3

Key the table at the right. Calculate the percent of change to two decimal places. Insert a totals row; sum this month's and last month's sales and calculate the total percent of change. Sort table in alphabetical order by last name. Add a double-line border and shade the first row. You decide other formatting features.

| MONTH-TO-MONTH SALES COMPARISON | | | |
|---|---|---|---|
| Salesperson | Last Month | This Month | % Change |
| Jim Harris | $112,456 | $105,696 | |
| Susan Loebb | $139,655 | $154,205 | |
| Paul Inez | $198,456 | $203,455 | |
| Sandra Davis | $90,452 | $85,430 | |
| Mary Clancy | $153,456 | $135,869 | |
| Rita Torina | $50,304 | $60,357 | |

## Table 4

Process the table at the right. Calculate the percent of budget used through March to two decimal places. Insert a totals row and determine the overall percent of budget used. Sort table by percent of budget used in ascending order. Use dotted lines with a double-line border. You decide other formatting features.

| BUDGET AND EXPENSES COMPARISON | | | | | |
|---|---|---|---|---|---|
| Item | Annual Budget Amount | January Expenses | February Expenses | March Expenses | % of Budget Used |
| Rent | $4,200 | $330 | $350 | $350 | |
| Utilities | $2,425 | $160 | $240 | $175 | |
| Auto Loan | $3,450 | $287 | $287 | $287 | |
| Insurance | $700 | $125 | | $65 | |
| Food | $1,800 | $200 | $220 | $240 | |
| Clothing | $900 | $75 | $200 | $85 | |
| Personal | $1,080 | $90 | $90 | $125 | |
| Savings | $750 | $65 | $65 | $70 | |

## Technique: Space Bar and Shift Keys

each line twice SS; DS between 4-line groups

**Goals**

- to reduce the pause between words
- to reduce the time taken to shift/strike key/release when making capital letters

Down-and-in spacing

Out-and-down shifting

**Space bar (Space *immediately* after each word.)**

1 so an if us am by or ox he own jay pen yam own may
2 she is in|am to pay|if he may|by the man|in a firm

3 I am to keep the pens in a cup by a tan mail tray.
4 Fran may try to fix an old toy for the little boy.

**Shift keys (Shift; strike key; release both quickly.)**

5 J. V., Dr. or Mrs., Ph.D. or Ed.D., Fourth of July
6 Mrs. Maria Fuente; Dr. Mark V. Quin; Mr. T. C. Ott

7 B. J. Marx will go to St. Croix in March with Lex.
8 Mae has a Ph.D. from Miami; Dex will get his Ed.D.

## 16E • 11
## Speed Building

each line twice SS (slowly, then faster); DS between 4-line groups

***Technique goals***

- quick-snap keystrokes
- quick joining of letters to form words
- quick joining of words to form phrases

**Key words and phrases (*Think, say,* and *key* words and phrases.)**

1 ox jam for oak for pay got own the lap via sob cut
2 make than with them such they when both then their

3 to sit|an elf|by six|an oak|did go|for air|the jam
4 to vie|he owns|pay them|cut both|the quay|for they

**Key sentences (Strike keys at a brisk, steady pace.)**

all letters learned

5 I may have six quick jobs to get done for low pay.
6 Vicky packed the box with quail and jam for Signe.

all letters learned

7 Max can plan to bike for just five days with Quig.
8 Jim was quick to get the next top value for Debby.

## R&e

1. Key each line once at a steady, easy pace to master reach-strokes.
2. Key each line again at a faster pace.

***Technique goals***

- keep fingers upright
- keep hands/arms steady

q/b

1 qa bf by quo but qt. quit both quad lube quid blow
2 Bob quickly won my squad over quip by brainy quip.

x/,

3 xs ,k sxs k,k ox ox, six six, flax flax, axle axle
4 I keyed ox, six, lox, mix, fox, fix, fax, and nix.

p/m

5 p; mj p.m. map amp pep mam mop imp camp ramp clump
6 Palma and her mom made peppy caps for my pep team.

v/y

7 vf yj ivy vary envy very wavy navy have many savvy
8 Levy may have to vary the way we serve and volley.

## Table 7

Open Table 1 and make the changes given at the right. Remove all rules from the table.

## Table 8

Process the table at the right. Calculate all totals, including totals for each salesperson in each quarter. You decide all formatting features, including the lines and borders.

**wp** note:

If your software allows you to select the type of number displayed (currency, accounting, percent, etc.), omit the $'s as you key. Insert them by choosing an appropriate type of display.

1. Add *3* singles and *1* home run for Mr. Sun.
2. Add *6* singles, *1* double, and *1* triple for Mr. Meyers.
3. Add *4* singles, *2* triples, and *3* home runs for Mr. Sanchez.
4. Arrange players' names in alphabetical order (last name).
5. Check accuracy of totals and, if needed, recalculate totals.

| SALES REPORT | | | | | |
|---|---|---|---|---|---|
| Month | John Dwyer | Mary Todd | Luis Manuel | Sarah Jerrod | Total |
| January | $5,567 | $6,623 | $7,659 | $6,902 | |
| February | $2,457 | $7,654 | $3,569 | $6,432 | |
| March | $6,930 | $3,096 | $5,792 | $8,790 | |
| Quarter 1 | | | | | |
| April | $4,783 | $5,091 | $4,390 | $5,402 | |
| May | $5,042 | $4,500 | $4,502 | $5,321 | |
| June | $5,430 | $5,781 | $5,781 | $6,023 | |
| Quarter 2 | | | | | |
| Total | | | | | |

# Tables with Math Applications

**Objectives:**

1. To process tables that require you to add, subtract, multiply, and divide.
2. To improve table formatting and decision-making skills.

## 208-209A • 5 (daily)
### Conditioning Practice

each line twice

| alphabet | 1 | Frank questioned me over the jazz saxophone at my new night club. |
|---|---|---|
| speed | 2 | If Jen signs the form, I may pay to dismantle the ancient chapel. |
| fig/sym | 3 | The #5346 item will cost Ford & Sons $921.87 (less 10% for cash). |

**gwam** 1' | 1 | 2 | 3 | 4 | 5 | 6 | 7 | 8 | 9 | 10 | 11 | 12 | 13 |

## **F** ORMATTING

### 208-209B • 45 (daily)

#### Table 1

Create the table at the right. Calculate the percent of discount off the regular price. You decide all formatting features, including the lines and borders.

| CELLULAR TELEPHONE SYSTEMS | | | |
|---|---|---|---|
| Model | Regular Price | Sale Price | Percent Discount |
| P-911 | $1,699 | $888 | |
| CP-243 | $1,749 | $925 | |
| XTZ | $1,924 | $975 | |
| ST-457 | $1,799 | $949 | |

# LESSON 17

## New Keys: Z and Colon (:)

**Objectives:**

**1.** To learn reach techniques for **Z** and **:** (colon).

**2.** To combine smoothly **Z** and **:** (colon) with all other learned keys.

---

### 17A • 7
### Conditioning Practice

each line twice SS; then a
1' writing on line 3; find
*gwam*

| | | |
|---|---|---|
| all letters learned | 1 | Jim won the globe for six quick sky dives in Napa. |
| spacing | 2 | to own \| is busy \| if they \| to town \| by them \| to the city |
| easy | 3 | She is to go to the city with us to sign the form. |

**gwam** 1' | 1 | 2 | 3 | 4 | 5 | 6 | 7 | 8 | 9 | 10 |

---

### 17B • 18
### New Keys: Z and :
### (Colon)

each line twice SS (slowly,
then faster); DS between
2-line groups; if time
permits, rekey lines 7-10

**z** *Left little* finger

**:** *Left Shift* and
strike **:** key

**LANGUAGE SKILLS** *cues:*

- Space twice after **:**
  used as punctuation.

- Capitalize the first
  word of a complete
  sentence following a
  colon.

Follow the *Standard Plan
for Learning New Keys*
outlined on p. 17.

**Learn z**

1 a a za za zap zap zap zoo zoo zip zip zag zag zany

2 za za zap zap zed zed oz. oz. zoo zoo zip zip maze

3 zap it, zip it, an adz, to zap, the zoo, eight oz.

**Learn : (colon)**

4 ; ; :: :: Date:  Time:  Name:  Room:  From:  File:

5 :; :; To:  File:  Reply to:  Dear Al:  Shift for :

6 Two spaces follow a colon, thus:  Try these steps:

**Combine z and :**

7 Zelda has an old micro with : where ; ought to be.

8 Zoe, use as headings: To:  Zone:  Date:  Subject:

9 Liza, please key these words:  zap, maze, and zoo.

10 Zane read:  Shift to enter : and then space twice.

## Table 3

Process the table at the right. Calculate the row average in Column F and the column average in Row 9, which must be inserted. You decide all formatting features.

| BUSINESS MATH GRADE BOOK | | | | | |
|---|---|---|---|---|---|
| Name | Test 1 | Test 2 | Test 3 | Test 4 | Average |
| Abel, P. | 78 | 85 | 72 | 78 | |
| Boggs, N. | 64 | 66 | 71 | 73 | |
| Carr, J. | 78 | 82 | 76 | 75 | |
| Mills, A. | 71 | 75 | 73 | 76 | |
| Pope, D. | 62 | 71 | 73 | 66 | |
| Wills, W. | 92 | 93 | 88 | 92 | |

## Table 4

Key the table at the right. Calculate the total hours in Column G. Calculate the gross pay in Cell I3 by multiplying G3 times H3. Copy this formula to find gross pay for other workers. Calculate the column average in Row 9, which must be inserted. You decide all formatting features.

| DAILY TIME SHEET | | | | | | Total Hours | Hourly Rate | Gross Pay |
|---|---|---|---|---|---|---|---|---|
| Employee | Mon | Tue | Wed | Thu | Fri | | | |
| Bates, G. | 8 | 8 | 8 | 8 | 8 | | $6.55 | |
| Cellings, M. | 9 | 7 | 8 | 8 | 8 | | $5.75 | |
| Gonzalez, P. | 8 | 8 | 8 | 9 | 8 | | $7.33 | |
| Hito, H. | 7 | 8 | 8 | 8 | 8 | | $5.78 | |
| Nestor, G. | 5 | 8 | 8 | 8 | 8 | | $6.51 | |
| Smithton, L. | 8 | 8 | 8 | 4 | 8 | | $6.25 | |

## Table 5

Create the table at the right. Calculate the total score in Column H. Calculate the column averages in Row 10, which must be inserted. You decide all formatting features, including changing the border.

Save Table 5 for use in the next activity.

| ALGEBRA II NINE-WEEK QUIZ SCORES | | | | | | | |
|---|---|---|---|---|---|---|---|
| Student | Quiz 1 | Quiz 2 | Quiz 3 | Quiz 4 | Quiz 5 | Quiz 6 | Total |
| Janet Adams | 89 | 91 | 88 | 97 | 95 | 95 | |
| Timothy Bell | 66 | 72 | 73 | 66 | 78 | 62 | |
| Shellie Eavey | 76 | 78 | 73 | 75 | 74 | 79 | |
| Pablo Menez | 88 | 91 | 82 | 85 | 87 | 91 | |
| Stuart Velez | 53 | 72 | 68 | 70 | 71 | 65 | |
| Frank Darr | 88 | 91 | 93 | 88 | 97 | 89 | |
| Alberto Juan | 88 | 91 | 82 | 85 | 87 | 91 | |

## Table 6

Revise Table 5 by adding the students' names and scores at the right and arranging all students' names in alphabetical order by last name.

| Gwendolyn Carney | 75 | 78 | 76 | 72 | 79 | 80 | |
|---|---|---|---|---|---|---|---|
| Dennis Trumpy | 72 | 74 | 75 | 65 | 64 | 70 | |

## 17C • 15
### New-Key Mastery

1. Key the lines once SS; DS between 2-line groups.
2. Key the lines again at a faster pace.

**Technique goals**
- curved, upright fingers
- quiet hands and arms
- steady keystroking pace

q/z
1 zoo qt. zap quo zeal quay zone quit maze quad hazy
2 Zeno amazed us all on the quiz but quit the squad.

p/x
3 apt six rip fix pens flex open flax drop next harp
4 Lex is apt to fix apple pie for the next six days.

v/m
5 vim mam van dim have move vamp more dive time five
6 Riva drove them to the mall in my vivid lemon van.

easy
7 Glen is to aid me with the work at the dog kennel.
8 Dodi is to go with the men to audit the six firms.

alphabet
9 Nigel saw a quick red fox jump over the lazy cubs.
10 Jacky can now give six big tips from the old quiz.

## 17D • 10
### Block Paragraphs

1. Key each paragraph (¶) once SS; DS between them; then key them again faster.
2. If your teacher directs, key a 1' writing on each ¶; find your *gwam*.

**Paragraph 1**                                            gwam 1'

The space bar is a vital tool, for every fifth or  10
sixth stroke is a space when you key.  If you use  20
it with good form, it will aid you to build speed.  30

**Paragraph 2**

Just keep the thumb low over the space bar.  Move  10
the thumb down and in quickly toward your palm to  20
get the prized stroke you need to build top skill.  30

gwam 1' | 1 | 2 | 3 | 4 | 5 | 6 | 7 | 8 | 9 | 10 |

1. Key each line once at a steady, easy pace to master reach-strokes.
2. Key each line again at a faster pace.

**Technique goals**
- keep fingers upright
- keep hands/arms steady

x/:.
1 xs :; | fix mix | Max:  Use TO: and FROM: as headings.
2 Read and key:  oxen, exit, axle, sixty, and sixth.

q/,
3 qa ,k | aqa k,k | quo quo, | qt. qt., | quite quite, | squat
4 Quen, key these:  quit, aqua, equal, quiet, quick.

p/z
5 p; za | ;p; zaza | zap zap | zip zip | size size | lazy lazy
6 Zip put hot pepper on his pizza at the zany plaza.

m/v
7 mj vf | jmj fvf | vim vim | vow vow | menu menu | move movie
8 Mavis vowed to move with a lot more vim and vigor.

# UNIT 44

LESSONS 206–211

## Process Tables with Math Applications

### LESSONS 206–207

## Tables with Math Applications

**Objectives:**
1. To process tables requiring calculation of sums, averages, and multiplication.
2. To improve table formatting and decision-making skills.

**206-207A • 5 (daily)
Conditioning Practice**

each line twice; then
1' writings on line 3 as time
permits

| alphabet | 1 | Weber excluded a quick jaunt to the big zoo from my travel plans. |
| speed | 2 | Their neighbor may pay the downtown chapel for the ancient ivory. |
| figures | 3 | My agents will sell 43 tables, 59 beds, 187 chairs, and 206 rugs. |

**gwam** 1' | 1 | 2 | 3 | 4 | 5 | 6 | 7 | 8 | 9 | 10 | 11 | 12 | 13 |

## F ORMATTING

**206-207B • 45 (daily)**

**Table 1**

Create the table at the right.
Calculate the total hits in
Column F and the column
totals in Row 8. You decide
all formatting features.
Save Table 1 for use later in
this lesson.

Indent the word "Total"
three spaces.

| STATISTICS OF THE TOP FIVE HITTERS | | | | | |
|---|---|---|---|---|---|
| Player | Singles | Doubles | Triples | Home Runs | Total Hits |
| Lu Che Sun | 53 | 5 | 9 | 1 | |
| Al Sandrey | 41 | 11 | 2 | 12 | |
| Bill Meyers | 17 | 19 | 0 | 19 | |
| Hector Ruiz | 25 | 5 | 8 | 3 | |
| Lee Horan | 22 | 6 | 2 | 8 | |
| Total | | | | | |

**Table 2**

Key the table at the right.
Enter **$125** in Cell E3 and
copy to other cells in
Column E.  Calculate the
row totals in Column F and
the column totals in Row 8,
which must be inserted.
You decide all formatting
features.

| APRIL PAY SCHEDULE | | | | | |
|---|---|---|---|---|---|
| Salesperson | Sales | Commission | Salary | Bonus | Total |
| Frederick Adams | $1,365 | $750 | $400 | | |
| Janice Brown | $1,735 | $954 | $425 | | |
| Carlos Cuez | $1,425 | $783 | $445 | | |
| Enrico Duarte | $1,357 | $746 | $450 | | |
| Lisa Ford | $1,285 | $706 | $375 | | |

**Objectives:**

**1.** To learn reach technique for **CAPS LOCK** and **?** (question mark).

**2.** To combine smoothly **CAPS LOCK** and **?** (question mark) with other learned keys.

### 18A • 7
### Conditioning Practice

each line twice SS; then a 1' writing on line 3; find *gwam*: total words keyed

| alphabet | 1 | Lovak won the squad prize cup for sixty big jumps. |
| z/: | 2 | To: Ms. Mazie Pelzer; From: Dr. Eliza J. Piazzo. |
| easy | 3 | He is to go with me to the dock to do work for us. |

**gwam** 1' | 1 | 2 | 3 | 4 | 5 | 6 | 7 | 8 | 9 | 10 |

### 18B • 16
### New Keys: CAPS LOCK and ? (Question Mark)

each line twice SS (slowly, then faster); DS between 2-line groups; if time permits, rekey lines 7-9

Depress the CAPS LOCK to key a series of capital letters. To release the CAPS LOCK to key lowercase letters: on computers, strike CAPS LOCK key again; on electronics, strike either Left or Right Shift key.

**CAPS LOCK**
*Left little* finger

**? (question mark)**
*Left Shift;* then *right little* finger

**Learn CAPS LOCK**

1 Hal read PENTAGON and ADVISE AND CONSENT by Drury.

2 Oki joined FBLA when her sister joined PBL at OSU.

3 Zoe now belongs to AMS and DPE as well as to NBEA.

**Learn ? (question mark)**

Space twice

4 ; ; ?; ?; Who? What? When? Where? Why? Is it?

5 Who is it? Is it she? Did he go? Was she there?

6 Is it up to me? When is it? Did he key the line?

**Combine CAPS LOCK and ?**

7 Did he join a CPA firm? I will stay on with NASA.

8 Is her dad still CEO at BSFA? Or was he made COB?

9 Did you read HOMEWARD? If so, try WHIRLWIND next.

## ACTIVITY 4:

1. Key the table at the right.
2. Calculate the totals and averages.
3. Format numbers in Columns C-G as dollars with 2 decimal places.
4. Select line and border style, other than default, that is attractive.
5. Move rows as needed to list group in alphabetical order within rooms.
6. Move Columns C through F so that the column headings are in alphabetical order.
7. You decide all other formatting features.

| FUNDRAISING REPORT | | | | | | |
|---|---|---|---|---|---|---|
| Room | Group | Posters | Binders | Notes | Pens | Total |
| 101 | Great One | 567.55 | 435.39 | 421.85 | 252 | |
| | Go-Fers | 378.35 | 298.95 | 622.75 | 424.95 | |
| | Best Ones | 453.55 | 375.41 | 698.45 | 542.42 | |
| | Runners | 364.76 | 235.98 | 635.21 | 456.87 | |
| | Total | | | | | |
| | Average | | | | | |
| 104 | Fivesome | 732.34 | 215.65 | 515.32 | 287.54 | |
| | Triumps | 452.54 | 458.35 | 219.65 | 356.37 | |
| | Funders | 421.56 | 195.92 | 824.35 | 421.56 | |
| | Schoolers | 561.32 | 327.59 | 367.61 | 542.45 | |
| | Total | | | | | |
| | Average | | | | | |
| 108 | Kickers | 532.86 | 253.69 | 321.52 | 498.19 | |
| | Winners | 324.69 | 482.91 | 724.56 | 268.34 | |
| | Rabbits | 563.21 | 682.43 | 145.61 | 392.,69 | |
| | Jaguars | 429.04 | 405.61 | 621.34 | 321.87 | |
| | Total | | | | | |
| | Average | | | | | |
| | Grand Total | | | | | |
| | Grand Average | | | | | |

## 18C • 18
### New-Key Mastery

1. Key lines once SS; DS between 2-line groups.
2. Key the lines again at a faster pace.
3. Key a 1' writing on line 11 and then on line 12; find *gwam* on each writing.

**TECHNIQUE** *cues:*

- reach *up* without moving hands away from you
- reach *down* without moving hands toward your body
- use CAPS LOCK to make ALL CAPS

**To find 1' gwam:**
Add 10 for each line you completed to the scale figure beneath the point at which you stopped in a partial line.

**Goal: finger-action keystrokes; quiet hands and arms**

| | | |
|---|---|---|
| CAPS LOCK/? | 1 | Did she join OEA?  Did she also join PSI and DECA? |
| | 2 | Do you know the ARMA rules?  Are they used by TVA? |
| z/v | 3 | Zahn, key these words:  vim, zip, via, zoom, vote. |
| | 4 | Veloz gave a zany party for Van and Roz in La Paz. |
| q/p | 5 | Paul put a quick quiz on top of the quaint podium. |
| | 6 | Jacqi may pick a pink pique suit of a unique silk. |
| key words | 7 | they quiz pick code next just more bone wove flags |
| | 8 | name jack flax plug quit zinc wore busy vine third |
| key phrases | 9 | to fix it\|is to pay\|to aid us\|or to cut\|apt to own |
| | 10 | is on the\|if we did\|to be fit\|to my pay\|due at six |
| alphabet | 11 | Lock may join the squad if we have six big prizes. |
| easy | 12 | I am apt to go to the lake dock to sign the forms. |

**gwam** 1' |  1  |  2  |  3  |  4  |  5  |  6  |  7  |  8  |  9  |  10  |

## 18D • 9
### Block Paragraphs

1. Key each paragraph once, using wordwrap (soft returns) if available. The lines you key will be longer than the lines shown if default side margins are used.
2. If time permits, key a 1' writing on one or two of the paragraphs.

**Goal:** Continuity (keep the cursor or print point moving steadily across the screen or paper).

**wp note:**

Clearing the screen from time to time between 1' writings avoids confusion when finding *gwam*. Learn how to clear the screen on your software.

**Paragraph 1**

**gwam** 1'

When you key lines of drills, strike the return or   10
enter key at the end of each line.  That is, use a   20
hard return to space down for a new line.            29

**Paragraph 2**

When you key copy in this form, though, you do not   10
need to strike return at the end of each line if a   20
machine has wordwrap or a soft return feature.       30

**Paragraph 3**

But even if your machine returns at line ends for    10
you, you have to strike the return or enter key at   20
the end of a paragraph to leave a line blank.        29

**Paragraph 4**

Learn now when you do not need to return at ends     10
of lines and when you must do so.  Doing this now    20
will assure that your copy will be in proper form.   30

**gwam** 1' |  1  |  2  |  3  |  4  |  5  |  6  |  7  |  8  |  9  |  10  |

## ACTIVITY 1:

**Move and Copy Rows, Columns, and Cells**

1. Read the copy at the right.
2. Learn how to move and copy rows, columns, and cells with your software.
3. Open TWP14-1 and rename it SWP14-1.
4. Follow the directions at the right to move and copy parts of a table.

Rows, columns, and cells in a table can be moved or copied by using cut, copy, and paste in the same manner as these features are used to move or copy text elsewhere in a document.

1. Copy Cell B3 to B4, B5, and B6.
2. Copy B7 to B8; B9 to B10 and B11.
3. Copy C5 to C6, C7 to C8, and C9 to C10 and C11.
4. Copy D10 to D11.
5. Move Column D to Column B.
6. Move rows as needed so soccer players are first, football second, golf third, and cross country last.
7. Keep SWP14-1 on the monitor for use in Activity 2.

## ACTIVITY 2:

**Delete and Edit Table Rules**

1. Read the copy at right.
2. Learn how to delete table lines and borders with your software.
3. Open SWP14-1 if it is not open and rename it NOLINES.
4. Follow the directions at the right to edit the lines in tables.

Most software permits you to delete or edit specific lines, or rules, or all vertical or horizontal rules within a table. In this activity you will delete all rules in a table and edit rules, or lines, and borders in various tables.

1. Delete all rules in the table.
2. Save table as NOLINES.
3. Open SWP14-1 and rename it SHADOW.
4. Edit the border to a shadow border.
5. Open SWP14-1 and rename it NEWLINES.
6. Change the rules to dotted lines.
7. Change the border to one that has double lines.
8. Save NEWLINES.
9. Save SHADOW.

## ACTIVITY 3:

**Formulas**

1. Read copy at the right.
2. Learn how to use formulas in a table with your software.
3. Follow the directions at the right to use formulas.

Formulas can be used in tables to perform calculations rapidly and accurately. In this activity you will use formulas to sum and average numbers in columns.

1. Open TWP14-3 and rename it FORMULAS.
2. In Cell B11, sum the values from B3:B10 (that is, starting with Cell B3 and ending with Cell B10).
3. Copy the formula in B11 to C11: E11 (or sum each of the columns separately and place in respective column in Row 11).
4. In Cell B12, average the values from B3:B10.
5. Copy the formula in B12 to C12: E12 (or average each of the columns separately and place in respective column in Row 12).
6. In F3, divide C3 by B3.
7. Copy the formula in F3 to F4:F11 (or divide each value in Column C by Column B for each row and place answer in respective row in Column F).
8 . Save table as FORMULAS.

**Objectives:**

**1.** To learn to use the **Tab key** to indent paragraphs.

**2.** To improve and check keying speed.

## 19A • 7
### Conditioning Practice

each line twice SS; then a 1' writing on line 3; find *gwam:* total words keyed

**Computers**

CAPS LOCK affects only the letter keys; shifted punctuation marks require the use of one of the shift keys.

**Electronics**

*Comma* and *period* as well as *colon* and *question mark* can be keyed when CAPS LOCK is on.

Fingers properly curved

alphabet 1 Zosha was quick to dive into my big pool for Jinx.

CAPS LOCK 2 Type these ZIP Codes:  OR, MD, RI, NV, AL, and PA.

easy 3 Ian kept a pen and work forms handy for all of us.

| gwam | 1' | 1 | 2 | 3 | 4 | 5 | 6 | 7 | 8 | 9 | 10 |

## 19B • 12
### Paragraph Indention

The **Tab key** is used to indent the first line of ¶s. Computer software and electronics use preset tabs (called default tabs). Usually, the first default tab is set 0.5" (5 spaces) to the right of the left margin and is used to indent ¶s (see copy below right).

See p. RG20 to learn to clear and set electronic tabs.

1. Locate the Tab key on your keyboard (usually at upper left of alphabetic keyboard).

2. Reach up to the Tab key with the left little finger; strike the key firmly and release it quickly. The cursor or print point will move 0.5" (5 spaces) to the right.

3. Key each ¶ once SS using wordwrap (soft returns) if available; DS between ¶s. As you key, strike the Tab key firmly to indent the first line of each ¶.

4. If you complete all ¶s before time is called, rekey them to master Tab key technique.

**Tab** key *Left little* finger

Tab ⟶ The tab key is used to indent blocks of copy such as these.

Tab ⟶ It should also be used for tables to arrange data quickly and neatly into columns.

Tab ⟶ Learn now to use the tab key by touch; doing so will add to your keying skill.

Tab ⟶ Strike the tab key firmly and release it very quickly.  Begin the line without a pause.

Tab ⟶ If you hold the tab key down, the cursor will move from tab to tab across the line.

## Skill Builder

each line 3 times (slowly, then faster, then in-between rate for control)

**Goal:** To keep hands quiet with keystroking action limited to fingers.

**Emphasize: Continuity and rhythm with curved, upright fingers**

N  Nora's niece and nephew can be tended by one new nanny on Monday.
O  One of four officers opposed opening offshore moorings for boats.
P  Peppy's playful puppy pulled the papers off the apples and pears.
Q  Quin quit questioning a requirement for bouquets at that banquet.
R  Rory and Larry arrived from a carriage ride over the rural roads.
S  Susana sat still as soon as Suno served sushi and sashini dishes.
T  Ted took title to two cottages the last time he went to the city.
U  Ursula usually rushes to help us unload the sugar from the truck.
V  Vera voted to review the vivid videos on my visit to the village.
W  Wib was waving wildly when the swimmer was wading into the water.
X  Tax experts explain that I am exempt from an existing excise tax.
Y  Young boys yearn to go yachting each year on my big yellow yacht.
Z  Zeno puzzled over a zealot who seized a bronze kazoo at a bazaar.

### Improve/Assess Keyboarding Skills

1. Key three 1' writings on each ¶; find *gwam*. Count errors. If errors are 2 or fewer on any writing, goal is to increase speed by one or two *gwam* on next writing. If errors on any writing are more than 2, goal is control (0-2 errors) on next writing.

2. Key two 3' writings on ¶s 1-3 combined; find *gwam* and count errors.

3. Key a 5' writing on ¶s 1-3 combined; find *gwam* and count errors.

| | gwam | 3' | 5' |
|---|---|---|---|

Being able to communicate well is one of the leading keys to the success of any business. Information must move outside a business and up, down, and sideways within a business so people can use acquired facts to make good decisions. The report is one medium that a business can use to relay information in internal and external directions.

| 4 | 2 | 42 |
| 8 | 5 | 45 |
| 12 | 8 | 48 |
| 17 | 10 | 50 |
| 21 | 13 | 53 |
| 23 | 14 | 54 |

A business report is generally thought to be a written message that is used to make business decisions. To be of value, the message must be based on factual information rather than fancy and should be presented in a format that is easy to read, consistent in style, neat, and free of keying and language skills errors.

| 27 | 16 | 56 |
| 31 | 19 | 59 |
| 35 | 21 | 61 |
| 39 | 24 | 64 |
| 44 | 26 | 66 |
| 44 | 26 | 67 |

Business reports can be done in many formats. Informal ones can utilize a letter or memo style. Progress, proposal, annual, or other major reports are often done in a formal style. These formal reports have a required style for margins, spacing, and headings and often have parts such as a title page, a table of contents, and an abstract.

| 48 | 29 | 69 |
| 52 | 32 | 72 |
| 57 | 34 | 74 |
| 61 | 37 | 77 |
| 65 | 39 | 79 |
| 67 | 40 | 80 |

gwam  3'  | 1 | 2 | 3 | 4 |
      5'  | 1 | 2 | 3 |

## 19C • 10
### Technique: Space Bar, Shift Keys, and CAPS LOCK

each pair of lines twice SS; DS between 4-line groups

Fingers upright

space bar
1 an me so en if em by he ox go am do is no or in to
2 She may go to the city if he can fix the old auto.

shift key
3 The best dancers are:  Ana and Jose; Mag and Boyd.
4 Did Ms. Paxon send us the letter from Dr. LaRonde?

CAPS LOCK
5 Masami saw the game on ESPN; Krista saw it on NBC.
6 The AMS meeting is on Tuesday; the DPE, on Friday.

## 19D • 14
### Speed Building

1. Key the lines once SS; DS between 2-line groups.
2. Key a 1' writing on each of lines 5-8; find *gwam* on each writing (1' *gwam* = total 5-stroke words keyed).
3. If time permits, key another 1' writing on line 7 and then on line 8 for speed.

**Key words and phrases (*Think, say,* and *key* words and phrases.)**

1 ad my we in be on at up as no are him was you gets
2 girl quay turn rush duty down maps rich laid spend

3 an ad|to fix|an oak|to get|the zoo|via jet|in turn
4 if they|to risk|by them|the duty|and paid|she kept

**Key easy sentences (Key the words at a brisk, steady pace.)**

5 He is to aid the girls with the work if they wish.
6 Jan may go to the city for the bid forms for them.

7 He may go to the lake by dusk to do the dock work.
8 I did all the work for the firm for the usual pay.

gwam 1'| 1 | 2 | 3 | 4 | 5 | 6 | 7 | 8 | 9 | 10 |

## 19E • 7
### Speed Check

1. Key each ¶ once SS using wordwrap if available; DS between ¶s.
2. Key a 1' writing on each ¶; find *gwam* on each writing (1' *gwam* = figure above the last word keyed).

Copy used to measure skill is triple-controlled for difficulty: E = easy; LA = low average; A = average.

    all letters used

.        2        .        4        .        6        .        8        .
    Be quick to excel in form and speed.  If you
  10      .       12       .      14       .       16       .       18       .
do, you can move back a word or two and watch the
  20      .       22       .      24       .      26       .       28
errors fall away.  Keep this in mind as you work.
         .        2        .        4        .        6        .        8        .
    You might be amazed how your speed will grow
  10      .       12       .      14       .       16       .       18       .
if you first push for speed and then level off to
  20      .       22       .      24       .      26       .       28
take control at just the right speed.  Try it now.

# Skill Builder

each line 3 times (slowly, then faster, then in-between rate for control)

**Goal:** To keep hands quiet with keystroking action limited to fingers.

**Emphasize:  Continuity and rhythm with curved, upright fingers**

A  After Al and Ann ate the pancake, each had an apple and a banana.
B  Bea became the best batter by being best at batting rubber balls.
C  Chris can use pictures of a raccoon and cactus in their calendar.
D  Did Red say he was a decoy doing deep runs to defeat the defense?
E  Eli, Eve, and Keene were elected to chaperon every evening event.
F  Fred figures fifty rafts floated from Fairfax to Fordstaff Falls.
G  Greg and Geof glanced at a gaggle of geese going over the garage.
H  Healthy habits and high hopes help them through the hockey match.
I  Jim will insist on sliding on the big icy path five or six times.
J  Jed objected to taking Jim's jeans and jogging jersey on the jet.
K  Kit kept Ki's knickknack in a sack in the keel of the knockabout.
L  Lolla and Lilly will fill all small holes in the left lane early.
M  Mia meets my mama most mornings at the mall in the summer months.

## Improve/Assess Keyboarding Skills

1. Key three 1' writings on each ¶; find *gwam*. Count errors.  If errors are 2 or fewer on any writing, goal is to increase speed by one or two *gwam* on next writing.  If errors on any writing are more than 2, goal is control (0-2 errors) on next writing.
2. Key two 3' writings on ¶s 1-3 combined; find *gwam* and count errors.
3. Key a 5' writing on ¶s 1-3 combined; find *gwam* and count errors.

| | gwam | 3' | 5' |
|---|---|---|---|

Character is often described as a person's combined moral or — 4 | 2 43
ethical strength.  Most people think it is like integrity, which — 8 | 5 46
is thought to be a person's ability to adhere to a code or a set — 13 | 8 48
standard of values.  If a person's values are accepted by society, — 17 | 10 51
others are likely to view her or him as having a somewhat high — 21 | 13 53
degree of integrity. — 23 | 14 54

You need to know that character is a trait that everyone — 27 | 16 57
possesses and that it is formed over time.  A person's character — 31 | 19 59
reflects his or her definition of what is good or just.  Most — 35 | 21 62
children and teenagers model their character through the words — 39 | 24 64
and deeds of parents, teachers, and other adults with whom they — 44 | 26 67
have regular contact. — 45 | 27 68

Existing character helps mold future character. It is im- — 49 | 29 70
portant to realize that today's actions can have a lasting effect. — 53 | 32 73
For that reason, there is no better time than now to make all — 57 | 34 75
your words and deeds speak favorably.  You want them to portray — 62 | 37 78
the things others require of people who are thought to possess a — 66 | 40 80
high degree of character. — 68 | 41 81

gwam  3' |  1  |  2  |  3  |  4
      5' |    1    |    2    |    3

# LESSON 20

## Skills Check

**Objectives:**

**1.** To demonstrate level of technique mastery.
**2.** To demonstrate level of keying speed attained.

### 20A • 7
### Conditioning Practice

each line twice SS; then a 1'
writing on line 3; find *gwam*

alphabet 1 Quig just fixed prize vases he won at my key club.

spacing 2 Marcia works for HMS, Inc.; Juanita, for XYZ Corp.

easy 3 Su did vow to rid the town of the giant male duck.

`gwam` 1' | 1 | 2 | 3 | 4 | 5 | 6 | 7 | 8 | 9 | 10 |

### 20B • 20
### Technique Check

each line twice SS; DS
between 6-line groups

Fingers
curved

Fingers
upright

Finger-
action
key-
stroking

Down-and-in spacing

Ask your teacher to
check your keyboarding
technique as you key the
following lines.

**Reach review (Keep on home keys the fingers not used for reaching.)**

1 old led kit six jay oft zap cod big laws five ribs

2 pro quo|is just|my firm|was then|may grow|must try

3 Olga sews aqua and red silk to make six big kites.

**Space bar emphasis (*Think*, *say*, and *key* the words.)**

4 en am an by ham fan buy jam pay may form span corn

5 I am|a man|an elm|by any|buy ham|can plan|try them

6 I am to form a plan to buy a firm in the old town.

**Shift key emphasis (Reach *up* and reach *down* without moving the hands.)**

7 Jan and I are to see Ms. Han.  May Lana come, too?

8 Bob Epps lives in Rome; Vic Copa is in Rome, also.

9 Oates and Co. has a branch office in Boise, Idaho.

**Easy sentences (*Think*, *say*, and *key* the words at a steady pace.)**

10 Eight of the girls may go to the social with them.

11 Corla is to work with us to fix the big dock sign.

12 Keith is to pay the six men for the work they did.

`gwam` 1' | 1 | 2 | 3 | 4 | 5 | 6 | 7 | 8 | 9 | 10 |

19. Key this references page on a separate page at the end of the report.
20. Spell-check, proofread, and check the format of the report.
21. Review the formatting requirements on p. 490 and complete them as needed to finish this report.

REFERENCES

Arnheim, Daniel D., and William E. Prentice. Principles of Athletic Training. 8th ed. St. Louis: Mosby Year Book, Inc., 1993.

Cylkowski, Greg J., M.A. Developing a Lifelong Contract in the Sports Marketplace. Little Canada, MN: Athletic Achievements, 1992.

Dictionary of Occupational Titles. 4th ed. Washington, D C: U.S. Department of Labor, 1991.

Mueller, Frederick O., and Allan J. Ryan. Prevention of Athletic Injuries: The Role of the Sports Medicine Team. Philadelphia: F.A. Davis Company, 1991.

"Sports Medicine." Compton's Interactive Encyclopedia. Version 2.01VW. Compton's New Media Inc., 1994.

Synowka, David P., Ph.D., ATC, Associate Professor of Sport Administration, Robert Morris College, Pittsburgh, PA. Personal interview. 26 June 1995.

22. Prepare a table of contents as directed at the right.
23. Prepare a title page using your name, your school name, and the current date.

**Table of Contents Directions**

Use usual formatting features with these additional directions.:

1. DS centered headings (first-level headings) at the LM.
2. DS side headings (second-level headings) at the first ¶ indention point.
3. SS ¶ headings (third-level headings) at the second ¶ indention point.
4. Include REFERENCES as a first-level heading in the table of contents.
5. Use leaders between the headings and the page numbers.
6. Use lowercase Roman numerals to number the table of contents pages. Begin with **ii**, centered, 1.0" from the bottom edge, since the title page is counted as page i, though not numbered.

## Speed Check: Sentences

1. Key a 30" writing on each line. Your rate in *gwam* is shown word-for-word above the lines.
2. Key another 30" writing on each line. Try to increase your keying speed.

**Goal:** At least 22 *gwam.*

| | 2 | 4 | 6 | 8 | 10 | 12 | 14 | 16 | 18 | 20 | 22 |

1 He bid for the rich lake land.

2 Suzy may fish off the dock with us.

3 Pay the girls for all the work they did.

4 Quen is due by six and may then fix the sign.

5 Janie is to vie with six girls for the city title.

6 Duane is to go to the lake to fix the auto for the man.

| | 2 | 4 | 6 | 8 | 10 | 12 | 14 | 16 | 18 | 20 | 22 |

If you finish a line before time is called and start over, your *gwam* is the figure at the end of the line PLUS the figure above or below the point at which you stopped.

## Speed Check: Paragraphs

1. Key a 1' writing on each paragraph (¶); find *gwam* on each writing.
2. Using your better *gwam* as a base rate, select a goal rate and key two 1' guided writings on each ¶ as directed below.

Copy used to measure skill is triple-controlled for difficulty: E = easy; LA = low average; A = average.

**E** all letters used     gwam 2'

| | . | 2 | . | 4 | . | 6 | . | 8 | . | |
Tab → How you key is just as vital as the copy you   5

| | 10 | . | 12 | . | 14 | . | 16 | . | 18 | . | |
work from or produce. What you put on paper is a   10

| | 20 | . | 22 | . | 24 | . | 26 | . | 28 | . | |
direct result of the way in which you do the job.   15

| | . | 2 | . | 4 | . | 6 | . | 8 | . | |
Tab → If you expect to grow quickly in speed, take   19

| | 10 | . | 12 | . | 14 | . | 16 | . | 18 | . | |
charge of your mind. It will then tell your eyes   24

| | 20 | . | 22 | . | 24 | . | 26 | . | 28 | . | |
and hands how to work through the maze of letters.   29

2' | 1 | 2 | 3 | 4 | 5 |

### Quarter-Minute Checkpoints

| gwam | 1/4' | 1/2' | 3/4' | Time |
| --- | --- | --- | --- | --- |
| 16 | 4 | 8 | 12 | 16 |
| 20 | 5 | 10 | 15 | 20 |
| 24 | 6 | 12 | 18 | 24 |
| 28 | 7 | 14 | 21 | 28 |
| 32 | 8 | 16 | 24 | 32 |
| 36 | 9 | 18 | 27 | 36 |
| 40 | 10 | 20 | 30 | 40 |

### Guided (Paced) Writing Procedure

#### Select a practice goal

1. Key a 1' writing on ¶ 1 of a set of ¶s that contain superior figures for guided writings, as in 20D above.
2. Using the *gwam* as a base, add 4 *gwam* to determine your goal rate.
3. Choose from Column 1 of the table at the left the speed nearest your goal rate. At the right of that speed, note the 1/4' points in the copy you must reach to maintain your goal rate.
4. Determine the checkpoint for each quarter minute from the word-count dots and figures above the lines in ¶ 1. (Example: Checkpoints for 24 *gwam* are 6, 12, 18, and 24.)

#### Practice procedure

1. Key two 1' writings on ¶ 1 at your goal rate guided by the quarter-minute calls (1/4, 1/2, 3/4, time).

**Goal:** To reach each of your checkpoints just as the guide is called.

2. Key two 1' writings on ¶ 2 of a set of ¶s in the same way.
3. If time permits, key a 2' writing on the set of ¶s combined, without the guides.

#### Speed level of practice

When the purpose of practice is to reach out into new speed areas, use the *speed* level. Take the brakes off your fingers and experiment with new stroking patterns and new speeds. Do this by:

1. Reading 2 or 3 letters ahead of your keying to foresee stroking patterns.
2. Getting the fingers ready for the combinations of letters to be keyed.
3. Keeping your eyes on the copy in the book.

The GED Scale is composed of three divisions: Reasoning Development, Mathematical Development, and Language Development. The description of the various levels of language and mathematical development is based on the curricula taught in schools throughout the United States. (Dictionary of Occupational Titles, 1012)

The general education needed by athletic trainers is reported in the following chart:

Athletic Training Competencies

The National Athletic Trainers' Association (NATA) has identified athletic training competencies and categorized them into six domains that parallel the duties and responsibilities of an athletic trainer:

- Prevention
- Recognition and evaluation
- Management and treatment and disposition
- Rehabilitation
- Organization
- Education and counseling

To be proficient in these six domains, students studying athletic training need formal instruction in the following subject areas in addition to the course work that will provide the needed general education foundation:

- Prevention and evaluation of athletic injuries and illnesses
- First aid and emergency care
- Therapeutic modalities and exercise
- Administration of athletic training programs
- Human anatomy and physiology
- Exercise physiology
- Kinesiology and biomechanics
- Nutrition
- Psychology
- Personal and community health

Additionally, courses in chemistry, physics, pharmacology, statistics, and research design are recommended. (Synovka)

14. Key the text at the right so that it follows the **General Education Requirements** section. You decide the bullet style.

15. Open file TPROFESS; insert the text below the **General Education Requirements** section.

16. Find *sport medicine* and replace it with *sports medicine* throughout the report.

17. Find *rehab* and replace it with *rehabilitation* throughout the report.

18. Insert a graphic (approximately 1.5" by 1.5") at the beginning of the **Sports Medicine** section and at the beginning of the **Athletic Trainers** section. You choose appropriate graphics and insert them at the left margin so that the tops are even with the first line of the first ¶ in each section.

# Language & Writing Skills 1

## Activity 1:

1. Study the spelling/definitions of the words in the color block at right.
2. Key line 1 (the **Learn** line), noting the proper choice of words.
3. Key lines 2-3 (the **Apply** lines), choosing the right words to complete the lines.
4. Key the remaining lines in the same way.
5. Check your accuracy; rekey lines containing errors.

### Choose the right word

| | |
|---|---|
| **do** (vb) to bring about; to carry out | **hear** (vb) to gain knowledge of by the ear |
| **due** (adj) owed or owing as a debt; having reached the date for payment | **here** (adv) in or at this place; at this point; in this case; on this point |

Learn  1  If you pay when it is due, the cost will be less.
Apply  2  (Do, Due) you expect the plane to arrive when it is (do, due)?
Apply  3  (Do, Due) you want me to indicate the (do, due) date of the invoice?

Learn  4  Did you hear the sirens while you were here in the cellar?
Apply  5  (Hear, Here) is the new CD you said you wanted to (hear, here).
Apply  6  To (hear, here) well, we should see if we can get seats (hear, here).

## Activity 2:

1. Read Sentence 1 to decide the correct word to complete the sentence.
2. Key Sentence 1, supplying the missing word.
3. Follow Steps 1-2 to complete the other sentences.
4. Check the accuracy of your work with the teacher; correct any errors you made.

### Proofread & correct

1  After a . at the end of a sentence, space _____.

2  After a ; used as punctuation, space _____.

3  After a . following an initial, space _____.

4  After a : used as punctuation, space _____.

5  After a , within a sentence, space _____.

6  After a . following an abbreviation, space _____.

## Activity 3:

1. Read Sentence 1 to decide the word to supply in the blank.
2. Key Sentence 1, inserting the word that correctly completes the sentence.
3. Follow Steps 1-2 to complete the other sentences.
4. Check the accuracy of your work with the teacher; correct any errors you made.

### Compose (think) as you key

1  All that glitters is not _____.

2  Do not cry over spilt _____.

3  A friend in need is a friend _____.

4  A new broom always sweeps _____.

5  A penny saved is a penny _____.

12. Key the table at the right so that it follows the last ¶ in the **Duties and Responsibilities** section.

| Reasoning Development | Mathematical Development | Language Development |
|---|---|---|
| Apply principles of logical or scientific thinking to define problems, collect data, establish facts, and draw valid conclusions. Interpret an extensive variety of technical instructions in mathematical or diagrammatic form. Deal with several abstract and concrete variables. | **Algebra:** Deal with system of real numbers; linear, quadratic, rational, exponential, logarithmic, angle, and circular functions, and inverse functions; related algebraic solution of equations and inequalities; limits and continuity, and probability and statistical inference.<br><br>**Geometry:** Deductive axiomatic geometry, plane and solid; and rectangular coordinates.<br><br>**Shop Math:** Practical application of fractions, percentages, ratio and proportion, mensuration, logarithms, practical algebra, geometric construction, and essentials of trigonometry. | **Reading:** Read novels, poems, newspapers, periodicals, journals, manuals, dictionaries, thesauruses, and encyclopedias.<br><br>**Writing:** Prepare business letters, expositions, summaries, and reports, using prescribed format and conforming to all rules of punctuation, grammar, diction, and style.<br><br>**Speaking:** Participate in panel discussions, dramatizations, and debates. Speak extemporaneously on a variety of subjects. |

13. Key the text at the right and on the next page so that it immediately precedes the table you prepared in Step 12 above.

General Education Requirements

The Dictionary of Occupational Titles identifies and describes (98, 1010, and 1011) the general education requirements needed by athletic trainers for satisfactory job performance. The general education is reported on a General Education Development (GED) Scale.

*(continued on next page)*

# UNIT 2

**LESSONS 21–24**

# Master Keyboarding/ Language Skills

## LESSON 21

### Keying Technique/Language Skills

**Objectives:**
1. To learn proper response patterns to gain speed.
2. To learn to capitalize appropriate words in sentences.

---

**21A • 5**
**Conditioning Practice**

each line twice SS; then a
1' writing on line 3; find
*gwam*

| | | |
|---|---|---|
| alphabet | 1 | Nat will vex the judge if she bucks my quiz group. |
| punctuation | 2 | Al, did you use these words:  vie, zeal, and aqua? |
| easy | 3 | She owns the big dock, but they own the lake land. |
| **gwam** | 1' | 1 \| 2 \| 3 \| 4 \| 5 \| 6 \| 7 \| 8 \| 9 \| 10 \| |

---

## S KILL BUILDING

**21B • 18**
**Technique: Response Patterns**

1. Key each pair of lines twice SS; DS between 4-line groups.

2. Key a 1' writing on line 10 and then on line 12; find *gwam* (total words keyed) on each writing.

3. Key another 1' writing on the slower line to increase your speed on more difficult copy.

**PRACTICE *cues*:**

**Balanced-hand lines:**
*Think, say,* and *key* the words by word response at a fast pace.

**One-hand lines:**
*Think, say,* and *key* the words by letter response at a steady but unhurried pace.

**Letter response**
Many one-hand words (as in lines 3-4) are not easy to key. Such words may be keyed letter-by-letter and with continuity (steadily without pauses).

**Word response**
Short, balanced-hand words (as in lines 1-2) are so easy to key that they can be keyed as words, not letter-by-letter. Think and key them at your top speed.

| | | |
|---|---|---|
| balanced-hand words | 1 | ah do so go he us if is of or to it an am me by ox |
| | 2 | ha for did own the for and due pay but men may box |
| one-hand words | 3 | as up we in at on be oh ax no ex my ad was you are |
| | 4 | ad ink get ilk far him few pop set pin far imp car |
| balanced-hand phrases | 5 | of it\|he is\|to us\|or do\|am to\|an ox\|or by\|is to do |
| | 6 | do the\|and for\|she did\|all six\|the map\|for the pay |
| one-hand phrases | 7 | as on\|be in\|at no\|as my\|be up\|as in\|at him\|saw you |
| | 8 | you are\|oil tax\|pop art\|you get\|red ink\|we saw him |
| balanced-hand sentences | 9 | The man is to go to the city and do the auto work. |
| | 10 | The girl is to go by bus to the lake for the fish. |
| one-hand sentences | 11 | Jimmy saw you feed a deer on a hill up at my mill. |
| | 12 | Molly sat on a junk in oily waters at a bare reef. |
| **gwam** | 1' | 1 \| 2 \| 3 \| 4 \| 5 \| 6 \| 7 \| 8 \| 9 \| 10 \| |

7. In the **Sports medicine clinics** ¶, delete from the fourth sentence: *and pay higher salaries than those paid by other employers of athletic training.*

8. Insert the copy at the right under **Duties and Responsibilities,** below the first ¶.

9. Open file T-PLACES; insert the text under **Places of Employment**, below the first ¶. Move **School districts** ¶ above **Secondary schools** ¶.

10. Open file TRELATIO; insert the text at the end of the **Places of Employment** section.

11. Move **Education** ¶ below **Counseling and guidance** ¶.

<u>Prevention of athletic injury.</u> One of the chief responsibilities of an athletic trainer is to make the competitive environment as safe as it can be in an effort to reduce the likelihood of injury. If injuries can be prevented, there is no need for first aid and subsequent rehabilitation. Athletic trainers prevent injury by working with other members of the sports medicine team to ensure the following items are carefully planned, implemented, and maintained for each athlete:

- Administration of physical examinations and preparticipation screenings.
- Appropriate training and conditioning programs.
- Selection, use, and maintenance of correct equipment that fits properly.
- Reduction and control of environmental hazards.

<u>Evaluation of athletic injuries and medical referral.</u> Most often an athletic trainer is the first sports medicine team member to tend to an athlete who has been injured. The athletic trainer must be able to evaluate the severity of an injury quickly and accurately, administer appropriate first aid to stabilize an injured athlete, and arrange for further treatment, if needed. Referrals for further treatment often involve making arrangements for transportation, appointments, billing procedures, and communication with an athlete's family.

*(continued on next page)*

## S KILL BUILDING

### 21C • 12
### Speed Building

**LS (line spacing):** DS

1. Key one 1' unguided and two 1' guided writings on ¶ 1 as directed on p. 54.

2. Key ¶ 2 in the same way.

3. As time permits, key one or two 2' unguided writings on ¶s 1-2 combined; find *gwam*.

1' *gwam* goals
▽ 17 = acceptable
☐ 21 = average
☉ 25 = good
◇ 29 = excellent

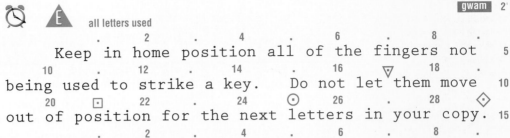

gwam 2'

all letters used

```
          .        2        .        4        .        6        .        8        .
     Keep in home position all of the fingers not      5
    10    .       12        .       14        .       16   ▽    .       18        .
being used to strike a key.    Do not let them move     10
    20    ☐    22            .       24   ☉    26        .       28        ◇
out of position for the next letters in your copy.     15
          .        2        .        4        .        6        .        8        .
     Prize the control you have over the fingers.      19
    10    .       12        .       14        .       16   ▽    .       18        .
See how quickly speed goes up when you learn that      24
    20    ☐    22            .       24   ☉    26        .       28        ◇
you can make them do just what you expect of them.     29
2' |      1      |      2      |      3      |      4      |      5      |
```

## L ANGUAGE SKILLS

### 21D • 15
### Capitalization

**LS (line spacing):** SS

**Standard Plan for Mastering Language Skills**

1. Read the first rule highlighted in color at right.

2. Key the Learn sentence below it, noting how the rule is applied.

3. Key the Apply sentence, supplying the needed capital letters.

4. Read and practice the other rules in the same way.

5. If time permits, key all Apply sentences again to quicken your decision-making skills.

Capitalize the first word in a sentence.

Learn 1 Mindy left her coat here.  Can she stop by for it?
Apply 2 do you plan to go today?  the game begins at four.

Capitalize personal titles and names of people.

Learn 3 I wrote to Mr. Katz, but Miss Dixon sent the form.
Apply 4 do you know if luci and lex bauer are with dr. tu?

Capitalize names of clubs, schools, organizations, and companies.

Learn 5 The Beau Monde Singers will perform at Music Hall.
Apply 6 lennox corp. now owns the hyde park athletic club.

Capitalize the days of the week.

Learn 7 Did you ask if the OEA contest is to be on Friday?
Apply 8 does FBLA meet on wednesday, thursday, and friday?

Capitalize the months of the year.

Learn 9 August was very hot, but September is rather cool.
Apply 10 they are to spend july and august at Myrtle Beach.

6. Under the heading **Practitioners**, insert this table below the third ¶. Align side margins of table with those of the report. Use full justification in the second column.

| Job Title | Position Description |
|---|---|
| Biomechanist | Biomechanists have expertise in analyzing the motions that athletes use to compete in their sports. Biomechanists advise athletes, coaches, and athletic trainers on matters relating to an athlete's movements so that faulty motions can be corrected, improving an athlete's ability and reducing the likelihood of injury. |
| Strength and Conditioning Coach | Strength and conditioning coaches are employed by some high schools and many colleges and universities and professional teams to advise athletes on in-season, off-season, and rehabilitation training and conditioning programs. |
| Sports Psychologist | Sports psychologists help athletes develop a healthy respect for their bodies; cope with injury; and understand the psychological aspects of injury and its effects on their social, emotional, intellectual, and physical dimensions. |
| Physical Therapist | Physical therapists supervise the rehabilitation process for injured athletes. |
| Exercise Physiologist | Exercise physiologists teach athletes and other members of the sports medicine team training and conditioning techniques, body composition analysis, and nutritional considerations. |
| Nutritionist | Nutritionists are frequently employed as consultants to plan eating programs geared to the needs of athletes in a particular sport and to provide nutritional counseling to athletes. |

*(continued on next page)*

**Objectives:**
1. To build skill on straight copy and script.
2. To learn to capitalize appropriate words in sentences.

**22A • 5**
**Conditioning Practice**

each line twice SS; then a
1' writing on line 3; find
*gwam*

| | | |
|---|---|---|
| alphabet | 1 | Wusov amazed them by jumping quickly from the box. |
| spacing | 2 | am to\|is an\|by it\|of us\|an oak\|is to pay\|it is due |
| easy | 3 | It is right for the man to aid them with the sign. |
| **gwam** | 1' | 1 \| 2 \| 3 \| 4 \| 5 \| 6 \| 7 \| 8 \| 9 \| 10 \| |

**S KILL BUILDING**

**22B • 18**
**Technique: Response Patterns**

1. Key each set of 3 lines twice SS (slowly, then faster); DS between 6-line groups.
2. Key a 1' writing on line 10, on line 11, and on line 12; find *gwam* on each; compare rates.
3. If time permits, rekey the slowest line.

> **Combination response**
> Normal copy (as in lines 7-9) includes both word- and letter-response sequences. Use *top* speed for easy words, *lower* speed for words that are harder to key.

| | | |
|---|---|---|
| | 1 | be in as no we kin far you few pin age him get oil |
| letter response | 2 | see him\|was nil\|vex you\|red ink\|wet mop\|as you saw |
| | 3 | Milo saved a dazed polo pony as we sat on a knoll. |
| | 4 | ox if am to is may end big did own but and yam wit |
| word response | 5 | do it\|to cut\|he got\|for me\|jam it\|an owl\|go by air |
| | 6 | He is to go to the city and to do the work for me. |
| | 7 | am at of my if on so as to be or we go up of no by |
| combination response | 8 | am in\|so as\|if no\|is my\|is up\|to be\|is at\|is up to |
| | 9 | Di was busy at the loom as you slept in the chair. |
| letter | 10 | Jon gazed at a phony scarab we gave him in a case. |
| combination | 11 | Pam was born in a small hill town at the big lake. |
| word | 12 | Keith is off to the lake to fish off the big dock. |
| **gwam** | 1' | 1 \| 2 \| 3 \| 4 \| 5 \| 6 \| 7 \| 8 \| 9 \| 10 \| |

**22C • 5**
**Handwritten Copy (Script)**

Key the lines once DS (2 hard returns); rekey the lines if time permits.

1 Script is copy that is written with pen or pencil.
2 Copy that is written poorly is often hard to read.
3 Read script a few words ahead of the keying point.
4 Doing so will help you produce copy free of error.
5 Leave proper spacing after punctuation marks, too.
6 With practice, you will key script at a good rate.

2. Open TLONGRPT.
3. Insert **Focus** as a side heading after the first ¶ in the **Sports Medicine** section of the report.
4. Under the **Sports Medicine** heading, insert the ¶ at the right as the third ¶.
5. Delete **(Cylkowski, 262)** in the ¶ that begins with the heading **Colleges and Universities**.

Proper

The best nutrition plays an important part in an athlete's preparation. Nutritionists have developed programs to tell help athletes eat foods and drink liquids that will provide good nutritional health balance and avoid harmful drugs stems. Proper equipment that fits correctly contributes to injury prevention. Athletic shoes for instance are continually improved to boost the athlete's speed, agility, ability to jump, and endurance while providing comfort health and protection. (from injury)

New materials that make sportswear more comfortable and protective while decreasing friction and other resistence assist athletes.

(to gain maximum proformance safely.)

*(continued on next page)*

## 22D • 10
## Speed Building

**LS:** DS

1. Key one 1' unguided and two 1' guided writings on ¶ 1 as directed on p. 54.
2. Key ¶ 2 in the same way.
3. As time permits, key one or two 2' unguided writings on ¶s 1-2 combined; find *gwam*.

**Quarter-Minute Checkpoints**

| gwam | 1/4' | 1/2' | 3/4' | Time |
|------|------|------|------|------|
| 16 | 4 | 8 | 12 | 16 |
| 20 | 5 | 10 | 15 | 20 |
| 24 | 6 | 12 | 18 | 24 |
| 28 | 7 | 14 | 21 | 28 |
| 32 | 8 | 16 | 24 | 32 |
| 36 | 9 | 18 | 27 | 36 |
| 40 | 10 | 20 | 30 | 40 |

all letters used                                                   gwam   2'

```
          .        2        .        4        .        6        .        8
      Are you one of the people who often look from       5
      10       .       12       .       14       .       16       .       18
  the copy to the screen and down at your hands?  If     10
  20       .       22       .       24       .       26       .       28       .
  you are, you can be sure that you will not build a     15
  30       .       32       .       34       .       36       .       38       .
  speed to prize.  Make eyes on copy your next goal.     20
          .        2        .        4        .        6        .        8
      When you move the eyes from the copy to check     24
      10       .       12       .       14       .       16       .       18
  the screen, you may lose your place and waste time     30
  20       .       22       .       24       .       26       .       28       .
  trying to find it.  Lost time can lower your speed     35
  30       .       32       .       34       .       36       .       38       .
  quickly and in a major way, so do not look away.      39
2' |      1      |      2      |      3      |      4      |      5      |
```

## L ANGUAGE SKILLS

## 22E • 12
## Capitalization

Follow the *Standard Plan for Mastering Language Skills* given in 21D, p. 57.

| | Capitalize names of holidays. |
|---|---|
| Learn 1 | Kacy and Zoe may visit their parents on Labor Day. |
| Apply 2 | gus asked if memorial day comes at the end of may. |

| | Capitalize the names of historic periods and events and special events. |
|---|---|
| Learn 3 | The Fourth of July honors the American Revolution. |
| Apply 4 | bastille day is in honor of the french revolution. |

| | Capitalize names of cities, states, and other important places. |
|---|---|
| Learn 5 | When you were in Nevada, did you visit Hoover Dam? |
| Apply 6 | did he see paris from the top of the eiffel tower? |

| | Capitalize geographic names, regions, and locations. |
|---|---|
| Learn 7 | Val drove through the Black Hills in South Dakota. |
| Apply 8 | we canoed down the missouri river near sioux city. |

| | Capitalize names of streets, roads, avenues, and buildings. |
|---|---|
| Learn 9 | Jemel lives at Bay Towers near Golden Gate Bridge. |
| Apply 10 | our store is now in midtown plaza on kenwood road. |

# REPORT PROJECT

**Objectives:**

1. To format a 17-page report containing three levels of headings, tables, textual citations, references, table of contents, and title page.
2. To follow directions and use problem-solving and decision-making skills.
3. To apply language skills rules.
4. To combine keyed and stored text (disk files) to create a document.

**Directions**

1. Read the objectives and formatting requirements at the right.

## Formatting Requirements

1. The report and all of its parts are to be formatted as an unbound report with textual citations.

2. A header should be placed on each page except page 1. Use the report title and the page number in the heading. Block the title at the left, key it in ALL CAPS, and place the page number flush right on the same line as the title. Do not number page 1.

3. Use 0.5" paragraph indention unless otherwise directed.

4. Use the Widow/Orphan feature and keep all headings with at least two lines of text that follow the heading.

5. Use the same font face throughout all report parts.

6. If possible, use 18 pt. for the report title (centered in ALL CAPS; omit underlines), 16 pt. for first-level headings (centered in initial caps), 14 pt. for second-level headings (blocked at left margin in initial caps), and 12 pt. for paragraph headings (third-level headings with first letter of first word capitalized). The body of the report should be keyed using 12-pt. font size.

7. Headings should be keyed in bold; paragraph headings should be bold and underlined.

8. Each table should appear on one page unless otherwise directed. Insert a page break above a divided table so that the table fills the newly created page. Then move text that follows the table to fill the "short" page before it. Afterwards, check that the text references to the table are still accurate. Bold and shade all column headings and use 14-pt. font size.

9. Bullets should begin at the left margin with text starting at first ¶ indention point. You decide the bullet style.

10. Enumerated items should be keyed in hanging indent style with the first line beginning at the ¶ indention point. About 0.25" should be between the period following the number and the first character in the text that will be blocked.

11. Use the Hyphenation feature and left justification throughout the document unless directed otherwise.

12. Check spelling and grammar and proofread all report parts carefully.

## LESSON 23   Keyboarding/Language Skills

**Objectives:**
1. To build straight-copy speed and control.
2. To learn to capitalize appropriate words in sentences.

**23A • 5**
**Conditioning Practice**

each line twice SS; then a
1' timed writing on line 3;
find *gwam*

alphabet 1 Marjax made five quick plays to win the big prize.
CAPS LOCK 2 Did you say to send the cartons by UPS or by USPS?
easy 3 I am to pay the six men if they do the work right.
gwam 1' | 1 | 2 | 3 | 4 | 5 | 6 | 7 | 8 | 9 | 10 |

**S KILL BUILDING**

**23B • 18**
**Technique: Response Patterns**

1. Key each set of 3 lines twice SS; DS between 6-line groups.
2. Key a 1' writing on line 10, on line 11, and on line 12 to increase speed; find *gwam* on each.

**Goal:** At least 24 *gwam* on line 12.

letter response 1 kilo beef ploy were only date upon gave milk rates
2 my car|oil tax|you are|was him|raw milk|as you see
3 We ate plump plum tarts in a pink cafe on a barge.

word response 4 also form town risk fuel auto goal pens iris visit
5 apt to|go for|is also|the goal|fix them|go for the
6 Roxie is also apt to go for the goal of good form.

combination response 7 an in of at is fix pop for him ham are pen far men
8 in the|at the|and tar|for him|due you|she saw them
9 An odor of wax and tar was in the air at the mill.

letter 10 Zac gave only a few facts in a case on wage taxes.
combination 11 He set off for the sea by dusk to see a rare loon.
word 12 It is right for them to audit the work of the men.
gwam 1' | 1 | 2 | 3 | 4 | 5 | 6 | 7 | 8 | 9 | 10 |

**23C • 10**
**Speed Building**

**LS:** DS

1. Key one 1' unguided and two 1' guided writings on ¶ 1 and then on ¶ 2, as directed on p. 54.
2. Key two 2' unguided writings on ¶s 1-2 combined; find *gwam* on each.

1' *gwam* goals
▽ 19 = acceptable
⊡ 23 = average
⊙ 27 = good
◇ 31 = excellent

all letters used     gwam 2'

```
          .    2    .    4    .    6    .    8    .
   The level of your skill is a major item when      5
 10    .   12    .   14    .   16    .   18   ▽
you try to get a job.  Just as vital, though, may    10
 20    .   22   ⊡  24    .   26   ⊙  28
be how well you can express ideas in written form.   15
          .    2    .    4    .    6    .    8    .
   It might amaze you to learn what it is worth      19
 10    .   12    .   14    .   16    .   18   ▽
to a company to find those who can write a letter    24
 20    .   22   ⊡  24    .   26   ⊙  28
of quality as they key.  Learn to do so in school.   29
2' |    1    |    2    |    3    |    4    |    5    |
```

continental cuisine and quality service. The Top-of-the-Mountain is open seven days a week for breakfast, lunch, and dinner. The adjoining Manor Lounge is perfect for relaxing conversation after a busy day. Later in the evening it's just the place to enjoy the greatest names in entertainment, which Clearview Manor provides each night of the week.

Recreational facilities. There's always something to do at Clearview Manor. Golf is available at the Manor's 18-hole golf course, and tennis can be played on the two indoor or five outdoor courts. Squash and racquetball can be played on air-conditioned indoor courts. In addition, resort guests can swim indoors or outdoors, and walk, jog, or hike for miles on well-marked trails. During the winter, guests can ski cross country on well-patrolled trails, ride for miles on a snowmobile, or skate on the indoor or outdoor rinks.

Travel Information

Clearview Manor is easily accessible by automobile or plane. If you are driving, you should use Exit 44 on Interstate 80 and follow the directional signs to Clearview Manor. If you are flying, use the Wilkes-Barre/Scranton Airport. Airport limousine, taxi, or automobile rental services are conveniently available.

---

**205B • 45**
**Reports: Sustained Practice**

**Time Schedule**

Plan and prepare ............. 5'
Timed practice ............... 30'
Proofread/compute
  n-pram ...................... 10'

1. Make a list of the reports to be processed:
   p. 479, Document 1
   p. 480, Document 2
   p. 482, Document 3
   p. 483, Document 1
2. Arrange materials for easy access. Process (in the order listed) the **first page** of as many of the reports as you can. Proofread and correct each document before beginning the next.
3. After time is called, proofread the final document and, if needed, print all completed work.
4. Identify uncorrected errors and compute n-pram:
   n-pram = words keyed − (15 x errors) divided by 30. Turn in work in order listed in Step 1.

## 23D • 11
## Difficult-Reach Mastery

1. Key each set of 4 lines once SS; DS between the 4-line groups.
2. Note the lines that caused you difficulty; practice them again to develop a steady pace.

**Adjacent (side-by-side) keys** (as in lines 1-4) can be the source of many errors unless the fingers are kept in an upright position and precise motions are used.

**Long direct reaches** (as in lines 5-8) reduce speed unless they are made without moving the hands forward and downward.

**Reaches with the outside fingers** (as in lines 9-12) are troublesome unless made without twisting the hands in and out at the wrist.

Fingers properly curved

Fingers properly aligned

**Adjacent-key letter combinations**

1 Rena saw her buy a red suit at a new shop in town.
2 Opal will try to stop a fast break down the court.
3 Jeremy knew that we had to pool our points to win.
4 Her posh party on their new patio was a real bash.

**Long direct reaches with same finger**

5 Herb is under the gun to excel in the second race.
6 My fervor for gym events was once my unique trait.
7 Music as a unique force is no myth in any country.
8 Lynda has since found many facts we must now face.

**Reaches with 3d and 4th fingers**

9 The poet will opt for a top spot in our port town.
10 Sam said the cash price for gas went up last week.
11 Zane played a zany tune that amazed the jazz band.
12 My squad set a quarter quota to equal our request.

## L ANGUAGE SKILLS

## 23E • 6
## Capitalization

Follow the *Standard Plan for Mastering Language Skills* given in 21D, p. 57.

Capitalize an official title when it precedes a name and elsewhere if it is a title of high distinction.

Learn 1 In what year did Juan Carlos become King of Spain?
Learn 2 Masami Chou, our class president, made the awards.
Apply 3 will the president speak to us in the rose garden?
Apply 4 mr. koch, our company president, chairs the group.

Capitalize initials; also capitalize letters in abbreviations if the letters would be capitalized when the words are spelled out.

Learn 5 Does Dr. R. J. Anderson have an Ed.D. or a Ph.D.?
Learn 6 He said that UPS stands for United Parcel Service.
Apply 7 we have a letter from ms. anna m. bucks of boston.
Apply 8 m.d. means Doctor of Medicine, not medical doctor.

Dining facilities. The center's master chef is prepared to provide an elegant cuisine for fine dining, informal buffets, nutritious snacks, and diet menus for a few to hundreds. The master chef also can provide many choices from the standard breakfast, lunch, dinner, and reception menus and will be happy to discuss special menus upon request.

General information. The Conference Center staff can provide special requests for entertainment, unusual decorations, and theme parties or meetings. Courier service can be provided for pickup or delivery of materials shipped via the rapid delivery services. Personnel for collecting tickets or staffing registration and information tables can also be provided. The state sales tax is 6 percent and will be added to all accounts. In addition, a gratuity of 15 percent will be charged on all food and beverage service.

The Resort

Clearview Manor's resort facilities provide everything necessary to make your stay pleasant and memorable. The resort offers top-quality accommodations, exceptional dining experiences, and a wide variety of entertainment and activities to choose from.

Lodging. Every room at Clearview Manor is spacious and professionally furnished with two double beds, a sofa, a table, and two chairs. Each room is equipped with a direct-dial telephone system, a safe, a refrigerator, color TV featuring cable and movie stations, and AM and FM radio with built-in alarm clock.

Dining and entertainment. Clearview Manor's popular Top-of-the-Mountain restaurant is known for its

(continued on next page)

## LESSON 24

# Keyboarding/Language Skills

**Objectives:**
1. To demonstrate proper keying technique.
2. To demonstrate skill on various kinds of copy.

### 24A • 5
**Conditioning Practice**

each line twice SS; then a 1' writing on line 3; find *gwam*

alphabet 1 Jack viewed unique forms by the puzzled tax agent.
? 2 Where is Elena?  Did she call?  Is she to go, too?
easy 3 Title to all of the lake land is held by the city.

gwam 1' | 1 | 2 | 3 | 4 | 5 | 6 | 7 | 8 | 9 | 10 |

### S KILL BUILDING

### 24B • 10
**Speed Building**

1. Key the lines once SS with a DS between 2-line groups.
2. If time permits, key the lines again to improve keying ease and speed.

**Technique goals**
- reach *up* without moving hands away from you
- reach *down* without moving hands toward your body
- use quick-snap keystrokes

ed/de 1 ed de led ode need made used side vied slide guide
2 Ned said the guide used a video film for her talk.

ju/ft 3 ju ft jug oft jet aft jug lift just soft jury loft
4 Judy left fifty jugs of juice on a raft as a gift.

ol/lo 5 ol lo old lot lob lox log sold loan fold long told
6 Lou told me that her local school loans old books.

ws/sw 7 ws sw was saw laws rows cows vows swam sways swing
8 Swin swims at my swim club and shows no big flaws.

ik/ki 9 ik ki kit ski kin kid kip bike kick like kiwi hike
10 The kid can hike or ride his bike to the ski lake.

za/az 11 za az zap adz haze zany lazy jazz hazy maze pizzas
12 A zany jazz band played with pizzazz at this plaza.

alphabet 13 Olive Fenz packed my bag with six quarts of juice.
14 Jud aims next to play a quick game with Bev Fritz.

gwam 1' | 1 | 2 | 3 | 4 | 5 | 6 | 7 | 8 | 9 | 10 |

### 24C • 14
**Speed Check:
Straight Copy**

**LS:** DS

1. Key one 1' unguided and two 1' guided writings on ¶ 1 and then on ¶ 2, as directed on p. 54.
2. Key two 2' unguided writings on ¶s 1-2 combined; find *gwam* on each.

**Goals**
1': At least 22 *gwam*.
2': At least 20 *gwam*.

E   all letters used                                     gwam 2'

```
          .       2       .       4       .       6       .       8
    You must realize by now that learning to key      5
  10      .    12      .    14      .    16      .    18
requires work.  However, you will soon be able to    10
20      .    22      .    24      .    26      .    28
key at a higher speed than you can write just now.   15
          .       2       .       4       .       6       .       8
    You will also learn to do neater work on the     19
  10      .    12      .    14      .    16      .    18
machine than you can do by hand.  Quality work at    24
20      .    22      .    24      .    26      .    28
higher speeds is a good goal for you to have next.   29
```

2' | 1 | 2 | 3 | 4 | 5 |

# LESSONS 204-205

## Reports: Sustained Practice

**Objectives:**
1. To process reports in pamphlet format.
2. To process reports under the pressure of time.

### 204-205A • 5 (daily) Conditioning Practice

each line twice

alphabet 1 Many plaques were just the right sizes for various duck exhibits.

speed 2 Karmela did lay the world map and rifle by the end of the mantle.

fig/sym 3 The ski oufit costs $358.41 (20% off), and she has only $297.60.

gwam 1' | 1 | 2 | 3 | 4 | 5 | 6 | 7 | 8 | 9 | 10 | 11 | 12 | 13 |

## FORMATTING

### 204B • 45

**Report in Parallel Column Format**

1. Key this information in 3" columns, moving from one column to another whenever a column becomes 7" deep. To keep the columns at 7", set top and bottom margins at 2". Use hyphenation and full justification.

2. You decide all other formatting features and the use of graphics.

3. Once the information has been keyed and formatted, it will be arranged in a three- or four-fold pamphlet.

---

CLEARVIEW MANOR
CONFERENCE CENTER

Situated 2,000 feet high on 2,700 acres of beautiful Pocono mountainside, Clearview Manor is a unique meeting, training, and resort facility for business and professional groups. Located two miles west of Mt. Pocono on Route 314, Clearview Manor provides an opportunity for groups to combine excellent conference facilities with outstanding resort facilities and activities.

The Conference Center

The center is known for its outstanding large and small meeting rooms with up-to-date computer and communication capabilities, spacious exhibit area, and elegant dining areas, which provide the necessary flexible space to meet the needs of groups from six to six hundred.

Meeting rooms. With nearly 6,000 square feet of meeting-room space, the Conference Center is a perfect choice for meetings. The space can be divided into eight separate, completely soundproof meeting rooms for groups ranging in size from 18 to 75. If larger rooms are required, the space can be divided to handle two large groups-- one of 376 and another of 262.

Exhibit area. The Conference Center can accommodate nearly 100 exhibitors in an unobstructed area of 15,000 square feet. Each exhibitor has access to alternating current, three-phase 60-cycle, 120/208-volt or 120-volt, single-phase current for both light and power circuits. Telephone, computer, radio, and closed-circuit television connections can be made. Exhibitors can make convenient delivery through a roll-up door (10 feet high by 11 feet wide) from a straight and level delivery drive.

*(continued on next page)*

## Corrected Copy (Rough Draft)

1. Study the proofreader's marks illustrated below and in the sentences.
2. Key each sentence DS, making all handwritten changes.
3. Rekey the lines to improve your correcting speed.

∧ = insert

\# = add space

∿ = transpose

⌦ = delete

⌒ = close up

≡ = capitalize

1 Rough draft is typed ~work~ _keyed copy_ with hand written changes.

2 Special marks _are_ may be used to show changes tobe made.

3 First, read a sentence notting changes; then ~type~ _key_ it.

4 Next, check to see ~if~ _that_ you made ~the~ changes _properly_ ~correctly~.

5 If not, correct your ~copy~ _work_ or key _the_ ~that~ sentence again.

6 Read rough draft _slightly_ ~a bit~ ahead of ~your~ _the_ keying p ɪ ont.

7 Doing _so_ ~this~ will help you _to_ make ~all~ the chang e right.

8 You _soon_ will key often from script and rough draft ~copy~.

---

## Skill Transfer: Straight Copy to Script and Rough Draft

1. Key each ¶ once SS; DS between ¶s.
2. Key a 1' writing on each ¶; find *gwam* on each writing; compare the three rates.

Your highest speed should be on ¶ 1 (straight copy); next highest on ¶ 2 (script); lowest on ¶ 3 (rough draft).

3. Key one or two more 1' writings on the two slowest ¶s to improve skill transfer.

### Recall

1' *gwam* = total words keyed

A standard word = 5 strokes (characters and spaces)

### Straight copy

`gwam` 1'

No matter what form the copy takes, keep the eyes on it    11

as you key.  If you look away from the copy, you lose a second    24

or two.  If you look away too often, your speed will drop by    36

a word or two.    39

### Script

*Fix your eyes on the copy now and keep them*    9

*there as you key this copy. Be quick to recognize*    19

*that looking away from the copy drops your speed.*    29

### Rough draft

Re ɛ d _a_ script and rough draft with _real_ ~great~ care to avɪod a    11

major error in _keying_ typing. Read \# _a bit_ ~slightly~ ahead of where _your_ ~the~ fingers    23

are key ing; that helps _to_ too.    29

**Document 3**
**Report with Inline Equation and Equation Boxes**
Process the test questions at the right in unbound report format. Use a 1" top margin; QS between questions. Use inline equation boxes for Questions 1-3; use an equation box for Question 4.

Student's Name: _____     Class Period: _____
Date: _____     Score: _____

_____

1. If *Regular Pay Rate* = $\dfrac{Regular\ Pay}{Regular\ Hours\ Worked}$ , is the equation

   *Hours Worked* = $\dfrac{Regular\ Pay}{Regular\ Pay\ Rate}$ correct? . . . . . . . . ____Yes ____No

2. If *Interest = Principal x Rate x Time*, is *Principal* = $\dfrac{Interest\ x\ Time}{Rate}$

   correct? . . . . . . . . . . . . . . . . . . . . . . . . . . . . . . . ____Yes ____No

3. Using *Interest = Principal x Rate x Time*, is *Rate* = $\dfrac{Interest}{Principal\ x\ Time}$

   correct? . . . . . . . . . . . . . . . . . . . . . . . . . . . . . . . ____Yes ____No

4. Is the equation listed below correct? . . . . . . . . . . . . . . . . ____Yes ____No

   *Hours Worked* = $\dfrac{Regular\ Pay}{Regular\ Pay\ Rate}$ + $\dfrac{Overtime\ Pay}{Overtime\ Pay\ Rate}$

5. Write an equation for finding Net Pay.

. . . . . . . . . . . . . . . . . . . . . . . . . . . . . . . . . . . . . . . . .

**Document 4**
**Report in Newspaper Format**

Open Document 2 (3-column newsletter) and add the article at the right. Compose a title and use at least one text box in the article, but you decide its content and format. If needed, you can adjust the bottom margin to get correct column endings and beginnings.

Appearance, which is often defined as the outward aspect of someone or something, is quite important to most of us and affects just about every day of our lives. We like to be around people and things we consider attractive. Because of this preference, appearance is a factor in almost every decision we make.

Appearance often affects our selection of food, the place in which we live, the clothes we purchase, the car we drive, and the vacations we schedule. For example, we usually do not eat foods that are not visually appealing or buy clothing that we realize may be unattractive to others who are important to us.

Appearance is important in business. People in charge of hiring almost always stress the importance of good appearance. Your progress in a job or career can be affected by how others judge your appearance. It is common for those who see but do not know you to evaluate your abilities and character on the basis of your personal appearance.

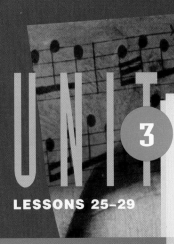

# UNIT 3

**LESSONS 25–29**

# Master Figure-Key Operation

## LESSON 25

### New Keys: 8 and 1

**Objectives:**

**1.** To learn reach technique for **8** and **1**.
**2.** To improve skill on straight-copy sentences and ¶s.

---

### 25A • 5
### Conditioning Practice

**LS:** SS
**SM:** defaults or 1.25"
each line twice (slowly, then faster); a 1' writing on line 3; find *gwam*

alphabet 1 Max was quick to fly a big jet plane over the frozen desert.

spacing 2 Any of them can aim for a top goal and reach it if they try.

easy 3 Nan is to go to the city hall to sign the land forms for us.

**gwam** 1' | 1 | 2 | 3 | 4 | 5 | 6 | 7 | 8 | 9 | 10 | 11 | 12 |

---

### 25B • 16
### New Keys: 8 and 1

each line twice (slowly, then faster); DS between 2-line groups; if time permits, key lines 5-7 again to build skill

**8** *Right middle* finger

**1** *Left little* finger

Follow the *Standard Plan for Learning New Keys* outlined on p. 17.

**Learn 8**

1 k k 8k 8k kk 88 k8k k8k 88k 88k Reach up for 8, 88, and 888.

2 Key the figures 8, 88, and 888.  Please open Room 88 or 888.

**Learn 1**

3 a a 1a 1a aa 11 a1a a1a 11a 11a Reach up for 1, 11, and 111.

4 Add the figures 1, 11, and 111.  Has just 1 of 111 finished?

**Combine 8 and 1**

5 Key 11, 18, 81, and 88.  Just 11 of the 18 skiers have left.

6 Reach with the fingers to key 18 and 188 as well as 1 and 8.

7 The stock person counted 11 coats, 18 slacks, and 88 shirts.

1. The articles below, the first two articles in a 3-column newsletter, are to be keyed with 1" margins, SS, hyphenation and full justification.

2. The main heading (title, volume, etc.) should be centered over all three columns and formatted appropriately.

3. Format article headings in large font size. Use 11-point font for body copy. You decide all other formatting features, including borders and graphics to be used.

# STRATEGIES FOR SUCCESS

**Vol. 6, No. 3 Spring, ----**

### Reputation and Choices

Reputation is the image people have aobut your standards of conduct; your ethical and moral principals. Most people think that a good reputation is needed to succeed in an job; and it is therefore, one of the most importnat personal assetts you can acquire in your life.

### A bad reputation can result from one misdeed.

A good reputation is a valued asset that requires time, effort, and discipline to develop and project. A bad reputation can be a longterm liability established in a short time. It can be a result from just one mis-

deed and can be a heavy burden to carry throughout life.

It is important to realize, therefore, that most of you have an opportunity to develope and protect the reputation you want. You have many chioces to make that will destroy or enhance the image you want to extned. The choices are hard; and honestly, loyalty, and dedicatoin are most often involved.

### Choices you make destroy or enhance your reputation.

### Learnig About People

Many aspects of a job present challenges to those who strive to do their best in all they do. The most critical challenge all workers face is being able to relate will with the many individuals with whom they have to work. It is common for workers to have dailty dealings with

bosses, peers, and subordinates. Also, most workers will interact with telephone callers and visitors from outside and inside the company daily.

### Relating well to others is a critical challenge.

While it is critical to learn all you can about your job and company, it is often just as critical to learn about the people with whom you will work and interact. Frequently, you can rely upon experienced workers for information that will help you analyze the formal and informal structures of the organization. What you learn may help you determine what an employer expects, likes, or dislikes, and will help you make a good adjustment to your workplace.

### Learn from experienced workers.

## New-Key Mastery

1. Key lines 1-12 once SS; DS between 2-line groups.
2. Key a 1' writing on line 13, then on line 14; find *gwam* on each writing.
3. If time permits, key a 1' writing on line 8 and then on line 12, trying to maintain your better rate in Step 2.

### Technique goals

- reach *up* without moving the hand forward
- reach *down* without twisting the wrists or moving the elbows in and out

**Row emphasis**

| | |
|---|---|
| figures | 1 The quiz on the 18th will be on pages 11 to 18 and 81 to 88. |
| | 2 Just 11 of the 118 boys got 81 of the 88 quiz answers right. |
| home/1st | 3 hand axe\|lava gas\|can mask\|jazz band\|lack cash\|a small flask |
| | 4 Ms. Hamm can call a cab, and Max can flag a small black van. |
| home/3d | 5 she quit\|with just\|that play\|fair goal\|will help\|they did go |
| | 6 Dru said you should try for the goal of top speed this week. |

**Response patterns**

| | |
|---|---|
| letter response | 7 as in re on we no ax up gas oil red mop fee hum are you were |
| | 8 You, in fact, saw him on a pump barge up at my mill at noon. |
| word response | 9 if so is do id go us me am by an ox and the for men end form |
| | 10 She is to go by the zoo to sign a work form for the six men. |
| combination response | 11 if as so in is re do on go we us no me ax am up by pi an kin |
| | 12 If she is at the inn, we may go by car to see a poppy field. |
| easy | 13 Ty is to pay for the eight pens she laid by the audit forms. |
| | 14 Keith is to row with us to the lake to fix six of the signs. |

| gwam | 1' | 1 | 2 | 3 | 4 | 5 | 6 | 7 | 8 | 9 | 10 | 11 | 12 |

## S KILL BUILDING

## Speed Building

1. Key a 1' writing on each ¶; find *gwam* on each writing.
2. Add 2-4 *gwam* to better rate in Step 1 for a new goal.
3. Key three 1' guided writings on each ¶ at new goal rate. (See p. 54 for procedure.)

### Quarter-Minute Checkpoints

| gwam | 1/4' | 1/2' | 3/4' | Time |
|---|---|---|---|---|
| 16 | 4 | 8 | 12 | 16 |
| 20 | 5 | 10 | 15 | 20 |
| 24 | 6 | 12 | 18 | 24 |
| 28 | 7 | 14 | 21 | 28 |
| 32 | 8 | 16 | 24 | 32 |
| 36 | 9 | 18 | 27 | 36 |
| 40 | 10 | 20 | 30 | 40 |

all letters used                                                                      gwam   2'

Do you think someone is going to wait around just for a          6

chance to key your term paper?  Do you believe when you get      12

out into the world of work that there will be someone to key     18

your work for you?  Think again.  It does not work that way.     24

Even the head of a business now uses a keyboard to send      29

and retrieve data as well as other information.  Be quick to     35

realize that you will not go far in the world of work if you     42

do not learn how to key.  Excel at it and move to the top.       47

| 2' | 1 | 2 | 3 | 4 | 5 | 6 |

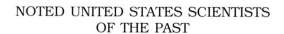

## NOTED UNITED STATES SCIENTISTS
## OF THE PAST

The scientists named in this report lived in the United States during the
last quarter of the 20th Century.  The scientist's name is in the first column,
and year of birth and year of death is in the second column. The third column indicates the accomplishment or area of expertise for which the scientist is noted.  The information is taken from The 1995 World Almanac and
Book of Facts, (Mahwah, NJ: Funk & Wagnalls, 1994), pp. 349–353.

| | | | |
|---|---|---|---|
| John Bardeen | 1908-1991 | The co-inventor of the transistor that led to modern electronics. | 110 116 |
| Max Delbruck | 1907-1981 | A pioneer in modern molecular genetics. | 128 129 |
| John F. Enders | 1897-1985 | A virologist who helped discover vaccines to fight polio, measles, and mumps. | 141 148 150 |
| Richard Feynman | 1918-1988 | A leading theoretical physicist of the postwar generation. | 162 167 |
| Julian Huxley | 1887-1975 | A biologist and gifted exponent and philosopher of science. | 179 184 |
| Edwin Land | 1900-1991 | Inventor of the Polaroid camera. | 195 |
| Robert N. Noyce | 1927-1989 | Inventor of the microchip that has revolutionized the electronics industry throughout the world. | 207 214 220 |
| Robert Norris Page | 1903-1992 | A physicist who served as research director of the U.S. Naval Research Laboratory and a leading figure in the development of radar technology. | 232 240 247 254 |
| Linus Pauling | 1901-1994 | A chemist who specialized in chemical bonds. | 266 268 |
| Roy Plunkett | 1922-1994 | A chemist who created Teflon™. | 280 |
| Isidor Issac Rabi | 1898-1988 | A physicist who pioneered atom exploration. | 291 294 |
| Albert B. Sabin | 1906-1993 | Developed the oral polio vaccine. | 306 |
| Roger Sperry | 1913-1994 | A brain expert who studied the relationship between the right and left sides of the brain. | 318 325 329 |
| Wernher von Braun | 1912-1977 | A pioneer in the development of rockets. | 342 344 |
| Sewall Wright | 1889-1988 | An evolutionary theorist. | 354 |

# LESSON 26

## New Keys: 9 and 4

**Objectives:**
1. To learn reach technique for **9** and **4**.
2. To improve language skills and skill transfer.

---

### 26A • 5
### Conditioning Practice

**LS:** SS
**SM:** defaults or 1.25"
each line twice; then a
1' writing on line 3; find
*gwam*

alphabet 1 Joby quickly fixed a glass vase and amazed the proud owners.

spacing 2 She told us to add the figures 11, 88, 18, 81, 118, and 881.

easy 3 Ciel may make a bid on the ivory forks they got in the city.

**gwam** 1' | 1 | 2 | 3 | 4 | 5 | 6 | 7 | 8 | 9 | 10 | 11 | 12 |

---

### 26B • 18
### New Keys: 9 and 4

each line twice SS (slowly,
then faster); DS between
2-line groups; if time
permits, key lines 5-7 again

**9** *Right ring* finger

**4** *Left index* finger

Follow the *Standard Plan for Learning New Keys* outlined on p. 17.

**Learn 9**

use the letter "l"

1 l l 9l 9l ll 99 l9l l9l 99l 99l Reach up for 9, 99, and 999.

2 Key the figures 9, 99, and 999.   Did the 9 and 99 finish it?

**Learn 4**

3 f f 4f 4f ff 44 f4f f4f 44f 44f Reach up for 4, 44, and 444.

4 Add the figures 4, 44, and 444.   Please study pages 4 to 44.

**Combine 9 and 4**

5 Key 44, 49, 94, and 99.   Only 49 of the 94 joggers are here.

6 Reach with the fingers to key 49 and 499 as well as 4 and 9.

7 My goal is to sell 44 pizzas, 99 tacos, and 9 cases of cola.

---

### 26C • 5
### New-Key Mastery

1. Key each of lines 1-3 twice SS (slowly, then faster); DS between 2-line groups.
2. If time permits, key each line again for speed.

**Figure sentences**

1 Keep the fingers low as you key 11, 18, 19, 48, 94, and 849.

use the figure "1"

2 On March 8, 1994, 14 people took the 4 tests for the 8 jobs.

3 He based his May 1 report on pages 449 to 488 of Chapter 19.

4. Study continues on security features 326
to prevent unauthorized (internal and external) 335
access to sensitive information. Stair discussed 345
the security risks as a disadvantage of net- 354
working (219). 357

5. As Fuller and Manning implied (193), 365
the sharing of resources that a LAN makes pos- 375
sible will make a major difference in the 383
department's workflow. Therefore, the Task 392
Force is beginning to outline procedural 400
changes that will be necessary. 407

6. Capron's comments (113) about 414
the shared resource advantage of networks sug- 422
gest that users will require training if the net- 432
work is to be used optimally. The Task Force is 442
beginning to identify training requirements. 451

Future Activities 455

Before networking the department's com- 462
puters, printers, and scanner, a complete phase- 473
in plan will be designed with the aid of an 481

independent consultant. The information 489
gathering should be completed within the next 499
six to eight weeks, with an implementation plan 508
to follow soon after. 513

Works Cited 515

Capron, H. L. Essentials of Computing. Red- 524
wood City, CA: The Benjamin/Cum- 531
mings Publishing Company, Inc., 1992. 539

Fuller, Floyd and William Manning. Comput- 547
ers and Information Processing. Boston: 556
Boyd and Fraser Publishing Company, 563
1994. 565

Ray, Charles, Janet Palmer, and Amy D. Wohl. 574
Office Automation: A Systems Approach. 582
2d ed. Cincinnati: South-Western Pub- 590
lishing Co., 1991. 594

Stair, Ralph M. Principles of Information Sys- 603
tems. Boston: Boyd and Fraser Publish- 612
ing Company, 1992. 615

---

## LESSONS 202-203

## Reports

**Objectives:**
1. To process reports that use columns, graphics, and border features.
2. To improve ability to key from rough-draft and script copy.

**202-203A • 5 (daily)**
**Conditioning Practice**

each line twice

alphabet 1 Que rejects my idea of having two dozen oak trees by the complex.

speed 2 Di and the eight sorority girls may handle half of the endowment.

figures 3 Flights leave for Chicago at 6:48 a.m., 12:09 p.m., and 5:37 p.m.

gwam 1' | 1 | 2 | 3 | 4 | 5 | 6 | 7 | 8 | 9 | 10 | 11 | 12 | 13 |

**F** ORMATTING

**202-203B • 45 (daily)**
**Reports**

**Document 1**
**Report in Parallel Column Format**

1. Process the copy on p. 484 as an unbound report. When keying the list of scientists, use the 3-column parallel feature. Make the first column about 1.5" wide, the second column about 1" wide, and third column about 3.5" wide. Leave about 0.5" between columns.

2. Place a border around the parallel columns.

## 26D • 12
### Script and Rough-Draft Copy

**LS:** DS
**SM:** defaults or 1.25"

1. Key each line once DS (2 hard returns between lines).
2. Rekey the rough-draft lines if time permits.

≡ = capitalize

∧ = insert

⟩ = delete

∿ = transpose

⟩# = delete space

# = add space

/ˡᶜ = lowercase

⊃ = close up

**Script**

1 Proofread: Compare copy word for word with the original.

2 Compare all figures digit by digit with your source copy.

3 Be sure to check for spacing and punctuation marks, also.

4 Copy in script or rough draft may not show exact spacing.

5 It is your job to insert correct spacing as you key copy.

6 Soon you will learn how to correct your errors on screen.

**Rough draft**

7 cap the first word an all proper nouns in every sentence.

8 For example:  pablo Mendez is from San juan, Puerto rico.

9 Ami Qwan and her parents will return to Taipie this summer.

10 our coffee comes is from Columbia; tea, from England or china.

11 How many of you have Ethnic origins ina for eign country?

12 Did you know which of the states once were part of mexico?

---

## L ANGUAGE SKILLS

### 26E • 10
### Number Expression

**Standard Plan for Mastering Language Skills**

1. Read the first rule highlighted in color.
2. Key the Learn sentence below it, noting how the rule is applied.
3. Key the Apply sentence, supplying the appropriate number expression.
4. Practice the other rules in the same way.
5. If time permits, key the Apply sentences again to improve number control.

**LANGUAGE SKILLS *cue*:**
No space is left before or after : when used with figures to express time.

Spell a number that begins a sentence even when other numbers in the sentence are shown in figures.

Learn 1 Twelve of the new shrubs have died; 48 are doing quite well.
Apply 2 14 members have paid their dues, but 89 have not done so.

Use figures for numbers above ten, and for numbers one to ten when they are used with numbers above ten.

Learn 3 She ordered 8 word processors, 14 computers, and 4 printers.
Apply 4 Did he say they need ten or 14 sets of Z18 and Z19 diskettes?

Use figures to express dates and times (except when used with the word *o'clock*).

Learn 5 He will arrive on Paygo Flight 418 at 9:48 a.m. on March 14.
Apply 6 Candidates must be in Ivy Hall at eight forty a.m. on May one.

Conclusion 865

The business faculty believes that this 873
DTP course must be added to the curriculum 881
so that the department can continue to equip 890
graduates with the up-to-date skills and knowl- 900
edge they need to enter and perform well in the 909
business world. 913

Truly, desktop publishing is a technology 921
whose time has come. It is having--and will 930
continue to have--a significant impact on the 939
way information is presented. It is a produc- 948
tivity tool in most businesses that is used to 958
increase output and decrease costs. 965

### ENDNOTES 967

[1]B. Lewis Keeling and Norman F. Kallaus, 975
Administrative Office Management, Abridged, 984
11th ed. (Cincinnati: South-Western Educa- 993
tional Publishing, 1996), p. 398. 1000

[2]Charles Ray, Janet Palmer, and Amy 1007
Wohl, Office Automation, 3d ed. (Cincinnati: 1016
South-Western Publishing Co., 1995), p. 134. 1026

[3]B. Lewis Keeling and Norman F. Kallaus, 1034
Administrative Office Management, 11th ed. 1043
(Cincinnati: South-Western Educational Pub- 1051
lishing, 1996), p. 457. 1056

[4]Keeling, Administrative Office Manage- 1064
ment, 11th ed., p. 511. 1070

### REFERENCES 1072

Keeling, B. Lewis, and Norman F. Kallaus. 1080
Administrative Office Management. 1087
Abridged. 11th ed. Cincinnati: South- 1095
Western Educational Publishing, 1996. 1103

Keeling, B. Lewis, and Norman F. Kallaus. 1111
Administrative Office Management. 11th 1119
ed. Cincinnati: South-Western Educa- 1127
tional Publishing, 1996. 1132

Ray, Charles, Janet Palmer, and Amy Wohl. 1141
Office Automation. 3d ed. Cincinnati: 1149
South-Western Publishing Co., 1995. 1156

.........................................................................................................................

**Document 3**
**MLA-Style Report**
Refer: pp. RG13-14

Process the report (use headers with page numbers) with Works Cited page. Use your name, your teacher's name, and the current date for the title information on p. 1. Instead of the course title, use **Public Relations and Advertising** in its place.

Networking--A Status Report 6

This report describes the status of the pro- 15
ject to network computers in the Public Rela- 23
tions and Advertising Departments. The 32
Networking Task Force has done much work and 40
some "rethinking" since the previous report. 50

Decisions Made 53

At last report, the Task Force had decided to 62
install a local area network (LAN); and that deci- 72
sion remains in place. The committee investigated 82
neural networks, described by Ray, Palmer, and 92
Wohl (565) as able "to learn by example and to 101
analyze incomplete, even inaccurate information, 111
so-called fuzzy data, including spoken words and 121
fingerprints." Neural networks are not yet practi- 131
cal for this organization, however. Therefore, a 141
classic star topology will be used for the LAN. 151

The director of computing obtained prices for a 160
host computer and network software, network 169

cards, cabling, etc., that meet specifications. 179
The price of the applications software, Suite Suc- 189
cess (network version), also has been obtained. 199

Current Activities 203

1. The choice of a graphics package in 211
line with the department's needs has been nar- 220
rowed to two: Double Verity from Bechtel and 230
BonaFide from RTR Labs. A choice will be made 239
within the next two weeks. 245

2. Four communication packages are un- 253
der consideration. Within the next month, one 262
of them will be identified as the best vehicle for 272
e-mail and Internet access in the department. 281

3. On the basis of price information, a 290
budget is being prepared. The first figures will 300
be released next month; the numbers are too 308
"soft" yet to be included with this report. 317

(continued on next page)

| | |
|---|---|
| **LESSON 27** | **New Keys: 0 and 5**  |

**Objectives:**
1. To learn reach technique for **0** and **5**.
2. To improve language skills and skill transfer.

### 27A • 5
### Conditioning Practice

**LS:** SS
**SM:** defaults or 1.25"
each line twice (slowly, then faster); DS between 2-line groups; then a 1' writing on line 3

alphabet 1 Roz may put a vivid sign next to the low aqua boat for Jack.
figures 2 Please review Figure 8 on page 94 and Figure 14 on page 189.
easy 3 Tien may fix the bus panel for the city if the pay is right.
gwam 1' | 1 | 2 | 3 | 4 | 5 | 6 | 7 | 8 | 9 | 10 | 11 | 12 |

### 27B • 18
### New Keys: 0 and 5

each line twice (slowly, then faster); DS between 2-line groups; if time permits, key lines 5-7 again

**0** *Right little* finger

**5** *Left index* finger

Follow the *Standard Plan for Learning New Keys* outlined on p. 17.

**Learn 0 (zero)**
1 ; ; 0; 0; ;; 00 ;0; ;0; 00; 00; Reach up for 0, 00, and 000.
2 Snap the finger off the 0.  I used 0, 00, and 000 sandpaper.

**Learn 5**
3 f f 5f 5f ff 55 f5f f5f 55f 55f Reach up for 5, 55, and 555.
4 Reach up to 5 and back to f.  Did he say to order 55 or 555?

**Combine 0 and 5**
5 Reach with the fingers to key 50 and 500 as well as 5 and 0.
6 We asked for prices on these models:  50, 55, 500, and 5500.
7 On May 5, I got 5 boxes each of 0 and 00 steel wool for her.

### 27C • 5
### New-Key Mastery

each line once DS (2 hard returns between lines)

**LANGUAGE SKILLS cues:**
- No space is left before or after : when used with figures to express time.
- Most nouns before numbers are capitalized; exceptions include page and line.

No space

1 Flight 1049 is on time; it should be at Gate 48 at 5:50 p.m.
2 The club meeting on April 5 will be in Room 549 at 8:10 a.m.
3 Of our 108 workers in 1994, 14 had gone to new jobs by 1995.
4 I used Chapter 19, pages 449 to 458, for my March 10 report.
5 Can you meet us at 1954 Maple Avenue at 8:05 a.m. August 10?
6 Of the 590 students, 185 keyed at least 40 wam by April 18.

## Course Description

| | words |
|---|---|
| | 195 |

The course provides students an opportunity to learn about desktop publishing and to use DTP software. Students write text; use graphics; decide font face, size, and style; and create the document design and layout for various business documents. Experience with laser printers and scanners is also acquired. Being a competent user of word processing and graphics software is a prerequisite for the course.

## Course Objectives

Students who complete the desktop publishing course will be able to:

- Define DTP, discuss DTP advantages and disadvantages, and identify DTP employment opportunities within the community.[4]

- Demonstrate competency in operating a microcomputer, laser printer, and scanner with DTP software.

- Design and process newsletters, certificates, business cards, letterheads, report covers, fliers, and directories using DTP software.

- Arrange and participate in a mock interview with a potential DTP employer.

## Teaching/Learning Strategies and Resources

Readings, lectures, demonstrations, and class discussions will be used for about 25 percent of the class time to accomplish the basic learning objectives. Students will spend the remaining class time applying what they have learned. During this time, they will use DTP software to acquire the competencies needed to produce the required documents.

Recommendation. A computer laboratory with computers, printers, and a scanner on a local area network is the recommended setting. Furthermore, class size should not exceed 25 students; and each student should have a computer work station. If this recommendation is accepted, the following equipment will be needed:

- Thirty Pentium-75MHz multimedia computers (25 for students, one for teacher, one to be used as file server, and three for backup). Each is to have an 850MB hard drive, 8MB RAM, double-speed CD-ROM drive, 16-bit stereo sound card and speakers, SRS stereo sound, and 1MB video RAM, one serial port, one parallel port, LAN board, and enhanced keyboard.

- Thirty VGA color monitors with VGA video adapters.

- Twenty-nine mouse or track-ball units.

- One desktop, flatbed design scanner with interface kit and scanner software.

- Three laser printers with 8 1/2" x 11" paper tray; one to be a color printer.

Cost and location. The estimated cost to purchase or upgrade hardware and software for this DTP course is $75,000 (maximum). The faculty recommends that the computing resources be located in Room 101 and that the room be named the Business Technologies Computer Laboratory. When equipped, this room will be able to support software instruction (word processing, database, graphics, spreadsheet, and communications) and student newspaper and yearbook production.

## Evaluation and Grading

Students will be evaluated according to their performance on written examinations, the quality and quantity of documents produced, and classroom participation. Written examinations will be given near the end of each grading period; unannounced quizzes will be given periodically during each grading period; and required documents will be due throughout the course.

Grades will be computed based on the following weighting:

1. Desktop publishing documents--50%.

2. Unannounced quizzes--10%.

3. Written examinations--30%.

4. Classroom participation--10%.

*(continued on next page)*

1. Key each ¶ once SS; DS between ¶s.
2. Key a 1' writing on each ¶; find *gwam* on each writing; compare the 3 rates.
3. Key one or two more 1' writings on the two slowest ¶s to improve skill transfer.

*stet* = no change

∧ = insert

⟩ = delete

# = add space

⊂ = close up

∿ = transpose

⊙ = insert period

### Straight copy

gwam 1'

It is up to you to proofread the copy you produce to    11

find any mistakes you may have made.  It is also up to you    22

to correct all the errors you find if the copy is to serve    34

a purpose other than to show that you have done the work.    46

| 1 | 2 | 3 | 4 | 5 | 6 | 7 | 8 | 9 | 10 | 11 | 12 |

### Script

It is vital to check your copy word for word against    11
the source copy from which you keyed. The words should    22
be in the same order, and each word must be spelled right.    34
A space should be left after each word or punctuation mark.    46

### Rough draft

Be quick to discover your errors even if you will not    11

correct them just now.  As soon as you begin to ap ply your    22

skill you may be taught easy ways to cor rect errors.  For now,    35

lern to excell in marking and finding them    44

## LANGUAGE SKILLS

27E • 10
### Number Expression

Use the *Standard Plan for Mastering Language Skills,* p. 67.

Use figures for house numbers except house number **One**.

Learn 1 My home is at 8 Vernon Drive; my office, at One Weber Plaza.
Apply 2 The Nelsons moved from 4059 Pyle Avenue to 1 Maple Circle.

Use figures to express measures and weights.

Learn 3 Glenda Redford is 5 ft. 4 in. tall and weighs 118 lbs. 9 oz.
Apply 4 This carton measures one ft. by nine in. and weighs five lbs.

Use figures for numbers following nouns.

Learn 5 Review Rules 1 to 18 in Chapter 5, pages 149 and 150, today.
Apply 6 Case 1849 is reviewed in Volume five, pages nine and ten.

to determine the best answers to "what- 285
if" questions. Electronic spreadsheets, for 294
example, allow decision makers to 301
analyze the impact of "what-if" financial, 310
marketing, or production alternatives.[2] 318

Expert system (ES). An ES is a computer 326
application program that "makes the knowl- 335
edge of experts available to others"[3] to assist 344
problem solving in areas where expert knowl- 353
edge is needed but not available. Information 363
stored in the application program includes the 372
data and decision rules pertaining to a special- 382
ized body of knowledge. There it is available 391
to nonexperts who need to perform at an 399
expert level in that knowledge area. 407

Executive information system (EIS). An 415
EIS is a computer application program used 423
by top-level managers to plot the course of a 433
business. An EIS allows a manager to look 441
quickly and accurately at summarized 449
business information to spot trends and 457
changes so that a timely reaction to business 466
conditions can be made.[4] 471

These computer applications are signifi- 479
cant enhancements to the functions of the com- 489
puter; and they, as well as newer applications, 498
are likely to become more and more prevalent 507
as a means to improve decision making. 514

[1]Ralph M. Stair, Principles of Information 523
Systems (Boston: Boyd and Fraser Publishing 532
Company, 1992), p. 5. 537

[2]Floyd Fuller and William Manning, Com- 545
puters and Information Processing (Boston: 554
Boyd and Fraser Publishing Company, 1994), 563
p. 281. 564

[3]Steven Alter, Information Systems (Read- 573
ing, MA: Addison-Wesley Publishing Company, 582
1992), p. 128. 585

[4]Fuller, Computers and Information Pro- 593
cessing, p. 282. 597

BIBLIOGRAPHY 599

Alter, Steven. Information Systems. Reading, 609
MA: Addison-Wesley Publishing Company, 617
1992. 618

Fuller, Floyd, and William Manning. Com- 626
puters and Information Processing. 635
Boston: Boyd and Fraser Publishing 642
Company, 1994. 644

Stair, Ralph M. Principles of Information Sys- 654
tems. Boston: Boyd and Fraser Publish- 662
ing Company, 1992. 666

- - - - - - - - - - - - - - - - - - - - - - - - - - - - - - - - - - - - - - - - - - - - - - - - - - - - -

**Document 2**
**Bound Report**
**with Endnotes**

Process the report (use headers, footers, and/or page numbering as appropriate) with endnotes
page, references page, table of contents, and title page.

A COURSE PROPOSAL 4

The business faculty have voted unani- 11
mously to offer a one-semester desktop publishing 21
(DTP) course beginning next September. 29
The course will be an elective course for all 38
students who have completed the existing word 47
processing or business computer applications 56
courses. 58

Rationale for the Course 63

Desktop publishing is one of the fastest- 72
growing computer applications because its use 81
saves businesses money and reduces the time 90

required to create professional-looking docu- 99
ments and presentation graphics.[1] Because of 108
the increased use and the resulting demand for 117
employees who can use DTP software, 124
the business faculty has a responsibility 133
to develop student competencies using 140
this technology.[2] 144

In addition to learning DTP applications, 153
students will apply writing, problem-solving, 163
decision-making, and creativity skills as 171
they prepare text, plan graphics, and lay out 180
the various documents they will process in 189
the course.[3] 191

(continued on next page)

# LESSON 28

## New Keys: 7 and 3

**Objectives:**

**1.** To learn the reach technique for **7** and **3**.

**2.** To improve keying speed and language skills.

### 28A • 5
### Conditioning Practice

**LS:** SS

**SM:** defaults or 1.25"

each line twice; DS between 2-line groups; then a 1' writing on line 3

alphabet  1  Gavin made a quick fall trip by jet to Zurich six weeks ago.

figures  2  Key 1 and 4 and 5 and 8 and 9 and 0 and 190 and 504 and 958.

easy  3  The man is to fix the big sign by the field for a city firm.

**gwam**  1' | 1 | 2 | 3 | 4 | 5 | 6 | 7 | 8 | 9 | 10 | 11 | 12 |

### 28B • 18
### New Keys: 7 and 3

each line twice SS (slowly, then faster); DS between 2-line groups; if time permits, key lines 5-7 again

**7**  *Right index* finger

**3**  *Left middle* finger

Follow the *Standard Plan for Learning New Keys* outlined on p. 17.

**Learn 7**

1  j j 7j 7j jj 77 j7j j7j 77j 77j Reach up for 7, 77, and 777.

2  Key the figures 7, 77, and 777.  She checked Rooms 7 and 77.

**Learn 3**

3  d d 3d 3d dd 33 d3d d3d 33d 33d Reach up for 3, 33, and 333.

4  Add the figures 3, 33, and 333.  Read pages 3 to 33 tonight.

**Combine 7 and 3**

5  Key 33, 37, 73, and 77.  Just 37 of the 77 skiers have come.

6  Please order 7 Model 337 computers and 3 Model 737 printers.

7  On August 7, the 33 bikers left on a long trip of 377 miles.

## S KILL BUILDING

### 28C • 7
### Technique:
### Response Patterns

1. Key each pair of lines once SS; DS between 2-line groups.

2. Key a 1' writing on line 2 and then on line 4; find *gwam* on each writing.

3. Rekey the slower line if time permits.

letter response  1  face pump ever milk area jump vast only save upon safe union

2  As we were in a junk, we saw a rare loon feast on a crawdad.

word response  3  quay hand also body lend hang mane down envy risk corn whale

4  Tisha is to go to the lake with us if she is to do the work.

combination response  5  with only|they join|half safe|born free|firm look|goal rates

6  I sat on the airy lanai with my gaze on the sea to the east.

**gwam**  1' | 1 | 2 | 3 | 4 | 5 | 6 | 7 | 8 | 9 | 10 | 11 | 12 |

# UNIT
## 43
# Process Reports

LESSONS 200–205

## LESSONS
## 200–201

## Reports

**Objectives:**
1. To process reports with footnotes, endnotes, or textual citations.
2. To process tables of contents and title pages.

---

**200-201A • 5 (daily)**
**Conditioning Practice**

each line twice; 1' writings
on lines 1 and 2 as time
permits

| | | |
|---|---|---|
| alphabet | 1 | Zack told Peg to be quiet and enjoy the first extra cowboy movie. |
| speed | 2 | Claudia is to land the giant dirigible by the busy downtown mall. |
| fig/sym | 3 | Ho's expenses are taxi--$59; airline--$260; auto--$37 (148 miles). |

**gwam** 1' | 1 | 2 | 3 | 4 | 5 | 6 | 7 | 8 | 9 | 10 | 11 | 12 | 13 |

---

## **F** ORMATTING

**200-201B • 45 (daily)**
**Reports**

Refer: pp. RG12-14

**Document 1**
**Unbound Report with Footnotes**

Process report including footnotes, with a bibliography, table of contents, and title page. Use appropriate headers or footers and/or page numbering.

---

| | words |
|---|---|
| COMPUTERS AND DECISION MAKING | 6 |

Computers have widespread use in today's world. Computers are used by workers who produce goods and services and by consumers who use goods and services. — 14, 23, 31, 37

Computers in Business — 42

People who pursue a career in business will learn that computers have helped reduce the cost of and time devoted to managing and processing information. Computers have no equal for computing, classifying, sorting, moving, editing, or storing information. — 50, 59, 68, 76, 86, 93

New Uses — 95

Computers are used to provide "accurate, complete, economical, reliable, simple, timely, and verifiable"[1] information to managers. This use is taking on a new dimension as innovative — 104, 113, 123, 132

computer applications are introduced. The new applications provide top-level managers with resources to improve decision making. Three such resources are decision support systems, expert systems, and executive information systems. — 142, 151, 160, 169, 177, 179

Decision support system (DSS). Decision support systems are computer applications that support the decision-making process. — 187, 197, 204

A DSS often helps managers choose among alternatives. A DSS includes a set of quantitative, modeling, and simulation programs. Together, these programs represent a set of mathematical, statistical, and graphic tools. They allow the DSS user to manipulate data in a variety of ways. . . . Many DSS's provide managers with the flexibility to look into the future — 211, 220, 227, 235, 244, 253, 261, 269, 278

*(continued on next page)*

## 28D • 8
## Speed Check

LS: DS

1. Key a 1' writing on ¶ 1 and then on ¶ 2; find *gwam* on each ¶.
2. Key two 2' writings on ¶s 1-2 combined; find *gwam* on each writing.

1' *gwam* goals
▽ 21 = acceptable
⊡ 25 = average
☉ 29 = good
◇ 33 = excellent

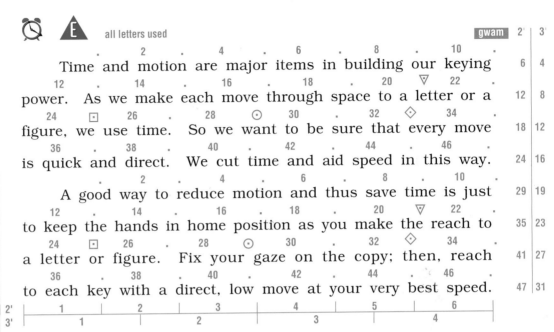

| all letters used | gwam | 2' | 3' |
|---|---|---|---|
| . 2 . 4 . 6 . 8 . 10 . | | | |
| Time and motion are major items in building our keying | | 6 | 4 |
| 12 . 14 . 16 . 18 . 20 ▽ 22 . | | | |
| power. As we make each move through space to a letter or a | | 12 | 8 |
| 24 ⊡ 26 . 28 ☉ 30 . 32 ◇ 34 . | | | |
| figure, we use time. So we want to be sure that every move | | 18 | 12 |
| 36 . 38 . 40 . 42 . 44 . 46 . | | | |
| is quick and direct. We cut time and aid speed in this way. | | 24 | 16 |
| . 2 . 4 . 6 . 8 . 10 . | | | |
| A good way to reduce motion and thus save time is just | | 29 | 19 |
| 12 . 14 . 16 . 18 . 20 ▽ 22 . | | | |
| to keep the hands in home position as you make the reach to | | 35 | 23 |
| 24 ⊡ 26 . 28 ☉ 30 . 32 ◇ 34 . | | | |
| a letter or figure. Fix your gaze on the copy; then, reach | | 41 | 27 |
| 36 . 38 . 40 . 42 . 44 . 46 . | | | |
| to each key with a direct, low move at your very best speed. | | 47 | 31 |

gwam 2' | 1 | 2 | 3 | 4 | 5 | 6 |
gwam 3' | 1 | 2 | 3 | 4 |

## 28E • 12
## Capitalization and Number Expression

Use the *Standard Plan for Mastering Language Skills*, p. 67.

Capitalize nouns preceding numbers (except **page** and **line**).

Learn 1 Please see Rule 30 in Unit 3, page 45, lines 17 and 18.
Apply 2 See Volume 13, section 48, page 574, lines 78 to 90.

Spell (and initial cap) names of small-numbered streets and avenues (ten and under).

Learn 3 I walked several blocks along Third Avenue to 54th Street.
Apply 4 At 7th Street she took a taxi to his home on 43d Avenue.

Spell indefinite numbers.

Learn 5 Joe owns one acre of Parcel A; that is almost fifty percent.
Learn 6 Nearly seventy members voted; that is nearly a fourth.

Apply 7 i read 3 items from COLLECTED POEMS by robert frost.
Apply 8 he arrives on Flight 175 at 8 a.m. on friday.
Apply 9 kim is to meet us on 58th street at 5th avenue.
Apply 10 she asked over 30 students; almost a 3d of us went.
Apply 11 we attended a meeting in room 193 of columbia hall.
Apply 12 i saw the quote on Page 173b of FAMILIAR QUOTATIONS.

# ACTIVITY 4:

**Borders**

1. Read the copy at right.
2. Learn how to add borders using your software.
3. Follow the directions at the right to add a border to a page, a paragraph, and a column.

Use the **Border** feature to add a border around a page, paragraph, or column.

Borders can be customized or chosen from a variety of predefined border styles.

**Border Around Page**

1. Use the following information to prepare a title page, including a border style of your choice. (See p. 368 for title page formatting guides.)

ADDING BORDERS TO DOCUMENTS

Your name

School name

Current date

2. Save the title page as WP13-4A.

**Border Around Paragraph**

1. Open WP13-1 if it is not open and rename it WP13-4B.
2. Place a border around each of the three ¶s, selecting a different border for each ¶. Shade the middle ¶.
3. Save the document (WP13-4B).

**Border Around Columns**

1. Open WP13-3B if it is not open and rename it WP13-4C.
2. Add the following centered title in a large font (approx. 24 point) 1" from the top: IMPORTANCE OF BUSINESS ETHICS.
3. Insert a centered horizontal line (about 6.5" long) between the title and the graphic.
4. Place a border around the page and between each pair of columns.
5. Save the document (WP13-4C).

# ACTIVITY 5:

**Printing**

1. Read the copy at right.
2. Learn how to make print selections using your software.
3. Follow the directions at right to print portions of a document.

Use **Options** from the Print menu to print the current page of a document, selected pages of the document, or selected portions of the document.

1. Open TWP13-5 and rename it WP13-5A.
2. Add page numbering at bottom center of each page.
3. Change font size to 16 point.
4. Keep lines of text together (protect text) appropriately.
5. Display last page of document on monitor.
6. Print the last page.
7. Print pages 1 and 4 of the document.
8. Print the first six lines of the second page of the document.

# LESSON 29

## New Keys: 6 and 2

**Objectives:**
1. To learn the reach technique for **6** and **2**.
2. To improve keying technique and speed.

---

### 29A • 5
### Conditioning Practice

**LS:** SS
**SM:** defaults or 1.25"

each line twice; DS between 2-line groups; then a 1' writing on line 3

alphabet  1  Jared helped Mazy quickly fix the big wood stove in the den.
figures   2  Bella lives at 1847 Oak Street; Jessi, at 5039 Duard Circle.
easy      3  They may make their goals if they work with the usual vigor.
**gwam** 1' | 1 | 2 | 3 | 4 | 5 | 6 | 7 | 8 | 9 | 10 | 11 | 12 |

---

### 29B • 18
### New Keys: 6 and 2

each line twice (slowly, then faster); DS between 2-line groups; if time permits, key lines 5-8 again

**6**  *Right index* finger

**2**  *Left ring* finger

Follow the *Standard Plan for Learning New Keys* outlined on p. 17.

#### Learn 6

1  j j 6j 6j jj 66 j6j j6j 66j 66j Reach up for 6, 66, and 666.
2  Key the figures 6, 66, and 666.  Did just 6 of 66 finish it?

#### Learn 2

3  s s 2s 2s ss 22 s2s s2s 22s 22s  Reach up for 2, 22, and 222.
4  Add the figures 2, 22, and 222.  Review pages 2 to 22 today.

#### Combine 6, 2, and other figures

5  Key 22, 26, 62, and 66.  Just 22 of the 66 scouts were here.
6  Reach with the fingers to key 26 and 262 as well as 2 and 6.

7  Key figures as units: 18, 26, 37, 49, 50, 62, 162, and 268.
8  The proxy dated April 26, 1997, was vital in Case No. 30584.

---

### 29C • 7
### New-Key Mastery

each line once SS

1  Lee has sold 16 elm, 28 ash, 37 oak, 49 pine, and 50 shrubs.
2  Flights 201 and 384 will be replaced by Flights 625 and 749.
3  Key as a unit:  10, 29, 38, 47, 56; two units, 162 and 4837.
4  In 1996, 26 of our 384 workers were moved to 507 Pecos Lane.

### Text Box

1. Open WP13-3A if it is not open; rename it WP13-3B.
2. With the cursor at the beginning of the second ¶, insert a text box that has a top and bottom line as a border.
3. Key **Written codes are being developed** in the text box, centered in bold italic print.
4. With the cursor at the beginning of the third ¶, insert a shaded text box that has a border on the top, bottom, left, and right.
5. Key **Workers must apply ethical standards** in the text box, centered in bold italic print.
6. Change format to newspaper columns.
7. Save the file (WP13-3B).

### Inline Equation Box

1. Create a new document and key the following information DS. Use the inline equation box style to create the equations.

The interest rate for a loan is calculated by the equation

$$Rate \; = \; \frac{Interest}{Principal \; x \; Time} \quad or \; R = \; \frac{I}{PT} \; . \; The \; principal \; of \; a \; loan \; is$$

calculated by the equation $Principal = \; \dfrac{Interest}{Rate \; x \; Time} \quad or \; P = \; \dfrac{I}{RT} \; .$

2. Save the document as WP13-3C.

### Equation Box

1. Open WP13-3C if it is not open and rename it WP13-3D.
2. Add the following text to the end of the file, using equation box style. Move the equation box so that it is centered below the last line of text.

The time of a loan can be determined by the equation given below:

$$Time = \; \frac{Interest}{Principal \; x \; Rate}$$

3. Save the updated file (WP13-3D).

## S KILL BUILDING

### 29D • 8
### Technique: Keying, Spacing, Shifting

1. Key each line once SS; DS between 2-line groups.
2. Key a 1' writing on line 7 and then on line 8 if time permits; find *gwam* on each.

quick-snap keystrokes
1 Ella may go to the soap firm for title to all the lake land.
2 Did the bugle corps toot with the usual vigor for the queen?

down-and-in spacing
3 Coy is in the city to buy an oak chair he wants for his den.
4 Jan may go to town by bus to sign a work form for a new job.

out-and-down shifting
5 Robb and Ty are in Madrid to spend a week with Jae and Aldo.
6 Are you going in May or in June?  Samuel is leaving in July.

easy
7 Rick paid for both the visual aid and the sign for the firm.
8 Glena kept all the work forms on the shelf by the big chair.

gwam 1' | 1 | 2 | 3 | 4 | 5 | 6 | 7 | 8 | 9 | 10 | 11 | 12 |

### 29E • 12
### Speed Check

**LS:** DS
**SM:** defaults or 1.25"

1. Key two 1' writings on each ¶; find *gwam* on each writing.
2. Key a 2' writing on ¶s 1-2 combined; find *gwam.*
3. Key a 3' writing on ¶s 1-2 combined; find *gwam.*

**Goals**

1': At least 24 *gwam.*
2': At least 23 *gwam.*
3': At least 22 *gwam.*

all letters used

gwam 2' | 3'

|  |  | 2 |  | 4 |  | 6 |  | 8 |  | 10 |  |  |  |
Success does not mean the same thing to everyone.  For | 6 | 4

12 . 14 . 16 . 18 . 20 . 22 .
some, it means to get to the top at all costs:  in power, in | 12 | 8

24 . 26 . 28 . 30 . 32 . 34 .
fame, and in income.  For others, it means just to fulfill | 18 | 12

36 . 38 . 40 . 42 . 44 . 46 .
their basic needs or wants with as little effort as required. | 24 | 16

. 2 . 4 . 6 . 8 . 10 .
Most people fall within the two extremes.  They work quite | 30 | 20

12 . 14 . 16 . 18 . 20 . 22 . 24
hard to better their lives at home, at work, and in the social | 36 | 24

. 26 . 28 . 30 . 32 . 34 . 36
world.  They realize that success for them is not in being at | 42 | 28

. 38 . 40 . 42 . 44 . 46 . 48
the top but rather in trying to improve their quality of life. | 48 | 32

gwam 2' | 1 | 2 | 3 | 4 | 5 | 6 |
3' | 1 | 2 | 3 | 4 |

## R&e

### Proofreading

1. Print a copy of the 3' writing you keyed in 29E.
2. Note the kinds of errors marked in the ¶ at right.
3. Note how proofreader's marks above the copy are used to mark errors for correction.
4. Proofread the printout of your 3' writing; mark each error for correction, using proofreader's marks.

# = space     ⋀ = insert     ⌒ = close up     ⌁ = delete     ∾ = transpose (tr)

Sucess does not mean the same thing to everyone.  For some,
it means to get to the top att all costs:  in power, in fame, and
in income.  For others, it means juts to fulfill their basic needs
or or wants wiht as little effort required.

| Line 1 | Line 2 | Line 3 | Line 4 |
|---|---|---|---|
| 1 Omitted letter | 1 Omitted word | 1 Misstroke | 1 Added word |
| 2 Failure to space | 2 Added letter | 2 Omitted comma | 2 Transposition |
| 3 Faulty spacing | 3 Faulty spacing | 3 Transposition | 3 Omitted word |

## ACTIVITY 2:

**Parallel Columns**

1. Read the copy at right.
2. Learn how to use the Parallel Columns feature of your software.
3. Follow the directions at right to format text in columns.

Parallel Columns

The **Parallel Column** feature groups text across the page in rows and is particularly useful in formatting resumes. The rows of text in the side-by-side columns need not be equal in length because the Parallel Columns feature begins the next row of text below the deepest column of the previous row.

1. Use default margins.
2. Activate the Parallel Columns feature so that text will be arranged in two columns—the first column 1.5" wide and the second, 5".
3. Key the following text with a 12-point font, using the Parallel Columns feature.

| | |
|---|---|
| NAME AND ADDRESS: | Frank E. Warren<br>2009 Riverside Dr.<br>Mt. Vernon, WA 98273-3816 |
| EDUCATION: | Mt. Vernon High School, graduated June ---- |
| SCHOOL ACTIVITIES: | Secretary, Student Council; Varsity Soccer; Business Club; Chorus; Computer Club |

4. Save file as WP13-2.

## ACTIVITY 3:

**Graphics**

1. Read the copy at right.
2. Learn how to add graphics using your software.
3. Follow the directions at the right to add graphics.

Use **Graphics** to add images, logos, charts, etc; to set off text; and to include equations in a document. Most wp programs use graphic style boxes for adding graphics. Different graphic box styles have different purposes. For example, to import a clip art image, use figure box style; to set off text, use text box style; and to include mathematical equations, use equation box style or inline equation box style.

**Figure Box**

1. Open WP13-1 if it is not open; rename it WP13-3A.
2. Change top and bottom margins to 2".
3. With the cursor at the left margin at the top of the document, insert a clip art file of your choice.
4. If needed, resize and move the graphic you inserted so that it is at the top of the first column and the same width as the column.
5. Save the revised file as WP13-3A.

*(continued on next page)*

# Skill Builder

## Practice Procedure

1. Key each line of a group (words, phrases, and sentences) three times: first, to improve keying technique; next, to improve keying speed; then, to build precise control of finger motions. DS between 3-line groups.

2. Take several 1' writings on the two sentences at the end of each set of lines to measure your skill on each kind of copy.

3. As time permits, repeat the drills, keeping a record of your speed scores to see how your skill grows.

Each of the 120 *different* words used in the drills is among the 600 most-used words in the English language. In a study of over two million words in personal and business communications, these 120 words accounted for over 40 percent of all word occurrences. Thus, they are important to you in perfecting your keying skill. Practice them frequently for both speed and accuracy.

### Balanced-hand words of 2-5 letters (Use word response.)

words
1 of is it he to by or us an so if do am go me the six and but
2 a box may did pay end man air own due big for they with when
3 make them also then such than form work both city down their
4 end they when wish hand paid name held down sign field world

phrases
5 to me│of us│and may│pay for│big box│the six│but due│own them
6 am to work│is to make│a big city│by the name│to do such work

sentences
7 He may wish to go to the city to hand the work form to them.
8 The city is to pay for the field work both men did for them.

gwam 1'│ 1 │ 2 │ 3 │ 4 │ 5 │ 6 │ 7 │ 8 │ 9 │ 10 │ 11 │ 12 │

### One-hand words of 2-5 letters (Use letter response.)

words
9 a in be on we up as my at no was you are him get few see set
10 far act war tax only were best date case fact area rate free
11 you act few ever only fact card upon after state great water

phrases
12 at no│as my│on you│we are│at best│get set│you were│only date
13 get you in│act on my case│you set a date│get a rate on water

sentences
14 Get him my extra tax card only after you set up a case date.
15 As you see, you are free only after you get a case date set.

gwam 1'│ 1 │ 2 │ 3 │ 4 │ 5 │ 6 │ 7 │ 8 │ 9 │ 10 │ 11 │ 12 │

### Double-letter words of 2-5 letters (Speed up double letters.)

words
16 all see too off will been well good miss feel look less call
17 too free soon week room fill keep book bill tell still small
18 off call been less free look need week soon will offer needs

phrases
19 a room│all week│too soon│see less│call off│need all│will see
20 see a need│fill a book│miss a bill│all will see│a good offer

sentences
21 It is too soon to tell if we will need that small book room.
22 They still feel a need to offer a good book to all who call.

gwam 1'│ 1 │ 2 │ 3 │ 4 │ 5 │ 6 │ 7 │ 8 │ 9 │ 10 │ 11 │ 12 │

### Balanced-hand, one-hand, and double-letter words of 2-5 letters

words
23 of we to in or on is be it as by no if at us up an my he was
24 and all war six see you men too are may get off pay him well
25 such will work best then keep were good been only city needs
26 make soon ever wish tell area name bill upon paid tell great

phrases
27 is too great│they will be│box was small│their offer was good
28 if at all│may get all│off the case│to tell him│to keep after

sentences
29 If you wish to get to the rate you set, keep the hand still.
30 All of us do the work well, for only good form will pay off.

gwam 1'│ 1 │ 2 │ 3 │ 4 │ 5 │ 6 │ 7 │ 8 │ 9 │ 10 │ 11 │ 12 │

## ACTIVITY 1:

### Newspaper Columns

1. Read the copy at right.
2. Learn how to use the Newspaper Columns feature of your software.
3. Follow the directions at right to format text in columns.

Newspaper Columns

Balanced Newspaper Columns

The **Columns** feature of wp software enables you to create newspapers, pamphlets, or other documents in which text is divided vertically. The **Newspaper Columns** feature arranges text from the top to the bottom of the first column, then top to bottom of the second column, etc., until all text has been keyed. The **Balanced Newspaper Columns** feature adjusts the text so that each column is the same or nearly the same length.

1. Set top and bottom margins at 4" and side margins at 1".
2. Activate the Newspaper Columns feature so that text will be arranged in three columns of equal width, and with equal space between columns.
3. Key the following text with a 12-point font, using the Newspaper Columns feature.

Ethics is a popular topic today. Many businesses that had written codes for ethical practice years ago, set them aside, and are now going back to them.

The main purpose of a code of ethics is to convey a company's values and business standards to all its workers. An organization is ethical to the extent that each person in it subscribes to and applies the standards. Far more than a list of do's and don'ts for office employees, ethics cuts across all lines of an organization. It involves how coworkers treat one another as well as how current and future customers, suppliers, and the general public are treated by the business.

Every job has an ethical aspect, and every person has values. When an individual's standards are in sync with the employer's, the situation is generally positive for both. If either of them is inclined to "take shortcuts" or "look the other way" now and then, an unhappy employer-employee relationship is likely.

4. With the cursor at the beginning of the first column, change from Newspaper Columns to Balanced Newspaper Columns.
5. Save file as WP13-1.

# Language & Writing Skills 2

## Activity 1:

1. Study the spelling/ definitions of the words in the color block.
2. Key line 1 (the **Learn** line), noting proper choice of words.
3. Key lines 2-3 (the **Apply** lines), choosing the right words to complete the sentences correctly.
4. Study/practice the other words in the same way.
5. Check your accuracy; rekey lines containing errors.

**Choose the right word**

| | |
|---|---|
| **hour** (n) the 24th part of a day; a particular time | **know** (vb) to be aware of the truth of; to have understanding of |
| **our** (adj) of or relating to ourselves as possessors | **no** (adv/adj/n) in no respect or degree; not so; indicates denial or refusal |

Learn  1  It is our intention to complete the work in an hour or two.
Apply  2  If I drive steadily, we should reach (hour, our) house in an (hour, our).
Apply  3  We should earn one credit (hour, our) for (hour, our) computer class.

Learn  4  Did you know that there are to be no quizzes this week?
Apply  5  If you (know, no) the chapter, you should have (know, no) fear of a quiz.
Apply  6  Did you (know, no) that they scored (know, no) touchdowns in the game?

## Activity 2:

1. Key each sentence once SS, capitalizing words according to the rules you have learned.
2. Check the accuracy of your application of those rules.
3. Rekey lines containing errors.

**Proofread & correct**

1  this stapler is defective.  please send a new one soon.
2  ask if alma and suzan took the trip with ms. diaz to zaire.
3  texas and mexico share the rio grande as a common border.
4  miss jackson is a field auditor for the irs in new mexico.
5  did alexis say that thanksgiving day is always on thursday?

6  our school year begins in late august and ends in early june.
7  is the dubois tower on sixth street or on oakland avenue?
8  marquis saw the play at lincoln center in new york city.
9  send these dental supplies to byron c. thompson, d.d.s.
10  do you know when senator metcalf asked to see the president?

## Activity 3:

Key each line once SS. In place of the blank line at the end of each sentence, key the word(s) that correctly complete(s) the sentence.

**Compose (think) as you key**

1  A small mass of land surrounded by water is a/an _____.
2  A large mass of land surrounded by water is a/an _____.
3  The earth rotates on what is called its _____.
4  When the sun comes up over the horizon, we say it _____.

5  When the sun goes down over the horizon, we say it _____.
6  A device used to display temperature is a/an _____.
7  A device used to display atmospheric pressure is a/an _____.
8  A device used to display time is a/an _____.

# Activity 3:

1. Read with care the credo of John D. Rockefeller, Jr., shown at the right.
2. Choose the statements with which you most agree (two or three, at least).
3. Compose/key a ¶ with one of the Rockefeller statements as its topic sentence. Expand that concept by giving examples of what it means to you.
4. Repeat Step 3 for each of the other statements you have chosen.

**Note:** This credo was written before the age of "political correctness." The word *man*, therefore, stands for *people* and *person.* You may substitute the appropriate word as you compose your ¶s.

**Compose (think) as you key**

## I BELIEVE

- I believe in the supreme worth of the individual and in his right to life, liberty, and the pursuit of happiness.

- I believe that every right implies a responsibility; every opportunity, an obligation; every possession, a duty.

- I believe that the law was made for man and not man for the law; that government is the servant of the people and not their master.

- I believe in the dignity of labor, whether with head or hand; that the world owes no man a living but that it owes every man an opportunity to make a living.

- I believe that thrift is essential to well-ordered living and that economy is a prime requisite of a sound financial structure, whether in government, business, or personal affairs.

- I believe that truth and justice are fundamental to an enduring social order.

- I believe in the sacredness of a promise, that a man's word should be as good as his bond; that character--not wealth, or power, or position—is of supreme worth.

- I believe that the rendering of useful service is the common duty and the greatness of the human soul set free.

- I believe in an all-wise and all-loving God, named by whatever name, and that the individual's highest fulfillment, greatest happiness, and widest usefulness are to be found in living in harmony with His will.

- I believe that love is the greatest thing in the world; that it alone can overcome hate; that right can and will triumph over might.

—John D. Rockefeller, Jr.

# UNIT 4

**LESSONS 30–31**

# Master Keyboarding/ Language Skills

## LESSON 30

### Keying Skills

**Objectives:**
1. To improve technique on individual letters.
2. To improve keying speed on 1', 2', and 3' writings.

---

### 30A • 5
**Conditioning Practice**

each line twice SS; then a 1' writing on line 3; find *gwam*

| | | |
|---|---|---|
| alphabet | 1 | Lopez knew our squad could just slip by the next five games. |
| figures | 2 | Check Numbers 267, 298, 304, and 315 were still outstanding. |
| easy | 3 | Dixie works with vigor to make the theory work for a profit. |

| gwam | 1' | 1 | 2 | 3 | 4 | 5 | 6 | 7 | 8 | 9 | 10 | 11 | 12 |

---

## S KILL BUILDING

### 30B • 30
**Technique Mastery: Individual Letters**

1. Key each line twice SS; DS between 2-line groups. Note the lines that were difficult for you.
2. Key those lines again.

**Technique goals**
- curved, upright fingers
- quick-snap keystrokes
- quiet hands and arms

A 1 Ana ate a salami sandwich and some papaya after a quick nap.
B 2 Bobby bought a beach ball and big balloons for the big bash.
C 3 Cora can serve cake and coffee to the cold campers at lunch.
D 4 David did all he could to dazzle the crowd with wild dances.
E 5 Elaine left her new sled in an old shed near the gray house.

F 6 Frank found a file folder his father had left in the office.
G 7 Gloria got the giggles when the juggler dropped his oranges.
H 8 Hugh helped his big brother haul in the fishing net for her.
I 9 Inez sings in a trio that is part of a big choir at college.
J 10 Jason just joined the jury to judge the major jazz festival.

K 11 Kurt makes kapok pillows for kayaks and ketches at the dock.
L 12 Lola left her doll collection for a village gallery to sell.
M 13 Myna asked her mom to make more malted milk for the mission.
N 14 Nadine knew her aunt made lemonade and sun tea this morning.
O 15 Owen took the book from the shelf to copy his favorite poem.

P 16 Pamela added a pinch of pepper and paprika to a pot of soup.
Q 17 Quent posed quick quiz questions to his quiet croquet squad.
R 18 Risa used a rubber raft to rescue four girls from the river.
S 19 Silas said his sister has won six medals in just four meets.
T 20 Trisha told a tall tale about three little kittens in a tub.

U 21 Ursula asked the usual questions about four issues you face.
V 22 Vinny voted for five very vital issues of value to everyone.
W 23 Wilt wants to walk in the walkathon next week and show well.
X 24 Xania next expects them to fix the extra fax machine by six.
Y 25 Yuri said your yellow yacht was the envy of every yachtsman.
Z 26 Zoella and a zany friend ate a sizzling pizza in the piazza.

# Language & Writing Skills 19

## Activity 1:

1. Study the spelling/definitions of the words in the color block at the right.
2. Key the **Learn** lines in the first set of sentences.
3. Key the **Apply** lines, choosing the right words to complete each sentence correctly.
4. Key the second set of lines in the same way.
5. Check your work; rekey lines containing word-choice errors.

### Choose the right word

**poor** (adj) having little wealth or value
**pore** (vb/n) to study carefully; a tiny opening in a surface, such as skin
**pour** (vb) to make flow or stream; to rain hard

**right** (adj) factual; true; correct
**rite** (n) customary form of ceremony; ritual
**write** (vb) to form letters or symbols; to compose and set down in words, numbers, or symbols

Learn 1 Pour the fertilizer over the poor soil before you till it.
Learn 2 As we pore over these formulas, others are playing football.
Apply 3 You can (poor/pore/pour) the soup for the (poor/pore/pour) men.
Apply 4 (Poor/Pore/Pour) over the fine print before you buy the policy.

Learn 5 I may write a paper on the tribal rite of passage into manhood.
Learn 6 You have a right to participate in the rite of graduation.
Apply 7 To succeed, (right/rite/write) in the (right/rite/write) way.
Apply 8 The processional is just one (right/rite/write) in the ceremony.

## Activity 2:

1. Read the ¶s given at the right, noting corrections needed in punctuation, word choice, and subject/predicate agreement.
2. Format/key the ¶s as an unbound report DS; use the title
   **KEYBOARDING ERGONOMICS**
3. As you key, correct errors in the copy given and also any errors you make.

### Proofread & correct

Several factors effect fatigue and eyestrain when you operate a computer.The computer monitor should be positioned so that you can look directly at it and their should be little or know reflection from it.

The keyboard should be placed in a position that is vary comfortable for you as your operating it. A good guide is to place the keyboard so that the tips of the fingers, the base of the hand and the lower arm is in alignment with the angle of the keyboard. This position of the keyboard results in reduced operating fatigue.

Another requirement related to position of the keyboard is an adjustable chair to make it easier to operate the keyboard and to sea the monitor. The fingers should be curved and upright, the eyes should view the screen at an angle of about ninety degrees.

Color of the screen background and of highlighted feature bars are another consideration, especially since certain colors are troublesum for the color blind. Currant monitors permit customizing color to avoid this problem. Sum workers think size, style and intensity of type is therefor more important then color of screen. These maybe the reel key to reading ease.

Although these are important ergonomic principals, the fact is that when we're in school or on the job we must except whatever equipment is available and adept ourselves to it. That's sad, perhaps, but true. Content yourself with the knowledge that in the days of manual typewriters much fine work was done on pour equipment--and carpal tunnel syndrome hadn't even been discovered.

## 30C • 15
## Speed Building:
## Guided Writing

1. Key one 1' unguided and two 1' guided writings on ¶ 1 and then on ¶ 2.
2. Key two 2' unguided writings on ¶s 1-2 combined; find *gwam* on each.
3. Key a 3' writing on ¶s 1-2 combined; find *gwam*.

1' *gwam* goals
▽ 23 = acceptable
⊡ 27 = average
⊙ 31 = good
◇ 35 = excellent

all letters used                                                      gwam  2' | 3'

.      2      .      4      .      6      .      8      .      10      .
When saying hello to someone is the correct thing to do,              6 | 4
12     .     14     .     16     .     18     .     20     .     22  ▽
make direct eye contact and greet the person with vitality           12 | 8
24     .     26   ⊡   28     .     30   ⊙   32     .     34  ◇
in your voice.  Do not look down or away or speak only in a          18 | 12
36     .     38     .     40     .     42     .     44     .     46   .
whisper.  Make the person feel happy for having seen you, and        24 | 16
48     .     50     .     52     .     54     .     56     .     58   .
you will feel much better about yourself as a consequence.           30 | 20

.      2      .      4      .      6      .      8      .      10
Similarly, when you shake hands with another person,                 35 | 23
12     .     14     .     16     .     18     .     20     .     22  ▽
look that person in the eye and offer a firm but not crushing        41 | 27
24     .     26   ⊡   28     .     30   ⊙   32     .     34  ◇
shake of the hand. Just a firm shake or two will do.  Next           47 | 31
36     .     38     .     40     .     42     .     44     .     46
time you meet a new person, do not puzzle about whether to           53 | 35
.    48     .     50     .     52     .     54     .     56     .     58
shake hands.  Quickly offer your firm hand with confidence.          59 | 39

gwam  2' |  1  |  2  |  3  |  4  |  5  |  6  |
      3' |     1     |     2     |     3     |     4     |

## **W**ORD PROCESSING

1. Read the information at the right; learn to use the wp features described.
2. Key the lines given below as shown; if necessary, ALL CAP underlined words and underline or ALL CAP italicized or bold titles.
3. Using available wp features, make the following changes in your lines:

**line 1**
In *4,589*, change *9* to *6*; in *2,576*, change *6* to *3*.
**line 2**
After *My*, insert *new*.
**line 3**
Change *He* to *Al*.
**line 4**
After *has*, insert *just*; change *Madrid* to *Berlin*.
**line 5**
After *is*, insert *now*.
**line 6**
Change *up* to *in*; *desk* to *door*.

**Insert Mode**
To insert new text into existing text, use Insert Mode, which is automatically on when you enter a software program. Move cursor to point of insert and key new text. Existing copy will move to right.

**Typeover Mode**
Typeover Mode allows you to replace current text with newly keyed text.

**Underline**
The Underline feature underlines text as it is keyed.

**Italic**
The Italic feature italicizes text as it is keyed.

**Bold**
The Bold feature prints text darker than other copy as it is keyed.

figures
1 Of these 4,589 voters, 2,576 marked Yes and 2,013 marked No.
2 My bank card number is 274 910; your card number is 562 838.

shift-key sentences
3 He and Vi crossed the English Channel from Hove to Le Havre.
4 J. W. Parker has left Madrid for Turin for some Alps skiing.

space-bar sentences
5 If it is up to me, tell the man to pay his part of the cost.
6 He is to sign up at the desk if he wants to go to the dance.

wp features
7 Effect is usually a noun; whereas, affect is used as a verb.
8 She keys each book title in CAPS, underlined, or in italics.

wp features
9 Kendra checked out a copy of *History of Art* by H. W. Janson.
10 I have an Edward Pixley update of **Invitation to the Theatre.**

A comparison of the course placements reveals a steady decline in the 282 / 296 / 309 / 322 / 337 / 345

percent and number of students needing to enter the Precollege Algebra course and a steady increase in the percent and number of students entering College Algebra and Calculus. This finding supports the contention that as SAT math scores increase, students will begin their college studies in higher-level courses.

This comparison will be reported to Dr. Theodore R. Ostrom, department head of mathematics in the School of Arts and Sciences. He and his faculty will then know that more and more business students are enrolling in higher-level math courses and that the number needing Precollege Algebra is decreasing. 357 / 371 / 386 / 399 / 406

I will distribute the comparison to all School of Business faculty so that they, too, will be aware of the increasing mathematical ability of the students entering that school. 421 / 435 / 442

Perhaps you would like to share this information with the dean of the School of Education since it provides further evidence of success in the education reform movement. 457 / 472 / 475

**Document 2**
**E-Mail Message**

Open T169B and rename it JMACKEY (or use the form in stationery pack) to prepare the e-mail message at the right.

F1-Help!    F2-Edit    F6-Handling    F7-Lists    F8-Options    F9-Send

**TO:** jmackey@johngillco.com
**FROM:** dckark@hudleycol.edu
**COPY:**
**SUBJECT:** BIOLOGY TEACHERS BULLETIN BOARD
**ATTACHMENT:**

─── MESSAGE ───

More than sixty biology teachers from a seven-county area subscribe to a biology bulletin board. Several teachers have requested that each subscriber recruit at least one biologist from
business, industry, or government who would be willing to join
this group. The members want an opportunity to discuss pertinent
issues with practicing biologists. To subscribe, e-mail a
message to this address: bioteachers@harrishi.edu.

**F**ORMATTING

**199B • 45**
**Process Correspon-dence: Sustained Practice**

**Time Schedule**

Plan and prepare ........... 5'
Timed practice ............. 30'
Proofread/compute
 *n-pram* ..................... 10'

1. Make a list of the memos and letters to be pro-cessed:
   p. 464, 194B, Document 1
   p. 466, 195B, Document 1
   p. 468, 196B, Document 1
   p. 470, 197B, Document 3
   p. 470, 197B, Document 4

2. Arrange materials for easy access. Process (in the order listed) as many of the documents as you can. Proofread and correct each document before beginning the next.

3. After time is called, proofread the final

document, and, if needed, print all completed work.

4. Identify uncorrected errors, and compute *n-pram*:
   *n-pram* = words keyed – (15 x errors) divided by 30.
   Turn in work in the order listed in Step 1.

## Keying/Language Skills

**Objectives:**
**1.** To improve skill on sentence and paragraph writings.
**2.** To improve capitalization and number expression skills.

### 31A • 5
### Conditioning Practice

each line twice SS; then a 1' writing on line 3; find *gwam*

| | | |
|---|---|---|
| alphabet | 1 | Jung quickly baked extra pizzas for the film festival crowd. |
| figures | 2 | I moved from 3748 Oak Street to 1059 Jaymar Drive on May 26. |
| easy | 3 | She paid the big man for the field work he did for the city. |

**gwam** 1' | 1 | 2 | 3 | 4 | 5 | 6 | 7 | 8 | 9 | 10 | 11 | 12 |

## S KILL BUILDING

### 31B • 30
### Technique Emphasis

1. Key the lines once SS as shown—DS between 3-line groups.
2. Key the lines again at a faster pace.
3. If time permits, key a 1' writing on each of lines 22, 23, and 24; find *gwam*.

**Technique goals**
- quick down-and-in spacing
- out-and-down reaches to shift keys
- curved, upright fingers
- quiet hands and arms
- unused fingers low over home keys

| | | |
|---|---|---|
| figures | 1 | a l ; 0 g 5 us 72 or 94 am 17 is 82 do 39 by 56 go 59 up 70; |
| | 2 | On June 18, 1997, 30 of them took a bus trip of 2,465 miles. |
| | 3 | We were billed for 3,650 bulbs, 1,278 shrubs, and 495 trees. |
| space bar | 4 | When you reach a goal you have set, set one a little higher. |
| | 5 | Kevin may sign the audit form in the city when he checks it. |
| | 6 | She said to turn in our term papers by the end of next week. |
| shift keys & CAPS LOCK | 7 | Did you see LA BOHEME at the Metropolitan Opera in New York? |
| | 8 | Mary Ann saw a new production of CAROUSEL at Lincoln Center. |
| | 9 | Keiko read LINCOLN by Vidal; Kermit read MEXICO by Michener. |
| double letters | 10 | Nell took a small drill from the tool box to drill the hole. |
| | 11 | Ann took off the desk a book of odd poems to keep at school. |
| | 12 | Tommy will tell the class how a little more effort paid off. |
| adjacent keys | 13 | Kerry opted to rent a silk suit instead of buying a new one. |
| | 14 | If we buy her coffee shop, should we buy the gift shop, too? |
| | 15 | We spent a quiet week at the shore prior to the open season. |
| long direct reaches | 16 | Jenny spun on the ice, jumped the curb, and broke her thumb. |
| | 17 | We once had many mussels, but not since the recent harvests. |
| | 18 | My niece has a chance to bring the bronze trophy back to us. |
| alphabetic sentences | 19 | Mae was quickly given the bronze trophy by six fussy judges. |
| | 20 | Quinto got six big jigsaw puzzles from the very daffy clerk. |
| | 21 | Roz fixed the crisp okra, while Jane made unique beef gravy. |
| easy sentences | 22 | Alfie is to go to work for the city to fix bus sign emblems. |
| | 23 | Did he rush the rotor of the giant robot to the island firm? |
| | 24 | The busy girl works with a fury to fix the signals by eight. |

**gwam** 1' | 1 | 2 | 3 | 4 | 5 | 6 | 7 | 8 | 9 | 10 | 11 | 12 |

# Correspondence (Sustained Practice)

**Objectives:**

**1.** To process correspondence under time pressure.

**2.** To process a two-page memo.

**198-199A • 5 (daily)
Conditioning Practice**

each line twice

alphabet 1 Zebb likely will be top judge for the exclusive quarter-mile run.

speed 2 Jamel is proficient when he roams right field with vigor and pep.

figures 3 This association has 16,873 members in 290 chapters in 45 states.

gwam 1' | 1 | 2 | 3 | 4 | 5 | 6 | 7 | 8 | 9 | 10 | 11 | 12 | 13 |

## FORMATTING

**198B • 45
Correspondence**

**Document 1
Long Standard Memo**
Prepare the memo at the right. Refer to p. 468 to review formatting a second and subsequent page heading.

words

TO:  Dorothy A. McIlvain, Dean, Semak School of Business  FROM:  **13**
Vincent R. Tedrow, Head, Freshmen Qualifications Committee  DATE:  **26**
June 15, ----  SUBJECT:  SCHOOL OF BUSINESS FRESHMEN MATH  **37**
SKILLS  **39**

At a recent meeting of the Freshmen Qualifications Committee, the Admis-  **53**
sions Department committee representative reported that freshmen  **66**
entering the Semak School of Business this year have higher  **78**
average SAT math scores when compared to the freshmen who entered the  **92**
School in each of the past five years.  **100**

Much discussion centered around the significance of the increase, and we  **115**
finally decided to compare the math placement records for these same  **129**
freshmen over the same time period.  By doing this, the committee believes  **144**
it can determine if students are being placed into higher-level math courses  **159**
during their first semester of study as a result of the increase in scores.  **174**

This study revealed the course placements that are reported below.  The  **189**
number reported in each course column is the percent of business  **202**
freshmen entering that course.  The number in parentheses is the actual  **216**
number of freshmen entering the course.  **224**

| Year | Precollege Algebra | College Algebra | Calculus I | |
|------|--------------------|-----------------|------------|---|
| | | | | **228** |
| | | | | **235** |
| 1993 | 26% (60) | 54% (123) | 20% (45) | **241** |
| 1994 | 23% (53) | 56% (127) | 21% (47) | **248** |
| 1995 | 21% (48) | 57% (128) | 22% (50) | **254** |
| 1996 | 18% (42) | 58% (136) | 24% (56) | **261** |
| 1997 | 16% (41) | 60% (149) | 24% (67) | **268** |

*(continued on next page)*

1. Key one 1' unguided and two 1' guided writings on each ¶.
2. Key two 2' unguided writings on ¶s 1-2 combined; find *gwam* on each.
3. Key a 3' writing on ¶s 1-2 combined; find *gwam*.

LA    all letters used                                    gwam  2' | 3'

When you need to adjust to a new situation in which new          6 | 4
people are involved, be quick to recognize that at first it     12 | 8
is you who must adapt.  This is especially true in an office    18 | 12
where the roles of workers have already been established. It    24 | 16
is your job to fit into the team structure with harmony.        30 | 20

Learn the rules of the game and who the key players are;        35 | 23
then play according to those rules at first.  Do not expect     41 | 27
to have the rules modified to fit your concept of what the      47 | 31
team structure and your role in it should be.  Only after you   53 | 36
become a valuable member should you suggest major changes.      59 | 39

gwam  2'  | 1 | 2 | 3 | 4 | 5 | 6 |
      3'    | 1 |  2  |  3  |  4  |

## R&e

**Language Skills Checkup**

1. Key each line given at the right, properly capitalizing words and expressing numbers.
2. Check your work and correct any lines containing errors in capitalization and number expression.

1  i know labor day is the first monday in september.

2  dr. j. d. wilkes got a d.d.s. from rutgers in may.

3  did ms. perez ask us to read THE CRADLE WILL FALL?

4  concordia bank is at mott street and laurel place.

5  was dr. eric b. roarke awarded an m.d. or ph. d.?

6  muriel getz, the club secretary, read the minutes.

7  condos 8 and 15 have 2 bedrooms; unit 9 has three.

8  the letter dated may 16 is vital in case no. 4809.

9  for the answer to problem 9, see unit 8, page 274.

10  of 63 workers, nine chose not to get the flu shot.

11  forty club members have signed up, but 8 have not.

12  did ms. ott say july 4 is always independence day?

## Document 2
### Modified Block Letter with ¶ Indentions

Prepare the letter at the right with mixed punctuation and full justification.

**wp users:**

Prepare an envelope with a POSTNET bar code above the address.

---

May 1, ----  Attention Science Department Head  East Tulsa High School  14
1016 N. Garnett Rd.  Tulsa, OK 74116-1016  Ladies and Gentlemen:  26
PHYSICS LABORATORY EQUIPMENT DONATION  34

AnTech Laboratories has up-to-date physics laboratory furniture and  47
equipment that it can donate to your high school.  We feel certain that your  63
physics teacher and students will derive great benefits from what we are  77
offering.  80

A list of the major items we can donate is enclosed.  All items will be avail-  94
able before the end of August.  100

Please call me at (918) 138-5000, and we will arrange a meeting for your  115
personnel to see the furniture and equipment.  124

Sincerely,  Jose L. Domingo  Public Relations  xx  Enclosure  136

---

## Document 3
### Block Letter

Prepare the letter at the right with open punctuation. Supply all missing letter parts. The letter is from:

**Lisa A. Hammersmith, Ph.D.
Superintendent**

**wp users:**

Prepare an envelope with a POSTNET bar code above the address.

---

May 15, ----  Mr. Jose L. Domingo  Public Relations  AnTech Laboratories  14
8201 E. Skelley Dr.  Tulsa, OK 74107-8201  22

This letter confirms East Tulsa High School's interest in the physics  40
laboratory furniture and equipment that AnTech Laboratories is able to  54
donate.  56

Three representatives of East Tulsa H. S. will meet with you and Dr. Rohn  70
Sams on May 23 at AnTech's offices at 3:15 p.m.  The representatives are  85
Dr. Mary St. George, principal; Ms. Marguerite Joseph, science department  100
head; and Mr. Frank Salopek, physics teacher.  109

Support such as this from business and industry is needed for today's  123
schools to prepare students for the changing world of work.  Your generosity  139
is greatly appreciated.  144

closing  155

---

## Document 4
### Simplified Block Letter

Supply all missing letter parts and design a letterhead logo for:

**TRT Hazardous Waste
  Removal
450 Bixler Rd.
Indianapolis, IN 46227-4481**
(phone no.) **317-555-2245**
The sender is:
**Mr. Leslie R. Rumbaugh
Service Manager**

**wp users:**

Prepare an envelope with a POSTNET bar code above the address.

---

May 17, ----  REGISTERED  SUSAN T KIPIN MD  404 E WASHINGTON ST  12
INDIANAPOLIS IN 46204-8201  CHANGE IN HAZARDOUS REMOVAL  23
CONTAINERS  25

The waste removal containers that we have located at your office will be re-  41
moved on May 30 and replaced with new containers that provide greater  55
safety for your patients, your employees, and you.  A brochure showing the  70
container dimensions is enclosed.  77

Our technician will fasten a container to the wall in each room you  90
designate.  Please be certain that your office manager knows the specific  105
locations.  107

Once the new containers have been installed, TRT technicians will  121
schedule a time when the waste can be removed daily.  131

closing  141

# Language & Writing Skills 3

## Activity 1:

1. Study the spelling/ definitions of the words in the color block at right.
2. Key line 1 (the **Learn** line), noting the proper choice of words.
3. Key lines 2-3 (the **Apply** lines), choosing the right words to complete the lines correctly.
4. Key the remaining lines in the same way.
5. Check your accuracy; rekey lines containing word-choice errors.

### Choose the right word

| | |
|---|---|
| **lead** (vb) to guide or direct; to be first | **choose** (vb) to select; to decide on |
| **led** (vb) the past tense of *lead* | **chose** (vb) the past tense of *choose* |

Learn 1 Max is to lead the parade; Pam led it last year.
Apply 2 The Falcons (lead, led) now; the Friars (lead, led) at the half.
Apply 3 Marj (lead, led) at the ninth hole, but she does not (lead, led) now.

Learn 4 Jose chose a Eureka computer; I may choose a Futura.
Apply 5 After he (choose, chose) a red cap, I told him to (choose, chose) blue.
Apply 6 Mae (choose, chose) you as a partner; Janice may (choose, chose) me.

## Activity 2:

1. Read the paragraph, noting errors in capitalization, number expression, and word choice.
2. As you key the paragraph, correct the errors you have noted.
3. Check your accuracy; correct any errors you may have made.

### Proofread & correct

over 20 of hour students, along with 4 sponsors, chose to take a trip to south america this summer.   they are to leave hear on june fifteen and are not do back until july 11.  all no that they must have valid passports and health cards as proof of required immunizations.  dr. elena diaz is the led sponsor of the tour.  they will tour capital cities in brazil, chile, peru, and venezuela.

## Activity 3:

Key each line once SS. At the end of each line, supply the information (noted in parentheses) needed to complete the sentence. In lines 3 and 6, also choose the correct article (*a* or *an*) to precede the information you supply.

### Compose (think) as you key

1 My full name is (first/middle/last).

2 I attend (name of school).

3 I am learning to key on a/an (brand of computer/typewriter).

4 My main goal has been to develop (technique/speed/accuracy).

5 My favorite class in school is (name of subject).

6 My career goal is to be a/an (name of job).

7 My main hobby is (name of hobby).

8 I spend most of my free time (name of activity).

**Document 3**
**E-Mail Message**

Send the e-mail message at the right to:

**alaron@brighton.com**

Open T169B and rename it ALARON (or use the form in stationery pack).

F1-Help!  F2-Edit  F6-Handling  F7-Lists  F8-Options  F9-Send

TO: alaron@brighton.com
FROM: vlopez@milldale.edu
COPY: mkish@milldale.edu
SUBJECT: CONFIRMATION OF DATES
ATTACHMENT:

——————————————— MESSAGE ———————————————

Thank you for letting me shadow you at Brighton Life Insurance Co. on the last Thursday and Friday of this month. I will be at your office by 8:30 a.m. and can stay until 5 p.m. I look forward to learning from you about being an actuary.

# LESSON 197  Memos and Letters

**Objectives:**
1. To process memos and letters.
2. To encode envelopes with bar codes.

## 197A • 5
### Conditioning Practice

each line twice

alphabet 1 Val needs a pretty gift box for the quartz clock I will send Jim.

speed 2 The busy auditor is to handle the problem when he works downtown.

fig/sym 3 Buy 23 monitors (#674-05-C) and 19 CPU's (#25-486-DX) at 15% off.

gwam 1' | 1 | 2 | 3 | 4 | 5 | 6 | 7 | 8 | 9 | 10 | 11 | 12 | 13 |

## F ORMATTING

## 197B • 45
### Memos and Letters

**Document 1**
**Standard Memo**

Process the information at the right in standard memo format.

words

TO: Harry R. Dobish, Vice President of Operations  FROM: Mudi A.  13
Mutubu, Chemistry Laboratory Manager  DATE: (Current date)  SUBJECT:  28
BIOCHEMISTRY LAB RENOVATIONS  33

I've met numerous times with the biochemistry lab technicians and research  48
biochemists who work in the Biochemistry Laboratories at the Madison site.  63
We've identified the renovations needed to meet proposed safety and access  78
regulations and new and replacement equipment required to maintain a  92
top-notch laboratory.  97

I'll have the architect prepare drawings showing changes to the facilities.  112
Also, I'll meet with a biochemistry salesperson from Hunter Research Labo-  127
ratory Equipment to get an equipment estimate.  137

When the drawings and estimate are available, I'll meet with you.  151

# UNIT 5

**LESSONS 32–34**

# Get Acquainted with Symbol Keys

## LESSON 32

### New Keys: /, $, %, and –

**Objectives:**
1. To learn reach-strokes for /, $, %, and –.
2. To combine /, $, %, and – smoothly with other keys.

---

**32A • 5**
**Conditioning Practice**

each line twice SS; then a 1' writing on line 3; find *gwam*

| | | |
|---|---|---|
| alphabet | 1 | Di will buy from me as prizes the six unique diving jackets. |
| figures | 2 | The January 17 quiz of 25 points will test pages 389 to 460. |
| easy | 3 | Both of us may do the audit of the work of a big title firm. |
| **gwam** | 1' | 1 \| 2 \| 3 \| 4 \| 5 \| 6 \| 7 \| 8 \| 9 \| 10 \| 11 \| 12 \| |

---

**32B • 16**
**New Keys: / and $**

each line twice SS (slowly, then faster); DS between 4-line groups; if time permits, practice the lines again

/ = diagonal
$ = dollar sign
Do not space between a figure and the / or the $ sign.

**Learn / (diagonal)**

1 ; ; /; /; ;; // ;/; ;/; 2/3 4/5 and/or We keyed 1/2 and 3/4.
2 Space between a whole number and a fraction:  7 2/3, 18 3/4.

**Learn $ (dollar sign)**

3 f f $f $f ff $$ f$f f$f $4 $4 for $4 Shift for $ and key $4.
4 A period separates dollars and cents:  $4.50, $6.25, $19.50.

**Combine / and $**

5 I must shift for $ but not for /:  Order 10 gal. at $16/gal.
6 Do not space on either side of /:  1/6, 3/10, 9 5/8, 4 7/12.
7 We sent 5 boxes of No. 6 3/4 envelopes at $11/box on June 2.
8 They can get 2 sets of disks at $49.85/set; 10 sets, $39.85.

**Document 1**
**Letter**

Modified block format with ¶ indentions; mixed punctuation; full justification; design an appropriate letterhead logo. The letter is from:

**Ms. Valerie E. Lopez**
**207 Brainard Rd.**
**Hartford, CT 06114-2207**

**Document 2**
**Long Letter**

Block format; open punctuation; full justification; design an appropriate letterhead logo for **Brighton Life Insurance Co.** Their phone number is **(203) 123-0095**. The street address is given in Document 1.

**Note:** A second and subsequent page heading of a letter or memo consists of the name of the addressee, page #, and date. SS this information at the left margin beginning at the default top margin. For example:

```
Ms. Valerie E. Lopez
Page 2
Current date
```

Second and subsequent pages are keyed on plain paper. Use the same side margins and other formatting features as used on the first page.

|  | words |
|---|---|
| (Current date)   Mr. Justin A. Alaron   Brighton Life Insurance Co.   I-84 & | 14 |
| Rt. 322   Milldale, CT 06467-9371   Dear Mr. Alaron: | 24 |

I am a senior student at Milldale High School and participate in the Shadow — 39
Experience Program (SEP).  My career objective is to become an actuary for — 54
an insurance company. — 59

SEP encourages students to "shadow" for one or two days a person who is — 73
working in their chosen career field.  I would like to "shadow" you so that — 87
I can learn firsthand what an actuary does. — 96

I can arrange to be with you at your office for one or two days during the — 111
coming month.  Please send your written response to me so that I can — 127
present it to Miss Michelle Kish, SEP Coordinator.  Thank you. — 137

Sincerely,  Ms. Valerie E. Lopez  SEP Member  xx — 146

---

(Current date)   Ms. Valerie E. Lopez   207 Brainard Rd. Hartford, CT 06114- — 15
2207  Dear Ms. Lopez   SUBJECT:  SHADOWING AT BRIGHTON LIFE — 26
INSURANCE CO. — 29

I'm pleased that you have chosen Brighton Life Insurance Co. as the place — 44
where you want to complete your shadow experience.  I believe that you will — 59
learn a great deal about being an actuary by spending two days at Brighton — 74
with me. — 76

To help you prepare for your visit, I have listed some of the things you should — 92
know about actuaries: — 96

- Gather and analyze statistics to determine probabilities of death, sick- — 111
  ness, injury, disability, unemployment, retirement, and property loss. — 125

- Specialize in either life and health insurance or property and casualty — 140
  insurance; or, specialize in pension plans or employee benefits. — 153

- Hold a bachelor's degree in a mathematics or business-related area, — 167
  such as actuarial science, finance, or accounting. — 178

- Possess excellent communication and interpersonal skills. — 190

Also, I have enclosed actuarial career information published by the Society — 205
of Actuaries (life and health insurance), Casualty Actuarial Society (prop- — 220
erty and casualty insurance), and American Society of Pension Actuaries — 234
(pensions).  These three associations offer actuaries professional certifica- — 249
tion through a series of examinations.  We can discuss the societies and the — 265
importance of obtaining the professional designations they offer. — 278

A good two-day period for you to be with me is the last Thursday and Friday — 293
of the month.  My activities on  those days will give you a good orientation. — 309
Can you be here from 8:30 a.m. to 5 p.m.  Casual business dress is appro- — 323
priate.  My office is on Floor 37 of the Brighton Building. — 336

Please tell me if these two days are good for you.  If you have e-mail, you — 352
can send your message to alaron@brighton.com. — 361

Sincerely  Justin A. Alaron  Senior Actuary  xx  Enclosures — 372

each line twice SS (slowly, then faster); DS between 4-line groups; if time permits, practice the lines again

% = percent sign
– = hyphen
Do not space between a figure and the %, nor before or after – or – – (dash) used as punctuation.

### Learn % (percent sign)

1 f f %f %f ff %% f%f f%f 5% 5% Shift for the % in 5% and 15%.

2 Do not space between a number and %: 5%, 75%, 85%, and 95%.

### Learn – (hyphen)

3 ; ; ; -; -; ;; -- ;-; ;-; 4-ply I use a 2-ply tire on my bike.

4 I gave each film a 1-star, 2-star, 3-star, or 4-star rating.

### Combine % and –

5 A dash is two unspaced hyphens--no space before or after it.

6 Kyle, send the parcel by fourth-class mail--a saving of 50%.

7 The prime rate may reach 9%--but he has no interest in that.

8 You need 40 signatures--51% of the members--on the petition.

**32D • 13**
**Skill Building**

1. Key lines 1-8 once SS.
2. Key a 1' writing on line 7 and then on line 8; find *gwam* on each sentence.
3. Key a 1' and a 2' writing on the ¶; find *gwam* on each writing.

/ and $
1 Key a series of fractions as figures:  1/4, 1/3, and 1 3/10.
2 The jacket was discounted from $172.99 to $128.99 to $98.99.

% and –
3 This outlet store gives discounts of 20%, 25%, 35%, and 50%.
4 We have 1-, 2-, and 3-bath condos--he wants a separate home.

all symbols learned
5 This 10 1/2% mortgage was rewritten at 8%--a $13,496 saving.
6 These 3-part forms--minus a 10% discount--cost $75/thousand.

easy sentences
7 Shana is to key all the forms for the city auditor by eight.
8 Six of the girls do work for me; eight do work for the city.

gwam 1' | 1 | 2 | 3 | 4 | 5 | 6 | 7 | 8 | 9 | 10 | 11 | 12 |

LA    all letters used                                      gwam 2'

       .    2   .   4   .   6   .   8   .   10

The computer came into personal use in the past decade    6

12     .     14     .     16     .     18     .     20     .     22

in a blaze of glory.  In schools and homes all over the coun-    12

24     .     26     .     28     .     30     .     32     .     34

try, it has quickly expelled the standard typewriter.  It is    18

36     .     38     .     40     .     42     .     44     .     46

used to learn, to play, to keep records, and to process all    24

48     .     50     .     52     .     54     .     56     .     58

sorts of information.  It is being used in major ways to ar-    30

60     .     62     .     64     .     66     .     68     .     70

range and compose music and to design art pieces of merit.    36

gwam 2' | 1 | 2 | 3 | 4 | 5 | 6 |

**Document 3**
Letter
(Merge)

1. Revise TSKAFORM as a letter in simplified block format. Use the letterhead logo from Lesson 194 (Document 3) for this and other letters in this lesson.
2. Revise MATHDATA so letter addresses are in USPS format by using Convert Case and

Name the revised file TSKBFORM.

Replace features. Name the revised form TSKBDATA.

3. Merge TSKBFORM with MATHDATA; name the merged file TSKBDOCS.

**Documents 4 and 5**
Memo and Letter

1. Create a simplified memo form file (TSKCFORM) using the information at the right. Add an appropriate closing ¶ for the memo.
2. Merge TSKCFORM with FACDATA; name the merged file TSKCDOCS.
3. Retrieve TSKCFORM and name it TSKDFORM.
4. Revise TSKDFORM as a letter in simplified block format.
5. Merge TSKDFORM with TSKBDATA; name merged file TSKDDOCS.

(Total average words in memo = 208)

(Total average words in letter = 221)

**Instructions:** Memo and letter are from **Dean Carolyn V. Pucevich, School of Technology**. Date correspondence **June 25**. Add memo and letter parts as appropriate.

The first meeting of the Mathematical Reasoning Skills Task Force was very productive. The discussion was stimulating and pertinent to the task force's charge.

While the meeting is still fresh in our minds, I think it would be wise if each of us reviewed the specific elements of the charge we agreed upon at the meeting. Please review each element below and note changes that are to be made. We will review the elements and suggested changes at the beginning of the next meeting.

- Document the mathematical content that is being taught or applied in each required general education course.
- Determine what mathematical content is to be taught or applied in each general education course.
- Propose a curriculum to ensure that all students acquire the desired level of competence in mathematical reasoning skills.

# LESSON 196

## Long Letters and E-Mail Messages

Objectives:
1. To process long letters.
2. To prepare simulated e-mail messages.

**196A • 5**
**Conditioning Practice**

each line twice

alphabet  1  Jacques puzzled over the outrageous amount of my worker tax.
speed  2  Eight ensigns and the airmen got the visual signal to turn right.
figures  3  Robert flew 3,670 miles in May; 2,980 in June; and 1,450 in July.

| gwam | 1' | 1 | 2 | 3 | 4 | 5 | 6 | 7 | 8 | 9 | 10 | 11 | 12 | 13 |

# LESSON 33

## New Keys: #, &, and ( )

**Objectives:**

**1.** To learn reach-strokes for **#**, **&**, and **( )**.
**2.** To combine **#**, **&**, and **( )** smoothly with other keys.

**33A • 5**
**Conditioning Practice**

each line twice SS; then a
1' writing on line 3; find
*gwam*

alphabet 1 Racquel just put back five azure gems next to my gold watch.

figures 2 Joel used a comma in 1,203 and 2,946 but not in 583 and 750.

easy 3 The auto firm owns the big signs by the downtown civic hall.

`gwam` 1' | 1 | 2 | 3 | 4 | 5 | 6 | 7 | 8 | 9 | 10 | 11 | 12 |

**33B • 16**
**New Keys: # and &**

each set of lines twice SS
(slowly, then faster); DS between groups; if time
permits, practice the lines
again

# = number/pounds
& = ampersand (and)
Do not space between # and
a figure; space once before
and after & used to join
names.

**Learn # (number/pounds)**

1 d d #d #d dd ## d#d d#d 3# 3# Shift for # as you enter #33d.

2 Do not space between a number and #: 3# of #633 at $9.35/#.

**Learn & (ampersand)**

3 j j &j &j jj && j&j j&j 7& 7& Have you written to Poe & Son?

4 Do not space before or after & in initials, e.g., CG&E, B&O.

**Combine # and &**

5 Shift for # and &.  Recall:  # stands for number and pounds.

6 Names joined by & require spaces; a # sign alone does, also.

7 Letters joined by & are keyed solid: List Stock #3 as C&NW.

8 I bought 20# of #830 grass seed from Locke & Uhl on March 4.

# Simplified Memos and Letters

**Objectives:**
1. To process memos and letters.
2. To improve skill in keying from rough-draft and script copy.

## 195A • 5
### Conditioning Practice
each line twice

| | | |
|---|---|---|
| alphabet | 1 | Quin, zip your jacket and fix your muffler to brave raging winds. |
| speed | 2 | Pa's neighbor may fish off the dock at the lake by the cornfield. |
| fig/sym | 3 | My policy (#31-407-X) paid $26.97 interest and a $47.58 dividend. |

**gwam** 1' | 1 | 2 | 3 | 4 | 5 | 6 | 7 | 8 | 9 | 10 | 11 | 12 | 13 |

## **F** ORMATTING

## 195B • 45
### Memos and Letters

**Document 1**
**Memo**

Prepare a simplified memo. Use the memo logo (delete headings and the rule) that you used in Lesson 194 (Document 1) for this and all other memos in this lesson.

words

June 12, ----   Dean Carolyn V. Pucevich   MATHEMATICAL REASONING   12
SKILLS TASK FORCE   16

All the faculty members and advisory committee members who attended   30
the June 2 informational meeting have agreed to join the Mathematical   44
Reasoning Skills Task Force.   50

I have acknowledged their acceptance and have told them you will notify   64
them shortly of the first task force meeting date.   74

Let me know the date, time, and location of the first meeting so that I can   90
welcome the group, if my schedule permits.   98

President Mary B. Tunno   103

**Document 2**
**Memo**
**(Merge)**

1. Create a form file (TSKAFORM) from the information at the right. Format it as a simplified memo. Date it **June 13** and supply a subject line. The sender is:
**Dean Carolyn Pucevich**
**School of Technology**

2. Merge TSKAFORM with FACDATA; name merged file TSKADOCS.

opening 19

President Mary B. Tunno has notified me that you have agreed to   31
become a member of the Mathematical Reasoning Skills Task Force. I am   45
pleased that you have decided to accept this important role and look   57
forward to working with you and other members of the task   69
force. The first meeting is scheduled for June 23 at   78
3:00 p.m. in Board Room C in Janis Hall. The main agenda   89
item will be to define the specific charges that the   100
task force is to address. ¶ I hope you can join us.   110

closing 119

## 33C • 16
### New Keys: ( and )

each set of lines twice SS (slowly, then faster); DS between groups; if time permits, practice the lines again

**SPACING** *cue:*

Do not space between ( ) and copy they enclose.

( = left parenthesis
) = right parenthesis

**Learn (**

use the letter "l"

1  l l (l (l ll (( l(l l(l 9( 9( Shift for the ( as you key (9.
2  As ( is the shift of 9, use the l finger to key 9, (, or (9.

**Learn )**

3  ; ; ); ); ;; )) ;); ;); 0) 0) Shift for the ) as you key 0).
4  As ) is the shift of 0, use the ; finger to key 0, ), or 0).

**Combine ( and )**

5  Hints: (1) depress shift; (2) strike key; (3) release both.
6  Tab steps: (1) clear tabs, (2) set stops, and (3) tabulate.
7  The new account (#594-7308) draws annual interest at 3 1/4%.

## 33D • 13
### Skill Building

1. Key lines 1-8 once SS.
2. Key a 1' writing on line 7 and then on line 8; find *gwam* on each sentence.
3. Key a 1' and a 2' writing on the ¶; find *gwam* on each writing.

& and #
1  Rios & Cho will try Case #947-285 and Case #960-318 in June.
2  DP&L sent Invoice #67-5849-302 to Ito & Brown on October 19.

( and )
3  Waltz (the plaintiff) and Ross (the defendant) are in court.
4  The note for five hundred dollars ($500) pays 8.5% interest.

basic symbols
5  Twenty-four (31%) of the owners voted for a $250 assessment.
6  Only 1/4 picked Yes, 1/2 picked No, and 1/4 did not respond.

easy sentences
7  Did the girl row to the dock for the clams and six big fish?
8  They wish to make an issue of the work she did for the city.

gwam  1' |  1  |  2  |  3  |  4  |  5  |  6  |  7  |  8  |  9  |  10  |  11  |  12  |

 **LA**  all letters used                                                    gwam  2'

.        2        .        4        .        6        .        8        .        10
When you key copy that contains both words and numbers,        6
12        .        14        .        16        .        18        .        20        .        22
it is best to key numbers using the top row. When the copy        12
24        .        26        .        28        .        30        .        32        .        34
consists primarily of figures, however, it may be faster to        18
36        .        38        .        40        .        42        .        44        .        46        .
use the keypad. In any event, keying figures quickly is a        24
48        .        50        .        52        .        54        .        56        .        58
major skill to prize. You can expect to key figures often        29
.        60        .        62        .        64        .        66        .        68        .        70        .
in the future, so learn to key them with very little peeking.        36

gwam  2' |        1        |        2        |        3        |        4        |        5        |        6        |

## Document 3
**Modified Block Letter with ¶ Indentions, Mixed Punctuation**

1. Using the Macro feature, create an appropriately sized replica of the following to use as a letterhead in this lesson.

**Sundy Junior College**
**711 Union St.**
**Nashville, TN 37219-2711**
**615-142-4311**

2. Prepare a form letter file (MATHFORM) using the body of Document 2 and date it **June 3, ----.** Insert text above right as the final ¶. **President Tunno**, who has a **Ph.D.** degree, is writing the letter.

3. Create a data file (MATHDATA) using the names and addresses at the right.

4. Merge MATHDATA and MATHFORM and name the merged file MATHDOCS.

Average words in opening lines: 25

It is very important that advisory committee members who employ Sundy   14
graduates are represented on this vital task force.  Your input is needed   29
and will be appreciated.   34

closing  43

---

✓ Mr. Clarence L. Daugherty, Data Consultants, I-65 & Hwy. 76, White House, TN 37188-3379

✓ Ms. Sheila Tronza-Toth, Mesko Productions, 201 Gifford Pl., Joelton, TN 37080-2010

✓ Mr. Peter Ebick, Tennessee Trucking, 3312 Dickerson Rd. Nashville, TN 37207-3381

✓ Mrs. Nedra Levy, Levy Paper Products, 1400 Brick Church Pike, Nashville, TN, 37207-4682

✓ Dr. Satish Dewan, Nashville Neurological Associates, Inc., 211 N. First St., Nashville, TN 37213-2770

✓ Mr. David S. Yoon, Compucon Imaging, 2345 Atrium Way, Nashville, TN 37214-2345

✓ Mrs. Helen T. Capri, Capri Glass Co., 1800 West End Ave., Nashville, TN 37203-1800

---

## Documents 4 and 5
**Standard Memo and Modified Block Letter with Block ¶s**

1. Create a memo form file (RQSTFORM) using the information at the right.

2. Merge RQSTFORM with FACDATA created for Document 2; name the merged file RQSTMEMO.

3. Open RQSTFORM and rename it COMFORM.

4. Reformat COMFORM: modified block format with a subject line, block ¶s, and open punctuation.

5. Merge COMFORM with MATHDATA; name merged file COMLTR.

Thank you for attending the June 2 meeting for the   11
a Mathematics Reasoning Task Force that I believe is sorely   23
needed at our institution It is apparent every one present   29
agrees that there is a need to resolve math issues in   38
the liberal arts curriculum.  The advisory committee validated   52
this in addressing the mathematical skills required in   64
today's workforce.   68

Please accept my formal invitation to serve on the   77
important task force.  Mark "Yes" on the enclosed reply card.   87

# LESSON 34

## New Keys: ' , " , __ , and *

**Objectives:**
1. To learn reach-strokes for ', ", _, and *.
2. To combine ', ", _, and * smoothly with other keys.

---

### 34A • 5
### Conditioning Practice

each line twice SS; then a 1' writing on line 3; find *gwam*

| | | |
|---|---|---|
| alphabet | 1 | Bowman fixed prized clocks that seven judges say are unique. |
| figures | 2 | Only 1,453 of the 6,280 members were at the 1997 convention. |
| easy | 3 | She lent the field auditor a hand with the work of the firm. |

**gwam** 1' | 1 | 2 | 3 | 4 | 5 | 6 | 7 | 8 | 9 | 10 | 11 | 12 |

---

### 34B • 16
### New Keys: ' and "

**Apostrophe:** ' is to the right of ; and is controlled by the right little finger.

1. Locate new symbol on appropriate keyboard chart; read technique statement below the chart.
2. Key twice SS the appropriate pair of lines given at right; DS between pairs.
3. Repeat Steps 1 and 2 for the other new symbol.
4. Key twice SS lines 5-8.
5. Rekey the lines with which you had difficulty.

**CAPITALIZATION *cue*:**
Capitalize first word and all other important words in titles of publications.

**Quotation mark:** Depress left shift and strike " (shift of ') with the right little finger.

**Note:** The appearance of single (apostrophe) and double quotation marks may differ according to type style and software program. Sometimes beginning and ending quotation marks differ in direction. Whatever their differences in appearance, they serve the same purpose.

**Learn ' (apostrophe)**

1 ; ; '; '; ;; '' ;'; ;'; it's he's I'm I've It's hers, I see.

2 I'm not sure if it's Hal's; but if it's his, I'll return it.

**Learn " (quotation mark)**

3 ; ; "; "; ;; "" ;"; ;"; "Keep on," she said, but I had quit.

4 I read "Ode on a Grecian Urn," "The Last Leaf," and "Trees."

**Combine ' and "**

5 "If it's Jan's or Al's," she said, "I'll bring it to class."

6 "Its" is an adjective; "it's" is the contraction of "it is."

7 Miss Uhl said, "To make numbers plural, add 's: 8's, 10's."

8 O'Shea said, "Use ' (apostrophe) to shorten phrases: I'll."

# Process Correspondence

## Standard Memos and Modified Block Letters

**Objectives:**
1. To process letters and memos.
2. To improve skill in keying from rough-draft and script copy.

### 194A • 5
### Conditioning Practice

each line twice; 1' writings on line 1 as time permits

alphabet 1 We realize expert judges may check the value of the unique books.

speed 2 The dorm officials may name six sorority girls to go to a social.

figures 3 A teacher will have 75 test items from pages 289-306 for Unit 41.

gwam 1' | 1 | 2 | 3 | 4 | 5 | 6 | 7 | 8 | 9 | 10 | 11 | 12 | 13 |

## FORMATTING

### 194B • 45
### Memos and Letters

**Document 1**
**Memo**

Create/save a file for memos in this lesson. Include standard memo headings, a full-width rule under the subject line, and a replica of this logo:

**Sundy Junior College**

Prepare a standard memo.

**Document 2**
**Memo (Merge)**

Create a data file (FACDATA) and a form file (FACFORM) and process this standard memo for each faculty member in the data file. Name the merged file FACDOCS.

**Data File:**

James Merritt, English
Paula Lapic, Food Service
Sam Larry, Psychology
Donald Green, Sociology
Diana Patsiga, Marketing
Lu Chang, Biology
Fred Stonfer, Mathematics
Betty Mahan, Engineering
Jim Malco, Nursing
Jane Steit, Avionics

words

TO: Dean Carolyn V. Pucevich  FROM:  President Mary B. Tunno  DATE: | 13
May 15, ----  SUBJECT:  MATHEMATICAL REASONING SKILLS TASK | 25
FORCE | 26

A meeting to discuss the formation of a Mathematical Reasoning Skills | 40
Task Force has been arranged for Tuesday, May 22, in my office at 2:30 | 54
p.m.  Vice President Gary Romeo will join us. | 64

The agenda for the meeting is to finalize the project description and to iden- | 80
tify faculty and advisory committee members who might join the task force. | 95

TO: Dr. (Name and subject area)    FROM: President  Mary B. Tunno   DATE: | 14
May 25, ----  SUBJECT:  MATHEMATICAL REASONING SKILLS TASK | 26
FORCE | 27

After discussions with members of the Presidential Planning Council, I be- | 42
lieve it is important that Sundy Junior College undertake a careful review | 57
of the curriculum that is intended to develop mathematical reasoning skills. | 72

To do so, I am establishing a task force composed of faculty from various | 87
disciplines and advisory committee members.  Dean Carolyn Pucevich will | 102
chair the task force. | 106

The broad charge to the task force is to determine what mathematical | 120
content is to be taught and applied in required general education courses, | 135
including required math courses. | 142

If you are interested in joining this task force, please attend an informa- | 157
tional meeting on June 2 at 2:30 p.m. in Board Room C. | 169

## 34C • 16
### New Keys: _ and *

**Underline:** Depress left shift; strike _ (shift of –) with right little finger.

**Asterisk:** Depress left shift; strike * (shift of 8) with right middle finger.

1. Locate new symbol on appropriate keyboard chart.
2. Key twice SS the lines given at right; DS between pairs.
3. Repeat Steps 1-2 for the other new key.
4. Key twice SS lines 5-8.

**wp note:**

Use the Underline feature (if you have one) to underline words as you key lines 5-7.

**Learn ___ (underline)**

1 ; ; _; _; ;; __ ;_; ;_; I _____ go there; she _____ go also.
2 They ___ to visit _____ aunt, but _____ cousin __ at school.

**Learn * (asterisk)**

3 k k *k *k kk ** k*k k*k She used * for a single source note.
4 All discounted items show an *, thus: 48K*, 588*, and 618*.

**Combine ___ and ***

5 Use an * to mark often-confused words such as <u>then</u> and <u>than</u>.
6 *Note: Book titles (like <u>Lorna Doone</u>) are often underlined.
7 I saw a review of "La Casa Verde" in <u>Latin American Fiction</u>.
8 Did you view <u>Hornblower</u>--a 12th Century African sculpture?

## **L** ANGUAGE SKILLS

### 34D • 13
### Capitalization

1. Read the first rule highlighted in color block.
2. Key the Learn sentences below it, noting how the rule has been applied.
3. Key the Apply sentences, supplying the appropriate capitalization.
4. Practice the other rule in the same way.
5. If time permits, key the Apply lines again at a faster pace.

Capitalize the first word of a direct quotation unless the quote is built into the structure of the sentence.

Learn 1 Yu-lan quoted the rule: "Spell the hour used with o'clock."
Learn 2 I didn't say that "making more errors makes us more human."

Apply 3 Kathleen quoted Pope: "to err is human, to forgive divine."
Apply 4 Ms. Ohms said to "Keep your eyes on the copy as you key."

Capitalize the first word of the first part of an interrupted quotation, but not the first word of the second part.

Learn 5 "To reduce errors," he said, "drop back slightly in speed."
Apply 6 "curve your fingers," she urged, "and keep them upright."

# ACTIVITY 3:

## Labels

1. Read the copy at right.
2. Learn how to prepare labels using your software.
3. Follow the directions at right to prepare labels.

Use the **Labels** feature to create mailing labels, file folder labels, diskette labels, and nametags. You can key the labels individually or use Merge to create labels from a data file. Most software has predefined labels so that you can choose the label definition that fits the labels and printer you are using.

1. Open TWP12-3 and rename it LABDATA.
2. LABDATA is a data file to be merged with a LABFORM file that you will create. The LABFORM file will contain these fields in USPS address format: <Name> <Street> <City> <ST> and <ZIP>.
3. Create the LABFORM file.
4. Merge LABDATA and LABFORM for labels that are 1" x 2.63" and to be printed on a laser printer.

# ACTIVITY 4:

## Nametags

Follow the directions at right to prepare nametags.

1. Open TWP12-3 if it is not open and rename it TAGDATA.
2. TAGDATA is a data file that will be merged with a TAGFORM file that you will create. The TAGFORM file will contain the <name> and <company>.
3. Create the TAGFORM file so that the person's name and company are in ALL CAPS in a large font, on two lines, separated by at least two blank lines, and centered on the nametag.
4. Merge TAGDATA and TAGFORM for nametags that are to be printed on a laser printer.
5. Save the nametags as TAGDOCS.

# ACTIVITY 5:

## Bar Code

1. Read the information at right about bar codes.
2. Learn how to prepare envelopes with bar codes using your software.
3. Follow the directions at right to address an envelope including a bar code. (Use your address or that of a friend.)

Most word processing software enables you to speed mail sorting, improve delivery accuracy, and lower mailing costs by printing a bar code on envelopes or mailing labels. The bar code created is a USPS POSTNET (**Post**al **N**umeric **E**ncoding **T**echnique) bar code and is based on the 5- or 9-digit ZIP Code that you key in the mailing address. When the document is printed, the software converts the digits into a combination of tall and short lines.

1. Prepare an envelope using your address as the mailing address.
2. Select the option to include a POSTNET bar code.
3. Print the envelope.
4. Compare the bar code on your envelope with that on other students' envelopes.

# UNIT 6

**LESSONS 35–37**

# Master Keyboarding/ Language Skills

## LESSON 35

### Keying/Language Skills

**Objectives:**
1. To improve keying speed and control.
2. To identify and construct simple sentences.

### 35A • 5
**Conditioning Practice**

each line twice SS; then a 1' writing on line 3; find *gwam*

alphabet 1 Linda may have Jack rekey pages two and six of the big quiz.

6/2 2 Our house at 622 Gold Circle will be paid for June 26, 2006.

easy 3 Jena is to go to the lake towns to do the map work for them.

gwam 1' | 1 | 2 | 3 | 4 | 5 | 6 | 7 | 8 | 9 | 10 | 11 | 12 |

### 35B • 10
**Skill Transfer**

1. Key a 1' writing on each ¶; find *gwam* on each.

2. Compare rates. On which ¶ did you have highest *gwam*?

3. Key two 1' writings on each of the slower ¶s, trying to equal your highest *gwam* in Step 1.

**Notes:**

1. Relative speeds on different kinds of copy:
   • highest—straight copy
   • next highest—script
   • lowest—statistical copy

2. To find *gwam*, use the 1' *gwam* scale for partial lines in ¶s 1 and 2, but count the words in ¶ 3.

**LA**   all letters/figures used                          gwam 1'

You should try now to transfer to other types of copy    11
as much of your straight-copy speed as you can.  Handwritten  23
copy and copy in which figures appear tend to slow you down.  35
You can increase speed on these, however, with extra effort.  48

An immediate goal for handwritten copy is at least 90%    11
of the straight-copy rate; for copy with figures, at least   23
75%.  Try to speed up balanced-hand figures such as 26, 84,  35
and 163.  Key harder ones such as 452 and 890 more slowly.   47

*Copy that is written by hand is often not legible, and*    11
*the spelling of words may be puzzling.  So give major attention*  23
*to unclear words.  Question and correct the spacing used*   35
*with a comma or period.  You can do this even as you key.*  47

1' | 1 | 2 | 3 | 4 | 5 | 6 | 7 | 8 | 9 | 10 | 11 | 12 |

**L**ANGUAGE SKILLS

### 35C • 10
**Number Expression**

1. Read each script line, noting where spacing and number-expression changes are needed.

2. Key each line once, making needed changes.

1 *15 voted for the amendment, but 12 voted against it.*

2 *Of the twenty divers, only three advanced to the state finals.*

3 *The curtain rises at eight thirty p.m. on Saturday, October ten.*

4 *My office is at ten Park Place; my home, at 1 Key Largo.*

5 *Buy one doz. eggs, two lbs. of butter, and 8 oz. of cream.*

# Word PROCESSING 12

## ACTIVITY 1:

**Shading**

1. Read the copy at right.
2. Learn how to add shading using your software.
3. Follow the directions at right to add shading.

Use the **Shading** feature of your software to customize documents by filling areas with varying shades of color (gray). The shading may cover a page; paragraph; cell, column, or row within a table; graphics text box or border. In this activity, you will cover a paragraph and a one-cell table with varying shades of gray.

1. Key the following paragraph using default margins; shade the paragraph. Save it as SHADE1A.

> This paragraph will be used to illustrate shading at 10%. If you select too high a percent, the text you are trying to highlight will not be easy to read. With experience, you will learn to select the percent that makes the shaded text stand out yet be easy to read.

2. Create a table with one column and one row (a one-cell table). If needed, add a single-line border around the table.
3. Adjust the table so that it is approximately 3" wide, is centered horizontally, and begins at the default TM.
4. Key FRANKLIN REALTY in the cell so that it is centered horizontally, with a blank line space above and below it.
5. Shade the table; use 20% shading.
6. Key the following memo heading in standard format, beginning about a DS below the shaded box:

TO:        Joseph Sandhu, Agent

FROM:      Jacquelyn Trembath, Owner

DATE:      October 21, ----

SUBJECT:   POTENTIAL LISTINGS

7. Save it as SHADE1B for use in the next activity.

## ACTIVITY 2:

**Horizontal Line**

1. Read the copy at right.
2. Learn how to insert a horizontal line using your software.
3. Follow the directions at right.

The **Horizontal Line** feature is a quick and easy method for adding horizontal lines to a document. Most software predefines the line's style, position, length, spacing, thickness, and color. You can, however, move, size, and edit the predefined line.

1. Open SHADE1B if it is not open.
2. Insert a horizontal line about 0.3" below the subject line.
3. Change the line style so that it is either a thick single line or a double line.
4. Key the following paragraph as the body of the memo about 0.3" below the horizontal line.

> Please see me as soon as possible for names, telephone numbers, and addresses of people you need to phone today or tomorrow. These people have expressed an interest in listing their homes with our agency in the very near future. They have been told that an agent will call them today or tomorrow to set up an appointment to discuss their property and explain what our agency has to offer.

5. Save the file as SHADE2.

## 35D • 12
### Skill Building

1. Key a 1' writing on each ¶; find *gwam*.
2. Key two 2' writings on ¶s 1-2 combined; find *gwam*.
3. Key a 3' writing on ¶s 1-2 combined; find *gwam*.

#### Quarter-Minute Checkpoints

| gwam | 1/4' | 1/2' | 3/4' | Time |
|------|------|------|------|------|
| 20 | 5 | 10 | 15 | 20 |
| 24 | 6 | 12 | 18 | 24 |
| 28 | 7 | 14 | 21 | 28 |
| 32 | 8 | 16 | 24 | 32 |
| 36 | 9 | 18 | 27 | 36 |
| 40 | 10 | 20 | 30 | 40 |
| 44 | 11 | 22 | 33 | 44 |
| 48 | 12 | 24 | 36 | 48 |

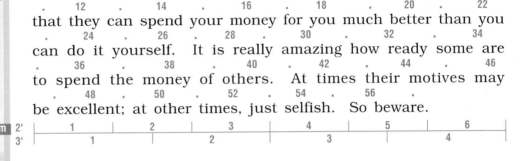

**LA**  all letters used                                    gwam  2' | 3'

Money is much harder to save than it is to earn.  Some-        6 | 4
body is always willing to help you spend what you make.  If   12 | 8
you confuse your needs and wants, you can quickly spend much  18 | 12
of it yourself.  Often, friends and relations can become an   24 | 16
additional major drain if you allow them to assist you.       29 | 19

And, of course, many politicians at all levels think          34 | 23
that they can spend your money for you much better than you   40 | 27
can do it yourself.  It is really amazing how ready some are  47 | 31
to spend the money of others.  At times their motives may     52 | 35
be excellent; at other times, just selfish.  So beware.       58 | 39

## L ANGUAGE SKILLS

### 35E • 13
### Simple Sentences

1. Study the guides in the color blocks and the sentences beneath them.
2. Key the Learn sentences as shown, noting the subjects and predicates.
3. Key the figure 1; opposite it key the subject and predicate of Sentence 1. Continue this procedure through line 8.

**Revise sentences:**

**9/10**

Combine the two sentences in each line into one simple sentence with two nouns as subject and one verb as predicate.

**11**

Combine the two sentences into one simple sentence with two nouns as subject and two verbs as predicate.

**12**

Combine the two sentences as in 9/10 above.

A *simple* sentence consists of one independent clause that contains a subject (noun or pronoun) and a predicate (verb).

Learn 1 Pam is president of her class.

Learn 2 Kevin walks to and from school.

Learn 3 Reading mystery novels is my favorite pastime.

Learn 4 The captain of the team is out with a badly sprained ankle.

A *simple* sentence may have as its subject more than one noun or pronoun (compound subject) and as its predicate more than one verb (compound predicate).

Learn 5 She bought a new bicycle.  (single subject/single predicate)

Learn 6 Marv and I received new bicycles.  (compound subject/single predicate)

Learn 7 Alice washed and waxed her car.  (single subject/compound predicate)

Learn 8 He and I cleaned and cooked the fish.  (compound subject and predicate)

Apply 9 Jorge read AURA by Fuentes.  Rosa read it, also.

Apply 10 Hamad cooks his own meals.  So does Janelle.

Apply 11 Mel chooses and buys his own training shoes. Suzy also chooses and buys hers.

Apply 12 Sara talked with Mona at the rock concert.  Lee talked with her, also.

# Skill Builder

## Statistical Copy

1. Key one 3' writing. Determine errors and *gwam*.
2. Select a goal: Control (if more than 6 errors in Step 1)—reduce errors by one on each writing. Speed (if 6 or fewer errors in Step 1)—Increase *gwam* by 3 on each writing.
3. Key three 3' writings; try to reach your goal on each writing.

The sales report for the quarter ending September 31 indicated   13 | 4 | 40

that sales for Easy-Korec Blue Correctable Film ribbon (Stock #B193)   26 | 9 | 44

were down by 40% while sales of all other ribbons were up by an   39 | 13 | 48

average of 15%.  To boost sales of B193 ribbons, the selling price   53 | 17 | 53

will be reduced during the next quarter from $7.50 to $4.49 per   65 | 22 | 57

ribbon (a 40% discount).  Also, a four-color display board empha-   79 | 26 | 62

sizing that the B193 ribbon can be used as a replacement ribbon   91 | 30 | 66

for TJK-133 and XRT-159 will be available to all salespersons in   104 | 35 | 70

the region.   106 | 35 | 71

gwam 1' | 1 | 2 | 3 | 4 | 5 | 6 | 7 | 8 | 9 | 10 | 11 | 12 | 13 |
     3' |    1    |     2     |     3     |    4    |

## Timed writings

1. Key three 1' writings on each ¶; find *gwam*. Count errors. If errors are 2 or fewer on any writing, goal is to increase speed by 1 or 2 words on next writing. If errors on any writing are more than 2, goal is control on next writing.
2. Key two 3' writings on ¶s 1-3 combined; find *gwam* and count errors.
3. Key a 5' writing on ¶s 1-3 combined; find *gwam* and count errors.

 all letters used

Appearance, which is often defined as the outward aspect of   4 | 2 | 41

someone or something, is quite important to most of us and af-   8 | 5 | 44

fects just about every day of our lives.  We like to be around   12 | 7 | 46

people whom and things that we consider attractive.  Because of   16 | 10 | 49

this preference, appearance is a factor in almost every decision   21 | 12 | 52

we make.   21 | 13 | 52

Appearance often affects our selection of food, the place in   25 | 15 | 54

which we live, the clothes we purchase, the car we drive, and the   30 | 18 | 57

vacations we schedule.  For example, we usually do not eat foods   34 | 20 | 60

that are not visually appealing or buy clothing that we realize   38 | 23 | 62

will be unattractive to others who are important to us.   42 | 25 | 64

Appearance is important in business.  People in charge of   46 | 27 | 67

hiring almost always stress the importance of good appearance.   50 | 30 | 69

Your progress in a job or career can be affected by how others   54 | 33 | 72

judge your appearance.  It is not uncommon for those who see but   59 | 35 | 74

do not know you to evaluate your abilities and character on the   63 | 38 | 77

basis of your personal appearance.   65 | 39 | 78

gwam 1' | 1 | 2 | 3 | 4 | 5 | 6 | 7 | 8 | 9 | 10 | 11 | 12 | 13 |
     3' |    1    |     2     |     3     |    4    |
     5' |      1      |      2      |     3     |

## LESSON 36

## Keying/Language Skills

**Objectives:**
1. To improve keying speed and control.
2. To identify and construct compound sentences.

### 36A • 5
### Conditioning Practice

each line twice SS; then a
1' writing on line 3; find
*gwam*

| | | |
|---|---|---|
| alphabet | 1 | Jacques could win a prize for eight more dives by next week. |
| figures | 2 | In 1995, we had only 240 computers; as of 1998 we owned 376. |
| easy | 3 | The girls paid for the eight antique urns with their profit. |
| **gwam** | 1' | 1 \| 2 \| 3 \| 4 \| 5 \| 6 \| 7 \| 8 \| 9 \| 10 \| 11 \| 12 \| |

### S KILL BUILDING

### 36B • 20
### Letter-Key Mastery

1. Key line 1 at a brisk pace. Note words that were awkward for you.
2. Key each of these words three times at increasing speeds.
3. Key line 2 at a steady, fluent rate.
4. Key each of the other pairs of lines in the same way.
5. If time permits, key again the lines in which you hesitated or stopped.

A/N
1 an and pan nap any nag ant man aunt land plan hand want sand
2 Ann and her aunt want to buy any land they can near the inn.

B/O
3 bow lob bog rob boy mob gob fob bob body robe boat born glob
4 Bobby bobbed in the bow of the boat as the boys came aboard.

C/P
5 cup cop cap pack copy cape cope pick pecks clips camps claps
6 Cap can clip a copy of the poem to his cape to read at camp.

D/Q
7 did quo quid ride quit road quiz paid aqua dude squid squads
8 The dude in an aqua shirt did quit the squad after the quiz.

E/R
9 or re ore per are her red peer here rent fore leer sore very
10 Vera read her book report to three of her friends at school.

F/S
11 if is fish fuss soft furs self fast fans sift surf fist fees
12 Floss said that fish on this shelf is for fast sale at half.

G/T
13 get got tag togs grit gilt gust tang right guilt fight ghost
14 Garth had the grit to go eight rounds in that fight tonight.

H/U
15 hue hut hub hurt shut shun huge hush brush truth shrug thugs
16 Hugh said four burly thugs hurled the man off the huge dock.

I/V
17 vie vim give view five vein dive vial vice vigor voice alive
18 Vivian made her five great dives with visible vim and vigor.

J/W
19 jay wow jet own jab town just will jest when joke what judge
20 Jewel jokes with your town judge about what and who is just.

K/X
21 oak fix kid fox know flax walk flex silk oxen park axle work
22 Knox fixed an oak axle on a flax cart for a kid in the park.

L/Y
23 lay sly try ply all pry lei ally only rely reply truly fully
24 Dolly truly felt that she could rely fully on only one ally.

M/Z
25 may zoo man zam zone make fuzz mama jazz maid jams game zoom
26 Zoe may make her mark in a jazz band jam session at the zoo.

# PHASE 6

## Extend Information Processing Skills

High school graduates often use keying, computer, and language skills to process information and prepare documents at work, college, or home. The primary purpose of Phase 6, therefore, is to extend your skill in these important areas. Science and math are subjects found often in the work you will do.

The first three units focus on correspondence, with many macros and merges; reports, with several "surprises"; and tables, with formulas you create to do math for you! Next is a special project—a longer-than-usual report with some "different" features. The following unit emphasizes news releases, meeting minutes (in a practical summary style), itineraries, and agendas. The fifth unit involves you in creating your own *functional resume* and other employment documents. Assessments and a word processing simulation complete Phase 6, which also offers these familiar "extras": *Word Processing*, *Language & Writing Skills*, and *Skill Builder* pages.

**In this phase, you will:**

1. Extend information processing skills.
2. Improve language and proofreading skills.
3. Integrate advanced word processing features and document processing knowledge and skills.
4. Apply your information processing skills to a challenging volunteer job in a community development organization (simulated).

## 36C • 12
### Skill Building

1. Key a 1' writing on each ¶; find *gwam.*
2. Key two 2' writings on ¶s 1-2 combined; find *gwam.*
3. Key a 3' writing on ¶s 1-2 combined; find *gwam.*

**LA** all letters used

| | gwam | 2' | 3' |
|---|---|---|---|

```
        .         2    .    4    .    6    .    8    .   10   .
It is okay to try and try again if your first efforts do          6    4
  12    .    14   .    16   .    18   .    20   .    22
not bring the correct results.  If you try but fail again and    12    8
 24    .    26   .    28   .    30   .    32   .    34    .    36
again, however, it is foolish to plug along in the very same     18   12
        38   .    40   .    42   .    44   .    46   .    48
manner.  Rather, experiment with another way to accomplish the   24   16
        50   .    52   .    54   .    56   .    58
task that may bring the skill or knowledge you seek.             30   20
        .         2    .    4    .    6    .    8    .   10   .
If your first attempts do not yield success, do not quit         35   23
  12    .    14   .    16   .    18   .    20   .    22    .
and merely let it go at that.  Instead, begin again in a bet-    41   28
 24    .    26   .    28   .    30   .    32   .    34    .
ter way to finish the work or develop more insight into your     47   32
 36    .    38   .    40   .    42   .    44   .    46   .    48
difficulty.  If you recognize why you must do more than just     54   36
        .    50   .    52   .    54   .    56   .    58   .    60
try, try again, you will work with purpose to achieve success.   60   40
```

| gwam 2' | 1 | | 2 | | 3 | | 4 | | 5 | | 6 | |
|---|---|---|---|---|---|---|---|---|---|---|---|---|
| 3' | | 1 | | | 2 | | | 3 | | | 4 | |

## L ANGUAGE SKILLS

### 36D • 13
### Compound Sentences

1. Study the guides in the color blocks and the sentences beneath them.
2. Key the Learn sentences, noting the words that make up the subjects and predicates of each sentence.
3. Key the figure 1; opposite it key the subject and predicate of each clause in Sentence 1. Continue this procedure through line 8.

**Revise sentences:**

In each of lines 9-12, combine the two sentences into a compound sentence. Choose carefully from the coordinating conjunctions *and, but, for, or, nor, yet,* and *so.*

> A *compound* sentence contains two or more independent clauses connected by a coordinating conjunction (*and, but, for, or, nor, yet, so*).

Learn 1 Jay Sparks likes to hike, and Roy Tubbs likes to swim.
Learn 2 The computer is operative, but the printer does not work.
Learn 3 You may eat in the hotel, or you may choose a cafe nearby.
Learn 4 The sky is clear, the moon is out, and the sea is very calm.

> Each clause of a compound sentence may have as its subject more than one noun/pronoun and as its predicate more than one verb.

Learn 5 Ben and I saw the game, and Bob and Marla went to a movie.
Learn 6 Nick dived and swam, but the others fished off the boat.
Learn 7 You may play solitaire, or you and Joe may play checkers.
Learn 8 Bobby huffed and puffed, but Erin scampered up the hill.

Apply 9 Karen listened to Ravel's BOLERO.  Matt read FORREST GUMP.
Apply 10 You may watch STAR TREK.  You and Edie may play dominoes.
Apply 11 Ken may play football or basketball.  He may not play both.
Apply 12 Linda skated to CABARET music.  Jon chose WEST SIDE STORY.

# ETHICS: The Right Thing to Do

From experience you know that many people use technology in ways we would not have imagined a few years ago. We use computers to do class assignments, pay bills and income tax, keep personal budgets, and find out what is new on the Internet. Faxes, e-mail, and interactive technology are widely used in homes, schools, and business.

When we use this technology, we depend upon software packages to make our study and daily life easier. Programmers spend hours designing and making software error-free. Companies pay programmers for their efforts. Company stockholders and programmers are paid from money earned from the sale of the software. Software is copyrighted to help prevent "pirating."

Because software is expensive and there is such a variety of it, individuals often lend and borrow software. In discussing a particular software package, a friend offers to lend it to you to use for a week. The software provides you with many practical applications as well as hours of enjoyment.

When you return the program, he/she tells you that it's easy to copy—and a copy can be made for you. You know that your friend has copied and distributed other software packages among your acquaintances. This is the first time your friend has offered to do this for you. You really like using the software and want a copy of your own. Letting your friend make a copy for you would save money you could use for other purposes. You know that your friend should not violate the software maker's license agreement. You also know that copying software defies the producer's copyright by denying that company a sale. You wonder what to do.

## ACTIVITIES

1. Read the material at the left.

2. Under the heading KNOWING WHAT TO DO, compose/key a short theme describing what you would do and why.
   Consider:
   a. Is your friend wrong to copy the software? Why?
   b. Are you equally wrong if you encourage her/him to make you a copy? Why?
   c. What is the penalty if you are caught? For you? For your friend?
   d. Should a possible penalty enter into your decision?
   e. What other of your experiences helped you decide?

# CULTURAL DIVERSITY

Like individuals and social groups, businesses know the importance of recognizing and accepting differences among people. Many businesses realize that to be successful in today's marketplace, they must meet the needs of customers not only in the United States but also throughout the world.

One company that is attempting to meet worldwide needs is a greeting card company. This company produces a series of greeting cards called *common threads*. These cards reflect a positive approach in dealing with the differences among people. This card company hopes that this respect for different cultures will enable people to share continually the good in every culture and encourage people to buy their cards.

Cards in the series contain artwork from many cultures. On the last side of all cards is the following statement: "For every difference that makes us unique, there is a common thread, which connects us all. We share the need for home and community, for love and respect. May these common threads form a beautiful world in which all people and all cultures are honored."

We know from our experience within our family, from our relationships with friends, and from working with classmates what the card message tells us. Some of the differences and similarities come from the persons we are; others come from our cultural heritage. To resolve inherent differences, we are challenged to work on common goals, using when possible the similarities as a bridge to greater understanding and acceptance.

## ACTIVITIES

1. Read the material at the left.

2. Divide into groups of 4 or 5 students each.

3. As a group, key lists of as many cultural similarities and differences in your group as you can identify.

4. As a group, classify the differences as hard to accept or easy to accept. Try to see yourself "walking in another's shoes."

5. Discuss how hard-to-accept differences can be made acceptable if everyone "gives" a little in an effort to understand them.

## LESSON 37 Keying/Language Skills

**Objectives:**

**1.** To check/improve keying speed and control.
**2.** To identify and construct complex sentences.

**37A • 5**
**Conditioning Practice**

each line twice SS; then a
1' writing on line 3; find
*gwam*

alphabet 1 Quig was just amazed by the next five blocks of his players.

figures 2 On October 14, 1997, the 281 members met from 5 to 6:30 p.m.

easy 3 Keith may hang the sign by the antique door of the big hall.

gwam 1' | 1 | 2 | 3 | 4 | 5 | 6 | 7 | 8 | 9 | 10 | 11 | 12 |

## S KILL BUILDING

**37B • 19**
**Technique Check**

1. Key each line once SS;
   DS between 3-line
   groups.
2. Key a 1' writing on each
   of lines 15, 18, and 21;
   find *gwam* on each.
3. If time permits, key
   another 1' writing on
   each of the two slower
   lines.

figures & symbols

1 and 163 sob 295 rid 483 fog 495 hen 637 lap 910 own 926 span

2 Case 10463 may be found in Volume 27, Section 108, page 592.

3 My note for $493 at 7.5% interest will be paid May 18, 2006.

shift keys & CAPS LOCK

4 GREAT AMERICAN SPEECHES did include King's "I Have a Dream."

5 THE ARTS by Tamplin is a history of 20th Century expression.

6 Simon & Schuster's OPERA is a quite complete reference work.

double letters

7 off odd zoo lee too door leek food hall good heel foot shall

8 Lee lost his footing and fell off a tall ladder in the mall.

9 Ella keeps a book of crossword puzzles in the school office.

adjacent keys

10 ruin part mere owes coin said true port buys flew stop point

11 Merv tried to buy a few old coins in that shop on the river.

12 Trudy said that her nephew tried out for a part in an opera.

letter response

13 dad hop few pop red you far kin gas oil vet mom get pin grew

14 As my case was set up, you saw him get only a few wage data.

15 Johnny read him rate cards on wage taxes set up at my union.

combination response

16 may few men saw pan tax ham get jam rest lend hulk bush gaze

17 A few of them ate jam tarts with the tea she served at dusk.

18 By noon they are to fix the pump at the oil rig on the hill.

word response

19 ox by got too off zoo odd lay but for fix pan with pair turn

20 Lana is to mend a map of the ancient lake town for the dorm.

21 Tish may sign a work form to aid the auditor of a soap firm.

gwam 1' | 1 | 2 | 3 | 4 | 5 | 6 | 7 | 8 | 9 | 10 | 11 | 12 |

# your PERSPECTIVE

## GLOBAL AWARENESS

To see or read with meaning and understanding news reports of what is happening in different parts of the world, it is necessary to have at least a general idea of the locations of those places. List A below includes some of the continents and regions that make up the globe of the world. List B below includes some of the countries that are often in the news on radio and TV and in newspapers and magazines.

Beneath the lists is a world map with double letters (such as AA) identifying the regions and continents and with single letters (such as A) identifying the locations of countries.

To check your global awareness, you will see how many of the items in Lists A and B you can properly match to appropriate letters on the map. ✳

### ACTIVITIES

1. Key the first item in List A; tab 4 times and key the letters on the map that show its location.

2. Key the remaining items, tabbing to align the letters of your response with ones above it.

3. Key the first item in List B; tab 4 times and key the letter on the map that shows its location.

4. Key the remaining items, tabbing to align the letter of your response with the one above it.

| List A | | List B | |
|---|---|---|---|
| Africa | North America | Brazil | Iraq |
| Asia | Persian Gulf | Canada | Israel |
| Australia | Scandinavia | China | Japan |
| Central America | South America | Egypt | Russia |
| Europe | Greenland | Great Britain | United States |

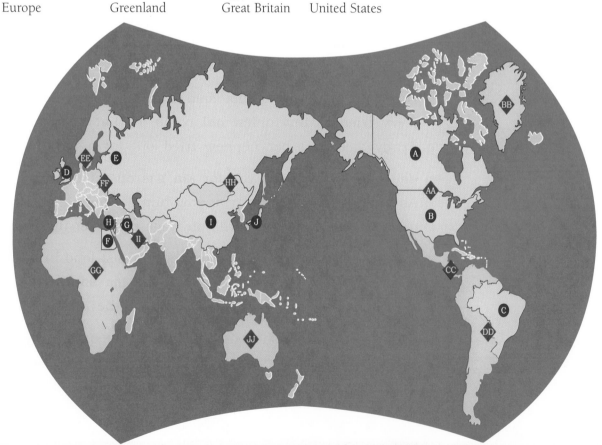

## 37C • 14
## Speed Check

1. Key a 1' writing on each ¶; find *gwam*.
2. Key two 2' writings on ¶s 1-2 combined; find *gwam*.
3. Key a 3' writing on ¶s 1-2 combined; find *gwam*.

### Quarter-Minute Checkpoints

| gwam | 1/4' | 1/2' | 3/4' | 1' |
|------|------|------|------|-----|
| 20 | 5 | 10 | 15 | 20 |
| 24 | 6 | 12 | 18 | 24 |
| 28 | 7 | 14 | 21 | 28 |
| 32 | 8 | 16 | 24 | 32 |
| 36 | 9 | 18 | 27 | 36 |
| 40 | 10 | 20 | 30 | 40 |
| 44 | 11 | 22 | 33 | 44 |
| 48 | 12 | 24 | 36 | 48 |
| 52 | 13 | 26 | 39 | 52 |
| 56 | 14 | 28 | 42 | 56 |

all letters used

|  | gwam 2' |
|---|---|
| What is it that makes one person succeed and another | 5 \| 4 |
| fail when the two seem to have about equal ability? Some | 11 \| 7 |
| have said that the difference is in the degree of motivation | 17 \| 11 |
| and effort each brings to the job. Others have said that an | 23 \| 16 |
| intent to become excellent is the main difference. | 28 \| 19 |
| At least four items are likely to have a major effect | 34 \| 22 |
| on our success: basic ability, a desire to excel, an aim | 40 \| 26 |
| to succeed, and zestful effort. If any one of these is ab- | 45 \| 30 |
| sent or at a low point, our chances for success are lessened. | 51 \| 34 |
| These features, however, can be developed if we wish. | 57 \| 38 |

| gwam | 2' | 1 | 2 | 3 | 4 | 5 | 6 |
|------|-----|---|---|---|---|---|---|
|  | 3' | 1 | 2 | 3 | 4 | | |

## L ANGUAGE SKILLS

## 37D • 12
## Complex Sentences

Use the procedure given in 36D, p. 90.

A *complex* sentence contains only one independent clause but one or more dependent clauses.

Learn 1 The book that you gave Juan for his birthday is lost.
Learn 2 If I were you, I would speak to Paula before I left.
Learn 3 Miss Gomez, who chairs the department, is currently on leave.
Learn 4 Students who use their time wisely usually succeed.

The subject of a complex sentence may consist of more than one noun or pronoun; the predicate may consist of more than one verb.

Learn 5 All who were invited to the party also attended the game.
Learn 6 If you are to join, you should sign up and pay your dues.
Learn 7 After she and I left, Cliff and Pam sang and danced.
Learn 8 Although they don't know it yet, Fran and Bret were elected.

Apply 9 My PSAT and SAT scores are high. I may not get into Yale.
Apply 10 They attended the symphony. They then had a light supper.
Apply 11 Mindy is to audition for the part. She should apply now.
Apply 12 You are buying a computer. You should also get software.

# Activity 3:

1. Read the account of destructive behavior given at the right.
2. Decide whether you believe the judge's ruling was right or wrong and list your reasons.
3. Decide whether you believe the parents' defense statements should have affected the judge's decision and list your reasons.
4. Compose/key two or three ¶s giving your assessment of the case; indicate whether you believe the judge's ruling was fair; give reasons in support of your opinion.

**Compose (think) as you key**

Three adolescent boys—one a resident of a condominium complex; the other two, overnight guests from other communities—were observed tossing poolside tables, chairs, and lounges into the unoccupied pool. The fenced pool was locked, but the resident boy had access to a key.

Because the resident boy and friends had been previously caught and warned several times for destructive behavior, the observer called the local police, who apprehended the boys. Being aware of the previous incidents and warnings, the police at the urging of the condo board of directors cited the boys to juvenile court. The boys were found guilty as charged, fined $50 each for damage to property, and severely warned by the judge against repetition of such acts.

The boys' parents defended their sons with such statements as: "Our boy would never do anything like that." "They're only boys." "Boys will be boys." "It's the first time he has ever done anything like this." "He has learning problems." "We both work and can't supervise him when he's not in school." "He had a difficult childhood." "He's a good boy who just got in with the wrong crowd."

Given the previous incidents of setting fire to grass alongside the pool house, breaking into the pool house and taking property, and pulling up flowers in community flower beds, among others, the judge believed something more than another warning was justified, and so ruled.

## ETHICS: The Right Thing to Do

Talk shows that deal with "how to put people down," "telling my friend what I really think," or "confronting my boss" fill the airwaves. Audiences encourage confrontation and seem disappointed when there is no pushing or shoving among a show's participants. With friends, we talk about the driver who cut us off and the person who moved ahead of us in line. We remember going to a movie where the people around us talked and laughed loudly, with no regard for those around them.

When we experience these behaviors, we ask ourselves: "Why do people behave and talk rudely to one another?" "Why don't people treat each other with more respect?"

Increasingly, it seems, people are not relating to each other with good manners, with civility. When we were young, family members taught us the behaviors we were to use in interacting with others. We were taught to say "please" when making a request and "thank you" when the request was fulfilled; "pardon me" when we bump into someone and "I'm sorry" if we offend someone.

Such expressions enable us to adapt our behavior so that we can interact smoothly and positively with others. An acceptable code of behavior increases communication and prevents problems from arising between people. The use of appropriate behavior is a glue that holds people together from varying backgrounds.

Such a system of accepted behaviors is called manners, etiquette, or civility. Whatever the term, these behaviors are everyday expressions of an ethical code—behaviors by which people interact with one another with courtesy, fairness, and justice.

Guide books on manners, such as those written by Amy Vanderbilt and Miss Manners, have become popular in the United States. People writing to Ann Landers express their pleasure when they see someone hold a chair for another person or help someone put on a coat. Interest in and reactions to such behavior patterns indicate that people are looking for ways to act in a considerate and ethical manner toward other people.

Good manners enable us to deal with others in courteous and positive ways that do not go unnoticed. Hold a door open for someone and see the look of appreciation on the person's face and hear the words "thank you." How do you think a student would respond if you helped pick up materials that perhaps you caused to be dropped? What would your reaction be if a person who offended you came to you and apologized?

Good manners are nothing more than a code of behaviors that involve treating others as you would have them treat you. Unless you follow such a code that shows respect for other people, you hardly have a right to demand respect for yourself. ✳

## ACTIVITIES

1. Read the paragraphs at the left dealing with good manners and their value in human relations.

2. Key a list of good manners that you observe in your dealings with others at home, at school, and in public.

3. Key a list of poor (if not bad) manners in which you engage more often than you should.

4. Compare your lists with those of a fellow student. Have her/him tell you if you do in fact follow the good manners *and* the poor manners on your lists. Then you do the same for her/him.

5. Finally, change your lists if needed as a result of Step 4 and key two new lists: (1) Good Manners I Usually Follow; (2) Poor Manners I Need to Change.

# Language & Writing Skills 18

## Activity 1:

1. Study the spelling/definitions of the words in the color block at the right.
2. Key the **Learn** line in the first set of sentences.
3. Key the **Apply** lines, choosing the right words to complete each sentence correctly.
4. Key the second set of lines in the same way.
5. Check work; rekey lines containing word-choice errors.

### Choose the right word

| | |
|---|---|
| **plain** (adj) with little ornamentation or decoration | **principal** (n/adj) a person in authority; a capital sum; main, primary |
| **plane** (n) an airplane or hydroplane | **principle** (n) a rule |

Learn 1 The seats of the plane were covered with plain beige fabric.
Apply 2 For the trip, she chose (plain/plane) skirts and lively blouses.
Apply 3 It was certain that the (plain/plane) would not leave on time.

Learn 4 The new principal is guided by the principle of fairness.
Apply 5 The (principal/principle) reason I'm here is to record his talk.
Apply 6 What (principal/principle) of law was applied in that case?

## Activity 2:

1. Read carefully the ¶s shown at the right, noting errors in punctuation, word choice, subject/predicate agreement, and noun/pronoun agreement.
2. Key the ¶s, making the needed corrections.
3. Proofread your work and correct any remaining errors you find.

### Proofread & correct

Two kinds of people, who never amount too much, are those who cannot do what they are told and those who can due nothing else. One of the things all word processing students must learn to do are to proofread and correct quickly and with care the work he or she produces at the keyboard. Copy with all errors corrected reflects a pride in work that is a credit to the person who produced it. Pride in work is highly sought in workplace personal.

It's important to find and correct all errors before a piece of work is given either to the teacher for grading or to an executive or a supervisor for office use. Sum people fail to detect and correct there errors because there careless. They don't realize the affect such errors have on those who see this work. Therefore its know wonder that employers value such workers less then they value workers who proofread with care.

# GLOBAL AWARENESS

Many animals you see in zoos throughout the country are said to be native to (indigenous to) certain continents or geographic regions. For example, the bison (a species of buffalo) is considered to be native to western North America.

To check your global awareness, you will see how many animals in List A you can match with their native region in List B.

| List A | List B |
|--------|--------|
| elephant | Africa |
| grizzly bear | Africa/Asia |
| ibex | Asia |
| iguana | Australia |
| koala | Central/South America |
| llama | India |
| rhesus monkey | North America |
| timber wolf | Northern Europe |
| water buffalo | South America |
| zebra | Southwestern North America |

## ACTIVITIES

1. Read paragraphs at left; study the two lists beneath them.
2. Key at left margin the first item of List A.
3. Tab 4 times; then key the continent(s) and/or region(s) to which the animal is considered native.
4. Key remaining items, tabbing to align the items in List B.
5. In groups of 3 or 4, compare answers and discuss reasons for choices made.

# CULTURAL DIVERSITY

Language is one index of the culture from which a person comes. In the United States, many languages are spoken. Among them are Chinese, French, German, Italian, Japanese, Korean, Spanish, Vietnamese, and, of course, many dialects of English.

One of the challenges when people of differing cultures interface lies in trying to understand what different people are really saying. Can you correctly match the English expressions in List A with the same expression in another language in List B and name the language represented by the expression?

| List A | List B |
|--------|--------|
| baby | bambino |
| girl | bon jour |
| good day | fille |
| good-bye | gracias |
| man | hai |
| no | hombre |
| plaza | nyet |
| please | piazza |
| thanks | por favor |
| yes | sayanara |

## ACTIVITIES

1. Read paragraphs at left; study the two lists beneath them.
2. Key at left margin the first item in List A.
3. Tab 4 times; key the expression in List B that matches the word(s) in List A; tab 4 more times and key in a third column the name of the language of the choice you made.
4. Key remaining items, tabbing to align the items in Columns 2 and 3.
5. Compare/discuss choices.

**Message from David Hofacre**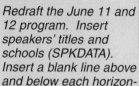

*Redraft the June 11 and 12 program. Insert speakers' titles and schools (SPKDATA). Insert a blank line above and below each horizontal rule.*

**Job 10**

**Message from Susan Synowka**

*Using information from Job 9 and variables in SPKDATA, compose a form letter to presenters. Give each speaker the date, time, and room for her or his presentation. Ask all presenters to arrive 15 minutes early to check audio-visual equipment and meet the person who will introduce them. Ask each presenter to fill out the (enclosed) registration form and to call me if he or she needs more information. Save the form letter, SPKFORM; merge and save the documents, SPKRDOCS.B.*

| JUNE 11 SCHEDULE | IASM CONFERENCE, ST. LOUIS | | |
|---|---|---|---|
| 4:30 p.m. | Registration--Ford Foyer | | |
| 7:00 p.m. | IASM Conference Welcome Reception--Grande I | | |
| 8:00 p.m. | General Session I: "Improving Leadership Practices and Strategies in Sport Management," Anthony Cannon--Grande II & III | | |

| JUNE 12 SCHEDULE | IASM CONFERENCE, ST. LOUIS | | |
|---|---|---|---|
| 8:00 a.m. | Registration--Ford Foyer | Exhibit Area Open (until 4:30 p.m.)--Ballroom A | |
| 8:30 a.m. | General Session II: "The Economics of Professional Sports," Helen P. Polk-Yeager--Grande I & II | | |
| 9:30 a.m. | Session 12-A: "Sport Sponsorship by Small Business," Don E. Ezzie--Regency | Session 12-B: "Satisfaction in Athletes," Bette L. Townsend--Park | Session 12-C: "Contracts in Sport Management," Cynthia Bagamery--River |
| 10:45 a.m. | Session 12-D: "Starting a Sports Recreation Business," Sue Hiatt-Locke--Regency | Session 12-E: "Delivering Community Sports," Henry L. Yu--Park | Session 12-F: "Sport and Minority Consumers," June F. Ford--River |
| Noon | IASM Award Luncheon--Grande I & II Presiding: Dr. Harriet G. Mills, IASM President | | |
| 1:30 p.m. | Session 12-G: "Social Justice via Sports," Ronald Beaver--Regency | Session 12-H: "College Athletic Directors' Leadership Styles," Ken P. Chan--Park | Session 12-I: "Skills Needed by Sport Management Interns," Arvn Quddus--River |
| 2:45 p.m. | Refreshment Break and Exhibits--Ballroom | | |
| 3:30 p.m. | General Session III: "Improving Leadership Practices and Strategies," Glena C. Free--Grande I & II | | |
| 4:30 p.m. | IASM Business Meeting and Election of Officers--Regency | | |

# Word Processing

Communication has often been called the nervous system of business and industry, sending and receiving signals to action all over world.

These signals start in the brain and move through the fingers to a keyboard that converts them into messages—memos, letters, reports, and the like. These may be transmitted as hard copy through the mail, or they may be sent electronically as e-mail or facsimile copies (faxes).

However transmitted, messages are prepared in specific arrangements (placement and spacing of messages parts) called "formats." In the lessons of Phase 2, you will learn how to process messages in the formats that are most often used. In addition, you will continue to improve your language skills.

No matter what career you choose or jobs you get along the way, a computer is likely to be the center of your communication functions. Learning now how to process messages properly and improving your language skills will give you a headstart on your future.

Rd., St. Louis, MO 63402-7730. Include a check or money order for $45 (U.S. funds) made payable to IASM. If additional information is needed, you can call me at (412) 162-8426, fax me at (412) 162-8494, or e-mail me at hofacre @ benzing . edu.

· · · · · · · ✂ · · · · · · ✂ · · · · · · ✂ · · · · · · ✂ · · · · · · ✂ · · · · · ·

| IASM GOLF OUTING REGISTRATION FORM | |
|---|---|
| Name: | Phone: |
| Address: | Fax: |
| | I need transportation: |
| E-mail address: | ☐ Yes ☐ No |
| Approximate handicap _____ or average score _____ | Name of preferred playing partner: |
| I need to rent clubs: ☐ Right-handed clubs ☐ Left-handed clubs | Paying $45 (U.S. funds) by: ☐ Check ☐ Money Order |

**Job 8**
**Data File Changes**

**Message from Susan Synowka**

Make these changes to the SPKRDATA file that you prepared earlier. Change the name of the revised file to SPKDATA.

✓ Change Yu's faculty rank from assistant professor to associate professor.

✓ Change Sue Hiatt's surname from Hiatt to Hiatt-Locke.

✓ Change Arvn Luddus' phone number from 172-5729 to 172-5792.

✓ Add these two individuals to the data file:

  ✓ Ms. Cynthia Bagamery, Instructor, Management Department, Welsh College, Johnson Hall, Bozeman, MT 59101-5583, (406) 152-5721

  ✓ Dr. Bette L. Townsend, Associate Professor, Sports Studies, Central Highlands University, Rollins Hall, Casper, WY 82601-5823, (307) 135-7093

# Learn Numeric Keypad Operation

## LESSON 38

### New Keys: 4/5/6/0

**Objectives:**

1. To learn reach-strokes for **4**, **5**, **6**, and **0**.
2. To key these home-key numbers with speed and ease.

---

### 38A • 5
### Numeric Keypad Arrangement

Figure keys 1-9 are in standard locations on numeric keypads of computers.

The zero (0 or Ø) key location may vary slightly from one keyboard to another.

The illustrations at the right show the location of the numeric keypad on selected computer keyboards.

Macintosh LCII numeric keypad

IBM PC

---

### 38B • 5
### Operating Position

1. Position yourself in front of the keyboard—body erect, both feet on floor for balance.
2. Place this book for easy reading—at right of keyboard or directly behind it.
3. Curve the fingers of the right hand and place them on the keypad:
   - index finger on 4
   - middle finger on 5
   - ring finger on 6
   - thumb on 0

**Note:** To use the keypad, the Num (number) Lock must be turned on.

Book at right of keyboard

Proper position at keyboard

TO:        David Hofacre

FROM:    Susan Synowka

DATE:    (Current date)

SUBJECT:  INFO FOR THE GOLF OUTING

Harry Ufko, the golf pro at Seven Hills Golf Course, called with the information you've been waiting for to prepare the Golf Outing Announcement and Registration Form.

IASM can have a shotgun start at 11:20 on June 11.  Up to 72 golfers can be involved in the outing.  The cost per golfer for the outing is $45.  The price includes the green and cart fees and a cookout (hot dogs, three cold salads, and soft drinks) at 4:30 p.m.  Left- and right-handed clubs can be rented for $10.

Mr. Ufko believes he has given me all the information you requested.  If not, he said for you to call him at 167-9324.

**Message from David Hofacre**  *D. Hofacre*

*Prepare this announcement and form. Single-space the text above the form. Use different font sizes, etc., to make it attractive.*

IASM  GOLF  OUTING
ANNOUNCEMENT  AND  REGISTRATION  FORM

The St. Louis IASM 18-hole golf outing will be held on Wednesday, June 11, at the well-known Seven Hills Golf Course. A shotgun start is scheduled at 11:20 a.m. Plan to be at the course, no later than 10:45 a.m. Roundtrip transportation from the Clark Hotel will be provided.

The cost for the outing is $45, and that includes green and cart fees and a cookout at 4:30 p.m. The outing will end in time for you to be at the IASM opening session at 7:30 p.m.

If you plan to participate in this event, complete the form below and return it by June 1 to Dr. David L. Hofacre, Sport Administration Department, Benzing College, North Hanley

*(continued on next page)*

## 38C • 40
## New Keys: 4/5/6/0 (Home Keys)

Complete the drills as directed below, entering the numbers in one continuous column on your wp software. The screen will fill quickly because numbers are listed vertically. Therefore, clear the screen after each drill.

1. Curve the fingers of your right hand; place them upright on the home keys:
   • index finger on 4
   • middle finger on 5
   • ring finger on 6
   • thumb on 0

2. Using the special Enter key (at right of keypad), enter data in Drill 1A as follows:

   4 Enter
   4 Enter
   4 Enter
   Strike Enter

3. Enter Columns B-F in the same way.

4. Using the special Enter key, enter data in Drill 2A as follows:

   44 Enter
   44 Enter
   44 Enter
   Strike Enter

5. Continue Drill 2 and complete Drills 3-5 in a similar way. In Drills 4 and 5, strike 0 with side of right thumb.

**Note:** When you can operate the keypad by touch—Lesson 40 completed—determine if your software contains a calculator accessory. If so, key each drill in Lessons 38-40 twice. (You may have to strike the + key before each number.) If the two totals of a single drill match, you have probably entered the data correctly.

### TECHNIQUE cue:
Strike each key with a quick, sharp stroke with the *tip* of the finger; release the key quickly. Keep the fingers curved and upright; the wrist low, relaxed, and steady.

**Drill 1**

| A | B | C | D | E | F |
|---|---|---|---|---|---|
| 4 | 5 | 6 | 4 | 5 | 6 |
| 4 | 5 | 6 | 4 | 5 | 6 |
| 4 | 5 | 6 | 4 | 5 | 6 |

**Drill 2**

| A | B | C | D | E | F |
|---|---|---|---|---|---|
| 44 | 55 | 66 | 44 | 55 | 66 |
| 44 | 55 | 66 | 44 | 55 | 66 |
| 44 | 55 | 66 | 44 | 55 | 66 |

**Drill 3**

| A | B | C | D | E | F |
|---|---|---|---|---|---|
| 44 | 45 | 54 | 44 | 55 | 66 |
| 55 | 56 | 46 | 45 | 54 | 65 |
| 66 | 64 | 65 | 46 | 56 | 64 |

**Drill 4**

| A | B | C | D | E | F |
|---|---|---|---|---|---|
| 40 | 50 | 60 | 400 | 500 | 600 |
| 40 | 50 | 60 | 400 | 500 | 600 |
| 40 | 50 | 60 | 400 | 500 | 600 |

**Drill 5**

| A | B | C | D | E | F |
|---|---|---|---|---|---|
| 40 | 400 | 404 | 406 | 450 | 650 |
| 50 | 500 | 505 | 506 | 540 | 560 |
| 60 | 600 | 606 | 606 | 405 | 605 |

**Message from
Susan Synowka** §§

*Format and print a form
from the one I have
roughed out at the right.
It will be enclosed in a
letter to the speakers.*

International Association for Sport Management Conference -- June 11-14, ---- | Complete and return this form by March 15, 19--

Name: | Col /Univ:

Check or List Audio-Visual Equipment Needed:

☑ Overhead projector with screen

☐ Slide projector with screen

☐ TV monitor with VCR

☐ Computer with LCD plate or projection screen

☐ Other (list in space at the right)

Exact Title of Presentation:

Short Description of Presentation:

**Message from
Susan Synowka** §§

*Check this letter for
errors. Set it up as a
form file. Use **Susan T.
Synowka, Ph.D.,
Program Co-Director**
in closing lines.*

*Use these fields for the
letter address:*
*<Name>*
*<Col/Univ>*
*<St/Bldg>*
*<City>, <State> <ZIP>*
*Save as SPKRFORM;
merge with SPKRDATA.
Save merged file as
SPKRDOCS.*

(Current date)

Dear **<Salutation>**

Congratulations on being selected by your peers to present a paper at the upcoming International Association of Sport Management Conference. The conference will be held in St. Louis from June 11-14, ----.

Please fill in and return the enclosed from so that the audio-visual equipment you need will be available. (Yes, IASM can provide computers that run software in a Windows environment). Add the exact title and a description of your presentation to help us dscribe the presentation correctly in the conference brochure.

Check the information that follows to make sure we have the correct spelling of your name and a accurate listing of your title and school. Write corrections on this copy and return it with the form.

**<Name>, <Faculty rank>, <Dept/Subj area>, <Col/Univ>, <St/Bldg>, <City>, <State> <ZIP>**

Please return the form by March 15. Such an important conference takes lots of preparation time.

# LESSON 39

## New Keys: 7/8/9

**Objectives:**

1. To learn reach-strokes for **7**, **8**, and **9**.
2. To combine quickly the new keys with other keys learned.

---

### 39A • 5
### Home-Key Review

Enter the columns of data listed at the right as directed in Steps 1-5 on p. 97.

| A | B | C | D | E | F |
|---|---|---|---|---|---|
| 4 | 44 | 400 | 404 | 440 | 450 |
| 5 | 55 | 500 | 505 | 550 | 560 |
| 6 | 66 | 600 | 606 | 660 | 456 |

---

### 39B • 45
### New Keys: 7/8/9

**Learn reach to 7**

1. Locate 7 (above 4) on the numeric keypad.
2. Watch your index finger move up to 7 and back to 4 a few times *without striking keys*.
3. Practice striking 74 a few times as you watch the finger.
4. With eyes on copy, enter the data in Drills 1A and 1B.

**Learn reach to 8**

1. Learn the middle-finger reach to 8 (above 5) as directed in Steps 1-3 above.
2. With eyes on copy, enter the data in Drills 1C and 1D.

**Learn reach to 9**

1. Learn the ring-finger reach to 9 (above 6) as directed above.
2. With eyes on copy, enter the data in Drills 1E and 1F.

**Drills 2-4**

Practice entering the columns of data in Drills 2-4 until you can do so accurately and quickly.

**Drill 1**

| A | B | C | D | E | F |
|---|---|---|---|---|---|
| 474 | 747 | 585 | 858 | 696 | 969 |
| 747 | 777 | 858 | 888 | 969 | 999 |
| 777 | 474 | 888 | 585 | 999 | 696 |

**Drill 2**

| A | B | C | D | E | F |
|---|---|---|---|---|---|
| 774 | 885 | 996 | 745 | 475 | 754 |
| 474 | 585 | 696 | 854 | 584 | 846 |
| 747 | 858 | 969 | 965 | 695 | 956 |

**Drill 3**

| A | B | C | D | E | F |
|---|---|---|---|---|---|
| 470 | 580 | 690 | 770 | 707 | 407 |
| 740 | 850 | 960 | 880 | 808 | 508 |
| 704 | 805 | 906 | 990 | 909 | 609 |

**Drill 4**

| A | B | C | D | E | F |
|---|---|---|---|---|---|
| 456 | 407 | 508 | 609 | 804 | 905 |
| 789 | 408 | 509 | 704 | 805 | 906 |
| 654 | 409 | 607 | 705 | 806 | 907 |
| 987 | 507 | 608 | 706 | 904 | 908 |

---

**R&e**

### For Calculator Accessory Users

Enter single, double, and triple digits in columns as shown, left to right.

| A | B | C | D | E | F |
|---|---|---|---|---|---|
| 4 | 90 | 79 | 4 | 740 | 860 |
| 56 | 87 | 64 | 56 | 64 | 70 |
| 78 | 68 | 97 | 78 | 960 | 900 |
| 90 | 54 | 64 | 60 | 89 | 67 |
| 4 | 6 | 5 | 98 | 8 | 80 |

half-price days, ladies' day), and special attractions (fire-

works, circus acts, parties).

   <u>Avid fans</u>.  While most of the promotions targeted for the

good fans *are likely to* ~~will also~~ work for avid fans, a new multiple-ticket

plan will help move the avid fans to the higher group.  This

plan will be named "theGOLDen 25" and will allow fans to buy

*mini-*season tickets for 25 games.  The only restriction on choice

*of games* is that the tickets purchased must include at least won game

with each opponent.

   <u>Best fans</u>.  Increasing the games attended is the primary

objective for fans in the best category.  To help accomplish

the goal, 30 free parking passes will be given to a person

ordering too season tickets ~~this coming year~~.  In addition,

season ticket holders will be given speical discounts on extra

tickets purchased during the season.

<u>Conclusion</u>

   *If the marketing efforts result in the addition of 25,000 fans the GOLD will have made a good market better. This better base will provide the financial support needed to field a competitive team in a world-class stadium.*

Bullaro, John J., and Christopher R. Edginton.  <u>Commercial Leisure Services</u>.  New York:  Macmillan Publishing Company, 1986.

Lewis, Guy, and Herb Appenzeller, eds.  <u>Successful Sport Management</u>.  Charlottesville, VA:  The Michie Company, 1985.

Rudolph, Barbara.  "Bonanza in the Bushes."  <u>Time</u>, 1 August 1987, 38-39.

**Lessons 189-193 • Sport Management Simulation** 451

# LESSON 40

## New Keys: 1/2/3

**Objectives:**
1. To learn reach-strokes for **1**, **2**, and **3**.
2. To combine quickly the new keys with other keys learned.

### 40A • 5
### Keypad Review

Enter the columns of data listed at the right as directed in Steps 1-5 on p. 97.

| A | B | C | D | E | F | G |
|---|---|---|---|---|---|---|
| 44 | 74 | 740 | 996 | 704 | 990 | 477 |
| 55 | 85 | 850 | 885 | 805 | 880 | 588 |
| 66 | 96 | 960 | 774 | 906 | 770 | 699 |

### 40B • 35
### New Keys: 1/2/3

**Learn reach to 1**
1. Locate 1 (below 4) on the numeric keypad.
2. Watch your index finger move down to 1 and back to 4 a few times *without striking keys*.
3. Practice striking 14 a few times as you watch the finger.
4. Enter the data in Drills 1A and 1B.

**Learn reach to 2**
1. Learn the middle-finger reach to 2 (below 5) as directed in Steps 1-3 above.
2. Enter data in Drills 1C and 1D.

**Learn reach to 3**
1. Learn the ring-finger reach to 3 (below 6) as directed above.
2. Enter data in Drills 1E, 1F, and 1G.

**Drills 2-4**
Enter data in Drills 2-4 until you can do so accurately and quickly.

**Drill 1**

| A | B | C | D | E | F | G |
|---|---|---|---|---|---|---|
| 414 | 141 | 525 | 252 | 636 | 363 | 174 |
| 141 | 111 | 252 | 222 | 363 | 333 | 285 |
| 111 | 414 | 222 | 525 | 333 | 636 | 396 |

**Drill 2**

| A | B | C | D | E | F | G |
|---|---|---|---|---|---|---|
| 114 | 225 | 336 | 175 | 415 | 184 | 174 |
| 411 | 522 | 633 | 284 | 524 | 276 | 258 |
| 141 | 252 | 363 | 395 | 635 | 359 | 369 |

**Drill 3**

| A | B | C | D | E | F | G |
|---|---|---|---|---|---|---|
| 417 | 528 | 639 | 110 | 171 | 471 | 714 |
| 147 | 280 | 369 | 220 | 282 | 582 | 850 |
| 174 | 285 | 396 | 330 | 393 | 693 | 936 |

**Drill 4**

| A | B | C | D | E | F | G |
|---|---|---|---|---|---|---|
| 77 | 71 | 401 | 107 | 417 | 147 | 174 |
| 88 | 82 | 502 | 208 | 528 | 258 | 825 |
| 99 | 93 | 603 | 309 | 639 | 369 | 396 |

### 40C • 10
### Numbers with Decimals

Enter the data in Columns A-F, placing the decimals as shown in the copy. **Note:** Use ring finger for entering the decimal.

| A | B | C | D | E | F |
|---|---|---|---|---|---|
| 1.40 | 17.10 | 47.17 | 174.11 | 1,477.01 | 10,704.50 |
| 2.50 | 28.20 | 58.28 | 285.22 | 2,588.02 | 17,815.70 |
| 3.60 | 39.30 | 69.39 | 396.33 | 3,996.03 | 20,808.75 |
| 4.70 | 74.70 | 17.10 | 417.14 | 4,174.07 | 26,909.65 |
| 5.80 | 85.80 | 28.20 | 528.25 | 5,285.08 | 30,906.25 |
| 6.90 | 96.90 | 39.30 | 639.36 | 6,396.06 | 34,259.90 |

| Fan Category | No. of Fans in Category | Average No. of Games Attended | Computed Total Attendance |
|---|---|---|---|
| Best Fans | 500 | 23 | 11,500 |
| Avid Fans | 1,050 | 14 | 14,700 |
| Good Fans | 14,500 | 3.5 | 50,750 |
| Computed Total Attendance | | | 76,950 |

Projected Attendance. The following strategies can be used to increase attendance for the coming season.

1. "Move" 10% of the avid fans into the best fans category; move 5% of the good fans into the avid category; and attract new fans to replace those who are "moved" or stop attending.

2. increase the average number of games attended in each category by 10%.

If these strategies work, the total attendance would climb almost 28% to 98,466, as shown in the table below.

| Fan Category | No. of Fans in Category | Average No. of Games Attended | Computed Total Attendance |
|---|---|---|---|
| Best Fans | 605 | 25.30 | 15,306 |
| Avid Fans | 1,775 | 15.40 | 27,335 |
| Good Fans | 14,500 | 3.85 | 55,825 |
| Computed Total Attendance | | | 98,466 |

Specific promotions

The ideas mentioned below are based on information in Lewis and Appenzeller (1985, 164-168) and an article that appeared in "Time" a number of years ago (Rudolph, 1987, 38-39).

Good fans. Since fans in the good category are not likely to be as near their satiation point as those in the avid and best categories, we plan to aim most of the promotion efforts at this group. The efforts include a continuation of the product give-away promotions already in place, the addition of quasi-price promotions (2 for 1's,

(continued on next page)

## Skill Builder

### Keypad Review
Enter the columns of data listed at the right.

### Speed/Control Building
Enter the data listed in each column of Drills 1-4.

**Note:** When using the calculator accessory, enter each column of data a second time (bottom to top). If you get the same total twice, you can "assume" it is correct. If you get a different total the second time, re-enter the data until you get two totals that match.

| A | B | C | D | E | F | G |
|---|---|---|---|---|---|---|
| 477 | 588 | 707 | 107 | 41.6 | 141.4 | 936.6 |
| 417 | 528 | 808 | 205 | 52.9 | 252.5 | 825.6 |
| 717 | 825 | 909 | 309 | 63.3 | 393.3 | 719.4 |

### Drill 1

| A | B | C | D | E | F | G |
|---|---|---|---|---|---|---|
| 5 | 77 | 114 | 5,808 | 1,936 | 9,300 | 6,936 |
| 46 | 89 | 225 | 3,997 | 2,825 | 8,250 | 3,896 |
| 3 | 78 | 336 | 9,408 | 3,796 | 10,475 | 7,140 |
| 17 | 85 | 725 | 5,650 | 8,625 | 7,125 | 4,874 |
| 28 | 98 | 825 | 3,714 | 9,436 | 12,740 | 2,515 |
| 9 | 69 | 936 | 2,825 | 8,514 | 12,850 | 8,360 |
| 10 | 97 | 704 | 6,796 | 4,174 | 9,674 | 1,794 |

### Drill 2

| A | B | C | D | E | F | G |
|---|---|---|---|---|---|---|
| 99 | 795 | 1,581 | 1,881 | 2,642 | 4,573 | 2,185 |
| 67 | 657 | 1,691 | 1,991 | 2,772 | 4,683 | 3,274 |
| 88 | 234 | 1,339 | 2,202 | 2,992 | 5,477 | 9,396 |
| 96 | 359 | 1,221 | 2,432 | 3,743 | 6,409 | 4,585 |
| 84 | 762 | 1,101 | 3,303 | 3,853 | 6,886 | 5,872 |
| 100 | 485 | 1,144 | 4,650 | 4,714 | 7,936 | 6,903 |

### Drill 3

| A | B | C | D | E | F |
|---|---|---|---|---|---|
| 1,077 | 3,006 | 5,208 | 7,104 | 1,774 | 7,417 |
| 1,400 | 3,609 | 5,502 | 8,205 | 2,885 | 8,528 |
| 1,700 | 3,900 | 5,205 | 9,303 | 3,996 | 9,639 |
| 2,008 | 4,107 | 6,309 | 7,407 | 4,174 | 3,936 |
| 2,500 | 4,400 | 6,600 | 8,508 | 5,285 | 5,828 |
| 2,805 | 1,704 | 6,900 | 9,609 | 6,396 | 4,717 |

### Drill 4

| A | B | C | D | E | F |
|---|---|---|---|---|---|
| 1.4 | 14.00 | 170.40 | 1,714.70 | 7,410.95 | 1,147.74 |
| 2.5 | 17.00 | 170.43 | 2,825.80 | 8,520.55 | 2,258.88 |
| 3.6 | 25.00 | 250.90 | 3,936.90 | 9,630.65 | 3,369.93 |
| 7.4 | 28.00 | 288.50 | 4,747.17 | 10,585.78 | 7,144.74 |
| 8.5 | 36.00 | 369.63 | 5,878.25 | 11,474.85 | 8,255.85 |
| 9.6 | 39.00 | 390.69 | 6,969.39 | 12,696.95 | 9,366.63 |

on the products and services that Madison <u>Gold</u> produces, the
plan centers on customers' needs and a~~j~~usting [d] products and
services to meet them. (Bullaro, 1986, 212) and Edginton
[# mark] [and Edginton added handwritten]

<u>Assumptions</u>

The plan has been constructed upon the following assumptions:

SS {

1.  Madison <u>Gold</u> is a mature sports organization with an
established base market.

2.  Madison <u>Gold</u>'s marketing strategy should be based on the
results of the market research conducted from the last two
years.

3.  Existing fans ~~will~~ Can account for the majority of increases in
attendance in the next ~~three~~ year ~~period~~.

<u>Internal Marketing</u>

DS {

The staff ~~believes~~ recommends adopting internal marketing techniques
in the next three years.  In <u>Successful Sport Management</u>, the
authors described internal marketing:

...a technique used to focus ma~~rk~~eting efforts on
existing customers first. . . .  Internal marketing has
shown to be cheaper and more effective at increasing total
attendance and/or participation levels.  In turn, more
satisified existing customers attract more non_consumers
so that internal marketing has added benefits.  (Lewis and
Appenzeller, 1985, 174)

DS {

In other words, internal marketing ~~rely~~ relies on increasing
attendance and involvement of current fans, while keeping fans
who will not or cannot increase their attendance.  Madison
GOLD will still need to attract some new fans who will attend
a few games during the season.

<u>Madison GOLD Fans</u>

Current fans fit into one of these categories:  good,
avid, and best.  A certain percentage of each group has been
targeted for "moving up."

<u>Existing attendance</u>.  Based on the information we have
~~garnered~~ gathered during the past three years, it has been determined
that Madison GOLD fans fall into the following categories (see
following table).

*(continued on next page)*

# Language & Writing Skills 4

## Activity 1:

1. Study the spelling/definitions of the words in the color block.
2. Key line 1 (the **Learn** line), noting the proper choice of words.
3. Key lines 2-3 (the **Apply** lines), choosing the right words to complete each sentence correctly.
4. Key the remaining lines in the same way.
5. Check your work; correct any errors you find.

### Choose the right word

| | |
|---|---|
| **its** (adj) of or relating to itself as the possessor | **than** (conj/prep) used in comparisons to show difference between items |
| **it's** (contr) it is; it has | **then** (n/adv) that time; at that time |

Learn 1 It's time for the dog to have its food.
Apply 2 Before (its, it's) time to bid, check (its, it's) number.
Apply 3 If (its, it's) not yours, return it to (its, it's) shelf.

Learn 4 If she is older than you, then I am older than you.
Apply 5 We (than, then) decided that two hours were more (than, then) enough.
Apply 6 Fewer (than, then) half the workers were (than, then) put on overtime.

## Activity 2:

1. Read the ¶, noting needed changes in capitalization, number expression, and word choice.
2. Key the ¶, making the needed changes. Correct any errors you make as you key.

### Proofread & correct

on our trip to san francisco, 10 of us had a delicious lunch at a restaurant called china doll: pork-stuffed dumplings, shrimp fried rice, and chinese vegetables. we than shopped 'til we dropped. we bought exquisite kimonos, faux ivory chopsticks, and an assortment of gifts of cloisonne, pearl, and jade. my good friend manuel bought his mother a beautiful chinese screen. with it's friendly atmosphere and unique shops, its no wonder chinatown attracts so many locals as well as tourists.

## Activity 3:

1. Key Items 1 and 2 as ¶ 1 of a short composition; at each set of parentheses, supply the information needed to complete each sentence.
2. Key Item 3 as ¶ 2, supplying the information noted in the parentheses.
3. Key Item 4 as ¶ 3, supplying the information noted in the parentheses.
4. Proofread, revise, and correct your composition. Look for misspelled words, improper capitalization, inaccurate information, and weak sentence structure.

### Compose (think) as you key

1 My name, (first/last), is (African/Asian/European/Oriental, etc.) in origin.

2 My mother's ancestors originated in (name of country); my father's ancestors originated in (name of country).

3 I know the following facts about the country of my (mother's/father's) ancestors:

   1. (enter first fact here)
   2. (enter second fact here)
   3. (enter third fact here)

4 If I could visit a country of my choice, I would visit (name of country) because (give two or three reasons).

**Job 2**
Letter

**Message from David Hofacre**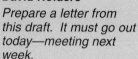

*Prepare a letter from this draft. It must go out today—meeting next week.*

---

BENZING COLLEGE | *From the Desk of David Hofacre* | BENZING COLLEGE

Mr. Carlos Bautista, Sales Manager, Clark Hotel, 4535 Washington Ave., St. Louis, MO 63042-4680

This letter confirms a meeting that Dr. Susan Synowka and I have with you next Friday afternoon at the Clark Hotel.

The primary purpose of the meeting is to tour areas of the hotel that will be used for sessions, exhibits, dining, and refreshment breaks at the International Association for Sport Management Conference (conference dates: June 11-14, ---- ).

In the session rooms, we need to see different (and other) seating arrangements and determine what audio-visual aids speakers can use. We will need a phone line to link a notebook computer with a remote computer in two other rooms. Each exhibitor must be able to use three electrical outlets at once. The exhibit area must be secured when not in use.

Susan and I will meet you in your office next Friday.

David L. Hofacre, IASM Program Co-Director

---

**Job 3**
Report

**Message from Susan Synowka** *SS*

*I received this fax from Sue Hiatt, one of the speakers. She sent this summary of her talk. We can use it as a model for other presenters. (All speakers' summaries will be compiled in a book.) Prepare a final draft in unbound report format with internal citations and a references page. Number all pages, including first, at bottom center. Check spelling and proofread carefully.*

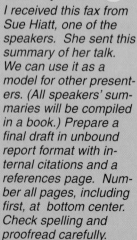

MARKETING A BASEBALL TEAM

Presented by:  Dr. Susan Hiatt, Holt Community College
    DS
    )— center
    QS

Madison GOLD's marketing staff ˆbased their marketing plan strategy on survey results and database information.  The staff analyzed 500 fans' responses to survey questions in the past ③ years and informations system data collected in the past 2 years. sp.

The marketing plan follows a trend among leisure service businesses that became popular in the 1980s   Instead of focusing

*(continued on next page)*

## ACTIVITY 1:

**Center**

1. Read the copy at right.
2. Learn the Justification features for your wp software.
3. Key the 6 lines at the right DS so that they are centered horizontally.

Justification refers to the horizontal position of a line of text. Use the **Center** feature to center one or more lines of text between the left and right margins as the text is keyed.

Conservation Laws

Newton's Law of Gravity

Relativity and the Nuclear Age

The Solar System

Elements, Compounds, and States of Matter

The Atmosphere and Meteorology

## ACTIVITY 2:

**Delete**

1. Read the copy at right.
2. Learn how to delete text using your wp software.
3. Key the ¶ at the right DS; underline and bold text as shown as you key.
4. Using the most efficient method, delete all text that is bolded or underlined.
5. Edit as needed to correct spacing.

The **delete** or **backspace** key may be used to correct simple keying errors. For deleting a word or phrase, however, a combination of keys and the mouse is faster. For example, in some wp packages the **Ctrl + Backspace** deletes a word and the **Ctrl + Delete** deletes a group of words.

John Homer, Naomi Kerrit, **Paul Desmond,** and Kay Ford were selected by the **five** geology faculty members to make a **short multimedia** presentation at the upcoming Delaware Valley Geological Society meeting on January 5 at the Harris Hotel in Clarks Summit. They will fly into Philadelphia from Columbus.

## ACTIVITY 3:

**Undelete and Undo**

1. Read the copy at right.
2. Learn how to use the Undo and/or the Undelete features of your wp software.
3. Key the ¶ at the right DS using bold as shown.
4. Read the ¶ you keyed and perform the undo and undelete (if applicable to your wp software) operations as directed in it.

Use the **Undo** feature to reverse the last change you made in text. (Some wp packages undo only the most recent editing change.) Undo restores text to its original location, even if you have moved the insertion point to another position. **Undelete**, a feature available on some wp packages, restores deleted text at the insertion point. The Undelete feature usually allows you to restore any or all of the last three deletions.

After keying **this** paragraph, delete **the** bolded words and restore them at their original place. Now: If your **wp** software has an Undelete feature, delete the words Now and Next (delete : too). Next: Restore the word Now (with :) at the beginning of the paragraph and the word Next before the last sentence. Correct spacing between sentences and after colons.

**F**ORMATTING

## 189-193B • 45 (daily)
## Work Assignments

🔍 **Proofreading alert:**
In all jobs correct any un-marked errors or errors you make.

### Job 1
### Data File

**Message from Susan Synowka** *SS*

*Here are business cards of ten educators who'll make presentations at the IASM conference. Create a data file. All have the title Dr. except Don Ezzie, who should be addressed as Mr. Use the person's title (Dr./Mr.) and last name for the salutation. Use parentheses before and after the area code in the telephone number and separate the exchange numbers from the last four digits with a hyphen. Use the following as the field names:*

*Name*

*Faculty rank*

*Dept/Subj area*

*Col/Univ*

*St/Bldg*

*City*

*State*

*ZIP*

*Phone*

*Salutation*

*Name and save this file as SPKRDATA.*

**ABRAHAM UNIVERSITY**
ABRAHAM UNIVERSITY
ABRAHAM UNIVERSITY
ABRAHAM UNIVERSITY

Anthony Cannon, Ph.D.   Professor, Health Education

Rock Rd., Wichita KS 67260-4471 (563) 156-9812
Internet: cannon@abraham.edu

**JOHNSON COLLEGE**

Dr. Henry L. Yu, Assistant Professor
Sport Administration Department
P.O. Box 1954, Erie, PA 16507-1954
(814) 157-3927    INTERNET: hlyu@johnson.edu

**Dr. Ronald Beaver, Professor**
*Kinesiology Department*
Tel: 603.161.7901   Fax: 603.161.7950

**Lawrence University**
**Granite Building**
**Nashua, NH 03051-1390**

**Helen P. Polk-Yeager, Ed.D.**

Associate Professor, Recreation
MOUNT MORRIS COLLEGE
Hull Avenue
Monaca, PA 15009-3529
(412) 555-9357

**HCC**
DR. SUE HIATT
Associate Professor
Sport Administration

**HOLT COMMUNITY COLLEGE**
**SMITH CENTER**
LaCrosse, WI 54601-5693
(608) 555-6920

**Springdale Technical Institute**
**Lock Hall, Room 3034**
**Plymouth, MA 02346-3797**

**Dr. June F. Ford, Professor**
Health Education Department
(508) 555-2334

**KEN P. CHAN, PH.D.**
**PROFESSOR, ATHLETIC MANAGEMENT**
**RUSSELL KADAR UNIVERSITY**
**Newton Center for Leadership**
**Oxford, OH 45056-3918**
**(513) 555-3792**
**Internet: chan@kadar.edu**

*Arvn Quddus, D.B.A.*
*Associate Professor, Economics*
**COLLEGE OF YORK**
**Harris Hall**
**Providence, RI 02920-4469**
**(401) 172-5729**

Dr. Glena C. Free
Assistant Professor of Recreation
• • • • • •
Sullivan University
858 S. Lewis, Tulsa, OK 74137-5498
(918) 199-8633

Mr. Don E. Ezzie, Instructor
Sport Studies
**Wingate College**
North Avenue
Syracuse, NY 10308-3396
(315) 172-5812   Fax: (315) 172-5822

<section></section>

## ACTIVITY 4:
### Blocked Text

1. Read the copy at right.
2. Learn how to block text using your wp software.
3. Retrieve TWP1-4.
4. Use the Block feature to italicize, underline, and bold the copy as shown at the right. Use Block to center line 5 and delete the last six words of line 6.

Use the **Block** feature to select a block of text on which various operations may be performed. The block is selected by using the cursor movement keys or mouse to highlight the text. Once blocked, the block of text can be bolded, italicized, underlined, deleted, centered, copied, moved, printed, saved, etc.

1. The office of **Best & Jones** *will be* relocated soon.
2. Mary *and* Jane confused <u>there</u> and <u>their</u> in the report.
3. Twelve **computers** *and* five **printers** <u>arrived</u> yesterday.
4. The students just started reading <u>A Man for All Seasons</u>.
5. *Death of a Salesman* was written by Arthur Miller.
6. Tom and Mary saw the parade and then went to the circus.
7. Most printers can print **bold**, *italics*, or <u>underlines</u>.

## ACTIVITY 5:
### Copy and Move

1. Read the copy at right.
2. Learn how to copy and move text using your wp software.
3. Retrieve TWP1-5.
4. Make a copy of the 1st ¶ and place it as the 5th ¶.
5. Move the 2d ¶ so it is the 4th ¶; move what is now the 3d ¶ so it becomes the 2d ¶.
6. Edit so ¶s are SS with DS between, with no ¶ indention.

After you have blocked text, you can use the Move or Copy feature. The **Move** feature removes (cuts) the blocked text from one location and places (pastes) it at another location. The **Copy** feature duplicates (copies) the blocked text and places (pastes) it in another, leaving the original unchanged.

The Move feature is commonly called "cut and paste," and the Copy feature is often called "copy and paste."

The Block feature is used in the move and copy commands in the same way it is used to bold, italicize, underline, center, or delete text.

Most word processing software has button bars that can be used to cut, copy, and paste text quickly.

The text will be moved or copied to the insertion point that is selected when the "paste" command is executed.

## ACTIVITY 6:
### Center Page

1. Read the copy at right.
2. Learn to center copy vertically using your wp software.
3. Open a new file. Set side margins at 2".
4. Use the Center Page feature.
5. Key the ¶s at the right DS.
6. Keep this text on the screen and proceed to Activity 7.

Use the **Center Page** feature to center lines of text between the top and bottom margins of the page. This feature leaves an equal (or nearly equal) amount of white space above and below the text.

A word processor is an excellent tool that can help you demonstrate your best writing skills. When you use a word processor to write papers for school, your final draft is likely to reflect your best effort.

The ease with which you can add, delete, and cut and paste copy with word processors encourages you to write a series of drafts until you know you have done your best.

The use of the word processor's spell checker, thesaurus, and grammar checker will "help" you to identify spelling, grammar, and punctuation errors; find and use the correct word; and identify style flaws.

# International Association for Sport Management: A Simulation

## Work Assignment

This unit is designed to give you the kinds of experiences you likely would have working in an administrative specialist position.

Assume that you are participating in a school-to-work program at your school and that you have been assigned to work part-time for Dr. Susan T. Synowka and Dr. David L. Hofacre, both of whom are professors of sport management at nearby Benzing College.

Dr. Hofacre and Dr. Synowka are serving as program directors for the upcoming 5th Annual International Association for Sport Management Conference that will be held at the Clark Hotel in St. Louis this coming June.

As an administrative specialist, your main duty is assisting Drs. Hofacre and Synowka in processing the documents they need to prepare for the upcoming conference.

You have completed an orientation program that focused on the general office policies, procedures, and routines that Professors Hofacre and Synowka have established for this project. To help you further, Drs. Hofacre and Synowka have written these guidelines for you to follow.

## Correspondence

1. Prepare all letters in block format with open punctuation; supply an appropriate salutation and complimentary close; use your reference initials; supply enclosure and copy notations as needed.
2. Prepare memorandums in standard format.

## Tables

1. Center tables horizontally and vertically; in reports, begin and end tables at the margins.
2. Use the Table format function of the software you are using and choose all formatting features.

## Reports

1. Format reports unbound.
2. Reference the cited works with textual citations and a separate references page.

## Other

1. Be alert to and correct errors in punctuation, capitalization, spelling, and word usage.
2. Drs. Synowka and Hofacre always use *Ph.D.* after their names in the closing lines of letters, instead of *Dr.* before their names. They do not use *Ph.D.* on memos.
3. If a formatting guide is not given, use your knowledge and judgment to format a document.
4. The telephone number is (412) 162-8426.

## International Association for Sport Management

**Objectives:**
1. To demonstrate ability to integrate your knowledge and skills.
2. To demonstrate your ability to make decisions.

### 189-193A • 5 (daily) Conditioning Practice

each line twice; 1' timings on lines 1-3 as time permits

| | | |
|---|---|---|
| alphabet | 1 | Hazel fixed the two pairs of jumper cables very quickly for Gwen. |
| speed | 2 | Did eighty firms bid on six authentic maps of the ancient island? |
| fig/sym | 3 | Expenses increased $82,965 (5%) and net profit fell $31,470 (6%). |

gwam 1' | 1 | 2 | 3 | 4 | 5 | 6 | 7 | 8 | 9 | 10 | 11 | 12 | 13 |

## ACTIVITY 7:

### View

1. Read the copy at right.
2. Learn how to preview a document using your wp software.
3. Preview the document from Activity 6 to see how it will look on a printed page. Notice that the top and bottom margins are nearly equal.

It is a good practice to see how your document will appear on paper before it is printed. Most wp software has a View (or Preview) feature that lets you do so. Thus you will not waste time and paper printing a document that is not correct. The view (or preview) mode will display a miniature model of each page of your document on your monitor. In some software, a document can be edited in this mode. Typically, the model is large enough for you to judge the appropriateness of the margin settings as well as the spacing above and below document parts. If needed, the "zoom" feature can be used to enlarge specific parts of a document for closer inspection.

## ACTIVITY 8:

### Envelope

1. Read the copy at right.
2. Learn how to prepare envelopes using your wp software.
3. Use the envelope (delivery) and return addresses given at the right to prepare two small envelopes. Key the envelope address in ALL CAPS without punctuation, as shown. Use default settings.

An envelope may contain a return (sender's) address besides the envelope (receiver's) address. You may need to specify the envelope size; type of paper feed for your printer; and other options, including a POSTNET bar code. The bar code is a machine-readable representation of the ZIP Code + 4 and other data that speeds mail sorting at the post office.

**Return address:**

**Envelope 1**

John Desilva
7904 Waverly Rd.
San Diego, CA 92120-2436

**Envelope 2**

Beth Murphy
467 Bradley St.
Portsmouth, VA 23701-9823

**Envelope address:**

MR HENRY JOHNSON
7894 FORBES ST
DAYTON OH 45405-4174

MS LAURA ANDERSON
4234 BINGHAM DR
PORTSMOUTH VA 23703-7103

## ACTIVITY 9:

### Apply What You Have Learned

Key the information at the right; 2 QS (seven blank lines) between keyed lines. Center it vertically and horizontally. Use bold, italic, and underline as shown.

A Book Report

on

***BLESS THE BEASTS AND CHILDREN***

by

Glendon Swarthout

Completed by:  Kenneth Greene

**Business Form 3**

Use the information at the right to prepare an invoice that will be sent to

**HALAS TOWING
9029 PEARL RD
STRONGSVILLE OH
44136-5572**

The date is **11/03/--** and the customer order number is **330956**.

(Total words = 72)

## 188C • 15
## Assess Straight-Copy Skills

Key two 5' writings on the ¶s at the right. Find *gwam* and number of errors on each. Record your better score.

---

Terms are **10/30, n/60**; shipper is **Newton's Shipping**; our order number is **3419604**; date shipped is **11/05/--**.   You are to compute the cost of the goods, sales tax at 8%, and the total amount due.

| | | | |
|---|---|---|---|
| 4 | 25" deep 4-drawer letter file/011-4562 | 79.99 | 319.96 |
| 1 | 26.5" deep 2-drawer letter file/011-4564 | 59.99 | 59.99 |
| 2 | 24.25" deep mobile tub file/0112-0945 | 89.99 | 179.98 |
| 1 | 18" deep lateral file/0111-6451 | 239.99 | 239.99 |

---

  all letters used

| | gwam | 1' | 5' |
|---|---|---|---|

Speaking before a group of people can cause a great deal of   12 | 2 | 60
anxiety for an individual.  This anxiety is so extensive that it   25 | 5 | 63
was ranked as the greatest fear among adults in a recent survey.   38 | 8 | 65
Such fear suggests that many people would rather perish than go   51 | 10 | 68
before the public to give a talk.  Much of this fear actually comes   65 | 13 | 71
from a lack of experience and training in giving public speeches.   78 | 16 | 73
People who excel in the area of public speaking have developed   90 | 18 | 76
this unique skill through hard work.   97 | 19 | 77

Planning is a key part to giving a good talk.  The talk should   13 | 22 | 80
be organized into three basic parts.  These parts are the intro-   25 | 24 | 82
duction, the body, and the conclusion.  The introduction is used   38 | 27 | 85
to get the attention of the audience, to introduce the topic of   51 | 30 | 87
the talk, and to establish the credibility of the speaker.  The body   64 | 32 | 90
of the speech is an organized presentation of the material   76 | 35 | 93
the speaker is conveying.  The conclusion is used to summarize   89 | 37 | 95
the main points of the talk.   95 | 38 | 96

Several things can be done to lower the level of anxiety   11 | 41 | 99
during a talk.  Learning as much as possible about the audience   24 | 43 | 101
prior to the talk can reduce uncertainty.  Advanced planning and   37 | 46 | 104
preparing are essential; the lack of either is a major cause of   50 | 48 | 106
anxiety.  Having the main points written on note cards to refer   62 | 51 | 109
to when needed is also helpful.  Using visual aids can also les-   75 | 53 | 111
sen the exposure a person feels.  These are but a few ideas that   88 | 56 | 114
may be used to develop better speaking skills.   97 | 58 | 116

| gwam | 1' | 1 | 2 | 3 | 4 | 5 | 6 | 7 | 8 | 9 | 10 | 11 | 12 | 13 |
|---|---|---|---|---|---|---|---|---|---|---|---|---|---|---|
| | 5' | | 1 | | | 2 | | | | 3 | | | | |

## ACTIVITY 10:

**Apply What You Have Learned**

1. Key the information at the right. Use 1.5 line spacing and italicize, bold, and underline text as you key.
2. Using the most efficient means, delete all text that is bolded, underlined, or italicized.
3. Delete the last sentence.
4. Restore the last sentence.

John, Mary, **Jim**, and George are going <u>to the show with me</u>.

Kara read the book, *Billy Budd*, by **author** Herman Melville.

We <u>very quietly</u> moved ahead by completing the **seven** steps.

**Matthew**, Tim, Rhonda, and I completed the *science* project.

Mary *just* completed making *four quality* cards for Marilyn.

The <u>64</u> rooms in the <u>major</u> hotel are reserved <u>for Thursday</u>.

Seven **of the eight** students recited the **long** poem quickly.

## ACTIVITY 11:

**Apply What You Have Learned**

1. Key the information directory at the right DS so that each line is centered horizontally.
2. Bold students' last names; italicize the class designation.
3. Copy "Bocktown," to the right of every name that does not have a residential area listed after it.
4. Delete each room number, including the word "Room" and the preceding comma.
5. Using Move, arrange the lines alphabetically by student's last name.
6. View the document to check formatting before printing or saving.

Scott Jewell, Bocktown, Sophomore, Room 101

Toby Jeffers, Broadhead, Junior, Room 102

Erica Johnson, Delmar, Sophomore, Room 101

Terry Jewell, Senior, Room 201

Pamela Lenhart, Sophomore, Room 101

Dino Leonetti, Delmar, Senior, Room 201

Manuel Peres, Freshman, Room 115

Kelli Means, Broadhead, Senior, Room 204

Michele Buyny, Freshman, Room 114

Mary Dutkovic, Junior, Room 102

## ACTIVITY 12:

**Apply What You Have Learned**

Prepare a No. 10 envelope for each address at the right. Use default settings.

**Return address for both envelopes:**

Mary Todorczuk
453 Spring Run Rd.
Kansas City, KS 66104-2041

**Mailing addresses:**

**Envelope 1**

MS HEATHER TOLLIS
509 BOSTON AVE
TULSA OK 74103-9861

**Envelope 2**

MR DAVID YAJKO
722 CHESTNUT DR
ST LOUIS MO 63101-1427

# Keyboarding and Business Forms Skills

**Objectives:**
1. To demonstrate ability to format and key invoices and purchase orders.
2. To demonstrate straight-copy skill.

## 188A • 5
### Conditioning Practice
each line twice

| | | |
|---|---|---|
| alphabet | 1 | Max and Jack have the best grades for the two philosophy quizzes. |
| speed | 2 | The neighbor may fix the rifle, bugle, and cycle for the visitor. |
| figures | 3 | I can call Shirley at 175-4093 on Friday or 168-9203 on Saturday. |

**gwam** 1' | 1 | 2 | 3 | 4 | 5 | 6 | 7 | 8 | 9 | 10 | 11 | 12 | 13 |

## 188B • 30
### Assess Business Forms Skills

**Time Schedule**

| | |
|---|---|
| Plan and prepare | 4' |
| Timed production | 20' |
| Proofread/compute n-pram | 6' |

**Business Form 1**
**Purchase Order**

Use the information at the right to prepare a purchase order that will be sent to

**ENGELS INDUSTRIES
3452 MACON RD
COLUMBUS GA 31970-4498**
Insert a total.

(Total words = 71)

**Business Form 2**
**Invoice**

Use the information at the right to prepare an invoice that is to be sent to

**BAKER ASSOCIATES INC
3257 LAS VEGAS BLVD
LAS VEGAS NV 89109-4467**

The date is **05/03/--** and the customer order number is **5924-14**.

(Total words = 78)

---

1. Format and key the business forms in the order given on this and the next page. Prepare as many forms as you can in 20'. Use PURORDER template for the purchase order and INVOICE template for the invoices (or use designated pages from stationery pack).

2. Compute *n-pram* and turn in your business forms arranged in form number order: *n-pram* = words keyed - (10 x errors) divided by 35.

PO number is **87-4529**; date is **July 15, ----**; terms are **15/30, n/45**; goods are to be shipped via **Jack's Shipping**.

| 3 | Overhead projector table/BRE29 (ea) | 79.95 | 239.85 |
|---|---|---|---|
| 4 | Printer stand/BRE36 (ea) | 79.95 | 319.80 |
| 1 | Yates 13" color TV/SHP13FM (ea) | 199.95 | 199.95 |
| 1 | Unis VHS camcorder/UNI1875 (ea) | 895.00 | 895.00 |
| 2 | Dilson VCR with remote/DIL45 (ea) | 299.00 | 598.00 |

Terms are **15/30, n/90**; shipper is **Rapid Transport**; our order number is **661704**; date shipped is **05/23/--**. You are to compute the cost of the goods, sales tax at 8%, and the total amount due.

| 12 | Phone rests/0203-2059 | 3.99 | 47.88 |
|---|---|---|---|
| 1 | Answering machine cassettes/0203-0332 | 35.45 | 35.45 |
| 5 | Modular phone jack/0203-5589 | 4.49 | 22.45 |
| 8 | 12' telephone handset cord/0201-7735 | 2.49 | 19.92 |
| 2 | Telephone untangler/0200-4823 | 27.48 | 54.96 |

# Learn to Center Lines/Documents

## LESSON 41

### Horizontal Centering

**O b j e c t i v e s :**
**1.** To learn to center lines horizontally (side to side).
**2.** To improve keying speed and control.

**41A • 5**
**Conditioning Practice**

each line twice SS; then a 1' writing on line 3; find *gwam*

| | | |
|---|---|---|
| alphabet | 1 | Jake led a big blitz which saved the next play for my squad. |
| fig/sym | 2 | Beth has ordered 26 5/8 yards of #304 linen at $7.19 a yard. |
| speed | 3 | Good form is the key if all of us wish to make the big goal. |
| **gwam** | 1' | 1 \| 2 \| 3 \| 4 \| 5 \| 6 \| 7 \| 8 \| 9 \| 10 \| 11 \| 12 \| |

**S KILL BUILDING**

**41B • 10**
**Technique Improvement**

1. Key the lines twice (slowly; then faster).
2. Key a 1' writing on each of lines 3, 6, and 9; find *gwam* on each.

| | | |
|---|---|---|
| | 1 | verb milk rare pomp were jump best limp grew hump fear union |
| letter response | 2 | saw him \| you are \| pop art \| join up \| gas pump \| milk cart \| best hump |
| | 3 | A union steward gets you a wage rate card after you join up. |
| | 4 | gowns their forms title ivory shall firms eight amend theory |
| word response | 5 | six forms \| the title \| for their \| and shall \| did amend \| work audit |
| | 6 | An audit of the work forms may end a fight for an amendment. |
| | 7 | is up to in for oil sit joy they grew work pump shall agreed |
| combination response | 8 | is up \| to be \| for joy \| the oil \| with milk \| they were \| the best man |
| | 9 | It is up to the union man to set a rate for the rest of you. |
| **gwam** | 1' | 1 \| 2 \| 3 \| 4 \| 5 \| 6 \| 7 \| 8 \| 9 \| 10 \| 11 \| 12 \| |

**41C • 10**
**Center Lines**
**Horizontally**

1. If equipment has AC (Automatic Centering) feature, learn to use it; then key Drills 1-3 DS on one page, each line centered horizontally; QS between drills.
2. If AC feature is not available, study p. RG19; then key Drills 1-3, each line centered horizontally.

| **1** | **2** | **3** |
|---|---|---|
| is | a | I |
| they | for | when |
| social | gowns | profit |
| problems | foreign | quality |
| amendments | processor | quantity |

## Table 2
**3-Column Table with Source Note from Rough-Draft Copy**

Key table at right; center horizontally and vertically; make Col. A about 2", Col. B about 1.75", and Column C about 1". Left-align Cols. A and B; center-align Col. C. Center-align all headings.

| OLDEST U.S. COLLEGES AND UNIVERSITIES | | | |
|---|---|---|---|
| Name | Location | Year Founded | |
| Harvard University | Cambridge, MA | 1636 | 21 |
| William and Mary College | Williamsburg, VA | 1693 | 30 |
| Yale University | New Haven, CNT | 1701 | 37 |
| Princeton University | Princeton, NJ | 1746 | 45 |
| University of Pennsylvania | Philadelphia, PA | 1756 | 62 |
| Brown University | Providence, RI | 1764 | 70 |
| Rutgers University | New Brunswick, NJ | 1766 | 78 |
| Dartmouth College | Hanover, NH | 1769 | 85 |
| Source: The World Book Encyclopedia, 1993. | | | 94 |
| Columbia College University | New York, NY | 1754 | 53 |

*Editing marks: "New Haven, CN" corrected to "CT"; "Pinceton" corrected to "Princeton"; arrow indicating row placement; "RH" corrected to "RI"; "Henover, ME" corrected to "Hanover, NH"; "Encyclopeadia" corrected to "Encyclopedia ^ 1993"; "Columbia College" changed to "Columbia University" and row circled to move above Source.*

Column heading words counts: 8, 9, 13

## Table 3
**4-Column Table**

Key table at right; center horizontally and vertically. You decide all formatting features, including the font face, style, size, and appearance.

| PRINTING BIDS RECEIVED | | | |
|---|---|---|---|
| Project: ---- Sales Catalog | | | |
| Firm Bidding | Contact Person | Telephone Number | Bid Received |
| DataPrint | Mr. John Wolf | 121-3300 | $30,970 |
| Beyer Printing | Mr. Sig Beyer | 129-6143 | $29,450 |
| Typeset Press | Miss E. V. Henry | 147-7000 | $29,250 |
| Reed & Park | Ms. A. J. Reed | 182-3633 | $28,540 |
| Publisher's Choice | Mr. Bob Arch | 141-8200 | $27,985 |
| Copy Mate | Ms. Val Mejeas | 143-8010 | $27,750 |
| VIP Press | Mrs. Peg Scott | 126-6700 | $25,450 |
| TrueType | Dr. Hal Reilly | 152-7856 | $24,975 |

Word counts for Table 3: 5, 10, 13, 22, 30, 39, 49, 58, 68, 76, 84, 92

## 41D • 25
## Center Lists and Announcements

**TM:** default (1")
**LS:** DS; 3 returns between problems

Problems 1-3 on 1 page
Problems 4-5 on 1 page
Problems 6-7 on 1 page

1. Read all directions before you begin.
2. Center horizontally each line of each problem.

**wp note:**

Before removing problems from screen, make the changes listed below.

**Problem 5**
Delete underline; show *Student Auditions* bold.

**Problem 6**
Bold the first line.

**Problem 7**
Change the play name to *"Fiddler on the Roof"*; raise each ticket price by $1.

∧ = insert
↗³ = delete/insert
∿ = transpose (tr)
⤶ = delete and close up
≡ = capitalize
⌗ = insert a space

---

**Problem 1**

CITY NAMES

Havana

Capetown

Port-au-Prince

Rio de Janeiro

Sault Sainte Marie

**Problem 2**

READING LIST
Lord of the Flies
To Kill a Mockingbird
A Raisin in the Sun

**Problem 3**

SPELLING DEMONS

accommodate

committee

immediately

judgment

recommendation

**Problem 4**

ENGLISH TO SPANISH

house:  casa

hotel:  hostal

airport:  aeropuerto

bank:  banco

train station:  tren estacion

---

**Problem 5**

ANNOUNCING

Student Auditions

for

Holiday Assembly Program

in

Student Activity Center

November 9

Actors at 9:00 a.m.

Vocalists at 10:30 a.m.

Instrumentalists at 1:00 p.m.

**Problem 6**

Health Service*s* Center

announces

MAKE-UP FLU ~~VACCINATIONS~~ *SHOTS*

November 2~~4~~ *3*

8:30-10:30 a.m.

Speca~~i~~l Events *Dining* Room

**Problem 7**

SCHOOL OF PERFORMMING ARTS

presents

"The Mouse that Roared"

on

January 21 *and 22*

2:30 a~~d~~ *n* 8:00 p.m.

Marx Theatre

Matinee:  $4.50; Evening:  $5.50

# LESSON 187

## Table Skills

**Objectives:**
1. To demonstrate ability to prepare tables.
2. To demonstrate ability to key from rough-draft and script copy.

**187A • 5**
**Conditioning Practice**

each line twice

| alphabet | 1 | A quick check of taxes on the big projects would amaze everybody. |
| speed | 2 | Eight rich airmen are to endow the chapel on a visit to the town. |
| fig/sym | 3 | Dan said, "Buy #3746 or #1098 at a 25% discount at Stitt & Sons." |

**gwam** 1' | 1 | 2 | 3 | 4 | 5 | 6 | 7 | 8 | 9 | 10 | 11 | 12 | 13 |

**187B • 45**
**Assess Table Skills**

**Time Schedule**

Plan and prepare .......... 3'
Timed production .......... 35'
Proofread/compute
   *n-pram* ...................... 7'

**Table 1**
**3-Column Table from Script Copy**

Key table at right; center horizontally and vertically; make Col. A about 1.75" and Cols. B and C about 1". Left-align Col. A; center-align Cols. B and C. Center-align all headings, including "Total" in the last row. Format numbers in Col. B as currency with 1 decimal place.

1. Format and key the tables in the order given on this and the next page. Complete as many tables as you can in 35'.

2. Compute *n-pram:*
*n-pram* = words keyed - (10 x errors) divided by 35.

Turn in your work arranged in table number order.

words

| TEN LARGEST AREA ADVERTISING AGENCIES | | | 8 |
|---|---|---|---|
| Ranked by Millions of Dollars in Billings | | | 16 |
| Name | Billings | Employees | 21 |
| Carlson Advertising | $ 118.5 | 202 | 27 |
| Robert Harn Agency | $ 104.0 | 158 | 33 |
| HARR Advertising | $ 55.8 | 95 | 38 |
| Rendar-Gazdacko | $ 21.0 | 25 | 44 |
| Crea, Peake, & Weiss, Inc. | $ 16.4 | 36 | 51 |
| Sundy Group | $ 13.5 | 35 | 55 |
| Park/Vladnoski | $ 13.3 | 24 | 60 |
| DeMark Communications | $ 12.0 | 42 | 67 |
| Cavicchia Group | $ 11.1 | 27 | 72 |
| Abdel Kamal Agency | $ 10.0 | 18 | 78 |
| Total | $ 375.6 | 662 | 81 |

## LESSON 42 Lists, Announcements, and Menus

**Objectives:**
1. To check and improve your keying skill.
2. To center lists, announcements, and menus.

### 42A • 5
### Conditioning Practice

each line twice SS; then key a 1' writing on line 3; find *gwam*

alphabet 1 Jacki had won first place by solving my tax quiz in an hour.

fig/sym 2 Our 1997 profit was $58,604 (up 23% from the previous year).

speed 3 Roddy may sign the six forms and work with the city auditor.

gwam 1' | 1 | 2 | 3 | 4 | 5 | 6 | 7 | 8 | 9 | 10 | 11 | 12 |

### 42B • 20
### Skill Assessment

1. Key a 1' writing on each ¶; find *gwam* on each writing.
2. Key two 2' writings on ¶s 1-2 combined; find *gwam* on each writing.
3. Key two 3' writings on ¶s 1-3 combined; find *gwam* and circle errors on each writing.

**Note:** If using wordwrap, ignore hyphens at line endings. Your line endings may differ from those in the textbook.

LA all letters used

|  | gwam 2' | 3' |
|---|---|---|

Each of us has to make choices, and each choice has its — 6 | 4

own results. You are not an exception. You choose all your — 12 | 8

friends; you decide which career you want to pursue; and you — 18 | 12

determine how you will act or behave in every situation. — 23 | 16

If you acquire friends who set goals for a high stan- — 29 | 19

dard of behavior, you will probably do so, too. Because each — 35 | 23

friend has a major effect on what we do and how we behave, we — 41 | 27

should choose carefully and prize each excellent choice. — 47 | 31

We are often drawn to those who appear to be a lot like — 52 | 35

we are, but we should not exclude everyone who has different — 58 | 39

interests and points of view. To extend our perspective, we — 65 | 43

ought to include friends who come from various cultures. — 70 | 47

gwam 2' | 1 | 2 | 3 | 4 | 5 | 6 |
3' | 1 | 2 | 3 | 4 |

in elevation between *l*ake*c* Erie and Ontario.  Most of the water    321
from the lakes drains into the St. Lawrence River, which flows    333
into the Atlantic Ocean.[2]    339

Depth⊙ The depth of the Great Lakes varies. *greatly too.* The deepest,    353
Lake Superior, is 1,333 feet (406 meters) deep. ^ Lake Erie, the    366
shallowest, is only 210 feet (64 meters) deep.[3]    376

Connecting Waterways    *DS*    380

Three sets of locks and canals make it possible for ships    392
to sail from one Great Lake to another and from Lake Ontario to    405
the Atlantic ocean, from which they can sail to any port in the    417
world. The canal*s* and the bodies of water they connect⊙ are listed    431
here. *DS*    432

1. Well*_*and Canal--connects Lake Erie and Lake Ontario.    444

2. Soo Canal*s*--connect*s* Lake Superior and Lake Huron.  *DS*    455

3. St. Lawrence Seaway--connect*s* Lake Ontario with the Atlan-    467
tic Ocean.  *DS*    470

Significance of the Lakes  *DS*    475

The five Great Lakes and the canals that link them together    487
make up the most important inland waterway in North America.    499
They provide the inexpensive transportation system needed to make    513
the Great Lakes region one of the most important industrial areas    526
in the United States.    530

← (Insert 1)

*DS* Although the Great Lakes (Lake Erie, Lake Huron, Lake Michigan,    147
Lake Ontario, and Lake Superior) were all formed by glacial activity    162
during the same period, they are quite different from one another.    176
The irregular movement of the glacier created variation in the    190
size, elevation, and depth of the lakes.    196

[2]The World Almanac and Book of Facts, 1995, s.v. "The    541
Great Lakes."    554

[3]The Information Please Almanac, 1994, s.v. "Large Lakes of    557
the World."    559

........................................................................

BIBLIOGRAPHY    3

"The Great Lakes."  The World Almanac and Book of Facts.  Mahwah,    16
NJ:  World Almanac Books, 1995.    23

"Great Lakes."  The World Book Encyclopedia.  Chicago, IL:  World    36
Book, Inc., 1993.    40

"Large Lakes of the World."  The Information Please Almanac.    52
Boston, MA:  Houghton Mifflin Company, 1994.    62

**Document 2**
**Bibliography**
Use the information at the right to prepare a bibliography.

**42C • 25**
**Center Lists, Announcements, and Menus**

**TM:** default (1")
**LS:** DS; 3 returns between problems

Problems 1-2 on 1 page
Problems 3-4 on 1 page
Problems 5-6, each on a separate page

1. Read all directions before you begin.
2. Center horizontally each line of each problem.

**wp note:**

Before removing problems from screen, make the changes listed below.

**Problem 1**
Remove underline and bold the heading.

**Problem 2**
Italicize the heading or underline it.

**Problem 3**
Change the day and date to *Friday, March 9*.

**Problem 4**
Change *35%* to *40%*; bold the shop name.

3. If time permits, center DS:

• your full name (ALL CAPS)
• your street address
• your city, state, ZIP Code
• your telephone number
• name of your school (ALL CAPS)
• name of your teacher
• name of your keyboarding textbook (capital and lowercase letters: C/lc) in italics or underlined

**Note:** See p. A15 for R & E activities for this unit.

---

**Problem 1**

National Honor Society
Joseph A. Emerik
Yuka Ito
Ricardo J. Mendosa
Billye Jean Peters
Christopher A. Thompson

---

**Problem 2**

SPANISH TO ENGLISH
por favor:  please
gracias:  thank you
da nada:  you are welcome
hasta luego:  see you later
hasta la vista:  I'll see you

---

**Problem 3**

ANNUAL FUND AUCTION
Student Activity Center
Lakeshore High School
Saturday, March 10
Dinner at 6:30 p.m.
Auction at 8:00 p.m.
Admission & Dinner:  $17.50 Per Person
Reservations Required:  555-4739

---

**Problem 4**

SUPER SAVER SALE
Up to 35% Off
Rings, Necklaces, Bracelets
at
THE GEM SHOP
December 1 through 15
10 a.m.-6 p.m.
Towne Shopping Center

---

**Problem 5**

RESTAURANTE LA BAMBA
Salon Buganvilea
ENTREMES
Queso Fundido con Chorizo Cantimpalo
SOPA
Crema de Elotes con Rajas
ENSALADA
Coliflor a la Vinagreta
ENTRADA
Camarones Gigantes al Mojo de Ajo
POSTRE
Rollo de Nuez con Crema

---

**Problem 6**

LA BAMBA RESTAURANT
Bougainvillea Room
APPETIZER
Grilled Cheese with Cantimpalo Sausage
SOUP
Cream of Corn with Green Chili Strips
SALAD
Cauliflower a la Vinegrette
ENTREE
Grilled Jumbo Shrimp with Garlic
DESSERT
Nut Roll in Cream Sauce

# LESSON 186

## Report Skills

**Objectives:**

1. To demonstrate ability to prepare unbound report with footnotes and bibliography.
2. To demonstrate ability to key from rough-draft and script copy.

### 186A • 5
### Conditioning Practice

each line twice

| | | |
|---|---|---|
| alphabet | 1 | Dean is a whiz at solving complex problems with formulas. |
| speed | 2 | The men may focus on their work if they are apt to make a profit. |
| figures | 3 | William's 169 stores in 48 states served over 320,750 last month. |

**gwam** 1' | 1 | 2 | 3 | 4 | 5 | 6 | 7 | 8 | 9 | 10 | 11 | 12 | 13 |

### 186B • 45
### Assess Report Skills

**Time Schedule**

Plan and prepare .......... 3'
Timed production .......... 35'
Proofread/compute
n-pram ...................... 7'

1. Format and key the report and bibliography (in that order) on this and the next page. Do as much of the documents as you can in 35'.

2. Compute n-pram and turn in your work arranged in document number order: n-pram = words keyed - (10 x errors) divided by 35.

**Document 1**
**Report with Footnotes**

Format the information at the right and on the next page as an unbound report with footnotes. Number all pages but the first.

words

THE GREAT LAKES  3

QS

The five Great Lakes are the largest group of fresh-water lakes, *in the world* 19

and they make up *the most important* an inland waterway in North America. *The* 46

*lakes formed more than 250,000 years ago during the Ice Age.*

A glacier moved south across the land of what is now  57

the Great Lakes region. The glacier dug out deep depres-  68

sions in the soft rocks of the region and picked up  79

great amounts of earth and rocks. The glacier withdrew  90

from 11,000 to 15,000 years ago, and the earth and rocks  101

blocked the natural drainage of the depressions. Water  112

from the melting glacier gradually filled in the depres-  124

sions and formed the Great Lakes.[1]  131

Physical Features (*Insert 1 from next page goes here.*)  135

Size. The Great Lakes have a combined area of 94,510  207

square miles (244,780 square kilometers). Lake Superior,  218

*only slightly* the largest of the lakes, is smaller than Maine; and Lake  233

*about* Ontario, the smallest of the lakes, is the size of New Jersey.  247

DS

DS

Elevation. The lakes vary *greatly* quite a bit in elevation.  257

Lake Superior, the highest, lies 600 feet (183 meters) above  269

sea level, while Lake Ontario, the lowest, lies just 245 feet  281

(75 meters) above sea level. There is an 325-foot difference  293

297

[1]The World Book Encyclopedia, 1977 *93,* ed., *s.v.* "Great Lakes."  308

*(continued on next page)*

# UNIT 9

## Master Keyboarding/ Language Skills

## LESSON 43

### Keyboarding/Language Skills

**Objectives:**
1. To improve keying speed and control.
2. To review/improve language skills (pronoun usage).

---

### 43A • 5
**Conditioning Practice**

each line twice SS; then a 1' writing on line 3; find *gwam*

| | | |
|---|---|---|
| alphabet | 1 | Pete quickly coaxed eight avid fans away from the jazz band. |
| fig/sym | 2 | Of $3,482.70 taxes paid, $956.10 went to the city and state. |
| speed | 3 | Vivian is to key the forms they wish to rush to the auditor. |

**gwam** 1' | 1 | 2 | 3 | 4 | 5 | 6 | 7 | 8 | 9 | 10 | 11 | 12 |

---

### 43B • 15
**Skill Building**

1. Key each line twice SS; DS between 4-line groups.
2. Select lines that were awkward or caused you to slow down; key each of those lines twice more.

**Note:** In lines 7-8, underline the words (do not use italics).

| | | |
|---|---|---|
| spacing | 1 | us by of an to am go in is on do my elm pay she may and they |
| | 2 | Kay is to pay the man for any of the film you buy from them. |
| shifting | 3 | Shep and Mark\|Jane or Ella\|J. Spence & Sons\|Apple & Kane Co. |
| | 4 | Dottie and Roby Park sang in the "Voice of Harmony" concert. |
| CAPS LOCK | 5 | UPS or USPS\|CNN and TNT\|NBC or CBS\|ZIP Codes\|SAN ANTONIO, TX |
| | 6 | I can use ALL CAPS for book titles; e.g., CAST OF THOUSANDS. |
| underline | 7 | <u>its</u>, not <u>it's</u>\|<u>than</u>, not <u>then</u>\|<u>four</u>, not <u>fore</u>\|<u>their</u>, not <u>there</u> |
| | 8 | He underlines magazine titles: <u>People</u> and <u>Education Digest</u>. |
| apostrophe & quotation | 9 | you don't\|he doesn't\|it's his\|I keyed "chose," not "choose." |
| | 10 | "To succeed," he said, "you must do your best at all times." |
| hyphen | 11 | co-op plan\|two-ply tire\|32-cent stamp\|self-esteem\|up-to-date |
| | 12 | Jay's just-in-time three-pointer gave us the half-time lead. |
| letter response | 13 | gave pink best ploy save only ever join vase edge pump facts |
| | 14 | You acted on a phony tax case only after a union gave facts. |
| word response | 15 | their field chair throw right visit risks world proxy eighty |
| | 16 | Lana may sign the form to pay for the giant map of the city. |
| combination response | 17 | paid link pair were hand only sign maps card also fast plump |
| | 18 | To get to be a pro, react with zest and care as the pros do. |

**gwam** 1' | 1 | 2 | 3 | 4 | 5 | 6 | 7 | 8 | 9 | 10 | 11 | 12 |

## Document 2
### Letter

modified block with ¶ indention; mixed punctuation; full justification; process envelope

(Current date) Dr. Henrietta L. Mateer  California College of Business  2806    14
Belden St.  Sacramento, CA 95815-1731  Dear Dr. Mateer:    26

I'm sending your official membership certificate for the Society for    40
Supervisors and Curriculum Developers.  Please display it in your office    55
or classroom so other educators and administrators will identify you as    69
participating in an organization that is shaping the future of our schools.    84

As a new member in the Society, you will receive a free subscription to    99
Leadership of the Nation's Schools, which is published each month,    112
September through May.  Members receive a large discount on texts    126
that the organization publishes each year.  Further, as a member you    139
will be able to register for next year's conference at a reduced rate.    154

I'm glad that you have decided to join the Society for Supervision and    168
Curriculum Developers, and I hope you will be an active member.    181

Sincerely,  Ms. Martha E. Ipolito  Executive Director  xx  Enclosure    194

## Document 3
### Letter Merge

1. Use the information below to prepare a data file, converting to USPS address style:

Name:  Mr. Hector Perez
St:  801 W. Champaign
City:  Rantoul
State:  IL
ZIP:  61866-5671
Sal:  Mr. Perez

Name:  Ms. Jo Popp
St:  3002 Stevenson Dr.
City:  Springfield
State:  IL
ZIP:  62703-4397
Sal:  Ms. Popp

Name:  Mrs. Sandra Newell
St:  220 Maine St.
City:  Quincy
State:  IL
ZIP:  62301-3366
Sal:  Mrs. Newell

2. Name and save the file MAGDATA.

3. Key the form file at the right in block letter format with open punctuation. Name and save the file as MAGFORM.

4. Merge MAGDATA and MAGFORM. Name and save the merged file as MAGDOCS. Provide keyboard input at the prompt as follows:

| Name | Magazine | Amount |
|------|----------|--------|
| Perez | The Newsflash | $33.59 |
| Popp | Week in Review | $28.94 |
| Newell | Breaking News | $43.92 |

**\<Current date\>**

**\<Name\>**
**\<St\>**
**\<City\> \<State\> \<ZIP\>**

Dear \<Sal\>      opening 17

You've enjoyed reading (*Name of magazine*) every week during the past year,    28
haven't you?  Those of us at Subscription Plus, Inc., want you to continue    43
receiving this ever-popular magazine when your subscription ends next    57
month.    58

To renew your subscription, send us a check for (*Amount*).  This small    72
amount will allow you to enjoy your favorite magazine every week for an-    86
other year.    89

Sincerely    91


Paula Riaz    93

xx    94

## 43C • 20
### Check/Improve Keying Skill

1. Key a 1' writing on each ¶; find *gwam* on each writing.

2. Key two 2' writings on ¶s 1-2 combined; find *gwam* on each writing.

3. Key two 3' writings on ¶s 1-3 combined; find *gwam* and circle errors on each writing.

**LA** all letters used | gwam | 2' | 3' |

A young man asked recently why he was required to take | 6 | 4

a course in keyboarding since he was sure that there would | 11 | 8

always be others to perform such tasks for him.  His false | 17 | 12

belief is common among males, particularly in high school. | 23 | 15

The work roles of men and women have changed quickly | 28 | 19

since the computer has become the major means of processing | 34 | 23

words and data.  As a result, all office workers are now ex- | 40 | 27

pected to bring keying and computer skills to the job. | 46 | 31

The old idea that in the office men think and direct | 51 | 34

while women merely type is no longer valid.  Now, everyone | 57 | 38

is expected to think, direct, and communicate through a key- | 63 | 42

board.  Learn these skills now; you will prize them highly. | 69 | 46

| gwam | 2' | 1 | 2 | 3 | 4 | 5 | 6 |
| | 3' | 1 | | 2 | | 3 | | 4 |

## L ANGUAGE SKILLS

## 43D • 10
### Pronoun Agreement

**SM:** 1" or defaults

**LS:** SS; DS between sets of lines

1. Read the first guide and study the applications in the Learn lines below it.

2. Key the Learn sentences, noting how the guide is applied.

3. Key the Apply sentences, using the correct pronoun shown in parentheses.

4. Practice the second rule in the same way.

5. If time permits, key the Apply lines again at a faster speed to quicken decision-making skill.

A personal pronoun (I, we, you, he, she, it, their, etc.) agrees in **person** (first, second, or third) with the noun or other pronoun it represents.

| first person | I, we | represents the speaker or writer |
| second person | you | represents the person(s) spoken/written *to* |
| third person | he, she, it, their | represents the person(s) spoken *about* |

Learn 1 Erica said, "I shall see the movie after I finish my project."  (1st person)
Learn 2 When you finish your homework, you may watch TV.  (2d person)
Learn 3 Malik said that he would drive his car to the hockey game.  (3d person)
Apply 4 Students who saw the exhibit said (he/she/they) were impressed.
Apply 5 After you run for a few days,  (one's/your) endurance increases.
Apply 6 Before I take the test, I want to review (our, my) class notes.

A personal pronoun agrees in **gender** (masculine, feminine, or neuter) with the noun or other pronoun it represents.

Learn 7 Ms. Wong will give her talk after the announcements.  (feminine)
Learn 8 The small boat lost its way in the dense fog.  (neuter)
Apply 9 Each mother will receive a corsage as she is given (her/its) award.
Apply 10 The ball circled the rim before (he/it) dropped through the hoop.

# UNIT 40
## LESSONS 185–188

# Assess Keyboarding/Document Processing Skills

## LESSON 185

### Keyboarding and Correspondence Skills

**Objectives:**
1. To demonstrate straight-copy skills.
2. To demonstrate ability to prepare letters and memos, including a letter merge.

---

**185A • 5**
**Conditioning Practice**

each line twice

alphabet 1 Mrs. Gaznox was quite favorably pleased with the market projects.

speed 2 The widow may visit the city to see the robot shape an auto body.

fig/sym 3 Book prices increased 17% from 05/01/96 to 08/30/97 in 42 stores.

gwam 1' | 1 | 2 | 3 | 4 | 5 | 6 | 7 | 8 | 9 | 10 | 11 | 12 | 13 |

---

**185B • 15**
**Assess Straight-Copy Skills**

1. Key two 5' writings on the ¶s in 188C, p. 445.

2. Find *gwam* and number of errors on each.

3. Record the better score.

---

**185C • 30**
**Assess Correspondence Skills**

**Time Schedule**
Plan and prepare .......... 3'
Timed production .......... 20'
Proofread/compute
n-pram ...................... 7'

**Document 1**
**Memo**

Prepare a memo in standard format. Use the current date and this subject line: **ACCESS RIGHTS**. Supply other memo parts as needed.

Format and key the letters and memos on this and the next page. Complete as many documents as you can in 20'. Compute *n-pram:*
*n-pram* = words keyed - (10 x errors) divided by 20.

Turn in your work arranged in the document number order.

words

TO:      Jim Kohl, Information Management Director

FROM:  Angela Roski, Vice President for Administration          opening 30

You are authorized to give Ray Allan access to these files on the NuTech          44
computer   system:   GETBIO.DAT,   CLASROST,   GRADES,   and          55
LOCATE.          57

Mr. Allan is authorized to access this information on the micro in his          71
office.   His authorization is limited to access; he is not permitted to          85
change or print the information stored in the files.          96

Please make the necessary changes so that Ray will be able to access          109
this material beginning the first of next month, the effective date of his          124
promotion to director of nursing certification.          135

# LESSON 44

## Keyboarding/Language Skills

**Objectives:**
1. To check/improve keying speed and control.
2. To review/improve language skills (pronoun usage).

### 44A • 5
### Conditioning Practice

each line twice SS; then a 1' writing on line 3; find *gwam*

alphabet 1 Spiro was amazed at just how quickly you fixed the big vans.
fig/sym 2 Of 26,374 citizens, 13,187 (50%) voted in the 1996 election.
speed 3 Diana may make a vivid sign to hang by the door of the hall.

gwam 1' | 1 | 2 | 3 | 4 | 5 | 6 | 7 | 8 | 9 | 10 | 11 | 12 |

### 44B • 15
### Skill Building

1. Key each line once SS; DS between 5-line groups.
2. Key each line again at increased speed.
3. If time permits, rekey lines that caused you to hesitate or stop.

A 1 Andy may carry a flag of orange and black in the big parade.
B 2 Bobbie lobbed the ball to the big boy for a baseline basket.
C 3 Chuck wrote a check to cover the cost of two cruise tickets.
D 4 Dondra made a mad dash from the deli for her third delivery.
E 5 Eduardo needs to relax and let his fingers make the reaches.

F 6 Flo will take off just after four for her first solo flight.
G 7 Gig ought to get as high a grade in algebra as in geography.
H 8 Heidi hopes she can help her brother with his math homework.
I 9 Irwin is to play a violin as well as a piano in the quintet.
J 10 Judy is a just judge who seeks justice from each major jury.

K 11 Keith checks skis and quickly marks each ski by worker name.
L 12 Lolly will lead the platoon in daily field drills this week.
M 13 Matt may be the top swimmer at my new swim club this summer.
N 14 Nadia has won many gymnastic events in this city and county.
O 15 Olaf hopes to work for a good company as an account manager.

P 16 Phyllis hopes to plan a peppy party for all the top players.
Q 17 Quig quietly quit the squad and quickly quelled the quarrel.
R 18 Roxanne is ready to write a report on her recent train trip.
S 19 Stan wants a seafood salad and a single glass of spiced tea.
T 20 Tess sent a letter to her state senator to protest his vote.

U 21 Utah urged our squad to unite to upset our ubiquitous rival.
V 22 Viva visited the old village for a vivid view of the valley.
W 23 Wes was weary of waiting on the windy wharf with the welder.
X 24 Xena, fax all six x-rays if he fixes the fax machine by six.
Y 25 Yorba says that day by day his keying ability must increase.
Z 26 Zazu dazzled us and puzzled the judges with zigzag footwork.

gwam 1' | 1 | 2 | 3 | 4 | 5 | 6 | 7 | 8 | 9 | 10 | 11 | 12 |

**Third row**

1 or up it us we you pop top rut rip wit pea tea wet pit were quiet
2 pew toe tie rep per hope pour rope quip your pout tore ripe quirk
3 tip out tar war per tour keep roar fret youth pretty yuppie puppy

**Home row**

4 ha has kid lad led last wash lash gaff jade fads half sash haggle
5 as dad add jug leg gas lads hall lass fast deal fall leafs dashes
6 at had sad jigs lash adds gall legs fish gash lakes halls haggles

**Bottom row**

7 ax can bam zag sax cab mad fax vans buzz knack caves waxen banana
8 ax ban man zinc clan band calm lamb vain back amaze bronze buzzer
9 box nab and bag lot name vane clam oxen main none climb mezzanine

gwam | 1 | 2 | 3 | 4 | 5 | 6 | 7 | 8 | 9 | 10 | 11 | 12 | 13 |

## Timed Writings

1. Key three 1' writings on each ¶; find *gwam*. Count errors. If errors are 2 or fewer on any writing, goal is to increase speed by 1 or 2 words on next writing. If errors on any writing are more than 2, goal is control on next writing.
2. Key two 3' writings on ¶s 1-3 combined; find *gwam* and count errors.
3. Key a 5' writing on ¶s 1-3 combined; find *gwam* and count errors.

| | | gwam | 1' | 3' | 5' |
|---|---|---|---|---|---|

| | 1' | 3' | 5' |
|---|---|---|---|
| Stress qualifies as either good or bad depending on the | 11 | 4 | 2 |
| circumstances and ability of people to cope.  It is good when it | 24 | 8 | 5 |
| has resulted from a pleasant event, such as a promotion.  In | 36 | 12 | 7 |
| addition, it may increase job performance if the pressure is not | 49 | 16 | 10 |
| too great.  On the other hand, stress is bad when caused by an | 62 | 21 | 12 |
| unpleasant event, such as being passed over for a prized promo- | 74 | 25 | 15 |
| tion.  Furthermore, it may interfere with the performance of a | 87 | 29 | 17 |
| task when the pressure is excessive. | 94 | 31 | 19 |
| The major point to recognize is that stress is quite normal | 12 | 35 | 21 |
| and will be experienced at times by all.  Avoiding stress is not | 25 | 40 | 24 |
| an issue, but learning to handle day-to-day stress in a proper | 38 | 44 | 26 |
| manner is.  A few methods that work are taking the time for | 50 | 48 | 29 |
| regular exercise, getting enough sleep, and eating well-balanced | 63 | 52 | 31 |
| meals.  These specific methods relate to personal habits.  In | 75 | 56 | 34 |
| addition, using some stress reducers that more directly relate to | 88 | 61 | 36 |
| the job also will be helpful. | 94 | 63 | 38 |
| A good way to reduce stress in the office is to use tech- | 11 | 66 | 40 |
| niques known to improve time management.  These include analyzing | 25 | 71 | 43 |
| the tasks performed to see if all are necessary, judging which | 37 | 75 | 45 |
| ones are most important so that priorities can be set, and using | 50 | 79 | 48 |
| most of the time to do the jobs that are most important.  Office | 63 | 84 | 50 |
| workers who do not use these procedures may expend considerable | 76 | 88 | 53 |
| energy on less valuable tasks and feel stressed when more impor- | 89 | 92 | 55 |
| tant ones go unfinished. | 94 | 94 | 56 |

| gwam | 1' | 1 | 2 | 3 | 4 | 5 | 6 | 7 | 8 | 9 | 10 | 11 | 12 | 13 |
|---|---|---|---|---|---|---|---|---|---|---|---|---|---|---|
| | 3' | | 1 | | | 2 | | | 3 | | | 4 | | |
| | 5' | | | 1 | | | | 2 | | | | 3 | | |

## 44C • 20
### Check/Improve Keying Skill

1. Key a 1' writing on each ¶; find *gwam* on each writing.

2. Key two 2' writings on ¶s 1-2 combined; find *gwam* on each writing.

3. Key two 3' writings on ¶s 1-3 combined; find *gwam* and circle errors on each writing.

**LA** all letters used

| | gwam | 2' | 3' |
|---|---|---|---|

There is a value in work, value to the worker as well as — 6 | 4
to the employer for whom one works.  In spite of the stress — 12 | 8
or pressure under which many people work, gainful work pro- — 18 | 12
vides workers with a feeling of security and self-esteem. — 23 | 16

Some people do not want to work unless they have a job — 29 | 19
of prestige; that is, a job that others admire or envy.  To — 35 | 23
obtain such a position, one must be prepared to perform the — 41 | 27
tasks the job requires.  Realize this now; prepare yourself. — 47 | 31

School and college courses are designed to help you to — 52 | 35
excel in the basic knowledge and skills the better jobs de- — 58 | 39
mand.  Beyond all of this, special training or work experi- — 64 | 43
ence may be needed for you to move up in your chosen career. — 70 | 47

gwam 2' | 1 | 2 | 3 | 4 | 5 | 6
3' | 1 | 2 | 3 | 4

## 44D • 10
### Pronoun Agreement

Follow the directions given in 43D, p. 111.

A personal pronoun agrees in **number** (singular or plural) with the noun or other pronoun it represents.

Learn 1 Tabitha drove her new car to New Orleans last week.  (singular)
Learn 2 The club officers made careful plans for their next meeting.  (plural)
Apply 3 All workers must submit (his/their) vacation requests.
Apply 4 The sloop lost (its/their) headsail in the windstorm.

A personal pronoun that represents a collective noun (team, committee, family, etc.) may be singular or plural, depending on the meaning of the collective noun.

Learn 5 Our men's soccer team played its fifth game today.  (acting as a unit)
Learn 6 The vice squad took their positions in the square.  (acting individually)
Apply 7 The Research Committee presented (its/their) reports at the meeting.
Apply 8 The jury will render (its/their) verdict at nine o'clock tomorrow.

# Activity 3:

The HELP WANTED notice shown at right has just been posted on the bulletin board in the Business Department of your high school.

1. Read the notice carefully.
2. List your qualifications in terms of the job duties.
3. Write a letter of application to Mrs. Morgan at your high school address asking to be considered as one of the six assistants selected. Be sure to include all the information Mrs. Morgan requests.
4. Ask for an interview appointment, give your home telephone number, and indicate the best time to call you.
5. Read your message carefully, revise it if necessary, and proofread/correct your work.

**Compose (think) as you key**

# COMPUTER CAMP ASSISTANTS NEEDED

**Six students are needed to assist three instructors who are to conduct two computer camps on the high school campus this summer.**

**Dates of the camps are as follows:**

**Camp 1:** July 5-11, 9:30 a.m.-noon. and 1:30-4 p.m.

**Camp 2:** August 1-7, 9:30 a.m.-noon. and 1:30-4 p.m.

**Qualifications:**  Keyboarding speed, 40 wam or more.
Ability to demonstrate good technique.
Experience with wp software.
Experience working with children.

**Job Duties:**  Observe and assist children (ages 11-13) as they learn to use computer software.

**Hourly Pay:**  $5.75

To become eligible for selection, write a letter of application to Mrs. Helen C. Morgan at the high school.  Tell her why you want the job, what your qualifications are, and at which of the two camps you wish to work.  Be sure to indicate how she can get in touch with you for an interview.

# UNIT 10
## Learn to Format Memos

**LESSONS 45–47**

### Format Guides: Memos

### Format Guides: Memos

Simplified Memo

Memorandums (memos) are written messages used by individuals within an organization to communicate with one another. They have often been described as "stripped down" letters because they omit certain letter parts. Memos may be formatted in two styles—simplified and standard—but both formats use the same margins.

| Top margin (TM): 2" (12 line spaces) |
| Side margins (SM): defaults or 1" |
| Page ending (PE): at least 1" |

In simplified format, begin all lines at the left margin unless some special part is to be centered. Quadruple-space (QS) between the date and the receiver's name and between the message (body) and the writer's name. Double-space (DS) between all other parts (including ¶s) unless otherwise specified.

In standard format, begin all lines (including headings) at the left margin unless otherwise specified.

TO:        Tab twice to key name.

FROM:    Tab once to key name.

DATE:    Tab once to key date.

SUBJECT: Tab once to key subject.

Double-space (DS) between *all* memo parts.

Compare the simplified model (p. 115) and the standard model (p. 117); note differences.

## LESSON 45    Simplified Memos

**Objectives:**
1. To learn to format simplified memos properly.
2. To process memos from arranged and semiarranged copy.

### 45A • 5
**Conditioning Practice**

each line twice SS; then a 1' writing on line 3; find *gwam*

alphabet 1 Five kids quickly mixed the prizes, baffling one wise judge.

fig/sym 2 Joe asked, "Is the ZIP Code 45209-2748 or is it 45208-3614?"

speed 3 The firms may make a profit if they handle their work right.

**gwam** 1' | 1 | 2 | 3 | 4 | 5 | 6 | 7 | 8 | 9 | 10 | 11 | 12 |

### 45B • 45
**Simplified Memos**

If equipment has a default top margin, enter a sufficient number of hard returns to leave a 2" top margin (12 line spaces).

1. Study the format guides given above and the model memo illustrating simplified format on p. 115. Note the vertical and horizontal placement of memo parts and the spacing between them.

2. Format/key Memo 1 shown on p. 115; do not correct your errors as you key. Center the name as shown.

3. Proofread your copy of the memo, marking for correction any errors you find.

4. Format/key the memo again from your marked copy, errors corrected.

5. Format/key Memos 2 and 3 on p. 116 in simplified format; correct any errors you make. Save as MEM45B1 a partially completed memo to finish later.

# Language & Writing Skills 17

## Activity 1:

1. Study the spelling/definitions of the words in the color block at the right.
2. Key the **Learn** line in the first set of sentences.
3. Key the **Apply** lines, choosing the right words to complete each sentence correctly.
4. Key the second set of lines in the same way.
5. Check your work; rekey lines containing word-choice errors.

### Choose the right word

**loan** (n) a sum of money lent with interest due

**lone** (adj) companionless; solitary

**lessen** (vb) to cause to decrease; to make less

**lesson** (n) something to be learned; a period of instruction; a class

Learn 1 The lone transaction in our office today was the loan she made.
Apply 2 He took a (loan/lone) to buy the (loan/lone) new car on the lot.
Apply 3 The (loan/lone) person in the lobby requested a (loan/lone).

Learn 4 This one lesson will lessen the time it takes you to do the job.
Apply 5 Failure to listen will greatly (lessen/lesson) your learning.
Apply 6 What I put into a (lessen/lesson) affects what I get out of it.

## Activity 2:

1. Read the letter given at the right, noting needed corrections in capitalization, punctuation, spelling, word choice, and subject/predicate agreement.
2. Format/key the letter in modified block style with open punctuation—all errors corrected.
3. Address the letter to:

   **Mr. Michael G. Verona, Office Manager**

   **Tri-State Life Insurance Co.**

   **20 Harper St.**
   **Pittsburgh, PA 15206-2183**

   Supply appropriate salutation.

4. As closing lines, use:

   **Sincerely yours**

   **Miss Tanya Papich, Sales Manager**

5. Add enclosure notation; use your initials as reference.

### Proofread & correct

It has often been said that "The spinal curve is directly related to the efficiency curve." In other words the "slump" of a seated worker leds to excessive fatigue and a "slump" in production. It is a matter of record, to that correct posture increases speed, reduces fatigue and improves efficiency and morale.

But don't take hour word for these statements. Just mail the enclosed postage free card for too knew publications that are of interest to any forward looking person. One publication discusses the value of correct sitting posture, the other describes the new Modern Posture Chair.

The Modern Posture Chair encourage sustained and accurate work. The self adjusting back gives the utmost in correct body support. What's more, their is a Modern posture Chair for every executive and general office need.

Be sure to male the card today. The too new publications will reach you promptly.

| | |
|---|---|
| Date | November 13, (Current year)   ▼   2" (or line 13) |

QS (4 hard returns)

| | |
|---|---|
| Addressee | <u>Periscope</u> Staff Members   DS |
| Subject | NEW WITHIN-SCHOOL MEMORANDUM FORMAT |

DS

Body   You asked me to suggest a simple message format to use when you write to one another and to others within the school about school newspaper business. This message is formatted as a

DS

SIMPLIFIED MEMORANDUM

DS

(1")    All lines begin at the left margin except for centered titles. A QS (4 hard returns) separates the date and receiver's name and the last paragraph and writer's name. All other parts, including paragraphs, are separated by a DS (2 hard returns). No personal title is used before a name, but an official title or department name may follow it.    (1")

DS

If a separate document (such as an edited article) is attached to the memo, the word <u>Attachment</u> is keyed at the left margin a double space below the writer's name; if the document is not attached, the word <u>Enclosure</u> is keyed instead.

DS

The simplified memo is easy to format and key. Use it for a few days and give me your reactions. I am attaching an annotated model for your initial guidance.

QS (4 hard returns)

*Keiko Sato*

| | |
|---|---|
| Writer | Keiko Sato, Sponsor |

DS

Attachment

Shown in 12-point (10-pitch) type,<br>
2" top margin, 1" side margins,<br>
photoreduced.

**Simplified Memorandum (Memo 1)**

Use the employee database forms in the stationery pack to complete forms in 184C.

**Note:** An Employee Database Form for each employee is completed and then periodically updated. This form serves as the hard copy record for an employee database maintained on a computer system.

**Employee Database Form 1**

Key the information in script at the right on an Employee Database Form.

(Total words = 69)

**Employee Database Form 2**

Key the information in script at the right on an Employee Database Form. Use the home telephone number for the emergency telephone number.

(Total words = 63)

---

| Date Completed: 02/05/-- | EMPLOYEE DATABASE FORM | |
|---|---|---|
| **Employee Name** | **Social Security Number** | **Birthdate** |
| Sarah White | 203-56-1199 | 01/14/64 |

| **Home Address** | **Work Address** |
|---|---|
| Apartment 31<br>9942 Adams Dr.<br>Tampa, Fl 33619-4459 | CPG Towers<br>2520 N. 50ᵗʰ St.<br>Tampa, FL 33619-5523 |

| **Home Telephone** | **Work Telephone** | **Emergency Telephone** |
|---|---|---|
| (813) 122-4121 | (813) 146-3200 | (813) 122-4121 |

| **Beginning Employment Date** | **Beginning Salary** | **Current Salary** |
|---|---|---|
| 06/15/84 | $9,500 | $20,450 |

| **Job Title** | **Job Classification** | **Immediate Supervisor** |
|---|---|---|
| Executive Assistant | Level 17 | Bill Brady |

| **Promotion Record with Dates** |
|---|
| 1. Secretary Level II on 9/84<br>2. Secretary Level III on 5/88<br>3. Executive Assistant on 8/94 |

---

Date Completed: 04/15/--          Employee Name: Harry R. Yount

Soc. Sec. No.: 193-67-9145          Birthdate: 06/05/68

Home Address:                       Work Address:

   4554 Woodson Rd.          1806 Ramada Blvd.
   St. Louis, MO 63042-4554   Collinsville, IL 62234-3691

Home Tel.: (314) 123-5642          Work Tel.: (618) 145-9823

Beginning Emp. Date: 08/01/90      Beginning Salary: $24,500

Current Salary: $29,750            Job Title: Partner

Job Classification: Level 20       Immediate Supervisor: Susan Huff

Promotions:  1. Architect on 09/01/94
            2. Project Director on 05/01/96
            3. Partner on 12/01/97

## Memo 2

1. Key in simplified format the memo shown at right.
2. Proofread your copy; correct any errors you find.

**Note:** Italics (rather than underlines) may be used wherever underlines appear in copy.

**wp note:**

Change the theme name from ALL CAPS to Caps/lowercase (C/lc) italic; delete *-in-chief* in last line.

---

words

November 14, (Current year)                                              4

All Class and Club Presidents                                           10

MEETING TO DISCUSS MIDWINTER ISSUE OF PERISCOPE                         19

The proposed theme for "Current Focus" in the midwinter issue of the    33
Periscope is                                                            36

HARMONY THROUGH INTERACTION                                             41

The goal is to highlight recent activities that you believe helped to foster    57
harmony among diverse groups in our school by getting them to interact          71
and to work together.  We would also like to report your suggestions for        86
future activities with this focus.                                              93

You are encouraged to attend a Periscope staff meeting at two o'clock on        108
Wednesday, November 27, in Room AC 8 of the Activities Center to help in        122
this effort.  In addition to a brief Guest Editorial, we want to include three  138
or four articles on this topic by some of you.                                  148

Please come and bring your ideas and suggestions with you.                     160

Joseph Costa, Editor-in-Chief                                                  166

---

## Memo 3

1. Key in simplified format the memo shown at right.
2. Color verticals indicate line endings in the opening and closing lines. Return at these points, but do not key the verticals.
3. Center the article title on a separate line; show it in C/lc enclosed in quotation marks.
4. Proofread your copy; correct all errors.

---

November 14, (Current year) | Sandra Alexander | PERISCOPE ARTICLE        11

Your proposed article for the midwinter issue of the Periscope should be a    26
winner.    I like the title INCLUSION VS. EXCLUSION                           36

The article is a few lines too long for the allocated space.  I have marked   51
some suggested cuts on the enclosed copy.  Please consider these cuts          65
along with the few other minor changes as you key your final copy.            79

Marcella Del Rio, Associate Editor | Enclosure                                88

---

# LESSON 46    Standard Memos

**Objectives:**
1. To learn to format standard memos properly.
2. To process standard memos from model and semiarranged copy.

---

## 46A • 5
### Conditioning Practice

each line twice SS; then a 1' writing on line 3; find *gwam*

| alphabet | 1 | Quincy worked six jigsaw puzzles given him for his birthday. |
| fig/sym | 2 | I deposited Hahn & Ober's $937.48 check (#1956) on March 20. |
| speed | 3 | Ellena may lend them a hand with the audit of the soap firm. |

gwam 1' | 1 | 2 | 3 | 4 | 5 | 6 | 7 | 8 | 9 | 10 | 11 | 12 |

## Format/Process New Employee Requisition Forms

Use the employee requisition forms in the stationery pack to complete forms in 184B.

**Note:** A New Employee Requisition Form is completed by a supervisor of a position when that supervisor is seeking approval to hire a replacement or additional employee.

### New Employee Requisition Form 1

Key the information in script at the right on a New Employee Requisition Form.

(Total words = 68)

### New Employee Requisition Form 2

Key the information in script at the right on a New Employee Requisition Form.

(Total words = 76)

---

**Date Completed:** 3/23/--

## NEW EMPLOYEE REQUISITION FORM

| Department | Budget and Account | Location |
|---|---|---|
| Secondary Mathematics | 3459-251 | Chicago Office |
| **Position Title** | **Job Level** | **Immediate Supervisor** |
| Production Editor | 15 | Janet Epson |

| Date Requested | Starting Date | Starting Salary Range |
|---|---|---|
| 3/23/-- | 5/1/-- | $22,500 - $26,000 |

**State any special or unusual qualifications required.**

Bachelor's degree is required; three or more years experience in publishing industry is preferred. Applicants must have demonstrated ability to work well with and lead others.

| Replacement for | Final Selection Made by | Position Authorized by |
|---|---|---|
| Phillip K. Wehner | Allen Swegal | Patricia Huffman |

---

Date: 04/24/--

Budget No.: 134-805

Position Title: Systems Analyst

Immediate Supervisor: Joan Huenza

Starting Date: 05/15/--

Department: Information Services

Location: Philadelphia Office

Job Level: IX

Date Requested: 04/24/--

Starting Salary Range: $25,500 — $27,850

Special or unusual qualifications required:

Bachelor's degree in computer, office, or management information systems. Must have above-average communication and interpersonal skills. Must have demonstrated ability to work well with and without direct supervision.

Replacement for: James Hurst

Final Selection Made by: Joan Huenza

Position Authorized by: Janet Yount

TO:  Tab  Tab  Faculty and Staff  2" (line 13)

DS (2 hard returns)

FROM:  Tab  Lenore M. Fielding, Principal

DS

DATE:  Tab  November 15, (Current year)

DS

SUBJECT: Tab STANDARD MEMO FORMAT

DS

At a recent meeting, department heads recommended that memos be processed on plain paper instead of preprinted forms.  This recommendation is a cost-cutting measure that requires only a little more effort on the part of the keyboard operator.

DS

The customary standard margins are used: 2" top margin; default (near 1") side margins; at least a 1" bottom margin.

DS

Standard double spacing separates memo parts, including paragraphs, which are individually single-spaced.  If someone other than the writer keys the memo, that person's initials should be keyed at the left margin a double space below the message.  If an attachment or enclosure is included, Attachment or Enclosure should be keyed at the left margin a double space below the message or the keyboard operator's initials (if any).

DS

Headings begin at left margin.  After TO: tab twice to key the name; after FROM: tab once to key the name; after DATE:  tab once to key the date; after SUBJECT: space twice (or tab once) to enter the subject (may be keyed in ALL CAPS or C/lc--Cap and lowercase).

DS

Please use this format for several days; then let me know if you experienced any difficulties.

DS

tbh

1"   1"

**Standard Memorandum (Memo 1)**

> Shown in 12-point (10-pitch) type, 2" top margin, 1" side margins, photoreduced.

## F ORMATTING

### 46B • 45
### Standard Memos

If equipment has a default top margin, enter a sufficient number of hard returns to leave a 2" top margin (12 line spaces).

1. Study the format guides given on p. 114 and the model above that illustrates standard memo format. Note the vertical and horizontal placement of memo parts and the spacing between them.

2. Key in standard format the memo shown above; do not correct errors as you key.

3. Proofread your copy of the memo, marking for correction any errors you find.

4. Format/key the memo again from your own copy, errors corrected.

5. Key Memos 2 and 3 on p. 118 in standard format. Save as MEM46B# any partially completed memo to be finished later.

| 36 | Ivory premium bond #60 paper/0601-10 | 8.99 | 323.64 |
| 20 | Designer stationery #24 paper/0602-11 | 4.99 | 99.80 |
| 15 | Letterhead #28 paper/0603-16 | 5.99 | 89.85 |
| 2 | Recycled computer paper/0605-19 | 19.99 | 39.98 |

You should compute the total cost of the paper, sales tax at 7%, and total invoice price including sales tax.

**Invoice 3**
Use the information at the right to prepare an invoice.

(Total words = 44)

Harrington Realty
399 Grove Ln.                                    Date: 5/15/--
Newton, MA 02162-7734            Customer Order No.: 3498-2

Terms: net 30  Shipped via: Customer pickup  Our order no.: 554301
Date shipped: 9/15/--
ETH41    Passport E-Class -- 4-door sedan  16,950 16,950
VIN: 163-BT46 DIDC-292477

You should compute the sales tax at 7% and total invoice price including sales tax.

**Invoice 4**

(Total words = 83)

1. Prepare an invoice for Purchase Order 2 on p. 430.

2. Date it **6/7/--**. Use **57056-A** as our order no., and **7/1/--** as shipping date. Compute tax at 8%.

3. All other needed information can be obtained from the purchase order.

# LESSON 184

## Business Forms

**Objectives:**

**1.** To format and process selected business forms.
**2.** To increase your ability to key from script copy.

**184A • 5**
**Conditioning Practice**

each line twice

alphabet 1 Ted and Vez saw pilots quickly taxi many big jets from the gates.
speed 2 Jen sat by the right aisle for the sorority ritual at the chapel.
figures 3 She sold 105 shirts, 28 belts, 94 skirts, 36 suits, and 47 coats.

| gwam | 1' | 1 | 2 | 3 | 4 | 5 | 6 | 7 | 8 | 9 | 10 | 11 | 12 | 13 |

## Memo 2

1. Key in standard format the memo at right. Use your initials as the keyboard operator.
2. Proofread your copy and correct all errors.

| | | words |
|---|---|---|
| TO: | Andrea Valdez, Head of Special Programs | 9 |
| FROM: | Marcus Ellerbee, Counselor | 16 |
| DATE: | November 16, (Current year) | 21 |
| SUBJECT: | ALAN WASHBURN | 25 |

After several informal testing activities with Alan Washburn, Ms. Davilos    40
and I believe he should be sent to the Clinical Learning Center at the    54
university for special testing and observation.    64

It appears to us that Alan exhibits not only deficient reading skills but    79
also short attention span and low motivation.  Any one of these factors    93
can result in poor performance.  Two or three of them in combination    107
certainly do.    110

Before we can make a referral, we must meet with Alan's parents and    124
get their approval.  Can you be available for such a meeting in the Guid-    138
ance Office at 4:30 next Wednesday?  The Washburns are available at    152
that time. | xx    155

## Memo 3

1. Key in standard format the memo shown at the right. Since you are keying the memo for Mr. Hardaway, show your initials above the enclosure notation.
2. Proofread your copy and correct all errors.

TO: Lenore M. Fielding, Principal    7
FROM: Jevon Hardaway, Business Department    16
DATE: November 16, (Current year)    21
SUBJECT: NEW MEMO PROCESSING PROCEDURE    28

I have used the plain-paper memo format for several years.  I    41
have found it quite satisfactory.  In fact, keying the head-    53
ings is easier than aligning copy on preprinted forms.  This    65
is especially true on computers because printers do not have    77
an aligning device.  Therefore, keyed copy often is slightly    89
above or slightly below the printed headings.    99

It is possible to create a computer template that when called    111
up will automatically take you to the points of copy entry.    123
You may wish to consider doing this if a sufficient number of    136
people have difficulty with the new format.  I'm enclosing a    148
disk containing such a template for you to try.    158

In any case, I favor cutting cost wherever possible.    169

Enclosure    171

## Invoices

**Objectives:**

1. To format and process invoices.
2. To improve ability to key from script copy and to follow directions.

### 183A • 5
### Conditioning Practice

each line twice

| | | |
|---|---|---|
| alphabet | 1 | Pamela will acquire eight dozen red vinyl jackets for an exhibit. |
| speed | 2 | Their visit may end the problem of the firm and make us a profit. |
| fig/sym | 3 | The next school dances will be on 04/29 and 06/18 at 07:35-10:50. |

**gwam** 1' | 1 | 2 | 3 | 4 | 5 | 6 | 7 | 8 | 9 | 10 | 11 | 12 | 13 |

## FORMATTING

### 183B • 45
### Format/Process Invoices

Use forms in the stationery pack to complete invoices in this lesson.

**Note:** An **invoice** is a form used by a business to charge for goods sold or services provided.

**Invoice 1**

Format and process the invoice shown at the right. Follow the alignment guides shown in color.

**Invoice 2**

Use the information at the right and on the next page to prepare an invoice.

(Total words = 69)

words

**Carr's Precision Lasers** 4621 Shelbyville Rd., Louisville, KY 40207-2359, Phone: (502) 146-8903

**INVOICE**

EISLER REALTY
1645 ARTHUR ST
LOUISVILLE KY 47137-1645

**Date:** 12/1/--    4
**Customer**    7
**Order No.:** 908274    14

| Terms | Shipped Via | Our Order No. | Date Shipped | |
|---|---|---|---|---|
| 10/15, n/30 | SafeWay, Inc. | 3570 | 11/30/-- | 22 |

| Quantity | Description/Stock Number | Price | | Total | | |
|---|---|---|---|---|---|---|
| 1 | Debco carry-on wheels/0403-12 | 59 | 99 | 59 | 99 | 31 |
| 3 | Velmar luggage cart/0404-23 | 20 | 96 | 62 | 88 | 39 |
| 1 | American briefcase/AB3826 | 69 | 99 | 69 | 99 | 47 |
| 4 | Make-A-Day planner/5211-17 | 10 | 99 | 43 | 96 | 56 |
| | | | | 236 | 82 | 57 |
| | Sales tax (6%) | | | 14 | 21 | 62 |
| | | | | 251 | 03 | 63 |

align

Mesko Stationery Company
4594 Quebec
Denver, CO 80216-9832

Date: 12/14/--
Customer Order No.: 23-5873

Terms are 10/10, n/45; shipped via FRF Delivery; our order no. is 3581; shipping date is 12/17/--.

(continued on next page)

# LESSON 47

## Simplified and Standard Memorandums

**Objectives:**
1. To check knowledge of simplified and standard memo formats.
2. To check the level of your memo processing skill.

---

### 47A • 5
**Conditioning Practice**

each line twice SS; then a 1' writing on line 3; find *gwam*

| | | |
|---|---|---|
| alphabet | 1 | Rex just left my quiz show and gave back a prize he had won. |
| fig/sym | 2 | Review reaches:  $40, $84, 95%, #30, 5-point, 1/6, B&O 27's. |
| speed | 3 | Di may profit by good form and a firm wish to make the goal. |

**gwam** 1' | 1 | 2 | 3 | 4 | 5 | 6 | 7 | 8 | 9 | 10 | 11 | 12 |

---

### 47B • 5
**Skill Building**

1. Center lines 1-3 DS.
2. Key lines 4-6 SS.
3. If equipment has the Italic feature, change all underlines to italics in lines 4 and 5.

1  FORMATTING MEMOS

centering  2  Simplified Memos

3  Standard Memos

4  Key newspaper names:  <u>Boston Globe</u>; <u>Erie Sentinel</u>; <u>Bay News</u>.

CAPS LOCK & underline  5  Key magazine names:  <u>Reader's Digest</u>; TIME; <u>Modern Maturity</u>.

6  Key abbreviations:  Atlanta, GA; NCAA title; U.S. Air Force.

---

## FORMATTING

### 47C • 40
**Memo Processing**

Key the memos shown at the right and on p. 120 as directed with each memo.

**Memo 1**
1. Key the copy at right as a simplified memo. Correct all errors.
2. Add an attachment notation.

words

November 17, (Current year)  —  4

Jonathon Eagle  —  7

ARTICLE FOR THE PERISCOPE  —  12

Attached is an annotated guide sheet for the preparation of your article reviewing the Native American Art Exhibit at Lakeview.  —  26 / 38

Because space in the <u>Periscope</u> is limited, we allocate that space before articles are written so that you, rather than the editors, hone your copy to fit the space.  —  52 / 68 / 71

As the guide sheet indicates, you may use two columns of 34 lines each plus the equivalent of 6 lines across the two columns for the title and by-line.  So you have 68 lines of approximately 40 characters each for your story.  If you key your copy using this line length, a quick line count will indicate whether cutting or expanding is needed.  —  85 / 100 / 115 / 130 / 140

Jacque Jordan, Associate Editor Attachment  —  149

## Purchase Order 2
Use the information at the right to prepare a purchase order that will be sent to

**LEWIS & KOHLER INC**
**4924 SUNSET RD**
**CHARLOTTE NC 28213-6812**

The letters *ea* in parentheses, meaning *each*, should follow each stock number.

Include a total for the purchases. Retain this PO (PO182B2) for use in 183B.

(Total words = 82)

## Purchase Order 3
Use the information at the right to prepare a purchase order that will be sent to

**OFFICE MART**
**845 BUSH RIVER RD**
**COLUMBIA SC 29210-5549**

The abbreviation (*ea*) follows each stock number. Include a total.

(Total words = 56)

## Purchase Order 4
Use the information at the right to prepare a purchase order that will be sent to

**CDMK**
**458 S BURLESON BLVD**
**FORT WORTH TX 76028-4496**

Include a total.

(Total words = 63)

## Purchase Order 5
Revise Purchase Order 3 by adding the two items described at the right. Include a new total.

(Total words = 80)

PO Number is **16489-X**; date is **May 30, ----**; terms are **15/15, n/30**; to be shipped via **TKL**.

| | | | |
|---|---|---|---|
| 2 | Panel, 60" x 72" / 0113-28 | 119.99 | 239.98 |
| 1 | Workstation, 29"h x 30"d x 60"w / 0113-29 | 139.99 | 139.99 |
| 1 | Return, 29"h x 24"d x 42"w / 0113-31 | 99.99 | 99.99 |
| 1 | Keyboard, 12"d x 24"w / 0113-34 | 49.99 | 49.99 |
| 2 | Bookshelf, 16"h x 12"d x 61"w / 0113-37 | 79.99 | 159.98 |
| 1 | Pedestal / 0113-39 | 169.99 | 169.99 |

PO Number is **745-2**; date is **June 5, ----**; terms are **20/15, n/30**; to be shipped via **SuperTrans**.

| | | | |
|---|---|---|---|
| 2 | Elwood 8130 multifunctional fax / 0205-247 | 1595.50 | 3191.00 |
| 4 | Portacomm personal-pager / 0204-113 | 99.99 | 399.96 |
| 3 | AnswerMate answering machine / 0205-357 | 79.99 | 239.97 |

PO Number is **5902**; date is **June 17, ----**; terms are **5/15, n/30**; to be shipped via **PGT Express**.

| | | | |
|---|---|---|---|
| 1 | No. 2 lead pencil / 1000-23 (pk) | 3.59 | 3.59 |
| 3 | Mechanical pencil / 1000-24 (pk) | 1.29 | 3.87 |
| 6 | Permanent marker / 1002-45 (pk) | 2.59 | 15.54 |
| 4 | Highlight markers / 1000-67 (set) | 3.19 | 12.76 |
| 3 | Ball-point pen / 1000-46 (pk) | 7.19 | 21.57 |

Order two Calcall desktop calculators (0202-459). Each costs $19.99. Also, purchase two Olympia voice-activated recorders. The item number is 0201-395 and each costs $119.98.

**Memo 2**

1. Key the copy at right as a standard memo. Correct all errors.
2. Add your initials as the keyboard operator.

| | | |
|---|---|---|
| TO: | Student Council Officers | 6 |
| FROM: | Lenore M. Fielding, Principal | 13 |
| DATE: | November 18, (Current year) | 18 |
| SUBJECT: | STUDENT BEHAVIOR AT ATHLETIC EVENTS | 27 |

Reports from a number of faculty and parents suggest that the behavior of 42
a few of our students at two recent athletic events violated the Code of 57
Student Conduct. 60

Only a few students were involved, and only three incidents were reported. 76
Even so, the reported behavior does not create the image Lakeview wants 90
to portray to members of our community or visitors from other commu- 104
nities. 105

Because you along with your fellow council officers monitor such events 120
and participate in the evaluation of Code of Student Conduct violations, I 135
want to meet with you and the assistant principals to review these reports 150
and their impact on our school image. 158

This meeting is scheduled for 2:30 this Thursday afternoon in Conference 173
Room B. Be prepared to tell us what you know about any such incidents 186
and what action you think we should take. | xx 195

**Memo 3**

1. Key the copy at right as a standard memo. Correct all errors.
2. Add an enclosure notation.

**Memo 4**

If time permits, reformat or rekey Memo 3 as a simplified memo. Correct all errors.

**Note:** See p. A16 for R & E activities for this unit.

To: Manuel Delgado, Community Services Coordinator 10
From: Lenore M. Fielding, Principal 18
Date: November 18, (Current year) 23
Subject: Community Clean-Up Campaign 30

Congratulations to you and your junior/senior workers on a 42
successful Community Clean-Up Campaign. 50

I have received many telephone calls and several letters from 63
people in the community conveying their thanks to and admira- 75
tion for these students. They freely gave their time and 86
effort to help the elderly and others in the community who 98
were physically unable to perform the needed work themselves. 111

Please share our compliments and gratitude with your work- 122
force. Their attitude and conduct during this campaign have 135
enhanced our image in the community. 142

I am enclosing an envelope containing some telephone messages 155
and letters for you to share with the students who partici- 166
pated. | xx 169

# UNIT 39

**LESSONS 182–184**

# Format/Process Business Forms

## LESSON 182

## Purchase Orders

### Objectives:
1. To format and process purchase orders.
2. To improve ability to key from script copy and to follow directions.

---

**182A • 5**
**Conditioning Practice**

each line twice; take 1'
writings on line 3 as time
permits

| | | |
|---|---|---|
| alphabet | 1 | Wixie plans to study my notes just before taking the civics quiz. |
| speed | 2 | The busy fieldhand kept the fox in a big pen to keep it in sight. |
| figures | 3 | Our soccer league had 3,650 boys and 2,478 girls playing in 1997. |

**gwam** 1' | 1 | 2 | 3 | 4 | 5 | 6 | 7 | 8 | 9 | 10 | 11 | 12 | 13 |

---

**F** ORMATTING

words

**182B • 45**
**Format/Process**
**Purchase Orders**

Review format guides for
forms on p. 313.

Use forms in the stationery
pack to complete forms in
this lesson.

**Note:** A **purchase order**
is a form used by a
business to order goods
or services from another
business.

**Purchase Order 1**

Format and process the
purchase order shown at
the right. Follow alignment
guides shown in color.

*Pet City*

1300 Veteran Memorial Dr.   Phone: (504) 165-2350
Kenner, LA 71109-3359       Fax:  (504) 165-2351

**Purchase Order**

| | |
|---|---|
| TROMBINO OFFICE SUPPLIES<br>1759 CANAL ST<br>NEW ORLEANS LA 70112-2443 | PO No.:  1547    6<br>Date:  May 23, ----    11<br>Terms:  2/10, n/30    19<br>Shipped Via:  Fast Xpress    21 |

| Quantity | Description/Stock Number | Price | | Total | | |
|---|---|---|---|---|---|---|
| 6 | Copy paper/0601-93 (rm) | 11 | 67 | 70 | 02 | 29 |
| 6 | Printer paper/0600-91 (rm) | 7 | 87 | 47 | 22 | 37 |
| 1 | Fax paper/0201-45 (pk) | 45 | 32 | 45 | 32 | 44 |
| 10 | Letterhead/0602-95 (pk) | 6 | 95 | 69 | 50 | 52 |
| 2 | Legal pads/0601-95 (pk) | 17 | 45 | 34 | 90 | 60 |
| | | | | 266 | 96 | 61 |

 align

By _____

# Skill Builder

**Keyboard Review**
1. Key each line twice SS; DS between 2-line groups.
2. If time permits, rekey lines that were awkward or difficult for you.

A/Z 1 Zoe had a pizza at the plaza by the zoo on a lazy, hazy day.

B/Y 2 Abby may be too busy to buy me a book for my long boat trip.

C/X 3 Zeno caught six cod to fix lunch for his six excited scouts.

D/W 4 Wilda would like to own the wild doe she found in the woods.

E/V 5 Evan will give us the van to move the five very heavy boxes.

F/U 6 All four of us bought coats with faux fur collars and cuffs.

G/T 7 Eight guys tugged the big boat into deep water to get going.

H/S 8 Marsha wishes to show us how to make charts on the computer.

I/R 9 Ira will rise above his ire to rid the firm of this problem.

J/Q 10 Quen just quietly quit the squad after a major joint injury.

K/P 11 Kip packed a backpack and put it on an oak box on the porch.

L/O 12 Lola is to wear the royal blue skirt and a gold wool blouse.

M/N 13 Many of the men met in the main hall to see the new manager.

figures 14 I worked from 8:30 to 5 at 1964 Lake Blvd. from May 7 to 26.

fig/sym 15 I quote, "ISBN #0-651-24876-3 was assigned to them in 1995."

**Timed Writings**
1. Key two 1' writings on each ¶; find *gwam* on each writing.
2. Key two 2' writings on ¶s 1-2 combined; find *gwam* on each writing.
3. Key two 3' writings on ¶s 1-2 combined; find *gwam* and circle errors on each writing.
4. If time permits, key 1' guided writings on each ¶ to improve speed or accuracy according to your needs.

all letters used

| | gwam | 2' | 3' |
|---|---|---|---|

As you work for higher skill, remember that how well you | 8 | 4

key fast is just as important as how fast you key. How well | 12 | 8

you key at any speed depends in major ways upon the technique | 18 | 12

or form you use. Bouncing hands and flying fingers lower the | 24 | 16

speed, while quiet hands and low finger reaches increase speed. | 31 | 20

Few of us ever reach what the experts believe is perfect | 36 | 24

technique, but all of us should try to approach it. We must | 42 | 28

realize that good form is the secret to higher speed with | 48 | 32

fewer errors. We can then focus our practice on the improve- | 54 | 36

ment of the features of good form that will bring success. | 60 | 40

gwam 2' | 1 | 2 | 3 | 4 | 5 | 6
3' | 1 | 2 | 3 | 4

**Table 6**

1. You decide column widths and alignments within cells.
2. You decide font face, size, style, and appearance.

| ALL CAPS Projected Population in World's Largest Countrys *ie* | | | | 10 |
|---|---|---|---|---|
| Country | Year | | | 11 |
| | 2000 | 2010 | 2020 | 15 |
| China | 1,199,400,000 | 1,302,100,000 | 157,150,000 | 25 |
| India | 1,042,500,000 | 1,166,200,000 | 1,379,600,000 | 35 |
| Indonesia | 223,800,000 | 238,800,000 | 278,200,000 | 54 |
| Pakistan | 149,100,000 | 180,700,000 | 275,100,000 | 63 |
| United States | 268,300,000 | 298,600,000 | 334,700,000 | 45 |
| Nigeria | Not Available | 162,000,000 | 246,000,000 | 72 |
| Brazil | 179,500,000 | 185,600,000 | 205,300,000 | 90 |
| Bangladesh | 146,600,000 | 164,800,000 | 211,200,000 | 81 |
| Iran | 75,700,000 | 106,800,000 | 161,900,000 | 98 |
| ~~Mexico~~ Russia | ~~107,200,000~~ Not Available | ~~118,500,000~~ 153,000,000 | ~~137,500,000~~ 152,300,000 | 107 |

# LESSON 181 · Tables (Sustained Practice)

**Objectives:**
1. To improve table formatting and processing skills.
2. To key tables efficiently and accurately under timed conditions.

## 181A • 5
## Conditioning Practice

each line twice

alphabet 1 Marvin will be expected to judge the quality of the tyke's kazoo.

speed 2 Ryan and my tidy neighbor may dismantle the shanty on the island.

fig/sym 3 Stopwatch (#93-408) and pedometer (#21-657) are on sale Saturday.

gwam 1' | 1 | 2 | 3 | 4 | 5 | 6 | 7 | 8 | 9 | 10 | 11 | 12 | 13 |

## 181B • 45
## Process Tables: Sustained Practice

**Time Schedule**

Plan and prepare ........... 5'
Timed practice ............. 30'
Proofread/compute
*n-pram* .................... 10'

1. Make a list of the tables to be processed:
   p. 422, 176B, Table 3
   p. 423, 177-178B, Table 1
   p. 424, 177-178B, Table 3
   p. 425, 177-178B, Table 6
   p. 425, 177-178B, Table 7
   p. 427, 179-180B, Table 5

2. Arrange materials for easy access. Process (in the order listed) as many of the tables as you can. Proofread and correct each table before beginning the next.

3. After time is called, proofread the final table and, if needed, print all completed work.

4. Identify uncorrected errors and compute *n-pram*:
   *n-pram* = words keyed - (10 x errors) divided by 20.

   Turn in work in order listed in Step 1.

**Lesson 181 • Format/Process Tables** 428

# Language & Writing Skills 5

## Activity 1:

1. Study the spelling/definitions of the words in the color block at right.
2. Key line 1 (the **Learn** line), noting the proper choice of words.
3. Key lines 2-3 (the **Apply** lines), choosing the right words to complete the lines correctly.
4. Key the remaining lines in the same way.
5. Check your work; correct or rekey lines containing word-choice errors.

### Choose the right word

| | |
|---|---|
| **your** (adj) of or relating to you or yourself as possessor | **for** (prep/conj) used to indicate purpose; on behalf of; because; because of |
| **you're** (contr) you are | **four** (n) the fourth in a set or series |

Learn  1  When you receive your blue book, you're to write your name on it.
Apply  2  (Your, You're) to write the letter using (your, you're) best English.
Apply  3  When (your, you're) computer is warmed up, (your, you're) to begin work.

Learn  4  All four workers asked for an appointment with the manager.
Apply  5  At (for, four) o'clock the lights went off (for, four) an hour.
Apply  6  The (for, four) boys turned back, (for, four) they feared the lightning.

## Activity 2:

1. Read the ¶ shown at the right, noting words that are misused or misspelled.
2. Key the ¶, correcting the errors you found.
3. Check your work to see if you have corrected all errors.
4. If your copy still contains uncorrected errors, rekey the ¶ to make the needed corrections.

### Proofread & correct

Its your duty as an officer of Student Council to monitor our students' behavior during school ours.  Your also expected to observe what they due at school-sponsored events after school hours, whether those events are hear or away.  If you don't no what happened when misconduct is reported, how can you decide if one remedy is better then another?  Hearsay evidence is not sufficient fore you to chose a remedy.

## Activity 3:

1. Read carefully the two creeds (mottos) given at the right.
2. Choose one as a topic for a short composition, and make notes of what it means to you.
3. Compose/key a ¶ or two indicating what it means to you and why you believe it would be (or would not be) a good motto for your own behavior.

### Compose (think) as you key

The following creeds were written by Edward Everett Hale for the

**Lend-a-Hand Society**

I am only one,
But still I am one.
I cannot do everything,
But still I can do something;
And because I cannot do everything,
I will not refuse to do the something
   that I can do.

**Harry Wadsworth Club**

To look up and not down,
To look forward and not back,
To look out and not in, and
To lend a hand.

**Table 4**

1. You decide column widths and alignments within cells.
2. Enlarge font size so that main and secondary headings are larger than column entries.
3. Bold session titles; underline or italicize room names.

| | | | | words |
|---|---|---|---|---|
| CHANGED SCHOOLS CONFERENCE | | | | 5 |
| Friday Afternoon's Schedule of Activities | | | | 14 |
| 1:00-1:55 | Making Classrooms Accessible (Huron Room) | Predictors of Academic Success (Erie Room) | The Active Student (Michigan Room) | 22<br>28<br>36<br>40 |
| 2:00-2:55 | | Using Information Technology (Erie Room) | New Tools for Teachers: The Internet and Digital Libraries (Ontario Room) | 46<br>51<br>57<br>62<br>65 |
| 3:00-3:25 | Exhibits (Grand Ballroom) | | | 72 |
| 3:30-4:25 | Keynote Address: Schools that Serve Society's Needs (Blue Room) | | | 85<br>87 |
| 4:30-5:25 | School and Business Partnerships (Huron Room) | Performance-Based Assessment (Michigan Room) | Service-Learning Projects (Superior Room) | 97<br>104<br>110<br>116 |
| 5:30-6:00 | Past Presidents' Reception (Blue Room) | | | 125 |

**Table 5**

1. Center horizontally and vertically on full sheet.
2. You decide column widths and alignments within cells.
3. You decide font face, size, style, and appearance.

| | | | | | | | |
|---|---|---|---|---|---|---|---|
| WEDNESDAY EVENING TELEVISION | | | | | | | 6 |
| | 7:00 | 7:30 | 8:00 | 8:30 | 9:00 | 9:30 | 12 |
| WLOR | Wilson Files 367783 | | "Groundhog Day" (PG, '93) 198813 | | | | 23 |
| KDFI | Evening News | Next Step 645019 | Sails 542134 | Ron 685132 | Tom Grant 863590 | Sports Review 452978 | 31<br>39<br>43 |
| WUJN | "Club Paradise" (PG-13, '86) 623958 | | | "Coneheads" (PG, '93) 412630 | | | 54<br>57 |
| SPRT | Sport Preview | College Basketball: Tillis State at Johnson University (Live) | | | | Sport Review | 68<br>76 |
| QDF | Press Room | America Today | Money and You 215096 | | Financial Planning 216834 | | 86<br>91 |
| MJOR | Daily Diary 529035 | | "Nothing but Trouble" (PG-13, '91) 361740 | | | | 103<br>104 |

# UNIT 11

## Learn Block Letter Format

**Format Guides:**
**Block-Style Letters**

Personal-Business Letter

Business Letter

When all parts of a letter (including paragraphs) begin at the left margin (LM), as shown in the models at left, the document is arranged in block format (style). Block format is widely used for both personal and business correspondence.

### Letter Margins

| | |
|---|---|
| **Side margins (SM):** defaults (1") | |
| **Top margin (TM):** 2" (line 13) | |
| **Page ending (PE):** at least 1" | |

Note: Letters may also be vertically centered, using the Center Page feature.

### Basic Parts of Letters

Basic letter parts are described below in order of their occurrence within letters.

**Return address.** In personal-business letters, the return address consists of a line for the street address and one for the city, state, and ZIP Code. In business letters, the letterhead (return address) includes a company name, street address, city, state, and ZIP Code (none of which must be keyed).

**Date.** In personal-business letters, key the month, day, and year on the line below the city, state, and ZIP Code. In business letters, key the date at the top margin.

**Letter address.** Key the first line of the letter address a QS below the date. A personal title (Miss, Mr., Mrs., Ms.) or a professional title (Dr., Lt., Senator) is typically used before the receiver's name.

**Salutation.** Key the salutation (greeting) a DS below the letter address.

**Body.** Begin the letter body (message) a DS below the salutation. SS and block the paragraphs (¶s) with a DS between them.

**Complimentary close.** Key the complimentary close (farewell) a DS below the last line of the body.

**Name of writer.** Key the name of the writer (originator of the message) a QS below the complimentary close. The name may be preceded by a personal title (Miss, Mrs., Ms.) to indicate how a female prefers to be addressed in a response. If a male has a name that does not clearly indicate his gender (Kim, Leslie, Pat, for example), the title Mr. may precede his name. A job title or department name may be keyed on the line with the writer's name, separated by a comma; or it may be keyed on the next line at the left margin.

### Special Parts of Letters

**Attention line.** If a letter is addressed to a company, the address may include an attention line (the first line of the address) to call the letter to the attention of a department or a job title.

**Subject line.** Sometimes a subject line is used to alert the reader immediately to the content of a letter. A subject line is keyed in ALL CAPS (or Caps and lowercase) at the left margin a DS below the salutation.

**Reference initials.** If someone other than the originator of the letter keys it, key the keyboard operator's initials in lowercase letters at the left margin a DS below the writer's name, title, or department.

**Attachment/Enclosure notation.** If another document is attached to a letter, the word Attachment is keyed at the left margin a DS below the reference initials. If the document is not attached, the word Enclosure is used instead. If reference initials are not used, Attachment or Enclosure is keyed a DS below the writer's name or title.

# FORMATTING

## 179-180B • 45
## Process Tables

center each table horizontally and vertically

**Electronics:** Your teacher will direct you in preparing Tables 1-6.

### Table 1
1. You decide column widths and alignments within cells.
2. Enlarge font size so that main heading is larger than column headings and column headings are larger than column entries.

### Table 2
1. You decide column widths and alignments within cells.
2. Enlarge font size so that main heading is larger than column headings and column headings are larger than column entries.

### Table 3
1. You decide column widths and alignments within cells.
2. Enlarge font size so that main heading is larger than column headings and column headings are larger than column entries.

| SCHOOL DISTRICT'S PROFESSIONAL PERSONNEL | | | | | | words |
|---|---|---|---|---|---|---|
| | Employment Status | | | | Average Years of Service | 8 / 11 / 13 |
| Position | Full Time | | Part Time | | | 21 / 22 |
| | Male | Female | Male | Female | | 27 |
| Administrative | 5 | 2 | 0 | 0 | 17.8 | 33 |
| Teachers | 36 | 64 | 1 | 2 | 15.8 | 37 |
| Others | 4 | 10 | 0 | 1 | 14.9 | 41 |

| AVERAGE SALARIES--FULL-TIME PROFESSIONAL EMPLOYEES | | | | | | | words |
|---|---|---|---|---|---|---|---|
| | Administrative | | Teachers | | Others | | 10 / 16 |
| Year | Number | Average Salary | Number | Average Salary | Number | Average Salary | 22 / 31 |
| Last | 6 | $59,313 | 98 | $41,215 | 12 | $43,166 | 38 |
| This | 7 | $62,786 | 100 | $43,275 | 14 | $45,324 | 46 |
| Next | 7 | $66,553 | 103 | $45,871 | 15 | $47,590 | 53 |

| STUDENT CHARGES AT SELECTED COLLEGES | | | | | | words |
|---|---|---|---|---|---|---|
| | Tuition and Fees | | | | Room and Board | 7 / 11 |
| College | Undergraduate | | Graduate | | | 18 / 19 / 23 |
| | In State | Out of State | In State | Out of State | | 29 |
| Boles | $11,100 | $11,100 | $10,500 | $10,500 | $5,424 | 38 |
| Curtis | $18,550 | $18,550 | $16,750 | $16,750 | $5,320 | 47 |
| Elser | $7,890 | $10,765 | NA | NA | $5,568 | 54 |
| Hult | $13,076 | $13,076 | $15,210 | $15,210 | $6,426 | 63 |
| Kerr | $15,765 | $15,765 | NA | NA | $5,765 | 69 |
| Obley | $5,460 | $10,980 | $ 5,350 | $10,500 | $3,585 | 78 |
| Shull | $7,400 | $14,500 | $ 8,500 | $15,500 | $5,450 | 86 |

**2" (or line 13)**

Return address: 1049 Michigan Ave. N.
Chicago, IL 60611-2273

Date: November 18, ---- (Current year)

QS (4 hard returns)

Letter address: Mr. Elden P. Carter
7257 Charles Plz.
Omaha, NE 68114-3219
DS

Salutation: Dear Elden
DS

Body: Your telephone call on Wednesday was a really pleasant surprise. Life for both of us since college has been exciting as well as challenging, it seems. I enjoyed the update.
DS

If you had taken keyboarding as I recommended when we were in high school, you wouldn't be asking me now for a model to use for your personal-business correspondence! But I am glad to supply this model in block format (all lines beginning at the left margin).
DS

1"        1"

Use the software default or 1" side margins. Begin the return address 2" (line 13) from the top of the paper. Key the date on the next line below the return address.
DS

All letter parts are separated by a double space (2 returns) with two exceptions: A quadruple space (4 returns) is left between the date and the letter address and between the complimentary close and the keyed name.
DS

I am attaching a page from a reference manual that includes an annotated model. Call again if you need more help.
DS

Complimentary close: Cordially QS (4 hard returns)

*Andrea Rialto*

Writer: Andrea Rialto
DS

Attachment notation: Attachment

> Shown in 12-point (10-pitch) type, 1" side margins, photoreduced.

**Personal-Business Letter in Block Format (Letter 1)**

**Table 6**

1. Make Columns A, C, and D, 1"; Column B, 1.5".
2. Center-align all headings and entries, except source note; left-align it.
3. Format Columns B and D as currency with 0 decimal places and Column C as percent with 2 decimal places.
4. Underline or italicize the title in source note.

| UNITED STATES HOUSING AFFORDABILITY | | | | words |
|---|---|---|---|---|
| Year | Median Priced Single-Family Home | Mortgage Rate | Median Family Income | 7 11 17 22 |
| 1975 | $35,300 | 8.35% | $13,719 | 27 |
| 1980 | $62,200 | 12.95% | $21,023 | 33 |
| 1985 | $75,500 | 11.74% | $27,735 | 38 |
| 1990 | $95,500 | 10.04% | $35,353 | 44 |
| Source:  Information Please Almanac, 1995. | | | | 52 |

**Table 7**

1. You decide column widths.
2. Center-align all headings and entries.
3. Insert the following text at the correct row based on the date:

**June 17, Richmond, Bragg House, (703) 160-2000**

**June 22, Chicago, Halsted, (708) 147-0994**

**June 20, Cincinnati, Montgomery, (513) 185-4356**

(Total words = 76)

| HOTEL RESERVATIONS | | | |
|---|---|---|---|
| Date | City | Hotel | Telephone |
| June 15 | Baltimore | Blackburn | (410) 160-1000 |
| June 16 | Norfolk | Dickens | (804) 161-1255 |
| June 18 | Morgantown | Riverview | (304) 198-2132 |
| June 19 | Columbus | Dublin | (614) 185-9797 |
| June 21 | Ft. Wayne | Washington | (219) 124-4590 |

## LESSONS 179-180

## Complex Tables

**Objectives:**

1. To make formatting decisions about table layout.
2. To make decisions about font, size, and appearance.

**179-180A • 5**
**Conditioning Practice**

each line twice

alphabet 1 Mack and Jebb expect high scores on every law quiz if they study.

speed 2 Gus, the man with the rifle, saw six turkeys by the lake at dusk.

figures 3 I wanted to have 175-4280 or 175-3690 as my new telephone number.

gwam 1' | 1 | 2 | 3 | 4 | 5 | 6 | 7 | 8 | 9 | 10 | 11 | 12 | 13 |

## Personal-Business Letters

**Objectives:**
1. To learn features of block-style letters.
2. To process personal-business letters in block format.

---

**48A • 5**
### Conditioning Practice

each line twice SS; then a 1' writing on line 3; find *gwam*

| | | |
|---|---|---|
| alphabet | 1 | Zoe just may have to plan a big, unique dance for next week. |
| fig/sym | 2 | Tami asked, "Can't you touch-key 65, 73, $840, and 19 1/2%?" |
| speed | 3 | Six of the big firms may bid for the right to the lake land. |

| gwam | 1' | 1 | 2 | 3 | 4 | 5 | 6 | 7 | 8 | 9 | 10 | 11 | 12 |
|---|---|---|---|---|---|---|---|---|---|---|---|---|---|

---

**48B • 45**
### Personal-Business Letters in Block Format

1. Study the format guides for letters on p. 123 and the model letter illustrating block format on p. 124. Note placement of letter parts and spacing between these parts.

2. Format/key Letter 1 (the model) on p. 124.

3. Proofread your copy and correct your errors; rekey if necessary to make all needed corrections.

4. Format/key Letter 2 shown below. Correct errors as you key.

5. If time permits, rekey the model letter to increase your input speed, especially on opening and closing lines.

---

**Letter 2**

As you key from semi-arranged copy, place letter parts properly and space correctly.

**wp note:**

Save any partially completed letter to be finished during the next class period. Suggested filename: LTR48B2, for example.

---

|  | words |
|---|---|
| 2165 Granada Ave. | 4 |
| San Diego, CA 92104-3710 | 9 |
| November 19, ---- (Current year) | 12 |
| | |
| Miss Maryann Figueroa | 17 |
| Human Services Director | 21 |
| Seaboard Office Products, Inc. | 28 |
| 200 Academy P1. | 31 |
| Seattle, WA 98109-2239 | 35 |
| | |
| Dear Miss Figueroa | 39 |

In a recent issue of <u>Office Careers</u>, I read with high interest your article — 55
about personal characteristics needed by successful office workers. Your — 69
examples seemed to suggest that you were speaking of workers who had — 83
been on the job for a number of years. — 91

Although these personal traits are important for beginning workers as — 105
well, I am also interested in the skills firms such as yours require for — 119
entry-level employment. — 124

The topic of my term paper for a business management class here at — 138
Sooner High School is "Landing That First Office Job." In it I want to — 152
highlight the major areas of skills required for entry-level office positions — 168
in modern companies like yours. — 174

If you have written an article on this topic, would you share it with me, — 189
please. Or you may prefer to list your thoughts for me in a letter. Either — 205
way, I shall appreciate your assistance. — 213

Sincerely yours — 216

Miss Rikki Samuels, President — 222
Business Education Club — 227

**Table 3**

1. Make all columns about 1.25".
2. Center-align all headings and entries.

| ATTENDANCE ANALYSIS | | | | words |
|---|---|---|---|---|
| | | | | 4 |
| Fan Category | Number of Fans in Category | Average Number of Games Attended | Computed Total Attendance | 6 / 11 / 16 / 24 |
| Best Fans | 500 | 23 | 11,500 | 29 |
| Avid Fans | 1,050 | 14 | 14,700 | 34 |
| Good Fans | 14,500 | 3.5 | 50,750 | 39 |
| Computed Total Attendance | | | 75,950 | 46 |

**Table 4**

1. Make all columns about 1.25".
2. Center-align headings and entries.

| PROMOTIONAL SCHEDULE FOR MAY, JUNE, AND JULY | | | | words |
|---|---|---|---|---|
| | | | | 9 |
| Date of Promotion | Promotional Event | Actual Cost to Club | Item Given to | 18 / 23 |
| May 7 | Bat Night | $6,000 | All fans under 16 | 25 / 31 |
| May 14 | Sportsbag Day | None* | First 5,500 fans | 34 / 40 |
| June 15 | Cap Night | $5,000 | All fans | 47 |
| June 30 | Calendar Day | None* | All fans under 21 | 49 / 56 |
| July 15 | Jersey Day | $3,000 | First 5,000 fans | 57 / 64 |
| *Corporate sponsor pays for promotional item. | | | | 73 |

**Table 5**

1. Make all columns about 1.25".
2. Center main, secondary, and column headings.
3. Left-align Column A; center-align Columns B-D.

| FACULTY LOAD REPORT | | | | words |
|---|---|---|---|---|
| | | | | 4 |
| Fall Semester | | | | 7 |
| Faculty | Regular Credits | Overload Credits | Total Credits | 11 / 18 |
| Abbott, F. | 12 | 3 | 15 | 22 |
| Bates, G. | 9 | 0 | 9 | 25 |
| Dobbs, B. | 12 | 1 | 13 | 28 |
| Howell, K. | 12 | 3 | 15 | 32 |
| Ruez, P. | 10 | 0 | 10 | 35 |

**Objectives:**
1. To improve letter processing skill.
2. To learn to format/key large and small envelopes.

**49A • 5**
**Conditioning Practice**

each line twice SS; then a 1' writing on line 3; find *gwam*

| | | |
|---|---|---|
| alphabet | 1 | Wayne froze the ball, having just made the six quick points. |
| fig/sym | 2 | Flo moved from 583 Iris Lane to 836 - 42d Avenue on 10/7/97. |
| speed | 3 | Suella may row to the small island to dig for the big clams. |

**gwam** 1' | 1 | 2 | 3 | 4 | 5 | 6 | 7 | 8 | 9 | 10 | 11 | 12 |

# FORMATTING

**49B • 35**
**Personal-Business Letters**

1. Key Letters 1 and 2 below, properly placed and spaced.

2. Proofread/correct any errors you made in arrangement or spacing.

3. If time permits, key Letter 2 again (at rough-draft speed) to increase input speed.

---

**Letter 1** words

| | |
|---|---|
| 1764 Seminole Dr. | 4 |
| Detroit, MI 48214-2176 | 8 |
| November 19, ---- (Current year) | 12 |
| | |
| Mr. Trevor L. Delong | 16 |
| 1371 King George Blvd. | 21 |
| Ann Arbor, MI 48104-2657 | 26 |
| | |
| Dear Trevor | 28 |

A news item in the <u>Detroit Free Press</u> indicates   38
that you will be graduated from the university   47
at midyear. With honors, no less! Congratu-   56
lations!   58

When you were a student at Hillside High,   67
I worried that you might never put your poten-   76
tial to work in a serious way. But evidently   85
you have been able to continue your athletic   94
goals and at the same time pursue an aca-   102
demic major successfully. I am glad you have   111
done credit to yourself and to us at Hillside.   121
We're proud of you.   125

What are your plans after graduation? What-   134
ever they may be, your former teachers at   142
Hillside wish you well. I would enjoy a note   152
from you that I can share with others on the   161
Hillside faculty.   164

Cordially yours   168

Mrs. Barbara Snodgrass   172

---

**Letter 2** words

| | |
|---|---|
| 4199 - 57th St. | 3 |
| Des Moines, IA 50310-4729 | 8 |
| November 19, ---- (Current year) | 12 |
| | |
| Mr. Thomas E. McCarthy | 17 |
| 2552 Madison Rd. | 20 |
| Cincinnati, OH 45208-3172 | 25 |
| | |
| Dear Tom | 27 |

Someone once said, "A friend in need is a   35
friend indeed," and I am in need.   42

When you were in Honors English at Hillside   51
High School, I recall your using <u>Cliff's Notes</u> to   61
help you through some of the more esoteric   70
reading assignments. Do you still have those   79
"Notes"?   81

Among our readings for second semester are   90
<u>Great Expectations</u> and <u>Hamlet</u>. <u>Cliff's Notes</u>   100
would be especially helpful for the latter, but   109
I'd appreciate having both. If you can lend me   119
these, I'll be forever grateful. Please let me   128
know if you can be of help.   134

Knowing you, I'm sure all is going well at   143
college.   145

Cordially   147

Kermit R. Dawkins   150

## Intermediate Tables

**Objectives:**

**1.** To improve ability to format and process tables.

**2.** To improve keying from script copy.

**177-178A • 5**
**Conditioning Practice**

each line twice

alphabet 1 To what extent was Kaz involved with my projects before quitting?

speed 2 Ken and my neighbor are to visit an ancient chapel on the island.

fig/sym 3 Runner #3019 was 1st (49' 35") and runner #1687 was 2d (50' 12").

gwam 1' | 1 | 2 | 3 | 4 | 5 | 6 | 7 | 8 | 9 | 10 | 11 | 12 | 13 |

## FORMATTING

**177-178B • 45**
**Process Tables**

center each table horizontally and vertically

**Electronics:** Key rules in Tables 1 and 2.

**Table 1**
1. Make columns about 1.25" wide.
2. Center headings.
3. Left-align Columns A and B; align Column C at the decimal point if possible; otherwise, right-align.

**Table 2**
1. Make Column A about 1.5"; Columns B-D about 1".
2. Center table and column headings.
3. Left-align Column A; right-align Columns B-D.

**Note:** Line up 1-, 2-, and 3-line column headings as shown (blank lines above the shorter headings).

words

| CONVERSION FACTORS | | | words |
|---|---|---|---|
| To Change | To | Multiply by | 9 |
| feet | meters | .3048 | 12 |
| meters | feet | 3.2808 | 16 |
| gallons | liters | 3.7853 | 21 |
| liters | gallons | .2642 | 25 |
| inches | millimeters | 25.4 | 30 |
| millimeters | inches | .0394 | 34 |

CONVERSION FACTORS = 4

| FOURTH-QUARTER ANALYSIS | | | | words |
|---|---|---|---|---|
| Department | Cost of Goods Sold | Operating Expenses | Profits | |
| Hardware | $ 33,758 | $ 32,753 | $ 31,655 | 25 |
| Lawn & Garden | $ 35,785 | $ 34,595 | $ 31,858 | 34 |
| Toys | $ 32,987 | $ 31,758 | $ 31,369 | 40 |
| Clothing | $ 45,878 | $ 36,549 | $ 37,337 | 47 |
| Appliances | $ 37,650 | $ 32,876 | $ 34,735 | 55 |
| Totals | $186,058 | $168,531 | $166,954 | 62 |

## 49C • 10
### Envelopes

1. Study the guides at right and the illustrations below.
2. Format a small (No. 6 3/4) and a large (No. 10) envelope for each of the addresses. Use your own return address on the small envelope.

MISS ARNELLA WILSON
C/O OASIS MANOR
106 FREMONT ST
LAS VEGAS NV 89101-2277

MR PHONG HO MANAGER
ELECTRONIC PRODUCTS INC
8746 LA JOLLA PKWY
SAN DIEGO CA 92136-3927

**Return address**
Use block style, SS, and Caps and lowercase or ALL CAPS. *Unless equipment has an Envelope function*, begin on line 2 from top of envelope, 3 spaces from left edge.

**Envelope address**
*Unless equipment has an Envelope function*, set a tab or tab over 2.5" from left edge of small envelope and 4" from left edge of large envelope.

Space down about 2" from top edge of envelope; begin address at tab position.

**USPS (postal service) style**
Use block style, SS. Use ALL CAPS; omit punctuation. Place city name, 2-letter state name abbreviation, and ZIP Code + 4 on last address line. One space precedes the ZIP Code.

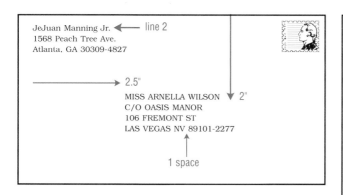

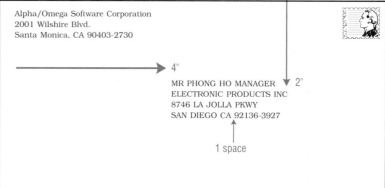

---

## LESSON 50    Personal-Business Letters

**Objectives:**
1. To achieve mastery of personal-business letter format.
2. To develop skill in processing personal-business letters.

### 50A • 5
### Conditioning Practice

each line twice SS; then a 1' writing on line 3; find *gwam*

| | | |
|---|---|---|
| alphabet | 1 | Vicky landed quite a major star for her next big plaza show. |
| fig/sym | 2 | Items marked * are out of stock: #139*, #476A*, and #2058*. |
| speed | 3 | Dodi is to handle all the pay forms for the small lake town. |

gwam  1' | 1 | 2 | 3 | 4 | 5 | 6 | 7 | 8 | 9 | 10 | 11 | 12 |

### F ORMATTING

### 50B • 45
### Personal-Business Letters

1. Key Letters 1-3, p. 128, properly placed and spaced; address an envelope for each letter.

2. Proofread/correct each letter before you save it or remove it from your machine.

3. If time permits, key Letter 1 again (at rough-draft speed) to improve input speed.

## Table 2

1. Make each column approximately 1.5" wide.
2. Center main and column headings.
3. Center-align each column.
4. Sort column entries by capacity in descending order.
5. Delete row for model 32436-D and insert the following text at the correct place:

**22678-D, 4264MB, $1,467.67**

(Total words = 52)

## Table 3

1. Make Column A about 2.25" and Columns B and C about 1".
2. Center table and column headings.
3. You decide alignment for column entries.
4. Sort column entries by code in ascending order.
5. Insert the following text at the correct place:

**Mountains, CDR63492, $29.87**

(Total words = 56)

## Table 4

You decide all formatting features (including font size and style, boldness of print, and alignment) in preparing the table at the right. Sort by outlets in descending order.

(Total words = 31)

| DISK DRIVES | | |
|---|---|---|
| Model | Capacity | Price |
| 22198-A | 1626MB | $1,039.87 |
| 41223-B | 2100MB | $1,189.56 |
| 19367-B C | 3020MB | $1,897.54 |
| 32436-D | 4294MB | $1,367.56 |
| 19917-E | 9090MB | $3,666.43 |
| 43256-B | 2100MB | $3,567.23 |
| [19754 -C | [3020 MB | $2,454.67 |
| 16737-D | 4264MB | $1,875.45 |
| 14573-A | 1626MB | $1,543.97 |

| TOP-SELLING SCIENCE CD-ROM | | |
|---|---|---|
| Title | Code | Price |
| Birds | CDR49657 | $15.97 |
| Butterflies | CDR33580 | $14.97 |
| Flowers | CDR49213 | $25.76 |
| Fruits and Vegetables | CDR79012 | $19.53 |
| Lakes and Rivers | CDR90312 | $24.97 |
| Trees and Leaves | CDR83214 | $18.88 |
| Underwater Life | CDR35460 | $17.65 |

| COMPUTER POWER PROTECTORS | | |
|---|---|---|
| Model | Outlets | Price |
| Back-UPS 200 | 2 | $ 89.82 |
| Back-UPS 300 | 2 | $ 99.53 |
| Back-UPS 400 | 4 | $144.38 |
| Back-UPS 500 | 6 | $175.81 |
| Back-UPS 600 | 6 | $199.85 |

**Letter 1**

2905 College Dr. | 3
Columbus, GA 31096-3628 | 8
November 20, ---- (Current year) | 12

Mr. Helmut E. Schultz | 16
Bucherer Watch Company | 21
730 Fifth Ave. | 24
New York, NY 10019-2046 | 29

Dear Mr. Schultz | 32

If anyone can repair a thinline Bucherer watch, you are the one.  So said | 47
Hermine Wolfe, manager of jewelry repair at Loring's here in Columbus. | 61

Ms. Wolfe has repaired my watch twice before, but she believes it now | 75
needs attention that only a licensed Bucherer shop can give.  In fact, she | 90
thinks the entire works may need to be replaced.   The case and band are | 105
of such value that I want to do whatever must be done to make the watch | 119
useful again. | 122

Please use the enclosed envelope to send me a rough estimate of the cost | 137
of repair and to tell me what I should do next.   The case number of the | 151
watch is 904618, in the event the number may be of use.  The watch was | 165
purchased in Geneva. | 170

Sincerely yours | 173

Kyle A. Karas | 176

Enclosure | 177

---

**Letter 2**

9248 Socorro Rd. | El Paso, TX 79907-2366 | | 8
November 20, ---- (Current year) | 12

Mrs. Susan L. Orr, Director | Graphic Arts | 20
Institute | 2099 Calle Lorca | Santa Fe, NM | 28
87505-3461 | Dear Mrs. Orr | 33

A graduate of your school, Ms. San-li Chou, | 42
has suggested that I write to you because of | 51
my interest in a career in graphic design. | 59

To keep my options open, I am taking a | 67
college-prep program.  All my electives, though, | 77
are being chosen from courses in art, design, | 86
and graphics--including photography.  I do | 95
unusually well in these courses. | 102

Can you send me a catalog that outlines the | 110
graphics programs now being offered by your | 119
school.  I shall appreciate your doing so. | 128

Cordially yours | Miguel Blanco | 134

---

**Letter 3**

4400 Coldwater Rd. | Fort Wayne, IN | 7
46825-3716 | November 20, ---- (Current year) | 13

Ms. Nina K. Medelin, Chair | Foreign Ex- | 20
change Committee | Rotary International | | 28
7800 S. Anthony Blvd. | Fort Wayne, IN | 35
46816-2250 | Dear Ms. Medelin | 41

Here are my completed application forms for a | 50
Rotary Foundation Scholarship to study one | 59
year in a South American country. | 66

I would especially like to study in Colombia | 75
because my mother has relatives in Bogota. | 83
Further, I visited Colombia with my family last | 93
year, and I liked the country and its people very | 103
much. | 104

As my application indicates, my minor course | 113
of study is Spanish. My career goal is to be- | 123
come a medical doctor and to serve in the His- | 132
panic community in one of our major cities. | 141

Sincerely yours | Sylvia LeClercq | Enclosures | 149

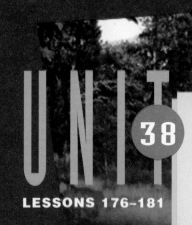

# UNIT 38

**LESSONS 176–181**

## Format/Process Tables

## LESSON 176

### Basic Tables

**Objectives:**
1. To format and process three-column tables.
2. To improve keying from rough-draft and script copy.

**176A • 5**
**Conditioning Practice**

each line twice

| | | |
|---|---|---|
| alphabet | 1 | Avoid fizzling fireworks because they just might explode quickly. |
| speed | 2 | It may be a big problem if both of the men bid for the dock work. |
| figures | 3 | He surveyed 3,657 women, 2,980 men, and 1,400 children last June. |

**gwam** 1' | 1 | 2 | 3 | 4 | 5 | 6 | 7 | 8 | 9 | 10 | 11 | 12 | 13 |

### F ORMATTING

**176B • 45**
**Tables**

center all tables horizontally and vertically

**Electronics:** Key Tables 1 and 2 without rules; key Tables 3 and 4 with rules; do *not* complete sorts, deletions, and insertions. Ignore direction to center-align column entries.

**Table 1**
1. Make each column approximately 1" wide.
2. Center main and column headings.
3. Left-align Column A; center-align Columns B and C.
4. Sort column entries by price in descending order.
5. Delete row for model YV945-521 and insert the following text at the proper place:

**UZ387-195, Wide, $585.64**

words

| COMPUTER PRINTERS | | | 4 |
|---|---|---|---|
| Model | Width | Price | 7 |
| ML420-134 | Narrow | $304.45 | 12 |
| ML421-134 | Wide | $427.45 | 17 |
| TX620-237 | Narrow | $354.86 | 22 |
| TX621-237 | Wide | $475.82 | 26 |
| TX690-237 | Narrow | $419.36 | 31 |
| UZ385-178 | Narrow | $449.54 | 36 |
| UZ386-178 | Wide | $576.32 | 41 |
| YR335-646 | Narrow | $509.96 | 46 |
| YA336-646 | Wide | $627.43 | 51 |
| YV945-521 | Narrow | $547.35 | 56 |
| YV947-524 | Narrow | $563.92 | 61 |
| YV994-491 | Wide | $657.38 | 65 |

# LESSON 51

## Business Letters

**Objectives:**
1. To learn features of business letters in block format.
2. To learn to format business letters in block format.

## 51A • 5
### Conditioning Practice

each line twice SS; then a 1' writing on line 3; find *gwam*

| | | |
|---|---|---|
| alphabet | 1 | Jacques worked to win the next big prize for my valiant men. |
| fig/sym | 2 | Rona's 1998 tax was $5,374, almost 2% ($106) less than 1997. |
| speed | 3 | Six of the eight girls may work for the auditor of the firm. |

**gwam** 1' | 1 | 2 | 3 | 4 | 5 | 6 | 7 | 8 | 9 | 10 | 11 | 12 |

## 51B • 45
### Business Letters in Block Format

Address an envelope for each letter processed in this lesson and remaining lessons in this unit.

**wp note:**

If an Envelope function is available, use it; otherwise, follow the procedure given on p. 127.

1. Study Letter 1 (the model) on p. 130; then format/key it, errors corrected.

2. Format/key Letter 2 below; correct any errors you make as you key.

3. If time permits, key the model letter again (at rough-draft speed) to improve your input speed.

**Letter 2**

words

| | |
|---|---|
| November 21, ---- (Current year) | 4 |
| Mr. Nigel P. Byers | 7 |
| Central High School | 11 |
| 65 Union Ave. | 14 |
| Memphis, TN 38103-2745 | 19 |
| Dear Mr. Byers | 22 |

Your question about the effect of word processing equipment on the need for keying accuracy is a good one.   36 / 43

Accuracy of documents processed is just as important now as ever before. The ease with which keying errors can now be corrected, however, has shifted the emphasis from number of input errors made to skill in finding and correcting these errors.   58 / 72 / 87 / 93

A major weakness of those who take employment tests is their inability to detect and correct the errors they make.  Therefore, we suggest that employee training should emphasize proofreading and error correction rather than error-free input.   107 / 121 / 135 / 141

A grading system rewarding efficient proofreading and correction skills instead of penalizing errors of initial input is worthy of your serious consideration.   156 / 171 / 174

| | |
|---|---|
| Sincerely yours | 177 |
| Ms. Leslie Bancroft, Office Manager | 184 |
| vk | 184 |

**Table 2**

1. Make all columns approximately 1".
2. Left-align entries in Column A; right-align all others. Center column heads.
3. Center and italicize *Totals* in Cell A7.
4. Bold *Totals* row.
5. Save as EXPENSES.

**WP note:**

Key $ as shown, using the general (default) number type.

| BUSINESS EXPENSE SUMMARY | | | | |
|---|---|---|---|---|
| **Quarter** | **Travel** | **Meals** | **Lodging** | **Other** |
| First | $5,753.59 | $2,308.54 | $1,987.45 | $678.98 |
| Second | 6,453.20 | 2,756.08 | 2,451.74 | 1,005.64 |
| Third | 5,642.05 | 2,645.02 | 3,002.50 | 1,105.99 |
| Fourth | 4,984.00 | 1,805.45 | 1,954.33 | 985.50 |
| *Totals* | **$22,832.84** | **$9,515.09** | **$9,396.02** | **$3,776.11** |

**Table 3**

1. You decide the width for columns.
2. Left-align entries in Column A and right-align all others. Center column heads.
3. Save as COLLEGE.

| CENTURY COLLEGE | | | | |
|---|---|---|---|---|
| School of Applied Science Enrollment | | | | |
| Program | Students Enrolled | | | |
| | Last Year | | This Year | |
| | Females | Males | Females | Males |
| Actuarial Sciences | 10 | 14 | 12 | 11 |
| Hospitality Management | 125 | 89 | 134 | 112 |
| Sports Management | 55 | 63 | 67 | 68 |
| Environmental Management | 85 | 74 | 78 | 68 |

# Kendal ■ Computers

■ **738 St. Louis St.**

■ **Baton Rouge, LA 77802-3615**

OFFICE: 504-555-1278
FAX: 504- 555-1998

Dateline　November 21, ---- (Current year)　　2" (or line 13)

QS (4 hard returns)

Letter
address　Mr. Julio M. Basanez, Manager
　　　　La Paloma Restaurant
　　　　224 Saint Louis St.
　　　　Baton Rouge, LA 77802-3615

DS

Salutation　Dear Julio

DS

Body　Your piquant black bean soup drew me back to the La Paloma yester-
　　　day.　We were taken promptly to our table, but we waited over ten
　　　minutes before menus were presented.

DS

Several times I provided clues to the server that I was hosting the
luncheon.　Without noting these clues or asking who should receive
the check, the server gave it to the man across from me.　Had the
check been placed upside down in the middle of the table, my client
wouldn't have been "put on the spot."

1"　　　　　　　　　　　　　　　　　　　　　　　　　　　　　　　　　　1"

DS

Several times a week someone from my company entertains clients at
La Paloma Restaurant.　Will you talk with your staff about greeting
diners promptly and about handling checks properly.　But please,
Julio, don't disturb the chef!

DS

Complimentary
close　Cordially　QS (4 hard returns)

*Mrs. Luanne Chang*

Writer　Mrs. Luanne Chang, President

DS

Reference
initials　mt

Shown in 12-point (10-pitch) type, 1" side
margins, photoreduced.

**Business Letter in Block Format (Letter 1)**

## ACTIVITY 4:

**Review Table Features**

1. Open file COUNTRYA.
2. Revise the table, following the directions at the right.
3. Spell-check the table.
4. Save as COUNTRYC.

**WP note:**

In Step 6, you may be able to increase the type size by selecting Large rather than choosing a point size larger than 12.

1. Change the font face of the entire table to one you select. Use 12-point size.
2. Change the column widths: Column A, about 1.25"; Columns B and C, 1.5".
3. Insert a column between Columns A and B (width, 1.5"). Key a column heading: **Approximate Population**. (Readjust the width of Column A, if necessary.)
4. Format Column B so that the numbers you enter will be right-aligned.
5. Beginning in Cell B2, key these numbers in Column B:

   B2  1,178,500,000    B7  149,000,000
   B3  896,400,000      B8  124,000,000
   B4  258,300,000      B9  122,400,000
   B5  187,600,000      B10 113,900,000
   B6  152,000,000      B11 95,100,000

6. Center the column headings horizontally and vertically; bold the type and increase the size of the font in this row.
7. Italicize the names of cities in Column D; bold the country name in A4.

## ACTIVITY 5:

1. Prepare Table 1 at right and Tables 2 and 3 on the next page.
2. Center each table horizontally and vertically.
3. Center and bold all main headings.
4. Change font size and face as desired.
5. Follow the additional directions provided for each table.

**Table 1**

1. Make Column A approximately 1.75"; Column B about 1.25"; Column C about 0.75".
2. Left-align entries in Column A; center-align Column B; and right-align Column C. Center column heads.
3. Save as TUNNELS.

| LAND VEHICULAR TUNNELS IN THE UNITED STATES | | |
|---|---|---|
| (Over 5,500 Feet in Length) | | |
| Name | Location | Length in Feet |
| E. Johnson Memorial | Colorado | 8,959 |
| Eisenhower Memorial | Colorado | 8,941 |
| Allegheny | Pennsylvania | 6,070 |
| Liberty Tubes | Pennsylvania | 5,920 |
| Zion National Park | Utah | 5,766 |
| Source: The World Almanac, 1995. | | |

## Business Letters

**Objectives:**
1. To review features of business letters in block format.
2. To process business letters in block format.

---

### 52A • 5
### Conditioning Practice

each line twice SS; then a 1' writing on line 3; find *gwam*

| | | |
|---|---|---|
| alphabet | 1 | Jarvis will take the next big prize for my old racquet club. |
| fig/sym | 2 | The Diamond Caper (Parker & Sons, #274638) sells for $19.50. |
| speed | 3 | A neighbor paid the girl to fix the turn signal of the auto. |

**gwam** 1' | 1 | 2 | 3 | 4 | 5 | 6 | 7 | 8 | 9 | 10 | 11 | 12 |

---

## F ORMATTING

### 52B • 45
### Business Letters in Block Format

**Letter 1**

Key Letters 1-3, at right and on p. 132, in block format; proofread and correct each letter before you save it or remove it from the machine.

words

| | |
|---|---:|
| November 22, ---- | 4 |
| | |
| Miss Rikki Samuels, President | 10 |
| Business Education Club | 14 |
| Sooner High School | 18 |
| 2165 Granada Ave. | 22 |
| San Diego, CA 92104-3710 | 27 |
| | |
| Dear Miss Samuels | 30 |

Thank you for giving me the opportunity to tell you the main things we look for in entry-level office workers. 45 / 53

First, we look for graduates who have specific skills we need:  in communications, keyboarding, word/data processing, accounting, and records management, to name a few.  A detailed personal data sheet will usually provide such information. 67 / 81 / 96 / 101

Next, we seek people who show pride in themselves--those who dress appropriately and are well groomed and who speak positively as well as forcefully about their educational background and related experiences. Usually these behavior patterns are observed in the job interview. 114 / 129 / 143 / 157

Finally, we seek people who show evidence that they can work well with others.  An effective application letter and data sheet will identify group activities in which the applicant has participated successfully and in what roles. 171 / 186 / 201 / 203

People with these qualifications have at least the potential to develop into valuable members of an office staff. 218 / 226

| | |
|---|---:|
| Sincerely yours | 229 |
| | |
| Miss Maryann Figueroa, Human Services Director | 237 |
| nt | 238 |

# ACTIVITY 3:

## Format and Align Numbers

1. Read the copy at right.
2. Determine if your wp software can format numbers and/or align them at the decimal point in a table. If your wp software can do neither, proceed to Activity 4.
3. Learn how your wp software formats numbers and aligns numbers at the decimal point.
4. Create a table using the information at the right.
5. Save table as NUMBER.

Many wp software packages have features that permit the operator to specify how numbers are to be displayed in a table (as dollars, percents, or negative numbers, for example). Most packages automatically align decimal numbers in tables at the decimal point, too. These features save time because the operator does not have to key $ or % signs, commas, parentheses (for negative numbers), or zeros after a decimal point or align decimal numbers.

1. Create the table below, making each column at least 1.25" wide. Center the table horizontally and vertically; center the main heading and column headings. Key all numbers exactly as shown; right-align the numbers.

| NUMBER FORMAT TYPE | | | |
|---|---|---|---|
| Commas | Currency | Accounting | Percent |
| 3566984 | 1234 | 1234 | .1 |
| 1456.7 | 12.34 | 12.34 | .01 |
| 378.98 | .12 | .12 | .001 |
| 1257.5673 | 1134.579 | 1134.579 | 1 |
| 1.36782 | 3.049 | 3.049 | -1.1 |

2. Reformat the numbers in Columns A-C so that they will be aligned at the decimal point. Right-align the numbers in Column D.
3. Format all numbers so that two decimal places are displayed.
4. Choose the number type as follows: Column A, Commas; Column B, Currency; Column C, Accounting; and Column D, Percent.
5. Compare your table with the illustration below. If you see variations in your table, try to change it using the features of your software.

| NUMBER FORMAT TYPE | | | |
|---|---|---|---|
| Commas | Currency | Accounting | Percent |
| 3,566,984.00 | $1,234.00 | $      1,234.00 | 10.00% |
| 1,456.70 | $12.34 | $      12.34 | 1.00% |
| 378.98 | $0.12 | $      0.12 | 0.10% |
| 1,257.57 | $1,134.58 | $      1,134.58 | 100.00% |
| 1.37 | $3.05 | $      3.05 | -110.00% |

**Letter 2**

**Note:** Line endings for opening lines are indicated by color verticals. Return at these points.

[wp] **note:**

Save this letter under the filename LTR52B2. You will be asked to retrieve it in a later lesson.

| | words |
|---|---|
| November 22, ---- | Mr. Pablo J. Lobos | 733 Marquette Ave. | | 11 |
| Minneapolis, MN 55402-2736 | Dear Mr. Lobos | 20 |

Congratulations! You are now the sole owner of the car you financed   33
through our bank. We also want to say thank you for choosing us to serve   48
your credit needs.   52

The original Certificate of Title and your Installment Loan Contract marked   67
"Paid in Full" are enclosed--evidence that you have fulfilled all the obliga-   83
tions of your automobile loan. File the papers in a safe place with your   97
other important records.   103

The promptness with which you made all monthly payments gives you a   116
preferred credit rating at our bank. Please let us know when we may be   131
of service to you again.   136

Sincerely yours | Ms. Ilya Lindgren, Auto Loan Department | hq |   148
Enclosures   150

**Letter 3**

**Note:** Do not key the diagonals; simply return at those points.

November 22, ----    4
Mrs. Glendora Ramos / 3716 Rangely Dr. /   11
Raleigh, NC 27609-4116 / Dear Mrs. Ramos   19

In these days of computers and other fancy office equipment,   31
the personal and friendly contact with people is sometimes   43
overlooked. We want you to know how much we appreciate your   55
past orders and this new opportunity to serve you.   65

The enclosed acknowledgment lists the four items you ordered   78
a few days ago. As in the past, we will carefully follow   89
your instructions for processing and shipping.   99

Although we appreciate receiving payment with an order, we   111
want to remind you that prepayment is not required. If you   123
prefer, you may simply enter your personal account number on   135
the order form, and we will send a bill later. Your account   147
number appears on your catalog address label.   156

Cordially yours / Miguel J. Maddox /   163
Mail Order Department / tm / Enclosure   170

## ACTIVITY 1:

### Insert and Delete Rows and Columns

1. Read the copy at right and learn how to insert and delete rows and columns in tables using your wp software.
2. Open TCOUNTRY and modify the table using the information at the right.
3. Save the table as COUNTRYA.

The **Table** feature can be used to edit or modify tables. Common modifications include the addition and deletion of rows and columns.

1. Insert a column between Columns B and C:
   Title (Cell C1): **LARGEST CITY**
   Cities (Cells C2-C6): **Shanghai, Greater Bombay, New York, Jakarta,** and **Sao Paulo**
2. Delete Column D (*Continent* column).
3. Bold the column headings.
4. Insert 5 rows below Row 6. Fill in with the following:

| Russia | Moscow | Moscow |
|------------|-----------|---------|
| Japan | Tokyo | Tokyo |
| Pakistan | Islamabad | Karachi |
| Bangladesh | Dhaka | Dhaka |
| Nigeria | Abuja | Lagos |

## ACTIVITY 2:

### Split Cells

1. Read the copy at right.
2. Learn how to split cells using your wp software.
3. Open COUNTRYA if it is not open.
4. Follow the directions at the right to reformat the table.
5. Save as COUNTRYB.

Use the Table feature to split a cell (divide one cell into two or more). This feature is useful for parting a joined cell. The split feature also is useful for creating forms because each row can be divided into a different number of cells of varying widths.

1. Insert a row above Row 1; join the cells of the new row.
2. Key in the new row: SELECTED COUNTRIES, CAPITALS, AND LARGEST CITIES.
3. Insert a row at the bottom of the table; join the cells of the new row.
4. Key in the new row: Source: MLS Library, 1997.
5. Insert a row below the source line; split the new row into three cells (columns).
6. Split the A cell in this row into two smaller cells; split the B cell into three; split the C cell into four cells.
7. Insert a row above the main heading; split the new row into three cells.
8. Split the A cell in this row into four cells; split the B cell into three; split the C cell into two cells.

# Block Letter Mastery

**Objectives:**
1. To improve skill on rough-draft copy.
2. To demonstrate mastery of correspondence formatting.

---

## 53A • 5
### Conditioning Practice

each line twice SS; then a
1' writing on line 3; find
*gwam*

alphabet 1 Belva had quickly won top seed for the next games in Juarez.

fig/sym 2 My income tax for 1996 was $4,870.62--up 3% over 1995's tax.

speed 3 Shana may make a bid for the antique bottle for the auditor.

gwam 1' | 1 | 2 | 3 | 4 | 5 | 6 | 7 | 8 | 9 | 10 | 11 | 12

---

## 53B • 10
### Skill Building

1. Key two 1' writings on the ¶; find *gwam* on each.
2. Key two 2' writings on the ¶; find *gwam* on each.

gwam 1' | 2'

As you learn to type, there is a time to work for speed 11 | 5

and a time to go for accuracy. Throughout the early weeks, 22 | 11

technique--not speed, not acuracy--is the main goal. Next, 35 | 17

spede through improved techniques becomes the primary focus 47 | 24

for a time. When you begin lerning to format documents, though, 60 | 30

acuracy of your copy (with erors corrected) is emphasized. 71 | 36

---

## **F** ORMATTING

## 53C • 35
### Correspondence in Block Format

**Document 1**

Key the copy as a simplified memo, all errors corrected.

words

November 18, ____  4

Adele Kliemens, Social Studies  10

STUDENT BEHAVIOR  13

Thank you for reporting the unpleasant incident you observed  25
at one of our recent athletic events.  33

This incident has been reviewed by officers of the Student  45
Council and by school administrators. The three students  57
involved have been identified and disciplined. We have also  69
set up procedures that we believe will prevent such incidents  81
from happening again.  86

The behavior of our students is of great importance to us,  98
not only for the image of our school but also as evidence  109
that our boys and girls are, through our help, growing into  121
well-behaved young men and women. Thank you for helping us  133
achieve our goal.  137

Lenore M. Fielding, Principal  142

# Activity 3:

1. Read the ¶s given at the right.

2. Review and analyze your own document processing performance by asking such questions as:

   - Do weak keying skills cause me to take longer than other students to process documents?

   - Have I memorized frequently required computer commands so that I don't have to look them up when needed?

   - Of the software features available, do I choose the ones that require the least time and effort to do the job?

   - Do my work habits indicate a minimum of "downtime"—time in which both the computer and I are idle?

3. Compose/key a ¶ identifying, on the basis of your analysis, areas in which your work performance can be improved.

4. Compose/key a second ¶ outlining a plan for working on those aspects of your performance that limit your production proficiency.

## Compose (think) as you key

Do you remember the old story of the crow and the pitcher of water? As the story goes, the crow was so thirsty he couldn't even caw. To make matters worse, there was plenty of water in the bottom of the pitcher, but try as he might the thirsty crow just couldn't reach it. Then the astute crow did something all of us should do more often. He set about solving this difficult problem. He spied some pebbles nearby, and they sparked the idea that was to save him from dying of thirst. One by one he began dropping the pebbles into the pitcher. With each pebble that he dropped into the pitcher, the water level rose. It wasn't long before the thirsty crow was drinking away to his heart's content.

\*\*\*

All of us can learn from this ancient fable. When we are faced with a problem to be solved, we should first be sure that we analyze the problem and do something about it. In using the computer, for example, you should start with a critical appraisal of how efficiently you use software features, how you organize your work, and the efficiency with which you do the actual processing of documents. Then, with this appraisal as the basis for practice, you can begin a campaign against wasted time and unneeded motions. If you have the right goals in mind and if you can reduce nonproductive time, you will be quite surprised at how quickly you reach expert performance.

**Document 2**

Key the copy as a business letter, block format, all errors corrected.

November 23, ---- | Miss Evangeline Norcross | 666 Walnut St. |   12
Des Moines, IA 50309-2661 | Dear Miss Norcross   21

Going places?   You will go twice as far in the new Gondola 2000 Compact.   35
Yes, one gallon of gasoline will take you 40 miles or more, even in city   50
driving.   And you'll do it in "smooth as silk" comfort.   61

Going places?   You will have money to spend if you invest in the best buy   76
of all compacts--the Gondola 2000.   The price is only $11,995.   You'll   90
have more money to spend, too, because the new Gondola 2000 is really   104
a miser with gasoline on the open road.   113

Going places?   Then go right to the nearest mailbox with the enclosed   127
postal card.   Just indicate the most convenient time for your free-trial   141
demonstration.   The supply of new Gondola 2000 Compacts is going fast,   155
so you'd better hurry.   160

Sincerely yours | Han Song Ki, Sales Manager | wh | Enclosure   171

**Document 3**

Key the copy as a personal-business letter, all errors corrected.

**Document 4**

If time permits, reformat or key Document 1 as a standard memo, all errors corrected.

**Note:** See p. A16 for R & E activities for this unit.

7706 Circle Dr. / St. Louis, MO 63121-4583 /   8
November 23, ---- /   12

Dr. Yolanda M. Flores / Director of Admissions /   21
LaRhonde School of Music / 1035 Bellevue   29
Ave. / St. Louis, MO 63121-2758 / Dear Dr. Flores   38

Please send me an application form for admission to the   49
LaRhonde School of Music.  I am to be graduated in June and   61
hope to enter college in September.   68

I shall appreciate information about scholarships that are   80
available and the procedure to follow in applying for one.   92
If I am to enter college in September, as I earnestly hope   105
to do, some financial aid is needed.   112

If an audition is required, when should I plan to come to   123
campus and what records should I bring with me?   133

Sincerely yours / Ivalee Moore   138

# Language & Writing Skills 16

## Activity 1:

1. Study the spelling/ definitions of the words in the color block at the right.
2. Key the **Learn** line in the first set of sentences.
3. Key the **Apply** lines, choosing the right words to complete each sentence correctly.
4. Key the second set of lines in the same way.
5. Check your work; rekey lines containing word-choice errors.

### Choose the right word

**knew** (vb) past tense of know; to have understood; to have recognized the truth or nature of

**new** (adj) novel; fresh; having existed for a short time; created in recent past

**personal** (adj) private; individual
**personnel** (n) employees

Learn 1 Ms. Uhl knew that new processing equipment would aid efficiency.
Apply 2 Why didn't she buy (knew/new) equipment if she (knew/new) that?
Apply 3 "What's (knew/new)?" I asked, even though I already (knew/new).

Learn 4 The personnel committee took a personal interest in all workers.
Apply 5 Max thought the case too (personal/personnel) to discuss openly.
Apply 6 The (personal/personnel) manager will mediate the dispute.

## Activity 2:

1. Read the letter given at the right, noting needed corrections in capitalization, punctuation, word choice, and subject/ predicate agreement.
2. Format/key the letter in block style, open punctuation—all errors corrected.
3. Address the letter to:
   **Ms. Jaye P. Neuman, Manager**
   **Western Tech Products, Inc.**
   **9574 S. Indiana Ave. Denver, CO 80201-2736**
   Supply an appropriate salutation.
4. As closing lines, use:
   **Sincerely yours**
   **Andre L. Dorlac, General Manager**
5. Use your initials as reference.

### Proofread & correct

Have you stayed at the Bayshore Inn lately?  We try to promote the inn as a sensible hotel for the busy executive whose stopping in Vancouver on business.  But, frankly, its been a losing battle because the Bayshore inn simply don't look like a sensible hotel.  It looks like a place you'd find in rio or Acapulco.

The Bayshore Inn is built on the lee shore of a yacht harbor and the mountains are so near you can smell the evergreens on there slopes. The inn is only fore blocks from the heart of Vancouver, but if you look out you're window,  you'd think you were in a mountain retreat. A walk in the gardens of the hotel is an adventure and lunch at the Traderhorn are a reward.

The only sensible thing about the Bayshore inn is the price:  single rooms start at $55.  Busy executives keep coming back hear again and again.  They tell us it is the sensible place to stay.  Perhaps you should stop at the inn the next time your in Vancouver.  We'd like the opportunity to pamper you, two.

# UNIT 12

## Master Keyboarding/ Language Skills

**LESSONS 54–55**

---

## LESSON 54

### Keyboarding/Language Skills

From this point forward, use 1" or default side margins.

**Objectives:**

**1.** To demonstrate mastery of capitalization and number expression.

**2.** To demonstrate your best technique, speed, and control.

---

### 54A • 5
**Conditioning Practice**

each line twice SS; then a 1' writing on line 3; find *gwam*

alphabet 1 Jacki next placed my winning bid for the prized antique red vase.

fig/sym 2 His sales this week are $28,193.50; that's an increase of 17.64%.

speed 3 They wish their neighbor to pay for half the land for the chapel.

gwam 1' | 1 | 2 | 3 | 4 | 5 | 6 | 7 | 8 | 9 | 10 | 11 | 12 | 13 |

---

### L ANGUAGE SKILLS

### 54B • 10
**Checkup**

1. Key each line, correcting errors in capitalization, number expression, and spacing.
2. Check accuracy of work.
3. Rekey each line in which you made errors.

1 the labor day parade begins at 1 elm street and ends at spruce.

2 we are inviting senator chavez to address our convention in july.

3 11 of 33 boys and nine of 27 girls scored 93 or more in english.

4 linda used the pope quote: "to err is human, to forgive divine."

5 sgt. p.t. simmons took the 911 call from merchants bank & trust.

6 myrna bought china service for 8 at the china plus gift shop.

7 kevin cruz earned his phi beta kappa key while at boston college.

8 i checked my data in volume 4, section 2, page 20, of sourcebook.

---

### S KILL BUILDING

### 54C • 15
**Technique**

1. Key the drill once SS; DS between 2-line groups.
2. Key a 1' writing on each of lines 6, 8, and 10; find *gwam* on each.
3. Key the drill again.

shift keys 1 Lana and Todd will go to a New Year's party with Tonya and Spiro.
2 R. J. Appel has been paid by the Apollo Insurance Co. of Jackson.

space bar 3 It is up to them to do their best in each try to make a new goal.
4 Andy may use his pen to sign the work form for a job in the city.

letter response 5 Only after you set a case date were oil tax rates set in my area.
6 You are free only after we get him set up on a gas tax rate case.

combination response 7 Polly may bid on the antique vase only if she regards it as rare.
8 You are to sign off on all the artwork he turns in for the union.

word response 9 He is to do the sign work for both of us, and she is to pay half.
10 The girl with the titian hair may own the title to the lake land.

gwam 1' | 1 | 2 | 3 | 4 | 5 | 6 | 7 | 8 | 9 | 10 | 11 | 12 | 13 |

## Skill Builder

**Technique: Difficult Reaches**

Key each line twice SS; DS between 2-line groups; rekey difficult lines as time permits.

**Consecutive direct reaches**

1 many much loan sold vice side cent code thus fund told wide price
2 golf slow gift grow delay chance checks manual fifty cloth demand
3 forums music brown enemy hence bright signed editor specific fold

**Adjacent finger**

4 this time find help give plan mail into sent item high file might
5 five vote else dues which plans claim giving during thanks always
6 fine inform plant blank civil light wishes single quality furnish

**Adjacent key**

7 same tire view rent true says ends spot bids sort aids cure suits
8 port wire open yule ruin stop merit other paper prior truck union
9 opera owner treat forty repay trucks corner citrus repair perhaps

| gwam | | 1 | 2 | 3 | 4 | 5 | 6 | 7 | 8 | 9 | 10 | 11 | 12 | 13 |

**Timed Writings**

1. Key three 1' writings on each ¶; find *gwam*. Count errors. If errors are 2 or fewer on any writing, goal is to increase speed by 1 or 2 words on next writing. If errors on any writing are more than 2, goal is control on next writing.

2. Key two 3' writings on ¶s 1-3 combined; find *gwam* and count errors.

3. Key a 5' writing on ¶s 1-3 combined; find *gwam* and count errors.

all letters used

|  | gwam | 3' | 5' |
|---|---|---|---|

Attempts to maximize the standard of living for humans | 4 | 2 | 41
through the control of nature and the development of new products | 8 | 5 | 44
have also resulted in the pollution of the environment. In some | 12 | 7 | 46
parts of the world, the water, air, and soil are so polluted that | 17 | 10 | 49
it is unsafe for people to live there because of the heightened | 21 | 13 | 52
risk from disease. | 22 | 13 | 52

Pollution of the air, land, and water has existed since | 26 | 16 | 55
people began to live in cities. People living in these early | 30 | 18 | 57
cities took their garbage to dumps outside the main part of the | 34 | 21 | 60
city or just put it into the streets or canals. Both of these | 39 | 23 | 62
disposal methods helped create the pollution process. | 42 | 25 | 64

Pollution is one of the most serious problems facing people | 46 | 28 | 67
today. Clean air, water, and land are needed by all living | 50 | 30 | 69
things. Bad air, water, and soil cause illness and even death | 54 | 33 | 72
to people and other living things. Bad water quickly kills fish | 59 | 35 | 74
and ruins drinking water; bad soil reduces the amount of land | 63 | 38 | 77
that is available for growing food. | 65 | 39 | 78

| gwam | 3' | | 1 | | 2 | | 3 | | 4 | |
|---|---|---|---|---|---|---|---|---|---|---|
| | 5' | | | 1 | | | 2 | | | 3 |

## 54D • 20
## Timed Writings

1. Key a 1' writing on each ¶; find *gwam* on each.

2. Key two 1' guided writings on each ¶ for speed. (See p. 54 for procedure.)

3. Key two 2' writings on ¶s 1-2 combined; find *gwam* on each.

4. Key two 3' writings on ¶s 1-2 combined; find *gwam* and count errors.

**Quarter-Minute Checkpoints**

| gwam | 1/4' | 1/2' | 3/4' | 1' |
|------|------|------|------|-----|
| 20 | 5 | 10 | 15 | 20 |
| 24 | 6 | 12 | 18 | 24 |
| 28 | 7 | 14 | 21 | 28 |
| 32 | 8 | 16 | 24 | 32 |
| 36 | 9 | 18 | 27 | 36 |
| 40 | 10 | 20 | 30 | 40 |
| 44 | 11 | 22 | 33 | 44 |
| 48 | 12 | 24 | 36 | 48 |
| 52 | 13 | 26 | 39 | 52 |
| 56 | 14 | 28 | 42 | 56 |

all letters used

|  | gwam | 2' | 3' |
|--|------|----|----|

As you build your keying power, the number of errors you make 6 | 4

is not very important because most of the errors are accidental and 13 | 9

incidental. Realize, however, that documents are expected to be 20 | 13

without flaw. A letter, report, or table that contains flaws is 26 | 17

not usable until it is corrected. So find and correct all errors. 33 | 22

The best time to detect and correct your errors is while the 39 | 26

copy is still on a monitor or in the machine. Therefore, just be- 45 | 30

fore you remove the copy from the screen or machine, proofread it 52 | 35

and correct any errors you have made. Learn to proofread carefully 59 | 39

and to correct all errors quickly. Up your production in this way. 65 | 44

---

## LESSON 55
# Keyboarding Check & Improvement

**Objectives:**

1. To check/improve keying speed on sentences.
2. To check/improve keying speed/control on paragraphs.

## 55A • 5
## Conditioning Practice

each line twice SS; then a 1' writing on line 3; find *gwam*

| | | |
|--|--|--|
| alphabet | 1 | Frazer may have a jinx on my squad, but we kept the big gold cup. |
| fig/sym | 2 | Lizzy asked, "Wasn't R&N's check #385367-0 deposited on 1/24/97?" |
| speed | 3 | When did the field auditor sign the amendment forms for the city? |

gwam 1' | 1 | 2 | 3 | 4 | 5 | 6 | 7 | 8 | 9 | 10 | 11 | 12 | 13 |

## 55B • 15
## Sentences

1. Key a 1' writing on each line; find *gwam* on each writing.

2. Compare rates and identify the 4 slowest lines.

3. Key a 1' writing on each of the 4 slowest lines.

4. As time permits in later lessons, key this drill again to improve speed.

| | | |
|--|--|--|
| fig/sym | 1 | Leland asked, "How much is due by June 30 on Account #4829-1657?" |
| figures | 2 | By October 5 in 1997, she had planted 320 trees and 1,648 shrubs. |
| one hand | 3 | My war on waste at a union mill was based only upon minimum data. |
| long reach | 4 | June said that I must curb at once my urge to glance at my hands. |
| adjacent key | 5 | Joi hoped for a new opal ring to wear to her next violin concert. |
| double letter | 6 | Bobby will sell them the cookbook for a little less than it cost. |
| combination | 7 | They may join us for tea at the big pool if they wish to see you. |
| balanced hand | 8 | Did they make the right land title forms for the eight big firms? |

gwam 1' | 1 | 2 | 3 | 4 | 5 | 6 | 7 | 8 | 9 | 10 | 11 | 12 | 13 |

| | words |
|---|---|
| SUMMARY MINUTES | 3 |
| HEALTH OCCUPATIONS ADVISORY COMMITTEE MEETING | 9 |
| | 12 |
| November 15, ---- | 16 |

Committee members present: Robert Dry-Kenich, Deborah Edington, Amy Lovetro, Ray Meucci, Rosemary Radmanich, Kenneth Ryave, Kim Van Aken, and Leo Yazzani. — 24, 33, 41, 47

School employees present: Mary Amaral, Drew Bowen, Larry Kaufmann, Fred Niklas, Carla Nilson, and Margaret Palmero. — 56, 65, 70

Recorder of minutes: Joseph Gloss. — 77

1. Amy Lovetro, committee chair, called the meeting to order at 11:15 a.m. and welcomed all to the meeting. Ms. Lovetro introduced Kim Van Aken, director of records, Hermanie Valley Hospital, as a new member of this committee. — 86, 94, 103, 111, 119, 124

2. The minutes from the May 14 meeting were read and approved. — 133, 137

3. Mr. Fred Niklas reported: — 143

   A. At least 125 students are presently enrolled in the health occupation programs, with medical records having the highest enrollment (35). — 152, 159, 167, 172

   B. Of the 53 health occupation students who were graduated last June, 28 are — 180, 188

employed in a health-related field, 15 have gone on to higher education, 3 entered the military, 5 are employed in an unrelated field, and 2 are unemployed. — 195, 203, 211, 218, 219

4. Unfinished business included passing a motion to recommend that Eastway AVTS students form a chapter of the Health Occupations Students of America. The committee members agreed to work closely with the students and the faculty sponsor. — 228, 235, 243, 250, 259, 267

5. New business included passing motions to support these three recommendations: — 276, 284

   A. All committee members be invited to participate in the AVTS's career fair. — 292, 300

   B. Two members of the committee (Deborah Edington and Kenneth Ryave) be appointed to the AVTS's Strategic Planning Committee. — 308, 315, 323, 326

   C. The advisory committee chair be appointed to the AVTS's School-to-Work Transition Committee. — 333, 341, 345

6. The next meeting was scheduled for May 15 at 11:15 a.m. — 355, 358

7. The formal meeting was adjourned at 12:35 p.m., and the committee members and school personnel moved to Gessey Dining Room for lunch and informal conversation. — 367, 374, 382, 390

**Document 3**
**News Release**

Format text at right as a news release. Use format guides for an unbound report DS with these additional guides:

- Key and center the letterhead information or use the designated sheet in stationery pack.

(Words in letterhead = 22)

- Key **News Release** flush left and **For Release:** . . . and **Contact:** . . . flush right.

- QS below the contact line and begin body.

- Center the symbols ### a DS below last line of the body to indicate the end of the release.

# East Harris County High School
### 458 Harris Rd. – Omaha, NE 68132-6459
### Tel: 401-196-4378 • Fax: 401-196-4379

| | words |
|---|---|
| News Release  For Release: Upon Receipt | 8 |
| Contact: Guy Madison | 12 |

OMAHA, NE, March 24, ----. Three East Harris County High School students, members of the EHC Business Club, will travel to Chicago to compete in the Business Olympics in May. — 25, 39, 48

Susan Marks, Juanita Perez, and John Lavic earned this honor by placing first in the statewide competition held at the Omaha Convention Center. Marks competed in telecommunications, Perez in marketing, and Lavic in accounting. Ms. Kelly Wyatt is the club's sponsor. ### — 61, 77, 91, 104

## 55C • 15
## Technique

1. Key lines 1-16 SS; DS between 2-line groups.

2. Key a 1' writing on each of lines 2, 4, and 6; find and compare *gwam* on the 3 writings.

3. If time permits, key additional 1' writings on the two slowest lines.

### *Technique goals*

- fingers deeply curved and upright
- quick-snap keystrokes
- hands/arms quiet, almost motionless
- unused fingers curved over home keys

| | | |
|---|---|---|
| word response | 1 | and for pen got map six they worn fish when risk than gowns ivory |
| | 2 | They may make the amendment to the title form for their neighbor. |
| letter response | 3 | my we in as you few join case upon areas onion reads union grades |
| | 4 | As you saw, my union drew upon a few area data in a gas tax case. |
| combination response | 5 | and you\|for him\|man was\|pay him\|they were\|with care\|to you or him |
| | 6 | It was up to you or him to read and amend the audit form by noon. |
| double letters | 7 | mall cuff will soon meek door need seeks books sells peeks little |
| | 8 | Ann will take all her old cookbooks to sell at the school bazaar. |
| adjacent keys | 9 | her top saw ore buy went open coin spot skew ruin soil trot build |
| | 10 | Jeremy was to open a coin shop in a new store in the town square. |
| long direct reaches | 11 | fun gym any ice gun nut sum nice must curb deck myth doubt humble |
| | 12 | Cecil had much fun at the gym and the new ice center this summer. |
| outside reaches | 13 | lop pow zoo spa caps pawn spot oars wasp maps span slow aqua slaw |
| | 14 | Silas won a prized spot on our last squad that took a town title. |
| shift keys & LOCK | 15 | Marla Apple and Pat Cox will play Nan Epps and Larry Sparks next. |
| | 16 | Sophie works in Boston for NBC; Paula works in Nantucket for CBS. |

gwam 1' | 1 | 2 | 3 | 4 | 5 | 6 | 7 | 8 | 9 | 10 | 11 | 12 | 13 |

## 55D • 15
## Timed Writings

1. Key a 1' writing on ¶ 1, then on ¶ 2; find *gwam* on each.

2. Key a 2' writing on ¶s 1-2 combined; find *gwam*, count errors.

3. Key a 3' writing on ¶s 1-2 combined; find *gwam*, count errors.

4. Key another 3' writing on the ¶s to increase speed or to reduce errors, according to your need.

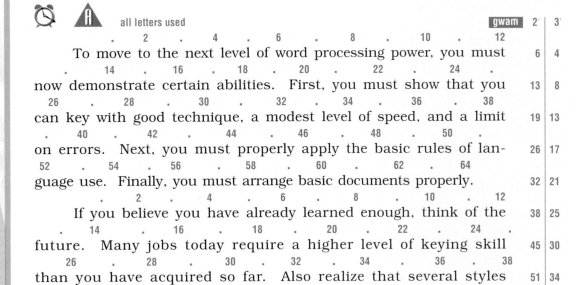

all letters used

|  | gwam | 2' | 3' |
|---|---|---|---|
| To move to the next level of word processing power, you must | | 6 | 4 |
| now demonstrate certain abilities.  First, you must show that you | | 13 | 8 |
| can key with good technique, a modest level of speed, and a limit | | 19 | 13 |
| on errors.  Next, you must properly apply the basic rules of lan- | | 26 | 17 |
| guage use.  Finally, you must arrange basic documents properly. | | 32 | 21 |
| If you believe you have already learned enough, think of the | | 38 | 25 |
| future.  Many jobs today require a higher level of keying skill | | 45 | 30 |
| than you have acquired so far.  Also realize that several styles | | 51 | 34 |
| of letters, reports, and tables are in very common use today.  As | | 58 | 39 |
| a result, would you not benefit from another semester of training? | | 64 | 43 |

gwam 2' | 1 | 2 | 3 | 4 | 5 | 6 |
3' | 1 | 2 | 3 | 4 |

**Document 1**
**Summary Minutes**
Format the text at the right as meeting minutes. Use format guides for an unbound report:

- Use 2" top margin.
- Use 1" side and bottom margins.
- DS between main and secondary heading.
- QS below secondary heading.
- SS and indent the body.
- DS above and below the side headings.
- You decide font face, size, and appearance; page numbering; and use of headers and/or footers.

words

WOODWARD HIGH SCHOOL BUSINESS CLUB                    7

March 2, ---- Meeting                    11

Participants:                                                           14

    All officers, committee chairs, and faculty sponsor attended.      27

Recorder of minutes:                                                   31

    Jerry Finley, secretary.                                         36

Call to order:                                                         39

    President Marcie Holmquist called the meeting to order at 2:45 p.m.   53

Reports:                                                               55

    Written reports from the following officers and committee chairs were      69
distributed, discussed, and approved or accepted (copies are retained      83
by the secretary):                                                     87

        Vice President/Membership Committee Chair--Accepted      98
        Treasurer--Approved                                    102
        Secretary--February meeting minutes were approved      112
        Fundraising--Accepted                                  116
        Community Service--Accepted                            122

Unfinished business acted upon:                                        128

  A.  Approved candy sale to begin May 1.                     136
  B.  Approved that Woodward High care for one mile of State Route      149
       163 as part of the community's Adopt-A-Highway Program.      161
  C.  Tabled the recommendation that the club help support an      173
       international student, pending availability of additional infor-   186
       mation.                                                187

New business discussed/acted upon:                                     194

  A.  President Holmquist appointed nominating committee (Sissy      207
       Erwin, Roberta Shaw, and Jim Vance).                   214
  B.  Approved officers to attend regional leadership conference at      228
       Great Valley Resort and Conference Center on April 12.      239

Next meeting and adjournment:                                          245

  A.  Next meeting is April 3 at 2:45 p.m. in Room 103.      256
  B.  Meeting adjourned at 4:10 p.m.                          263

**Document 2**
**Summary Minutes**

Format the minutes on the next page as an unbound report. Follow the format guides given for Document 1 above.

# Language & Writing Skills 6

## Activity 1:

1. Study the spelling/definitions of the words in the color block at right.
2. Key line 1 (the **Learn** line), noting the proper choice and spelling of words.
3. Key lines 2-4 (the **Apply** lines), choosing the right words to complete the lines correctly.
4. Key lines 5-8 in a similar manner.
5. Check the accuracy of your copy; rekey lines that still contain word-choice/spelling errors.

### Choose the right word

**their** (pron) belonging to them
**there** (adv/pron) in or at that place; word used to introduce a sentence or clause
**they're** (contr) a contracted form of *they are*

**to** (prep/adj) used to indicate action, relation, distance, direction
**too** (adv) besides; also; to excessive degree
**two** (pron/adj) one plus one in number

Learn 1 They're to be there to present their plans for the new building.
Apply 2 Were you (their/there/they're) for the large fireworks display?
Apply 3 Do you believe (their/there/they're) going to elect her as mayor?
Apply 4 In (their/there/they're) opinion, the decision was quite unfair.

Learn 5 Is it too late for us to go to the two o'clock movie today?
Apply 6 I am (to/too/two) give everyone (to/too/two) bowls of beef soup.
Apply 7 We are going (to/too/two) the opera; Stan is going, (to/too/two).
Apply 8 She thought that (to/too/two) workers were (to/too/two) many.

## Activity 2:

1. Read the ¶ shown at the right, noting errors in spelling and word choice.
2. Key the ¶, changing all words necessary to make the ¶ correct.
3. Check your copy for accuracy; correct any remaining errors you find.

### Proofread & correct

That all individuals want others two respect them is not surprising. What is surprising is that some people think their do respect even when there own behavior has been unacceptable or even illegal. Key two the issue is that we respect others because of certain behavior, rather then in spite of it. Its vital, than, to no that what people due and say determines the level of respect their given by others. In that regard, than, respect has to be earned; its not hour unquestioned right too demand it.

## Activity 3:

1. Read the ¶ and decide whether the student's action was right or wrong (legal, ethical, or moral). Decide if stealing for any reason can be justified.
2. Compose a ¶ stating your views and giving your reasons.
3. Revise, proofread, and correct your ¶.
4. Key the ¶ at right as ¶ 1; key your corrected ¶ as ¶ 2.

### Compose (think) as you key

A student sees a designer jacket hanging over the door of a locker. No one seems to be around. The student tries it on; it looks great. He likes it and wants it. He reasons that if the owner can afford an expensive jacket, he can afford another one. So quickly the student puts it in his gym bag and walks away.

(Last Name) 3    412

Works Cited    414

Cook, S., ed. <u>Domestic Travel in Review</u>. Proc. of Travel    426

     Review Conference, 1986. Washington, DC: U.S. Travel    437

     and Tourism Administration, 1987.    444

Dorsey, J. "Survey: U.S. Residents Will Take Shorter Trips    456

     Here and Abroad." <u>Travel Weekly</u>, 27 May 1991: 6.    467

Crossley, John C., and Lynn M. Jamieson. <u>Introduction to</u>    479

     <u>Commercial and Entrepreneurial Recreation</u>. 2d ed.    489

     Champaign, IL: Sagamore, 1993.    495

**Document 3**
**Prepare a Report in MLA Style**

Reformat Document 1 (Career Planning report) in 170C, p. 403 in MLA style.

Key the footnotes as parenthetical references; key a Works Cited page, adapting

the BIBLIOGRAPHY to the style shown above.

---

## LESSONS 174-175

## Reports, Minutes, and News Release

**Objectives:**
**1.** To process reports during sustained timing.
**2.** To prepare meeting minutes and news releases.

**174-175A • 5**
**Conditioning Practice**

each line twice

alphabet 1 Beth Vegas excluded quick jaunts to the town zoo from many plans.

speed 2 The man is to visit the widow when he works by the mall downtown.

fig/sym 3 Kaitlin renewed Policies #23-4598 (truck) and #65-9107-44 (auto).

**gwam** 1' | 1 | 2 | 3 | 4 | 5 | 6 | 7 | 8 | 9 | 10 | 11 | 12 | 13 |

**174B • 35**
**Process Reports: Sustained Practice**

**Time Schedule**
Plan and prepare ........... 5'
Timed practice .............. 25'
Proofread/compute
     n-pram ..................... 5'

1. Make a list of the reports to be processed:
p. 403, 170C, Document 1
p. 406, 171C, Document 1
2. Arrange materials for easy access. Process (in the order listed) as much of the two reports as you can. *Do not key footnotes or their*

*superscript numbers; convert the footnotes to textual citations.* Proofread and correct each document before beginning the next.
3. After time is called, proofread the final document and, if needed, print all completed work.

4. Identify uncorrected errors and compute *n-pram:*
*n-pram* = words keyed – (10 x errors) divided by 25.
Turn in work in order listed in Step 1.

# ACTIVITY 1:

**Flush Right**

1. Read the copy at right.
2. Learn the Flush Right feature on your wp software.
3. Key your name so that it ends at the right margin.
4. Key the lines in each group at the right, following the directions at the beginning of each group.

Use the **Flush Right** feature when you want a line of text (or part of a line) to end even with the right margin. Flush Right can be activated before or after text is keyed. If turned on before text is keyed, the text will "back up" from the right margin as you key.

1. Use Flush Right, then key each line.

This line is keyed with flush right activated.

This line uses flush right so that it ends at the right.

2. Key each line at left margin as shown, select (highlight) the four lines, and use Flush Right to align them at the right margin.

Massey Hall

Room 315

Phone: (715) 167-8045

Fax: (715) 167-8145

3. Key each line (begin at left margin); use Flush Right to place only the ZIP + 4 at the right margin.

375 Baker Street, Jamestown, New York 14701-7598

960 Pembroke Street, New Rochelle, New York 10801-3127

# ACTIVITY 2:

**Learn to Use Tabs**

1. Read the copy at right.
2. Learn how to clear and set tabs (left, right, and decimal tabs) with your wp software.
3. Clear the preset tabs.

Most wp software has left tabs already set at half-inch (0.5") intervals from the left margin. These preset tabs can be cleared and reset. Most wp software lets you set:

**Left tabs**
Left tabs align all text evenly at the left by placing the text you key to the right of the tab setting. Left tabs are commonly used to align words.

**Right tabs**
Right tabs align all text evenly at the right by placing the text you key to the left of the tab setting. Right tabs are commonly used to align whole numbers.

**Decimal tabs**
Decimal tabs align all text at the decimal point or other align character that you specify. If you key numbers in a column at a decimal tab, the decimal points will "line up," regardless of the number of places before or after the decimal point.

*(continued on next page)*

take long vacations together.  As a result, weekend and long    222

weekend trips now account for just over 50% of vacation    234

travel (Dorsey .6).    238

The following table gives figures for business and plea-    250

sure travel that were reported by Cook (15-24) in 1987.    261

These figures serve as a benchmark for industry personnel to    273

compare today's business and pleasure travel with that of    285

"yesteryear."  Figures are reported for male and female    296

travel, mode of travel, and lodging accommodations of    307

travelers for both business and personal travel.    317

DS

Table 1    318
DS

Comparison of Business and Pleasure Travel    327
DS

---------------------------------------------------------------    340
DS

| Category | Business Travel | Pleasure Travel |    |
|----------|-----------------|-----------------|----|
|          |                 |                 | 348 |

DS

---------------------------------------------------------------    361

DS

| Men | 61% | 50% | 364 |
| Women | 39% | 50% | 366 |
| Personal car | 50% | 73% | 371 |
| Plane | 42% | 21% | 373 |
| Rental car | 15% | 6% | 377 |
| Stayed in hotel/motel | 71% | 39% | 383 |
| Stayed in private home | 18% | 48% | 389 |
| Other (R.V., condo, etc.) | 11% | 13% | 396 |

---------------------------------------------------------------    409

[wp] **note:**
Using the Table format feature, specify no rules, or lines, to make your table look like the original.

(continued on next page)

4. Set a left tab at 1.5", a right tab at 3.5", and a decimal tab at 4.5".
5. Key the first 3 lines using these tab settings.
6. Reset tabs: left tab at 2", right tab at 5", decimal tab at 6".
7. Key the last 3 lines, using the Step 6 tab settings.

| Left tab at 1.5" | Right tab at 3.5" | Decimal tab at 4.5" |
|---|---|---|
| Mary Hale | 45,789 | 1345.9076 |
| Susan Huff | 5,632 | 1.09 |
| Jim Rust | 45 | 23.07689 |

| Left tab at 2" | Right tab at 5" | Decimal tab at 6" |
|---|---|---|
| Gwen Russell | 9,010 | .056 |
| Brit Trent | 143,978 | 243.1 |
| John Oravetz | 2,587 | 1.1 |

# ACTIVITY 3:

## Paragraph and Hanging Indent

1. Read the copy at right.
2. Learn how to key indented items using your wp software.
3. Key the ¶ at the right below three times SS: first without indention; then indented; finally, hanging indented.

Use the **Paragraph Indent** feature to move a complete paragraph one tab position to the right. When the Paragraph Indent feature is used, your text will wrap around to this tab position, instead of to the left margin. Use the **Hanging Indent** feature to move all but the first line of a paragraph one tab stop to the right. The first line begins at the left margin, but all other lines in the paragraph wrap around to the tab position.

| Blocked (Unindented Text) | This example shows text that is not indented from the left margin. All lines begin at the left margin. Xxxxxxxxxxxxxxxxxxxxxxxxxxxxxxxxxxxxxxxxxxx xxxxxxxxxxxxxxxxxxxxxxxxxxxxxxxxxx. |
|---|---|
| Indented Text (Paragraph Indent) | This example shows text that is indented from the left margin. Notice that all lines begin at the indention point. Xxxxxxxxxxx xxxxxxxxxxxxxxxxxxxxxxxxxxxxxx. |
| Hanging-Indented Text | This example shows hanging indent. Notice that the first line begins at the left margin but the remaining lines begin at the indention point. Xxxxxxxxxxxxxx xxxxxxx. |

This paragraph is the one you are to key three times. The first time, key it without indenting (1" SMs and SS). The second time you key it, indent all lines so that they begin evenly at the first (default) tab setting. The third time you key the paragraph, use hanging indent so that the first line begins at the left margin and all others begin at the first (default) tab setting.

**Document 2**
**Report in MLA Style**
1. If needed, review the content of the outline in Document 1.
2. Key the information at the right and on the next two pages, including the "Works Cited" page, as a report formatted in MLA style.
3. Correct errors.

(Last Name) 1                    2

First and Last Name                    7

Your Teacher's Name                    11

United States History                    14

8 April ----                    17

## Growth and Development of the Travel Industry    26

Growth in the travel industry has paralleled the growth    37
in the transportation industry.  Developments in the transpor-    50
tation industry have cut travel time and increased comfort    62
greatly in the past 200 years.    68

In the early 1800s, a business person would spend about    79
one month traveling by boat from New York to London or Paris.    92
Not only did this travel consume a great deal of time, but it    104
also often involved discomfort.  Today, business people can    116
travel in comfort between North America and Europe in a mat-    128
ter of hours by jet.    133

Pleasure travel has also seen remarkable growth and now    144
accounts for nearly 80% of all travel, according to Crossley    156
and Jamieson (220).  Notably, this percentage is up from    167
about 50% in 15 years.    172

A major social trend of the past 20 years has been the    183
increase in the number of married women who have entered the    195
workforce.  Many "two-career families" cannot find time to    207

*(continued on next page)*

# ACTIVITY 4:

## Hard Page Break

1. Read the copy at right.
2. Learn how to insert and delete a hard page break.
3. Key the ¶s at the right DS, inserting a hard page break at the end of each ¶, except the last ¶.
4. Use View to verify that you have four pages. If you do not, use Reveal Code or View to check that you inserted hard page breaks after each ¶.
5. Save the four-page document (WP2ACT4) or leave it open for use in the next activity.

Word processing software has two types of page breaks: **soft** and **hard**. Both a soft and hard page break signal the end of a page and the beginning of a new page. The software inserts a soft page break automatically when the current page is full. You insert hard page breaks manually when you want a new page to begin before the current one is full. When a hard page break is inserted, the wp software adjusts any following soft page breaks so that those pages will be full before a new one is started. Hard page breaks do not move unless you move them. If you want to change the location of a hard page break, you can either delete it and let the wp software insert soft page breaks at appropriate places, or insert a new page break(s) where you want.

Send the membership roster to each student in the sixth, seventh, and eighth grades. Direct students to return the roster with their dues within 15 days.

Collect the candy sale money from the members in Homerooms 101, 102, 105, and 203. Deposit the money in the Club's savings account.

Invite all teachers to the Club's annual open house in the main auditorium on Friday evening at 7:30 and Saturday morning at 9:30.

Send thank-you notes to the local business leaders who donated food and clothing for the Club's annual drive for needy children in the school district.

# ACTIVITY 5:

## Numbering Pages

1. Read the copy at right.
2. Learn how to number (and suppress page numbers) with your wp software.
3. Retrieve the document created in Activity 4.
4. Number all four pages with the page number in the upper-right corner (flush right), without the word "Page."
5. Suppress the number on page 1.
6. Use View to verify that the page numbers have been added (pages 2-4) or suppressed (page 1).

Use **Page Numbering** to select the type of page numbers you want and to place them in specific locations on the printed page. Most wp software permits the use of text with the number (such as *Page 2*) and allows you to select the kind of number or letter (Arabic numerals—1, 2, 3, etc.; lowercase Roman numerals—i, ii, iii, etc.; uppercase Roman numerals—I, II, III, etc.; uppercase letters–A, B, C, etc; or lowercase letters–a, b, c, etc.). You can usually place numbers at the top or bottom of the page aligned at the left margin, center, or right margin. Often you will need to keep a number from printing on a page (such as the first page of a school report). The feature that keeps a page number from printing (or appearing in view) is called **Suppress** or **Hide**.

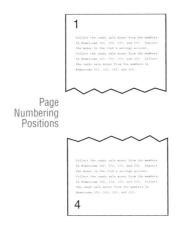

Page Numbering Positions

# Reports (MLA Format)

**Objectives:**

**1.** Prepare an outline in MLA format.

**2.** Learn to prepare a report using MLA format.

## 173A • 5
### Conditioning Practice

each line twice

| | | |
|---|---|---|
| alphabet | 1 | Kay Gazbo is not exempt from equal justice if she violated a law. |
| speed | 2 | To their dismay, the haughty man kept the dog by the city kennel. |
| figures | 3 | Order monitor 4103, printer 5278, and CPU 3956 for the registrar. |
| **gwam** | 1' | 1 \| 2 \| 3 \| 4 \| 5 \| 6 \| 7 \| 8 \| 9 \| 10 \| 11 \| 12 \| 13 \| |

## **F** ORMATTING

## 173B • 45

**Document 1**
**MLA-Style Outline**

1. Prepare the text at the right as an outline, TM 1", DS all lines. Ensure that the outline fits one page.

2. Read and study the information presented for use in Documents 2 and 3.

| | words |
|---|---|
| MAJOR FEATURES OF MLA STYLE | 6 |

I.   Margins — 8

   A.   All pages--top margin is 0.5" (last name and page #). — 20

   B.   All pages--side and bottom margins are 1". — 29

II.   Spacing--double-space entire report, including long quotations, enumerations, and list of works cited (references). — 43 / 54

III.   Indentions — 57

   A.   Paragraphs--indent first line 0.5" from left margin (or use first default tab setting). — 70 / 75

   B.   Long quotations--indent 1" from left margin (or use second default tab setting). — 88 / 93

IV.   Page numbers — 97

   A.   Location--place in upper-right corner on each page on line 3 (or use default top margin) flush right. — 109 / 117

   B.   Contents--key your last name and the page number (on a word processor, set up a header for this). — 130 / 139

   C.   Spacing--double-space below the page number and begin or continue the text (automatic if a header is used). — 150 / 161

V.   Tables within reports — 167

   A.   Placement--place table as near as possible to the part of the text that it illustrates. — 178 / 185

   B.   Identification--identify table with a title and number (Table 1) and a caption (heading). — 196 / 204

   C.   Location--key title and number and caption above the table flush left using initial caps and double spacing. — 215 / 226

VI.   Binding--secure all pages at the upper left. — 235

## ACTIVITY 6:

**Speller**

1. Read the copy at right.
2. Learn to use your wp software's Speller.
3. Open TWP2-6.
4. Use the Speller to identify words spelled incorrectly and words not in your speller's dictionary. Correct all errors detected by editing or selecting a replacement offered by the Speller.
5. Proofread after Speller is used to verify accuracy of copy. Correct any errors detected.

Use the **Speller** to check words, documents, or parts of documents for misspellings. A Speller checks a document by comparing each word in the document to words in its dictionary(ies). If the Speller finds a word in your document that is not identical to one in its dictionary(ies), the word is displayed in a dialog box. Usually the Speller lists words it "believes" are likely corrections (replacements) for the displayed word. When a word is displayed, you must make a selection:

1. Retain the spelling of the word as it is displayed in the dialog box and add it to the Speller's dictionary.
2. Replace a misspelled word that is displayed with a correctly spelled word offered by the Speller.
3. Replace a misspelled word that is displayed by editing it if the Speller does not list the correctly spelled replacement.

Spellers often use similar procedures for checking repeated words and/or irregular capitalization.

**Note:** The copy in TWP2-6 contains 11 errors. Can the Speller find all of them? Can you?

## ACTIVITY 7:

**Apply What You Have Learned**

Key the information at the right as shown DS.

| | |
|---|---|
| Harvey Bubb-Clark | Associate Professor of History |
| Mary Deerfield | Professor of Education |
| Jose Emanuel | Assistant Professor of Computer Science |
| Maria Spanola | Professor of Quantitative Science |

## ACTIVITY 8:

**Apply What You Have Learned**

1. Set LM at 2"; clear tabs.
2. Set a left tab at 3.5", a right tab at 4.5", and a decimal tab at 6".
3. Key the text at right DS, striking **Tab** or **Enter** as shown to move to the next column.
4. Reset LM at 1"; clear tabs.
5. Set a left tab at 2.25", a right tab at 3.25", and a decimal tab at 4.75".
6. Rekey the columns.

| | | | | | | |
|---|---|---|---|---|---|---|
| Hydrogen | (Tab) | H | (Tab) | 1 | (Tab) | 1.008 |
| Helium | (Tab) | He | (Tab) | 2 | (Tab) | 4.003 |
| Titanium | | Ti | | 22 | | 47.9 |
| Silver | | Ag | | 47 | | 107.87 |
| Lead | | Pb | | 82 | | 207.2 |
| Radium | | Ra | | 88 | | 226.03 |
| Uranium | | U | | 92 | | 238.03 |

(Enter appears after 1.008 and 4.003)

☎ The importance of honesty.    543

○ The consistent leader.[2]    549

Styles.  Styles of leadership, ranging from    558
autocratic to democratic, will be presented and    567
than role-played in the seminar.  Participants    577
will be encouraged to try all styles and to adapt    587
leadership style to given situations rather than    597
to adopt one "best" style.    602

Much of this material will be based on the    611
work of Yukl, who explains leadership as:    619

. . . processes affecting the interpretation    628
of events for followers, the choice of    636
objectives for the group or organization,    645
the organization of work activities to    652

accomplish the objectives, the motiva-    660
tion of followers to achieve the objectives,    669
the maintenance of cooperative rela-    676
tionships and teamwork, and the enlist-    684
ment of support and cooperation from    691
people outside the group or organiza-    699
tion.[3]    700

_____    704

[2]Patsy J. Fulton, Office Procedures and    712
Technology, 10th ed. (Cincinnati:  South-    720
Western Publishing Co., 1994), pp. 372-374.    729

[3]Gary Yukl, Leadership in Organizations,    738
3d ed. (Englewood Cliffs, NJ:  Prentice Hall,    747
1994), p. 5.    749

---

**Document 2**
**Bibliography**
Format the bibliography at the right as the last page of the report in Document 1.

BIBLIOGRAPHY    3

Fulton, Patsy J.  Office Procedures and Technology.  10th ed.  Cincinnati:    18
South-Western Publishing Co., 1994.    25

Keeling, B. Lewis, and Norman F. Kallaus.    Administrative Office    39
Management.  11th ed.  Cincinnati: South-Western Educational    51
Publishing, 1996.    55

Gary Yukl.  Leadership in Organizations.  3d ed.  Englewood Cliffs, NJ:    70
Prentice Hall, 1994.    74

---

**Documents 3 and 4**
**Table of Contents and Title Page**
1. Prepare a table of contents for Document 1. Use side and ¶ headings as entries.  Insert dot leaders between the entry and its page number.
2. Prepare a title page for Document 1; use your name, school, and today's date.

TABLE OF CONTENTS

LEADERSHIP SEMINAR PROGRESS REPORT

Harry Owens

West Beatty High School

September 20, ----

## ACTIVITY 9:

**Apply What You Have Learned**

1. Using Paragraph Indent, key the text at the right. (It represents a long quotation in a report.)
2. Using Hanging Indent, key the (encyclopedia) reference.
3. Use Speller; then proofread for additional errors.

---

Literature has two main divisions: fiction and nonfiction. *Fiction* is writing that an author creates from imagination. The author may include facts about real persons or events, but combines these facts with imaginary situations. Most fiction is narrative writing, such as novels and short stories. Fiction also includes drama and poetry. *Nonfiction* is factual writing about real-life situations. The chief forms of nonfiction include the essay, history, biography, autobiography, and diary.

"Literature." *The World Book Encyclopedia.* Vol. 12. Chicago: Field Enterprises Educational Corporation, 1993.

---

## ACTIVITY 10:

**Apply What You Have Learned**

1. Key each test essay question at the right at the top of a separate page SS.
2. Number all pages with "Page" preceding the number. Number page 1 at bottom center; all others at top right.
3. Use Speller to detect errors, then proofread.
4. Use View to verify that there are four pages.

---

Explain why people read literature; then explain why you do or do not enjoy reading literature.

Most every literary work includes four major elements: (1) characters; (2) plot; (3) theme, or statement; and (4) style. Briefly describe at least three of the elements.

Writers may use four kinds of discourse to tell readers what they want them to know: (1) exposition, (2) argument, (3) description, and (4) narration. Define each of the four discourses.

Essays, histories, biographies, autobiographies, and diaries are forms of nonfictional writing. Define each of the forms.

---

## ACTIVITY 11:

**Review Centering**

1. Center the lines at right vertically and horizontally. Use DS.
2. Use Speller and View to check your work before proofreading.

---

INFORMATIONAL BOOKS/GEOGRAPHY

Where in the World Do You Live?--Al Hine and John Alcorn

The Globe for the Space Age--Carl S. Hirsch

The Ashanti of Ghana--Sonia Bleeker

My Village in Brazil--Sonia and Tim Gidal

All About the Arctic and the Antarctic--Armstrong Sperry

This Is Hong Kong--Miroslav Sasek

---

## ACTIVITY 12:

**Review Move and Copy**

1. Set a right tab at 4" and 5" and a left tab at 6". Key the roster at right DS.
2. Select the words *Defensive Back*, including the space before them.
3. Copy the words on each remaining line of the roster.
4. Using Move, arrange the lines in alphabetical order by players' last names.

---

| Brandon James | (Tab) | 175 | (Tab) | 22 | (Tab) | Defensive Back | (Enter) |
| Bobby Lake | (Tab) | 165 | (Tab) | 16 | (Tab) | | (Enter) |
| Harry Schmidt | | 155 | | 37 | | | |
| Larry Schloat | | 135 | | 25 | | | |
| Jerry Packard | | 140 | | 26 | | | |

Use DS and standard formatting guides for margins, vertical spacing, and placement of report parts. Choose the font style and size, indentions, bolding, headers, footers, etc.

**Note:** To place footnotes using a typewriter, see the procedure on p. RG20.

**Proofreading alert:** There are 8 errors unmarked in the report body. Find and correct them and any errors you may make as you key.

|  | words |
|---|---|
| LEADERSHIP SEMINAR PROGRESS REPORT | 7 |

Development of the leadership seminars for supervisors and first-line managers is progressing on schedule. One seminar will be conducted at each of the 4 Indiana plant sights. The primary objectives of the seminars is to have the participants understand the following points: — 16, 25, 35, 43, 53, 61, 63

☞ The importance of having leaders at all levels of the corporation. — 70, 77

☞ The definition of leadership and how leadership traits are developed for use within the corporation and the community. — 84, 91, 99, 101

☞ That various styles of leadership exist and that there is no one best leadership style. — 108, 116, 119

**Seminar Presenter** — 123

Three staff members observed training sessions conducted by five professional training and development companies before selecting the firm to conduct these leadership seminars. — 131, 141, 149, 159

Selection. Derme & Associates, Inc., a local consulting firm specializing in career enhancement seminars, has been selected to develop and conduct the four seminars. — 167, 177, 185, 193

Reason. One reason for selecting Derme & Associates is that they will develop the content of the seminars around Keeling and Kallaus' definition of leadership,[1] which we want to emphasize with employee's. — 201, 211, 219, 228, 235

**Seminar Development** — 239

We have had two meeting with partners of Derme & Associates since the signing of the agreement two weeks ago. — 247, 256, 261

Meeting #1. The first meeting was held so that we could learn about the contnet of leadership seminars that Derme & Associates, Inc., has presented for other clients. — 269, 278, 287, 295

Meeting #2. The specific content of the four seminars were identified at the second meeting. Also, we decided to use the prepared content for each seminar except for the changes we suggest. These suggestions will be based on the feedback we get from the participants at the end of each seminar. — 304, 312, 321, 330, 339, 347, 355

**Seminar Dates** — 358

The first seminar will be on October 15 at the Logansport Plant; the second will be at the Muncie Plant on October 22; the third meets at the Fort Wayne Plant on October 29; and the fourth will be at the Evansville Plant on November 5. The 85 employees who are to attend will be notified of the dates and times by the end of this week. Instructions will be given for arranging coverage during the attendees' absences. — 367, 376, 385, 394, 403, 412, 421, 430, 439, 443

**Seminar Content** — 446

The seminars will focus on leadership characteristics and styles that are applicable to most work and community environments. — 454, 463, 471

Characteristics. The following four characteristics will be targeted for development: — 480, 489

✻ Social and environmental responsibility. — 498

✈ International awareness. — 504

— 507

_____

[1] B. Lewis Keeling and Norman F. Kallaus, Administrative Office Management, 11th ed. (Cincinnati: South-Western Educational Publishing, 1996), p. 46. — 515, 524, 533, 537

_(continued on next page)_

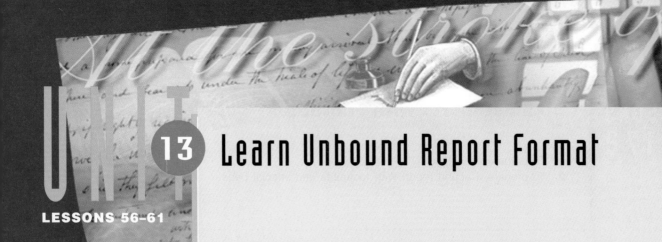

# Learn Unbound Report Format

## Format Guides: Unbound Reports

[report image]

Page 1

[report image]

Page 2

**Note:** If you do *not* have an Automatic Centering feature, use the back-space-from-center (manual) method to center report headings. (See p. RG19.)

Short reports are often prepared without covers or binders. If they consist of more than one page, the pages are usually fastened together in the upper left corner by a staple or paper clip. Such reports are called **unbound reports**.

## Standard Margins

Unbound reports have standard margins.

| First page: | |
|---|---|
| Side margins: | defaults (or 1") |
| Top margin: | default + 6 hard returns (or 2"–line 13) |
| Bottom margin: | at least 1" (6 lines) |
| Page number: | often not used |
| **Second page and subsequent pages:** | |
| Side margins: | defaults (or 1") |
| Top margin: | default (or 6 hard returns–line 7) |
| Bottom margin: | at least 1" (6 lines) |
| Page number: | top right (at default top and right margins; or 1"–line 7) |

## Internal Spacing of Reports

QS (4 hard returns) between report title and first line of body. DS multiple-line titles.

DS between side headings and following text and between paragraphs. Key paragraphs DS unless otherwise directed.

DS between page number and text on the second and subsequent pages.

## Textual (Within Text) Citations

References used to give credit for paraphrased or quoted material are cited in parentheses in the report body. The

textual citation method is rapidly replacing the footnote method because it is easier and quicker to use. Textual citations include the name(s) of the author(s), the year of publication, and the page number(s) of the material cited.

Quotation marks are used for direct quotes of up to three lines within text but not for paraphrased material or a long quotation (four lines or more) set apart from text. Key such long quotations SS, block them at paragraph point, and run the lines to the right margin. Use an ellipsis (. . .) to indicate any material omitted from a quotation:

```
The ability to proofread accu-
rately is one of the most im-
portant skills for . . . daily
activities that involve working
with written communication.
(Jones and Kane, 1990, iii)
```

## Reference Lists

All references cited in a report are listed alphabetically by author surnames at the end of a report (often on a separate page) under the heading REFERENCES (or BIBLIOGRAPHY or WORKS CITED). QS between the heading and the first reference.

Use the same margins as for the first page of the report, but key a page number at the default top and side margins (on line 7 at 1" right margin).

SS each reference; DS between references. Begin first line of each reference at left margin; indent other lines to paragraph point.

If the reference list appears on the last page of the report body, QS between the last line of text and REFERENCES.

# LESSONS 171-172

## Bound Reports with Footnotes

**Objectives:**
**1.** To prepare an outline.
**2.** To prepare a bound report with footnotes and special pages.

### 171-172A • 5
**Conditioning Practice**

each line twice

alphabet 1 Jimmy wants seven pens and extra clips in a kit for the big quiz.

speed 2 A goal of the proficient tutor is to quantify the right problems.

fig/sym 3 I sold 56 advertisements for $3,780 between 12/14/96 and 1/30/97.

gwam 1' | 1 | 2 | 3 | 4 | 5 | 6 | 7 | 8 | 9 | 10 | 11 | 12 | 13 |

### F ORMATTING

### 171B • 10
**Outline**

Key the information at the right in outline form. Correct errors.

|  | words |
|---|---|
| LEADERSHIP SEMINAR PROGRESS REPORT | 7 |

I. INTRODUCTION — 10

II. SEMINAR PRESENTER — 15

   A. Selection--Derme & Associates Selected — 23
   B. Reason--Derme & Associates' Definition of Leadership — 35

III. SEMINAR DEVELOPMENT — 40

   A. Meeting #1--Learned About Content of Previous Derme — 51
     Seminars — 53
   B. Meeting #2--Decided the Content of the Four Scheduled — 64
     Seminars — 66

IV. SEMINAR DATES AND LOCATIONS — 72

   A. October 15--Logansport — 78
   B. October 22--Muncie — 82
   C. October 29--Fort Wayne — 87
   D. November 5--Evansville — 92

V. SEMINAR CONTENT — 96

   A. Leadership Characteristics--Social and Environmental — 108
     Responsibility, International Awareness, Honesty, and — 118
     Consistency — 121
   B. Leadership Styles--Autocratic to Democratic — 130

2" TM

Title                ELECTRONIC KEYBOARDING APPLICATIONS

QS (4 SS; 2 DS)

Report body         Learning to key is of little value unless one applies it in preparing a useful document--a letter, a report, and so on.  Three basic kinds of software are available to assist those with keying skill in applying that skill electronically.

DS

Side heading    Word Processing Software

DS

        Word processing software is specifically designed to assist in the document preparation needs of individuals or businesses.  Word processing software permits the user to "create, edit, format, store, and print documents."  (Fulton and Hanks, 1996, 152)  The software can be used to process a wide variety of documents such as memos, letters, reports, and tables.

Textual citation

        This software has special features such as automatic center-ing and wordwrap that reduce time and effort.  It also permits easy error correction, format and sequence changes, and insertion of variables "on screen" before a copy is printed.  These features increase efficiency by eliminating document rekeying.

1" LM

1" RM

DS

Side heading    Database Software

DS

        A database is any collection of related items stored in com-puter memory.  The data in a database may be about club members, employee payroll, company sales, and so on.  Database software allows the user to enter data, arrange it, retrieve and change it, or select certain data (such as an address) for use in documents.

Textual citation    (Tilton, et al, 1996, 112-113)

At least 1"

**Unbound Report with Textual Citations**

(continued on next page)

3. Technical skills or work content skills that are ~~required to perform a specific job. These skills may 281
include keyboarding, accounting, computer operation, 306
and language arts skills.[3] *such things as* 310

Interests. "Interests are best described as activities you 385
enthusiastically engage in and find most attractive."[5] By 397
listing and analyzing *your interests,* them you should be able to identify a de- 412
sirable wrok environment. For example, your list is likely to 424
*reveal* indicate if you like to work with things or people, work along or 437
with others, lead or follow others, *or be* being indoors or outdoors. 450

Values. *Values* These are your priorities in life, and you should 322
identify them *stet* early so that you can pursue a career that will 335
*improve* enhance your chances to *acquire* achieve them. Some of the more obvious 348
*values* considerations include the importance you place on family, 358
security, wealth, prestige, creativity, power, independence, 370
and glamour.[4] 373

**Document 2**
**Bibliography**
Prepare a bibliography from the information given at the right as page 3 of the report keyed as Document 1. Use same format as that used for the report (Document 1) and continue using the same header and footer.

BIBLIOGRAPHY 3

Cunningham, William H., Ramon J. Aldag, and Stanley B. Block. <u>Business</u> 17
<u>in a Changing World</u>. 3d ed. Cincinnati: South-Western Publishing 31
Co., 1993. 33

Parks, Janet B., and Beverly R. K. Zanger. <u>Sport Fitness Management</u>. 48
Champaign, IL: Human Kinetics Books, 1990. 57

Scheele, Adele. "Deciding What You Want to Do." <u>Business Week Careers</u>, 72
1988 ed. 74

VanHuss, Susie, and Willard R. Daggett. <u>Electronic Office Systems</u>. 88
Cincinnati: South-Western Publishing Co., 1992. 98

2
DS

Side heading

<u>Spreadsheet Software</u>

A spreadsheet is an electronic worksheet made up of columns and rows of data.  Spreadsheet software allows the user to "create, calculate, edit, retrieve, modify, and print graphs, charts, reports, and spreadsheets" necessary for current business operations

Textual citation

and in planning for the future.  (Fulton and Hanks, 1996, 156)

Employment personnel look favorably upon job applicants who

(1" LM)

are familiar with these kinds of software and how they are used.

(1" RM)

QS (4 SS; 2 DS)

REFERENCES
QS

Fulton, Patsy, J., and Joanna D. Hanks.  <u>Procedures for the Office</u>

List of references

<u>Professional</u>. 3d ed.  Cincinnati:  South-Western Publishing Co., 1996.
DS
Tilton, Rita S., et al.  <u>The Electronic Office:  Procedures &</u> <u>Administration</u>. 11th ed.  Cincinnati:  South-Western Publishing Co., 1996.

# LESSON 56

## Unbound Report Model

**Objectives:**
1. To learn format features of unbound reports.
2. To process a two-page unbound report in proper format.

### 56A • 5
### Conditioning Practice

each line twice SS; then a 1' writing on line 3; find *gwam*

alphabet 1 Six boys quickly removed the juicy lamb from a sizzling stew pot.

fig/sym 2 Lenz & Company's phone number has been changed to (382) 174-9560.

speed 3 Six big firms may bid for the authentic map of an ancient island.

| gwam | 1' | 1 | 2 | 3 | 4 | 5 | 6 | 7 | 8 | 9 | 10 | 11 | 12 | 13 |
|------|----|---|---|---|---|---|---|---|---|---|----|----|----|----|

### 56B • 45
### Unbound Report

1. Read the format guides on p. 144; study the model report on p. 145 and above.

2. Key the model report using the spacing guides given on the model; proofread and correct errors.

3. Key the report again (at rough-draft speed) to increase your input speed.

## 170C • 35
## Process Reports

**Document 1**
**Unbound Report**

1. Key the text at the right and on the next page as an unbound report. Make changes as indicated; correct errors.

2. Insert footnotes listed below on the same page as the corresponding superscript number(s) in the text.

3. Insert your name (beginning at LM) and Page # (flush right) on all pages as a footer.

4. Insert the report title as a header on page 2 (beginning at LM in ALL CAPS).

**Electronics:**
Refer to p. RG20 to learn to format and place footnotes at the bottom of a page when wp software is not being used.

*Footnotes:*
[1] Janet B. Parks and Beverly R. K. Zanger, <u>Sport Fitness Management</u> (Champaign, IL: Human Kinetics Books, 1990), p. 140.
(Words = 25)

[2] William H. Cunningham, Ramon J. Aldag, and Stanley B. Block, <u>Business in a Changing World,</u> 3d ed. (Cincinnati: South-Western Publishing Co., 1993), p. 701.
(Words = 32)

[3] Adele Scheele, "Deciding What You Want to Do," <u>Business Week Careers,</u> 1988 ed., p. 7.
(Words = 18)

[4] Susie VanHuss and Willard R. Daggett, <u>Electronic Office Systems</u> (Cincinnati: South-Western Publishing Co., 1992), p. 529.
(Words = 25)

[5] Parks and Zanger, <u>Sport Fitness Management</u>, p. 141.
(Words = 11)

---

Career Planning *— bold & enlarge*   3

*QS*

Career planning is an important, ongoing process. It is   15

important because the career you ~~follow~~ *choose* will affect ~~your~~ *the* quality   27

of life and will help determine the respect and recognition you   40

~~will~~ receive. Throughout your lifetime you are likely to make   55

career changes (three or more) ~~times~~.[1]   58

Establish a Career Objective *— bold, enlarge*   64

One important ~~and early aspect of career~~ *early step in the* planning *process* is to   76

define *your* career objective.   83

Your skills and your knowledge would probably be useful in any of   96

several jobs. So, if opportunities for a particular job dry up,   109

*SS* you may be able to find another job elsewhere. The U. S. Office   122

of Education has identified 15 so-called "career clusters." Each   135

career cluster is a group of related jobs. When preparing for a   148

career, it may help to think in terms of career clusters.[2]   160

Complete a Personal Inventory *bold, enlarge*   166

Another useful step in ~~the~~ career planning is to develop a   177

personal profile of your skills, (values) and (interests).   188

Skills. An ~~analyses~~ of your skills is likely to reveal that   201

you *have* *many* different kinds ~~of skills~~   207

1. Functional skills ~~that~~ determine how well you manage   218

   time, communicate, motivate people, write, etc.   228

2. Adaptive skills ~~that~~ determine how well you will fit   *SS*  240

into a specific work environment. These skills include personal   253

traits such as flexibility, reliability, efficiency, thorough-   265

ness, and enthusiasm for the job. *D.S.*   272

*(continued on next page)*

# LESSON 57

## Unbound Reports

**Objectives:**

**1.** To process a play review in unbound report format.

**2.** To process an unbound report with references.

---

### 57A • 5
### Conditioning Practice

each line twice SS; then a
1' writing on line 3

alphabet 1 Dorn was quickly given a big prize for completing six high jumps.

fig/sym 2 Item #329 was sold by Zahn & Co. for $875.46 (less 10% for cash).

speed 3 A key is to name the right goals and to work for them with vigor.

gwam 1' | 1 | 2 | 3 | 4 | 5 | 6 | 7 | 8 | 9 | 10 | 11 | 12 | 13 |

---

### 57B • 45
### Unbound Reports

**Report 1**
**Play Review**

Process the play review
shown at the right as a DS
unbound report. Correct
errors as you key.

|  | words |
|---|---|
| PLAY REVIEW | 2 |
| by | 3 |
| Denise Jackson | 6 |

Carousel, the Rodgers and Hammerstein classic musical, has 18
been revived in a stunning new production at Omnibus University. 31

Students of Rodgers and Hammerstein's work will note the fresh 44
approach from the opening curtain.   Gone is the traditional park scene. 58
In its stead is a cleverly staged "mill" workroom complete with a 72
gigantic loom.   The scene rapidly changes to an amusement park with 85
a modern multicolored spinning carousel.   Also new in this production 99
are nonspecific ethnic casting, streamlined musical numbers, and 112
updated dialogue. 116

Carousel is one of the genre's first to use a serious theme.   The 129
story recounts the life of Billy Bigelow, a "barker" for the carousel. 144
Billy falls in love with Julie Jordan, a worker at the mill, shunning 158
the advances of the aging carousel owner, Nellie Fowler.   Billy then 172
loses his job, marries Julie, and becomes a "worthless bum," in the 185
opinion of Julie's friends.   Julie's pregnancy, the turning point in the 200
plot, forces Billy to evaluate his worthiness for parenthood. 212

Billy decides to turn to thievery rather than to work to get money 226
to support his family.   An ill-fated robbery attempt ends with Billy 240
killing himself to avoid being arrested.   The next scene finds Billy in 254
heaven, repentant and determined to return to earth to undo some 267
of the harm he has caused.   Upon his surrealistic return, he awkwardly 282
but effectively touches the lives of Julie and his daughter. 294

Critics have called this musical "out of date and out of touch" 307
because of its treatment of women.   Most notable is that Billy actually 321
strikes his wife and his daughter.   Their reaction to being hit is that 335
"it's only his way of showing affection."   In spite of this apparent 349
flaw, Carousel has found new life in this newly staged, artfully performed 364
production. 366

# UNIT 37

**LESSONS 170–175**

# Format/Process Reports

## LESSON 170

### Unbound Reports

**Objectives:**
1. To prepare an outline.
2. To prepare an unbound report with footnotes and bibliography.

---

**170A • 5**
**Conditioning Practice**

each line twice; then 1'
writing on each line

alphabet 1 Myra's expensive black racquet is just a wrong size for children.

speed 2 Claudia saw my hand signal to go right when she got to the field.

figures 3 Order 97-341 for 20 Series 568 storm windows was faxed on May 25.

**gwam** 1' | 1 | 2 | 3 | 4 | 5 | 6 | 7 | 8 | 9 | 10 | 11 | 12 | 13 |

---

**170B • 10**
**Outline**

Format and process the outline at the right. Correct any errors as you key.

**Notes:**
- Key Level 1 heads in ALL CAPS; DS.
- Key Level 2 heads with caps and lowercase; SS.
- Use 2" TM; 1" LM.

words

ELECTRONIC INFORMATION EQUIPMENT                7

I.   INPUT EQUIPMENT                                        10

     A.  Intelligent Data Entry Devices                     17

     B.  online terminal-oriented system                    25

II.  DIRECT-ENTRY EQUIPMENT                                 30

     A.  Optical Character Recognition (OCR)                38

     C.B. Magnetic Ink Character Recognition (MICR)         53

     B.C. Optical Character Readers                         44

III. PROCESSING EQUIPMENT                                   58

     A.  Mainframes                                         61

     B.  Minicomputers                                      64
     C.  Microcomputers                                     68
IV.  OUTPUT EQUIPMENT                                       72
     A.  Impact Printers                                    76
     B.  Nonimpact Printers                                 80
     C.  Computer Output Microfilm Equipment                88

1. Process the report as a DS unbound report. Correct all errors as you key.
2. Then, make the following changes:
   a. Bold the title.
   b. Format the references as a separate page.
   c. If Italic is available, convert book titles in the references list to Italic; delete the underlines.

words

PROOFREADING AND EDITING | 5

Proofreading is the process of finding and marking for correction any mechanical and content errors in a document. Mechanical and content errors include improper capitalization, excessive or inadequate punctuation, faulty number expression, faulty agreement of subjects and verbs, misuse of personal and possessive pronouns, inaccurate facts, and misleading statements. | 18 / 31 / 46 / 59 / 72 / 79

Editing, by contrast, is the process of checking a document for "wordiness, cliches, hackneyed expressions, logical sequence, avoidance of passive voice, improper spelling and use of words, and other things to make weak writing better." (Amsbary, 1994, 90) | 94 / 108 / 123 / 131

Proofreading Alone | 135

Usually you will proofread a document by yourself. If you are checking a paper copy, place that copy and the source copy side by side for easy comparison. Use a card on the source copy to keep you "on line" and use one index finger on the second copy to guide your eyes word by word. Pronounce the words as words, but read figures, symbols, punctuation marks, and capitals one by one. Read the copy once for mechanical errors, again for meaning. | 148 / 162 / 177 / 191 / 206 / 220 / 226

When you proofread copy on screen, use a card as a line-by-line guide on the source copy and use an index finger to guide the eyes along the lines on the screen. Read the copy twice: once for mechanical errors, again for meaning. Check all format features. | 240 / 254 / 268 / 278

Team Proofreading | 282

Team proofreading involves two people: One person reads from the source copy aloud; the other person reads and marks the other copy. This method is especially effective when statistical and technical copy must be checked. (Jones and Kane, 1990, 8) | 295 / 310 / 325 / 332

The person who reads the source copy should read each special symbol and punctuation mark individually. Figures, however, should be read in groups: Read 3891 as thirty-eight ninety-one. Read 2,845 as two-comma-eight-forty-five. Read the figure 0 (zero) as <u>oh</u> and the decimal point as <u>point</u>. Read .05 as point-oh-five. | 345 / 360 / 373 / 388 / 397

Proofreading is an essential skill for all business workers. Editing is an essential skill for writers and editors. The person who can do both well will be a highly prized employee. | 411 / 427 / 434

REFERENCES | 436

Amsbary, George S.   <u>Proof It!</u>   Cincinnati: South-Western Publishing Co., 1994. | 450 / 452

Jones, Ellis, and David Kane.   <u>Proofreading & Editing Precision.</u> Cincinnati: South-Western Publishing Co., 1990. | 465 / 474

## ACTIVITY 6:
**Superscript and Subscript**

1. Read the copy at right.
2. Learn how to key superscript and subscript text with your wp software.
3. Key the lines at right, inserting superscript and subscript text as you key.

A format frequently used in documents is keying text (letters, symbols, and/or numbers) in superscript or subscript position. **Super-** **script** places text slightly above the normal baseline ($x^2 + y^3$). **Subscript** places text slightly below the baseline ($H_2O$).

1 I needed to solve this problem: $(a^2 - 2ab + b^2)$ $(a - b)$.

2 I need to key $^{A}B_{C\ and\ D}E^{F}$ in this manner.

3 The radius of the sun is $6.96 \times 10^8$ m.

4 Calcite is $CaCO_3$; magnesite is $MgCO_3$; and gypsum is $CaSO_4 . H_2O$.

## ACTIVITY 7:
**Prepare an Outline**

Use the Outline feature to prepare the outline below.

### HIRING EMPLOYEES

I. ESTABLISH GOALS, AIMS, PURPOSES OF THE POSITION

   A. Consult Staff Members
   B. Determine Company Trends
   C. Establish Position Requirements

II. ADVERTISE NEW POSITION

   A. Professional Journals
   B. Area Newspapers
      1. Daily papers
      2. Weekly papers
      3. Sunday papers
   C. Personal Calls
   D. Placement Services

III. FORM SCREENING COMMITTEE

   A. Evaluate Applicants' Vitae
   B. Identify Top Candidates
      1. Contact candidate
      2. Check references
      3. Check credentials
   C. Invite Top Candidates for Interview
   D. Seek Committee's Recommendation

IV. MAKE OFFER

   A. Decide Top Candidate
   B. Make Offer
   C. Set Response Deadline

## ACTIVITY 8:
**Process a Report**

1. Open T-METRIC and use it and the directions below to process an unbound report.
2. Bold the main and side headings. Increase the size of the main heading by about 6 points; side heading by about 4 points.
3. Underline paragraph headings.
4. Format enumerated items as SS ¶s.
5. Insert these two footnotes at the places designated:

**Footnote 1** (at end of ¶ 1)

[1] Roswell E. Fairbank, Robert A. Schultheis, and Raymond M. Kaczmarski, Applied Business Mathematics, 13th ed. (Cincinnati: South-Western Publishing Co., 1990), p. 167.

**Footnote 2** (at end of main heading for table)

[2] The Information Please Almanac (Boston: Houghton Mifflin Co., 1994), pp. 426-428.

6. Use the Thesaurus feature to find suitable replacements for:
   - *instruction* in ¶ 2.
   - *activities* in ¶ 3.
   - *goals* in first ¶ after **Instructional Strategies** side heading.
7. As a header, insert the title (beginning at LM) on pages 2 and 3. As a footer on all pages, insert your name (beginning at LM) and "Page #" (flush right).
8. Protect Goals of the Instruction and following sentence from being separated by a page break.

# Book Report from Rough Draft

**Objectives:**
1. To key a book report in unbound report format.
2. To improve skill in keying from rough draft.

**58A • 5**
**Conditioning Practice**

each line twice SS; a
1' writing on line 3; find
*gwam*

| | | |
|---|---|---|
| alphabet | 1 | Zelma quickly put on a down jacket and gloves to fix her bicycle. |
| fig/sym | 2 | The rug costs $758.14 (with a 20% discount), but I had only $639. |
| speed | 3 | She may turn down the foggy lane by the shanty to their big lake. |

**gwam** 1' | 1 | 2 | 3 | 4 | 5 | 6 | 7 | 8 | 9 | 10 | 11 | 12 | 13 |

# **F** ORMATTING

**58B • 45**
**Book Report**

1. Review the proofreader's marks shown below.
2. Format/key the book report as a DS unbound report.
3. Key the reference list below the last line of the report body.
4. Then (wp only) make these changes:
   a. Use your own name in the byline.
   b. Italicize name of book in report body and reference list if Italic is available; delete the underlines.
5. If you finish before time is up, key the lines in 59B, p. 150.

∧ insert

— underline

⊂ close up

# add space

↑ insert comma

/ᵃ replace letter

≡ cap

∿ transpose

/ˡᶜ lowercase

∨ insert apostrophe

|  | words |
|---|---|
| BOOK REVIEW | 2 |
| by } DS | 3 |
| Colin Barker | 6 |

Homeland, John Jakes' formidable novel about the final explo- | 18

sive events of the *nineteenth* 19th century, is the first in a series that | 32

will focus attention on a new "Jakes " family, the Crowns. | 43

*Multiple* Many characters and settings are the norm for Jakes; how- | 55

ever, this story *rivets* focuses primary attention on Paul Crown, a young | 68

german immigrant. Paul leaves behind a Germany of cholera, pov- | 81

erty, and political upheaval only to face problems of equal magni- | 94

tude in america. | 98

Undaunted by a dificult ocean crossing, Paul arrives at Ellis | 111

island penniless but niavely optimistic about his future. He makes | 124

his weary way to the opulant home of his uncle, Joe Crown, a well | 137

established brewer in Chicago. Jakes used the Chicago setting as | 151

a back drop for his "class struggle" motive which is central to | 163

the plot of his story. | 168

Paul's uncle, Joe, and cousin, Joe Jr., are foils in this | 179

class struggle that ultimately fractures the Crown family and | 192

forces Paul to leave his Uncle's home tofind work on his own. | 205

The behavior and work ethic of Joe jr. who is born to wealth and | 218

pivilege in America, is justaposed with that of imigrant Paul. | 231

*Jakes portrays* The author pictures Joe Jr. as spoiled and without focus, espe- | 242

cially when compared to Paul's mature approach to life and work. | 255

*(continued on next page)*

## ACTIVITY 3:
### Protect Text

1. Read the copy at right.
2. Learn to protect text with your wp software.
3. Open files and protect the text as directed at the right.
4. View the documents to verify that all pages begin and end correctly.

Use the **Protect Text** features to keep text together on one page. (Some wp software provides Conditional End of Page and Block Protect features to protect text.) **Conditional End of Page** is especially useful when you want to keep a side heading and at least two lines of following text together. **Block Protect** is useful when you want to keep selected text from being divided by a page break. Block Protect is useful when a table or a table and its source note are to be on one page.

**Protect Text**

1. Open T-TRADE if it is not open and then ensure that the side heading <u>Other Trade Restrictions</u> is not separated by a page break from the text that follows it. Use the Conditional End of Page feature to keep the side heading with the sentence that follows it.
2. Open T-PROTEC and then use a Protect Text feature to ensure that the table appears on one page.

## ACTIVITY 4:
### Thesaurus

1. Read the copy at right.
2. Learn to use your wp software's Thesaurus feature.
3. Open T-TRADE if it is not open and find synonyms as directed for the words at the right.
4. Save document as THESAURU.

Use **Thesaurus** feature to search for synonyms (words with the same meaning) and antonyms (words with the opposite meaning) of words that appear in your text. If you find one that improves the precision and/or variety of your writing, the software will let you select it to replace the existing word in your text.

For these words in the "International Trade" report, use the Thesaurus feature to find synonyms for the following words. Replace each word listed below with a suitable synonym:

*market* (¶ 1)          *restrict* (¶ 3)
*restrictions* (¶ 2)    *limit* (¶ 5)
*device* (¶ 3)

## ACTIVITY 5:
### Footnotes

1. Read the copy at right.
2. Learn to use your wp software's Footnote feature.
3. Open T-TRADE if it is not open and insert the footnotes at the right in the designated places.
4. Keep text together as needed.
5. Save document as FOOTNOTE.

Use the **Footnote** feature to list sources or to provide detailed information about information in your text. Word processing software will print each footnote at the bottom of the same page as the reference to it. Word processing software permits you to edit, add, or delete footnotes and will make the necessary changes in numbering and formatting automatically.

1. Insert footnote reference at end of long quotation:

    [1] <u>Encyclopedia of Business and Industry</u>, Vol. 5 (Kansas City, MO: Landmark Incorporated, 1996), p. 401.

2. Insert footnote reference at end of 5th paragraph following the period after the word *employment*:

    [2] Parker Knepper, <u>Essentials of Modern Marketing</u> (Seattle, WA: Opportunity Press, 1996), p. 53.

3. Insert footnote reference at end of the last paragraph:

    [3] Alice B. Gardonio, <u>Dictionary of Common Business Terms</u> (Seattle, WA: Opportunity Press, 1994), p. 62.

Jakes utilizes the character of Paul to introduce the reader 267

to the flegling business of moving pictures.  Paul is facinated 281

with this new "art form" which involves him in many adventures in- 294

cluding war, a brush with daeth, and marrying his first love. 307

This first novel of the Crown sereis does a credible job in 319

setting the stage for future adventures of Paul Crown and his bud- 332

ding new family. 336

REFERENCE 338

Jakes, John. Homeland. New York: Bantam Books, 1994. (Paper- 351
back Edition) 353

# LESSON 59

## Unbound Report with Listed Items

**Objectives:**
1. To learn how to format listed items in reports.
2. To improve skill in processing reports.

### 59A • 5
### Conditioning Practice

each line twice SS; a
1' writing on line 3; find
*gwam*

| | | |
|---|---|---|
| alphabet | 1 | Quick, lively jumps of a gray fox will amaze both giddy children. |
| fig/sym | 2 | The 164 copies (priced at $18.75) may be shipped on May 29 or 30. |
| speed | 3 | Vivian may wish to make an apricot gown for the big civic social. |

gwam  1'  |  1  |  2  |  3  |  4  |  5  |  6  |  7  |  8  |  9  |  10  |  11  |  12  |  13  |

### 59B • 10
### Skill Building

1. Key each line once SS; DS between 2-line groups.
2. Key a 1' writing on each of lines 2, 4, and 6 for high speed.

| | | |
|---|---|---|
| space bar | 1 | of go by at in to am so me if on man buy pan yen can tam men buoy |
| | 2 | Any of you can go by the inn for a cool swim in the pool at noon. |
| word response | 3 | both dorm they with name pens turn flap mend when girl torn their |
| | 4 | I shall make them a big name panel to hang by a door of the hall. |
| combination response | 5 | they were them pump lend gave make gear pans jump form were ivory |
| | 6 | Six of you may join my trade panel at the big union hall at noon. |
| double letters | 7 | will soon meet door took sell week book heed hall cook zoom abbey |
| | 8 | Allen said a little more effort from week to week is needed, too. |
| outside reaches | 9 | well play game next walk past spot caps toss lost next pans plaza |
| | 10 | Lowell gave his old football jersey to a happy young man at camp. |
| long direct reaches | 11 | curb must brim gyms fume much cent nice runs myth guns lace lunch |
| | 12 | Brenda was under the gun to take a bronze in the county gym meet. |

gwam  1'  |  1  |  2  |  3  |  4  |  5  |  6  |  7  |  8  |  9  |  10  |  11  |  12  |  13  |

# ACTIVITY 1:

**Outline**

1. Read the copy at right.
2. Learn to use the Outline feature of your wp software.
3. Key the outline at the right using the Outline feature.

Use the **Outline** feature to organize and reorganize your ideas before you write the first draft of a report or research paper. Word processing software usually gives you choices for identifying the level of the ideas in your outline. For example, you can usually elect to use a predefined outline definition. Two common outline definitions are: (1) a combination of Roman and Arabic numbers and (2) uppercase and lowercase letters (I, A, 1, and a, etc.).

## EAR

I. PARTS OF THE EAR

    A.   The Outer Ear
       1.   The auricle
       2.   The external auditory canal
    B.   The Middle Ear
       1.   Auditory ossicles
       2.   Malleus
       3.   Hammer
    C.   The Inner Ear
       1.   The vestibule
       2.   The semicircular canals
       3.   The cochlea

II. HOW WE HEAR

    A.   How Sounds Reach the Inner Ear
    B.   The Inner Ear Sends Sounds to the Brain

III. CARE OF THE EAR

    A.   Preventing Ear Infections
    B.   Preventing Ear Injury

# ACTIVITY 2:

**Headers and Footers**

1. Read the copy at right.
2. Learn to insert headers and footers with your wp software.
3. Open T-TRADE and insert the header and footer at the right into the report.
4. View the pages to see the header and footer.
5. Save document as HDR-FTR.

A **header** or **footer** is text or a graphic (a chapter title, date, filename, person's name, company name, and/or company logo) that is printed at the top (header) or bottom (footer) of a paper. When formatting reports, headers are omitted on page 1. You can see the header and/or footer when you view the page or when the document is printed. Page numbers can be added to the header or footer (as you will do in this activity). You can edit and change the format of headers or footers (see *options* in dialog boxes).

1. Insert this header on p. 2 (name ends at right margin):

Summers High School              A History Report by Henry Settler

2. Insert this footer on both pages (page no. is flush right):

December ----              Page #

**59C • 35**
**Unbound Report with Listed Items**

1. Process the report in DS unbound format, all errors corrected.
2. Block the listed items on page 2 at ¶ point; let them run to the right margin.
3. After you complete the report, proofread it and make any additional corrections.
4. Place the references on a separate sheet.
5. Then (wp only) make these changes:
   a. Bold the title.
   b. Italicize book and newspaper names in the references list; delete the underlines.

words

THE VALUE OF WORK EXPERIENCE 6

A summer or part-time job pays more than money. Even though 18
the money earned is important, the work experience gained has a 31
greater long-term value when one applies for a full-time job after gradua- 46
tion from school. Job application documents (the application blank and 60
the personal data sheet) ask you to list jobs you have held and to list as 75
references the names of individuals who supervised your work. (Gieseking 90
and Plawin, 1994, 22) 94

As one young person was heard to remark, "You can't get a job with- 108
out experience, and you can't get experience without a job." That dilemma 122
can be overcome, however, by starting work early in life and by accepting 137
simpler jobs that have no minimum age limit and do not require experience. 152

Jobs Teens Can Do 156

Begin early at jobs that may not pay especially well but help to estab- 170
lish a working track record: delivering newspapers, babysitting, mowing 185
lawns, assisting with gardening, and the like. Use these work experiences 200
as springboards for such later jobs as sales clerk, gas station attendant, 215
fast-food worker, lifeguard, playground supervisor assistant, and office staff 231
assistant (after you have developed basic office skills). As you progress 246
through these work exploration experiences, try increasingly to get jobs that 261
have some relationship to your career plans. If, for example, you want a 276
career involving frequent contact with people--as in sales--seek part-time 291
and summer work that gives you experience in dealing with people. 305
(Hamel, 1989, 10) 308

How to Handle Yourself on the Job 315

Whatever the job you are able to get, the following pointers will help 330
you succeed in getting a good recommendation for the next job you seek. 344

1. Be punctual. Get to work on time and return from lunch and 357
other breaks promptly. 362

2. Get along well with others. Do your job well and offer to assist 376
others who may need help. Take direction with a smile instead of a 390
frown. 391

3. Speak proper English. Teenage jargon is often lost on the adults 406
who are likely to be your supervisors. 414

4. Dress the part. Observe the unwritten dress code; dress as 427
others on the job do. Always be neat and clean. 437

REFERENCES 439

Gieseking, Hal, and Paul Plawin. 30 Days to a Good Job. New York: 453
Simon & Schuster, 1994. 458

Hamel, Ruth. "Making Summer Earnings Work for You." USA Weekend, 471
2-4 June 1989, 10-11. 475

```
F1-Help!    F2-Edit    F6-Handling    F7-Lists    F8-Options    F9-Send

                    TO:  lesikar@gitnet
                  FROM:  morton@gitnet
                  COPY:  stickles@gitnet
            BLIND COPY:  gunther@gitnet
               SUBJECT:  NEWTON PROPOSAL
           ATTACHMENTS:  NWTNPROP.WPD
          --------------------MESSAGE---------------------

    Attached is the final draft of the Newton Proposal.  I will be
    presenting the proposal to Newton's Vice President for Business
    Affairs next Tuesday at Newton's Louisville home office.

    Please note that Newton has 30 days in which to accept or reject
    the proposal.  After 30 days, the price will be increased to
    reflect our new pricing structure that was adopted last week.
```

**Message 3**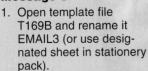

1. Open template file T169B and rename it EMAIL3 (or use designated sheet in stationery pack).
2. Simulate creating an e-mail message by keying the information at the right using the file (or sheet).

|  |  | words |
|---|---|---|
| TO: | ray@smtp {ray@psu.edu}, pena@smtp{pena@ovh.com} | 11 |
| FROM: | dillon@ritnet | 15 |
| COPY: | nolty@smtp {nolty@swp.edu} | 21 |
| SUBJECT: | USING E-MAIL | 26 |
| ATTACHMENT: | | |

————————————— MESSAGE —————————————    39

Here is more information about e-mail.  Most e-mail systems can auto-    52
matically read the address in the FROM line and use it to send a reply    66
back to the sender.  This feature eliminates the need to rekey the    80
address.    82

The reply feature is another time-saver on most e-mail systems.  When    96
reply is used, the message received (original) is displayed in an upper    110
window so that you can view a message as you respond to it.  The reply    124
message header (TO, FROM, and SUBJECT) is automatically completed    138
from the information of the original message, thus eliminating the need    152
for keying.    155

You can key a reply in a window displayed for the response or key it at    169
appropriate points within the text of the original message.  The latter makes    187
it easy for the reply recipient to reference your reply to the original text.    200

**L ANGUAGE SKILLS**

**169C • 15 Proofreading**

**(Word processing users only)**

1. Open template file T169C and rename it HILLSDAL.
2. Format the copy as a bound report.
3. Proofread the text carefully, making necessary corrections and changes.
4. Use software to check spelling and grammar. Save your final draft as HILLSDAL.

**Objectives:**

**1.** To process an unbound report with listed items.

**2.** To format a separate references page.

**60A • 5**

**Conditioning Practice**

each line twice SS; a
1' writing on line 3; find
*gwam*

| alphabet | 1 | Jane very quickly called them before swimming a dozen extra laps. |
|---|---|---|
| fig/sym | 2 | Debit her account (#73658) for $290.14 for December 10 purchases. |
| speed | 3 | Pepe may go to the shelf for the forms and then hand me the clay. |

**gwam** 1' | 1 | 2 | 3 | 4 | 5 | 6 | 7 | 8 | 9 | 10 | 11 | 12 | 13 |

## FORMATTING

**60B • 45**

**Unbound Report
with Listed Items and
Separate References
Page**

1. DS the report, at right
and on p. 153, as an
unbound report, all
errors corrected.

2. Block listed items at ¶
point and run them to the
right margin.

3. Place the reference list
on a separate sheet.

**wp** note:

You may, if you wish, bold
the title and reference list
heading. You may also
italicize book and periodical
titles in the reference list,
instead of underlining.

words

EFFECTIVE STUDY — 3

Effective learning depends upon good study skills, but "Many — 15
students--both traditional and nontraditional--entering college have — 29
few, if any, practical study skills." (Huber, 1994, 29) Good study skills — 44
do not simply occur; they must first be learned and then applied — 57
consistently. Efficient study strategies include a preset time, a desirable — 73
place, and a well-designed plan for study. — 81

A Time for Study — 85

Many of us think we have more to do than we have time to do, — 97
and studying gets shortchanged. It is important to prepare a schedule — 111
of daily activities that includes time slots for doing the studying you — 126
have to do. Within each study slot, write in the specific study activity; — 140
for example, "Read Unit 6 in Modern Writing, answer Questions 1-10." — 154
Keep the schedule flexible so that it can be modified if you meet your — 169
study goals early--or late. — 174

A Place to Study — 178

Choose the best place to study and use the same time each day. — 191
Doing so will help to put you in a study mood when you enter that — 204
place. Choose a place that has the fewest distractions: people traffic, — 219
conversation, telephone, TV, and outside noises. Usually study is best — 233
done alone in the absence of sights and sounds that distract the eye and — 248
ear. Force the mind to focus intently on the study task. (Silver, 1992, 26) — 263

A Plan for Study — 267

Research on the effects of specific study skills on student perfor- — 280
mance suggests that the following study tactics help to improve academic — 295
performance. (Dansereau, 1985, 39) — 302

1. Skim a unit or a chapter, noting headings, topic sentences, — 315
key words, and definitions to clue you to what you are going to study. — 329

2. As you read the material, convert the headings into questions; — 343
then seek answers to those questions as you read. — 353

*(continued on next page)*

# LESSON 169

## E-mail Messages

**Objectives:**
1. To learn about electronic mail.
2. To create e-mail messages.

### 169A • 5
### Conditioning Practice

each line twice

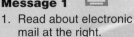

alphabet 1 Packy thought Dom's long joke about the next quiz was very funny.

speed 2 Eight was the divisor for half the problems Nancy did on the bus.

figures 3 The listing on June 5, 1996, had 87 cars, 24 vans, and 30 trucks.

gwam 1' | 1 | 2 | 3 | 4 | 5 | 6 | 7 | 8 | 9 | 10 | 11 | 12 | 13 |

### 169B • 30
### E-mail

**Message 1**

1. Read about electronic mail at the right.
2. Open template file T169B and rename it EMAIL1 (or use designated sheet in stationery pack).
3. Simulate creating an e-mail message by keying the information in the model on p. 398 using the file or sheet.

Electronic mail (e-mail) enables you to use a computer for sending and receiving messages, without printing them, that have a format similar to that of a memo. Most e-mail systems allow you to send multiple copies of a message to several people; reply to messages received; send priority, 1st or 2d class, and certified messages; and view, edit, print, delete, and save messages in much the same way as you do when using wp software.

E-mail is a network application. It is only available when you are logged into a network and have been assigned a mail account. The mail account authorizes you to send and receive messages, gives you a message address for sending and receiving messages, and provides disk space to hold your messages.

E-mail is part of the information highway that allows you to send e-mail messages from your computer to anyone who has an e-mail address on a system that your network can reach. This ability to connect networks makes it possible for you to use your computer to communicate with millions of people throughout the world.

While many different programs are used to create e-mail messages, most have certain features in common to facilitate the transmission of the messages from one network to another. A typical e-mail message includes a FROM line (the sender's e-mail address), a TO line (the recipient's e-mail address), a SUBJECT line (a short description of the message), and the body of the message. Many programs also include lines to identify the persons who are to receive copies or blind copies and to reference computer files (word processing, spreadsheet, or other computer files) that are to be sent along with the message as an attachment. The spelling and punctuation must be correct in the TO and FROM lines or the message will be returned to the sender.

**Message 2**

1. Open template file T169B and rename it EMAIL2 (or use sheet in stationery pack).
2. Simulate creating an e-mail message by keying the information at the right using the file (or sheet).

|  |  | words |
|---|---|---|
| TO: | burns@smtp {burns@psu.edu}, goth@smtp {goth@ovh.com} | 12 |
| FROM: | dillon@ght.com | 17 |
| COPY: | nolty@smtp {nolty@swp.edu} | 25 |
| SUBJECT: | NEED TO PROOFREAD | 30 |
| ATTACHMENT: | CHPTR5.WPD | 35 |

————————————— MESSAGE ————————————— 48

Proofread the attached file (CHPTR5.WPD) within the next ten days. Pay 62
particular attention to the text relating to each of the new figures (5.2, 5.4, 78
5.7, & 5.14) planned for this edition of APPLIED PHYSICAL SCIENCE. 92

Send list of recommended changes and corrected CHPTR5.WPD copy via 105
e-mail to each author and the editor. 113

3. If you own the book, use color markers to highlight important ideas: headings, topic sentences, special terms, definitions, and supporting facts. Otherwise, make notes of these.

4. After reading the material, review the highlighted items (or your notes that contain them).

5. Using the headings stated as questions, see if you can answer those questions based on your reading.

6. Test yourself to see if you recall definitions of important terms and lists of supporting facts or ideas.

A high correlation exists between good study habits and good grades for courses taken in school.

## REFERENCES

Dansereau, D. F. "Learning Strategy Research." Thinking and Learning Skills. Vol. 1. Hillsdale, NJ: Lawrence Erlbaum, 1985.

Huber, Rose. "Teaching Students How to Study." Eastside Weekend, September 1-7, 1994.

Silver, Theodore. Study Smart. New York: Villard Books, 1992.

## LESSON 61 — Three-Page Unbound Report

**Objectives:**
1. To process a multiple-page report.
2. To improve speed/accuracy in processing reports.

### 61A • 5
### Conditioning Practice

each line twice SS; a 1' writing on line 3; find *gwam*

| | | |
|---|---|---|
| alphabet | 1 | Buck can relax if he passed the major quiz with a very high mark. |
| fig/sym | 2 | You gave us 10% discount on Model #4736-A; 20%, on Model #8295-C. |
| speed | 3 | Roz may make a big profit if she owns the title to the lake land. |
| gwam | 1' | 1 | 2 | 3 | 4 | 5 | 6 | 7 | 8 | 9 | 10 | 11 | 12 | 13 |

### F ORMATTING

### 61B • 45
### Unbound Report

1. Process the report in DS unbound format, all errors corrected.
2. Place the reference list on a separate sheet.

**wp note:**

You may, if you wish, bold the title and reference list heading. You may also italicize book and periodical titles in the reference list, instead of underlining.

words

ETHICS, MORALS, AND THE LAW    6

The words "ethical," "moral," and "legal" are often misunderstood and misused. The terms are similar in that each refers to a human behavioral code. Human behavior is complex and thus no one term is sufficient to describe it. Ethical, moral, and legal issues also intertwine to create our entire understanding of behavior as it relates to our sense of right and wrong.

To further complicate matters, each civilization and culture (past and present) has its own notion of what is ethical, moral, or legal. Therefore,

*(continued on next page)*

**Document 2**
**Form (Primary) File**

1. Use the information at the right to create a form file that will be used in a merge that requires keyboard input.
2. Use block format with mixed punctuation.
3. Save the form file as PAGEFORM.
4. Merge PAGEFORM and PAGEDATA and save the merged file as PAGE-DOCS.

<Date>

FIELD<Name>
FIELD<Street>
FIELD<City,> FIELD<State> FIELD<ZIP>

Dear FIELD<Sal:>

The Accounts Receivable Department informs me that it has been unsuccessful in its efforts to collect (Enter balance here) due us for purchases made by you (Enter # of months here) months ago.

At the suggestion of our legal staff, we are writing to urge you to bring this matter to a satisfactory conclusion by sending us the balance due before the end of the month. Use the enclosed return envelope.

Please give this matter your prompt attention.

Sincerely,


Louis P. Page, Collections Manager

xx

Enclosure

---

**168C • 10**
**Process Letter**

1. Use block format; open punctuation, and full justification.
2. Send letter to **Mrs. Vera L. Bowden, 3491 Ross St., Minneapolis, MN 55441-5781**.
3. Supply letter parts as needed.

words
opening 17

What a pleasant surprise it was to find your $50 donation to Beta Xi in my mail this morning. I think it is great that you thought of Beta Xi and decided to help members of your local chapter serve those who are less fortunate. | 33 / 48 / 62 / 65

Your contribution will be used to purchase food and clothing for young children in our community as part of Community Day. As you know, Beta Xi, Minnesota Epsilon Chapter, conducts a fall drive to support this event. | 79 / 92 / 107 / 108

I have heard about the success you are having in microbiology. Perhaps you would return to speak to our Beta Xi members? Please let me know if you can. | 123 / 137 / 139

Yours truly   Miss Amelia R. Carter, Sponsor   Beta Xi, Minnesota Epsilon Chapter   xx   Enclosure   (postscript) A receipt is enclosed since your contribution is tax deductible. | 153 / 166 / 171

one cannot arrive at a simple, clear definition of what each term means. 125
The "meaning" of the terms is often dependent upon who is defining 138
them. 139

## Ethics 141

Many people who write about ethics use the term when referring 154
to the most general codes by which humankind lives; that is, those 167
codes of behavior that, for the most part, transcend time, culture, 181
and geography. In simple terms, ethics is the study of people's concept 195
of right and wrong. 199

Therefore, we use the word "ethical" when we are speaking of that 213
general code of right and wrong recognized by enlightened civilizations 227
from the beginning of time. When we ask the question "Was that act or 241
decision ethical?" we are asking if it meets the test of what is accepted as 257
universally <u>right</u>. Writers suggest that we consider such basic concepts 272
as honesty, fairness, and compassion as universal ethical values. 285
(Josephson, 1989, 42) 290

## Morals 291

The term "moral" speaks to issues that concern a community of people 305
rather than humankind in general. The study of morals also concerns 319
itself with right and wrong but more directly in terms of specific groups 334
of people. One may consider morals as specific rules of right and wrong 348
based on universal ethical truths. 355

Thus, we use the word "moral" when we refer to behavior that may 368
be acceptable for one society but not for another. Some people consider 383
as moral issues such things as treatment of children, the aged, animals, 398
and the environment along with questions about marriage and other 411
human relationships. (Purple, 1989, 66) 419

## Legal 420

Just as <u>moral</u> can be seen as more specific than <u>ethical</u>, <u>legal</u> is seen 435
as the most specific of the three terms. Laws are codified behaviors 449
for members of a society enacted by a specific lawful authority. (Gifis, 464
1991) The law may have as its foundation moral rules and ethical 477
truths, but it is closely allied with politics. As a result, it suffers from 493
greater subjectivity than do ethics and morals. Laws differ not only 507
from society to society but also from town to town. What is legal in Los 522
Angeles, for example, may be punishable in Portland. Laws are more 535
temporary than morals or ethics, often changed by simple majority vote 550
or by decree. 553

We use the word "legal" when judging an act by the most specific set 567
of local laws that have been codified by local authority. Issues as univer- 583
sal as theft and as specific as jaywalking are subject to local law. (Elliott, 599
1992, 28-35) 601

The terms "ethical," "moral," and "legal" are similar in the sense that 616
each refers to the interpretation of right and wrong. Their differences 630
depend upon how explicit and specific a description we use to interpret a 645
set of behaviors. 649

**REFERENCES**

Elliott, Carl. "Where Ethics Comes from and What to Do About It." <u>Hastings Center Report</u>, July-August 1992.

Gifis, Steven. <u>Law Dictionary</u>. New York: Barrons, 1991.

Josephson, Michael. "Ethical Dilemmas." <u>New Age Journal</u>, July-August 1989. (Adapted from Bill Moyers' "A World of Ideas." Public Affairs Television, 1989.)

Purple, David E. <u>The Moral and Spiritual Crisis in Education</u>. New York: Bergen and Garvey, 1989.

**Note**: See p. A17 for R & E activities for this unit.

## 167B • 45
### Letters: Sustained Practice

**Time Schedule**

Plan and prepare .......... 5'

Timed production .......... 30'

Proofread/compute

   *n-pram* ...................... 10'

1. Make a list of documents to be processed:
   - p. 391, 164B, Letter 3
   - p. 391, 165B, Letter 1
   - p. 393, 166B, Document 2
   - p. 394, 166B, Document 4
   - p. 392, 165B, Letter 3
   - p. 390, 164B, Letter 1

2. Process (in the order listed) as many of the letters as you can in 30'. Proofread and correct each document before beginning the next.

3. After time is called, proofread the final document and, if needed, print all completed work.

4. Identify uncorrected errors; compute *n-pram* (uncorrected errors times 10 subtracted from number of words keyed; divide result by production time). Put documents in order listed in Step 1.

---

# LESSON 168

## Letter Merge

**Objectives:**

1. To create a form file containing variables.
2. To perform a merge that requires keyboard input.

---

## 168A • 5
### Conditioning Practice

each line twice

alphabet  1  Sixty glazed rolls with jam were quickly baked and provided free.

speed  2  The auditor cut by half the giant goal of a sorority's endowment.

figures  3  Ted was born 1/7/42, Mel was born 3/9/64, and I was born 5/18/80.

**gwam** 1' | 1 | 2 | 3 | 4 | 5 | 6 | 7 | 8 | 9 | 10 | 11 | 12 | 13 |

---

## **F** ORMATTING

## 168B • 35
### Complete Letter Merge

**Electronics users:**
See Note below.

**Computer users only:**

**Document 1**
**Data (Secondary) File**

1. Use the information at the right to prepare a data file that will be used in the merge.

2. Use the following fields:
   - Name
   - Street
   - City
   - State
   - ZIP
   - Sal(utation)

3. Save data file as PAGEDATA.

**Note to electronics users:**
Use the information in the top two blocks at right to process the form letter (next page) to Ms. Kenney and Mr. Weisner.

---

**Ms. Paula Kenney**
**459 Rosegarden Rd.**
**Long Beach, CA 98766-4259**

*Dear Ms. Kenney*
*Balance: $576.50*
*Purchased: six months ago*

**Mr. Allan R. Weisner**
**935 Harper Rd.**
**Forest Hills, NY 10467-1298**

*Dear Mr. Weisner*
*Balance: $945.65*
*Purchased: ten months ago*

**Mr. Lawrence R. Aamont**
**523 Howard St., W.**
**Wichita, KS 67207-9183**

*Dear Mr. Aamont*
*Balance: $753.95*
*Purchased: nine months ago*

**Mrs. Wilamen A. Gross**
**543 Winterhaven Rd.**
**Pasadena, CA 91107-6173**

*Dear Mrs. Gross*
*Balance: $249*
*Purchased: four months ago*

*(continued on next page)*

## Skill Builder

### Skill Building

1. Key each line once SS; DS between 2-line groups.

**Goal:** No pauses between letters and words.

2. Key a 1' writing on each of lines 4, 6, 8, and 10; find *gwam* on each.

3. If time permits, rekey the 3 slowest lines.

| | | |
|---|---|---|
| space bar | 1 | am by an in ham urn buy ran dim any turn many dorm gown plan buoy |
| | 2 | All the men on the quay may go via bus to the lake towns to work. |
| shift keys | 3 | Jaime and Aida\|Rosa or Pablo\|Han & Fong, Inc.\|the J. P. Spitz Co. |
| | 4 | Alma and Max left with Rob and Juana on a trip to Padua and Rome. |
| adjacent keys | 5 | as guy are spot were open last part rent bids walk soil suit trim |
| | 6 | Luis was the last guy to weigh in before stadium practice opened. |
| long direct reaches | 7 | my any run sum ice gym nut gum tune much nice many curb vice guns |
| | 8 | Wyn broke my record to receive a bronze medal at the county meet. |
| word response | 9 | foam land corn lent risk town with pans when rock name than eight |
| | 10 | Both of them may wish to make a formal bid for the big auto firm. |

gwam 1' | 1 | 2 | 3 | 4 | 5 | 6 | 7 | 8 | 9 | 10 | 11 | 12 | 13 |

### Timed Writings

1. Key a 1' writing on each ¶; find *gwam* on each one.

2. Key two 2' writings on ¶s 1-2 combined; find *gwam* on each writing.

3. Key two 3' writings on ¶s 1-2 combined; find *gwam* and count errors on each writing.

4. If time permits, key two 1' guided writings on each ¶: one for speed; one for control (accuracy).

#### Quarter-Minute Checkpoints

| gwam | 1/4' | 1/2' | 3/4' | 1' |
|---|---|---|---|---|
| 24 | 6 | 12 | 18 | 24 |
| 28 | 7 | 14 | 21 | 28 |
| 32 | 8 | 16 | 24 | 32 |
| 36 | 9 | 18 | 27 | 36 |
| 40 | 10 | 20 | 30 | 40 |
| 44 | 11 | 22 | 33 | 44 |
| 48 | 12 | 24 | 36 | 48 |
| 52 | 13 | 26 | 39 | 52 |
| 56 | 14 | 28 | 42 | 56 |

all letters used

gwam 2' 3'

What is a job?  In its larger sense, a job is a regular duty, | 6 | 4 | 60

role, or function that one performs for pay.  Therefore, when you | 13 | 8 | 64

apply for and accept a job, you accept responsibility for complet- | 19 | 13 | 69

ing a series of specified tasks such as data entry, recordkeeping, | 26 | 17 | 73

and word processing. | 28 | 19 | 74

What is a career?  A career is a broad field in business, pro- | 34 | 23 | 78

fession, or public life that permits one to progress in successive | 41 | 27 | 83

steps up the job ladder.  Whatever the tasks performed, one may | 47 | 31 | 87

have a career in law, in health services, in education, or in busi- | 54 | 36 | 92

ness, for example. | 56 | 37 | 93

It should be very clear that a career may include many jobs, | 62 | 41 | 97

each with different ability requirements.  Realize, however, that | 69 | 46 | 101

many of the jobs leading to increasing success in most careers are | 75 | 50 | 106

better done with greater ease by people who have built a high level | 82 | 55 | 110

of keying skill. | 84 | 56 | 112

gwam 2' | 1 | 2 | 3 | 4 | 5 | 6 |
3' | 1 | 2 | 3 | 4 |

1. Use the following information:
**TO:** Mary Huarte
**FROM:** Bill Morgan
**DATE:** May 1, ----
**SUBJECT:** CAREER FAIR

2. Supply other memo parts as needed.

| | words |
|---|---|
| | opening 17 |

The Annual Career Fair will be held May 15 from 9 a.m. to 12:30 p.m. in Gymnasium A. A list of the 20 employers who will attend is enclosed. The employers represent many different industries, and each has a variety of career opportunities to offer our graduates.

Please announce the career fair in your classes and urge all junior and senior students to attend and speak to as many of the employers as possible. To ensure that your students speak to many employers, have them get signatures of the employers they visit and turn them in to you.

It is important that students dress and act appropriately for the career fair. Standard or casual business dress is suggested, and students should have up-to-date resumes for the employers. Also, remind your students that using correct grammar, speaking in a clear voice, and avoiding the use of slang will help them create a favorable first impression.

| | |
|---|---|
| | 27 |
| | 38 |
| | 49 |
| | 59 |
| | 70 |
| | 82 |
| | 94 |
| | 106 |
| | 118 |
| | 127 |
| | 139 |
| | 150 |
| | 162 |
| | 174 |
| | 186 |
| | 198 |
| | closing 201 |

# LESSON 167

## Letter Review

**O b j e c t i v e s :**
1. To improve correspondence keying and formatting skills.
2. To improve proofreading skills.

**167A • 5**
**Conditioning Practice**

each line twice

alphabet  1  Zelda was quite naive to pack two big boxes with just fresh yams.
speed  2  Pamela kept the emblem and shamrock in the fir box on the mantle.
figures  3  Flight 4365 will leave Runway 28L at 10 p.m. with 297 passengers.

**gwam** | 1' | 1 | 2 | 3 | 4 | 5 | 6 | 7 | 8 | 9 | 10 | 11 | 12 | 13 |

# Language & Writing Skills 7

## Activity 1:

1. Study the spelling/ definitions of the words in the color block at right.
2. Key line 1 (the **Learn** line), noting the proper choice of words.
3. Key lines 2-3 (the **Apply** lines), choosing the right words to complete the lines correctly.
4. Key the remaining lines in the same way.
5. Check your work; correct or rekey lines containing word-choice errors.

**Choose the right word**

**vary** (vb) change; make different; diverge

**very** (adj/adv) real; mere; truly; to a high degree

**passed** (vb) past tense of *pass*; already occurred; gave an item to someone

**past** (adv/adj/prep/n) gone or elapsed; time gone by; moved by

Learn 1 Marquis said it is very important that we vary our attack.
Apply 2 The (vary/very) nature of skill is to (vary/very) the response.
Apply 3 As you (vary/very) input, you get (vary/very) different results.

Learn 4 In the past we passed the zoo before we marched past the library.
Apply 5 We filed (passed/past) the desk as we (passed/past) in our tests.
Apply 6 In the (passed/past) month, I (passed/past) up two job offers.

## Activity 2:

1. **Lines 1-7:** As you key each line, select the words that correctly complete the sentence.
2. **Lines 8-14:** As you key each line, supply capitalization where needed.
3. **Lines 15-21:** As you key each line, express numbers correctly.

**Proofread & correct**

1 (Its/It's) up to them to (do due) the work required by the job.
2 She is (to/too/two) small (to/too/two) play on the varsity team.
3 He (passed/past) the ball as the receiver ran (passed/past) me.
4 I (know/no) that team (lead/led) by (to/too/two) touchdowns.
5 More (than/then) an (hour/our) had (passed/past) by (than/then).
6 (Choose/Chose) the right one, since (your/you're) the leader.
7 I was (hear/here) when the boys sang (their/there/they're) song.

8 ms. pardo saw the eiffel tower in paris when she was in france.
9 the senior class had its prom at the skirvin hotel last year.
10 lucia, carlos, and ana comprise this year's prom committee.
11 we had a labor day picnic in hyde park, followed by a ball game.
12 "how often," she asked, "do you watch the boston celtics on TV?"
13 did you write the check to stephen p. kendall, d.d.s.?
14 we took wilshire boulevard to the beverly wilshire hotel today.

15 12 Drama Club members attended the meeting; 4 did not.
16 I took the six thirty a.m. shuttle; he met me at Gate fifty-one.
17 Towne Center is at 1 Oak Street; Sloan Tower, at 6 Kyles Lane.
18 Her article appeared on pages three and four of the last issue.
19 Answer Questions 1-10 on page nine and Questions 1-5 on page 18.
20 Our committee met in Room ten at two p.m. on November twentieth.
21 Mai-li checked the data in Volume two, Section five, page 293.

## Activity 3:

1. Study the quotations, considering the relationship between honesty and truth.
2. Compose/key a ¶ to show your understanding of honesty and truth. Describe an incident in which *honesty* and *truth* should prevail but often don't in real life.

**Compose (think) as you key**

Honesty's the best policy.
                    --Cervantes

To be honest . . . here is a task for all that a man has of fortitude.
                    --Robert Louis Stevenson

Piety requires us to honor truth above our friends.
                    --Aristotle

The dignity of truth is lost with much pro- testing.
                    --Ben Jonson

## LESSON 166

## Letters and Memos

**Objectives:**
1. To process letters and memos using various formats and parts.
2. To improve script-copy skill.

### 166A • 5
**Conditioning Practice**
each line twice

alphabet 1 Quent packed an extra big jar of very zesty wild apples for them.

speed 2 The ensign works with the busy official to right the big problem.

fig/sym 3 I tried this equation:  $7(12X + 140) + 5(X - 6) = 3(X + 50) - 98.$

gwam 1' | 1 | 2 | 3 | 4 | 5 | 6 | 7 | 8 | 9 | 10 | 11 | 12 | 13 |

## **F** ORMATTING

### 166B • 45
**Letters/Memos**

**Document 1**
**Letter—Simplified Block**
Format the letter with listed enclosures and postscript. Use full justification.

words

(Today's date)   MR YEZDI AMRAM   3903 NORMAN BLVD   BALTIMORE MD   12
21216-6513   REVIEW OF 1985 POLICY   19

It was a pleasure speaking with you this morning about your Provident   33
American life insurance policy.   39

Enclosed is a form that you can use to change the beneficiary on your 1985   54
policy.  Provide the needed information, sign, and return the form to me as   69
soon as possible.   73

I have also sent information on a new policy that we are recommending to   88
grandparents who want to help provide for their grandchildren's education   103
after high school.   107

ROBERT J. TRUE, AGENT   xx   (listed enclosures)  Form 1060-A   EduPro Policy   118
Pamphlet   (postscript)  I will be happy to review your son-in-law's in-   130
surance program.  I will call him to set up an appointment.   142

**Document 2**
**Memo—Simplified Format**

**Note:** See Memo Distribution Lists on p. 189, if necessary, for keying the receivers' names.

**Document 3**
**Memo—Standard Format**
Reformat Document 2 in standard memo format.

October 12, ----    Ted Kennesaw, Joe Porto, Joan Stewart   BUDGET   13
CORRECTIONS AND TRANSFERS   18

Ted, there is a need to make transfers from 126-862 to reflect correct   32
expenditures.   35

1.  June 25--$311.40 expense for Premiere should be charged to 133-862.   50

2.  July 14--$861.25 expense for Kelly Office Supplies should be charged to   65
998-821.   67

3.  July 29--$81.34 expense for Ace Lithographing and Printing should be   82
charged to 742-863.   86

Call me if you have questions about these transfers.   97

Mrs. Juanita R. Santos, Sales Manager   xx   104

# UNIT 14

## LESSONS 62–67

# Learn Simple Table Format

**Format Guides: Tables**

Three-Column Table with Source Note

 **note:**

The Table format software function is introduced on p. 299.

## Parts of a Simple Table

A table is a systematic arrangement of data (words/numbers) in rows and columns. Tables range in complexity from those with only two columns and a main heading to those with several columns and special features. The tables in this unit are limited to those with the following parts:

1. Main heading (title) in ALL CAPS.

2. Secondary heading in Capital and lowercase letters (C/lc).

3. Column headings (blocked).

4. Body (column entries).

5. Source note (at left margin).

6. Total line (indented 5 spaces).

The first tables in this unit consist of only a main heading and two columns of data. Later tables progress in complexity so that, finally, they include three columns and several of the parts listed above.

## Format Features of Simple Tables

The following table summarizes format features of tables and their parts.

| Margins | |
|---|---|
| Top: | 2" |
| Side: | equal |
| Bottom: | variable |
| **Line spacing** | |
| Headings: | DS below |
| Body: | usually DS; may be SS |
| Totals (if any): | DS above |
| Divider rule (if any): | DS above/below |
| Source note (if any): | SS; DS above |
| **Column spacing** | 0.4"-1.6" (4-16 spaces) |

## Centering Tables

For a table to be centered horizontally (side to side), the side margins must be about equal. Vertically (top to bottom), a table may be centered (about equal top and bottom margins), or it may begin a standard distance from the top edge of the paper. Tables in Lessons 62-67 will be formatted with a standard 2" top margin.

*If Automatic Centering feature is available,* use the keyline method of horizontal centering:

1. Center/key the keyline (the longest item in each column plus spaces to be left between columns).

2. Record the position of first character in each column; then delete the keyline.

3. Center main and secondary headings.

4. Reset left margin for first column at first position recorded in Step 2.

5. Clear all tabs and set needed tabs at other positions recorded in Step 2.

6. Key entries, tabbing from column to column.

Example (in 10-pitch monospace)

|  | 1.0" |  |
|---|---|---|
| correspondence | (10 sp.) | installation |
| 2.4" |  | 4.5" |

*If Automatic Centering feature is not available,* see Manual Centering Method on p. RG19.

## Aligning Data in Columns

Words in columns are aligned at the left. Figures, however, are usually aligned at the right or at the decimal point.

## Letter 2

Block format; open punctuation. Address the letter to **Ms. Paulette Humphrey, 9459 Darby Pl., Baton Rouge, LA 70802-8941.** Use today's date and an appropriate salutation.

|  | words |
|---|---|
| opening | 19 |

Mr. Marcus Hughes told me that you made an excellent presentation — 33
describing the activities of Wilson High School's Community Service — 46
Club at last week's Baton Rouge Chamber of Commerce luncheon meeting. — 60

You should be proud of this accomplishment.  One major benefit of — 74
it is that you have made a presentation to business and community — 87
leaders--an experience that should help you in your future professional and — 102
personal activities. — 106

I'm proud that you enhanced the reputation of Wilson High, and I hope — 120
you found the presentation rewarding. — 128

Sincerely   Ms. Janet T. Phlog, Principal   xx   c Mr. Marcus Hughes — 141

# L ANGUAGE SKILLS

## Letter 3

1. Modified block format, ¶ indention, mixed punctuation, and full justification.
2. Use today's date and address the letter to the attention of financial planners at **InVestPro, 3344 Reed St., Toronto, Ontario M5V 3B1 CANADA.**
3. Use an appropriate salutation and closing lines. The letter was written by **Mrs. Mary  L. Poe, Marketing Manager**.
4. Proofread and then use wp software to check grammar, if possible.

**Proofreading alert:**

The revised copy contains 8 unmarked errors; find and correct them as you process the letter.

1. Use a dictionary to check whether a compound term is one word, two words, or hyphenated.
2. Check for incorrect or inconsistent number expression.
3. Proofread text at least twice—once for content, again for mechanics.
4. Check subject-verb agreement.

## Letter 4

Reformat Letter 2 in simplified block format, supplying an appropriate subject line.

|  | opening | 24 |
|---|---|---|

InTrack is a sophisticated ^yet easy-to-use ~~investment man-~~ *financial* — 34
~~agement~~ *planning software* package with a version designed for Canada's *ian* financial — 49
planners.  The software ~~posts~~ *records* all client ^transactions^, *investment* track — 64
commissions, dividends, and interest earned; and create^*s* value and — 77
tax projections.  It ~~will~~ print^ *s and charts* reports on investment perfor- — 91
mance, portfolio values, capitol gains, and investment income. — 104

The mouse-supported menu-driven ~~user~~ *system* are powerful and easy — 195
to learn.  New users can complete the 5 practice ~~sessions~~ *lessons* to get — 209
started quickly and **than** use the Help menu^ *whenever the need arises* — 223

InTrack has over 50 specialized reports, each with full — 115
customization options and printing support.  InTrack ~~permits~~ *lets you* im- — 128
porting and export~~ing~~ files to^ *many* other financial planning software. — 141

InTrack can be used on any computer system that operates in — 153
a windows environment.  The computer must have^ *at least* a 486 processor, — 169
2 MB of memory, ~~and~~ 5 MB of available hard disk space, and^ *a* VGA — 180
graphics card. — 183

I have enclosed a demonstration disc that you can use to — 234
learn first hand how this software will make your enterprize more — 247
efficient^ *and profitable*. — 252

|  | closing | 264 |
|---|---|---|

| Keyline | Photography/Layout 2" | 1.0" (10 sp.) | Malik Fredericks 4.8" |
|---------|-----------------------|---------------|------------------------|

| Main heading | | NEW PERISCOPE STAFF | 2" (or line 13) |
|--------------|--|---------------------|----------------|
| | | | DS |
| | Editor | Kristi Stojko | |
| | | | DS |
| | Associate Editor | Brian Poole | |
| | | | DS |
| Body | Business Manager | Anita Solena | |
| | | | DS |
| | Photography/Layout | Malik Fredericks | |
| | | | DS |
| | Advertising/Sales | Xen Chueng | |
| | | | DS |
| | Advisor | Marcella Proust | |

Shown in 10-pitch monospace, photoreduced

**Two-Column Table Centered Horizontally (Table 1)**

---

## LESSON 62 — Simple Two-Column Tables

**Objectives:**
1. To learn placement/arrangement of basic table parts.
2. To format tables using the keyline method.

**62A • 5**
**Conditioning Practice**

each line twice SS; key a 1' writing on line 3; find *gwam*

| alphabet | 1 | Wex just received a quite sizable check from a big paper company. |
|----------|---|------------------------------------------------------------------|
| fig/sym | 2 | Invoice #14729 was paid by Gibb & Byron's check (#6058) on May 3. |
| speed | 3 | Roz may go to the ancient island city by the lake to work for us. |

| gwam | 1' | 1 | 2 | 3 | 4 | 5 | 6 | 7 | 8 | 9 | 10 | 11 | 12 | 13 |

**62B • 45**
**Two-Column Tables**

1. Study the format guides for tables on p. 157.
2. Learn to center horizontally, using the method appropriate for your equipment (see p. 157).

3. Study the model above: margins, column spacing, and line spacing.
4. Key the model, guided by the keyline and spacing callouts. Proofread and correct errors.

5. Key Tables 2-3 on p. 159 as directed there; correct errors.
6. If time permits, reformat the model above leaving 1.6" (16 spaces) between columns.

## Letter 3

Process letter in modified block format; no ¶ indention; open punctuation.

**Note:** When multiple enclosures are referred to in a letter (or memo), follow the word *Enclosures* with a colon. The enclosures are left-aligned about two spaces to the right of the colon.

## Letter 4

Reformat Letter 3 in block format and full justification; open punctuation. Send it to **Mr. Eduardo J. Camino, 2395 Duss Dr., Atlanta, GA 30349-2710**.

| | words |
|---|---|
| (Today's date)   Mr. Joseph P. Campuata   347 Lakeshore Dr.   Vancouver, WA | 14 |
| 98660-4296   Dear Mr. Campuata | 20 |
| | |
| Your copy of the consultant's report is enclosed.  Overall, the report is very | 36 |
| favorable; I am certain the few expressed concerns can be addressed | 49 |
| quickly. | 51 |
| | |
| Also enclosed is a copy of the matrix that the consultant has recom- | 65 |
| mended.   I agree with this recommendation and, therefore, request you | 79 |
| to complete the matrix for your area.  Return the completed matrix to | 93 |
| me by next Tuesday. | 97 |
| | |
| Thanks for your cooperation throughout this project. | 108 |
| | |
| Sincerely   Ms. Carla F. Evans, Director   Planning Group D   xx   Enclosures: | 122 |
| Consultant's Report   Matrix | 127 |

---

# LESSON 165 — Letters with Unmarked Errors

### Objectives:
1. To use a blind copy notation.
2. To improve revised-copy skill.

## 165A • 5
### Conditioning Practice

each line twice

| | | |
|---|---|---|
| alphabet | 1 | Jaxie amazed the partial crowd by kicking five quick field goals. |
| easy | 2 | Their visit may end the problems and make the firm a tidy profit. |
| figures | 3 | Call 375-4698 by April 27 to set the 10 a.m. meeting with Sandra. |

**gwam** 1' | 1 | 2 | 3 | 4 | 5 | 6 | 7 | 8 | 9 | 10 | 11 | 12 | 13 |

## **F** ORMATTING

## 165B • 45
### Process Letters

**Letter 1**
Block format; open punctuation

**Note:** When a copy of a letter is to be sent to someone without disclosing that fact to the addressee of the letter, a blind copy (bc) notation is used. When used, bc and the name of the person receiving the blind copy (for example, **bc Ms. Pat Day**) are keyed at the left margin a DS below the last letter part on all copies of the letter *except* the original.

| | words |
|---|---|
| (Today's date)   REGISTERED   Mr. Rick T. Parks   Gossett Junior College | 13 |
| 356 Ward St. Long Island City, NY 11101-3755 Dear Rick | 24 |
| SPORT ADMINISTRATION ARTICULATION AGREEMENT | 33 |
| | |
| Enclosed is an agreement for articulating Gossett's two-year sport manage- | 44 |
| ment associate's degree program with our four-year bachelor's degree | 62 |
| program.  Please review and return it within 30 days. | 73 |
| | |
| If you have recommended changes, Rick, note them on the copy you will | 87 |
| return to me.  If items need to be discussed before preparing a final draft, | 102 |
| I will call you to set up a meeting. | 110 |
| | |
| Sincerely   Henry J. Key, Registrar   xx   Enclosure   bc Mary L. Butera, | 123 |
| Attorney-at-Law | 126 |

## Table 2
Center table horizontally, 1.0" (10 sp.) between columns; DS throughout. Proofread and correct errors.

## Table 3
Center table horizontally, 1.2" (12 sp.) between columns; DS throughout. Proofread and correct errors.

## Table 4
See p. 158, Step 6.

| SPELLING DEMONS | | words |
|---|---|---|
| | | 3 |
| adequate | customer | 7 |
| appropriate | electrical | 11 |
| categories | eligible | 15 |
| compliance | employees | 20 |
| compliment | implemented | 24 |
| correspondence | installation | 30 |
| corporate | monitoring | 34 |

| MORE SPELLING DEMONS | | 4 |
|---|---|---|
| opportunity | prior | 8 |
| permanent | pursuant | 12 |
| personnel | received | 15 |
| participants | reference | 20 |
| patient | similar | 23 |
| possibility | successful | 28 |
| previously | sufficient | 32 |

---

## LESSON 63    Tables with Secondary Headings

**Objectives:**
1. To learn to center and space secondary headings in tables.
2. To format two-column tables with secondary headings.

### 63A • 5
### Conditioning Practice

each line twice SS; key a 1' writing on line 3; find *gwam*

alphabet 1 Cooks brought piquant flavor to exotic foods with zesty marjoram.

fig/sym 2 Orr's order (#30-967) is for 42 maps, 15 atlases, and 8 almanacs.

speed 3 The chair did signal the man to name an auditor for the big firm.

gwam 1' | 1 | 2 | 3 | 4 | 5 | 6 | 7 | 8 | 9 | 10 | 11 | 12 | 13 |

### **F** ORMATTING

### 63B • 45
### Tables with Secondary Headings

1. Review the procedure for centering tables horizontally (p. 157). Remember to have a 2" top margin on all tables.

2. Format/key the tables on p. 160 using the directions given with each table.

3. **Note:** Be sure to proofread and correct each table before saving it or removing it from the machine.

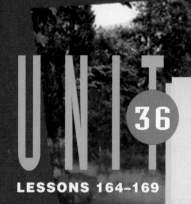

# UNIT 36
## Format/Process Communications

### LESSON 164

## Business Letters with Listed Enclosures

**Objectives:**

1. To list multiple enclosures.
2. To review block and modified block letter formats.

---

**164A • 5**
**Conditioning Practice**
each line twice; take 1'
writings on lines 1 and 2 as
time permits

| | | |
|---|---|---|
| alphabet | 1 | If Margorie has extra help, jigsaw puzzles can be solved quickly. |
| speed | 2 | The busy maid is to rush the clay to the eight girls in the dorm. |
| fig/sym | 3 | Tom mailed checks #398 & #401 to show he paid for Model #325-769. |

**gwam** 1' | 1 | 2 | 3 | 4 | 5 | 6 | 7 | 8 | 9 | 10 | 11 | 12 | 13 |

---

## F ORMATTING

**164B • 45**
**Process Letters**

**Letter 1**
Process letter in block
format with open punctua-
tion. Address it to **Mr.
Jason P. Curtiss, 233
Rhodes Ave., Detroit, MI
48226-5327**. Use today's
date.

words

opening 15

Dear Mr. Curtiss   I am pleased to inform you that you are likely to qualify 30
for Great Lakes College's advanced placement program. 41

According to your  transcript, you should qualify for advanced placement in 56
at least one beginning science course.  A final determination will be made 71
when your final transcript is received. 79

Please speak to me about your advanced placement options when you at- 93
tend the freshmen orientation program this summer. 103

Sincerely   Susan J. Hawthorne, Ph.D.   Head, Science Department 116
xx   Enclosure 118

---

**Letter 2**
Process letter in modified
block format with indented
¶s. Use mixed punctuation.
Address it to **Ms. Kim A.
Gimbel, 452 West St.,
Tulsa, OK 74105-3549**.
Use today's date.

opening 13

Dear Ms. Gimbel   The Forge Laboratories' Strategic Planning Committee 27
has been established, and subcommittees are now being formed. 40

You have been recommended for membership on the Chemistry Laboratory 57
Operations Subcommittee.  This subcommittee will establish a meaningful 71
linkage with laboratory workers and the Strategic Planning Committee. 83

I hope you will accept!  Your expertise in operations and keen interest in 98
planning are needed to plan a bright future. 107

Sincerely   Norm Landers   Vice President for Operations   xx 118

## Table 1
### Table with Secondary Heading
DS the table throughout, 1.0" (10 sp.) between columns

| OLDEST AMERICAN UNIVERSITIES | | 6 |
|---|---|---|
| (Founded Before 1750) | | 10 |
| Harvard | 1636 | 13 |
| Yale | 1701 | 15 |
| Pennsylvania | 1740 | 18 |
| Denver | 1743 | 21 |
| Princeton | 1746 | 24 |
| Washington and Lee | 1749 | 29 |

## Table 2
### Table from Script
DS the table throughout, 1.2" (12 sp.) between columns.

| FEDERAL SERVICE ACADEMIES | | 5 |
|---|---|---|
| (By Year Founded) | | 9 |
| U.S. Military Academy | 1802 | 14 |
| U.S. Naval Academy | 1845 | 19 |
| U.S. Coast Guard Academy | 1876 | 25 |
| U.S. Merchant Marine Academy | 1943 | 32 |
| U.S. Air Force Academy | 1954 | 37 |

## Table 3
### Table with Source Note from Rough Draft
1. Read the table, noting changes to be made.
2. Format/key the table DS, 1.4" (14 sp.) between columns.
3. DS above and below the divider line.

**Note:** A divider line is a series of 15 underlines (about 1.5"); DS above and below it.

## Table 4
If time permits, reformat Table 3 with 1.0" (10 sp.) between columns.

| ALL-TIME TOP GRAMMY WINNERS | | 6 |
|---|---|---|
| (With Total Awards won) | | 10 |
| Sir George Solti | 30 | 14 |
| Quincy jones | 26 | 17 |
| Vladimir Horowitz | 52 | 22 |
| Henry Mancinni | 20 | 25 |
| Steve Wonder | 17 | 28 |
| Loenard Bernstein | 16 | 33 |
| Paul Simon | 1 6 | 35 |
| John Williams | 16 | 39 |
| DS ←_____ | | 42 |
| Source: USA Today, March 3, 1994. | | 49 |

## ACTIVITY 7:

**Create a document doing the following:**
1. Open T-MARGIN and rename it JUSTIFY.
2. Change the 1st ¶ of JUSTIFY to full justification with initial caps.
3. Change the 2d ¶ to left justification with uppercase letters and a monospace font (10 or 12 cpi.).
4. Change the 1st sentence of ¶ 3 to a large font (15 pt. or higher) and bold it.
5. Change the 2d sentence of ¶ 3 to a small font (10 pt or lower) and italicize it.
6. Change ¶ 3 to left justification.
7. On or near the 6" line, key your name in italics so that it ends evenly with the right margin.
8. On the 7" line, center your school's name in bold print.
9. On the 8" line, use all justification (or center, if all justification is not available) and key the current day and date in shadow print.

## ACTIVITY 8:

Reference: p. 266.

1. Use the information below to prepare a data file:

Name: **Mr. Max R. Rice**
Street: **23 Oak St.**
City: **Schiller Park**
State: **IL**
ZIP: **60176-6932**
Sal: **Mr. Rice**

Name: **Ms. Diana P. Boni**
Street: **6450 Trouy Ave.**
City: **Chicago**
State: **IL**
ZIP: **60648-4712**
Sal: **Ms. Boni**

Name: **Mrs. Carol I. Yao**
Street: **600 E. Lake St.**
City: **Addison**
State: **IL**
ZIP: **60101-3492**
Sal: **Mrs. Yao**

Name: **Mr. Yoon-Yin Cheng**
Street: **1900 Manheim Rd.**
City: **Melrose Park**
State: **IL**
ZIP: **60611-6671**
Sal: **Mr. Cheng**

2. Name and save the file as HLTHDATA.
3. Key the form file below in modified block letter format with indented paragraphs and mixed punctuation. Save the file as HLTHFORM.
4. Merge HLTHDATA and HLTHFORM. Name and save the merged file as HLTHDOCS. Provide keyboard input as follows:

| Name | Coverage | Premium |
| --- | --- | --- |
| Rice | individual | $147.12 |
| Boni | individual | $147.12 |
| Yao | family | $290.25 |
| Cheng | family plus | $368.00 |

<Date>

<Name>
<Street>
<City,> <State> <ZIP>

Dear <Salutation:>

If the health plan you chose last year has not delivered everything you thought it would, we have some good news for you. Health Plus, the area's largest HMO, is now available to you during this open enrollment period.

Health Plus gives you access to the area's best doctors and medical facilities. Join now and you will be given (At the prompt, insert type of coverage here) coverage for only (At the prompt, insert premium here) a month.

To enroll, simply complete the enclosed application and return it to your benefits office within 30 days.

Sincerely,

Ms. Peg Murphy
Account Specialist

xx

Enclosure

**Objectives:**
1. To learn to format tables with blocked column headings.
2. To improve skill in processing two-column tables.

## 64A • 5
### Conditioning Practice

each line twice SS: a
1' writing on line 3; find
*gwam*

| | | |
|---|---|---|
| alphabet | 1 | Puma quit cutting flax when big jet clouds covered the azure sky. |
| fig/sym | 2 | I paid a $72.41 premium on a $5,000 travel policy (dated 6/3/98). |
| speed | 3 | Eighty of the city firms may form a panel to handle the problems. |

**gwam** 1' | 1 | 2 | 3 | 4 | 5 | 6 | 7 | 8 | 9 | 10 | 11 | 12 | 13 |

## F ORMATTING

## 64B • 45
### Two-Column Tables with Multiple Features

Format/key the tables as directed.

**Table 1**
**Table with Column Headings**

1. Key the table DS, 0.8" (8 sp.) between columns.
2. Block column headings at left of columns.
3. Correct any errors you make as you key.

**Table 2**
**Table with Multiple Features**

1. Key the table DS, 1.0" (10 sp.) between columns.
2. Block column headings at left of columns.
3. Correct any errors you make as you key.

| | | words |
|---|---|---|
| SUMMER READING LIST | | 4 |
| (Read at Least Three) | | 8 |
| Author | Selection | 12 |
| Dante Alighieri | The Divine Comedy | 20 |
| Charles Baudelaire | Les Fleurs du Mal | 26 |
| Robert Frost | The Road Not Taken | 33 |
| Victor Hugo | Les Miserables | 38 |
| Niccolo Machiavelli | The Prince | 44 |
| William Shakespeare | Measure for Measure | 52 |

| | | words |
|---|---|---|
| WINNERS OF MOST ACADAMY AWARDS *(E)* | | 6 |
| *(Since 1950)* | | 9 |
| Actor | Years | 11 |
| Marion Brando | 1954/1972 | 16 |
| Sally Feild | 1979/1985 | 21 |
| Jane Fonda | 1971/1978 | 25 |
| Jody Fostor | 1988/1991 | 29 |
| Tom Hanks | 1993/1994 | 33 |
| Katherine Hepbrun | 1967/1968/1981 | 40 |
| Dustin Hofman | 1979/1988 | 45 |
| Glenda jackson | 1970/1937 | 50 |
| Elizabeth Taylor | 1960/1966 | 55 |
| DS ―――――――― | | 59 |
| Source: The World Almanac, 1996. | | 65 |

## ACTIVITY 4:

**File Manager**

1. Read the copy at right.
2. Learn about using the file manager to retrieve and rename files with your software.
3. Follow the directions at the right to retrieve and rename a file.

All word processing packages have tools for managing files. These **file managers** typically enable you to list, view, open, copy, move, rename, delete, print, and/or change to another directory temporarily. In this activity, you use the file manager to retrieve (open) an existing document and to rename the document.

1. Access your file manager.
2. Open file T-CHECK.
3. Change the filename T-CHECK to GRAMMAR.
4. Leave monitor on for use in Activity 5.

## ACTIVITY 5:

**Grammar Check**

1. Read the copy at right.
2. Learn about using your software's Grammar Check feature.
3. Follow the directions at the right to use Grammar Check.

Use the **Grammar Check** feature to check documents for spelling, grammar, and punctuation errors and style flaws. You can determine how strictly the Grammar Check observes grammar and style rules by selecting the degree of formality to which your writing will be compared (formal, standard or business, or informal or casual).

When an error or style flaw is identified, the Grammar Check will suggest replacements or improvements. Some Grammar Checks allow you to compare the document's style to acceptable writing styles used when writing business letters, business or technical reports, fiction, and newspaper articles.

1. Open the file named GRAMMAR if it is not open.
2. Access the **Grammar Check** feature.
3. Compare the file text to business/standard writing.
4. Use Grammar Check to check for spelling, grammar, and punctuation errors and style flaws. Correct all spelling, grammar, and punctuation errors and revise the text so that suggested style changes are made when you believe they will improve the material.
5. Proofread the document and make necessary changes not identified by the Grammar Check feature.
6. Save your revision as GRAMREV.

## ACTIVITY 6:

**Merge with Keyboard Input**

1. Read the copy at right.
2. Learn to provide keyboard input for merged documents.
3. Complete Steps a-d at right to provide keyboard input.

While **merging information** from a data file into a form file, you may sometimes have to key information into the form file because the needed information is not in the data file. (A variable account balance in a form letter is an example of such information.)

A **merge code** inserted in the form file stops the merge process at the point the keyed insertion is needed, prompts and/or enables you to key the information, and then continues the merge process until the next form file needs the insertion.

a. Use data file named TMRGDATA and form file named TMRGFORM to complete a merge.
b. Open TMRGFORM and make this change: Delete the xxx in line 1 of the letter body and insert the keyboard input command after the $ and include this prompt: **Key the contribution amount here**.
c. Merge the four documents providing the following $ amounts from the keyboard when prompted.

| Letter | Amount |
| --- | --- |
| Miller | **275** |
| de los Ortiz | **325** |
| Russin | **125** |
| Valcho | **50** |

d. Save the merged file as MRGDOCS.

Table 3

**Table 3**

1. Format/key the table DS, 1.2" (12 sp.) between columns.
2. As you key, make indicated changes and correct any errors you make as you key.

**Table 4**

If time permits, reformat Table 3 with 1.4" (14 sp.) between columns.

|  | | words |
|---|---|---|
| LONGEST-RUN BROADWAY PLAYS | | 5 |
| *Performances Through July 17, 1994* | | 12 |
| <u>Play</u> | <u>Perf.</u> | 15 |
| Chorus Line | 6,137 | 19 |
| Oh, Calcutta (revival) | 5,959 | 25 |
| Cats | 4,917 | 27 |
| 42d Street | 3,486 | 31 |
| Grease | 3,388 | 33 |
| Fiddler On The Roof | 3,224 | 38 |
| Life with father | 3,224 | 43 |
| Tobaco Road | 3,182 | 47 |
| Les Miserables | 3,005 | 51 |
|  | | 54 |
| DS Source: The World Almanac, 1995. | | 61 |

# LESSON 65

## Three-Column Tables with Multiple Features

**Objectives:**

1. To learn to format three-column tables with multiple features.
2. To build skill in processing tables from rough draft.

**65A • 5**
**Conditioning Practice**

each line twice SS; a 1' writing on line 3; find *gwam*

| alphabet | 1 | Hal just picked a bouquet of six vivid flowers growing at my zoo. |
|---|---|---|
| fig/sym | 2 | He said, "A quiz over pages 35-149 and 168-270 will be on May 5." |
| speed | 3 | Ellena is to pay the six auto firms for all the bodywork they do. |

**gwam** 1' | 1 | 2 | 3 | 4 | 5 | 6 | 7 | 8 | 9 | 10 | 11 | 12 | 13 |

**F ORMATTING**

**65B • 45**
**Three-Column Tables**

**Table 1**
**Three-Column Table with Multiple Features**

1. Format/key the table DS, 0.6" (6 sp.) between columns.
2. Correct all errors.

| | | | words |
|---|---|---|---|
| PULITZER PRIZES IN POETRY | | | 5 |
| (Since 1990) | | | 8 |
| <u>Year</u> | <u>Poem or Collection</u> | <u>Author</u> | 15 |
| 1990 | The World Doesn't End | Charles Simic | 23 |
| 1991 | Near Changes | Mona Van Duyn | 29 |
| 1992 | Selected Poems | James Tate | 35 |
| 1993 | The Wild Iris | Louise Gluck | 42 |
| 1994 | Neon Vernacular | Yusef Komunyakaa | 49 |
| | | | 53 |
| Source: <u>Information Please Almanac</u>, 1995. | | | 61 |

# Word PROCESSING 9

## ACTIVITY 1:

### Justification

1. Read the copy at right.
2. Learn the justification features for your wp software.
3. Key the information at the right using the justification indicated.

**Use justification to align text. Left Justification** aligns text evenly along the left margin only and produces a "ragged right" margin. **Right Justification** aligns text evenly along the right margin and produces a "ragged left" margin. **Full Justification** aligns text along both the left and right margins. **Center Justification** centers each line of text between the left and right margins. **All Justification**, if available on your wp software package, lets you evenly space characters from the left margin to the right margin.

**Left Justification**

Format this line with left justification.

**Right Justification**

Format this line with right justification.

**Center Justification**

Format this line with center justification.

**All Justification (if available)**

Format this line with all justification.

**Full Justification**

Key these lines with full justification. With this feature, the lines will begin evenly at the left margin and end evenly at the right margin (as shown here). The space between words is adjusted to provide the even right margin.

## ACTIVITY 2:

### Change Fonts

1. Read the copy at right.
2. Learn about changing fonts on your wp software and printer.
3. Format the five lines at the right as directed in each line.

The **Font** is the typeface in which your document will be printed. The font consists of three elements: the typeface used (such as Times Roman, Courier, or Prestige); appearance (such as bold, italic, or shadow), and size (such as 10 cpi. or 12 pt.). The letters **cpi** stand for *characters per inch* and indicates that a monospace font is being used; **pt** stands for *point* and indicates that a variable space font is being used. Variable space fonts are often scalable; that is, the typeface selected can be printed in almost any point size. The number and size of fonts you can use are dependent on your printer and the word processing package you are using. You can change fonts before or after keying text.

1 Key this line using a 10-cpi. font and bold the last word.
2 Key this line using a 12-pt. font in italic print.
3 Key this line using a 15-pt. font in regular appearance.
4 Copy line 1; change the last four words to a 15-pt. font.
5 Copy line 2; change it to a regular 10-cpi. font.

## ACTIVITY 3:

### Convert Case

1. Read copy at right.
2. Learn to convert case using your wp software.
3. Key the lines at right.
4. Format each line as directed in each line.

Use **Convert Case** to change selected text to uppercase letters, lowercase letters, or initial caps. When converting from uppercase to lowercase, most word processors will retain a capital letter for the first word in the sentence. Some word processors offer a case sensitive feature that retains uppercase letter "I" for the word "I" and words starting with "I" followed by an apostrophe (such as "I'm" and "I'd"). When changing to initial caps, or title case, some word processors will not use initial caps for words such as "and" and "the."

1 Change this line of text to all uppercase letters.
2 CHANGE THIS LINE OF TEXT TO ALL LOWERCASE LETTERS.
3 Change this line of text to initial caps (uppercase and lowercase).
4 CHANGE THESE SENTENCES TO LOWERCASE. TOM AND I WILL GO TO THE SHOW TODAY.

## Table 2
**Three-Column Table from Rough Draft**

1. Format/key the table DS, 0.6" (6 sp.) between columns.
2. Make all indicated changes and correct any errors you make as you key.

words

JOHN WOODEN AWARD WINNERS    6
(Collegiate Basketball)    11

| Year | Player | College | |
|------|--------|---------|---|
| | | | 15 |
| 1990 | Lionel Simmons | La Salle | 21 |
| 1991 | Larry Johnson | UNLV | 26 |
| 1992 | Christian Leattner | Duke | 31 |
| 1993 | Calvert Chaney | Indiana | 37 |
| 1994 | Glen Robinson | Perdue | 42 |
| 1995 | Ed O'Bannon | UCLA | 47 |
| | | | 50 |

Source: The World Almanac, 1996.    57

## Table 3
**Three-Column Table from Rough Draft**

1. Format/key the table DS, 0.4" (4 sp.) between columns.
2. Make all indicated changes and correct any errors you make as you key.

## Table 4
Reformat Table 2 DS, 0.8" (8 sp.) between columns, all errors corrected.

WORLD CHAMPION FIGURE SKATERS    6
1990 - 1995    8

| Year | Men | | Women | |
|------|-----|---|-------|---|
| | | | | 12 |
| 1990 | Kurt Browning (Canada) | | Jill Trenary (U.S.) | 21 |
| 1991 | Kurt Browning (Canada) | | Kristi Yamaguchi (U.S.) | 32 |
| 1992 | Viktor Petrenko (Unified Team) | | Kristi Yamaguchi (U.S.) | 44 |
| 1993 | Kurt Browning (Canada) | | Oksana Baiul (Ukraine) | 54 |
| 1994 | Elvis Stojko (Canada) | | Yuka Sato (Japan) | 63 |
| 1995 | Elvis Stojko (Canada) | | Chen Lu (China) | 71 |
| | | | | 75 |

Source: Information Please Almanac, 1996.    83

---

## LESSON 66   Tables with Multiple Features

**Objectives:**

1. To build skill in processing two- and three-column tables.
2. To improve skill in processing rough-draft tables.

## 66A • 5
## Conditioning Practice

each line twice SS; a 1' writing on line 3; find *gwam*

| | | |
|---|---|---|
| alphabet | 1 | Al criticized my six workers for having quick tempers on the job. |
| fig/sym | 2 | Order #45-1073 from Wilson & Co. totals $198.56, less 2/10, n/30. |
| speed | 3 | To lend a hand to a visitor to the city is the wish of all of us. |

| gwam | 1' | 1 | 2 | 3 | 4 | 5 | 6 | 7 | 8 | 9 | 10 | 11 | 12 | 13 |

# Activity 3:

1. Read carefully the ¶s given at the right.
2. Review your work habits and attitudes in the courses you are currently taking.
3. List some instances in which you have done less well than you believe you are capable.
4. Compose/key a ¶ identifying instances in which you have done less than your best and indicate why that was so.
5. Compose/key another ¶ in which you explain why you agree or disagree with the Chesterfield quote and describe a plan to improve your own work habits and attitudes about work.

**Compose (think) as you key**

Chesterfield said, "Whatever is worth doing at all, is worth doing well." This quotation can be the guide by which to judge everything you do. Use it for just one week, and you will realize how often your performance is "all right" but not your best. If you can't be superior in everything you do, you can work with the certainty that if it is worth doing at all, it is worth doing as well as you can do it.

Have you made maximum use of your time in learning to read and write, doing math calculations, performing science experiments, drawing and painting, and even operating a keyboard? You are the only one who can answer these questions with certainty. Only you can know if you have done the work as well as you could. If you have not done as well as possible, you probably do not believe that "Whatever is worth doing at all, is worth doing well."

There is magic in believing, if to the belief you hold you add the work you should do. "Faith without works is dead" is often quoted, but work without faith is equally dead. Work and belief in it are necessary if you want to achieve your highest potential. What you get out of life depends on you: on the work you do and the magic to believe that whatever you do is worth doing well.

## 66B • 45
## Tables with Multiple Features

**Table 1**
**Table with Column Headings**
Format/key the table DS, 0.8" (8 sp.) between columns, all errors corrected.

**Table 2**
**Table with Multiple Features**

1. Fomat/key the table DS, 0.8" (8 sp.) between columns.
2. Make indicated changes and correct any errors you make as you key.

**Table 3**
**Table with Multiple Features**
Use same directions as for Table 2.

**Table 4**
If time permits, reformat Table 2 DS, 0.6" (6 sp.) between columns, errors corrected.

| | | words |
|---|---|---|
| WINTER LISTENING LIST | | 4 |
| Selection | Composer | 9 |
| Brandenberg Concertos | Johann Sebastian Bach | 17 |
| Symphonie Fantastique | Hector Berlioz | 25 |
| Jupiter Symphony | Wolfgang Amadeus Mozart | 33 |
| Finlandia | Jean Sibelius | 38 |
| The Rite of Spring | Igor Stravinsky | 45 |
| Manfred Symphony | Piotr Ilyich Tchaikovsky | 53 |

| | | | words |
|---|---|---|---|
| PULITZER PRIZES IN DRAMA | | | 5 |
| Since 1990 | | | 7 |
| Year | Play | Author | 11 |
| 1990 | The Piano Lesson | August Wilson | 18 |
| 1991 | Lost in Yonkers | Neil Simon | 25 |
| 1992 | The Kentucky Cycle | Robert Schenkan | 33 |
| 1993 | Angles in America/Millenium | Tony Kushner | 42 |
| 1994 | Three Tall Women | Edward Albee | 49 |
| | | | 52 |
| Source: Information Please Almanac, 1996. | | | 61 |

| | | | words |
|---|---|---|---|
| HEISMAN TROPHY WINNERS | | | 5 |
| Collegiate Football | | | 9 |
| Year | Player | College | 13 |
| 1990 | Tye Detmer | Brigham Young | 19 |
| 1991 | Desmond Howard | Michigan | 25 |
| 1992 | Gino Toretto | Miami (Fla.) | 31 |
| 1993 | Charlie Ward | Florida State | 38 |
| 1994 | Marshall Faulk | San Diego State | 45 |
| 1995 | Rasham Salaam | Colorado | 50 |
| | | | 54 |
| Source: The Universal Almanac, 1996. | | | 61 |

## Activity 1:

1. Study the spelling/definitions of the words in the color block at the right.
2. Key the **Learn** line in the first set of sentences.
3. Key the **Apply** lines, choosing the right words to complete each sentence correctly.
4. Key the second set of lines in the same way.
5. Check work; rekey lines containing word-choice errors.

**Choose the right word**

**complement** (n) something that completes or makes up a whole

**compliment** (n) an expression of praise or congratulation

**fair** (adj) just, equitable, visually beautiful or admirable

**fare** (n) a transportation charge

Learn 1 Jo's compliment to Dan was that his tie complemented his suit.
Apply 2 The laser printer is a (complement/compliment) to the system.
Apply 3 Gloria accepted Kevin's (complement/compliment) with a smile.

Learn 4 Mary knew that the taxi fare was not fair for such a short trip.
Apply 5 With a shrug and a sigh, Lucia said, "Life is not (fair/fare)."
Apply 6 The round-trip airline (fair/fare) seemed (fair/fare) to me.

## Activity 2:

1. Read carefully the letter given at the right; note needed corrections in capitalization, punctuation, and word choice.
2. Format/key the message as a personal-business letter. Use your own address as the return address.
3. Address the letter to:
   **Dr. Lee J. Carr, President**
   **Justin Academy**
   **Richmond, VA 23251-4322**
   Supply missing letter parts.
4. Key your own name as the writer of the letter.

**Proofread & correct**

Many of us who have achieved even a small measure of success can identify a few important mileposts in life.  For me, one vary significant mileposts was when I entered justin academy, much too young and ignorant to no that failure was possible.  I was protected, I think by the "shield of faith" and encouraged I know, by the understanding of the faculty.

Many schools may be known for there superior physical plant, strict discipline or they're exacting curriculum, but I think more about the lives you reach then of the facts you teach at Justin.  You seem always too be able to plant the seeds of expectancy in all your students.

Its a proud feeling to have been a student at Justin and I am grateful for the personel guidance and the mental discipline that I received when these were most needed.

On this fiftieth anniversary of the founding of the school of which you are the distinguished and honored head I send congratulations and best wishes.

# Tables with Totals and Footnotes

**Objectives:**
1. To learn to format tables with totals and footnotes.
2. To format tables with single-spaced entries.

**67A • 5**
**Conditioning Practice**

each line twice SS: a
1' writing on line 3; find
*gwam*

| alphabet | 1 | The quick jabs and deft parries amazed several wary young boxers. |
| fig/sym | 2 | She gave him numbers and prices:  #16392, $48.30; #14593, $75.95. |
| speed | 3 | To handle the problem with proficiency and vigor is a civic duty. |

**gwam** 1' | 1 | 2 | 3 | 4 | 5 | 6 | 7 | 8 | 9 | 10 | 11 | 12 | 13 |

**F** ORMATTING

**67B • 45**
**Tables with Totals and Footnotes**

**Table 1**
1. Format/key the table SS, 0.6" (6 sp.) between columns, all errors corrected.
2. Underline the entire width of the amount columns.
3. Indent the word *Totals* 0.5" (5 sp.) from left margin.
4. Key the footnote as if it were a source note,  a DS below the divider line.

**Table 2**
Follow the directions given for Table 1.

**Table 3**
If time permits, reformat Table 1 with all lines DS.

**Note:** See p. A18 for R & E activities.

words

LAKEVIEW STUDENT GOVERNMENT — 6

Budget for Year ----/----* — 11

| Item | Amount | Up/Dn. | |
|---|---|---|---|
| | | | 15 |
| Student Government Awards Night | $2,850 | $150 | 24 |
| Grub Day Scholarships | 750 | 50 | 30 |
| Photocopy Services | 475 | –25 | 35 |
| Operation Youth | 375 | 35 | 40 |
| State Assn. of Student Councils | 350 | 15 | 48 |
| National Honor Society Awards | 350 | –50 | 55 |
| Student Government Pizza Night | 240 | 20 | 63 |
| Frosh Hot Dog Night | 195 | 15 | 68 |
| Student Clubs | 185 | 20 | 72 |
| Fall Picnic | 175 | 25 | 76 |
| Executive Board Trip | 165 | 15 | 83 |
| Totals | $6,110 | $270 | 87 |
| | | | 90 |

*Information obtained from school financial office. — 100

HILLSIDE ALUMNI ASSOCIATION — 6

Financial Statement, June 30, ---- — 13

| Activity | Revenue | Expense | |
|---|---|---|---|
| | | | 18 |
| Class Reunion | $ 5,385 | $ 4,323 | 24 |
| Softball Tournament | 5,272 | 4,216 | 31 |
| Golf Classic | 3,840 | 3,050* | 36 |
| Basketball League | 3,500 | 3,100 | 42 |
| Newsletter | 2,950 | 2,135 | 46 |
| Spring Dance | 2,062 | 1,583 | 51 |
| Interest Income | 137 | ----- | 57 |
| President's Reception | ----- | 1,176 | 63 |
| Operations and Meetings | ----- | 814 | 70 |
| Advertising/Public Relations | ----- | 722 | 80 |
| Totals | $23,146 | $21,119 | 84 |
| | | | 88 |

*Some expenses still to be paid. — 94

# Skill Builder

**Technique:
Keystroking Patterns**

Key each line twice SS; DS between 2-line groups; rekey difficult lines as time permits.

**Adjacent key**

1 are ire err her cash said riot lion soil join went wean news
2 pew art sort try tree post upon copy opera three maker waste
3 sat riot coil were renew forth trade power grope score owner

**One hand**

4 ad bar car deed ever feed hill jump look null noon poll upon
5 him joy age kiln noun loop moon bear casts deter edges facet
6 get are save taste versa wedge hilly imply phony union yummy

**Balanced hand**

7 go aid bid dish elan fury glen half idle jamb lend make name
8 oak pay hen quay rush such urus vial works yamen amble blame
9 cot duty goal envy focus handy ivory lapel oriel prowl queue

gwam 1' | 1 | 2 | 3 | 4 | 5 | 6 | 7 | 8 | 9 | 10 | 11 | 12 |

## Timed Writings

1. Key three 1' writings on each ¶; find *gwam*. Count errors. If errors are 2 or fewer on any writing, goal is to increase speed by 1 or 2 words on next writing. If errors on any writing are more than 2, goal is control on next writing.

2. Key two 3' writings on ¶s 1-3 combined; find *gwam* and count errors.

3. Key a 5' writing on ¶s 1-3 combined; find *gwam* and count errors.

all letters used

|  | gwam | 3' | 5' |
|---|---|---|---|
| There are many opportunities for jobs in the physical fitness | | 4 | 2 42 |
| industry. The first step for many people is to be a fitness in- | | 8 | 5 45 |
| structor in a fitness center or program. A genuine interest in the | | 13 | 8 48 |
| field as well as evidence of a personal commitment to good fitness | | 17 | 10 50 |
| are frequently the major things needed to land a job as a fitness | | 22 | 13 53 |
| instructor. | | 22 | 13 54 |
| Another opportunity in the fitness industry is to become a | | 26 | 16 56 |
| strength coach for an athletic team. This person works to make the | | 31 | 19 59 |
| team members fit and strong at the same time the athletic coach | | 35 | 21 61 |
| works to maximize their skills. A college degree in physical | | 39 | 24 64 |
| education or a related field is usually needed for this kind of job. | | 44 | 26 66 |
| Others in the fitness field often get a job in a big company | | 48 | 29 69 |
| or hospital as a fitness program director. These directors run | | 52 | 31 71 |
| programs that improve the fitness and overall health of the people | | 57 | 34 74 |
| who work in the hospital or company. Directors usually need a | | 61 | 37 77 |
| college degree and a lot of training in fitness skills, health | | 65 | 39 79 |
| promotion, and business. | | 67 | 40 80 |

gwam 3' | 1 | 2 | 3 | 4 |
5' | 1 | 2 | 3 |

# Skill Builder

## Speed Building

1. Key each line once SS; DS between 2-line groups.
   **Goal:** No pauses between letters and words.
2. Key a 1' writing on each of lines 4, 6, 8, and 10; find *gwam* on each.
3. If time permits, rekey the three slowest lines.

| | | |
|---|---|---|
| space | 1 | city then they form than body them busy sign firm duty turn proxy |
| bar | 2 | Jan may do key work for the six men on the audit of the big firm. |
| shift | 3 | Lake Como \| Hawaii or Alaska \| Madrid and Bogota \| Sparks & Mason, Inc. |
| keys | 4 | Karl left for Bora Bora in May; Nan goes to Lake Worth in August. |
| adjacent | 5 | same wire open tire sure ruin said trim went fire spot lids walks |
| keys | 6 | We opened a shop by the stadium to offer the best sporting goods. |
| long direct | 7 | vice much many nice once myth lace cents under check juice center |
| reaches | 8 | Eunice brought a recorder to the music hall to record my recital. |
| word | 9 | their right field world forms visit title chair spent towns usual |
| response | 10 | They wish to go with the girl to the city to make the visual aid. |

gwam 1' | 1 | 2 | 3 | 4 | 5 | 6 | 7 | 8 | 9 | 10 | 11 | 12 | 13 |

## Timed Writings

1. Key a 1' writing on each ¶; find *gwam* on each one.
2. Key two 2' writings on ¶s 1-2 combined; find *gwam* on each writing.
3. Key two 3' writings on ¶s 1-3 combined; find *gwam* and count errors on each writing.
4. If time permits, key two 1' guided writings on each ¶: one for speed; one for control (accuracy).

all letters used

gwam 2' | 3'

In deciding upon a career, learn as much as possible about ... 6 | 4 | 57
what individuals in that career do. For each job class, there are ... 12 | 8 | 62
job requirements and qualifications that must be met. Analyze ... 19 | 13 | 66
these tasks very critically in terms of your personality and what ... 25 | 17 | 70
you like to do. ... 27 | 18 | 71

A high percentage of jobs in major careers demand education or ... 33 | 22 | 76
training after high school. The training may be very specialized, ... 40 | 27 | 80
requiring intensive study or interning for two or more years. You ... 47 | 31 | 85
must decide if you are willing to expend so much time and effort. ... 53 | 35 | 90

After you have decided upon a career to pursue, discuss the ... 59 | 39 | 93
choice with parents, teachers, and others. Such people can help ... 66 | 44 | 97
you design a plan to guide you along the series of steps required ... 72 | 48 | 102
in pursuing your goal. Keep the plan flexible and change it when- ... 79 | 52 | 106
ever necessary. ... 80 | 53 | 107

gwam 2' | 1 | 2 | 3 | 4 | 5 | 6 |
3' | 1 | 2 | 3 | 4 |

## Quarter-Minute Checkpoints

| gwam | 1/4' | 1/2' | 3/4' | 1' |
|---|---|---|---|---|
| 24 | 6 | 12 | 18 | 24 |
| 28 | 7 | 14 | 21 | 28 |
| 32 | 8 | 16 | 24 | 32 |
| 36 | 9 | 18 | 27 | 36 |
| 40 | 10 | 20 | 30 | 40 |
| 44 | 11 | 22 | 33 | 44 |
| 48 | 12 | 24 | 36 | 48 |
| 52 | 13 | 26 | 39 | 52 |
| 56 | 14 | 28 | 42 | 56 |

## 163B • 45
## Itinerary and Agenda

**Document 1**
**Itinerary**

1. Review Itineraries section on p. 369; refer to model on p. 369.
2. Process the itinerary at the right.

**Document 2**
**Agenda**

1. Review Agendas section on p. 369; refer to model on p. 369.
2. Process the agenda at the right.

words

|  |  | |
|---|---|---|
| | ITINERARY | 2 |
| | Ronald T. Melrose | 6 |
| | American Sport Management Association } DS | 13 |

August 23 — 15

| 2:47 p.m. | Depart Wichita on West Air--Flight ß85 for | 26 |
| | Louisville, KY. | 29 |
| 6:14 p.m. | Arrive Louisville; take Caldwell Shuttle to | 40 |
| | Caldwell Hotel, 572 Sage Street. | 47 |
| 7:30 p.m. | Dinner with Felicia Gomez, ASMA Conference director; | 68 |
| | Caldwell Hotel in Pastels Dining Room. | 70 |

August 24

| 8:15 a.m. | Register for ASMA Conference, meetings until | 81 |
| | 4:30 p.m.  Attend Joe Stead's session at 2:15 | 90 |
| | p.m. 15 | 91 |
| 12 noon | Lunch with Ito Hua in First Cafe, Caldwell Hotel | 103 |
| 5:30 p.m. | Dinner with Leo Lynch; Caldwell Hotel in Heritage | 115 |
| | Room. | 116 |
| 9:45 p.m. | Reception for ASMA Executive Board, Hardy Suite, | 130 |

August 25 | Floor 15. | 133 |

| 8:30 a.m. | Attend conference meetings. | 156 |
| | 7:30 am. Breakfast with Tom Evans at Larkins | 142 |
| | Restaurant, 590 Sage Street. | 148 |
| 11:45 a.m. | Lunch with Mary Dilt in First Cafe, Caldwell | 168 |
| | Hotel | |
| 2:15 p.m. | Depart hotel via Caldwell Shuttle for Louisville | 180 |
| | Airport for 3:30 p.m. West Air--Flight 259 to | 189 |
| | Wichita. | 191 |
| 4:33 p.m. | Arrive Wichita | 196 |

AGENDA — 1

AAPD Board Meeting -- February 8, ---- — 9

DS

| 1. Call to Order . . . . . . . . . . . | Sally Kurt, President | 24 |
| 2. Approval of January Minutes . . . . . | John Green, Secretary | 40 |
| 3. Treasurer's Report . . . . . . . . | Mary Perez, Treasurer | 55 |
| 4. Strategic Planning Report . . . . . | Debbie Turk | 70 |
| 5. Education Committee Report . . . . | Juan Quinnes | 86 |
| 6. ADC Report . . . . . . . . | Elizabeth Joshua | 101 |
| 7. Unfinished Business . . . . . . | Sally Kurt | 117 |
| 8. New Business . . . . . . . . | Sally Kurt | 132 |
|    Sale of Helton Property | | 137 |
|    Adopt-A-Lot Project | | 141 |
| 9. Adjournment | | 144 |

# Language & Writing Skills 8

## Activity 1:

1. Study the spelling/ definitions of the words in the color block at the right.
2. Key the **Learn** line, noting the proper choice of words.
3. Key the **Apply** lines, choosing the right words to complete each line correctly.
4. Check your accuracy; rekey lines containing errors in word choice.

## Activity 2:

1. Read the ¶ at the right, noting words that are used incorrectly or misspelled.
2. Key the ¶, correcting the errors you noted.

## Activity 3:

1. Read the ¶ at the right based on a survey of people in your age group.
2. On the basis of your own experience in viewing movies and TV, compose a ¶ indicating whether you agree or disagree with the survey results, giving reasons why or why not.

### Choose the right word

| | |
|---|---|
| **buy** (n/vb) a bargain; to purchase; to acquire | **some** (n/adv) unknown or unspecified unit or thing; to a degree or extent |
| **by** (prep/adv) close to; via; according to; close at hand; at/in another's home | **sum** (n/vb) the whole amount; the total; to find a total; summary of points |

Learn  1  She stopped by a new shop on the square to buy the new CD album.
Apply  2  We are to go (buy/by) bus to the ski lodge to (buy/by) ski togs.
Apply  3  Did you (buy/by) the new novel (buy/by) Margaret Atwood?

Learn  4  The problem was to find the sum, but some students couldn't.
Apply  5  He said, "In (some/sum), both ideas are true to (some/sum) degree."
Apply  6  I bought (some/sum) pears and apples for the (some/sum) of $4.30.

### Proofread & correct

Sum people think that because their good at sum sport, music, or other activity, there entitled to respect and forgiveness for anything else they chose to do.   Its not uncommon, than, when such people break the law or violate sum code of conduct, four them too expect such behavior two be overlooked buy those whose job it is to enforce the law or too uphold an established code of conduct.   Sum parents, as well as other members of society, think that a "star's" misbehavior should be treated less harshly because of that person's "celebrity" status; but all people are the same under the law.

### Compose (think) as you key

A mid-decade poll of young people revealed that U.S. youths thought current TV and movie fare glamorizes violence and sex without portraying the negative consequences of immoral behavior.  Over sixty percent of youths surveyed said that such glamorizations on the screen influenced them to engage in such behavior.

_____

Source:  Armstrong Williams, <u>USA Today</u>, March 2, 1995.

## Form 2
### Invoice

Format the invoice at right. Proofread and correct errors.

**Clarke Floors**
206 Glen Club Dr.
Stone Mountain, GA 30087-3451

Phone: 404-179-4566
Fax: 404-179-4563

# I N V O I C E

| HARDT CONCORD AND VERDE | Date: October 29, ---- | 8 |
| 25 INTERNATIONAL BLVD | Customer | 13 |
| ATLANTA GA 30354-4312 | Order No.: 358-9824-X | 19 |

| Terms | Shipped Via | Our Order No. | Date Shipped | |
|---|---|---|---|---|
| 2/10, n/90 | Xpress Carry | 24-45-97 | 10/29/-- | 28 |

| Quantity | Description/Stock No. | Unit Price | | Total | | |
|---|---|---|---|---|---|---|
| 1 | Computer operator chair/RG-33 | 99 | 99 | 99 | 99 | 36 |
| 2 | Architect chair/SF-341 | 135 | 95 | 271 | 90 | 44 |
| 6 | Folding chair/ACF-01 | 19 | 99 | 119 | 94 | 51 |
| 3 | Folding table/AFS-2472 | 49 | 95 | 149 | 85 | 59 |
| 4 | Contoured stack chair/CS-216 | 65 | 99 | 263 | 96 | 68 |
| 1 | Executive chair/EX-52 | 314 | 95 | 314 | 95 | 76 |
| | | | | 1220 | 59 | 77 |
| | Sales tax {6%} | | | 73 | 24 | 82 |
| | | | | 1293 | 83 | 83 |

## Form 3
### Invoice

1. Format an invoice for the purchase order that was processed as Form 1.

2. Use **November 2, ----** as the date.

3. The terms are **3/30**, **n/60**; the shipper is **Free Way**

**Express**; the order number is **3-58-67**; the date shipped is **11/1**; and sales tax is **6%**. Use

PO No. for the Customer Order No., and delete (ea) after each item.

# LESSON 163

# Special Documents

**O b j e c t i v e s :**
1. To format an itinerary and agenda.
2. To improve keying on rough-draft and script copy.

## 163A • 5
## Conditioning Practice

each line twice

| alphabet | 1 | Both weary girls were just amazed by the five quick extra points. |
| speed | 2 | The antique bowl she saw at the downtown mall is authentic ivory. |
| fig/sym | 3 | JR & Sons used P.O. #7082-B35 to order 154 chairs (Style LE-196). |

| gwam | 1' | 1 | 2 | 3 | 4 | 5 | 6 | 7 | 8 | 9 | 10 | 11 | 12 | 13 |

# UNIT 15

**LESSONS 68–71**

## Assess Keyboarding/ Application Skills

### LESSON 68 — Assessment Preparation

**Objectives:**
1. To improve keying speed and control.
2. To review format features of major documents.

---

**68A • 5**
**Conditioning Practice**

each line twice SS; DS
between 2-line groups;
a 1' writing on line 3

| | | |
|---|---|---|
| alphabet | 1 | Five or six people jogged quickly along the beach in a warm haze. |
| fig/sym | 2 | This Chu & Son's May 17 check should be $45.39 instead of $62.80. |
| speed | 3 | Lana and he may cycle to the ancient city chapel by the big lake. |

**gwam** 1' | 1 | 2 | 3 | 4 | 5 | 6 | 7 | 8 | 9 | 10 | 11 | 12 | 13 |

---

**68B • 10**
**Skill Building**

1. Key each line once SS; DS between 2-line groups. Do not substitute italic for underlines in lines 1 and 2.

2. If time permits, key a 1' writing on each of lines 10, 12, and 14; find *gwam* on each.

| | | |
|---|---|---|
| underline & CAPS LOCK | 1 | <u>Ballet & Modern Dance</u>; <u>The Encyclopedia of Film</u>; <u>American Theatre</u> |
| | 2 | Marilou has bought TEN OF THE BEST of the <u>Reader's Digest</u> series. |
| shift keys | 3 | The Royal Ballet; Nederlands Dans Theater; London Festival Ballet |
| | 4 | Balanchine and Kirstein founded the New York City Ballet in 1948. |
| apostrophe & quotes | 5 | Masefield's "The Dauber"; Kipling's "Gunga Din"; Bronte's "Hope"; |
| | 6 | We'll read Sandburg's "Chicago" and Frost's "The Road Not Taken." |
| alphabet | 7 | hope very quit mark axle zone cord boat sign four gown such major |
| | 8 | Six able men have quietly walked off good jobs at our city plaza. |
| letter response | 9 | date upon ever only care jump sets pink fear join were milk defer |
| | 10 | As you are aware, my trade union acted upon only a few age cases. |
| combination response | 11 | fish were duty ever risk fear goal fast they safe sign hulk ivory |
| | 12 | You are to refer the big wage case to an auto union panel of six. |
| word response | 13 | then form their eight world visit title chair firms signal profit |
| | 14 | A city auditor is to sign all the work forms for the civic panel. |

**gwam** 1' | 1 | 2 | 3 | 4 | 5 | 6 | 7 | 8 | 9 | 10 | 11 | 12 | 13 |

---

**68C • 35**
**Preparation for Assessment**

To prepare for assessment, key selected problems from those listed at the right. Make a list of page numbers to avoid having to return to this page as you work.

Simplified memo, p. 115
Personal-business letter, p. 124
Business letter, p. 130
Unbound report, pp. 145-146

Study the placement and spacing of document parts as a review.

## 162B • 15
## Basic Skill Check

1. Three 1' writings on ¶1; find *gwam*; circle errors.
2. Practice ¶s 2 and 3 in same manner.
3. Two 5' writings on ¶s 1-3 combined; find *gwam*; find errors.

all letters used | gwam 3' | 5'

Sleep is a very important element of staying healthy. Many people who do not get the proper amount of sleep quickly become edgy, fatigued, and tired. In addition, people who do not get enough sleep are more likely to be attacked by various diseases. It is, therefore, important that you get the amount of sleep that your body needs.

Science knows very little about sleep. There is evidence that the amount of sleep each individual needs to maintain good health varies. Some believe that the amount of sleep people need lessens with age. For example, children below four years of age frequently need to sleep about half of each day while teenagers need just eight to ten hours each day to perform adequately.

Most people realize that a good mattress, one that is neither too hard nor too soft; a quiet room; and darkness are conditions that help them get enough sleep to restore body power. Also helpful are covers and electric blankets that are warm but not too heavy. It is also helpful to avoid excitement and heavy eating before going to sleep.

## FORMATTING

## 162C • 30
## Purchase Order and Invoices

### Form 1
**Purchase Order**

1. Review the Forms section on p. 369.
2. Prepare the purchase order at right.

| | | | | words |
|---|---|---|---|---|
| MAINLINE VIDEO SUPPLY INC | | PO No.: 34-57239 | | 7 |
| EIGHT MERRILL ST | | Date: October 23, ---- | | 14 |
| DETROIT MI 48202-5610 | | Terms: 3/10, n/30 | | 21 |
| | | Shipped Via: A & M Express | | 23 |
| 2 | Video tables/LT-2389 (ea) | 98.95 | 197.90 | 31 |
| 1 | TV/VCR security system/GR-0322 (ea) | 549.50 | 549.50 | 42 |
| 6 | Videotape racks/LT-20-V (ea) | 27.95 | 167.70 | 51 |
| 6 | Safety straps/LT-RS (ea) | 28.95 | 173.70 | 59 |
| 3 | Ceiling mounts/BR-TV27 (ea) | 158.45 | 475.35 | 68 |
| | | | 1564.15 | 69 |

# Assess Keyboarding & Correspondence Skills

**Objectives:**

**1.** To build/assess keying skills.

**2.** To assess correspondence knowledge and skills.

---

**69A • 5**

## Conditioning Practice

each line twice SS; DS between 2-line groups; a 1' writing on line 3

alphabet 1 Jack saw five prime quail and a big fox down by the old zoo lake.

fig/sym 2 The cabinet (36" x 59" x 14 1/2") is now on sale for just $78.50.

speed 3 The busy auditor may work with vigor to form the key audit panel.

gwam 1' | 1 | 2 | 3 | 4 | 5 | 6 | 7 | 8 | 9 | 10 | 11 | 12 | 13 |

---

**69B • 10**

## Assessment: Keying Skill

1. Key a 1' writing on each ¶; note *gwam*.

2. Key a 2' writing on ¶s 1-3 combined; find *gwam*.

3. Key a 3' writing on ¶s 1-3 combined; find *gwam*, count errors.

all letters used

gwam  2'  3'

.  2  .  4  .  6  .  8  .  10  .  12

For many people during a large part of the past century, stay-  6  4  57

.  14  .  16  .  18  .  20  .  22  .  24

ing in the same job with a single company or institution for their  13  9  62

26  .  28  .  30  .  32  .  34  .  36  .  38  .

entire productive lives was not uncommon.  Now it is thought that  19  13  66

.  40  .  42  .  44  .  46  .  48  .  50  .

many fledgling workers will switch jobs several times in their  26  17  70

52  .  54

working lives.  27  18  71

.  2  .  4  .  6  .  8  .  10  .  12

The pace of change in the national job arena today requires  33  22  75

.  14  .  16  .  18  .  20  .  22  .  24

that all people prepare themselves to move upward or outward in the  40  27  80

26  .  28  .  30  .  32  .  34  .  36  .  38

same company or from firm to firm.  Such moves demand widened ex-  46  31  84

.  40  .  42  .  44  .  46  .  48  .  50  .

perience and education.  Often the moves result in better pay and  53  35  88

52  .

benefits.  54  36  89

.  2  .  4  .  6  .  8  .  10  .  12

So do not envision your diploma or your initial job as the end  60  40  93

.  14  .  16  .  18  .  20  .  22  .  24  .

of anything.  Recognize that they are merely milestones in the on-  67  45  98

26  .  28  .  30  .  32  .  34  .  36  .  38

going process of preparing for a richer, more responsible life.  73  49  102

.  40  .  42  .  44  .  46  .  48  .  50  .

Living is a process of becoming rather than a state of being.  79  53  106

gwam 2' | 1 | 2 | 3 | 4 | 5 | 6 |
3' | 1 | 2 | 3 | 4 |

**Table 2**

Center table; CS: 0.5"
(6 sp.); DS; center headings.

| | | | | words |
|---|---|---|---|---|
| FIRST-QUARTER STATEMENT | | | | 5 |
| Department | Cost of Goods Sold | Operating Expenses | Operating Profits | 10 / 19 |
| Electrical | $4,652 | $3,987 | $ 665 | 26 |
| Auto Supply | 5,983 | 4,710 | 1,273 | 32 |
| Household | 3,756 | 3,254 | 502 | 37 |
| Plumbing | 6,041 | 4,984 | 1,057 | 42 |

**Table 3**

Center table, CS: 0.5"
(6 sp.); DS; center headings.

| | | | | words |
|---|---|---|---|---|
| CHEMICAL ELEMENTS | | | | 4 |
| (1950s and 1960s Discoveries) | | | | 10 |
| Chemical Element | Atomic Symbol | Weight | Year Discovered | 14 / 21 |
| Rutherfordium | Rf | 261 | 1969 | 26 |
| Lawrencium | Lr | 260 | 1961 | 31 |
| Nobelium | No | 259 | 1958 | 35 |
| Mendelevium | Md | 258 | 1955 | 40 |
| Fermium | Fm | 257 | 1953 | 44 |
| Einsteinium | Es | 254 | 1952 | 49 |
| Californium | Cf | 251 | 1950 | 54 |
| | | | | 57 |
| Source: The World Almanac. | | | | 62 |

**Table 4**

Center table; CS: 0.5"
(6 sp.); DS; center headings.

| | | | words |
|---|---|---|---|
| PLAYERS WITH .300+ BATTING AVERAGE | | | 7 |
| Player | Games Played | Batting Average | 10 / 15 |
| Hector Juarez | 10 | .415 | 19 |
| Bill Green | 15 | .378 | 23 |
| Andy Vladski | 9 | .349 | 27 |
| Pete Lenci | 13 | .305 | 31 |

## LESSON 162 — Business Forms

**Objectives:**
1. To format purchase orders and invoices.
2. To improve straight-copy skill.

**162A • 5**
**Conditioning Practice**

each line twice

alphabet 1 Julie passed the extra keyboarding quiz as we got back from Vail.

speed 2 Nancy may sign the usual proxy if they make an audit of the firm.

fig/sym 3 Mary's house at 267 Weston Drive was appraised at $153,490 (+8%).

gwam 1' | 1 | 2 | 3 | 4 | 5 | 6 | 7 | 8 | 9 | 10 | 11 | 12 | 13 |

## 69C • 35
### Assessment:
### Correspondence Skills

Format/key the documents as directed below.

**Document 1**
**Simplified Memo**
**SM:** defaults (or 1")
**Date:** current year
**Errors:** corrected

November 26, ---- | Members of Lakeview Chorale | REHEARSALS FOR "SOUNDS OF LAKEVIEW" — 11 / 16

On December 1, formal rehearsals for our holiday program, "Sounds of Lakeview," will begin. — 30 / 35

These rehearsals will be held in the auditorium at 2:30 on Monday, Wednesday, and Friday afternoons. Each rehearsal is scheduled for two hours. Make plans now for transportation home. If someone is to pick you up, be sure he or she is here no later than 4:45 p.m. — 48 / 62 / 75 / 89

We have an exciting program planned, so arrive on December 1 in good voice and with your usual enthusiasm. — 102 / 110

Cecilia Valdez, Choral Director | xx — 117

**Document 2**
**Personal-Business Letter**
**SM:** defaults (or 1")
**Format:** block
**Date:** current year
**Errors:** corrected

2299 Riverside Dr. | Tulsa, OK 74105-3896 | November 26, ---- | Miss Amanda Monaco | Fallsington Hall for Women | 500 Ash St. | Houston, TX 77044-2145 | Dear Amanda — 12 / 23 / 30

How great it will be to have the "college grind" over for several days, starting December 20. I look forward to seeing you during the holidays. — 45 / 58 / 60

Remembering how much we enjoyed participating in the musical events at Mohawk High School, I acquired two tickets for this year's holiday program on December 23. I hope you will be my guest. — 73 / 87 / 98

I'm sure many of our mutual friends will attend. Seeing them again should be great fun for both of us. Please say you'll go. — 112 / 124

Cordially | Adrian Forbes — 129

**Document 3**
**Business Letter**
**SM:** defaults (or 1")
**Format:** block
**Date:** current year
**Errors:** corrected

November 26, ---- | Mrs. Evelyn M. McNeil | 4582 Campus Dr. | Fort Worth, TX 76119-1835 | Dear Mrs. McNeil — 11 / 20

The new holiday season is upon us, and we invite you to beat the rush and visit our exciting Gallery of Gifts. Gift-giving can be a snap this year because of our vast array of gifts "for kids from one to ninety-two." — 34 / 48 / 62 / 64

What's more, many of our gifts are prewrapped for presentation. All can be packaged and shipped from right here in the store. — 77 / 89

A catalog of our hottest gift items and a schedule of holiday hours for special charge-card customers are enclosed. Please stop in and let us help you select that special gift, or call us if you wish to shop by phone. — 104 / 118 / 132 / 133

We wish you happy holidays and hope to see you soon. — 144

Cordially yours | Ms. Carol J. Suess, Manager | xx | Enclosures — 155

**Table 2**

Center table; CS: 0.5" (6 sp.); DS; center column headings.

**Note:** Parentheses indicate negative numbers.

**Table 3**

Reformat Table 2; CS: 0.75" (8 sp.); SS.

|  |  |  |  | words |
|---|---|---|---|---|
| WEST VALLEY SPORTS CLUB | | | | 5 |
| Quarterly Cash-Flow Statement | | | | 11 |
| Item | July | August | September | 17 |
| Net Revenues | 12,000 | 15,300 | 16,700 | 24 |
| Expenses | 13,500 | 15,000 | 14,500 | 30 |
| Monthly Cash Flow | (1,500) | 300 | 2,200 | 37 |
| Cumulative Cash Flow | (1,500) | (1,200) | 1,000 | 46 |
| Cash--Start of Month | 3,000 | 1,500 | 300 | 53 |
| Cash--End of Month | 1,500 | 300 | 1,300 | 60 |

## LESSON 161 — Tables: Multiple-Line Column Headings

**Objectives:**

**1.** To format tables with multiple-line headings.
**2.** To format tables with source notes.

### 161A • 5
**Conditioning Practice**

each line twice

| | | |
|---|---|---|
| alphabet | 1 | Lizzie checked the liquid oxygen just before moving down the pad. |
| speed | 2 | Did eight firms bid for title to the authentic map of the island? |
| fig/sym | 3 | Her fax (25-473) was $256.98 and his 1200 baud modem was $175.59. |

**gwam** 1' | 1 | 2 | 3 | 4 | 5 | 6 | 7 | 8 | 9 | 10 | 11 | 12 | 13 |

## FORMATTING

### 161B • 5
**Drill: Centered Multiple-Line Column Headings**

**(Electronics Only)**

▶ 1. Refer to procedures for centering column heads on p. RG19.

▶ 2. Center the multiple-line column headings at right by longest item, whether it is one of the column heading lines or a column-entry line. Key headings 2" from top edge; CS: 0.5" (6 sp.); SS; do not correct errors.

| Warehouse Center | Center Director | Inventory Last Quarter | words |
|---|---|---|---|
| | | | 5 |
| | | | 12 |
| North | Mary Harter | 125,000 | 17 |
| South | Bart Justine | 95,000 | 22 |

### 161C • 40
**Format Tables: Multiple-Line Headings**

**Table 1**

Center table: CS: 0.75" (8 sp.); DS; center column headings.

| THE GREAT LAKES | | | | 3 |
|---|---|---|---|---|
| Great Lake | Length (Miles) | Breadth (Miles) | Area (Square Miles) | 8 / 16 |
| Erie | 241 | 57 | 32,630 | 20 |
| Huron | 206 | 183 | 74,700 | 24 |
| Michigan | 307 | 118 | 67,900 | 29 |
| Ontario | 193 | 53 | 34,850 | 34 |
| Superior | 350 | 160 | 81,000 | 38 |
| | | | | 42 |
| Source: The World Almanac. | | | | 47 |

## LESSON 70

# Assess Report Skill

**Objectives:**
1. To build/assess keying skills.
2. To assess report knowledge and skills.

---

### 70A • 5
### Conditioning Practice

each line twice

alphabet 1 Six monks in the park quietly saw a fat lizard devour juicy bugs.

fig/sym 2 Rates varied from 14.25% to 17.50% on loans from $298 to $36,500.

speed 3 Keith may make an authentic map of the ancient city for the firm.

**gwam** 1' | 1 | 2 | 3 | 4 | 5 | 6 | 7 | 8 | 9 | 10 | 11 | 12 | 13 |

---

### 70B • 5
### Assessment:
### Keying Skill

1. Key a 3' writing on ¶s of 69B, p. 169; find *gwam*.

2. Proofread your 3' writing and count/record errors.

---

### 70C • 40
### Assessment:
### Report Skills

Format/key the document shown at right and on p. 172 as a three-page unbound report, errors corrected. Place the references list on a separate sheet—as page 4. Save as RPT70C1.

words

ENHANCE YOUR REPORT IMAGE                                    5

Whether in school or on the job, you must prepare and present re-    18
ports.  Written reports create an image of you--on paper.  To achieve the    33
most positive image, written reports must be prepared carefully and pre-    47
sented forcefully.                                                          51

To prepare an excellent report, Clippinger (1995, 11-12) suggests five    66
equally vital steps that must be taken in the order listed:    (1) plan;    80
(2) draft;  (3) revise;  (4) edit;  (5) format.                              89

Plan the Report                                                             92

To plan, ask:  What is my purpose for writing, and what is the    105
reader's purpose for reading what I write?  The answers become the core    120
of the message.  Compose and key the core idea.  Then as they come to    134
mind through listening, reading, and thinking, jot (on the computer screen)    149
ideas and facts that are related to the core idea.  Next, check the list for    165
missing items (and add them), unneeded items (and delete them), and    178
redundant items (and combine them).  Put the items in psychological or-    193
der (main point followed by details, usually) and arrange them logically (in    208
chronological, geographical, or importance order, for example).  Finally,    223
check the list to see that the items are tied together and related to the core    239
idea.  When appropriate, use tables, charts, or graphs to condense data;    253
then list only summaries of what the visuals reveal in greater detail.    268

*(continued on next page)*

# LESSON 160 — Tables: One-Line Column Headings

**Objectives:**
1. To format tables with single-line blocked headings.
2. To format tables with single-line centered headings.

## 160A • 5
### Conditioning Practice

each line twice

| | | |
|---|---|---|
| alphabet | 1 | We moved quickly to pack an extra dozen lanyards Bif just bought. |
| speed | 2 | Both of the men risk a big penalty if they dismantle their autos. |
| fig/sym | 3 | I sold 22 at $45 less 13%, 8 at $69 less 5%, & 16 at $70 less 8%. |

**gwam** 1' | 1 | 2 | 3 | 4 | 5 | 6 | 7 | 8 | 9 | 10 | 11 | 12 | 13 |

## FORMATTING

## 160B • 10
### Blocked Column Headings

1. Review Tables on p. 368, and refer to table model (block headings), p. 157.
2. Horizontally and vertically center the table at right. Insert current year in the main heading. **CS:** 0.5" (6 sp.); DS; block column headings.

**wp note:**
When using the Table feature, disregard these directions: Column spacing (CS) and line spacing (DS or SS).

|  | | words |
|---|---|---|
| MONTHLY HOME BUDGET FOR ---- | | 6 |
| Joe and Mary Wood | | 9 |
| Budget Item | Amount | 14 |
| Food and household supplies | $575 | 16 |
| Home mortgage and taxes | 635 | 23 |
| Payments—Automobile | 345 | 28 |
| Utilities | 245 | 33 |
| Clothing and gifts | 250 | 36 |
| Gas, lunches, and entertainment | 300 | 40 |
| Savings | 225 | 47 |

## 160C • 5
### Drill: Centered Column Headings
(Electronics Only)

► 1. Review Centering column headings section on p. RG19.

► 2. Center the column headings and entries at right by the longest line, whether heading or entry. Key headings 2" from top of sheet; CS: 0.5" (6 sp.); DS data; do not correct errors.

| Microcomputer | Capacity | Rating | |
|---|---|---|---|
| Expo 688 | High | *** | 7 |
| Star | Medium | *** | 10 |
| Captain | Low | * | 13 |
| World | Medium | ** | 19 |

## 160D • 30
### Centered Column Headings

**Table 1**

Center table; CS: 0.75" (8 sp.); DS; center column headings. Use **BILL WAVERLY'S COURSE SCHEDULE** as the main heading.

| Course | Period | Room | |
|---|---|---|---|
| | | | heading 6 |
| | | | 11 |
| Applied Mathematics I | 1 | East--134 | 17 |
| Consumer Economics | 2 | South--114 | 24 |
| Sophomore English | 3 | East--201 | 30 |
| Physical Education | 4 | North--Gym | 36 |
| Document Processing II | 6 | South--104B | 44 |
| Principles of Technology | 7 | West--101 | 51 |
| World Cultures | 8 | South--205 | 56 |

## Draft the Message

words
273

To draft or compose the message, pretend that the reader is sitting before you. Write (at the keyboard) as you would talk with that person (level of vocabulary, degree of formality, and so on). Focus on the core of your message as you follow your listed items. Ignore for now such things as grammar, spelling, and style. Complete the entire report in one work session, if possible. If that is not possible, finish at least a major section without stopping (to gain continuity).

## Revise the Copy

To revise, read and study what you wrote. Try to read the text as the reader will--without knowing what you meant to say. Ask again and again: Does it do what I set out to do--to get the message from my mind into the reader's mind in a favorable way? If not, why not? Check for and eliminate cliches, faulty logic, irrelevant facts or ideas, lack of examples, or vague statements. Revise the message until it cannot be misunderstood.

## Edit the Text

To edit, study the revised draft and analyze how you said what you wrote, looking at each word, phrase, and sentence. Put yourself in the reader's place again. Ask these questions: Is the text interesting? Did I use active verbs? Do sentences vary in length and structure? Do the ideas flow evenly and smoothly and support the core idea or theme? Rid the text of common defects: excess words, impressive-sounding words and technical jargon, passive verbs, indefinite words, long words, short choppy sentences or complicated ones, and ill-chosen words or lack of transitional words or phrases. For a "proof of the pudding" check, have the text read by another set of eyes and revise the text again if any part of the message is unclear or confusing. Excellent reports result from multiple revisions. (Harcourt, and others, 1996, 76)

## Format the Report

To format or present the report, leave blank space around the text and between parts. Use a standard report format for placement and spacing. Use emphasis devices for items you want to stress: bold, italic, underline, and bullets. Use such devices judiciously because if you emphasize everything, you emphasize nothing.

You may choose a distinctive typeface of larger size for the report title. Generally, though, use 10- or 12-point type for the body copy and one or two emphasis devices to highlight different levels of internal headings (ALL CAPS, bold, italic, underline). Such final touches make the report appear inviting, well organized, and easy to read.

Finally, support your report with a list of references from which you paraphrased or directly quoted. Quoting or paraphrasing without giving credit is illegal; further, supporting your report with relevant references helps to authenticate what you have said.

## REFERENCES

Baugh, L. Sue. How to Write Term Papers and Reports. Lincolnwood, IL: VGM Career Horizons, 1993.

Clippinger, Dorinda A. "Write This Way." The Small Business Journal, March 1995.

Harcourt, Jules, and others. Business Communication. Cincinnati: South-Western Publishing Co., 1996.

Sorrenson, Sharon. Webster's New World Student Handbook. 2d ed. New York: Prentice-Hall, Inc., 1992.

## Proofreading alert:

1. Check the document format. Are all parts included? Are top, bottom, and side margins appropriate and consistent? Is vertical spacing between parts accurate? Is the text attractive and readable?

2. Proofread special parts of the document. For example, on reports, check the headings, enumerated items, endnotes, and references.

3. Read slowly and proofread text at least twice—once for content and again for mechanics.

**Document 2**
**Endnotes Page**

1. Review Endnotes page in the Report Documentation section on p. 368; refer to endnotes page model on p. 368 and p. RG13.

2. Format endnotes page for Document 1 at right in bound format. Include an appropriate heading.

**Document 3**
**Bibliography**

1. Review Reference list/ bibliography in the Report Documentation section on p. 368; refer to bibliography model on p. 368 and p. RG13.

2. Format bibliography for Document 1 at right in bound format.

**Document 4**
**Title Page**

---

Educational Opportunities | 226

In 1993, about 29 colleges and universities offered bachelor's degree | 240
programs in health services administration. Sixty-four schools had | 254
programs leading to the master's degree in health services adminis- | 267
tration. . . .[3] | 270

Bachelor's degree programs. Health services managers are often re- | 284
cruited from the college or university from which they were graduated. In | 299
larger hospitals, they are often recruited to fill assistant department head | 314
positions. In smaller hospitals, they may be able to enter at the depart- | 329
ment head level.[4] | 333

Additional Information | 338

The organizations listed below will be contacted to gather information | 352
about academic programs in health services management. These organi- | 366
zations will be asked to recommend a curriculum design expert who could | 380
assist in developing the courses in the major. | 390

1. American College of Healthcare Executives, 840 North Lake Shore | 403
   Dr., Chicago, IL 60611-7516. | 409
2. Association of University Programs in Health Administration, 1911 | 423
   Fort Meyer Dr., Ste. 503, Arlington, VA 22209-2937. | 434
3. National Health Council, Health Careers Programs, 70 West 40th | 447
   St., New York, NY 10018-5914. | 454
4. American College of Health Care Administrators, P.O. Box 5890, | 467
   8120 Woodmont Ave., Ste. 200, Bethesda, MD 20814-3219. | 478

..........................................................................................

heading 2

[1] United States Department of Labor, Bureau of Statistics, Occupa- | 15
tional Outlook Handbook, 1994-1995 ed. (Washington, DC: U.S. Gov- | 29
ernment Printing Office, April 1994), p. 44. | 38

[2] Carol Kleinmann, 100 Best Job$ for the 1990's & Beyond (Chicago: | 52
Dearborn Financial Publishing, Inc., 1995), pp. 197-228. | 63

[3] United States Department of Labor, Bureau of Statistics, p. 44. | 76

[4] Carol Kleinmann, p. 204. | 81

..........................................................................................

BIBLIOGRAPHY | 3

Kleinmann, Carol. 100 Best Job$ for the 1990's & Beyond. | 14
Chicago: Dearborn Financial Publishing, Inc., 1995. | 25

United States Department of Labor, Bureau of Statistics. Occu- | 38
pational Outlook Handbook. 1994-1995 ed. Washington, | 49
DC: U.S. Government Printing Office, April 1994. | 59

..........................................................................................

1. If needed, review Title page section in Other    Report Pages on p. 368.    2. Prepare a title page for Document 1.

# Assess Keyboarding & Table Skills

**Objectives:**
1. To build/assess keying skill.
2. To assess table knowledge and skills.

**71A • 5**
**Conditioning Practice**

each line twice SS; DS between 2-line groups; a 1' writing on line 3

alphabet 1 Jacques asked to be given one week to reply to the tax quiz form.

fig/sym 2 The damaged carton (#29-403-567) was returned on June 18 to AF&T.

speed 3 Doris may sign the proxy form if they make an audit of the firms.

| gwam | 1' | 1 | 2 | 3 | 4 | 5 | 6 | 7 | 8 | 9 | 10 | 11 | 12 | 13 |

**71B • 10**
**Assessment: Keying Skill**

1. Key a 1' writing on each ¶; find *gwam* on each.
2. Key a 2' writing on ¶s 1-3 combined; find *gwam*.
3. Key a 3' writing on ¶s 1-3 combined; find *gwam*, count errors.

all letters used

| | gwam | 2' | 3' |

Workers on the job have to plan their workdays and organize    6  4  72
their work so that all duties are done in a timely fashion.  As a   13  8  76
result, much is being said about teaching students to prioritize   19 13  81
work.  The truth is that novice office workers have only limited   26 17  85
opportunities to set their own priorities; rather, priorities are   32 21  89
often set for them.    34 23  91

For example, in a word processing center a supervisor receives   40 27  95
the work from various document writers.   He or she then assigns the   47 31  99
work to keyboard operators on the basis of their work loads and in   54 36 104
the sequence of immediacy of need.   Even a private secretary is   60 40 108
often told by the "boss" which work is urgent and which may not be   67 45 112
needed immediately.    69 46 114

As workers develop on the job and are given a greater variety   75 50 118
of tasks to perform, the need to set priorities increases.  By   81 54 122
then, however, they will have learned through their supervisors   88 59 126
which types of tasks take priority and which ones can be put off.   94 63 131
Realize that priorities grow out of the immediacy or timeliness   101 67 135
of need.    102 68 136

| gwam | 2' | 1 | 2 | 3 | 4 | 5 | 6 |
| | 3' | 1 | 2 | 3 | 4 |

## Document 2
### References Page

1. Review Report Documentation on p. 368; refer to reference list model, p. RG13.

2. Format references at right as page 3 for Document 1. Include an appropriate heading.

### Documents 3 and 4
### Title Page and Table of Contents

|  | words |
|---|---|
|  | heading 2 |

Fulton, Patsy J. *Office Procedures and Technology*. Cincinnati: South-Western Publishing Co., 1994. — 17, 23

Jaderstrom, Susan, and Leonard B. Kruk. *Administrative Support Systems and Procedures*. Cincinnati: South-Western Publishing Co., 1992. — 37, 51

VanHuss, Susie H., and Willard R. Daggett. *Electronic Office Systems*. Cincinnati: South-Western Publishing Co., 1992. — 65, 76

1. Review Other Report Pages on p. 368. Refer to title page and table of contents models on p. RG14.

2. Format and key a table of contents and title page for Document 1.

---

## LESSON 159 — Bound Reports

**Objectives:**

1. To format a bound report.
2. To format an endnotes, bibliography, and title page.

### 159A • 5
### Conditioning Practice

each line twice

alphabet 1 Fay's bright jacket has an amazing weave and exceptional quality.

speed 2 If they go to the social with us, they may visit the eight girls.

fig/sym 3 The computer (486-SX) was $2,159 and printer (Elon 370) was $259.

gwam 1' | 1 | 2 | 3 | 4 | 5 | 6 | 7 | 8 | 9 | 10 | 11 | 12 | 13 |

## L ANGUAGE SKILLS

### 159B • 45
### Bound Report Processing

#### Document 1
#### Report with Long Quotation

1. Review Report Margins on p. 367; refer to bound report model, p. 367 and pp. RG 13-14.

2. Format the copy at right and on p. 377 in bound format; DS.

3. Key second line of enumerations flush with the first letter in the first line (hanging indent format).

**Proofreading alert:**
The report copy contains 6 errors. Locate and correct them as you key.

| | words |
|---|---|

HEALTH SERVICES MANAGEMENT PROGRAM — 7

This report gives information about opportunites in health services management. A proposal to have Heritage University develope and offer a health services management curriculum at the undergraduate level likely will be submitted within six months. — 21, 35, 50, 57

Employment Opportunities — 62

Opportunites for employmnet in health services are numerous and growing. Health care promises strong employment into the next century. — 75, 90

Places of employment. People who manage health services are needed in a wide variety of work settings. The most common place of employment for these individuals is hospitals, followed by the offices of pyhsicians, dentists, and other health-related practioneers.[1] — 102, 117, 131, 144

Employment outlook. Careers in the health-care area are included in the 100 Best Job$ for the 1990's & Beyond.[2] Demand for health services managers is expected to be strong as the country's population ages and needs more health-care services. Also, demand for managers will increase as the providers of health care become more oriented to the bottom line because of competition. — 157, 172, 186, 201, 216, 221

*(continued on next page)*

**Table 1**

Using standard placement, format/key the table DS with 1.0" (10 sp.) between columns; correct errors.

**Table 2**

Using standard placement, format/key the table DS with 1.0" (10 sp.) between columns; make indicated changes and correct any errors you make as you key.

**Table 3**

Format/key the table DS with 0.6" (6 sp.) between columns; correct errors.

**Table 4**

If time permits, format/key Table 1 again, substituting your favorite novels/authors.

| | | words |
|---|---|---|
| MY ALL-TIME FAVORITE NOVELS | | 6 |
| Title | Author | 9 |
| East of Eden | Steinbeck | 13 |
| Grapes of Wrath | Steinbeck | 19 |
| The Old Man and the Sea | Hemingway | 25 |
| The Red Badge of Courage | Crane | 32 |
| The Yearling | Rawlings | 36 |

| | | words |
|---|---|---|
| MOST VISITED CIVIL WAR SITES | | 6 |
| (Managed by National Park Service) | | 13 |
| Site | Mil. | 15 |
| Gettysburg, PA | 1.4 | 19 |
| Chickamauga-Chatanooga, GA-TN | 1.0 | 26 |
| Vicksburg, ~~VA~~ MS | 1.90 | 30 |
| Kennesaw, GA | 0.9 | 33 |
| Manasas, VA | 0.6 | 36 |
| | | 40 |
| Source: U.S. NEWS & WORD REPORT, April 10, | | 49 |
| 1995. | | 50 |

| | | | words |
|---|---|---|---|
| ALL-TIME BEST-SELLING MUSIC ALBUMS | | | 7 |
| Title | Artist | Sold | 11 |
| Thriller | Michael Jackson | 24 m. | 17 |
| Rumours | Fleetwood Mac | 17 m. | 23 |
| Boston | Boston | 15 m. | 27 |
| Eagles Greatest Hits | Eagles | 14 m. | 34 |
| Born in the U.S.A. | Bruce Springsteen | 14 m. | 43 |
| Total Sales | | 84 m. | 46 |
| | | | 49 |
| Source: USA Today, May 5, 1995. | | | 56 |

## 158B • 45
## Unbound Report Processing

**Document 1**
**Unbound Report with Textual Citations**

1. Review Reports on p. 367; refer to unbound report model on p. RG12.

2. Format the copy at right in unbound format; DS. Do NOT replace underlines with italics.

3. Key second and subsequent lines of enumerated items even with the ¶ indention point.

4. Proofread and correct errors before printing (or removing from typewriter).

**🔍 Proofreading alert:**

1. Assume the text has errors before you begin proofreading.

2. Become familiar with commonly misspelled words and sound-alike word pairs (personal/personnel).

3. Check for errors in spacing with punctuation marks, especially quotation marks and apostrophes.

4. Be sure quotation marks, parentheses, and brackets occur in pairs. Omitting the closing mark is a common error.

**Note:** A single explanatory note in a report may be indicated by an asterisk (*) with a matching asterisk preceding the note at the foot of the page.

If two or more explanatory notes occur in a report, matching superscript figures are used to number them.

|   |   |
|---|---|
| TELEPHONE SKILLS | 3 |

Next to face-to-face communication, the telephone is the most popular | 17
means of exchanging information in business. (Jaderstrom and Kruk, | 31
1992, 201) It is important, therefore, that all employees realize that a | 46
business will be more successful if every employee can use the phone | 59
more efficiently and effectively. | 66

Telephone Techniques | 71

People who have good telephone techniques can turn complaining | 83
callers into satisfied ones; create a very good image for the business with | 99
its customers, clients, and suppliers; and get more done each day because | 114
they handle callers properly. | 120

Processing incoming calls. Incoming calls should be answered | 132
promptly. (Fulton, 1994, 209) The employee answering the call should | 146
identify himself or herself immediately and speak in a tone that is relaxed | 162
and low-pitched. A writing pad should be kept near the phone so that | 176
all important parts of the conversation can be recorded. The caller should | 191
be thanked at the end of the conversation. | 200

Processing outgoing calls. These techniques should be used to | 212
improve the process of placing calls: | 220

1. Group calls and make them during set times each day to reduce | 233
   the amount of idle chatter. | 239

2. Place calls in order of importance or urgency. | 249

3. Identify yourself as the caller as soon as the call is answered. | 263

4. If necessary, request the name and extension number of the person | 277
   with whom you are speaking in the event a second call must be made. | 290

5. Outline the major points of each call and place needed reference | 304
   material at hand before placing a call. (Jaderstrom and Kruk, 1992, 203) | 319

Telephone Procedures | 323

Employees must know how to screen calls, transfer calls, and to place | 337
callers on hold properly if calls are to be processed effectively. | 351

Screening calls. Callers are screened by identifying who is calling | 365
and by asking the purpose of the call so that the person answering can | 379
decide to process the call or transfer it to another person. | 391

Transferring calls. Since having calls transferred can be an exasper- | 406
ating experience* for callers, the person transferring the call should be | 420
certain the caller speaks to the correct person on the first transfer. | 435

Holding calls. Calls should be placed on hold only when necessary, | 449
for short periods of time, and in a courteous manner. If calls need to be | 464
put on hold for more than a minute or two, callers should be given | 477
the option of being called back. (VanHuss and Daggett, 1992, 285) | 490

_____ | 494

*Repeated transfers may be exasperating because callers must explain | 507
the purpose of the call each time the call is transferred. | 519

# Twin Cities Youth Camp for Fine & Performing Arts

**TWIN CITIES
YOUTH CAMP**

**(A Keyboarding
Simulation)**

## Setting and Organization

This coming summer Twin Cities University (TCU) will sponsor a Twin Cities Youth Camp for Fine & Performing Arts. The camp is made possible by grants from the Carnegie Foundation and the National Endowment for the Arts. A committee of local high school teachers will assist in planning and coordinating the camp.

The purpose of the camp is to give approximately 40 qualified high school seniors in the Minneapolis-St. Paul area an opportunity to study and work with outstanding performers in the fields of art, music, theater, and dance. The camp will be limited to 8-10 students in each of those categories.

The study program will include formal classes, demonstrations, individualized coaching, and workshop-style performances of both students and teachers. Campers will also visit art galleries and museums and attend evening events in which professionals perform in recital or concert.

You have been chosen to work as a part-time office assistant to Ms. Twyla Winfrey, of Lake Como High School, who chairs the high school teacher committee. She works directly with Dr. Jorgi Franco of TCU, who chairs the university planning committee.

In addition to answering the telephone, filing correspondence and other records, and entering/retrieving information using the computer, you will process memos, letters, reports, and other documents. Even though your keyboarding teacher has verified that you know how to process documents in standard formats, Ms. Winfrey gives you the following excerpts from the *Formatting Manual* used by the Twin Cities Youth Camp office personnel.

You are to consult the excerpts if you have format questions.

## Format Guides

### Letters

1. Stationery: camp letterhead/envelopes.
2. Format: block style, open punctuation.
3. SM: defaults (or 1").
4. TM: 2" (or Center Page feature).
5. Spacing: QS (3 blank line spaces) between date and letter address and between complimentary close and writer's name; DS (1 blank line space) between all other parts.

### Memos

1. Stationery: camp letterhead.
2. Format: standard.
3. SM: defaults (or 1").
4. TM: 2".
5. Spacing: DS (1 blank line space) between all parts; SS ¶s, DS between them.

### Announcements and Tables

1. Stationery: plain paper.
2. TM: 2" (or Center Page feature).
3. Spacing: DS throughout; EXCEPTION: SS 2-line headings, source notes, and grouped items within tables.

### Reports

1. Stationery: plain paper.
2. SM: defaults (or 1").
3. TM: 2", page 1 and references page, if separate; otherwise, 1".
4. PE: at least 1" bottom margin.
5. Spacing: QS (3 blank line spaces) between title and body; DS all other lines.
6. Page numbers: page 1, not numbered; other pages, at top right margin.

**157B • 45**
**Standard and Simplified Memos**

**Memo 1**

1. Review Standard format on p. 367 and refer to standard memo model on p. RG9.
2. Format memo at right in standard format.

**Memo 2**

1. Review Simplified format on p. 367 and refer to simplified memo model on p. RG9.
2. Format memo at right in simplified format.

**Memo 3**

Format the memo at right in simplified format.

**Memo 4**

Reformat Memo 3 in standard format.

words

TO: Olivia Dunoon | FROM: Mona Egan | DATE: September 30, ---- |    12
SUBJECT:   INTERVIEW SCHEDULE    17

Mr. Glenn Dodge and Ms. April Grant have been selected to return for a    32
second interview for the position of administrative assistant.    44

You are to interview Mr. Dodge at 10:30 a.m. on October 4 and Ms. Grant    59
at 1:30 p.m. on October 5. Both interviews will take place in your office    74
and should last about 45 minutes. Mrs. Cyd Trent will accompany each    88
candidate. | xx    90

October 3, ---- | Jim Tudor, Human Resources Director | ADVERTISING    13
A NEW POSITION    16

This memo is to inform you that the vice president for operations has    30
approved a new position in the Accounting Department and that we will be    44
advertising the position in the major newspapers and at the placement    58
offices of local colleges and universities.    67

The position is approved for December 1; therefore, we want to begin re-    82
cruiting soon. Please tell me the deadline I must meet to have an ad appear    97
in next Sunday's newspaper.    103

Bryan Epler, Senior Accountant | xx    110

October 4, ---- | Perry de los Santos, Regional Sales Manager | CLIENT    13
ENTERTAINMENT GUIDELINES    18

Attached are the recently approved guidelines for entertaining clients,    33
which I mentioned at last week's meeting. All sales reps and account    47
managers are to use them immediately.    55

Please fax them to all the sales reps and account managers in your region    69
by tomorrow.    72

John Wilde, VP Sales | xx | Attachment | c Accounting Department    84

---

**LESSON 158**

## Unbound Reports

**Objectives:**
1. To format an unbound report with textual citations.
2. To format a reference page, title page, and table of contents.

**158A • 5**
**Conditioning Practice**

each line twice

alphabet 1 June quickly wraps the five dozen macaroons and six big cupcakes.

speed 2 If I go to the city to visit them, I may go to the spa and dorms.

fig/sym 3 I got 25% off on orders over $83,900 because of contract #41-6-7.

**gwam** 1' | 1 | 2 | 3 | 4 | 5 | 6 | 7 | 8 | 9 | 10 | 11 | 12 | 13 |

# A Keyboarding Simulation

**Objectives:**

**1.** To apply keying skills in a work setting.

**2.** To work under direction but with few *specific* directions.

**72A-75A • 5**
**Daily Warmup**

| | | |
|---|---|---|
| alphabet | 1 | The judge quizzed my expert witness before making the vital call. |
| fig/sym | 2 | Both started today (6/7):   Tina at $421.89/wk.; Vic at $10.53/hr. |
| speed | 3 | A city panel may work with the six big firms to fix the problems. |
| **gwam** | 1' | 1 \| 2 \| 3 \| 4 \| 5 \| 6 \| 7 \| 8 \| 9 \| 10 \| 11 \| 12 \| 13 \| |

**F**ORMATTING

**72B-75B • 45**
**Simulation**

**Document 1**
**Standard Memo**

*From the desk of:*
*Ms. Winfrey*

**TO:** Members of Youth Camp Planning Committee

**FROM:** Twyla Winfrey, Chair, H.S.

**DATE:** January 5, ----

**SUBJECT:** Youth Camp Participant Selection Process

**Document 2**
**Summary Report in Unbound Format**

*From the desk of:*
*Ms. Winfrey*

**Format:** Unbound DS report; bold the title; italicize side headings (if Italic is available)

**Purpose:** To promote summer youth camp

Here is a first draft of a summary of the selection process to be used in choosing students for the Twin Cities Youth Camp for Fine & Performing Arts to be held at Twin Cities University this summer.

I believe the decisions reached at our last joint meeting are accurately reflected in the summary.  To be sure, please read the summary carefully and note any changes you think should be made.

After I receive your feedback, I'll prepare a revised summary to be included in a packet of material to be given to prospective participants and their parents.

xx | Enclosure

TWIN CITIES YOUTH CAMP FOR FINE & PERFORMING ARTS

July 9-22, ----

The Twin Cities Youth Camp for Fine & Performing Arts on the Twin Cities University campus is scheduled for two weeks, from Sunday afternoon, July 9, to Saturday night, July 22.  Made possible by grants from the Carnegie Foundation and the National Endowment for the Arts, the camp will give approximately forty students a rare opportunity to study and work with outstanding specialists in the fields of art, music, theater, and dance.  The camp can accommodate up to ten students in each of these fields.

Art Camp

Up to ten art students will be chosen on the basis of their entries in a competitive art exhibit to be held at Roseville High School on Saturday, May 13.  Entries will be judged by an art professor from TCU, an art teacher from a local high school, and an art critic from the Minneapolis Institute of Art.  Each student must enter at least three but not more than five pieces--at least one in oils, one in watercolor, and one in charcoal.  Other categories include sculpture and computer graphics.

Music Camp

As many as ten music students will be chosen based on their performance at competitive auditions to be held at Hiawatha High School on Saturday, May 13.

*(continued on next page)*

## 156B • 15
### Letters: Script Copy

**Letter 1**

1. Format letter in block format, open punctuation.
2. Address the letter to:
   **Mr. Maxwell G. Clay
   Wren Corporation
   984 Lily Rd.
   South Bend, IN 46637-7051**
3. Date the letter **May 1,----;** include a salutation and complimentary close. (**Tom Welty, Secretary**, is the writer.)
4. Use **OFFICE AUTOMATION CONVENTION NEEDS** as a subject line. Insert current year at ----.
5. Include other letter parts as needed.

🔍 **Proofreading alert:**

The letter contains 8 unmarked errors; find and correct them as you key the letter.

**Letter 2**

Reformat the letter at right in simplified block format.

|  | words |
|---|---|
|  | opening 27 |

The ---- Regional Office Automation Convention will be | 38
held at the hotel morris here in South Bend on May 25. We are | 51
planing to give demonstrations of the McGregger 6000 computer, the | 65
Pro Copier 690, and the Park 7000 color printer. President Koontz | 78
suggested that personnel from the Wren Corporations Information | 91
Processing Division (IPD) give demonstrations at the convention. | 104
Would it be possible for you to assist us by providing IPD personal? | 118
We will, of course provide the equipment. | 127

If so, we would like the individuals you select to be specialists | 140
with the equipment who can present the professional image that is | 154
critical to advance are sells efforts. I'll call you within a few days to | 169
give you details about the convention. | 177

|  | closing 183 |
|---|---|

## 156C • 30
### Letters: Sustained Practice

**Time Schedule**

| | |
|---|---|
| Plan and prepare | 3' |
| Timed production | 20' |
| Proofread/compute *n-pram* | 7' |

1. Make a list of documents to be processed:
   page 372, 155C, Letter 1
   page 371, 155B, Letter 2
   page 370, 154B, Letter 2
   page 371, 155B, Letter 1
2. Arrange materials for easy access. Process (in the order listed) as many of the letters as you can in 20'. Proofread and correct each letter before beginning the next.
3. After time is called, proofread the final document and, if requested, print all documents.
4. Identify uncorrected errors; compute *n-pram* (number of words keyed, minus the number of errors times 10; divided by production time). Put letters in the order listed in Step 1.

---

## LESSON 157 — Simplified and Standard Memos

**Objectives:**
1. To format standard and simplified memos.
2. To process memos with additional memo parts.

## 157A • 5
### Conditioning Practice

each line twice

| | | |
|---|---|---|
| alphabet | 1 | Elvira enjoyed the amazing water tricks of six quick polar bears. |
| speed | 2 | The man paid a visit to the downtown firm to sign the work forms. |
| figures | 3 | Tom flew 2,467 miles in June; 3,158 in July; and 1,905 in August. |
| gwam | 1' | 1 \| 2 \| 3 \| 4 \| 5 \| 6 \| 7 \| 8 \| 9 \| 10 \| 11 \| 12 \| 13 \| |

The judges will include two professors of music from TCU, two music teachers from local high schools, and two music critics (one from the Star Tribune, the other from the Pioneer Press). Both vocalists and instrumentalists may enter the competition. For the first time, a computerized synthesizer may be used for accompaniment.

Theater Camp

Eight to ten theater students will be chosen on the basis of their performance at competitive auditions to be held at Richfield High School on Saturday, May 20. Judges will include two professors of drama and theater from TCU, two class play directors from local high schools, and one drama/theater critic from each of our local newspapers. Musical theater students may enter as actors, vocalists, or both.

Dance Camp

Up to ten dance students will be selected on the basis of their performance at a dance competition to be held at Falcon Heights High School on Saturday, May 13. Judges will be specialists in ballet and modern dance from TCU, a dance theater critic from the Star Tribune, and the director of Twin Cities Dance Company. Entrants may dance solo, in pairs, or in groups.

Living Accommodations

All students will live in campus dormitories. Each group will be mentored by a TCU faculty member and a high school teacher. Meals will be provided for all youth campers in the Student Center cafeteria. Student living costs are covered by the grants.

**Document 3**
Youth camp
faculty list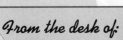

*From the desk of:*
*Ms. Winfrey*

**Format:** 3-column table; SS body, but DS between departmental groups— *open File TCAMP3*

**TM:** 2" (or Center Page feature)

**CS:** 0.6" (6 sp.)

**Purpose:** To include in promotion packet for students/parents

YOUTH CAMP FOR FINE & PERFORMING ARTS
*Participating TCU Faculty & Staff*

| Name | Function | Department |
|------|----------|------------|
| Dr. John M. Lenz | Coordinater | Art |
| Ms. Lucia del Rio | Instructor | Art |
| Mr. Frederick Marx | Instructor | Art |
| Miss Bella Spear | Coach | Art |
| Mr. Paul Mehta | coach | Dance |
| Miss Ana de Avila | Coordinator | Dance |
| Mr. Ari Baccus | Instructor | Dance |
| Ms. Tamara Jones | Instructor | Dance |
| Mr. Darius Brown | Cordinator | Music |
| Mr. Felix Ardello | Instructor | Music |
| Ms. Anita Fry Carr | Instructor | " |
| Miss Susan Parish | Coach | " |
| Dr. Olivia Habjan | Coordinator | Theatre |
| Ms. Serena Conte | Instructor | " |
| Mr. Henri DeLong | Instructor | " |
| Mr. Cyril Pierce | Coach | " |

## Format Letters with Additional Letter Parts

**Letter 1**

1. Review letter parts and spacing guides on p. 366 and p. RG8.
2. Key letter at right in block format with open punctuation.

**Letter 2**

Key letter at right in modified block format with indented ¶s; use mixed punctuation.

| | words |
|---|---|
| September 25, ---- | REGISTERED | Mr. John G. Hale | Best Equip- | 12 |
| ment | 4095 Kentucky Ave. | Denver, CO 80219-7851 | Dear Mr. Hale | | 24 |
| REQUEST FOR REPLACEMENT EQUIPMENT | 30 |

The photocopier (Model X-279-5Z) has needed service calls for six different   46
problems since it was installed on July 25.   55

The person who serviced the machine on the last visit reported to my office   70
manager that there is a defect in the mechanism that secures the main   84
roller.   86

This letter is notification that I expect you to honor our state's "Lemon Law"   101
and replace this photocopier with an equivalent one within the next ten   116
days.   117

Sincerely | MILAN, INC. | Ms. Mary L. Bandan, President | xx | c Bill   130
James, Attorney   133

---

September 25, ---- | Attention Office Manager | Yarnell Co. | 25 Cory   13
Dr. | Bowie, MD 20720-1497 | Ladies and Gentlemen: | A DIFFERENT   25
SOLUTION   26

Within the next four weeks, VOX, INC. will begin selling and servicing   40
its excellent lines of office equipment and supplies in and around Bowie.   55

VOX carries a complete line of computers, monitors, scanners, and print-   69
ers. The VOX3997 computer with state-of-the-art CD-ROM drives was voted   82
the best in its class by Office Equipment Review this past   96
month. This model as well as others are described in the enclosures.   110

Mrs. Juanita B. Forge, the Bowie Office sales manager, will call you soon   125
to set up an appointment to explain why you should consider VOX for   139
your office equipment needs. Please give us this opportunity to serve you.   154

Sincerely, | Ms. Carla Fargo | Eastern Regional Manager | xx | Enclo-   166
sures | As an introductory bonus, VOX will discount your equipment   179
purchases 18 percent for three months after Juanita meets with you.   193

# LESSON 156

## Letters from Script

**Objectives:**
1. To format a letter from script copy.
2. To build letter-processing skills.

### 156A • 5
## Conditioning Practice

each line twice

| | | |
|---|---|---|
| alphabet | 1 | Jake will buy very good quality zinc from experts at the auction. |
| speed | 2 | Nancy may go with me to visit them by the cornfield and big lake. |
| fig/sym | 3 | Al's gas bill was $98.35 (+6%); his office bill was $40.17 (-2%). |

**gwam** 1' | 1 | 2 | 3 | 4 | 5 | 6 | 7 | 8 | 9 | 10 | 11 | 12 | 13 |

**Document 4**
Announcement

---

*From the desk of:*
*Ms. Winfrey*

**Format:** 2" TM; DS; center each line, bold the main heading
**Purpose:** To place on high school bulletin boards

---

**Document 5**
Final Event Program

---

*From the desk of:*
*Ms. Winfrey*

**Format:** 2-column table; DS body
**TM:** 2" (or Center Page feature)
**CS:** 0.8" (8 sp.)
**Purpose:** To include with letter inviting parents to final event

---

**Document 6**
Proposed Letter to Parents

---

*From the desk of:*
*Ms. Winfrey*

**Format:** Block style, open punctuation
**TM:** 2" (or Center Page feature)
**Date:** January 6, ----
**Address:** Mr./Mrs. John C. Dunn, 178 Royal Oak Blvd., Brooklyn Center, MN 55430-4322
**Salutation:** Dear Mr./Mrs. Dunn
**Complimentary close:** Cordially
**Signature:** Miss Adele Chiodi, Chair Invitation Committee
**Purpose:** To invite parents of participating students to final event

---

TWIN CITIES UNIVERSITY *AND* MINNEAPOLIS/ST. PAUL

anounce

Twin Cities Youth ~~Cared~~ *Camp* for Fine & Performing Arts

TCU Campus *July 9-22*

for

High School *Student* Artists, Musicians, Actors, and Dancers

Participants Determined by Competitive *Exhibits/* Auditions

*Admission* Attendance: *&* Free

Courtesy Carnegie Foundation and National Endowment for the Arts

Further Information to be Available Soon!

---

VOICES OF HARMONY
Youth Camp ~~Main~~ *Final* Event

| Theme | Focus |
|---|---|
| Voices of Freedom | Gospel music/drama |
| Voices of Expression | Hispanic music/~~drama~~ *dance* |
| Voices of the Spirit | Native American poetry/~~cadence~~ *rhythm* |
| Voices of Jazz | African-American jazz/dance |
| Voices of Movement | Oriental music/~~drama~~ *dance* |
| Voices of Tradition | Classical/folk music |
| Voices of the American Stage | Tribute to american musicals |
| Voices of ~~Youth~~ *Hope* | Youth looks toward the future |

---

You are invited to attend the Final Event of the Twin Cities Youth Camp for Fine & Performing Arts. This exciting event, "Voices of Harmony," will be held in Nokomis Auditorium on the TCU campus at 7:30 p.m., July 22. Admission for parents is free.

A copy of the preliminary program is enclosed. You will note the multicultural focus of the program, which reflects the theme of the two-week camp in which the student participants will be engaged. The youth campers are highlighted, but some TCU faculty and students are included when necessary to supplement the cast.

In addition to the variety of music, drama, and dance that comprise the program, you will enjoy viewing the artwork of the Art Campers that will be exhibited in the foyer of the auditorium.

The Final Event is designed to delight you, to surprise you, and to expand your perspective. Please come and bring other members of your family (if any) to support these happy campers. | xx

## 154C • 10
### Drill: Letter Parts

Use Letter 1 copy, block format and open punctuation, to complete this drill.

1. Three 1' writings on the opening lines (date through salutation) and as much of the letter body as time permits. Try to improve by 1 or 2 words with each writing.

2. Three 30" writings on the last line of the body and closing lines (complimentary close through initials). Try to improve by 1 or 2 words with each writing.

3. A 3' writing on the entire letter.

## LESSON 155

# Personal-Business and Business Letters

**Objectives:**

**1.** To process letters in block and simplified block formats.

**2.** To format letters with additional letter parts.

## 155A • 5
### Conditioning Practice

each line twice

| | | |
|---|---|---|
| alphabet | 1 | Jay asked four zany questions before each good example was given. |
| speed | 2 | The men may pay for a big emblem of the chapel with their profit. |
| figures | 3 | My mutual fund fell 4.87 points to 65.92 on Friday, May 30, 1996. |

**gwam** 1' | 1 | 2 | 3 | 4 | 5 | 6 | 7 | 8 | 9 | 10 | 11 | 12 | 13 |

## F ORMATTING

### 155B • 20
### Personal-Business and Business Letters

#### Letter 1

1. Review Block format for letters on p. 366; refer to personal-business format model, p. 124 and p. RG9.

2. Key personal-business letter at right in block format with mixed punctuation.

#### Letter 2

1. Review Simplified block format section on p. 366; refer to simplified block format model on p. 366 and p. RG10.

2. Key the business letter at right in simplified block format.

|  | words |
|---|---|
| 110 Ball Rd. | Anaheim, CA 92805-2214 | September 15, ---- | Ms. Greta | 13 |
| Hazlett | Admissions Counselor | Anaheim College | 1125 Cerritos | 25 |
| Ave. | Anaheim, CA 92805-6179 | Dear Ms. Hazlett: | 34 |

Thank you for sending the information about the various scholarships that 49
are awarded at Anaheim College. 55

Please send the application for the Gant Scholarship to me. I am confident 71
that I meet the criteria for this $2,500 award. 80

I am pleased I can be considered for additional financial aid. 93

Sincerely, | Juan P. Lucera 98

| | words |
|---|---|
| September 15, ---- | MS SUE CHADRON | BTM OFFICE SYS- | 10 |
| TEMS | 4827 CATOMA ST | JACKSONVILLE FL 32210-6592 | | 19 |
| ACKNOWLEDGMENT OF BID | 24 |

We have received your company's bid for the office equipment that we plan 38
to purchase. 41

My staff and I will consider all bids soon and will make a recommendation 56
to our senior officers by November 15. We plan to purchase all the equip- 71
ment before December 31. 76

Thank you for sending your quotation. It meets the specifications and 90
deadlines stated in the request for proposals and will be considered. 104

MISS CATHY C. CLAYTON | xx 109

*From the desk of:*
*Ms. Winfrey*

**Format:** 3-column table; SS body of table, but DS below data for each gallery
**TM:** 2" (or Center Page feature)
**CS:** 0.4" (4 sp.)
**Purpose:** To include in promotion packet for students/parents

**Document 8**
Letter to Judge of
the Dance Contest

*From the desk of:*
*Ms. Winfrey*

**Format:** Block style, open punctuation
**TM:** 2" (or Center Page feature)
**SM:** defaults (or 1")

**Documents 9-11**
Letters to Judges of Other
Competitions

*From the desk of:*
*Ms. Winfrey*

Process the message of Document 8 to each addressee listed at the right. Change the salutation as appropriate; make needed changes in ¶ 1 as indicated below the addresses. Use your initials as the keyboard operator.

HIGHLIGHTS OF ART MUSEUM TOUR

New Perspectives

| Gallery | Artist | Subject |
|---|---|---|
| African-American Gallery | A Collection | Prints |
| | Robert Scott Duncanson | Murals |
| Hispanic Gallery | Julio Larraz | Sketches |
| | Rafael Ortiz | Abstracts |
| Main Gallery | Thomas Sierak | Sketches |
| | Camille Pissaro | Landscapes |
| Oriental Gallery | Tat Shinno | Florals |
| | Sherrie McGraw | Still Life |

January 7, ----

Mr. Alexi Kosov
Star Tribune
800 N. First St.
Minneapolis, MN 55401-3627

Dear Mr. Kosov

How fortunate we are to have you join the panel of judges who will select the winners of the dance contest to be held at Falcon Heights High School at 2 p.m. on May 13.

You will be joined on the panel by selected faculty members from Twin Cities University and local high schools. It is especially fitting, though, to have a professional critic on the panel.

Your insistence on serving without honorarium is most commendable. Please know how grateful we are.

As the contest date nears, I'll send a friendly reminder.

Cordially yours

Ms. Twyla Winfrey, Chair
Planning Committee, H.S.

xx

**Ms. LuAnn Chang**
**Pioneer Press**
**345 Cedar St.**
**St. Paul, MN 55101-2266**

¶ 1, line 2: *art contest;*
*Roseville High School*

**Mr. Anton Navarro**
**Star Tribune**
**800 N. First St.**
**Minneapolis, MN 55401-3627**

¶ 1, line 2: *music contest;*
*Hiawatha High School*

**Mrs. Nadia Horowitz**
**Pioneer Press**
**345 Cedar St.**
**St. Paul, MN 55101-2266**

¶ 1, line 2: *drama contest;*
*Richfield High School*
¶ 1, line 3: *May 20*

# Simple Letters

**Objectives:**

**1.** To format block and modified block letters.

**2.** To use open and mixed punctuation.

## 154A • 5
## Conditioning Practice

each line twice; then 1'
writings on line 2

| | | |
|---|---|---|
| alphabet | 1 | Zac, be a good fellow and keep extra quiet to enjoy these movies. |
| speed | 2 | Pamela and Susi may fix the penalty box when they visit the city. |
| fig/sym | 3 | He arrived at 12:43 p.m. on Flight #80-7 (Gate 6) with 59 others. |

**gwam** 1' | 1 | 2 | 3 | 4 | 5 | 6 | 7 | 8 | 9 | 10 | 11 | 12 | 13 |

# **F** O R M A T T I N G

## 154B • 35
## Block and Modified Block Letters

### Letter 1

1. Review Letters on p. 366; refer to block letter format model, p. 366 and p. RG9.
2. Review Punctuation Styles on p. 367.
3. Key letter at right in block format with open punctuation.
4. Retain copy for use in 154C.

words

September 5, ---- | Dr. Louis L. Elmore | Medical Park Dr. | Birmingham,    13
AL 35213-2496 | Dear Dr. Elmore    19

The next meeting of the Wright Observatory Amateur Astronomers Club is    34
scheduled for 7:30 p.m. on Friday, September 23, in Room 102 of the Wright    49
Observatory.    51

The primary purpose of the meeting is to plan next year's schedule of events.    67
As usual, the events are likely to include a lecture series and one or two    82
star parties. A project to involve high school students in astronomy needs    97
to be planned and approved.    103

Please mark your calendar for this important meeting. If you are unable to    118
attend, please call me at 148-9351.    126

Sincerely | Richard Clavijo | Assistant Director of Committee | xx    138

### Letter 2

1. Refer to modified block letter format model, p. 366 and p. RG10.
2. Key letter at right in modified block format with block ¶s and mixed punctuation.

### Letter 3

Reformat Letter 2 in block format with open punctuation.

### Letter 4

Reformat Letter 1 in modified block format with ¶ indention and mixed punctuation.

September 5, ---- | Miss Helen Pritchard | Modern Office Systems | 1255    13
Riverview Ave. | Wilmington, DE 19805-5612 | Dear Miss Pritchard:    26

Congratulations on the excellent presentation you made at the Wilmington    40
Office Systems Association on August 18, ----. Your method for configuring    56
microcomputer networks will apply to many of our operations.    68

As we agreed at the reception, you are to speak on October 23 to students    83
in the Office Information Class that I am teaching at Concord College.    97

The class meets in Franklin Hall, Room 203, from 6 p.m. to 8:50 p.m.    111
You may begin your presentation at 7:30 p.m. and end at 8:50 p.m. I    125
will have the large-screen projection device that you can use with    138
your portable microcomputer.    144

Sincerely, | Raphael Naranja, Ph.D. | Professor | xx    153

# *your* PERSPECTIVE

## ETHICS: The Right Thing to Do

Robert Frost once said, "Good fences make good neighbors." This statement reflects the common practice of erecting fences, walls, and other barriers to human interaction. Walls and fences are often erected to keep people *out*, but sometimes they are erected to keep people *in*.

A fence can be erected around a yard to keep pets in and to provide a safe place for children to play. On the other hand, a fence may be erected to keep out the neighbors' children and pets as well as other invaders of privacy. Walls and fences surround prisons to keep inmates in and to control who on the outside can have direct contact with those on the inside.

We see walls and fences used to protect the privacy and property of those inside; at other times, we see them used to protect the lives and property of those on the outside. In other situations, we see them used merely to keep out or to keep in the unwanted.

Walls and fences can be *invisible* as well as *physical*. Invisible walls and fences may take the form of qualifications for membership in a club or other organization, as expressed in bylaws. They may be unwritten or outwardly unspoken preferences or attitudes of one group of people toward another group.

Thus, we see that walls or fences erected to protect one group may seem positive to those included, but to those in the excluded group may seem restrictive and negative. This is often especially evident in the behavior of rival gangs, but it is at least subtly apparent in the attitudes and behaviors of various factions in clubs, schools, churches, and communities.

Richard Lovelace, in *"To Althea, from Prison,"* said: "Stone walls do not a prison make, nor iron bars a cage." He added that so long as his mind was innocent and free, he enjoyed liberty even though in prison.

Edwin Markham, speaking of invisible fences used to shut out others, wrote in "Outwitted":

> He drew a circle that shut me out—
> Heretic, rebel, a thing to flout.
> But love and I had the wit to win;
> We drew a circle that took him in. ✳

## ACTIVITIES

**1.** Read carefully the comments at the left about physical and invisible walls and fences people use to include or exclude others.

**2.** Key a list of the kinds of walls and fences used to include and protect in a positive way those within.

**3.** Key a list of the kinds of walls and fences (or circles) used to exclude people in a negative way.

**4.** Using your lists as background, compose a short theme on the positive (good) and negative (bad) effects of walls and fences (physical and invisible) and how you deal with them.

**Purchase Order**

**Invoice**

**Itinerary**

**Agenda**

5. A source note, if needed, is placed in the row below the last column entry. (Join the cells of that row.) On electronics, DS below the last entry; key a 1.5" divider line; DS and key the source note.

**Horizontal placement.** A table is usually arranged so that the left and right margins are nearly equal. Centering is an option when the Table Format feature is used. On electronics, use the Center key and create a keyline: (1) On scrap paper, key the longest item in each column (whether an entry or the heading) and the spaces to be left between the columns; (2) record the position of the first character in each column; (3) key and center the main (and secondary) heading; (4) clear all tabs and set the LM and tabs at positions recorded in Step 2.

**Vertical placement.** A table may be centered so that the top and bottom margins are nearly equal—using the software's Center Page feature. Otherwise, to center a table vertically, subtract the number of lines of text needed for all the lines of the table (including blank lines) from the number of lines available on the sheet (usually 66) and divide the difference by 2. The quotient is the number of lines to leave in the top margin. If the quotient has a fraction, disregard it. **Note:** Tables may have a 2" TM instead of being centered.

**Centering column headings that are shorter or longer than the longest column entry.** The Table Format feature allows text in any cell to be centered—including column headings. If you are using an electronic, see centering procedure on p. RG19.

## Forms

See the purchase order and invoice at top left. Word processing users who use a forms utility will find that many of the following procedures are done automatically.

**Margin and tab stops.** Set the left margin and tab stops for the entries to be keyed in the columns so that the entries (except those in the description column) are approximately centered under the form's

column headings. The description column entries begin 1 or 2 spaces to the right of the vertical line that marks the beginning of the description column.

**Heading entries.** When appropriate, use the margin and tab stops set for the column entries as the beginning point for the information that is to be keyed to the right of the preprinted words on the heading portion of a form. For example, the address lines on many forms can begin at the tab set for the quantity or the description column. USPS style is preferred for address lines.

**Column entries.** SS the information to be keyed in the columns. Begin the first entries a DS below the horizontal rule under the column headings.

**Column amounts.** When amounts in a column are totaled, underline the amount for the last entry; then DS and key the total. On business forms, large numbers may be keyed with or without commas.

## Special Documents

A model of each special document appears at left.

**Itineraries.** Itineraries are often formatted as tables on plain paper with equal left and right margins. The space left between columns should be enough to separate the information but should not be so large as to make reading difficult (about 0.5" recommended).

Itineraries can be centered vertically on the paper or formatted with a 2" top margin for one-page itineraries or 1" top margin for longer ones.

**Agendas.** Depending on the length of the agenda, it is formatted with a 1" (multi-page) or 2" (one-page) top margin. Side and bottom margins are 1". Agenda headings and text are typically DS. Sub-topics are generally SS and indented .5" from the left margin; DS after subtopics to item below.

Leaders are often used to connect the agenda topic at the left to the name of the person responsible for the topic. The names can begin at the same position (left-aligned), or they may be right-aligned.

# GLOBAL AWARENESS

Climate, in addition to other factors, causes different countries to produce or manufacture certain products by which those countries are often identified. Although the United States produces many of these same products, it is not especially noted for doing so. In fact, the United States often imports the products in List B from the countries in List A.

To check your global awareness, you will see how many countries/products you can match correctly.

| List A | List B |
| --- | --- |
| Australia | coffee/cocoa |
| Brazil | corn/wheat products |
| China | cotton/textiles |
| Cuba | electric/electronic products |
| Ecuador | diamonds/gold |
| Egypt | oil products |
| Japan | rice/silk |
| Mexico | sugar products |
| Saudi Arabia | tropical fruits |
| South Africa | wheat/wool |

## ACTIVITIES

1. Read paragraphs at left; study lists below them.

2. Key at left margin the first country in List A.

3. Tab 4 times and key the item(s) in List B with which that country is most closely associated.

4. Key remaining items in the same way, tabbing to align items in List B.

5. Compare/discuss answers and reasons for choices.

# CULTURAL DIVERSITY

Many countries have national holidays of celebration to honor or remember special people or events in their history. One of those in the United States is Independence Day, or the Fourth of July, which commemorates the breakaway of the original thirteen Colonies from British rule.

How many of the national holidays in List A can you match with the country of their observance as given in List B?

| List A | List B |
| --- | --- |
| Bastille Day | Canada |
| Buddha's Birthday | France |
| Confucius' Birthday | Great Britain |
| Commonwealth Day | Kenya |
| Constitution Day | Korea/Japan |
| Guy Fawke's Day | Mexico |
| Jamburi Day | Japan |
| Joan of Arc's Day | Taiwan |
| National Foundation Day | |
| Victoria Day | |

## ACTIVITIES

1. Read paragraphs at left; study lists below them.

2. Key at left margin the first item in List A.

3. Tab 4 times; key name of country you believe celebrates that holiday.

4. Key remaining items in the same way, tabbing to align items in List B.

5. Compare/discuss answers and reasons for choices.

Endnotes Page

Bibliography

Table with Centered Column Heads

"run-over" line(s) flush with the number. If hanging indent format is used, key the first stroke of "runover" lines flush with the first letter of the first word in the first line.

### Report Documentation

**Short quotations.** Direct quotations occupying fewer than four lines of text begin and end with quotation marks (" ") and have the same line spacing as the report body.

**Long quotations.** Direct quotations occupying four or more lines are SS and indented from the left margin to the ¶ indention point (usually 0.5"). Quotation marks are not used.

**Textual citation.** Textual citations, the simplest way to document report information, include the name(s) of the author(s), the year of publication, and the page number(s) of the material cited. This information is keyed in parentheses following the ending punctuation mark(s). If possible, use the author's name in the context of the report, followed immediately by the publication year and page number in parentheses. For example: . . . *With an output speed of ten pages per minute, an acceptable office standard reported by Brindza (1988, 106), a large volume of work can be processed by one printer.*

**Endnotes page.** Endnotes may be used instead of textual citations to document a report. An endnotes page uses the same margins as the first page of the report, except a page number is keyed at the top of the page in the same manner as it was for the second and subsequent pages.

A QS separates the title and the first line of the first endnote. SS the endnotes; DS between them. The first line of each endnote is indented 0.5" and a superscript endnote number precedes it. "Runover" lines begin at the left margin.

**Reference list/bibliography.** References (one for each source cited) are listed alphabetically by author surnames on a separate page a QS under the title REFERENCES or BIBLIOGRAPHY at the end of a report. Such a list is essential, whether textual citations, endnotes, or footnotes (presented in Unit 37) are used in the report.

If the reference list/bibliography fits on the last page of a report, use a QS to separate the title from the last line of the report text.

If the reference list/bibliography is keyed on a separate page, use the margin settings that were used for the first page of the report, except key a page number at the top of the page in the same manner as it was for the second and subsequent pages.

SS the entries; DS between them. Begin the first line of each entry at the left margin and indent the second and subsequent lines 0.5" from the left margin.

### Other Report Pages

**Title page.** Use the same side margins as the first page of the report. Center each line horizontally: report title in ALL CAPS 2" from the top, your name 5" from the top, school name a DS below your name, and current date 9" from the top. Electronics users see p. RG20.

**Table of contents** (see model on p. RG14). Use the same side and top margins as the first page of the report. Key TABLE OF CONTENTS as the main heading, then QS to list side and ¶ headings of the report. DS side headings beginning at left margin; indent and SS ¶ headings with a DS above and below them. Key page number for each entry at the right margin.

## Tables

A table is an arrangement of information in rows and columns. Tables often include these parts.

1. A main heading is centered and keyed in ALL CAPS.

2. A secondary heading is centered (DS) below the main heading. Capitalize the first letter of each main word in a secondary heading.

3. Column headings may be blocked at the left side of each column or centered over the column. Column headings are placed in the row below the preceding heading (DS on electronics). Multiple-line column headings are SS and aligned at the bottom.

4. Each column entry is placed in the next row. On electronics, DS above the first column entry and DS or SS (as directed) between entries. The width of columns may vary (Table Format feature). The space between columns (electronics) may vary between 0.25" and 1".

## Improve Keyboarding, Formatting, and Language Skills

This part of the textbook will enable you to improve present skills. Some activities will help you improve keying techniques, which can lead to higher speed and greater accuracy. Language skills can be improved, too, by familiar Read/Learn/Apply activities.

The thrust of Phase 3 is on improving your ability to format documents. After reviewing the formats for memos, letters, reports, and tables, you will apply your skill to longer, slightly harder forms of these documents. Then you will "go to work" again, applying your learning to work place situations.

Many documents involve topics you might find in a social studies course; for example, economics, geography, government, and history. Preparing these documents should remind you that ". . . people in all walks of life employ a computer keyboard. . . ."

**In the 37 lessons of this phase, you will:**

1. Refine keying techniques.
2. Improve language skills.
3. Improve keying skill on rough-draft and script copy.
4. Improve formatting skills on memos, letters, reports, and tables.
5. Gain work experience in a (simulated) travel agency.
6. Assess keying and formatting skills.

**Standard Memo**

**Simplified Memo**

**Unbound Report**

**Bound Report with Long Quotation and Enumerated Items**

## Punctuation Styles

**Open.** No punctuation follows the salutation or complimentary close.

**Mixed.** A colon follows the salutation and a comma follows the complimentary close.

Either punctuation style may be used with block or modified block formats. However, open punctuation is typically used with block format and often used with modified format.

## Memos

**Standard format** (see model at left and p. RG9). All lines begin at the left margin and guide words (TO:, FROM:, DATE:, SUBJECT:) are keyed in the order given here. The information keyed to the right of each guide word is started at the second default tab setting (generally 10 spaces from the left margin.)

The first guide word, TO:, is keyed at the left margin 2" from the top edge of the paper. DS between the guide words and between the last guide word and the first ¶. SS the ¶ lines and DS between ¶s:

Key reference initials a DS below the last ¶ line and then, if needed, key the enclosure (or attachment) notation a DS below the reference initials.

Key the copy notation a DS below the reference initials or enclosure (or attachment) notation, if used.

**Simplified format** (see model at left and p. RG9). All lines begin at the left, but no guide words are used in the simplified memo. This format is similar to a simplified block letter without a letter address.

Use 1" or default left and right margins. Key the date 2" from the top edge of the paper. QS below the date and key the name(s) or title(s) of the memo recipient(s).

A copy notation, if needed, is placed after the reference initials or enclosure/attachment notation, if one is used, in the same manner as they are keyed when standard memo format is used.

Key a subject line in ALL CAPS a DS below the memo recipient and DS to start the first ¶. SS the ¶ lines and DS between ¶s.

Key the memo writer's name and title a QS below the last ¶ line.

Reference initials are keyed a DS below the writer's name and enclosure (or attachment) notation, if used, is keyed a DS below the reference initials.

## Reports

Refer to the models at bottom left of this page and at left on p. 368 as needed while reading this section. Also, see pp. RG12-14.

### Report Margins

**Side margins.** Use default or 1" left and right margins for unbound reports and 1.5" left margin and default or 1" right margin for bound reports.

**Top margin.** Begin first line (usually the report title) on page 1, 2" from top edge of paper; begin first line of second and subsequent pages (usually the page number) at default top margin or 1" from the top edge of the sheet. The report text begins a DS below the page number.

**Bottom margin.** Use default or 1" margin.

### Report Spacing

**Body.** ¶ lines of a report are usually DS, but they may be SS.

**Report title.** Center in ALL CAPS 2" from top edge of paper followed by QS to the first ¶. Multiple-line titles are DS.

**Side headings.** Key at the left margin with a DS above and below the heading. Initial cap main words and underline the heading.

**Paragraph headings.** Begin ¶ headings at ¶ indention point, underline, and end with a period. Capitalize the first letter of only the first word.

**Page numbers.** The first page need not be numbered. When numbered, center the number 0.5" from the bottom edge of paper. For second and subsequent pages, place numbers at default top margin or 1" from top edge of paper even with the right margin.

**Enumerated items.** SS each item and DS between them. Key the number at the ¶ indention point used in the report. Key lines to the right margin of the report. If block format is used, key the first stroke of

# UNIT 17 Improve Keyboarding Skills

**LESSONS 76-77**

## LESSON 76

### Keying Technique/Language Skills

**O b j e c t i v e s :**
1. To improve and assess keying techniques.
2. To improve and assess keying speed and control.

**76A • 5**
**Conditioning Practice**

each line twice SS; then two 1' writings on line 2; find *gwam;* clear screen

| | | |
|---|---|---|
| alphabet | 1 | Jack Gomez will be our equipment manager for the next seven days. |
| speed | 2 | Their neighbor on the island is the chair of the sorority social. |
| fig/sym | 3 | She paid Invoice #382 ($6.79 with a 5% discount) with Check #104. |

gwam  1' | 1 | 2 | 3 | 4 | 5 | 6 | 7 | 8 | 9 | 10 | 11 | 12 | 13 |

**S KILL BUILDING**

**76B • 15**
**Technique:**
**Letter Keys**

each line twice; rekey the lines that are most difficult for you

**Goal:** To keep keystroking action limited to the fingers.

**Emphasize continuity and rhythm with curved, upright fingers.**

A After Diana Aaron ate the pancake, she had an apple and a banana.

B Barbi Babbitt became a better batter by batting big rubber balls.

C Chi Chang from Creekcrest Circle can catch a raccoon for Chelcia.

D Did Dave and Don decide to delay the date of departure for a day?

E Ed and Eileen were elected to chaperone every late evening event.

F Fred figured fifty fast rafts floated from Fairfax to Ford Falls.

G Gary and Gregg glanced at the gaggle of geese on the green grass.

H His haphazard shots helped them through half of the hockey match.

I I think Ike insisted on living in Illinois, Indiana, or Missouri.

J Jackie just objected to taking Jay's jeans and jersey on the jet.

K Ken kept Kay's knickknack in a knapsack in the back of the kayak.

L Large and small holes in the lane by her dwelling will be filled.

M Mike meets my mom most mornings at the mall in the summer months.

gwam  1' | 1 | 2 | 3 | 4 | 5 | 6 | 7 | 8 | 9 | 10 | 11 | 12 | 13 |

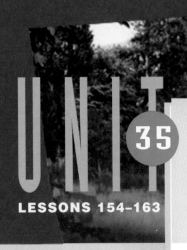
**Format Guides:**

Block Format

Modified Block Format

Simplified Block Format

## Letters

**Block format.** *Every* line begins at the left margin. This format is highly recommended because of its efficiency. See model at left and on p. RG9.

When a personal-business letter is arranged in block format, key a return address (street, city, state, ZIP) at the left margin on the lines preceding the date. See model, p. RG9.

**Modified block format.** Begin the date and signature block lines at the horizontal center. Paragraphs (¶s) may be blocked at the left margin or indented 0.5" (generally 5 spaces). All other lines begin at the left margin. See model at left and on p. RG10.

**Simplified block format.** Like the block format, all lines begin at the left margin. The simplified block format omits the salutation and complimentary close, includes a subject line, and uses the USPS-style letter address. See model at left and on p. RG10.

## Letter Parts and Spacing

**Side margins.** Use default or 1" left and right margins.

**Date.** Key the month, day, and year (or the first line of the return address in a personal-business letter) 2" from the top edge of the paper. If a word processor's Center Page feature is used, key the date (or the first line of the return address in a personal-business letter) on the first line of writing.

**Mailing notation.** Mailing notations (such as *Registered* and *Special Delivery*) may be included on the letter and the envelope in ALL CAPS. If used, key the notation on the letter a DS below the date; DS below the notation to key the first line of the letter address. On the envelope, key the notation below the stamp about 0.5" above the envelope address.

**Letter address.** SS the letter address a QS below the date.

**Attention line.** If used, key as the first line of the letter address (Attention *department or job title*) and use Ladies and Gentlemen as the salutation.

**Salutation.** If used, key the salutation a DS below the last line of the letter address.

**Subject line.** If used, place the subject line a DS below the salutation in ALL CAPS.

**Body.** Begin the letter body a DS below the preceding letter part (usually the salutation). SS the lines of a ¶ and DS between ¶s.

**Complimentary close.** If used, key the complimentary close a DS below the last line of the letter body.

**Company name.** If used, key the company name in ALL CAPS a DS below the complimentary close.

**Writer's name and title.** Key the name of the writer a QS below the preceding letter part (usually a complimentary close). The writer's title may follow the name on the same line, preceded by a comma, or may be keyed on the next line.

**Reference initials.** If used, key the reference initials in lowercase letters a DS below the writer's name or title.

**Enclosure notation.** If an enclosure notation is needed, key the word *Enclosure* (or *Enclosures*) a DS below the reference initials.

**Copy notation.** If a copy notation is needed, key the letter *c* followed by a space and the recipient's name a DS below the preceding letter part (usually the reference initials or enclosure notation).

**Postscript.** If used, key it a DS below the last letter part in the same format as the ¶s, without the abbreviation *P. S.*

## 76C • 10
### Singular Verbs

1. Read the first rule.
2. Key the Learn sentences below it (with number and period), noting how the rule has been applied.
3. Key the Apply sentences using the correct verb shown in parentheses.
4. Read and practice the other rules in the same way.

Use a singular verb with a singular subject.

Learn  1. The administrative assistant has left for lunch.
Learn  2. Marshall has already finished the assignment.
Apply  3. The author (has, have) already finished the manuscript.
Apply  4. She (is, are) leaving for college next Friday.

Use singular verbs with indefinite pronouns (**each, every, any, either, neither, one,** etc.) used as subjects.

Learn  5. One of the members is expected to vote.
Learn  6. Each of the girls has been given an assignment.
Apply  7. Either of the two candidates (is, are) a good choice.
Apply  8. Neither of the artists (is, are) very good.

## S KILL BUILDING

## 76D • 20
### Skill Check

1. A 1' writing on ¶ 1; determine *gwam*.
2. Add 2-4 *gwam* to the rate attained in Step 1, and note quarter-minute checkpoints from table below.
3. Take three 1' guided writings on ¶ 1 to increase speed.
4. Practice ¶ 2 in the same way.
5. Two 3' writings on ¶s 1 and 2 combined; determine *gwam* and find errors.

### Quarter-Minute Checkpoints

| gwam | 1/4' | 1/2' | 3/4' | 1' |
|------|------|------|------|-----|
| 28 | 7 | 14 | 21 | 28 |
| 32 | 8 | 16 | 24 | 32 |
| 36 | 9 | 18 | 27 | 36 |
| 40 | 10 | 20 | 30 | 40 |
| 44 | 11 | 22 | 33 | 44 |
| 48 | 12 | 24 | 36 | 48 |
| 52 | 13 | 26 | 39 | 52 |
| 56 | 14 | 28 | 42 | 56 |
| 60 | 15 | 30 | 45 | 60 |

all letters used  gwam 3' | 5'

Many options are available for people to ponder as they  4 | 2 | 39
invest their money.  Real estate, savings accounts, money market  8 | 5 | 41
accounts, bonds, and stocks are but a few of the options that  12 | 7 | 44
are open to those who wish to invest their extra money.  Several  17 | 10 | 46
factors will determine which type of investment a person will  21 | 12 | 49
choose.  These factors pertain to the expected rate of return, the  25 | 15 | 52
degree of liquidity desired, and the amount of risk a person is  29 | 18 | 54
willing  to  take.  30 | 18 | 55

An investor who seeks a high rate of return and who is  34 | 20 | 57
willing to take a high degree of risk often considers the stock  38 | 23 | 59
market.  Stock markets or stock exchanges are organizations that  43 | 26 | 62
bring investors together to buy and sell shares of stock.  Stock  47 | 28 | 65
represents a share in the ownership of a company.  Since more  51 | 31 | 67
risk is associated with an investment that has a high rate of  55 | 33 | 70
return, judgment must be exercised by those thinking about the  60 | 35 | 72
purchase  of  stock.  61 | 36 | 72

gwam 3' | 1 | 2 | 3 | 4
5' | 1 | 2 | 3

1. Two 1' writings on each ¶ for speed; find *gwam*.
2. Two 1' writings on each ¶ for control; circle errors.
3. Two 3' writings on all ¶s combined; find *gwam*, circle errors.
4. Record your better 3' *gwam* and compare to the 151C score you recorded.
5. One 5' writing on all ¶s combined; find *gwam*, circle errors. Compare your 5' score to your 3' score.

all letters used

| | gwam | 3' | 5' |
|---|---|---|---|

The citizens of our country have a higher level of interest · 4 | 2 | 51

in sports now than at any time in the past. The interest contin- · 8 | 5 | 54

ues to grow in spite of the problems that have been present in the · 13 | 8 | 56

recent past. The problems include long and short strikes, bad · 17 | 10 | 59

attitudes and poor behavior on the part of many players, lack of · 21 | 13 | 62

competitive balance, low quality of play, and questionable prac- · 26 | 15 | 64

tices of many owners. · 27 | 16 | 65

Many believe that people become fans because it is easy to · 31 | 19 | 67

understand most sports. That is, most people can grasp the object · 35 | 21 | 70

or purpose of the game and develop a rooting interest in it very · 40 | 24 | 73

quickly. Another reason may be that sports give fans a sense of · 44 | 26 | 75

continuity since much is written and spoken daily about the his- · 48 | 29 | 78

tory of many sports, the outcomes of yesterday's games, and the · 53 | 32 | 80

future of various sports. · 54 | 33 | 81

One other major theory states that people favor sports · 58 | 35 | 83

because the sports event is a tranquil event for people who live · 62 | 37 | 86

in an otherwise uncertain world. For example, people know if a · 67 | 40 | 89

ball is dropped, if a player is out of bounds, when a play is · 71 | 42 | 91

over, and which team wins. Contrast this with the larger public · 75 | 45 | 94

where there is not much certainty about government, economic, · 79 | 47 | 96

foreign, and domestic policies. · 81 | 49 | 97

gwam 3' | 1 | 2 | 3 | 4
5' | 1 | 2 | 3

**Objectives:**

**1.** To improve and assess keying techniques.
**2.** To improve and assess keying speed and control.

**77A • 5**
**Conditioning Practice**

each line twice

alphabet   1 Jay Zuvella had two questions to complete before taking the exam.

speed   2 Their neighbor may dismantle the ancient shanty in the big field.

figures   3 Jim's score was 86 percent; he missed Numbers 17, 29, 35, and 40.

gwam 1' | 1 | 2 | 3 | 4 | 5 | 6 | 7 | 8 | 9 | 10 | 11 | 12 | 13 |

## SKILL BUILDING

**77B • 15**
**Technique:**
**Letter Keys**

each line twice; rekey the lines that are most difficult for you

**Goal:** To keep keystroking action limited to the fingers.

**Emphasize continuity and rhythm with curved, upright fingers.**

n Norman's niece and nephew can be tended by a new nanny on Monday.

o One of our boys opposed opening more offshore moorings for boats.

p Peter's playful puppies pulled the paper wrapping off the apples.

q Quinten quit questioning the quantity of bouquets at the banquet.

r Robert and Rae arrived after a carriage ride over the rural road.

s Sue sat still as soon as Sam served his sushi and sashimi dishes.

t Ty took title to two tiny cottages the last time he went to town.

u Uko usually rushes uptown to see us unload the four sugar trucks.

v Val voted to review the vivid videos when she visits the village.

w Will was waving wildly when a swimmer went wading into the water.

x Six tax experts explained that he was exempt from the excise tax.

y Your younger boy yearns to see the Yankees play in New York City.

z Zeno puzzled over a zealot who seized a bronze kazoo at a bazaar.

gwam 1' | 1 | 2 | 3 | 4 | 5 | 6 | 7 | 8 | 9 | 10 | 11 | 12 | 13 |

**77C • 5**
**Speed Forcing Drill**

Each line once at top speed; then, try to complete each sentence on the call of 15", 12", or 10" writing as directed. Force speed to higher levels as you move from line to line.

**Emphasis: high-frequency balanced-hand words**

| | gwam | 15" | 12" | 10" |
|---|---|---|---|---|
| Sue owns the chair in the shanty by the big field. | | 40 | 50 | 60 |
| The girl will hand the sorority emblem to the visitors. | | 44 | 55 | 66 |
| The handyman is to go to the field to cut ivy for the bowls. | | 48 | 60 | 72 |
| Their goal is to surprise the four city officials during a visit. | | 52 | 65 | 78 |

gwam 1' | 1 | 2 | 3 | 4 | 5 | 6 | 7 | 8 | 9 | 10 | 11 | 12 | 13 |

1. Set a goal of *speed (add 4 gwam to 151C rate)* if you did not exceed 6 errors on the 3' writing in 151C; *control (subtract 4 gwam)*

if you made more than 6 errors.
2. Take a 1' writing on each ¶ of 151C. Find *gwam* or errors.

3. Take a 5' writing on ¶s of 151C. Find *gwam* and circle errors.

# LESSON 153  Keyboarding Skills

**Objectives:**
**1.** To improve keyboarding skill.
**2.** To inventory straight-copy speed and control.

## 153A • 5
### Conditioning Practice
each line twice

| | | |
|---|---|---|
| alphabet | 1 | Pam will acquire two dozen red vinyl jackets for the big exhibit. |
| speed | 2 | They may sign the usual proxy if they make an audit of the firms. |
| figures | 3 | The library has 95,684 books, 1,205 periodicals, and 3,457 tapes. |

gwam 1' | 1 | 2 | 3 | 4 | 5 | 6 | 7 | 8 | 9 | 10 | 11 | 12 | 13 |

## S KILL BUILDING

## 153B • 15
### Skill Building
each line twice SS; DS between 2-line groups; rekey difficult lines as time permits.

**Adjacent-key words**

1 are ire err ask gas sag saw ion poi riot soil went news sort fort
2 opt top try say tree post spot ruin quip talk chalk tackle anklet
3 pot ends aids week knew part true poem stop sleds quickly booklet
4 ewe weave renew report citrus pounds pocket reopen liquid premium

**One-hand words**

5 are ace ill bar lip cat mom dad nil ear oil fad pop cab were upon
6 beg rag hip sat hop sew ink tag joy tea mop wax pin web noun seat
7 cab area hook beef join drab jump edge look fact moon nylon gates
8 egg rare imply saga jolly star onion tear phony weave union zebra

**Near-balanced hand words**

9 vote many loan this same much time sure sold mail sale five loans
10 cent into tire thus high rent told does true wide grow fine plant
11 grow five says gold vote went gift else bids slow tube sort blank
12 rose tenth chance plans cities forty giving informs trucks editor

**Balanced-hand words**

13 aid bug cob cut dig elf fit got ham iris jams kept lake meld name
14 owl own pro pay quay roam sick soap than curl vial wish yang meld
15 rue also body city disk elan foam goal half idle jape kale laughs
16 oak usual mantle naught orient papaya quench enrich social theory

gwam 1' | 1 | 2 | 3 | 4 | 5 | 6 | 7 | 8 | 9 | 10 | 11 | 12 | 13 |

## 77D • 10
## Singular Verbs (continued)

Follow the Learn/Apply procedure in 76C, p. 184.

Use a singular verb with singular subjects linked by *or* or *nor*. *Exception*: If one subject is singular and the other is plural, the verb agrees with the closer subject.

| Learn | 1. | Neither Jan nor Alice was invited to the banquet. |
| Learn | 2. | Either the council members or the chair has the agenda. |
| Apply | 3. | Neither Bill nor Jim (is, are) going to the game. |
| Apply | 4. | Either the cabinet members or the President (has, have) the gift. |

Use a singular verb with a singular subject that is separated from the verb by phrases beginning with *as well as* and *in addition to*.

| Learn | 5. | The teacher as well as the students is going to attend. |
| Apply | 6. | The shirt as well as the dresses (has, have) to be ironed. |

Use singular verbs with collective nouns (*committee, team, class, jury,* etc.) if the collective noun acts as a unit.

| Learn | 7. | The social committee has made the necessary arrangements. |
| Apply | 8. | The team (has, have) a game on Friday. |
| Apply | 9. | The jury (has, have) been sequestered. |

## S KILL BUILDING

## 77E • 15
## Skill Check

1. A 1' writing on ¶ 1; determine *gwam*.

2. Add 2-4 *gwam* to the rate attained in Step 1, and note quarter-minute checkpoints from the table below.

3. Take three 1' guided writings on ¶ 1 to increase speed.

4. Practice ¶ 2 in the same way.

5. One 3' writing on ¶s 1 and 2 combined; determine *gwam* and find errors.

### Quarter-Minute Checkpoints

| gwam | 1/4' | 1/2' | 3/4' | 1' |
|------|------|------|------|----|
| 28 | 7 | 14 | 21 | 28 |
| 32 | 8 | 16 | 24 | 32 |
| 36 | 9 | 18 | 27 | 36 |
| 40 | 10 | 20 | 30 | 40 |
| 44 | 11 | 22 | 33 | 44 |
| 48 | 12 | 24 | 36 | 48 |
| 52 | 13 | 26 | 39 | 52 |
| 56 | 14 | 28 | 42 | 56 |
| 60 | 15 | 30 | 45 | 60 |

all letters used        gwam 3' | 5'

|  | 3' | 5' |
|---|---|---|
| The value of an education has been a topic discussed many | 4 | 2 | 36 |
| times with a great deal of zest. The value is often measured in | 8 | 5 | 39 |
| terms of costs and benefits to the taxpayer. It is also judged in | 13 | 8 | 42 |
| terms of changes in the individuals taking part in the educational | 17 | 10 | 44 |
| process. Gains in the level of knowledge, the development and | 21 | 13 | 47 |
| refinement of attitudes, and the acquiring of skills are believed | 26 | 15 | 49 |
| to be crucial parts of an education. | 28 | 17 | 51 |
| Education is a never-ending process. A person is exposed to for- | 32 | 19 | 53 |
| mal and informal education throughout his or her life. Formal learning | 37 | 22 | 56 |
| takes place in a structured situation such as a school or | 41 | 25 | 59 |
| a college. Informal learning occurs from the experience gained | 45 | 27 | 61 |
| from daily living. We are constantly educated from all the types | 50 | 30 | 64 |
| of media with which we come in contact each day as well as by each | 54 | 32 | 66 |
| person with whom we exchange ideas. | 57 | 34 | 68 |

| | | |
|---|---|---|
| alphabet | 1 | Jim avoids fizzling fireworks because they often explode quickly. |
| speed | 2 | Nancy works in the big cornfield down by the lake with the docks. |
| fig/sym | 3 | Runner #3019-A was first (49' 35"); runner #687-D was last (62'). |

gwam   1' | 1 | 2 | 3 | 4 | 5 | 6 | 7 | 8 | 9 | 10 | 11 | 12 | 13 |

## S KILL BUILDING

**152B • 10**
**Skill Check: Script**

each line three times SS;
DS between 3-line groups;
rekey difficult lines as time
permits

words

| | | | |
|---|---|---|---|
| 3d row | 1 | *Witt requested that Roy report your errors to the authority.* | 12 |
| 3d row | 2 | *Rory said Perry will quit work at the pet store early today.* | 12 |
| 1st row | 3 | *Have Zane make Buxton a black bag. Mack can make a handbag.* | 12 |
| 1st row | 4 | *Can Zane and Vax both come? Mack and Cazi may be back soon.* | 12 |
| home/1st | 5 | *Hans and Lana had a black bag, small can, and half a banana.* | 12 |
| home/3d | 6 | *The fire at the store spread at a real high speed yesterday.* | 12 |

**152C • 25**
**Skill Check: Script ¶s**

1. Three 1' writings on each ¶ for speed; find *gwam*.
2. Three 1' writings on each ¶ for control; circle errors.
3. Two 3' writings on both ¶s combined; find *gwam* and circle errors.

**A**   all letters used

gwam   1'   3'

*Some people seem to have a greater level of job stress than* 12 4 58
*others, and the reason for the differences may not be revealed* 25 8 62
*by just a quick observation. Without taking time to analyze a* 37 12 68
*situation, one may assume that the jobs of highly stressed people* 50 17 70
*are much more demanding; but a close examination may point* 62 21 75
*out that the real discrepancy is in the way people react to a* 75 25 79
*potentially stressful situation.* 81 27 81

*For example, some job-related problems, such as the quality* 93 31 85
*of work performed by coworkers, cannot be resolved by the office* 106 35 89
*worker. The reaction of one person may be to recognize and ac-* 119 40 93
*cept the situation, whereas the reaction of another may be to* 131 44 97
*worry about the dilemma. The person whose attitude is to make* 144 48 101
*the best of such a plight will likely become less stressed than* 157 52 106
*the one who worries.* 161 54 107

## ACTIVITY 1:

**Date Text and Date Code**

1. Read the copy at right.
2. Learn the Date Text and Date Code features for your wp software.
3. Key the information at the right using the Date Text and Date Code features as indicated.

The current date can be inserted into a document by using the **Date Text** feature. The **Date Code** feature also inserts the current date into the document. However, the Date Code feature replaces the previous date with the current date each time the document is opened or printed. The date and time on your computer must be current in order for the date to be correct.

**<Date Text>**

Mr. Jason Winchell
428 North 500 West
Salt Lake City, UT 84103-8321

**<Date Code>**

Ms. Rochelle Wilson
351 Parkwood Cir.
Anderson, SC 29621-8256

## ACTIVITY 2:

**Automatic Hyphenation**

1. Read the copy at right.
2. Learn to activate the Hyphenation feature.
3. Key the text at the right with hyphenation off.
4. Key the text again with hyphenation on.

The **Automatic Hyphenation** feature divides (hyphenates) words that would normally wrap to the next line. This gives the right margin of the document a more attractive appearance.

A very useful feature in most of today's best word processing software packages is the feature that automatically hyphenates long words at the right margin. This feature will automatically divide such words rather than wrap them to the next line. By dividing these words automatically, the hyphenation feature makes the right margin less "ragged."

## ACTIVITY 3:

**Cursor Move**

1. Read the copy at right.
2. Learn to move the cursor using **Home**, **End**, **PgUp**, **PgDn**, and **Home (Ctrl)** + arrow key *or* + arrow key combinations.
3. Key Sentence 1; edit as instructed in Sentences 2, 3, and 4 using the cursor move keys.

The **Home**, **End**, **PgUp**, and **PgDn** keys can be used to move the cursor quickly from one location to another location in a document.

The **Home** or **Ctrl** key in combination with the arrow keys can also be used to move the cursor to various locations.

1. Key the following.

Ellen will be in New York on Monday.

2. Make the following changes, using the cursor move keys.

Ellen will be in New York on Monday.

3. Make these additional changes, utilizing the cursor move keys.

Ellen Castino will be in Albany, New York, on Monday, June 25.

4. Make these changes.

Ms. Ellen J. Castino, the new manager, will be in Albany, New York, on Tuesday, June 26, from 11 a.m. to 3 p.m.

**151C • 30**
**Skill Check**

1. Three 1' writings on each ¶ for speed; find *gwam*.
2. Two 1' writings on each ¶ for control; circle errors.
3. Two 3' writings on all ¶s combined; find *gwam*, circle errors.
4. Record and retain your better 3' *gwam* and error count for use in 152D.

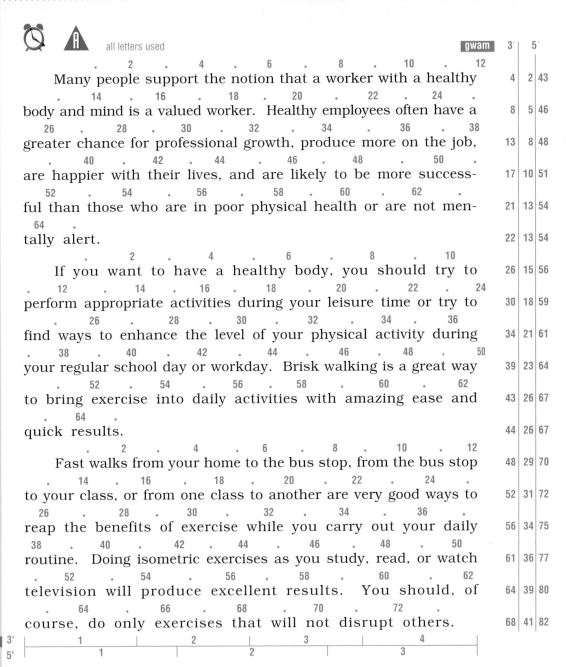

all letters used

| | gwam | 3' | 5' |
|---|---|---|---|

    •    2    •    4    •    6    •    8    •    10    •    12

Many people support the notion that a worker with a healthy    4   2 | 43

    •   14    •   16    •   18    •   20    •   22    •   24    •

body and mind is a valued worker. Healthy employees often have a    8   5 | 46

  26    •   28    •   30    •   32    •   34    •   36    •   38

greater chance for professional growth, produce more on the job,    13   8 | 48

    •   40    •   42    •   44    •   46    •   48    •   50    •

are happier with their lives, and are likely to be more success-    17   10 | 51

  52    •   54    •   56    •   58    •   60    •   62    •

ful than those who are in poor physical health or are not men-    21   13 | 54

  64    •

tally alert.    22   13 | 54

    •    2    •    4    •    6    •    8    •    10

If you want to have a healthy body, you should try to    26   15 | 56

    •   12    •   14    •   16    •   18    •   20    •   22    •   24

perform appropriate activities during your leisure time or try to    30   18 | 59

    •   26    •   28    •   30    •   32    •   34    •   36

find ways to enhance the level of your physical activity during    34   21 | 61

    •   38    •   40    •   42    •   44    •   46    •   48    •   50

your regular school day or workday. Brisk walking is a great way    39   23 | 64

    •   52    •   54    •   56    •   58    •   60    •   62

to bring exercise into daily activities with amazing ease and    43   26 | 67

    •   64    •

quick results.    44   26 | 67

    •    2    •    4    •    6    •    8    •    10    •    12

Fast walks from your home to the bus stop, from the bus stop    48   29 | 70

    •   14    •   16    •   18    •   20    •   22    •   24    •

to your class, or from one class to another are very good ways to    52   31 | 72

  26    •   28    •   30    •   32    •   34    •   36    •

reap the benefits of exercise while you carry out your daily    56   34 | 75

  38    •   40    •   42    •   44    •   46    •   48    •   50

routine. Doing isometric exercises as you study, read, or watch    61   36 | 77

    •   52    •   54    •   56    •   58    •   60    •   62

television will produce excellent results. You should, of    64   39 | 80

    •   64    •   66    •   68    •   70    •   72    •

course, do only exercises that will not disrupt others.    68   41 | 82

gwam   3'     |———1———|———2———|———3———|———4———|
      5'         |—————1—————|—————2—————|—————3—————|

# LESSON 152

## Keyboarding Skills

**O b j e c t i v e s :**
1. To improve keyboarding techniques.
2. To inventory script-copy speed and control.
3. To improve straight-copy speed and control.

## ACTIVITIES 4&5:

### Zoom and Save As

1. Read the copy at right.
2. Learn to use the Zoom and Save As features of your software.
3. Open the letter keyed in Lesson 52 (LTR52B2).
4. Use the Zoom feature to increase and decrease the amount and size of text on the screen.
5. Make the changes outlined at the right; save the document as WHITMAN.

The **Zoom** feature allows you to manipulate the amount and size of text appearing on the screen. The feature can be used to view the entire page by decreasing the print size or can be used to view a portion of the page more clearly by enlarging the print size.

**Address the letter to:**

Ms. Jessica Whitman
561 Woodcliff Dr.
Atlanta, GA 30350-8821

**Change salutation to:**

Dear Ms. Whitman

The **Save As** feature is used to save an existing file under another filename, thus keeping the original document intact. This feature is frequently used when a document is opened and changes are made. To be able to open the original document as well as the revised document, the revised document should be saved under another filename using the Save As feature.

## ACTIVITY 6:

### Macro

1. Read the copy at right.
2. Learn to define macros using your software.
3. Define a macro for **Thompson Floral & Greenhouse.**
4. Key the text at the right using the macro key each time *Thompson Floral & Greenhouse* appears in the text.

The **Macro** feature of a software package allows the operator to save (record) keystrokes and retrieve (playback) them at a later time. For example, if the headings for a standard memo (TO:, FROM:, DATE:, and SUBJECT:) were saved as a macro, the operator could depress the defined macro keys instead of keying the headings each time a standard memorandum was created.

Thompson Floral & Greenhouse sells fresh cut bouquets.

Thompson Floral & Greenhouse delivers balloon bouquets.

Thompson Floral & Greenhouse sells green plants.

Thompson Floral & Greenhouse delivers fruit baskets.

Thompson Floral & Greenhouse has silk and dry arrangements.

Thompson Floral & Greenhouse has beautiful wedding flowers.

Thompson Floral & Greenhouse has flowers for all occasions.

Thompson Floral & Greenhouse is your full flower center.

# UNIT 34
**LESSONS 151–153**

## Inventory/Improve Keyboarding Skills

### LESSON 151

## Keyboarding Skills

**Objectives:**
1. To inventory keyboarding techniques.
2. To inventory straight-copy speed and control.

**151A • 5**
**Conditioning Practice**

each line twice; then 1'
writing on each line

alphabet 1 To what extent was Kazu involved with my project before quitting?

speed 2 To my dismay, the official kept the fox by the dog in the kennel.

figures 3 A van with License No. A982-457 is parked in Space 103 in Lot 16.

gwam 1' | 1 | 2 | 3 | 4 | 5 | 6 | 7 | 8 | 9 | 10 | 11 | 12 | 13 |

**151B • 15**
**Technique:**
**Response Patterns**

1. Key each line twice SS; DS between 2-line groups.
2. Take 1' writing on each group as time permits.

**Letter response**

1 at ad be ho we him age ill awe pop cabs hull deaf junk mill areas

2 as we up in be at pin up see him look upon were traded phony beef

3 my ink red car pink nylon sets free join union fast reader awards

4 Extra reserved seats set up in my area at noon served only a few.

5 Rebecca served a plump, sweet plum dessert on my terrace at noon.

**Word response**

6 by to do or it am bus key off cog cod rot hep make clap bury risk

7 of so is if me cot sit fig zoo jam yang zori thru make wick virus

8 to roam rush it six pairs sight land may mend cozy flame the fork

9 Dirk is due to dismantle the worn antique chair in the dorm hall.

10 My busy neighbor is to go downtown to the giant mall to visit me.

**Combination**

11 xi mu pi nu eta chi rho tau phi psi beta zeta kappa sigma phi eta

12 see far eye him jump fast hand held save this they fish do it now

13 dials six queue up right hand look at him men and girls profit by

14 The six beggars deserved a better neighbor than the neurotic man.

15 As a visitor, you may see my hilly island area better by bicycle.

gwam 1' | 1 | 2 | 3 | 4 | 5 | 6 | 7 | 8 | 9 | 10 | 11 | 12 | 13 |

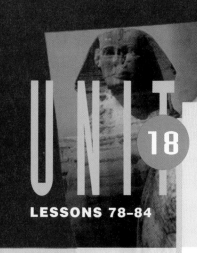

## Format Guides

**Modified Block with Indented ¶s and USPS Letter Address**

**Second-Page Heading**

**Distribution List: Horizontal**

**Distribution List: Vertical**

Two variations of the block letter format presented in Unit 11 are the modified block and the simplified block formats. The following guidelines present the changes required for formatting these two styles of letters.

## Modified Block Letter Format

"Modified block" (illustrated on p. 193) simply means that the block format has been modified. The date and the closing lines (complimentary close, writer's name, and writer's job title or department) start near the horizontal center of the paper instead of at the left margin. Use the default tab at 4" position.

**Paragraphs.** The paragraphs of a letter formatted in the modified block style may be indented, or they may be blocked at the left margin.

**Open and mixed punctuation.** The modified block letter may be formatted with open or mixed punctuation. A letter formatted with mixed punctuation has a colon following the salutation and a comma following the complimentary close. A letter formatted with open punctuation has no punctuation following the salutation or the complimentary close.

## Simplified Block Letter Format

The simplified block letter format (illustrated on p. 199) is another variation of the block letter format. The salutation (Dear Mr. Visquel:) and the complimentary closing (Sincerely yours,) are omitted. A subject line is always included. The writer's name and title are keyed in ALL CAPS a QS below the final paragraph of the letter.

## Second-Page Headings

Leave a 1" top margin above the second-page heading of a letter or memo. Key

the heading SS in block format at the left margin. Include the name of the addressee, the page number, and the date. DS between the heading and the body. (See illustration at left.) If the document is going to multiple individuals, use a name that describes the group of individuals collectively; for example, *Managers, Executive Board,* or *Planning Committee.*

## Memo Distribution Lists

When a memo is sent to several individuals, a distribution list is used. The simplified memo uses the horizontal listing; the standard format uses the vertical listing. (See illustrations at bottom left.)

## Special Letter Parts

**Subject line.** The subject line specifies the topic discussed in the letter or memo. Key the subject line in ALL CAPS, a DS below the salutation (or letter address for simplified letter format).

**Attention line.** When an attention line, such as *Attention Human Resources Manager,* is used in a letter addressed to a company, key it as the first line of the letter and envelope address. When an attention line is used, the correct salutation is "Ladies and Gentlemen." (An attention line is used ONLY when the person's name is unknown to the letter writer.)

## USPS Letter Address Style

The letter address for any letter format may be keyed with uppercase and lowercase letters, or it may be keyed in ALL CAPS with no punctuation (USPS Style). See illustration at top left.

## Assess and Improve Information Processing Skills

The purpose of Phase 5 is to extend information processing skills. The first two units focus on refining keying skills and reviewing formats of correspondence, reports, tables, and business forms.

The next five units present formats for multipage letters, reports with footnotes (and a review of MLA style), e-mail messages, meeting minutes, news releases, and complex tables. These lessons are followed by skill assessments.

A work place simulation caps Phase 5. A sport management office conveys the health, physical education, and environment topics found also in many other documents in this phase.

**In this phase, you will:**

1. Integrate word processing technology and formatting skills to create a variety of professional-looking documents.
2. Increase keyboarding skill on straight, rough-draft, and script copy.
3. Improve language skills and work methods (planning, organizing, designing, and evaluating).

## LESSON 78 — Letters/Memos Review

**Objectives:**
1. To review letter and memo formatting.
2. To increase proficiency in keying opening and closing lines of letters.

### 78A • 5
**Conditioning Practice**

each line twice SS; then two 1' writings on line 2: find *gwam*; clear screen

alphabet 1 Jasper Markowitz, the tax manager, believed he could not qualify.

speed 2 A formal social for the girl is to be held in the ancient chapel.

figures 3 Pat quickly found the total of 8.25, 9.16, and 10.43 to be 27.84.

gwam 1' | 1 | 2 | 3 | 4 | 5 | 6 | 7 | 8 | 9 | 10 | 11 | 12 | 13 |

### F ORMATTING

### 78B • 45
**Letters and Memos**

**Document 1**
**Personal-Business Letter**
Review the model personal-business letter on p. 124. Format and key in block style the letter shown at the right. Italicize or underline *The Wall Street Journal* and *Business Week;* bold **International Partnerships**.

**wp note:**

Wherever you see underlined words, you may use italic if you prefer. Do NOT use both underline and italic, though.

words

910 Longbrook Ave./Bridgeport, CT 06497-2325/May 17,----/Mr. Yorick  14
Kelsey/First National Bank/2995 Mt. Pleasant Dr./Bridgeport, CT  27
06611-2301/Dear Mr. Kelsey  32

¶ Thank you for taking time to speak to our FBLA chapter.  43
Your comments were most appropriate for our members.  54

¶ During your presentation you referred to articles appearing  66
in The Wall Street Journal and Business Week. Do you remember  79
in which issues those articles appeared? I'm preparing a  91
report for my social studies class on trade barriers; I believe  104
the articles you referred to would be excellent sources of  115
information for the report. Are you aware of other sources  127
that would be appropriate for the topic?  136

¶ Thank you again for sharing your expertise. Your  146
talk on International Partnerships made us realize the  157
importance of American business abroad.  165
Sincerely/Miss Jessica A. Kelley/FBLA Member  174

# GLOBAL AWARENESS

During the time you have spent in this class, in addition to learning keyboarding, you have met other students that you may have only seen in the hallway or at school activities. Some students you have met may now be your friends. Other students you may be getting to know better through conversations you have before and after class.

Friendships that have developed or are developing come about because people decided to talk (communicate) with each other. The communication may have begun by sharing how to complete a keying task. From this beginning you may have shared thoughts about a movie or feelings regarding a team's victory in the last game. From these initial conversations, you may have moved on to how your families celebrate certain holidays or to conversations that had a more personal meaning.

In good communication we begin to share our deeper thoughts and feelings. It is from this deeper level of communication that we begin to realize that though differences exist among people, important similarities exist as well. Thus we begin to understand that differences need not be a stumbling block in a relationship but rather a gift that can enrich it.

In addition to talking (face to face or by telephone), we also can communicate through the written word. Letters, e-mail, and faxes are ways that can be used to stay in touch locally, across the nation, and throughout the world.

To understand and appreciate other people and other cultures takes time, and it requires communication—both oral and written.

## ACTIVITIES

Assume that you are to be the mentor for an exchange student in your school next year—"to show her/him the ropes."

You want to get to "know" the student before he/she arrives. You decide to do so by letter.

Compose/key a letter to this imaginary person from the country of your choice. Welcome the student and include comments about your school, family, town, interests, and hobbies. Include a list of questions for her/him to answer in response: goals, fears, interests, etc.

# CULTURAL DIVERSITY

The foods eaten and avoided by people of different lands provide clues to the culture from which individuals come. In general, people eat foods that are native to their own country and avoid foods that are unfamiliar or perhaps are forbidden in certain cultures. For example, the eating of pork is forbidden in Arab countries and discouraged by certain groups in others. Beef is forbidden as human food in India because the cow is considered sacred. Shellfish, too, are forbidden in some cultures.

Although not forbidden, white bread, popcorn, ketchup, roast turkey, and watermelon (common American foods) are avoided by people of some cultures. Corn on the cob—one of our favorite summer foods—is considered in Europe to be food for animals and not fit for human consumption.

Often an uninformed or thoughtless host is embarrassed when certain guests are unable to eat the only entree and several of the hors d'oeuvres offered at a luncheon or dinner party.

Perhaps the statement "We are what we eat" is not farfetched, after all.

## ACTIVITIES

Assume that your school has several new exchange students. At least one student is from each of the following countries: Israel, China, Mexico, Italy, Saudi Arabia, and Nigeria.

The student council is planning a picnic to welcome these students. Your job is to plan the menu for the picnic.

In groups of 3 or 4, list foods some of these students cannot eat; then list foods from which each of them could acceptably choose.

Prepare a menu of selected appetizers, entrees, salads, vegetables, and desserts that would appeal to these diverse tastes.

**Document 2**
**Business Letter**

Format and key the text at the right as a business letter in block format with open punctuation (see p. 130 to review).

words

May 18, ---- | Miss Jessica A. Kelley | 910 Longbrook Ave. | Bridgeport, 13
CT 06497-2325 | Dear Miss Kelley 20

Speaking to your FBLA chapter was my pleasure. I particularly en- 33
joyed responding to the questions of your members after the pre- 46
sentation. 48

I have enclosed copies of the articles in The Wall Street Journal and 62
Business Week about which you inquired. Perhaps the article that appeared 77
in last week's Time magazine, "Let's Talk Trade," will also assist you 92
in preparing your report. 97

Representatives from our bank always enjoy speaking to student groups. 112
If you need presenters in the future, please let me know. 123

Sincerely | Yorick Kelsey | Customer Relations | xx | Enclosures 135

**Document 3**
**Standard Memo**

Format and key the text at the right as a standard memo (see p. 117 to review). Save to open later. Filename: MEM78B3.

TO: Department Managers | FROM: Rhett Canton, Human Resources | 12
DATE: June 15, ---- | SUBJECT: MANAGING CONFLICT SEMINAR 23

Last week President Simonson attended a seminar on managing conflict. 37
She was so impressed with the seminar that she would like all department 52
managers to take part in a future seminar. 61

The one-day seminar is geared to help you deal constructively with 74
conflicts that arise in the normal operations of your department. 87
Ms. Simonson believes that each department manager who participates 101
in a seminar will be more effective in dealing with conflicts. She thinks 116
that you will be able to build and maintain stronger departmental 129
relationships. 132

Two seminars are scheduled for next month. The first is scheduled 146
for July 12 in Milwaukee. The second is scheduled for July 23 and will 160
be held in Madison. Please let me know which seminar you would like 174
to attend, and I will make the necessary arrangements. | xx 185

**Document 4**
**Simplified Memo**

Format and key the text at the right as a simplified memo (see p. 115 to review).

February 2, ---- | Word Processing Department | SELECTION OF NEW 12
WORD PROCESSING DEPARTMENT MANAGER 19

As you may have heard by now, Diane Chi announced her plans to retire at 33
the end of March. The position will be advertised both internally and exter- 48
nally. 51

For those interested in applying for the position, a resume and letter 65
of application should be sent to Director Rhett Canton, Human Resources 79
Department, by February 16. Interviews will be conducted the following 93
week so that the new manager can be hired by March 1. This schedule 107
will allow the new manager to work with Ms. Chi for a month prior to 121
her retirement. 124

Ms. Kathy Lind | Human Resources | xx 131

# *your* PERSPECTIVE

## ETHICS: The Right Thing to Do

• *Fables, anecdotes, and stories have been used over the ages in various cultures to teach lessons in*
• *honesty and truth.  One such story is the following one from Ethiopia.*

Long ago Truth, Falsehood, Fire, and Water were journeying together and came upon a herd of cattle.  They discussed how to distribute the herd and decided it would be fairest to divide the herd into four parts so that each could take home an equal share.  But Falsehood was greedy and schemed to get more for himself.

"Listen to my warning," he whispered, pulling Water to one side.  "Fire plans to burn all the grass along your banks and drive your cattle away across the plains so he can have them for himself.  If I were you, I'd extinguish him now, and then we can have his share for ourselves."  Water was foolish enough to listen to Falsehood, and he dashed himself upon Fire and put him out.

Next, Falsehood crept toward Truth.  "Look what Water has done," he whispered.  "He has murdered Fire and taken his cattle.  We should not consort with the likes of him.  We should take all the cattle and go to the mountains."  Truth believed Falsehood and together they drove the cattle into the mountains.

"Wait for me!" Water called, and he hurried after them; but of course he could not run uphill.  So he was left all alone in the valley below.

When they reached the top of the highest mountain, Falsehood turned to Truth and laughed.  "I've tricked you, stupid fool," he shrieked.  "Now you must give me all the cattle and be my servant, or I'll destroy you."

"Yes, you have tricked me," Truth admitted, "but I will never be your servant." And so they fought; and when they clashed, thunder rolled back and forth across the mountaintops.  Again and again they threw themselves together, but neither could destroy the other.

Finally they decided to call upon the Wind to declare a winner of the contest.  So Wind came rushing up the mountain slopes, and he listened to what they had to say.  "It is not for me to declare a winner in this fight," he told them.  "Truth and Falsehood are destined to struggle. Sometimes Truth will win, but other times Falsehood will prevail, and then Truth must rise up and fight again.  Until the end of the world, Truth must battle Falsehood and must never rest or let down his guard, or he will be finished once and for all."

And so Truth and Falsehood are fighting to this day. ✳

## ACTIVITIES

1. Read the material at the left.

2. Discuss what it means to be honest and to tell the truth.

3. Through discussion with family and friends, try to discover any story that has been handed down through generations that demonstrates the tradition of honest behavior.  Share these with the class.  What ideas seem to be common in all such stories shared?

4. Compose/key a definition of honesty and describe what it means to you.

5. Compose/key a list of ways that the expectation of honesty affects your behavior at school, at home, and at work (if you have a job).

---

**Source:** Bennett, William J. (ed.).  *The Book of Virtues:  A Treasury of Great Moral Stories.*  New York: Simon and Shuster, 1993.

**Objectives:**
**1.** To format business letters in modified block style.
**2.** To use word processing features to edit documents.

### 79A • 5
### Conditioning Practice
each line twice

alphabet 1 Zac Jurkovic was quite eager for the next two games to be played.

speed 2 The girl and man may signal the proficient maid with a big flame.

fig/sym 3 The 11% tax on Order #624 is $13.80; for Order #209 it is $37.50.

gwam 1' | 1 | 2 | 3 | 4 | 5 | 6 | 7 | 8 | 9 | 10 | 11 | 12 | 13 |

### 79B • 35
### Modified Block Letters

1. Study the modified block letter format guides on p. 189 and the model letter illustrating modified block on p. 193. Note the differences between the block letter and the modified block letter format.

2. **Letter 1**: Format and key the letter on p. 193. Correct your errors as you key. Proofread the document. On screen use the View feature to check the format of the letter before saving the letter under the filename CORLESS.

3. **Letter 2**: Retrieve (or rekey) the letter and format it as a modified block letter with the following changes:

   a. Address the letter to:
      **MR BRANDON SMOLTZ**
      **HOILAND PLASTICS**
      **876 KENILWORTH AVE**
      **PONTIAC MI 48058-8723**

   b. Delete the subject line.

   c. Include the following sentence at the end of the first paragraph: **The paragraphs of a modified block letter may or may not be indented.**

   d. Use SMOLTZ for the filename.

### 79C • 10
### Editing Text

Either key copy or open MEM78B3 (or rekey Document 3, p. 191) and make the changes outlined at the right to the first two paragraphs of the memo.

Last week President Simonson ^and I attended a seminar on managing conflict. ^We were so impressed ~~with the seminar~~ that ^we would like ^to have all department managers, ~~to take part in a future seminar~~ , "You Can Manage Conflict,"

The one-day seminar ^is geared to help you deal constructively with conflicts that arise in the ^day-to-day ~~normal~~ operations of your department. Ms. Simonson ^and I believes that each department manager who participates in a seminar will ^become ~~be~~ more effective in dealing with conflicts. ^We ~~She~~ thinks that ~~you will be able to~~ ~~build and maintain~~ stronger departmental ^and interdepartmental relationships ^will exist if all managers attend.

**Table 1**
DS; CS: 0.5"; center column headings

**Table 2**
1" margins; block column headings; DS

**Table 3**
1" margins; center column headings; DS between entries

words

## SPEAKERS OF THE HOUSE OF REPRESENTATIVES
### 1947–Present

| Speaker | Party | State | Tenure | |
|---------|-------|-------|--------|---|
| | | | | 8 |
| | | | | 11 |
| Speaker | Party | State | Tenure | 17 |
| Joseph W. Martin Jr. | R | Massachusetts | 1947-1949 | 27 |
| Sam Rayburn | D | Texas | 1949-1953 | 33 |
| Joseph W. Martin Jr. | R | Massachusetts | 1953-1955 | 42 |
| Sam Rayburn | D | Texas | 1955-1961 | 48 |
| John W. McCormack | D | Massachusetts | 1962-1971 | 57 |
| Carl Albert | D | Oklahoma | 1971-1977 | 63 |
| Thomas P. O'Neill Jr. | D | Massachusetts | 1977-1987 | 73 |
| James Wright | D | Texas | 1987-1989 | 79 |
| Thomas S. Foley | D | Washington | 1989-1995 | 87 |
| Newt Gingrich | R | Georgia | 1995- | 93 |

96

Source: The World Almanac and Book of Facts, 1994.    107

## COMPUTER SUPPORT SERVICES    5
### Support Telephone Numbers    10

| Application | Phone | |
|-------------|-------|---|
| Application | Phone | 14 |
| Spreadsheets | 4902 | 27 |
| Graphics | 3067 | 39 |
| Word Processing | 2935 | 51 |
| | 2937 | 52 |
| Database | 6574 | 64 |
| E-mail | 8201 | 76 |
| Network | 6528 | 89 |
| DOS | 6723 | 101 |
| Windows | 4598 | 113 |
| Software Installation | 6573 | 125 |

*Bold company names*

## COMPUTER PRODUCT DEALERS    5
*June 25, ----*    8

DS

| Name | Address & Phone | |
|------|-----------------|---|
| Name | Address & Phone | 12 |
| Computer Sales and Service | 8210 Lakeland Dr. | 21 |
| | 182-9412 | 23 |
| Computer Systems | 830 Robindale Dr. | 30 |
| | 127-3856 | 32 |
| PC Tailors | 129 Pawtucket Dr. | 38 |
| | 171-5674 | 40 |
| Micro Solutions | 1445 Antique St. | 46 |
| | 127-8520 | 48 |
| Office Products | 920 Carolina Ave. | 55 |
| | 171-8301 | 57 |
| Software Specialists | 8231 Algonquin Dr. | 65 |
| | 171-8396 | 66 |

*Indent phone nos. 0.5" (5 spaces)*

**DOCUMENT PROCESSING SPECIALISTS**
6652 Remington St.
New Haven, CT 06517-1498
(203) 555-8215

Dateline

March 27, ---- · 2" TM or center page

QS

Letter
address

Miss Anne Corless
Asturia Technologies
5409 Bayview Dr.
Miami, FL 33160-8682 DS

Salutation

Dear Miss Corless: DS

Subject line

MODIFIED BLOCK LETTER FORMAT/BLOCKED PARAGRAPHS DS

Body of
letter

This letter is arranged in modified block format with blocked paragraphs. The only difference between this letter format and the block format is that the dateline and the closing lines (complimentary close, keyed name of the originator, and his or her title) begin at the horizontal center point. DS

1"

Mixed punctuation (a colon after the salutation and a comma after the complimentary close) is used in this letter. If an enclosure is mentioned in the body of the letter, the word Enclosure is keyed a double space below the reference notation, flush with the left margin. Copy notations are placed a double space below the enclosure notation or below the reference initials if no enclosure has been indicated. DS

1"

A copy of the block format letter is enclosed so that you can compare the two formats. As you can see, either format presents an attractive appearance. DS

Complimentary
close

Sincerely yours, QS

*Troy Williams*

Keyed name
Official title

Troy Williams
Word Processing Consultant
DS

Reference
initials

ph DS

Enclosure
notation

Enclosure DS

Copy
notation

c Ms. Kimberlee Rodriguez

**Letter in Modified Block Format (Letter 1)**

**Endnotes Page**

Prepare an endnotes page from the information at the right.

**Document 2**
**Title Page**

Format a title page for the report. Use your name, school name, and the current date.

**Document 3**
**References Page**

Prepare a references page from the information at the right.

| | words |
|---|---|
| 3 7. Graphics software. *that will run on the network* | 245 |
| 4. A ~~micro~~computer *capable of* ~~to~~ serve *ing* as the host computer. | 257 |
| 5. Furniture to *accommodate* ~~fit~~ the equipment that will be pur- | 269 |
| chased. | 271 |
| *DSH* Advantages. The *main* ~~chief~~ advantage of *share* networking is that | 282 |
| the department's 25 *computer* ~~micro~~ users will ~~use computer~~ files, | 292 |
| software packages, a scanner, and computer printers.²³ Shar- | 304 |
| ing will *increase* ~~improve~~ the quantity *and quality* of the documents and presenta- | 319 |
| tions. | 320 |
| *DSH* Disadvantages. Most sources list network manaegment as *one of* | 333 |
| the major problem in running a network. Installing the Ad- | 345 |
| vertising Department's network will require hiring another | 357 |
| person to coordinate the network. Even though it is not as | 372 |
| difficult as it was six years ago, finding and hiring a com- | 386 |
| petent person to maintain *and maintain* the network is not going to be | 397 |
| easy.³⁴ *technically* | 399 |

ENDNOTES — 401

¹John A. Boyer, "Networking--A Preliminary Report," — 411
(Pittsburg: Office Network, Inc., 1990), p. 5, photocopied. — 426

²Mark G. Simkin, *Computer Information Systems for Business* — 438 *Consultants*
(Dubuque, *IA* ~~Iowa~~: Wm. C. Brown Publishers, 1987), p. 161. — 449

³"The future, According to Wang," *The Office*, June, *1988* p. 40. — 462

⁴Barry Gerber, "1995's Hottest Networking Issues," *Network* — 474
*Computing*, December 1994, p. 136. — 481

---

**LESSON 150**   **Assessment: Tables**

**Objective:**
To assess table formatting skill.

**150A • 5**
**Conditioning Practice**

set 0.5" SMs
each line twice

alphabet 1 After a wild jump ball, the guards very quickly executed a zone press.

speed 2 If they do the work for us, I may go to the city and then to the lake.

figures 3 The ZIP Code for Jay's new address at 3497 Cedar Street is 87105-2628.

gwam 1' | 1 | 2 | 3 | 4 | 5 | 6 | 7 | 8 | 9 | 10 | 11 | 12 | 13 | 14 |

**150B • 8**
**Skill Check**

1. Key a 5' writing on 148C, page 354.
2. Find *gwam* and number of errors.
3. Record score.

**Objectives:**
**1.** To format letters in modified block style.
**2.** To increase proficiency in keying opening and closing lines of letters.

## 80A • 5
### Conditioning Practice

set 0.5" SMs; each line twice

alphabet   1   Nan was to have completed the required textbook for the zoology major.

speed   2   She may work with the men on their problem with the city turn signals.

fig/sym   3   Blake Realty sold the houses on Lots #3 & #6 for $87,950 and $104,200.

**gwam**   1'  | 1 | 2 | 3 | 4 | 5 | 6 | 7 | 8 | 9 | 10 | 11 | 12 | 13 | 14 |

## **F** ORMATTING

## 80B • 7
### Drill: Modified Block Letter

1. Two 1' writings on opening lines (date through ¶ 1) of modified block letter on p. 193. Concentrate on letter parts. Add 2 words on the second writing.

2. Two 1' writings on closing lines (¶ 3 through copy notation) of modified block letter on p. 193. If you finish before time is called, DS and begin

again. Focus on correct placement of letter parts. Add about two words (10 keystrokes) on the second writing.

## 80C • 33
### Modified Block Letters

**Letter 1**
**Business Letter**
modified block format, blocked ¶s; open punctuation

**wp** note:

Save to open later (LTR80C1).

words

| | |
|---|---:|
| December 12, ----  \|   Ms. Lindsay Magnus  \|   NEA Convention Chair  \| | 12 |
| 819 Country Club Dr.  \|   Largo, FL 34641-5639  \|   Dear Ms. Magnus | 23 |

Here is the printout of individuals registered with **Speakers, Speakers,** *38*
**Speakers** who have listed economic issues as a topic on which they *51*
give presentations. The printout provides a brief description of their *65*
presentations along with the fees charged. *74*

If you decide you are interested in learning more about any of the *87*
speakers after reviewing the printout, let us know. We can provide you *101*
with a videotape of a portion of your selected speaker's presentation. *116*
This allows you and your committee to become familiar with a speaker's *130*
presentation and style. *135*

Given the fees being charged by speakers today, we think this preview *149*
gives you the opportunity to learn as much as possible about the *162*
speaker before making a final selection. Much of the uncertainty is *176*
eliminated. Let us know which videos you would like, and we will *189*
send them out today. *193*

Sincerely  \|   Ms. Kim Khatib  \|   Manager  \|   xx  \|   Enclosure *202*

# Assessment: Reports

**Objective:**
To assess report formatting skill.

| | | |
|---|---|---|
| alphabet | 1 | Gavin expects the banks to formalize quite a few details in July. |
| speed | 2 | The ancient maps may aid them when they do the work for the city. |
| figures | 3 | Is the charge on Order No. 5304, dated June 19, $28.67 or $28.76? |

**gwam** 1' | 1 | 2 | 3 | 4 | 5 | 6 | 7 | 8 | 9 | 10 | 11 | 12 | 13 |

**149B • 45**
## Assess Report Skills

**Document 1**
**Report from Rough Draft**

1. Format and key the report in bound style.
2. When you finish, proofread your copy.

words

STATUS REPORT     3

Advertising Department Network Project     11

The purpose of this report is to ~~inform~~ *update* you ~~of~~ *on* the ~~sta~~ *current* sta-     23

tus of the project to network the ~~micro~~computers *in* ~~assigned to~~     33

the Advertising Department.     38

Decisions Made     42

Based on the recommendations ~~made~~ in the report, *John Boyer's* ~~(Boyer,~~     52

~~5, 1990)~~ it has been decided to install a star network:     62

One of the most popular ways of creating local area net-     73
works is with physical coaxial and a host computer. The     85
cables physically connect to the central host computer and     96
thus "hardwire" the network. This is often called a star     108
network because workstation connections (nodes) radiate     119
from the host computer like the many points of a star.     131

The decision has been made to network 25 computers, 5     141
printers; *, and a scanner* to purchase a higher level graphics package; and     156
to include a *an electronic* mail system.     164

Current Activities     168

The director of computing is ~~seeking~~ *requesting* prices *quotes* on the     180
following items that are needed to install the network.     191

1. Network software, network cards, active and passive     203
hubs, cabling, etc.     207

2. Network versions of *existing* word processing, desktop publish-     220
ing, data base, spreadsheet, and workflow applications     231
packages. *software*     235

*(continued on next page)*

**Letter 2**
**Business Letter**
modified block; indented ¶s;
mixed punctuation

**note:**
Save to open later
(LTR80C2).

February 3, ---- | Mr. Rori M. Conseco | NEA President | 3890 Northcliffe    14
Manor Dr. | Houston, TX 77066-9365 | Dear Mr. Conseco:    24

As a member of the San Francisco Convention Bureau, I am pleased to    38
extend an early welcome to the National Economics Association.  San    51
Francisco is a great convention city.    59

My company, **Tours Unlimited**, works with organizations such as yours to    73
customize tours of the sights of San Francisco.  We provide the enclosed    88
listing of the most frequently visited sights; you select the ones your mem-    103
bership would like to see.  We will take care of making sure your members    118
see everything they desire while in San Francisco.  It is as simple as that.    133

I will give you a call early next week to see if you are interested in having    149
**Tours Unlimited** assist with your convention plans.    159

Sincerely,  |  Ms. Ashton Sheridan  |  Tour Consultant  |  xx  |  Enclosure    171

**Letter 3**
**Personal-Business Letter**
modified block format;
blocked ¶s; mixed
punctuation

930 Main St. | Cartersburg, IN 46114-8930 | June 6, ---- |    11
Attention Software Manager | McCarty Computer Products |    21
382 Mayhew Dr. | Indianapolis, IN 46227-8762 | Ladies    31
and Gentlemen: | USER'S MANUAL    39

Last week when I was in Indianapolis, I    47
purchased the "Fingertip Geography" software package    58
from your store. Today when I tried to use the software,    69
I found that a user's manual was not included.    79

Please send a copy of the manual as soon as    88
possible so that I will be able to install the software and    100
start using it. I've enclosed a copy of the receipt that    111
contains the identification numbers for the software.    122
Sincerely yours, | Richard LaFayette | Enclosure    131

**80D • 5**
**Editing Text**
Either open LTR80C2 or
rekey Letter 2 and make the
changes outlined at the right
to the second paragraph.

My company, **Tours Unlimited,** works with organizations such as yours
to customize tours of the sights of San Francisco.  ~~We provide~~ *from* the
enclosed listing of the most frequently visited sights; you select
*those* the ones your membership would like to see.

**Letter 2**

Format and key the text at the right in simplified block letter format. Address the letter to:

**Ms. Annette Young, Principal East High School**
**2650 Old Orchard Ln.**
**Montgomery, AL 36117-2341**

Use **January 17,----** for the letter date. The subject line is **MULTIMEDIA COMPUTER SYSTEM SEMINAR.** The letter is from **Jared C. Scott, Technology Consultant.**

Add an enclosure notation.

**148C • 8**
**Skill Check**

1. One 5' writing.
2. Determine *gwam* and number of errors.
3. Record score.

| | words |
|---|---|
| | opening 29 |

Multimedia computer systems play a significant role in enhancing the educational environment. If you plan to purchase a multimedia system in the near future, you won't want to miss the seminar on February 25 entitled "Selecting Your Multimedia Computer System Components." — 44 / 58 / 73 / 84

The seminar will present the various components of a reasonably priced ($1,700 to $2,500) system. Included in the presentation will be a discussion of: — 98 / 113 / 115

| | words | | words |
|---|---|---|---|
| ✓ operating systems | 125 | ✓ memory (RAM) requirements | 125 |
| ✓ microprocessors | 131 | ✓ disk drives | 131 |
| ✓ CD-ROM drives | 137 | ✓ monitors | 137 |
| ✓ video cards | 142 | ✓ speakers | 142 |
| ✓ sound cards | 148 | ✓ telecommunication | 148 |
| | | connection requirements | 153 |

Time will be available for questions from the audience. Thus, issues not covered during the formal presentation can be addressed. — 168 / 180

Fill out and return the enclosed card to reserve your seat at the workshop. The number of seminar participants is limited to 15 so that we can meet individual needs. — 195 / 209 / 213

closing 223

 all letters used

| | gwam | 1' | 5' |
|---|---|---|---|

Office productivity refers to the ratio of office input, or — 12 / 2 / 52
the cost of equipment, office space, supplies, and labor, to the — 25 / 5 / 55
output of the office work force. The ability of an organization — 38 / 8 / 57
to increase output at a faster rate than operating costs are ris- — 51 / 10 / 60
ing is vital to its success and possibly to its survival. Most — 64 / 13 / 62
people agree that improving productivity is crucial, but the — 76 / 15 / 65
puzzle is how to go about doing so. Perhaps the first step is to — 89 / 18 / 67
dispel a myth that many people believe--that is, they must work — 102 / 20 / 70
harder to exceed their present rate of production. The better — 115 / 23 / 73
idea is that they must work smarter at their jobs, not harder. — 127 / 25 / 75

To determine how to work smarter, one might first analyze — 12 / 28 / 77
the daily routine to see if some tasks that are being done manu- — 24 / 30 / 80
ally might be performed more efficiently with the aid of tech- — 37 / 33 / 82
nology. Through office automation, many jobs can be done more — 49 / 35 / 85
quickly and more accurately. Often, information that is complete — 63 / 38 / 88
and up to date can be provided only through automated systems, as — 76 / 41 / 90
some information becomes obsolete by the time it can be produced — 89 / 43 / 93
manually. However, care must be exercised to ensure that auto- — 101 / 46 / 95
mation is not used to generate too much of the wrong kind of — 114 / 48 / 98
data, as has been the case sometimes. — 121 / 50 / 99

| gwam | 1' | 1 | 2 | 3 | 4 | 5 | 6 | 7 | 8 | 9 | 10 | 11 | 12 | 13 |
|---|---|---|---|---|---|---|---|---|---|---|---|---|---|---|
| | 5' | | 1 | | | 2 | | | | 3 | | | | |

# LESSON 81 — Standard Memos

## Objectives:
**1.** To format standard memos with a distribution list.
**2.** To format a two-page memo.

### 81A • 5
### Conditioning Practice

each line twice

alphabet 1 Jake will become the quality supervisor for Guzzo Food next year.

speed 2 The official paid the men for the handiwork they did on the dock.

figures 3 The packages were sent to 312 Birch, 4069 Lake, and 578 Hastings.

gwam 1' | 1 | 2 | 3 | 4 | 5 | 6 | 7 | 8 | 9 | 10 | 11 | 12 | 13 |

## FORMATTING

### 81B • 35
### Standard Memos

**Memo 1**

Format and key the text at the right as a standard memo.

**wp note:**

Create a macro for standard memo headings (see p. 188).

**Note:** Electronic typewriter users can store the standard memo headings.

|  | words |
|---|---|
| TO: All Employees \| FROM: Justin Reed, Accounting Department \| DATE: | 13 |
| June 5, ---- \| SUBJECT:  EXPENSE FORMS | 21 |

Please start using the attached expense form when you submit your June / 35
expenses.  Your suggestions for improving the form were very helpful.  We / 50
are confident that you will find the form easier to complete. / 62

We were able to accommodate those of you who requested that the form be / 76
put on the computer.  You can access the form on the network by retrieving / 92
the EXPNFORM file.   Of course, we encourage all of you to use the comput- / 106
erized form, if possible; most of the delays in processing the expense forms / 122
are a result of illegible writing. / 129

If you encounter any problems with the form, please call Mary Nen / 142
(Extension 2871). \| xx \| Attachment / 148

**Memo 2**

Format and key the text at the right as a standard memo. Review how to format memo distribution lists and two-page memo headings in the format guides on p. 189.

| | words |
|---|---|
| TO:  Marsha Mastin, Accounting Manager \| Kent Van Noy, Market- | 12 |
| ing Manager \| Rebecca Etheridge, Finance Manager \| Shelby | 23 |
| Fuller, Word Processing Manager \| Kari Hefner, Personnel | 34 |
| Manager \| Cori Goodwin, Graphics Manager \| Christine Bennett, | 45 |
| Public Relations Manager \| FROM:  Edward G. Nolta, Vice | 56 |
| President \| DATE:  October 12, ---- \| SUBJECT:  EMPLOYEE PERFOR- | 67 |
| MANCE REVIEWS | 70 |

It's almost time again for annual performance reviews, a pro- / 83
cess that you may not anticipate eagerly.  As we discussed / 94
last summer at our meeting, employees and managers often look / 107
upon these conferences as a time to discuss all the things / 118
employees have done wrong during the past year. With this / 130
approach to performance reviews, tension is high; and / 141
neither the managers nor the employees feels good at the / 152

*(continued on next page)*

# UNIT 33

## Assess Document Formatting Skills

### LESSON 148

## Assessment: Letters

**Objective:**
To assess letter formatting skill.

### 148A • 5
**Conditioning Practice**

each line twice

| | | |
|---|---|---|
| alphabet | 1 | Jackson believed she might maximize profits with a quality force. |
| speed | 2 | If it is so, they may go with me to the city by the lake to work. |
| figures | 3 | In 1996, we had 287 office chairs, 143 desks, and 50 work tables. |

**gwam** 1' | 1 | 2 | 3 | 4 | 5 | 6 | 7 | 8 | 9 | 10 | 11 | 12 | 13 |

### 148B • 37
**Assess Letter Skill**

**Letter 1**

Format and key the text at the right as a two-page letter in block format with mixed punctuation. Use the USPS letter address style and send the letter to:

**MS ROWANDA SMITH**
**MEMORIAL HIGH SCHOOL**
**375 BEACON ST N**
**BOSTON MA 02135-3882**

Use **January 14, ----** for the letter date; supply an appropriate salutation and complimentary closing. The letter is from **Ms. Janice F. Etheridge, Instructor**.

words
opening 22

You are right!  Keeping up with today's rapidly developing technologies  36
can be a nightmare.  We often struggle with these issues at the university.  52

In your letter you asked for my opinion about upgrading your computer lab  66
versus replacing as much of the old computer equipment as possible with  81
newer technologies.  On a short-term basis, upgrading may be satisfactory.  96
By investing in newer technology, however, you will be able to do much more  111
than you can with your current equipment.  120

I have enclosed a copy of an article written by Odvard Egil Dyrli and Daniel  135
E. Kinnaman in the January, 1995, issue of Technology & Learning.  They  150
state that only by investing in the newer technology will you and your stu-  165
dents be able to:  169

• Use complex graphical environments to control the machines.  181

• Take advantage of the newest hypertext and hypermedia software.  195

• Learn to use "photographic-quality," high-resolution graphics and video.  210

• Play and record speech, stereo music, and sound effects.  222

• Use online help features to learn about software and computer systems.  237

• Use worldwide telecommunications information services and tools with  251
  help from graphical interfaces such as Mosaic.  260

• Benefit from the newest generation of high-quality educational software  275
  delivered on high-density disks and CD-ROM.  284

If you are planning to use the computers only as word processors, upgrad-  299
ing to accommodate the new software you plan to purchase is sufficient.  313
However, if you want to utilize some of the newer technologies that are now  329
available and that will become available in the near future, you may wish to  344
start replacing some of your machines.  There is not a simple answer to your  359
question.  361

closing 371

completion of the review.  Further, the overall produc- | 163
tivity of the company seems to suffer, at least for a | 174
few weeks. | 176

I have talked over with President Vermillion the concerns | 186
that were expressed at our summer meeting.  He recog- | 199
nizes that improvements need to be made to our perfor- | 209
mance appraisal procedures.  He feels so strongly about | 221
wanting to improve our review procedures that he has | 231
agreed to bring in two or three outside consultants to | 242
work with us for two or three days. | 250

The three consultants ~~who~~ *who* I am considering bringing in | 261
are Dr. Mitch Carlson, Dr. Charlayne Winger, and Mr. | 271
Roul Mikva. | 281

*All three individuals have an extensive background in the area of employee appraisals.*

Dr. Carlson is the personnel director for a California- | 292
based firm, Integrated Technologies.  During his eight | 303
years at Integrated Technologies, the turnover rate has | 314
been cut in half--we all know what that means in terms | 325
of training costs.  He has also given numerous workshops | 337
throughout the United States and Canada. | 345

Dr. Winger is a management professor at ~~the~~ Brickley | 356
State University.  She is the author of several articles | 367
dealing with employee motivation and evaluation in some | 379
of the leading management journals.  She also has con- | 389
ducted a number of seminars. | 395

I believe the time that these individuals spend with us | 459
will be most productive.  Plans call for each of the | 470
three consultants to make a short lecture-type presen- | 481
tation.  This will be followed by a videotape presenta- | 492
tion illustrating positive and negative performance | 502
appraisals.  Time is also being set aside for a discus- | 513
sion with the consultants on the problems encountered in | 525
performance appraisals.  Finally, we plan to have a | 539
videotaped role-playing session that will be critiqued | 547
and discussed by the consultants. | 553

The consultants will be with us on November 3 and 4. | 564
Please arrange to have your schedule free on both days. | 575

*Mr. Mikva has international experience in the area of* | 406
*employee evaluation. He completed graduate work on* | 417
*the topic at a university in England. He has done* | 427
*consulting work in Germany, Japan, and Mexico. He* | 437
*should be able to offer an international perspective.* | 448

**Table 1**
DS; CS: 1"; center
column headings

**wp** note:
Right-align both figure
columns.

| | | words |
|---|---|---|
| | | |

FOREIGN VISITORS TO THE U.S., 1990 — 7

| Country of Origin | Visitors (Millions) | Expenditures Per Visitor | |
|---|---|---|---|
| | | | 13 / 20 |
| Australia | 0.5 | $2,279 | 24 |
| Canada | 17.3 | 330 | 28 |
| France | 0.7 | 1,703 | 31 |
| Germany | 1.2 | 1,778 | 35 |
| Italy | 0.4 | 1,973 | 38 |
| Japan | 3.2 | 2,381 | 41 |
| Mexico | 6.8 | 592 | 44 |
| Netherlands | 0.3 | 1,422 | 48 |
| New Zealand | 0.2 | 2,181 | 53 |
| United Kingdom | 2.2 | 1,596 | 58 |

61

Source: World Almanac, 1993. — 67

**Table 2**
DS; CS: 1.5"; center
column headings

**Table 3**
Format and key
Document 1, 129B, p. 310.

**Table 4**
Arrange Table 1 in descending order by Expenditures Per Visitor. Bold the main heading and change column spacing to 0.5".

CAST FOR
THE FUGITIVE — 2 / 4

| Characters | Actor/Actress | |
|---|---|---|
| | | 10 |
| Biggs | Daniel Roebuck | 23 |
| Dr. Anne Eastman | Julianne Moore | 36 |
| Samuel Gerard | Tommy Lee Jones | 49 |
| Helen Kimble | Sela Ward | 63 |
| Dr. Richard Kimble | Harrison Ford | 76 |
| Newman | Tom Wood | 89 |
| Dr. Charles Nichols | Jeroen Krabbe | 102 |
| Poole | L. Scott Caldwell | 115 |
| Cosmo Renfro | Joe Pantoliano | 129 |
| Sykes | Andreas Katsulas | 142 |

## 81C • 10
## Singular Verbs
## (continued)

Follow the Learn/Apply procedure in 76C, p. 184.

Use singular verbs with the pronouns **all** and **some** (and with fractions and percentages) when used as subjects if their modifiers are singular. Use plural verbs if their modifiers are plural.

Learn   1.  All of the manuscript is at the publishers.
Learn   2.  Some of the girls have already left for spring break.
Apply   3.  All of the materials (has, have) been purchased.
Apply   4.  Some of the watermelon (is, are) left.

Use a singular verb when **number** is used as the subject and is preceded by **the**; use a plural verb if **number** is preceded by **a**.

Learn   5.  A number of clients have moved to Colorado.
Learn   6.  The number of men passing the CPS exam has increased.
Apply   7.  The number of games on the schedule (has, have) decreased.
Apply   8.  A number of individuals (is, are) going to the meeting.

# LESSON 82

## Simplified Block Letters

**Objective:**
To learn to format letters in simplified block style.

## 82A • 5
## Conditioning Practice

each line twice

alphabet  1  Putting on the extravaganza was quite a big job for Lydia Camack.

speed  2  Enrique and the girls may go downtown to pay for the six emblems.

figures  3  He sold 1,307 units on Monday, 954 on Tuesday, and 862 on Friday.

**gwam**  1' | 1 | 2 | 3 | 4 | 5 | 6 | 7 | 8 | 9 | 10 | 11 | 12 | 13 |

## 82B • 37
## Simplified Block Letters

### Letter 1
Study the format guides for the simplified block letter on p. 189 and the model letter on p. 199. Format and key the letter on p. 199.

### Letter 2
Format and key the text at the right in simplified block format.

**wp note:**

Save this document (LTR82B2) for later use.

words

June 21, ---- | MR ANTHONY KENSINGTON | 8288 NEWCASTLE   10
LN | ALBANY GA 31701-9326 | NEW PHONE SYSTEM   18

To provide better customer service, Fair Oaks Credit Union will begin   32
using a new phone system on July 1. Although the new system requires   46
changing most Fair Oaks Credit Union phone numbers, it provides our   60
customers with direct access to all of our departments.   71

The attached listing is enclosed for your convenience. For numbers not   86
listed, dial 186-2222. We are confident that this new system will provide   101
you with better banking services.   108

MS. JULIE A. NOTTINGWOOD, CUSTOMER SERVICE | xx | Attachment   119

of the seven wonders of the electronic world."[2]  E-mail is     242

the sending, storing, and delivering of ^written messages electroni-  255

cally.  ~~According to~~ Reiss ^and Donlan[3] ~~there are~~ ^identify two categories  265

of electronic mail services:  271

    1.  In-house electronic mail.  (E-mail ~~which~~ ^that is run on  282
    a firm's computer system.)  287

2.  Commercial electronic mail.  (E-mail ~~which~~ ^that is supplied by  300
organizations such as General Electric Information Services  312
and MCI Communications.)  317

<u>Summary</u>  319

    Desktop publishing and electronic mail are but ②ˢᵖ of the  330

changes that are shaping the future of information process-  342

ing.  Each year ^new technology enhances the ability of personnel  355

to produce ^quality information ⌐in less time  364

- - - - - - - - - - - - - - - - - - - - - - - - - - - - - - - - - - - - -

heading   2

[1] Mary Ellen Oliverio and others, <u>The Office Procedures</u>  14
<u>and Technology</u> (Cincinnati: South-Western Publishing Co.,  26
1993), p. 291.  29
[2] Robert Wiggins, "The Remote E-Mail Checklist,"  42
<u>Mobile Office</u>, August 1994, p. 32.  49
[3] Levi Reiss and Edwin G. Dolan, <u>Using Computers:</u>  59
<u>Managing Change</u> (Cincinnati: South-Western Publishing  70
Co., 1989), p. 529.  73

**Document 2**
On a separate page, prepare an endnotes page from the information at the right.

**Document 3**
Format a title page for the report. Use your name and school name and the current date.

---

## LESSON 147    Prepare for Assessment:  Tables

**O b j e c t i v e :**
To prepare for assessment of tables.

**147A • 5**
**Conditioning Practice**

each line twice

alphabet   1   Kevin justified his lowest quiz score by explaining his problems.
speed   2   She may lend the ancient map to us if the city pays for the work.
fig/sym   3   Is Check #9084 for $76.52, dated June 13, made out to Chen & Chi?

**gwam**   1' | 1 | 2 | 3 | 4 | 5 | 6 | 7 | 8 | 9 | 10 | 11 | 12 | 13 |

# Communication ◑ Concepts Inc.

*178 S. Prospect Ave.* ▪ *San Bernardino, CA 92410-4567* ▪ *(714) 186-7934*

**Dateline**    August 13, ----   2" TM or center page
                QS

**Letter address**    MR CARL VISQUEL
            382 OLD MURFREESBORO RD
            NASHVILLE TN 37217-8902 DS

**Subject line**    SIMPLIFIED BLOCK LETTER FORMAT DS

**Body of letter**    This letter is arranged in simplified block format. Several differences distinguish this format from the block and modified block styles. DS

The **salutation** is omitted; it is replaced by a subject line. The **subject line** is keyed below the letter address in ALL CAPS. A double space is left above and below it. DS

The letter format is further streamlined by the omission of the **complimentary close**. The **writer's name** and **title** (or department) are keyed a quadruple space below the body of the letter in ALL CAPS. The name and title are separated by a comma. DS

Notice that the letter address of this letter is keyed in the style recommended by the U.S. Postal Service for OCR processing: ALL-CAP letters with <u>no</u> punctuation. As with the other letter formats, it would also be appropriate to use cap-and-lowercase letters with punctuation for the letter address. DS

Many organizations have decided to use this particular style. Their opinion is that the salutation and complimentary close serve little purpose and are obsolete. Other organizations still prefer the traditional block or modified block format. QS

*Mrs. Caroline Martinez*

**Writer's name and title**    MRS. CAROLINE MARTINEZ, WORD PROCESSING SPECIALIST DS

**Reference initials**    hpj

**Letter in Simplified Block Format**

Review the format guides on p. 268. Note the placement of the subject line, company name, copy notation, and postscript. Format and key:

113B, Document 3, p. 270.
114C, Letter 2, p. 272.
115C, Letter 2, p. 274.

## LESSON 146

# Prepare for Assessment:  Reports

**O b j e c t i v e :**
To prepare for assessment of reports.

**146A • 5**
**Conditioning Practice**

each line twice

alphabet 1 Jacques planned a very sizable agenda for the meetings next week.

speed 2 Glen did the work for us, but the city officials will pay for it.

fig/sym 3 Their bill was $74.05 ($68.12 for paper and $5.93 for envelopes).

gwam 1' | 1 | 2 | 3 | 4 | 5 | 6 | 7 | 8 | 9 | 10 | 11 | 12 | 13 |

## F ORMATTING

**146B • 45**
**Review Report Formats**

**Document 1**

1. Review the format guides for reports on pp. 211-212.
2. Format the report in unbound style; use **TODAY'S OFFICE** for the report heading.

words

opening   3

*DS ¶*  A person returning to the office environment after a 25-   14
year absence would have a difficult time coping with the   26
changes that have taken place during that time.  Changing tech-   38
nology would best describe the challenges facing today's office   51
worker.  Two "buzzwords" currently being used in the office are   64
electronic desktop publishing and electronic mail.   74

Electronic Desktop Publishing *(DTP)*   80

    Desktop publishing is the process of integrating text and   93

graphics by utilizing computer soft ware to produce *professional-* a profes-   106

sion looking document without using profesional services.   117

    A primary reason for using DTP is the enhanced   127
appearance of finished documents.  Almost anything that   138
can be typeset by a professional printer can be produced   149
using a DTP system:  announcements, business cards, let-   160
terheads, newsletters, etc.[1]   166

Since *today's* firms are *more* concerned *than ever* about creating the proper   181

image, it is expected that *a* greater number of firms will turn   194

to *desktop* publishing to enhance their images.   203

Electronic Mail   207

    The second "buzz word" being used extensively in the modern   217

office is electronic mail (e-mail).  "Electronic mail is one   230

*(continued on next page)*

Letter 3
Business Letter

Format and key the text at the right in simplified block format.

words

November 10, ---- | MS MICHELE YOUNG | 491 BROOKSIDE DR | FORT — 11
COLLINS CO 80526-3977 | COMMUNICATION PRESENTATION — 21

After hearing you make a few comments at the Business Education — 34
Advisory Council meeting, I knew you were an effective communicator and — 48
would be an excellent guest speaker for my business communication — 62
class.  My initial assessment was confirmed by your presentation — 75
yesterday. — 77

The students and I appreciated your taking time to share your thoughts — 91
with us.  After you left, we took a few minutes to discuss some of — 105
your comments.  The students were in complete agreement that you — 118
were an excellent role model of what we have been discussing during — 131
the semester.  Many of your remarks reinforced points that had previously — 146
been made in class.  The students are looking forward to testing some — 160
of your suggestions when they give their presentations. — 171

Thank you again for bringing your expertise to Lincoln High School. — 185

CHAD ANDERSON, INSTRUCTOR | xx — 191

## 82C • 8
### Editing Copy

Open LTR80C1 (or rekey Letter 1, p. 194). Reformat the letter in simplified block format with the changes to the second paragraph outlined at the right. Use CONVENTION SPEAKERS for the subject line.

Should
If you decide you ~~are interested in learning more~~ would like additional information about any of

listed on
the speakers ~~after reviewing~~ the printout, ~~let us know.~~ complete the enclosed card. We

cassette
can provide you with a video~~tape~~ of a portion of your selected
free of charge

can
speaker's presentation. ~~This allows~~ you and your committee ~~to~~

acquainted                                           before making a decision
become ~~familiar~~ with a speaker's presentation and style.

# LESSON 83

## Letters and Basic Skill Practice

**O b j e c t i v e s :**
1. To increase skill at processing letters in various formats.
2. To increase straight-copy keying skill.

## 83A • 5
### Conditioning Practice

each line twice

| | | |
|---|---|---|
| alphabet | 1 | Listing the exact job requirements for Eve will keep Zelda happy. |
| speed | 2 | They may visit the big chapels in the dismal towns on the island. |
| fig/sym | 3 | Warren McKinley paid me $736,000 for the 8,460 acres on 12/15/96. |

gwam 1' | 1 | 2 | 3 | 4 | 5 | 6 | 7 | 8 | 9 | 10 | 11 | 12 | 13 |

# UNIT 32

**LESSONS 145–147**

## Prepare for Assessment

### LESSON 145

## Prepare for Assessment: Letters

**O b j e c t i v e :**
To prepare for assessment of letters.

**145A • 5**
**Conditioning Practice**

set 0.5" SMs
each line twice

alphabet  1  The quick example Ozzie gave of adjectives and verbs was very helpful.

speed  2  He or she may work with us to make a profit for the eighty auto firms.

fig/sym  3  The cost of Model #80-93 is $425 plus 6% sales tax and 17% excise tax.

| gwam | 1' | 1 | 2 | 3 | 4 | 5 | 6 | 7 | 8 | 9 | 10 | 11 | 12 | 13 | 14 |

**145B • 13**
**Skill Check**

Key two 5' writings; calculate *gwam* and determine errors.

all letters used

| | gwam | 3' | 5' |

An education is becoming more important in our society.  More  `4 | 2 42`
jobs will be open to the skilled person with fewer jobs open to  `8 | 5 45`
the unskilled or less educated person.  Future jobs will require  `13 | 8 47`
people who can communicate and who have basic math and reading  `17 | 10 50`
skills.  It is predicted that there will be a large number of new  `21 | 13 52`
jobs available to those with the appropriate training who want to  `26 | 15 55`
work in an office.  These jobs will require the skills listed  `30 | 18 58`
above and an ability to process office documents.  `33 | 20 60`

To quickly process quality office documents will take a great  `37 | 22 62`
deal of training.  A person must be able to key rapidly, format a  `42 | 25 65`
variety of documents, make decisions, follow directions, recognize  `46 | 28 67`
all types of errors, and apply language skills.  In addition to  `50 | 30 70`
these skills, the best office workers will be willing to put forth  `55 | 33 73`
an extra effort.  You should begin to put forth an extra effort  `59 | 36 75`
today to get the training needed to become one of the skilled  `63 | 38 78`
workers in the labor force of the future.  `66 | 40 79`

| gwam | 3' | 1 | 2 | 3 | 4 | 5 |
| | 5' | 1 | | 2 | | 3 |

**83B • 33**

**Letter 1**
**Personal-Business Letter**
Format and key the letter shown at the right in modified block style with indented paragraphs and mixed punctuation. Save as LTR83B1.

words

928 Big Horn Ave. | Moorcroft, WY 82721-8329 | August 25, ---- |   12
Ms. Kellee Martinson | Section of Vital Statistics | 2120 Capitol   24
Ave. | Cheyenne, WY 82001-8821 | Dear Ms. Martinson:   34

Several weeks after the birth of our son, **Keith Mathews Anderson**, we   48
received a letter asking for verification of Keith's name. His middle name,   63
**Mathews**, was misspelled on that form. It was incorrectly spelled as   77
Matthews with two "t's" instead of **Mathews** with one "t." My maiden name   92
is **Mathews** (one "t"), and it is important to me to have it spelled correctly.   107

We made the requested correction on the original verification form and re-   122
turned it on June 17 along with a $12 check for two copies of the birth   136
certificate. Now we have been sent a "Request for Name Change" form. We   151
do <u>not</u> want to change his name. We just want the error corrected.   165

Sincerely, | Ms. Mary Mathews Anderson   172

**Letter 2**
**Business Letter**
Format and key the text at the right as a business letter in block format with open punctuation.

August 15, ---- | Mr. Steven Swenson | 280 Westridge Dr. | Halifax, NS   13
B3M 3K8 | CANADA | Dear Mr. Swenson   19

The degree program plan you submitted for a Master of Science degree in   34
business education was approved on August 14. A copy of the plan with   48
the required signatures is enclosed. Any changes to the approved program   63
will require submission of the **Program Change Form**, which is available in   77
the Graduate Office.   82

In your recent letter, you mentioned that you were planning to complete   96
your degree next summer. Please remember that you will need to register   111
for the written comprehensive examination the first week of the semester in   126
which you plan to take the exam. A complete listing of other important   141
dates for you to be aware of is included on **Summer Graduation Dates**   155
**Form** (enclosed).   157

If you have questions about any of the dates or if we can be of assistance   172
to you as you complete your degree requirements, please stop by our office.   187

Sincerely | Jason R. Edwards | Assistant Dean | xx | Enclosures   198

**Letter 3**
**Personal-Business Letter**
Open LTR83B1 (or rekey Letter 1 above). Change the format to block format with open punctuation. Include the text at the right as the last paragraph of the letter.

*Please verify when this correction has been made. Let us know, also, when we will get the birth certificate copies that we paid for two months ago.*

**Timed Writings**

1. A 1' writing on each ¶ for speed; find *gwam*.
2. A 1' writing on each ¶ for control; determine errors.
3. A 3' writing on ¶s 1-3 combined; find *gwam*; determine errors.

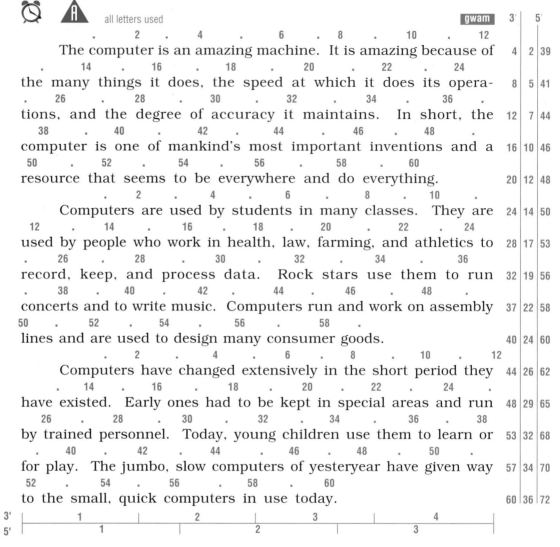

all letters used

| | gwam | 3' | 5' |
|---|---|---|---|

The computer is an amazing machine. It is amazing because of the many things it does, the speed at which it does its operations, and the degree of accuracy it maintains. In short, the computer is one of mankind's most important inventions and a resource that seems to be everywhere and do everything.

Computers are used by students in many classes. They are used by people who work in health, law, farming, and athletics to record, keep, and process data. Rock stars use them to run concerts and to write music. Computers run and work on assembly lines and are used to design many consumer goods.

Computers have changed extensively in the short period they have existed. Early ones had to be kept in special areas and run by trained personnel. Today, young children use them to learn or for play. The jumbo, slow computers of yesteryear have given way to the small, quick computers in use today.

gwam 3' 1 2 3 4
5' 1 2 3

**L** ANGUAGE SKILLS

**Number Expression**
Key each sentence, supplying the correct form of number expression.

1. The center is seven ft. 6 in. tall and weighs 230 lbs.
2. The technology meetings will be held in Rooms five and nine.
3. 2 of the board members will be out of town on March second.
4. He was scheduled on Flight fifty-three, which leaves at four p.m.
5. Nearly 60 members voted for Sue; that is about 3/4.
6. Problems four and five from Chapter four dealt with networks.
7. The two file servers will be connected tomorrow by nine a.m.
8. The servers were purchased at 1 State Street and 28 Lori Lane.
9. Exactly 1/2 of the computers have multimedia capabilities.
10. The play is scheduled for April third at six p.m. in Room 28.

**Letter 4**
**Business Letter**

Format and key the text at the right as a business letter in modified block format with mixed punctuation. Use the USPS style for the letter address.

| | words |
|---|---|
| March 28, ---- | Mr. and Mrs. Jason Verde | 8203 Martin Luther King | 13 |
| Blvd. | Boston, MA 02119-2698 | Dear Mr. and Mrs. Verde: | 24 |

Stearns Associates is pleased to announce that your financial planner, 38
Mr. Martin Lancaster, CFP, has qualified to join an elite group of highly 53
skilled professionals designated as **Master Planners**. Only <u>2</u> percent of all 68
financial planners are accorded this status. 77

Mr. Lancaster, as a **Master Planner**, will now have access to a wider assort- 92
ment of financial planning resources and tools. This access will allow 106
him to address your needs with a greater degree of personalization and 120
timeliness. 123

If you are interested in having Mr. Lancaster review your existing portfolio, 139
please contact him to set up an appointment. 148

Sincerely, | Jay S. Chang | Senior Vice President, Marketing | xx 160

## S KILL BUILDING

### 83C • 12
### Skill Check

1. Key a 3' writing on ¶s 1 and 2 combined; determine *gwam* and number of errors.
2. Key a 1' writing on each ¶; determine *gwam* and number of errors.
3. Key another 3' writing on ¶s 1 and 2 combined; determine *gwam* and number of errors.

**wp note:**
Use wordwrap instead of dividing words at the end of lines.

 all letters used

| | gwam | 3' | 5' |
|---|---|---|---|

. 2 . 4 . 6 . 8 . 10 . 12
The quality of life is a reflection of the quality of think- 4 | 2 | 41
. 14 . 16 . 18 . 20 . 22 . 24
ing. Just contemplate what the quality of life on this earth 8 | 5 | 43
. 26 . 28 . 30 . 32 . 34 . 36 .
would be today without the high-quality thinking done by famous 12 | 7 | 46
38 . 40 . 42 . 44 . 46 . 48 . 50
inventors. Imagine what it would be like without electricity. 17 | 10 | 48
. 52 . 54 . 56 . 58 . 60 . 62
If the phone didn't exist, consider the impact on your life. Do 21 | 13 | 51
64 . 66 . 68 . 70 . 72 . 74 . 76
you realize how your existence would change if horses were still 25 | 15 | 53
. 78 . 80 . 82 . 84 . 86 . 88 .
the primary mode of transportation? Would your life be the same 30 | 18 | 56
90 . 92 . 94 . 96
if the computer had not been invented? 32 | 19 | 57

. 2 . 4 . 6 . 8 . 10 .
High-quality thinking has impacted the quality of life 36 | 22 | 60
12 . 14 . 16 . 18 . 20 . 22 . 24
on this earth. By the same token, the quality of an individual's 40 | 24 | 62
. 26 . 28 . 30 . 32 . 34 . 36
existence is a reflection of the quality of an individual's 44 | 27 | 65
. 38 . 40 . 42 . 44 . 46 . 48
thinking. You need to think about school and how you can be a 48 | 29 | 67
. 50 . 52 . 54 . 56 . 58 . 60 .
better student. You need to examine career options and plan 53 | 32 | 70
62 . 64 . 66 . 68 . 70 . 72 .
instructional training that will allow you to pursue the career 57 | 34 | 72
74 . 76 . 78 . 80 . 82 . 84 . 86
of your choice. You need to contemplate the future; the quality 61 | 37 | 75
. 88 . 90 . 92 . 94
of your life hinges on such thoughts. 64 | 38 | 76

| gwam | 3' | 1 | | 2 | | 3 | | 4 | |
|---|---|---|---|---|---|---|---|---|---|
| | 5' | 1 | | | 2 | | | 3 | |

## Skill Builder

### Tabulation
1. Set tabs 1", 2.5", and 4" from the left margin.
2. Key the text at the right.
3. Key three 1' writings.

**Goal:** Increase amount of text keyed on each writing.

| | | | | words |
|---|---|---|---|---|
| North Carolina | North Dakota | Ohio | Oklahoma | 8 |
| Raleigh | Bismark | Columbus | Oklahoma City | 16 |
| Oregon | Pennsylvania | Rhode Island | South Carolina | 26 |
| Salem | Harrisburg | Providence | Columbia | 33 |
| South Dakota | Tennessee | Texas | Utah | 40 |
| Pierre | Nashville | Austin | Salt Lake City | 48 |
| Vermont | Virginia | Washington | West Virginia | 56 |
| Montpelier | Richmond | Tacoma | Charleston | 64 |
| Wisconsin | Wyoming | | | 67 |
| Madison | Cheyenne | | | 71 |

### Keying Technique
1. Key each line once.
2. Key a 1' writing on each even-numbered line.

**Alphabetic**
1 zebra extra vicious dozen happen just quick forgot way limp exact
2 Everyone except Meg and Joe passed the final weekly biology quiz.

**Fig/sym**
3 Account #2849 | 10% down | for $6,435.70 | Lots #8 & #9 | $250 deductible
4 The fax machine (#387-291) is on sale for $364.50 until March 21.

**Bottom row**
5 modem zebra extinct moving backbone moon vacate exam computerized
6 Zeno's vaccine injection for smallpox can be given in six months.

**Third row**
7 you tip rip terror yet peer quit were pet tire terrier pepper out
8 Our two terrier puppies were too little to take to your pet show.

**Double letters**
9 footnote scanner less process letters office cell suppress footer
10 Jill, my office assistant, will process the four letters by noon.

**Balanced hands**
11 wish then turn us auto big eight down city busy end firm it goals
12 If the firm pays for the social, the eight officials may also go.

**Shift keys**
13 The New York Times | Gone with the Wind | Chicago Tribune | WordPerfect
14 Alan L. Martin finished writing Planning for Changing Technology.

**Adjacent keys**
15 were open top ask rest twenty point tree master merge option asks
16 The sort option was well received by all three new group members.

**Space bar**
17 it is fix and fox go key do by box men pen six so the to when big
18 Did they use the right audit form to check the city busline?

| gwam | 1' | 1 | 2 | 3 | 4 | 5 | 6 | 7 | 8 | 9 | 10 | 11 | 12 | 13 |

## Letters and Language Skills

**Objectives:**
1. To learn to format second-page heading for letters.
2. To increase proficiency at processing letters.
3. To improve language skills (verbs).

### 84A • 5
### Conditioning Practice

each line twice

alphabet 1 Quite possibly Juarez will be the next city making a fuel device.

speed 2 The proficient man was kept busy with the problem with the docks.

figures 3 Of the 14,650 disks that we purchased on May 29, only 387 remain.

**gwam** 1' | 1 | 2 | 3 | 4 | 5 | 6 | 7 | 8 | 9 | 10 | 11 | 12 | 13 |

## FORMATTING

### 84B • 7
### Drill: Simplified Block Letter

1. Two 1' writings on opening lines (date through ¶ 1) of modified block letter on p. 193. Concentrate on letter parts. Add 2 words (10 keystrokes) on second writing.

2. Two 1' writings on closing lines (¶ 3 through copy notation) of modified block letter on p. 193. If you finish before time is called, DS and begin

again. Focus on correct placement of letter parts. Add 2 words on second writing.

### 84C • 28
### Letter Formats

**Letter 1**
**Personal-Business Letter**
Format the text at the right as a personal-business letter in block format with open punctuation.

words

8329 Elmwood Dr. | Minot, ND 58701-4367 | August 4, ---- | 11
Ms. Tammy LaConte | Apartment #292 | 3891 West Ocotillo Rd. | 22
Glendale, AZ 85303-2883 | Dear Tammy 29

Congratulations on your new job with **Technology Specialists**! It sounds 43
very exciting. I am glad to hear that you are using all the skills you 58
gained from the Keyboarding and Computer Applications course. I am 71
particularly gratified to hear that you are using the database concepts 86
you learned in class. I remember how you struggled with this part of 100
the class and considered dropping the course. It is evident that your 114
persistence paid off! 119

Our department continues to make changes. Our new networked lab 132
is now complete. We are teaching a new desktop publishing class as 145
well as offering additional sections of the Keyboarding and Computer 159
Applications course. I am teaching full time this year. 171

I really appreciate receiving your letter. Many students leave school 185
and that is the last we hear from them. Please keep in touch and think 199
of us next winter when you see our weather reports. 210

Sincerely | Mrs. Janet Jamison 215

# Activity 3:

1. Read the account of the hapless job applicant as given at the right.
2. Compose/key a ¶ indicating why you believe the applicant didn't get the job.
3. Compose/key another ¶ indicating why you believe you could have had a successful interview and gotten the job.

**Compose (think) as you key**

I have just had my first job interview and now realize how totally unprepared I was for it. I hadn't given much thought to identifying my interests and even less to determining my competence. I didn't expect to be given a "once over" to see how I was dressed. I wanted a job. More truthfully, I wanted a paycheck; so I had to get a job to get my cash.

Before I could see the personnel manager with whom I had an appointment, I was asked to fill in an application blank. I wrote as carefully as possible, but I did a messy job. I didn't have my social security card or number. I didn't have a record of my school marks or the names and addresses of my references. I was totally unprepared.

I didn't expect the interview to be as interesting as it was. I was asked questions about my school- and church-related activities, my hobbies and personal habits, the books I have enjoyed, and the plays I have seen and concerts I have attended recently. Throughout the questioning, I felt very sure I was being "sized up" as a person rather than as a worker.

There was a test, of course. It covered some English, spelling, and math. There was also a timed writing on difficult copy. I was asked to key accurately and not to try for maximum speed. The document processing included a two-page letter with special features, a simplified memo, and a five-column table with columnar headings to be centered. All errors in documents were to be found and corrected. Who'd have thought I'd have to do all that?

It's too bad I hadn't had some work experience before going for the interview and test. It's too bad that I had not followed up on the hints my teachers had given me about what to expect in a job interview and employment test and what to do to prepare for them. It's too bad that I shrugged off as punishment my teachers' frequent directions to "proofread and correct" all work. When I go for my next interview and test, I'll be prepared; then I won't have to say "It's too bad."

## Letter 2
### Second Page of Letter
Format and key the text at the right as the second page of a business letter (see format guide, p. 189). Use block format and open punctuation.

Ms. Charla Whitaker | Page 2 | April 15, ---- — 8

Finally, you need to be aware of two changes the committee members have — 23
planned for the final issue of The Historical Review. The publication dead- — 38
line has been changed from March 1 to April 1. The committee has decided — 53
to add a new feature to each issue of the Review. It will be called "My — 68
Perspective--Historically Speaking." They have invited Dr. DeWitt Danforth — 83
to share his perspective for the first featured article. If either of these — 98
changes does not meet with your approval, you should contact the chair of — 113
the committee, Margaret Ryan, immediately. — 122

I believe that I have covered all the major items of the meeting. The min- — 137
utes of the meeting should be available within the next two weeks. After — 152
you have had an opportunity to review them, call me if you have questions. — 167

Sincerely yours | Lamar B. Santana | Executive Director | xx — 178

## Letter 3
### Business Letter
Format and key the text at the right as a business letter in simplified block format.

**Note:** Additional documents for letters/memos can be found on pp. A19-A20.

October 15, ---- | MRS ANNA ALVAREZ | 3950 CALLE PACIFICO | — 11
SANTA FE NM 87505-9321 | SATISFACTION GUARANTEED — 20

We hope you and your family are enjoying the living-room furniture you — 35
purchased at **Villa Furniture**. Oakwood is an excellent line of furniture — 49
that should last for many years. If, however, there is any reason you are — 64
not pleased with the furniture, let us know. We will take the necessary — 79
steps to guarantee your satisfaction. — 87

**Villa Furniture** has been in business for over 100 years because of satis- — 101
fied customers. We are committed to keeping customer satisfaction high by — 116
offering quality furniture at reasonable prices. — 126

We appreciate our loyal customers and hope you will remain one of them. — 141
Please let me know when we can be of further service. — 152

MISS JOYCE BUTTERFIELD, FURNITURE CONSULTANT | xx — 161

## L ANGUAGE SKILLS

### 84D • 10
### Plural Verbs
Follow the Learn/Apply procedure in 76C, p. 184.

Use a plural verb with a plural subject (noun or pronoun).

| | | |
|---|---|---|
| Learn | 1. | The students have completed the assignment. |
| Learn | 2. | They are ready for the examination. |
| Apply | 3. | The participants (is, are) ready to begin the race. |
| Apply | 4. | She (is, are) the first member of her family to graduate. |

Use plural verbs with compound subjects joined by **and**.

| | | |
|---|---|---|
| Learn | 5. | Ms. Jensen and her daughter have purchased the play tickets. |
| Learn | 6. | The president and the secretary are reviewing the minutes. |
| Apply | 7. | Jane and Ted (is, are) going to the convention. |
| Apply | 8. | Mr. Black and Ms. Linton (has, have) been nominated. |

# Language & Writing Skills 14

## Activity 1:

1. Study the spelling/definitions of the words in the color block at the right.
2. Key the **Learn** line in the first set of sentences.
3. Key the **Apply** lines, choosing the right words to complete each sentence correctly.
4. Key the second set of lines in the same way.
5. Check work; rekey lines containing word-choice errors.

### Choose the right word

**cents** (n) specified portion of a dollar

**sense** (n/vb) meaning intended or conveyed; perceive by sense organs; ability to judge

**since** (adv/conj) after a definite time in the past; in view of the fact; because

**cite** (vb) use as support; commend; summon

**sight** (n/vb) ability to see; something seen; a device to improve aim; observe or examine by taking a sight

**site** (n) the place something is, was, or will be located

Learn 1 Since you ask, I sense that this is a dollars-and-cents issue.
Apply 2 I have only a few (cents/sense/since) left out of my allowance.
Apply 3 Do you (cents/sense/since) a change (cents/sense/since) he left?
Apply 4 How long has it been (cents/sense/since) you were graduated?

Learn 5 Did you cite the article about keying by sight?
Apply 6 We visited the Olympics (cite/sight/site) on our tour.
Apply 7 Did the attorney (cite/sight/site) the case law on that issue?
Apply 8 The tournament (cite/sight/site) is now in (cite/sight/site).

## Activity 2:

1. Read carefully the letter shown at the right, noting errors in capitalization, punctuation, number expression, and word choice.
2. Format/key the message as a personal-business letter, using the current date and your own return address.

   Address the letter to:

   **Mr. Carlos F. Aquila**
   **A.G. Marshall & Sons**
   **2533 N. 117 Ave.**
   **Omaha, NE 68164-2263**

   Supply an appropriate salutation and closing.
3. Correct all errors, including those you make as you key.

### Proofread & correct

Your advertisement in sundays <u>Enquirer</u> for summer assistants in you're information processing center interests me very much. Please consider me an applicant for one of these positions.

A focus of my training during the passed 2 years were courses in Information Processing. As a result, I am skilled as a keyboard operator, are adept in the use of several software packages and have a good working knowledge of spreadsheets and databases.

Supervisors of my previous part time and summer jobs have said that I take direction positively and work well with others. In addition, they have told my teachers that I show initiative and readily step in to help others with there work.

After you review the enclosed data sheet may I please have an appointment for an interview? You can reach me at the address and telephone number shown on the data sheet.

# Language & Writing Skills 9

## Activity 1:

1. Study the spelling/ definitions of the words in the color block at the right.
2. Key the **Learn** line in the first set of sentences.
3. Key the **Apply** lines, choosing the right word to complete each sentence correctly.
4. Key the second set of lines in the same way.
5. Check work; rekey lines containing word-choice errors.

**Choose the right word**

**sew** (vb) to fasten by stitches
**so** (adj/conj) in the same manner or way; in order that; with the result that
**sow** (vb) to plant seed; scatter; disperse

**raise** (vb/n) to lift up; to collect; an increase in amount, as of wages
**rays** (n) beams of energy or light; lines of light from a bright object
**raze** (vb) to tear down; to demolish

Learn 1 He can sew the bags so that we can use them to sow the grass seed.
Apply 2 I can have them (sew/so/sow) the oats if you say (sew/so/sow).
Apply 3 The design is intricate, (sew/so/sow) I can't (sew/so/sow) it now.
Apply 4 She is to (sew/so/sow) in the words "(Sew/So/Sow) seeds of kindness."

Learn 5 The sun's rays caused the flowers to raise their heads.
Learn 6 If we raise the price, will they raze the old building this month?
Apply 7 The (raise/rays/raze) of the sun will (raise/rays/raze) the fog.
Apply 8 After they (raise/rays/raze) the gym, work on a new arena can begin.

## Activity 2:

As you key the lines shown at the right, select and key the proper verb shown in parentheses.

**Proofread & correct**   Subject/Predicate agreement

1 The debate team (has/have) won the city championship.
2 Ms. Yamaguchi and her mother (is/are) now American citizens.
3 Either the coach or an assistant (is/are) to present the award.
4 Two aides in addition to the President (was/were) to attend.
5 The planning committee (is/are) to present its proposal today.
6 The dancers as well as the orchestra (was/were) late.
7 Some of the students (has/have) chosen to do acrylic paintings.
8 The number of applicants (is are) greater this year.
9 All of the lasagna (was/were) eaten by the hungry campers.
10 A number of our workers (is/are) to receive proficiency awards.

## Activity 3:

As you key the lines shown at the right, use appropriate capitalization and number expression (words or figures).

**Proofread & correct**   Capitalization/Number expression

1 "the jury," said the judge, "must reach a unanimous decision."
2 for what percentage of total sales is mrs. rhodes responsible?
3 i need a copy of the dictionary of composers and their music.
4 miss valdez told us to go to room eight of corbett hall.
5 the institute of art is at fifth avenue and irving place.
6 "don't you agree," he asked, "that honesty is the best policy?"
7 is the tony award show to be shown on tv on april seventeen?
8 dr. robin j. sousa is to address fbla members in orlando.
9 see page 473 of volume one of encyclopedia americana.
10 here is pbc's check #2749 for $83 (less ten percent discount).

Please fax the attached note to Lynelle Montgomery at the Carrington Hotel.

The final counts for the meal functions are as follows:

| Lunch | August 8 | 238 |
| Breakfast | August 9 | 179 |
| Lunch | August 9 | 255 |

I will be arriving on August 7 around 4 p.m. Would it be possible for us to meet for 20-30 minutes to go over any last-minute details? I've appreciated all the help you have given us. You have a very professional staff at the Carrington.

**Job 14**

Please send the attached thank-you letter to each of the Denver Symposium presenters at their work addresses.

\<Date\>

\<Title\> \<First Name\> \<Last Name\>
\<Address\>
\<City,\> \<State\> \<ZIP\>

Dear \<Title\> \<Last Name\>

Thank you for presenting at our symposium last week. Your topic, \< Title of Presentation\>, was an important part of "A Technology Vision." Many of the participants remarked that your presentation was excellent.

**P**rofessional **S**ymposium **S**pecialists is very fortunate to be able to provide speakers with your expertise at our symposiums. I hope that we can include your name on future programs that we sponsor dealing with technology.

You should receive a check from our main office within the next week to cover your honorarium and expenses.

Sincerely

Ms. Katelynn Eastwick
Western Branch Manager

xx

# Activity 4:

1. Read the case of the 'extra change' error at the right.
2. After considering the comments and suggestions of your friends, what would you do in this situation?
3. Compose/key a paragraph to indicate your choice, how you made it, and why?
4. As a group, discuss the decision(s) reached by various members of the class in terms of *honesty*, *fair play*, and *caring* about others.

**Compose (think) as you key**

You are looking forward to this weekend because you and your friends have arranged to go to dinner together before separating for other activities: a ball game, a movie, and a "mixer." To pay for the dinner, you have collected money from each friend.

The restaurant is upscale, the food very good, and the service excellent. Your server has been friendly and has quickly met all your needs. Your server has not rushed you to finish, so you and your friends have enjoyed conversation and laughter long after the meal ended. It is great that all of you get along so well.

When it is time to go, you ask your server for the check and pay it. When you receive your change and are leaving a tip, you notice that your change is ten dollars more than you should have received.

A discussion takes place among the six of you regarding this error. Various comments and suggestions are made:

1. Keep the money; the server will never know to whom the extra change was given.

2. Are you lucky! This never happens to me.

3. You have to return the money. If you don't, the server will have to make up the loss of money at the end of the evening.

Several thoughts go through your mind as you listen to the comments of your friends. You know it would be great to have ten extra dollars to share with your friends. What will my friends think if I return the money, or if I keep it? The server has been very pleasant and has worked hard this evening. If I keep the money, is it right to make the server pay for the error? How would I want to be treated if I made the same mistake at my job?

### Instructions from Katelynn Eastwick
### July 15

Format and key a references list from the following information.

**Manning, George, and Kent Curtis. <u>Group Strength: Quality Circles at Work</u>. Cincinnati: South-Western Publishing Co., 1988.**

**Rader, M. H., and Linda A. Kurth. <u>Business Communication</u>. Cincinnati: South-Western Publishing Co., 1994.**

to the effective functioning of every facet of the operations of a business." (Rader and Kurth, 1994, p 2) ~Although~ Numerous areas of communication could be explored, ~Although~ Effective business presentations ~will~ could be the emphasis for the first communication symposium.

<u>Recommendations</u>

The following recommendations are offered as a means to increase the earnings of *the Western Branch of* Professional Symposium Specialists.

1. Expand into Phoenix and Santa Fe. At least one symposium will be offered in each state in the Western Region. (Originally this was a long-term goal to be achieved next year.)

2. Offer a one-day fee for those *wishing to* attending *only* on Saturday's session.

3. Increase *two-day registration* fee to $350 for each symposium.

4. *Offer* ~Give~ reduced rates for organizations sending five or more individuals.

5. Offer more than one symposium per year in the more lucrative markets.

### Instructions from Katelynn Eastwick
### July 20

Send the attached form letter to the work address of the speakers. The information for the Date:, Time:, Topic:, and Room: can be taken from Job 7. Merritt listed a **computer** and **Color LCD Data Projection** for **AV Equipment**. Dozier listed a **Whiteboard with Marker**. The rest of the speakers listed an **Overhead Projector**.

&lt;Date&gt;

&lt;Title&gt; &lt;First Name&gt; &lt;Last Name&gt;
&lt;Company Name&gt;
&lt;Address&gt;
&lt;City,&gt; &lt;State&gt; &lt;ZIP&gt;

Dear &lt;Title&gt; &lt;Last Name&gt;

Plans for the August symposium, "A Technology Vision," are being finalized. You are scheduled for:

Date: &lt;Date&gt;
Time: &lt;Time&gt;
Topic: &lt;Topic&gt;
Room: &lt;Room&gt;
AV Equipment: &lt;AV Equipment&gt;

DS

We are pleased to have you play an important role in assisting Professional Symposium Specialists with the symposium. Call me at 503-139-4877 if you have any questions regarding the symposium.

Sincerely

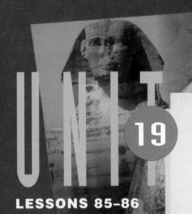

# UNIT 19

**LESSONS 85–86**

# Improve Keyboarding Skills

## LESSON 85

### Keying Techniques/Language Skills

**Objectives:**
1. To improve/refine technique and response patterns.
2. To increase speed on straight copy.
3. To improve language skills (verbs).

**85A • 5**
**Conditioning Practice**

set SMs for 0.5"; each line twice

| | | |
|---|---|---|
| alphabet | 1 | Max Braatz always rejected the idea of taking over the equipment firm. |
| speed | 2 | Diana and the visitor may handle the problems of the eighth amendment. |
| figures | 3 | Sections 1, 2, and 3 of ECON 405 had 68, 67, and 69 students enrolled. |

**gwam** 1' | 1 | 2 | 3 | 4 | 5 | 6 | 7 | 8 | 9 | 10 | 11 | 12 | 13 | 14 |

## S KILL BUILDING

**85B • 15**
**Keying Skill: Speed**

1. A 30" writing on each line; find *gwam* on each.
2. Compare rates on lines 2–6 with the rate on line 1.
3. Two 30" writings on each of the slower lines.

| | | |
|---|---|---|
| balanced hand | 1 | Orlando is apt to make the men go to the island for the coalfish. |
| double letters | 2 | Looking for food, three little rabbits were hopping between rows. |
| adjacent keys | 3 | Three of our territory reporters were told to type their reports. |
| long direct reaches | 4 | I went to a symphony concert; he decorated for a secret ceremony. |
| outside reaches | 5 | Paul Quixote won all six prizes last season for his zealous play. |
| one hand | 6 | Gregg saw a deserted cat on a battered crate in a vacated garage. |

**gwam** 1' | 1 | 2 | 3 | 4 | 5 | 6 | 7 | 8 | 9 | 10 | 11 | 12 | 13 |

**85C • 8**
**Techniques: Figures/Tab**

**CS:** 0.5"
Key the drill twice (slowly, then faster); correct errors you make as you key.

**Concentrate on figure location; quick tab spacing; eyes on copy.**

| 3296 | 3209 | 1287 | 6504 | 1389 | 2309 | 7808 | 134 |
|------|------|------|------|------|------|------|-----|
| 3673 | 1029 | 3658 | 6145 | 7807 | 6577 | 2140 | 907 |
| 4308 | 1586 | 4584 | 1069 | 3215 | 8452 | 9961 | 823 |
| 4162 | 4545 | 6759 | 2309 | 4207 | 8211 | 6743 | 609 |

revenues and expenses of the three first-time symposiums (Cheyenne, Sacramento, and ~Eugene~ *Billings*) are deleted from the figures, expenses are 46 percent of revenues.

New Topics for Next Year *Symposium*

Evaluations include a section in which participants suggest topics for future symposium. The most frequently list*ed* topics include:

1. Implementing Quality Circles at Work.
2. Organizational Communication.

Quality Circles. The quality circle concept has become more popular during the past few years. The philosophy behind quality circles is the belief that specific job-related problems can best be solved by those employees who are closest to the problem area.

George Manning and Kent Curtis have done *extensive* work in the area of work groups and would be excellent symposium facilitators. Part Two of there book, Group Strength (1988, 55) ~would~ provide an excellent basis for a symposium. The areas explored include:

1. The management philosophy behind quality circles.

2. The social nature of people and why work groups are important.

3. How different systems of worker governance reflect a continuum of employee involvement.

4. The principles of business management and employee relations that helped Japan create a post-World War II economic success story.

5. The need for quality circles.

6. The value of quality circles.

Communication. The area of communication is always a popular seminar topic. The Chairman and Chief Executive Office*r* of The BFGoodrich Company *, John D. Ong,* states that "Communication is basic

(continued on next page)

**85D • 10**
**Verbs (continued)**

Follow the Learn/Apply
procedure in 76C, p. 184.

> When used as the subject, the pronouns *I*, *we*, *you*, and *they*, as well as plural nouns, require the plural verb *do not* or the contraction *don't*.

Learn    1. I do not want to participate in the activity.
Learn    2. The painters don't want to work on Saturday.
Apply    3. They (don't doesn't) want to revise the report.
Apply    4. The actors (do not, does not) want another dress rehearsal.

> When used as the subject, the pronouns *he*, *she*, and *it*, as well as singular nouns, require the singular verb *does not* or the contraction *doesn't*.

Learn    5. Judy doesn't want the design changed.
Learn    6. The quote does not include labor for installing the carpet.
Apply    7. She (don't, doesn't) like the new contract.
Apply    8. The new paint (do not, does not) match the old paint.

**S** KILL BUILDING ················································

**85E • 12**
**Straight Copy**

1. A 3' writing on ¶s 1-2 combined; find *gwam* and number of errors.
2. A 1' writing on ¶ 1, then on ¶ 2; find *gwam* and number of errors on each.
3. Another 3' writing on ¶s 1-2, trying to increase your *gwam* by 2 *gwam* over first 3' writing.
4. Record your better 1' and 3' *gwam* for use in 86B.

all letters used

|  | gwam | 3' | 5' |
|---|---|---|---|

Many firms feel that their employees are their most valuable | 4 | 2 | 45
resources. Excellent companies realize that people working toward | 9 | 5 | 47
common goals influence the success of the business. They are also | 13 | 8 | 50
aware of the need to hire qualified people and then to create a | 17 | 10 | 53
work environment to allow the people to perform at their highest | 22 | 13 | 55
potential. Firms that believe that the main job of managers is | 26 | 16 | 58
to remove obstacles that get in the way of the output of the | 30 | 18 | 60
workers are the firms that do, in fact, achieve their goals. | 34 | 20 | 63

Not only do executives and managers in the most successful | 38 | 23 | 65
firms admit to themselves the value of their employees, but they | 42 | 25 | 68
also reveal this feeling to their workers. They know that most | 46 | 28 | 70
people enjoy being given credit for their unique qualities. They | 51 | 31 | 73
also know that any action on their part that aids the workers in | 55 | 33 | 75
realizing their own self-worth will lead to a higher return for | 59 | 36 | 78
the firm, since such people are self-motivated. When leaders do | 64 | 38 | 81
not have to be occupied with employee motivation, they can devote | 68 | 41 | 83
their energy to other vital tasks. | 70 | 42 | 85

| gwam | 3' | 1 | 2 | 3 | 4 |
|---|---|---|---|---|---|
|  | 5' | 1 | 2 | 3 | |

*Instructions from Katelynn Eastwick July 15*

Format and key the attached information as an unbound report. Please proofread again for any errors I may have missed.

WESTERN BRANCH UPDATE > Center

January-June, ---- QS

¶The first half of this year has been excellent.  Many of the goals ~~we set~~ *established* for the Western branch have been ~~completed~~ *accomplished*. Our goal of delivering a symposium every 15 days has been achieved.  As of July 1, fourteen symposiums were completed in 14 cities.  11 of the symposiums were *financial* successes.  The three that did not break~~e~~ven were first-time ventures into new markets.  Based on past performance, we anticipate*d* *in new markets* that we would likely recover around 50 percent of the expenses.  Revenues generated from the *three* new markets covered 79 percent of the expenses.  We was very pleased with these percentages. A complete analysis of each symposium is shown in the following table.

| Location | Expenses | Revenues |
|---|---|---|
| San Francisco | $ 50,750 | $109,400 |
| Portland | 40,690 | 82,500 |
| Seattle | 48,750 | 130,800 |
| Boise | 37,820 | 59,400 |
| Salt Lake City | 42,740 | 69,900 |
| Las Vegas | 43,690 | 95,700 |
| Los Angeles | 49,690 | 140,100 |
| San Diego | 47,280 | 107,400 |
| Spokane | 41,390 | 75,900 |
| Denver | 43,660 | 97,500 |
| Cheyenne | 26,590 | 19,800 |
| Sacramento | 34,220 | 28,800 |
| Eugene | 39,380 | 78,000 |
| Billings | 33,750 | 26,100 |
| | $580,400 | $1,131,300 |

*Alphabetize* | *align $*

Note that the expenses and revenues do no include meal functions.  However, the expenses column does include a *or entertainment* charge of $4,700 for each symposium location to cover office salaries and office expenses.  Expenses were *approximately* 51.3 percent of revenues.  This is slightly higher than the 50 percent goal that had been established.  However, when the

*(continued on next page)*

# LESSON 86

## Keying Techniques

**Objectives:**
**1.** To improve/refine technique and response patterns.
**2.** To increase speed on straight copy.

### 86A • 5
### Conditioning Practice

each line twice

| | | |
|---|---|---|
| alphabet | 1 | Marie Vasquez was probably sick during the last six days of June. |
| speed | 2 | She may blame the girls for the problem with the neighbor's auto. |
| figures | 3 | Tables 8, 9, and 16 are in Chapter 12 on pages 379, 395, and 405. |

gwam 1' | 1 | 2 | 3 | 4 | 5 | 6 | 7 | 8 | 9 | 10 | 11 | 12 | 13 |

### 86B • 18
### Skill Check

1. Three 1' writings on ¶ 1 of 85E. Strive to increase rate recorded previously for 85E by 4 gwam.

2. Repeat Step 1 using ¶ 2.
3. Two 3' writings using both ¶s.

4. Determine better 3' gwam and record.

## S KILL BUILDING

### 86C • 15
### Keying Techniques

1. Key each line twice.
2. Key three 1' writings on line 3; first for accuracy, then for speed, then again for accuracy.
3. Repeat Step 2 for lines 6 and 9.

**Shift keys**

1 Kim, Sue, Nan, and I all live on Fenton Avenue, four blocks away.

2 We visited Texas, Colorado, New Mexico, New York, and New Jersey.

3 Janet S. Glavine, manager of Pizza Del Rio, lives on Park Avenue.

**Space bar**

4 Thomas will go to the city next week to buy a car for his mother.

5 Jana, Mike, and I will leave next week to see our aunt and uncle.

6 I will not be able to fix all ten of the tires by noon on Friday.

**Balanced-hand sentences**

7 To the right of the lake is the dismal shanty with the six ducks.

8 The maid may go with them when they go to the city for the gowns.

9 The box with a shamrock and an iris is by the door of the chapel.

gwam 1' | 1 | 2 | 3 | 4 | 5 | 6 | 7 | 8 | 9 | 10 | 11 | 12 | 13 |

### 86D • 12
### Techniques: Figures/Tab

**CS:** 0.5"

1. Key copy given at the right.
2. Key two 1' writings.

|  |  |  | words |
|---|---|---|---|
| 7820 Oakview Dr. | 392 Fairland St. | 390 Marsh St. | 10 |
| 892 Hemlock St. | 2031 Ferris Ave. | 1290 Knox Rd. | 19 |
| 9284 Fawn Dr. | 9986 Cedar St. | 982 King Ave. | 28 |
| 9301 Dixie Ct. | 567 Acorn Ct. | 9021 Hart Ln. | 36 |
| 5638 Ivy Dr. | 8290 Grand Cir. | 1092 Allen Ct. | 45 |
| 1892 Forrest Dr. | 2956 Boyd St. | 8256 Butler Ln. | 54 |

I have written in the rest of the information for the speaker list. Please make the changes and print a final copy.

# "A TECHNOLOGY VISION"

## Speaker List

| Name | Home Address | Work Address |
|------|--------------|--------------|
| Jon Mathis (Dr.) | 310 Buckeye St. Toledo, OH 43611-1234 *419-186-8921* | 4290 Brooklawn Dr. Toledo, OH 43623-8102 419-132-83~~6~~*(62)* |
| Rose LaJardin (Dr.) | 8290 Quonset Ave. Warwick, RI 02889-9867 401-156-3819 | 2930 Lighthouse Dr. Warwick, RI 02889-5714 401-139-3865 |
| Anne Harper (Dr.) | *207 Churchill Way Hartford, CT 06111-2856 203-165-1285* | P.O. *of* Box 321 Staford, CT 06075-8332 203-159-3825 |
| Stan Dozier (Dr.) | 3290 Craig Cir. Ogden, UT 84404-4237 801-186-1929 | 1320 Lorl Ln. Ogden, UT 84404-1209 801-125-7692 |
| Ann Merritt (Ms.) | 3286 Hanover Dr. Pueblo, CO 81007-8348 719-120-5656 | 631 Monterrey St. Pueblo, CO 81006-8460 719-121-2301 |
| Chad Chadwick (Mr.) | 4920 Hickory Dr., N. Boise, ID 83704-2839 208-130-6210 | 2956 Demark St. Boise, ID 83705-2243 208-160-2380 |
| Lindon York (Dr.) | *8490 Glenhill Rd. El Cajon, CA 92020-8382 714-129-4544* | 3847 Park Hyde St. Orange, CA 92668-8382 714-133-8767 |

# Word PROCESSING 4

## ACTIVITY 1:

### Search

1. Read the copy at right.
2. Learn the Search to Find and Search to Replace features for your software.
3. Key the ¶ at the right.
4. Use the Search to Find feature to determine how many times the word *are* appears in the ¶.
5. Use the Search to Replace feature to replace the word *month* with **pay period**.
6. Replace the word *assessments* with the word **taxes**.

The **Search to Find** feature is used to locate a specified series of keystrokes or word(s) in a document. The **Search to Replace** feature locates a specified series of keystrokes or word(s) in a document and replaces them with another series of keystrokes or word(s).

An individual has to pay a number of assessments. FICA assessments are the assessments that support the Social Security system and are deducted from your check each month. Federal income assessments are also deducted from your check each month. Assessments that are not deducted from your check each month include property assessments and sales assessments.

## ACTIVITY 2:

### Orphan/Widow

1. Read the copy at right.
2. Learn the Orphan/Widow feature for your software.
3. Open RPT70C1. Turn on the feature.

The **Orphan/Widow** feature ensures that the first line of a paragraph does not appear by itself at the bottom of a page (**orphan line**) or that the last line of a paragraph does not appear by itself at the top of a page (**widow line**).

1. In RPT70C1 search to find the words . . . *greater detail.*

2. Add these sentences at the end of the paragraph: **Do not put in visuals just to pad the report or decorate the pages. Choose visuals that support and clarify the text.**
3. Search to find: *Excellent reports.* Delete the entire sentence.
4. Note how the feature reforms the text to prevent an orphan or widow line.

## ACTIVITY 3:

### Review wp Features

1. Key Sentences 1-5; underline, *italicize*, and **bold** text as you key.
2. Key Sentences 6-10. *Do not bold, italicize, or underline the copy as you key. After keying the sentences, go back and underline, italicize, and bold existing text. In this activity, do not substitute italics for underline.*
3. Use the Block Delete feature to delete lines 4, 6, and 9.

1 *Ted* saved **$25** in May, **$50** in June, and **$35** in July; *Linda* saved **$20** in May, **$40** in June, and **$60** in July.

2 Agreement **#82-789** was signed on January 18, 1997.

3 He misspelled **absence**, **calendar**, and **mortgage** on the quiz.

4 Dr. Romanski included **Chapters 8, 9,** and **11** on the exam.

5 The **Boston Symphony Orchestra** performed **Britten's** *Four Sea Interludes* and **Beethoven's** *Symphony No. 7.*

6 One of his favorite classics was **Dvorak's** *Symphony No. 9 in E Minor* from "**The New World**" Second Movement.

7 The bronze medal went to **Maria Boxmeyer**, the silver medal went to **Clinton Pizzaro**, and the gold medal went to **Charlene Biden**.

8 At **2:45 p.m.**, the team from **China** will play the **German** team.

9 The movie Major League II stars **Charlie Sheen, Tom Berenger, Corbin Bernsen,** and **Bob Uecker.**

10 The class discussed the **Indent** feature on Monday, the **Merge** feature on Wednesday, and the **Table** feature on Friday.

### Instructions from Katelynn Eastwick July 14

Format and key the attached information in an attractive format. Use "A TECHNOLOGY VISION" for the main heading.

**August 8**

| Presenter | Topic | Time | Room |
|---|---|---|---|
| Chadwick | Networking--*An* Overview | 9:30-11:00 | Senate A |
| ~~Kemp~~ *LaJardin* | What Databases Can Do | 9:30-11:00 | Senate B |
| Mathis | Technology "Risk Takers" | 1:30-3:00 | *Colorado Ballroom* ~~Senate A~~ |
| York | Turning A Technology *into Opportunity* | 11:30-12:30 | Senate A |

**August 9**

| | | | |
|---|---|---|---|
| Dozier | Boot Camp for Would-Be *Internet Users* | 1:30-3:00 | Senate B |
| Harper | Client-Server Architectures | 1:30-3:30 | Senate A |
| Merritt | Taking Control of *Information* | 9:00-1:00 (2) | Senate A |

**Professional Symposium Specialists**
429 Kentwood Dr.
Eugene, OR 97401-8392
503-139-4877

**Purchase Order**

FRIENDSHIP OFFICE SUPPLY
7830 PIEDMONT AVE NW
SALEM OR 97304-6767

PO No.: 138A
Date: July 14, ----
Terms: 2/10, n/30
Shipped Via: Western Freight

| Quantity | Description/Stock Number | Price | | Total | |
|---|---|---|---|---|---|
| 10 | Name badge/G240-A96 (6x) | 11 | 50 | 115 | 00 |
| 5 | Red dry erase markers/D115-001 (ea) | 1 | 69 | 8 | 45 |
| 5 | Blue dry erase markers/D115-002 (ea) | 1 | 69 | 8 | 45 |
| 5 | Green dry erase markers/D115-005 (ea) | 1 | 69 | 8 | 45 |
| 5 | Dry marker eraser (ea) | 5 | 45 | 27 | 25 |
| | | | | 167 | 60 |

By _____

**Format Guides:
Reports**

THE ENVIRONMENT

Textual Citations in Report

REFERENCES

References Page

## Report Classification

Reports can be classified in a variety of ways. A few of the ways reports can be classified are by formality (formal or informal), by purpose (analytical or informative), by type (feasibility, progress, justification, periodic), by setting (internal and external), and by format (bound or unbound).

## Unbound Reports

Many short reports are prepared without covers or binders. Such reports are called unbound reports (see model on pp. 145 and 146). If they consist of more than one page, the pages are fastened together in the upper-left corner by a staple or paper clip.

## Bound Reports

Longer reports are generally prepared with covers or binders. Such reports are called bound reports and require a larger left margin (1.5") to accommodate the binding.

## Standard Margins

With the exception of the left margin (1" for unbound and 1.5" for bound), all margin settings are the same for the unbound and bound reports. The right margin is 1". A top margin of 2" and a bottom margin of 1" are customarily used on the first page of reports. All remaining pages are keyed with 1" top and bottom margins. Since the internal spacing of report parts varies, a bottom margin of exactly 1" is often not feasible. For that reason, a bottom margin of 1" to 1.5" is acceptable. On electronics, vary the bottom margin to prevent: a side heading or first line of a paragraph from printing as the last line on a page (orphan); or the last line of a paragraph from occurring at the top of a new page (widow). The Widow/Orphan feature of word processing software may be used to prevent these problems.

## Page Numbering

The first page of a report is usually not numbered. However, if a page number is used on the first page, center it at the bottom of the page. On the second and subsequent pages, place the page number 1" from the top of the page at the right margin. A DS is left between the page number and the text of the report. The page number for endnotes and reference pages should also be placed 1" from the top of the page at the right margin.

## Spacing

A QS is left between the report title and the first line of the body. Multiple-line titles are DS. A DS is left above and below side headings and between paragraphs, which are usually DS but may be SS (when directions specify). The paragraphs are indented 0.5" (generally 5 spaces).

**Long quotes.** Quoted material of four or more lines should be SS and indented 0.5" from the left margin. The right margin for quoted material remains at 1". Double-space above and below the quoted material.

**Enumerated items.** Indent enumerated items 0.5" from the left margin; block the lines at that point. The right margin for enumerated items remains at 1". Single-space individual items; DS between items as well as above and below a series of items.

**Job 4**

*Instructions from Katelynn Eastwick July 7*

Format and key the attached information as a flyer to be distributed at the symposium. Consider some type of border.

**Job 5**

*Instructions from Katelynn Eastwick July 8*

Please format the attached text as a letter to the convention manager of the Carrington Hotel. List each enclosure separately.

**Job 6**

*Instructions from Katelynn Eastwick July 14*

Please fax the attached note to Lynelle Montgomery at the Carrington Hotel.

*Exhibitors* — DS

Telephone Specialists, Inc.
ECL Communication Systems
Computer Networking
Business Computer Connections
Computer Systems Design
HMG Computer Consultants
Mobile Communications
Telecommunications Consultants
The FAX IT Company
Teleconferencing Solutions
Freelance Computing
Micros in Action

*Resource Systems*
*Voice Connections*

*Alphabetize*

Enclosed is a copy of our symposium brochure. The schedule is printed on the inside cover.

A copy of the contract for our keynote speaker, who will present on Friday, August 8, from 1:30-3:00, is also enclosed. Approximately 250 participants will attend this session. The requirements that would pertain to the hotel setup are listed under the "Additional Terms and Considerations" section. Please let me know if you will be able to accommodate his requests.

Are you still planning for this session to be held in the Colorado Ballroom? As indicated on the contract, he would like the participants to be seated at tables.

Will July 20 fit your schedule for meeting with my assistant and me to discuss final details for the symposium? Please give me a call to confirm a meeting time.

*I still have not received a copy of your audio-visual request list. Please fax me a copy ASAP.*

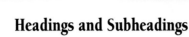

## Headings and Subheadings

**Main heading.** Center the main heading in ALL CAPS over the line of writing.

**Side headings.** Begin side headings at the left margin. Capitalize the first letter of the first word and all other main words in each heading. Underline side headings.

**Paragraph headings.** Indent paragraph headings 0.5" from the left margin. Capitalize the first letter of the first word only, underline the heading, and follow the heading with a period.

## Title Page

A cover or title page is prepared for many reports. To format a title page, center the title in ALL CAPS 2" from the top. Center your name in capital and lower-case letters 5" from the top. The school name is centered a DS below your name. The date should be centered 9" from the top. Electronics: see p. RG20.

## Documentation

**Textual citation.** Documentation is used to give credit for published material that is quoted or closely paraphrased (slightly changed). One form of documentation is the textual citation method. This method includes the name(s) of the author(s), the date of the referenced publication, and the page number(s) of the material cited as part of the actual text:

(Kirkpatrick, 1996, 275)

When the author's name is used in the text introducing the quotation, only the year of publication and the page number(s) appear in parentheses:

Kirkpatrick (1996, 275) said that . . . .

**Endnotes.** Another method of documentation is the endnotes method. When using this method, a reference cited in the text is identified by a superscript number . . . .[1]

The complete documentation for the reference is placed at the end of the report in a section labeled ENDNOTES. The references listed in the ENDNOTES section are placed in the same order they appeared in the report and have the corresponding superscript number that identifies the reference in the text.

The ENDNOTES page has the same top and side margins as the first page of the report, except that it has a page number 1" from the top at the right margin. Each reference is single-spaced with a double space between references. The first line of each reference is indented 0.5" from the left margin (keyed to a superscript endnote number); all other lines begin at the left margin.

[1]Richard G. Harris, "Globalization, Trade, and Income," Canadian Journal of Economics, November 1993, p. 755.

**References.** Complete information about the material cited is placed in a separate section called the reference section (also referred to as the bibliography or works cited section). All references cited are listed alphabetically by author surnames under the heading REFERENCES (or BIBLIOGRAPHY or WORKS CITED). The REFERENCES page has the same top and side margins as the first page of the report, but a page number is keyed 1" from the top at the right margin. Each reference is single-spaced with a double space between references. The first line of each reference begins at the left margin; all other lines are indented 0.5" from the left margin.

**Note:** Both the textual citation and endnote method of documentation require a REFERENCES page. It follows an ENDNOTES page.

Superscripts in Report

Endnotes Page

Title Page

Format the attached text as a two-page form letter. Eventually the letter will be sent to the Region 6 database. To check to make sure the merge will work, merge the letter with the following two addressees.

Mr. Douglas Smith
Hoyle Glass Company
308 Folsom St.
Boulder, CO 80302-0467

Ms. Kara Timms
The Printer's Company
480 Orchard Ct.
Golden, CO 80403-7512

<Date>

<Title> <First Name> <Last Name>
<Company Name>
<Address>
<City,> <State> <ZIP>

Dear <Title> <Last Name>

Plan now to attend "A Technology Vision" symposium on August 8-9 in Denver, Colorado. As today's technology continues to evolve, it becomes increasingly important for business executives to take an active leadership role in determining the role technology will play in their organizations.

Prominent technology presenters from throughout the United States will be in Denver to share their expertise with symposium participants from the Western Region. Time during the symposium will be dedicated to informal small-group discussions in which participants will be able to meet with other executives in their job-related fields to share ideas.

Dr. Jon Mathis from the Devlin Institute of Technology will be the keynote speaker. His presentation will focus on technology "Risk Takers" and the impact they have had on their organizations. The program will be completed with other prominent business and educational experts in the field of technology.

One of the suggestions from last year's symposium was to have some type of entertainment arranged for the group during the evening. On Friday night, arrangements have been made to attend a Colorado Rockies' baseball game. Saturday night's entertainment features a performance of the Denver Symphony. Of course, Denver offers a variety of other types of entertainment options for those who do not want to participate in the group functions.

Complete the enclosed form to ensure your meeting and hotel reservations at this year's symposium.

Sincerely

The newly renovated Carrington Hotel in downtown Denver is the location for the symposium. The hotel is located a block from the capitol building and is within walking distance of many fine restaurants, shopping, and entertainment. The check-in time is 7:30 a.m. in the main lobby of the hotel. A complimentary continental breakfast will be served in Conference Room 22 from 7:45 - 9:00.

**Objectives:**
1. To format an unbound report with enumerated items.
2. To review capitalization guides.

### 87A • 5
### Conditioning Practice

each line twice SS; then two
1' writings on line 2; find
*gwam*; clear screen

| | | |
|---|---|---|
| alphabet | 1 | Jay Klugman awarded Bob sixth place for his very high quiz score. |
| speed | 2 | The auditor on the panel did not sign a key element of the audit. |
| fig/sym | 3 | The checks written on 12/4 ($57.90 and $36.80) were not recorded. |

gwam 1' | 1 | 2 | 3 | 4 | 5 | 6 | 7 | 8 | 9 | 10 | 11 | 12 | 13 |

## L ANGUAGE SKILLS

### 87B • 10
### Check Capitalization

Key the sentences at the
right, supplying the needed
capital letters.

1. lake powell and lake mead are both located in arizona.
2. fbla is the abbreviation for future business leaders of america.
3. the largest cities in idaho are boise, pocatello, and idaho falls.
4. our next delta pi epsilon meeting will be held friday, may 2.
5. is the grand canyon national park located in arizona?
6. the green bay packers will play the dallas cowboys on sunday.
7. robert e. lee and ulysses s. grant signed the treaty at appomattox.
8. the grade school is located on tyler; the high school, on cedar.
9. this year thanksgiving will be on thursday, november 24.
10. kim told dr. dean that he had lessons 8 and 9 completed.

## F ORMATTING

### 87C • 35
### Unbound Report

**Document 1**
**Report from Rough Draft**

1. Review the format guides for reports on pp. 211-212.
2. Format the report in unbound style; use **THE ENVIRONMENT** for the heading of the report.
3. When you finish, use the spell check and proofread your copy.

words

heading 2

Our environment is a topic that receives a great deal of 13
attention. The environment has been the basis of numerous televi- 27
sion and radio commentaries as well as a multitude of newspaper 39
and magazine articles. The environment is even the foundation for many 54
political debates addressing issues and the concerns about what 66
is happening and what will happen to the environment over the 78
next several years. A look at the past is will be helpful in 89
understanding the present concern. 96

Prior to 1955 99

Comparatively speaking, little emphasis was placed on ecology 112
(the study of the relationship of plants and animals to their environment) 127
prior to 1955. Air pollution (as we know it today), toxic 134
waste, marine pollution, pesticides, oil spills, acid rain, etc., 147
are relatively new problems that are taking their toll on the environment. 162

*(continued on next page)*

**Job 2**

Instructions from
Katelynn Eastwick
June 5

Format and key the attached presenter information sheet; attach a copy to the Mathis letter. I have given some formatting guidelines. Let's plan on a two-page format. Use fonts and shading if available.

## "A Technology Vision" Symposium

### August 8-9, ----

#### SYMPOSIUM PRESENTER INFORMATION SHEET

Name: _____

Home Address: _____

City: _____ State: _____ ZIP: _____

Telephone Number: _____ *Social Security Number* _____

**Please return this form and your biographical sketch (p. 2) by June 15, ---, to Ms. Katelynn Eastwick, Professional Symposium Specialists, 429 Kentwood Dr., Eugene, OR 97401-8392.**

* * * * *

**Please write a brief description of your presentation as you would like it to appear in the symposium program.**

2"

**Please indicate the audio visual equipment that will be required for your presentation.**

_____ Overhead Projector
_____ Screen
_____ 35 MM Slide Projector
_____ Color LCD Data Projection
_____ VCR and Monitor
_____ Flipchart
_____ Laser Pointer
_____ Computer
_____ Compact Disc Player
_____ Easel
_____ Whiteboard with Marker
_____ Speaker Phone
_____ Interactive Teleconference Hookup
_____ Power Strip
_____ *Extension Cord*

*PRESENTER INFORMATION SHEET*
*Page 2*

*Please give a brief biographical sketch for your symposium introduction.*

**Note:** Indent the enumerated items 0.5" to the right of the left margin; let the lines run to the right margin.

**Document 2**
Use the following information to create a REFERENCES list on a separate page (p. 3).

Bascietto, John. "Ecotoxicity and Ecological Risk Assessment." <u>Environmental Science & Technology</u>. Washington, DC, January 1990.

Talbot, L. M. "Man's Role in Managing the Global Environment." <u>Changing the Global Environment</u>. Boston:   Harcourt Brace Jovanovich Publishers, 1989.

| | words |
|---|---|
| <u>Since 1955</u> | 164 |

Since 1955, *however,* our interest in protecting the environment has    178
been kindled by recognition of these environmental problems.    190
Studies of change in the environment have led to efforts to    202
protect it.    205

    <u>Environmental Changes</u>.   Changes to the environment have    216
been significant over the past 35 years.   Talbot (1989, 21-22)    229
listed these major changes:    235

1.   The human population has almost doubled, from fewer    246
than three billion to more than five billion people.    256

2.   Half the world's tropical forests have been lost.    268

3.   The processes of overgrazing and desertification have    279
greatly increased.    283

4.   Chemical pollution has become pervasive and few species    295
or lands escape its effects.    301

5.   New hazardous wastes, not even mentioned in 1955, now    313
represent a major problem worldwide.    321

6.   Acid rain and carbon dioxide buildup have resulted    332
from increased industrialization throughout the world.    343

    <u>Environmental Protection</u>.   As the seriousness of environmen-    355
tal problems has been recognized, governmental agencies, *and* as well    367
as nongovernmental organizations have been established to deal    379
with them.   (Talbot, 22, 1989)   In 1955 there were only a few    391
nongovernmental environmental organizations; today there are    403
thousands.   In 1955 no government had environmental agencies;    416
today virtually all nations have ~~such institutions~~ *them*.   The purpose    426
of the agencies is to identify, quantify, and reduce adverse    438
impacts on the environment. (Bascietto, 1990, 14)    449

    A clean environment is a global problem, ~~but~~ a problem that    460
is going to take all the inhabitants of the earth to solve.   For    473
*the* Earth to be habitable by future generations, today's generations    487
must take care of it.    491

# Professional Symposium Specialists

**Objectives:**
1. To improve your document processing skills by keying from rough draft and script.
2. To improve your ability to read and follow directions.
3. To improve your ability to detect and correct unmarked errors.

**139-144A 5 (daily)**
**Conditioning Practice**

each line twice

alphabet 1 Dr. Jurwin gave both of them excellent marks on the physics quiz.

speed 2 She may sign the form by proxy if they make an audit of the firm.

fig/sym 3 Jay & Cey wrote Check #99 for $425.76 and Check #100 for $380.75.

gwam 1' | 1 | 2 | 3 | 4 | 5 | 6 | 7 | 8 | 9 | 10 | 11 | 12 | 13 |

**139-144B • 45 (daily)**
**Work Assignments**

**Job 1**

*Instructions from*
*Katelynn Eastwick*
*June 5*

Two additional speakers have agreed to present at the Denver Symposium. Please send the attached letter to them. Do NOT include the script paragraph with the letter you send to Chadwick.

Dr. Jon Mathis
310 Buckeye St.
Toledo, OH 43611-1234

Mr. Chad Chadwick
4920 Hickory Dr., N.
Boise, ID 83704-2839

<Date>

<Title> <First Name> <Last Name>
<Address>
<City,> <State> <ZIP>

Dear <Title> <Last Name>

Thank you for agreeing to be a speaker for Professional Symposium Specialists. As we discussed on the telephone, the symposium is scheduled for August 8 and 9 at the Carrington Hotel in Denver, Colorado. The theme for the symposium is "A Technology Vision."

Your presentation is scheduled for Friday, August 8, at 1:30 p.m. A presenter form is enclosed for you to complete and return to me by June 15. The information you provide will be used for the symposium program and for your introduction. A copy of one of the pages from last year's program is enclosed to give you an idea of the short descriptions that were used last year.

I am looking forward to meeting you on August 8. If you have questions before I contact you again, please call me at 503-139-4877.

*I checked with the home office in Boston; they gave me permission to increase the honorarium to $2,500. Your expenses, of course, will be covered by our company.*

# Unbound Report from Rough Draft

**Objectives:**

**1.** To format and key an unbound report with a table.

**2.** To improve language skills (verbs).

## 88A • 5
## Conditioning Practice

each line twice

alphabet **1** Extensive painting of the gazebo was quickly completed by Jerrod.

speed **2** The rich widow and the maid may make the usual visit to the dock.

figures **3** Train 236 left 40 minutes after the 7:45 departure of Flight 819.

**gwam** 1' | 1 | 2 | 3 | 4 | 5 | 6 | 7 | 8 | 9 | 10 | 11 | 12 | 13 |

## **L** ANGUAGE SKILLS

## 88B • 8
## Verbs

1. Read the guide at the right.
2. Key the Learn sentences below it.
3. Key the Apply sentences supplying the correct verb.

If there is confusion whether a subject is singular or plural, consult a dictionary.

Learn **1.** A few alumni are planning to attend the banquet.

Learn **2.** The criteria for evaluating the projects have been identified.

Apply **3.** An analysis of that type (is, are) very time consuming.

Apply **4.** Parentheses (is, are) used to enclose the textual citation.

Apply **5.** The basis of a democratic state (is, are) liberty.   --Aristotle

## **F** ORMATTING

## 88C • 27
## Unbound Reports

**Document 1**
**Unbound Report with a Table**

Format and key the copy shown at the right as an unbound report. Correct the errors marked on the copy and any you make as you key.

**Note:** Use the keyline method to determine tab positions for the table.

**wp note:**

Students completing the **wp activity** on the next page should delay printing the document until the changes outlined in the **wp activity** are made. Save the file for later use.

words

LISTENING   2

One of the most ~~important~~ critical skills that an individual   12

acquires is the skill of communicatnig. Studdies indicate that   25

a person spends 70 percent to 80 percent of ~~their~~ his/her time communi-   38

cating. A break down for the average individual of ~~the~~ time   58

Nixon and West (1989, 28) give the following

spent communicating ~~includes (Nixon and West, 1989, 28):~~   62

DS

Writing          9%        center   64
Reading          16%       Leave 1.5" between columns   67
Speaking         30%       69
listening        45%       72

DS

Since ~~most~~ almost half of the time spent communicating is spent listening,   86

it is important to overcome any obstacles that obstruct our   98

ability to listen and to learn new ways to improve our listening   111

ability.   113

*(continued on next page)*

# Professional Symposium Specialists
# [A School-to-Work Simulation]

Table with Clip Art

Forms with Script Font and Shading

## Work Assignment

You have accepted a position with Professional Symposium Specialists (PSS) as an assistant to the branch manager. PSS sponsors professional business meetings designed to enhance the expertise of those attending the meetings. A broad range of timely topics—technology, motivation, communication, leadership, etc.— are covered at the meetings. Each symposium features short addresses from well-recognized authorities on the topic. These speakers are brought in from throughout the United States.

You will work for Katelynn Eastwick, who is the branch manager for the Western Region of PSS. As an executive assistant, you will assist Ms. Eastwick in coordinating the symposiums. Currently Ms. Eastwick is working on a technology symposium being held in the Western Region. The documents you create for this simulation all relate to the technology symposium that will be held in Denver, Colorado, on August 8 and 9.

During your training program, you were instructed to use the unbound format for all reports and the block format with open punctuation for all company letters. Ms. Eastwick likes all her letters closed as follows:

```
Sincerely

Ms. Katelynn Eastwick
Western Branch Manager
```

General processing instructions from Ms. Eastwick will be attached to each document you are given to process. Use the date included on the instructions for all documents requiring a date. You are to use your decision-making skills to arrange the documents in an attractive format. Since PSS has based its word processing manual on the Century 21 textbook, you can also use the text as a reference to assist you in making formatting decisions and learning how to enhance your documents.

**Enhanced appearance.** Utilize the features of your equipment/wp software to enhance the appearance of the documents. When enhancing the appearance, make sure that it is "tastefully" done, but not overdone. Consider such things as borders, font face, font size, bolding, and underlining. Use your creativity (see illustrations at left).

**Notation for multiple enclosures.** For documents with multiple enclosures, use the following enclosure notation format:

```
Enclosures:  Presenter Form
             Previous Program
```

**Word processing features.** You are expected to use the word processing features covered during your training period to decrease the amount of time required for document processing and to enhance the appearance of the documents you produce. Since time did not allow for all the features to be covered, you are expected to learn some of the features on your own. Review the Word Processing Features in the special index (p. 14) to determine which features can be used to facilitate the processing of the documents at PSS.

**Business card for convention manager.** When you met with the convention manager of the Carrington Hotel, she provided you with her business card.

Montgomery, Lynelle (Ms.)
Convention Manager
Carrington Hotel
310 Union Blvd.
Denver, CO 80228-8764

FAX: (303) 189-5555
Phone: (303) 189-5554
e-mail: montgolm@carringt.com

# Barriers to Listening

Anything that interferes with our ability to listen ~~can be~~ is    128

classified as a barrier to listening.  Barriers that obstruct    141

[            ] our ability to listen can be divided into two basic    151

categories--external and internal barriers.    160

    Internal Barriers. *(lc)*  Internal barriers are those barriers that deal    174

with the mental or psychologcal *(i)* aspects of listening.  The    186

perception of the importance of the message, the emotional    197

state, and the tuning in and out of the speaker by the listener    210

are a few examples of internal barriers.    219

    External Barriers. *(lc)*  External barriers are barriers other    230

than those that deal with the mental and psychological make up of the    244

listner *(e)* that tend to keep *(#)* the listener from devoting full attention to    258

what is being said.  Telephone interruptions, uninvited visitors, noise,    273

and the physical environment are examples of external barriers.    286

Ways To *(lc)* Improve Listening    291

    Barriers to listening can be overcome.  However, it does    303
take a sincere effort on the part of the listener.  Neher and    315
Waite (1993, 83-84) suggest the following:    324

1.  Be aware of the barriers that are especially troublesome for    337
you.  Listening difficulties are individualistic.  Developing    349
awareness is an important step in overcoming such barriers.    362

2.  Listen as though you will have to paraphrase what is being    374
said.  Listen for ideas rather than for facts.    384

3.  Expect to work at listening.  Work at overcoming distrac-    396
tions, such as the speaker's delivery or nonverbal mannerisms.    409

4.  Concentrate on summarizing the presentation as you listen.    422
If possible, think of additional supporting material that would    434
fit with the point that the speaker is making.  Avoid trying to    447
refute the speaker.  Try not to be ~~too~~ turned off by remarks you    459
disagree with.    462

*(continued on next page)*

**WP** activity:
Use the Search to Find feature to determine how many times the word *communicating* appears in the report.
  Use the Search to Replace feature to replace the word *barriers* with the word *obstacles*.

1. A 5' writing on ¶s 1-3
   combined; find *gwam*,
   determine errors.
2. Two 1' writings on each
   ¶; find *gwam*, determine
   errors.
3. Another 5' writing on
   ¶s 1-3 combined; find
   *gwam*, determine errors.

**Additional Skill Building**
1. Key a series of 1' guided
   writings on each of the
   3 ¶s.
2. Key additional 5' writings
   to check skill increases.

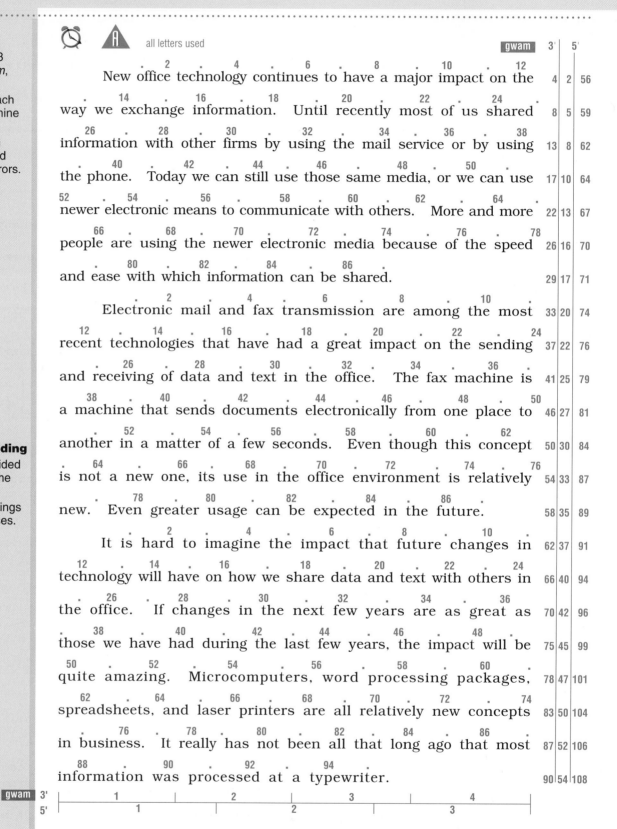

all letters used

| | gwam | 3' | 5' |

New office technology continues to have a major impact on the — 4 | 2 | 56

way we exchange information. Until recently most of us shared — 8 | 5 | 59

information with other firms by using the mail service or by using — 13 | 8 | 62

the phone. Today we can still use those same media, or we can use — 17 | 10 | 64

newer electronic means to communicate with others. More and more — 22 | 13 | 67

people are using the newer electronic media because of the speed — 26 | 16 | 70

and ease with which information can be shared. — 29 | 17 | 71

Electronic mail and fax transmission are among the most — 33 | 20 | 74

recent technologies that have had a great impact on the sending — 37 | 22 | 76

and receiving of data and text in the office. The fax machine is — 41 | 25 | 79

a machine that sends documents electronically from one place to — 46 | 27 | 81

another in a matter of a few seconds. Even though this concept — 50 | 30 | 84

is not a new one, its use in the office environment is relatively — 54 | 33 | 87

new. Even greater usage can be expected in the future. — 58 | 35 | 89

It is hard to imagine the impact that future changes in — 62 | 37 | 91

technology will have on how we share data and text with others in — 66 | 40 | 94

the office. If changes in the next few years are as great as — 70 | 42 | 96

those we have had during the last few years, the impact will be — 75 | 45 | 99

quite amazing. Microcomputers, word processing packages, — 78 | 47 | 101

spreadsheets, and laser printers are all relatively new concepts — 83 | 50 | 104

in business. It really has not been all that long ago that most — 87 | 52 | 106

information was processed at a typewriter. — 90 | 54 | 108

gwam 3' | 1 | 2 | 3 | 4
5' | 1 | 2 | 3

Neher, William W., and David H. Waite. The Business and Profes-   13
   sional Communicator.  Needham Heights, MA:  Allyn and Bacon,   23
   1993.   27

Nixon, Judy C. and Judy F. West.  "Listening--The New Com-   38
   petency."  The Balance Sheet, January/February 1989, 27-29.   50

### 88D • 10
**Editing Text**

Open the report keyed for
88C. Delete the text
following **Ways to Improve
Listening**. Replace the text
with the two ¶s at the right;
prepare a new references
page that includes the
references in Document 2
and the new reference at the
right. Print page 2 and the
REFERENCES page.

Ways to Improve Listening

   _stet_ Obstacles to listening can be overcome/; _lc_ However, it does

take a conscientious effort on the part of the listener.  A good

listener will try to maintain eye contact _with the speaker_ and work to avoid

tuning the speaker out.  Removing as many external distractins

as possible is another means for improving listening.

   Listening is also improved by directing attention to the

message rather than _to_ on the speaker. _'s appearance and mannerisms_ Focusing on the main points

being made by the speaker and taking notes, if appropriate, are

ways of directing attention to the message. _(Rader and Kurth, 1994, 510)_

_Rader, M. H., and Linda A. Kurth. Business Communication
with Contemporary Issues and Microcomputer
Applications. Cincinnati: South-Western Publishing
Co., 1994._

## LESSON 89 — Bound Report

**Objectives:**
1. To format a bound report.
2. To review number expression.

### 89A • 5
**Conditioning Practice**

each line twice

alphabet  1  Judge Bezdorf quickly approved the law for the maximum penalties.

speed  2  Enrique may wish for vigor when he duels with a haughty neighbor.

figures  3  Invoices 639, 640, and 758 were paid on May 12 with Check No. 94.

gwam  1' |  1  |  2  |  3  |  4  |  5  |  6  |  7  |  8  |  9  |  10  |  11  |  12  |  13  |

# Skill Builder

## Keying Technique

1. Key each line once.
2. Key a 1' writing on each even-numbered line.

### Alphabetic

1 bug pair cute was fox hair very just zoo kite quiet long den moon
2 Jack Dover was extremely happy after completing the biology quiz.

### Fig/sym

3 3/4" bolt|June 28, 1996|check for $25.17|5:30 p.m.|6.0% tax|$3.84
4 Your invoice (#392-587) for $31,286.00 was paid by check (#1544).

### Bottom row

5 box can fax man van zoo came cozy main brain exact amount minimum
6 Maxine Zorn came by my vacant barn just moments ago to buy my ax.

### Third row

7 out top up it tree yet pet were wet you trip quiet ripe troop pop
8 Reporter Wes Porter will take three tip top trees to the top row.

### Space bar

9 say no may yet nice can day next boy up yell not box pins sin den
10 It will be a very nice day if I can get all my work done by noon.

### Double letter

11 need grass cell afford better wood pebbles will dessert penniless
12 Betty and Bill will be attending the Phillies next baseball game.

### Combination response

13 the bear|may exceed|their puppy|they created|and eggs|oak dresser
14 Gregg Kaufman stated the dreaded due dates of my eight tax forms.

### Word response

15 men of owns firm end keys eight six wish visit so their town such
16 The firms may form a panel to handle the dismal problem downtown.

| gwam | 1' | 1 | 2 | 3 | 4 | 5 | 6 | 7 | 8 | 9 | 10 | 11 | 12 | 13 |

## Tabulation

1. Clear tabs; set tabs 1", 2.5", and 4" from the left margin.
2. Key the text at the right.
3. Take three 1' writings.

**Goal:** Increase amount of text keyed in each writing.

words

| Kentucky | Louisiana | Maine | Maryland | |
| *Frankfort* | *Baton Rouge* | *Augusta* | *Annapolis* | 7 / 15 |
| Massachusetts | Michigan | Minnesota | Mississippi | 24 |
| *Boston* | *Lansing* | *St. Paul* | *Jackson* | 30 |
| Missouri | Montana | Nebraska | Nevada | 37 |
| *Jefferson City* | *Helena* | *Lincoln* | *Carson City* | 45 |
| New Hampshire | New Jersey | New Mexico | New York | 54 |
| *Concord* | *Trenton* | *Santa Fe* | *Albany* | 60 |

**Document 1**
Format the copy as a bound
report (review p. 211).

**Document 2**
Prepare a REFERENCES page
on a separate sheet (p. 4).

words

### EFFECTIVE COMMUNICATORS — 5

Communication is the thread that binds our — 13
society together. Effective communicators are — 23
able to use the thread (communication skills) — 32
to shape the future. To be an effective com- — 41
municator, one must know how to put words — 49
together that communicate thoughts, ideas, — 58
and feelings. These thoughts, ideas, and feel- — 67
ings are then expressed in writing or delivered — 77
orally. Some individuals are immortalized — 86
because of their ability to put words together. — 95
A few examples of those who have been immor- — 104
talized are Patrick Henry, Nathan Hale, — 112
Abraham Lincoln, and Winston Churchill. — 120
Consider the impact of their messages. — 128

### Patrick Henry — 131

Words will move people to action. Patrick — 140
Henry's words were a moving force behind one — 149
of the sparks that ignited the Revolutionary War — 159
in 1775. The impact of that revolution is well — 168
known to all Americans. Many Americans are — 177
familiar with his speech to the Second Virginia — 187
Convention on March 23, 1775. The most — 195
familiar part of his speech is "I know not what — 204
course others may take; but as for me, give me — 214
liberty or give me death!" (North American — 223
Biographies, 1994, 92) — 227

### Nathan Hale — 230

Words show an individual's commitment — 237
and can be very inspirational. Nathan Hale — 246
(Ubbelohde, 1993, 710) needed only these 14 — 255
words to show his commitment to his cause: "I — 264
only regret that I have but one life to lose for — 274
my country." These words are committed to — 283
memory by many and are still inspiring. — 291

### Abraham Lincoln — 294

One of the most famous speeches ever de- — 302
livered was Lincoln's Gettysburg Address. Kane — 312
(1989, 100) refers to the speech as an immortal — 322
address. It is debatable as to whether the — 331

words

opening lines "Four score and seven years ago, — 340
our fathers brought forth on this continent a — 349
new nation, conceived in liberty, and dedicated — 359
to the proposition that all men are created — 368
equal" or the closing lines " . . . and that gov- — 378
ernment of the people, by the people, for the — 387
people shall not perish from the earth" are most — 396
familiar to Americans. — 401

### Winston Churchill — 405

Another speech of significant magnitude was — 414
delivered by Winston Churchill. (1940, 572) — 423
His words not only lifted the spirits of the — 432
British but also were motivational to those com- — 442
mitted to the Allied cause. — 447

We shall go on to the end, we shall fight — 456
in France, we shall fight on the seas and — 464
oceans, we shall fight with growing confi- — 473
dence and growing strength in the air, we — 481
shall defend our island, whatever the cost — 490
may be, we shall fight on the beaches, we — 498
shall fight on the landing grounds, we shall — 507
fight in the fields and in the streets, we shall — 517
fight in the hills; we shall never surrender, — 526
and even if, which I do not for a moment — 534
believe, this island or a large part of it were — 544
subjugated and starving, then our Empire — 552
beyond the seas, armed and guarded by the — 560
British fleet, would carry on the struggle, — 569
until in God's good time, the New World, — 577
with all its power and might, steps forth to — 586
the rescue and the liberation of the old. — 595

### Summary — 597

The power of the written and spoken word — 605
can have a significant impact on the lives of — 614
those who hear or read it. Developing a skill at — 624
using the spoken and written word is impor- — 633
tant to a person's success. Not everyone can — 642
be immortalized by their words, but everyone — 651
can have an impact on those with whom they — 660
associate by being skilled at using the written — 669
and spoken word. — 672

*(continued on next page)*

# LESSON 138

## Process Interview Follow-Up Letters

**Objectives:**
1. To learn/apply guides for formatting follow-up letters.
2. To compose an interview follow-up letter.

---

### 138A • 5
### Conditioning Practice

each line twice

| | | |
|---|---|---|
| alphabet | 1 | Bo kept examining the size and quality of the very choice jewels. |
| speed | 2 | When the eight towns amend the maps, the visitor problem may end. |
| fig/sym | 3 | Add a tax of 5% to Sales Slip #437-92 to make a total of $182.60. |

**gwam** 1' | 1 | 2 | 3 | 4 | 5 | 6 | 7 | 8 | 9 | 10 | 11 | 12 | 13 |

---

### 138B • 30
### Follow-Up Letters

**Document 1**

Format and key the follow-up letter at the right to **Ms. St. John** as a personal-business letter from **Teresa A. Teasdale**. Refer to pages 324 and 325 for Ms. Teasdale's and Ms. St. John's addresses. Use **May 25, ----** for the date; supply missing letter parts. Use modified block format with mixed punctuation.

**Document 2**

Study the guides for interview follow-up letters on p. 323. Assume that you interviewed for the job you applied for in 135B, Document 2. Compose a follow-up letter; edit and prepare a final copy.

words

opening   35

Thank you for discussing the secretarial opening at Regency Insurance   49
Company. I have a much better understanding of the position after meet-   63
ing with you and Ms. Meade.   69

Ms. Meade was extremely helpful in explaining the specific job responsibili-   84
ties. My previous jobs and my business education classes required me to   99
complete many of the tasks that she mentioned. With minimal training, I  113
believe I could be an asset to your company.  123

Even though I realize it will be a real challenge to replace a person like Ms.  138
Meade, it is a challenge that I will welcome. If there is further infor-  153
mation that would be helpful as you consider my application, please let me  168
know.  170

closing  176

---

### **L**ANGUAGE SKILLS

### 138C • 15
### Compose at the Keyboard

1. During an interview, applicants are often asked to respond to questions similar to those shown below. Select three of the questions and compose your responses to each. Number your responses and DS between paragraphs.
2. Compose three questions that you would ask the interviewer during the interview.
3. Edit your copy, marking corrections and changes to improve sentence structure and organization.

1. What would you like to be doing five years from now?
2. Give three reasons why our firm should hire you.
3. Do your grades accurately reflect your ability? Explain why or why not.
4. Are you considering further education? Explain why or why not.
5. What are your greatest weaknesses?
6. What hourly wage should you be paid during the first year?
7. What are your major accomplishments in life?
8. What have you learned from previous employment?

| REFERENCES | words 675 |
| --- | --- |

Churchill, Winston. "We Shall Fight in the Fields and in the Streets." London, June 4, 1940. Quoted by William J. Bennett, <u>The Book of Virtues</u>. New York: Simon & Schuster, 1993.

683
691
697
705
711

Henry, Patrick. "Liberty or Death." Richmond, VA, March 23, 1775. Quoted in <u>North American Biographies</u>, Vol. 6. Danbury, CT: Grolier Education Corporation, 1994.

721
729
737
744
745

Lincoln, Abraham. "The Gettysburg Address." Gettysburg, PA, November 19, 1863. Quoted by Joseph Nathan Kane, <u>Facts About the President</u>, 5th ed. New York: The H. W. Wilson Company, 1989.

754
761
769
777
783

Ubbelohde, Carl. "Hale, Nathan." <u>The Encyclopedia Americana International Edition</u>. Danbury, CT: Grolier Incorporated, 1993.

792
801
808
809

## L ANGUAGE SKILLS

**89C • 10**
**Number Expression**

Key the sentences at the right, supplying the correct form of number expression.

1. The store was on the corner of 4th Avenue and 26th Street.
2. Almost 50 of our former students passed the CPA exam.
3. The publisher plans for Volume Two to be finished by June 7.
4. The new baby is twenty-one inches long and weighs 6 lbs. 5 oz.
5. Only 4 of the twenty applicants applying for the job will be hired.
6. Fifteen of the delegates voted for Steele; twenty voted for Myers.
7. The address of the Utah Historical Society is 1 Main Street.
8. Rules 7-10 are presented in Chapter four; Rules 11-13 in Chapter 5.
9. Of Tom's twenty-three hits, nine of them were for extra bases.
10. The office of Baker & Ortiz is located at Eight Brackett Avenue.

# LESSON 90 Bound Report with Endnotes

**Objectives:**
**1.** To format and key a bound report with long quotation and numbered list.
**2.** To improve language skills (commas).

**90A • 5**
**Conditioning Practice**

set 0.5" SM;
each line twice

alphabet 1 Brzycki Excavating Company quit projecting when they will be finished.

speed 2 Make the panel suspend the pay of their city officials as the penalty.

figures 3 Only 6,398 of the 14,652 students scored above 70 percent on the test.

gwam 1' | 1 | 2 | 3 | 4 | 5 | 6 | 7 | 8 | 9 | 10 | 11 | 12 | 13 | 14 |

## S KILL BUILDING

**90B • 5**
**Rough Draft**

Take three 1' writings on the ¶, making the marked changes. Try to increase your speed on each writing.

words

Year after year employers express there desire to hire 11

employee who have skills. those with the expertise to organize 28

and deliver ideas in writen or oral form are an asset to their 41

firm; those who do have this ability quickly become aliability. 55

If you plan on enterign the job market in the near future, you 68

want to refine skills so that you wil be an asset not a liability. 85

¶ _Preparing Physically_                                                              278

Preparing physically also plays an important part in planning         290

                     successful
for a⌃interview.   The interviewee should learn about appropri-       305

                                         prior to the interview
ate company dress and grooming standards⌃.   The interviewer has      322

                                                      a
to be able to picture the job applicant as⌃person who would          335

                                      Extreme  lc              image
fit in well with current employees.⌃ Differences in ~~appearance~~    349

between current employees and the applicant make it difficult         361

                                          p
for the interviewer to picture the applicant as an employee of        374

his/her
~~their~~ company.                                                    377

---

## 137C • 7
### Employment Test: Timed Writing

1. A 5' writing on all ¶s.
2. Find *gwam* and number of errors.

| | gwam | 3' | 5' |
|---|---|---|---|

all letters used

Something that you can never escape is your attitude.   It    4 | 2 | 44

will be with you forever.   However, you decide whether your   8 | 5 | 47

attitude is an asset or a liability for you.   Your attitude   12 | 7 | 49

reflects the way you feel about the world you abide in and    16 | 9 | 52

everything that is a part of that world.   It reflects the way you   20 | 12 | 54

feel about yourself, about your environment, and about other peo-   25 | 15 | 57

ple who are a part of your environment.   Oftentimes, people with   29 | 17 | 59

a positive attitude are people who are extremely successful.   33 | 20 | 62

At times we all have experiences that cause us to be   36 | 22 | 64

negative.   The difference between a positive and a negative per-   41 | 24 | 66

son is that the positive person rebounds very quickly from a bad   45 | 27 | 69

experience; the negative person does not.   The positive person is   49 | 30 | 72

a person who usually looks to the bright side of things and   53 | 32 | 74

recognizes the world as a place of promise, hope, joy, excite-   58 | 35 | 77

ment, and purpose.   A negative person generally has just the   62 | 37 | 79

opposite view of the world.   Remember, others want to be around   66 | 40 | 82

those who are positive but tend to avoid those who are negative.   70 | 42 | 84

| gwam | 3' | 1 | 2 | 3 | 4 |
|---|---|---|---|---|---|
| | 5' | 1 | | 2 | 3 |

## F ORMATTING

## 90C • 30
## Bound Report

Save Documents 1-3 for later use.

### Document 1
**Bound Report with Long Quotation and Numbered List**

Format and key the copy as a bound report.

**Note:** Quoted material of four or more lines should be SS and indented 0.5" from the left margin. The right margin for quoted material remains at 1". Double-space above and below the quoted material.

### Document 2
**Endnotes Page**

Using the same margins as for p. 1 of the report, format and key the following endnotes on a separate page (p. 3).

¹David J. Rachman and Michael H. Mescon, Business Today (New York: Random House, 1987), p. 529.

²Greg Anrig, Jr., "Making the Most of 1988's Low Tax Rate," Money, February 1988, pp. 56-57.

### Document 3
**References Page**

Use the information from the endnotes page to key a REFERENCES page (p. 4). See examples of book and article references on p. 153. Follow these examples to change endnotes into references.

TAXES — 1

Americans are taxed in order to raise revenues to finance — 13
governmental activities. Taxation has never been popular. — 25
Much time and energy have been devoted by the legislature — 36
trying to devise a system that requires everyone to pay his/ — 49
her fair share. Taxes are generally based on the benefits — 60
received and/or on the ability to pay. Two of the most — 72
common revenue-raising taxes are the personal income tax and — 84
the sales tax. — 87

Personal Income Tax — 91

The personal income tax is the tax individuals are re- — 102
quired to pay on their earnings. Employers deduct this tax — 114
from employees' paychecks. When employees file their income — 126
tax returns, they will either receive a refund for any excess — 139
that has been paid or they will have to pay the balance due. — 151

Personal income taxes have been the Federal Government's — 162
largest single source of revenue and a major source of — 173
state revenues as well. On the federal level, the per- — 184
sonal income tax is a graduated tax, which means the — 195
more you make, the higher the percentage of your income — 206
you pay in taxes.¹ — 210

With the Tax Reform Act of 1986, the highest tax an — 221
individual will pay is 33 percent. The amount an individual — 233
pays changes with each tax reform. In the past, the top tax — 245
rate has been as high as 70 percent.² — 253

Sales Tax — 255

The sales tax is another tax with which most people are — 266
familiar. It is a tax that is added to the retail price of — 278
goods and services. Two examples of this particular type of — 290
tax are as follows: — 295

1. General Sales Tax. The general sales tax is a tax — 306
levied by most states on goods and services. The amount — 317
of tax and the specific goods and services that are — 327
taxed varies by state. ⌇ vary — 332

2. Excise Tax (Selective Sales Tax). The excise tax — 343
is a state tax levied against specific items. Examples — 354
of items with an excise tax include tobacco, alcoholic — 365
beverages, and gasoline. — 370

While the income tax is a tax based on an individual's ability to — 384
pay, the general sale tax and the excise tax are based on bene- — 396
fits received. For example, Taxes collected on gasoline are used for high- — 411
ways. individuals purchasing gasoline are those who benefit — 424
from the construction and maintenance of highways. — 434

**Document 3**
Report
1. Process the copy at the right as a bound report with textual citations.
   Use **THE JOB INTERVIEW** for the title of the report.
2. Using the information given below, prepare a references list on a separate sheet.

**Reynolds, Caroline.** Dimensions in Professional Development. 4th ed. Cincinnati: South-Western Publishing Co., 1993.

**Hirsch, Maurice L., Rob Anderson, and Susan Gabriel.** Accounting and Communication. Cincinnati: South-Western Publishing Co., 1994.

|  |  |  | words |
|---|---|---|---|
| TELEPHONE PROFESSIONAL*S* |  |  | 5 |
| *Consulting* Staff |  |  | 8 |
| Consultant | Specialty | Phone | 14 |
| Ken Allen | Teleconferencing | 137-3897 | 21 |
| Jared Austin | Specialty Training | 137-3787 | 30 |
| Marsha Barber | Phone Systems | 137-3891 | 37 |
| Grant Chi | Voice Mail | 137-3792 | 43 |
| Felipe Cruz | Phone Systems | 137-3880 | 50 |
| Tiffani Daniels | Customized Services | 137-3884 | 59 |
| Greg Grant | Voice Mail | 137-3894 | 66 |
| Sharon Norton | Intercom Systems | 137-3781 | 74 |
| Christian Ryan | Sound Paging | 137-3888 | 81 |

heading 4

A successful letter of application and data sheet will result 16

in an invitation from a *potential* employer for a*n* interview. Prepar*ing* 30

for the interview is just as important in obtaining employment 43

as developing an effective application letter and data sheet. 56

The interviewers first impression of the applicant is 67
crucial to the success of the interview. This impression, 78
which may take as little as 60 seconds to form, determines 90
whether the interviewer is interested in learning more about 102
the potential employee. Therefore, the prospective employee 115
must make a special effort to ensure a positive first impres- 127
sion. Reynolds (1993, 57-61) suggested that to make that 138
positive first impression the applicant must be prepared men- 151
tally as well as physically. 157

Preparing Mentally DS 161

Preparing mentally includes learning as much *as possible* about the 174
*prior to the interview* Company and anticipating questions that the employer may ask 191
*person applying for the job* during the interview. The interviewee should also formulate 206
*ask during the interview to* questions to learn as much as possible about the position and 224
the co. An interview should be considered as an interpersonal 238
conversation in which one person elicits information from 249
another. Both parties should gain some knowledge about the 261
other. (Hirsch, Anderson, and Gabriel, 1994, 164) 274

*(continued on next page)*

## 90D • 10
## Comma

Follow the Learn/Apply procedure on p. 184.

Use a comma after (a) introductory phrases or clauses and (b) words in a series.

| | | |
|---|---|---|
| Learn | 1. | When you finish keying the report, please give it to Mr. Kent. |
| Learn | 2. | We will play the Mets, Expos, and Cubs in our next home stand. |
| Apply | 3. | If you attend the play, take Mary Jack and Tim with you. |
| Apply | 4. | The last exam covered memos simple tables and unbound reports. |

Do not use a comma to separate two items treated as a single unit within a series.

| | | |
|---|---|---|
| Learn | 5. | Her favorite breakfast was bacon and eggs, muffins, and juice. |
| Apply | 6. | My choices are peaches and cream brownies or ice cream. |
| Apply | 7. | Mary ordered ham and eggs toast and milk. |

Use a comma before short direct quotations.

| | | |
|---|---|---|
| Learn | 8. | The man asked, "When does Flight 787 depart?" |
| Apply | 9. | Mrs. Ramirez replied "No, the report is not finished." |
| Apply | 10. | Dr. Feit said "Please make an appointment for next week." |

# LESSON 91

# Bound Report Project

**Objectives:**
1. To format and key a bound report.
2. To improve language skills (commas).

## 91A • 5
## Conditioning Practice

each line twice

| | | |
|---|---|---|
| alphabet | 1 | The exclusive photo of a mosque by Dru Jenkins was quite amazing. |
| speed | 2 | The official goal of the spa downtown is to get my body in shape. |
| figures | 3 | Order No. 8479 was dated May 30; it was for 26 pies and 15 cakes. |

**gwam** 1' | 1 | 2 | 3 | 4 | 5 | 6 | 7 | 8 | 9 | 10 | 11 | 12 | 13 |

## 91B • 10
## Editing Text

Open the report keyed for 90C; make the changes outlined at the right to the first ¶ of the report. Change the endnotes and references to include the new reference (below).
**Electronics:** Key only the portion of the report shown at right and the endnotes and references pages.

[1]**Peter D. G. Thomas, Tea Party to Independence** (New York: Oxford University Press, 1991), p. 14.

Print all pages.

Americans are taxed in order to raise revenues to finance governmental activities. Taxation has never been popular. ~~Much~~ ~~time and energy have been devoted by~~ the legislature *(has devoted a great deal of time and energy)* trying to devise a system that requires everyone to pay his/her fair share.

*The Boston Tea Party (a result of the 1773 Tea Act)[1] was one of the earliest indicators of just how unpopular taxes can be to Americans.*

## LESSON 136   Process Employment Application Forms

**Objectives:**
1. To identify typical information on job application forms.
2. To complete an application form.

### 136A • 5
### Conditioning Practice
each line twice

alphabet   1   As a freezing wave hit, the explorers quickly adjusted the beams.

speed   2   I may make the goal if I work with vigor and with the right form.

fig/sym   3   The balance due on Account #4982 after the 10% payment is $5,673.

gwam   1' | 1 | 2 | 3 | 4 | 5 | 6 | 7 | 8 | 9 | 10 | 11 | 12 | 13 |

### 136B • 45
### Job Application Forms

**Document 1**

Key (or neatly print) the job application form on p. 327, using the form in stationery pack or one supplied by your teacher. Correct any errors you make as you key the copy.

**Document 2**

Complete an application for employment form to apply for the position you selected in Document 2, 135B. You should review the form and make a few notes before entering your personal data on the form.

## LESSON 137   Office Employment Test

**Objectives:**
1. To identify typical tasks in an office employment test.
2. To complete a simulated employment test.

### 137A • 5
### Conditioning Practice
each line twice

alphabet   1   Those men were amazed by the quick, lively jumps of the gray fox.

speed   2   She may pay the men for the work and then go with us to the city.

fig/sym   3   Was Check #3657 for $98.40, dated May 21, 1996, made out to Matt?

gwam   1' | 1 | 2 | 3 | 4 | 5 | 6 | 7 | 8 | 9 | 10 | 11 | 12 | 13 |

### **F** ORMATTING

### 137B • 38
### Employment Test

**Document 1**
**Letter**

Format the text at the right as a letter in block format with mixed punctuation. Use the current date.

|  | words |
|---|---|
| Ms. Carol Parker | Facilities Manager | Presido Industries | 8290 | 12 |
| Rockdale Dr. | Dallas, TX 75220-0396 | Dear Ms. Parker: | 22 |

You have probably heard the saying "Time is money." If you are concerned   37
about your company's time and money, you will be interested in hearing   51
how the **T**elephone **P**rofessionals can save your company both **Time** and   65
**Money**.   66

Improved technology continues to change the way a telephone can enhance   81
your business operations. Specialized business phone systems, call for-   95
warding, three-way calling, voice mail, and calling cards are only a few of   110
the options available today.   116

Please contact me at 137-3828 to arrange for one of our "**T**elephone **P**rofes-   131
sionals" to update you on your telephone options.   141

Sincerely, | Jason Hawthorn | New Accounts Manager | xx   151

## 91C • 10
## Comma (continued)

Follow the Learn/Apply procedure in 76C on p. 184.

Use a comma before and after word(s) in apposition.

Learn | 1. Andrea, the assistant manager, will chair the next meeting.
Apply | 2. Greg Mathews a pitcher for the Braves will sign autographs.
Apply | 3. The personnel director Marge Wilson will be the presenter.

Use a comma to set off words of direct address.

Learn | 4. I believe, Tom, that you should fly to San Francisco.
Apply | 5. Finish this assignment Mary before you start on the next one.
Apply | 6. Please call me Erika if I can be of further assistance.

Use a comma to set off nonrestrictive clauses (not necessary to the meaning of the sentence); however, do not use commas to set off restrictive clauses (necessary to the meaning of the sentence).

Learn | 7. The manuscript, which I prepared, needs to be revised.
Learn | 8. The manuscript that presents banking alternatives is complete.
Apply | 9. The movie which won top awards dealt with human rights.
Apply | 10. The student who scores highest on the exam will win the award.

## FORMATTING

## 91D • 25
## Report Formatting

Begin formatting and keying the report (92C) on pp. 223-225.

You will start keying the report for 91D and will complete it for 92C.

---

## LESSON 92
# Bound Report Project and Topic Outline

**Objectives:**
1. To format and key a bound report.
2. To improve language skills (commas).

## 92A • 5
## Conditioning Practice

each line twice

alphabet 1 Jack said that Dr. Weiberg plans on requiring five zoology exams.

speed 2 The eight signs are downtown by the chapel by the big city docks.

figures 3 Since 1987, 352 of our guests were from Utah; 460 were from Iowa.

gwam 1' | 1 | 2 | 3 | 4 | 5 | 6 | 7 | 8 | 9 | 10 | 11 | 12 | 13 |

## APPLICATION FOR EMPLOYMENT

*PLEASE PRINT WITH BLACK INK OR USE TYPEWRITER*                    *AN EQUAL OPPORTUNITY EMPLOYER*

| NAME (LAST, FIRST, MIDDLE INITIAL) | SOCIAL SECURITY NUMBER | CURRENT DATE |
|---|---|---|
| Teasdale, Teresa A. | 368-56-2890 | May 22, ---- |

| ADDRESS (NUMBER, STREET, CITY, STATE, ZIP CODE) | HOME PHONE NO. |
|---|---|
| 310 Royal Oak Ct. Daytona Beach, FL 32017-1157 | (904)136-7289 |

| REACH PHONE NO. | U.S. CITIZEN? YES X  NO | DATE YOU CAN START June 8,---- |
|---|---|---|

| ARE YOU EMPLOYED NOW? | IF SO, MAY WE INQUIRE OF YOUR PRESENT EMPLOYER? |
|---|---|
| Yes | Yes |

| TYPE OF WORK DESIRED | REFERRED BY | SALARY DESIRED |
|---|---|---|
| Secretarial | Ms. Anna Cruz | $ Open |

IF RELATED TO ANYONE IN OUR
EMPLOY, STATE NAME AND POSITION

| DO YOU HAVE ANY PHYSICAL CONDITION THAT MAY PREVENT YOU FROM PERFORMING CERTAIN KINDS OF WORK? | YES | NO X | IF YES, EXPLAIN |
|---|---|---|---|

| HAVE YOU EVER BEEN CONVICTED OF A FELONY? | YES | NO X | IF YES, EXPLAIN |
|---|---|---|---|

| E D U C A T I O N | EDUCATIONAL INSTITUTION | LOCATION (CITY, STATE) | DATES ATTENDED FROM MO. YR. | DATES ATTENDED TO MO. YR. | DIPLOMA, DEGREE, OR CREDITS EARNED | CLASS STANDING (CHK QUARTER) 1 | 2 | 3 | 4 | MAJOR SUBJECTS STUDIED |
|---|---|---|---|---|---|---|---|---|---|---|
| | COLLEGE | | | | | | | | | |
| | HIGH SCHOOL Jefferson High School | Daytona Beach, FL | 8 93 | 5 97 | Diploma | X | | | | Business Ed. |
| | GRADE SCHOOL | | | | | | | | | |
| | OTHER | | | | | | | | | |

### LIST BELOW THE POSITIONS THAT YOU HAVE HELD (LAST POSITION FIRST)

| 1. NAME AND ADDRESS OF FIRM | DESCRIBE POSITION RESPONSIBILITIES |
|---|---|
| Fischer Studio 839 Franklin Dr. Daytona Beach, FL 32019-8321 | Studio Assistant. Schedule appointments, maintain customer database, respond to customer inquiries. |
| NAME OF SUPERVISOR Mr. Jeremiah Fischer | |
| EMPLOYED (MO-YR) FROM: 8/95   TO: Present | REASON FOR LEAVING |

| 2. NAME AND ADDRESS OF FIRM | DESCRIBE POSITION RESPONSIBILITIES |
|---|---|
| The Printing Press 289 Seminole Ave. Daytona Beach, FL 32019-7585 | Bookkeeper. Processed accounts receivable and reconciled bank statements. |
| NAME OF SUPERVISOR Ms. Ruth Stewart | |
| EMPLOYED (MO-YR) FROM: 5/94   TO: 7/95 | REASON FOR LEAVING Started a new job. |

| 3. NAME AND ADDRESS OF FIRM | DESCRIBE POSITION RESPONSIBILITIES |
|---|---|
| Camp Clearwater P.O. Box 382 Lake City, FL 32055-1749 | Camp Assistant. Assisted Ms. Ramirez with various camp activities for 8- and 9-year-olds. |
| NAME OF SUPERVISOR Ms. Carmen G. Ramirez | |
| EMPLOYED (MO-YR) FROM: 6/93   TO: 8/93 | REASON FOR LEAVING Summer employment. |

*Teresa A. Teasdale*
SIGNATURE OF APPLICANT

## 92B • 10
### Comma (continued)
Follow the Learn/Apply procedure in 76C on p. 184.

Use a comma to separate the day from the year and the city from the state.

| | | |
|---|---|---|
| Learn | 1. | On November 19, 1863, Lincoln delivered the Gettysburg Address. |
| Learn | 2. | I attended the "Stadium of Fire" fireworks display in Provo, Utah. |
| Apply | 3. | The next meeting was scheduled for January 3 1995 in Detroit Michigan. |
| Apply | 4. | One of the Federal Reserve banks is located in Minneapolis Minnesota. |

Use a comma to separate two or more parallel adjectives (adjectives that could be separated by the word **and** instead of a comma).

| | | |
|---|---|---|
| Learn | 5. | The rude, discourteous fan was told to leave the game. |
| Learn | 6. | Hank Aaron autographed the small brown bat. (no comma needed) |
| Apply | 7. | Mary bought a small oval mirror for her room. |
| Apply | 8. | Ms. Marichal was a dependable skilled manager for our firm. |

Use a comma to separate (a) unrelated groups of figures that occur together and (b) whole numbers into groups of three digits each. (**Note**: Policy, year, page, room, telephone, and most serial numbers are keyed without commas.)

| | | |
|---|---|---|
| Learn | 9. | By the end of 1995, 2,500 troops were stationed here. |
| Learn | 10. | The telephone number for Room 1828 is 137-2932. |
| Apply | 11. | The serial number on the computer in Room 1215 is 28B6389. |
| Apply | 12. | During the summer of 1995 285670 people attended the play. |

## F ORMATTING

### 92C • 25
### Bound Report
Complete the report (below and on pp. 224 and 225) begun in 91D.

**Document 1**
Format and key the copy as a bound report.

**Document 2**
Prepare an ENDNOTES page on a separate sheet. Supply page number.

**Document 3**
Prepare a title page; review format guides, p. 212.

|  | words |
|---|---|
| GLOBALIZATION | 3 |

Today, more than ever before, the term globalization is being used. According to Harris,[1] the term is being used in a variety of contexts. In a very broad context, media use it almost daily to refer to a wide variety of political, sociological, environmental, and economic trends.

The business world, however, uses this term in a much narrower context to refer to the production, distribution, and marketing of goods and services at an international level. Everyone is impacted by the continued increase of globalization in a variety of ways. The types of food we eat, the kinds of clothes we wear, the variety of technologies that we utilize, the modes of transportation that are available to us, and the types of jobs we pursue are directly

| | words |
|---|---|
| | 11 |
| | 20 |
| | 29 |
| | 38 |
| | 47 |
| | 57 |
| | 60 |
| | 68 |
| | 77 |
| | 86 |
| | 95 |
| | 104 |
| | 114 |
| | 124 |
| | 133 |
| | 143 |
| | 152 |

linked to "globalization." Globalization is changing the world we live in.

### Causes of Globalization

Harris[2] indicates that there are three main factors contributing to globalization. These factors include:

* The reduction in trade and investment barriers in the post-World War II period.

* The rapid growth and increase in the size of developing countries' economies.

* Changes in technologies.

### Trade Agreements

Originally, each nation established its own rules governing foreign trade. Unfair

| | words |
|---|---|
| | 161 |
| | 168 |
| | 173 |
| | 182 |
| | 191 |
| | 194 |
| | 202 |
| | 211 |
| | 220 |
| | 227 |
| | 233 |
| | 236 |
| | 244 |
| | 253 |

(continued on next page)

Check this application letter against the guidelines on p. 323. Note the kinds of information in each paragraph.

have been able to apply what I learned in these courses at Fischer Studio, where I have worked as a studio assistant for almost two years.

My work experience and school activities have given me the opportunity to work with people to achieve group goals. Participating in FBLA has given me an appreciation of the business world.

The opportunity to interview with you to discuss the possibility of employment will be greatly appreciated. Please call me at 136-7289 to arrange an interview.

Sincerely, | Ms. Teresa A. Teasdale | Enclosure

| | words |
|---|---|
| | 176 |
| | 189 |
| | 203 |
| | 218 |
| | 227 |
| | 242 |
| | 257 |
| | 260 |
| | 268 |

**Document 2**

Review the application letter guidelines on p. 323. Compose at the keyboard a rough-draft letter applying for one of the positions shown at the right. Edit/revise your letter; then process it in final form.

# POSITIONS AVAILABLE

## Office Work

Immediate opening for a dependable person to assist office manager. General office duties. Must be able to follow directions, key at least 55 wpm, and possess good telephone skills.

Should enjoy working with the public. Send data sheet and application letter to

**Perry Sabato**
**Personnel Director**
**Blanchard Construction**
**310 Coronado St.**
**Anaheim, CA 92806-9276**

## Office Assistant

Small printing company has full-time position for an office assistant. Applicant must be able to key 45 wpm, process client orders, perform basic math operations, and project professional telephone image.

Apply to:

Jonathan Ryan
8290 Mercedes Dr.
Biloxi, MS 39531-0286

## Word Processing

Rhodes Consulting Services has an opening in the Word Processing Department for a detail-oriented individual with excellent document processing skills.

Word processing training desirable. Must have keyboarding skill of 50 wpm.

Send letter of application and data sheet to

Ms. Christine Jackson
Rhodes Consulting Services
3498 Plymouth Rd.
Hartford, CT 06119-2411

## Receptionist/Secretary

Small company seeks outgoing individual to do general office work. Responsibilities include answering phone, receiving clients, distributing mail, filing, and processing documents.

Interested applicants must have a minimum keyboarding skill of 55 wpm. Experience preferred, but will consider applicants with no previous experience who possess excellent keyboarding skills.

To apply, send letter of application and data sheet to
**Director of Human Resources**
**Brooks Financial Services**
**482 Rosswood Ct.**
**Louisville, KY 40291-8329**

words

regulations and tariffs were often the outcome, leading to the tariff wars of the 1930s. As a result:

Nations have found it convenient . . . to agree to rules that limit their own freedom of action in trade matters, and generally to work toward removal of artificial and often arbitrary barriers to trade.[3]

Many trade agreements exist in the world today. Three of those agreements (General Agreement on Tariffs and Trade [GATT], the European Community, and the North American Free Trade Agreement [NAFTA]) have had or will have a significant impact on the United States.

GATT. The first trade agreement of major significance was the General Agreement on Tariffs and Trade. GATT was aimed at lowering tariff barriers among its members. The success of the organization is evidenced by its membership. Originally signed by 23 countries in 1947, the number of participating countries continues to grow.

The Uruguay Round of GATT is the most ambitious trade agreement ever attempted. Some 108 nations would lower tariff and other barriers on textiles and agriculture goods; protect one another's intellectual property; and open their borders to banks, insurance companies, and purveyors of other services.[4]

The European Community. The European Community is another example of how trade agreements impact the production, distribution, and marketing of goods and services. The 12 member nations of the European Community have dismantled the internal borders of its members.

Dismantling the borders, however, was only the first step toward an even greater purpose--the peaceful union of European countries. This first step was accomplished by the Paris and Rome treaties, which established the European Community and consequently removed the economic barriers. The treaties called for members to establish a common market; a common customs tariff; and common economic, agricultural, transport, and nuclear policies.[5]

NAFTA. A trade agreement that will have a significant impact on the way business is conducted in the United States is the North American Free Trade Agreement. This trade agreement involves Canada, the United States, and Mexico. Proponents of NAFTA claim that the accord will not only increase trade throughout the Americas, but it will also moderate product prices and create jobs in all three of the countries.[6]

Over the years a number of trade agreements have been enacted that promote trade. The result of all of these agreements has been an enhanced quality of life because of the increased access to goods and services produced in other countries.

Growth in Developing Countries' Economies

The growth in developing countries' economies is another major reason for globalization. According to Jacob, the global surge means more consumers who need goods and services. These needs appear because of the increase in per capita incomes of the developing countries.

According to the U.S. Department of Commerce, the world's ten biggest emerging markets include:

* Argentina        * Mexico
* Brazil           * Poland
* China            * South Africa
* India            * South Korea
* Indonesia        * Turkey

Of these emerging markets, the most dramatic increase is in the East Asian countries. Estimated per capita incomes rose at an annual rate of 6.5 percent from 1983 to 1993. In China alone, incomes grew 8.5 percent annually.[7]

Changes in Technologies

Recent technological developments have also contributed to globalization. Because of these developments, the world is a smaller place; communication is almost instant to many parts of the world. The extent of the technological developments can be sensed in Engardio's comments:[8]

Places that until recently were incommunicado are rapidly acquiring state-of-the-art telecommunications that will let them foster both internal and foreign investment. It may take a decade for many

(continued on next page)

# LESSON 134

## Process Data Sheets

**Objectives:**

1. To learn/apply guides for formatting a data sheet.
2. To compose a personal data sheet.

### 134A • 5
### Conditioning Practice

each line twice

alphabet  1  Wexford enjoyed checking the problems on the quiz he gave Friday.

speed  2  Sign the form for the firm to pay the men for their work with us.

figures  3  On May 20, 1997, I moved from 468 Oak Street to 5371 Glenn Drive.

gwam  1' | 1 | 2 | 3 | 4 | 5 | 6 | 7 | 8 | 9 | 10 | 11 | 12 | 13 |

### 134B • 45
### Data Sheets

**Document 1**
Format and key the data sheet on page 324.

**Document 2**
Compose at the keyboard a rough-draft data sheet for yourself using the guidelines on p. 323 and the model on p. 324. Edit; then key a final copy.

---

# LESSON 135

## Process Application Letters

**Objectives:**

1. To learn/apply guides for formatting an application letter.
2. To compose an application letter in response to job ads.

### 135A • 5
### Conditioning Practice

each line twice

alphabet  1  Kevin justified his low quiz score by explaining his unusual problems.

speed  2  She and the neighbor may go downtown to sign the form for the auditor.

figures  3  Of the 830 surveyed, only 256 knew the importance of December 7, 1941.

gwam  1' | 1 | 2 | 3 | 4 | 5 | 6 | 7 | 8 | 9 | 10 | 11 | 12 | 13 | 14 |

## **F**ORMATTING

### 135B • 45
### Application Letters

**Document 1**

Format and key the application letter for Ms. Teresa A. Teasdale. Format as a personal-business letter in modified block with mixed punctuation. If necessary, refer to the illustration on p. 124. Use the data sheet on p. 324 for the return address for Ms. Teasdale.

words

opening  10

May 10, ---- | Ms. Jenna St. John | Personnel Director | Regency Insur-  23
ance Company | 4291 Imperial Dr. | Daytona Beach, FL 32017-3856 |  35
Dear Ms. St. John:  39

Ms. Anna Cruz, my information processing instructor, informed me of the  54
secretarial position with your company that will be available June 15. She  69
speaks very highly of your organization. After learning more about the  83
position, I am confident that I am qualified and would like to be considered  98
for the position.  102

Currently I am completing my senior year at Jefferson High School. All of  117
my elective courses have been in the information processing area. I have  132
completed the advanced course in document formatting, the database and  146
spreadsheet applications course, and the business procedures course. I  161

*(continued on next page)*

countries in Asia, Latin America, and 1032
Eastern Europe to unclog bottlenecks in 1040
transportation and power supplies. But by 1048
installing optical fiber, digital switches, and 1058
the latest wireless transmission systems, 1066
urban centers and industrial zones from 1074
Beijing to Budapest are stepping into the 1083
Information Age. Videoconferencing, elec- 1091
tronic data interchange, and digital 1098
mobile-phone services already are reaching 1107
most of Asia and parts of Eastern Europe. 1116

All of these developing regions see 1123
advanced communications as a way to 1130
leapfrog stages of economic development. 1138

## Summary 1140

The world continues to become more glo- 1148
balized. The trend will continue because of 1157
three main factors: new and improved trade 1166
agreements, rapid growth rates of developing 1175
countries' economies, and technological ad- 1183
vances. All of these factors foster globalization. 1193

### ENDNOTES 1195

[1]Richard G. Harris, "Globalization, Trade, 1204
and Income," Canadian Journal of Economics, 1213
November 1993, p. 755. 1217

[2]Harris, p. 763. 1221

[3]Encyclopedia Americana, Vol. 26 1228
(Danbury, CT: Grolier Incorporated, 1993), 1237
p. 915. 1238

[4]Louis S. Richman, "Dangerous Times for 1246
Trade Treaties," Fortune, September 20, 1993, 1256
p. 14. 1257

[5]"Fact Sheet: European Community," Vol. 1265
4, No. 7, Washington, DC: U.S. Department 1274
of State Dispatch, February 15, 1994, p. 89. 1284

[6]Mario Bognanno and Kathryn J. Ready, 1291
eds., North American Free Trade Agreement 1300
(Westport, CT: Quorum Books, 1993), p. xiii. 1309

[7]Rahul Jacob, "The Big Rise," Fortune, 1317
May 30, 1994, pp. 74-75. 1321

[8]Pete Engardio, "Third World Leapfrog," 1330
Business Week, May 18, 1994, p. 47. 1338

 **activity:**

Before printing the report, use the Search to Replace feature to replace the word *agreements* with the word **accords** in the GLOBALIZATION report.

---

## 92D • 10
## Topic Outline

1. Review the information at the right.
2. Format and key the outline.

**Note:** If you prefer less space after periods, set tabs instead of using default tabs. Use the hanging indent style for items that run longer than one line.

See pp. A21-A23 for additional R & E report activities.

SPACING TOPIC OUTLINES QS

1st Tab   2d Tab   3d Tab

I.   VERTICAL SPACING DS
     A.   Title of Outline
          1.   Two-inch top margin
          2.   Followed by three blank line spaces (QS)
     B.   Major Headings
          1.   First major heading preceded by a QS; all others preceded by one blank line space (DS)
          2.   All major headings followed by a DS
          3.   All subheadings single-spaced (SS) DS

II.  HORIZONTAL SPACING DS
     A.   Title of Outline Centered over the Line of Writing
     B.   Major Headings and Subheadings
          1.   Identifying Roman numerals aligned at one-inch left margin (periods aligned), followed by a tab
          2.   Identifying letters and numbers for each subsequent level of subheading aligned below the first word of the preceding heading, followed by a tab

**Teresa A. Teasdale**
310 Royal Oak Ct.
Daytona Beach, FL 32017-1157
(904) 136-7289


EDUCATION

Senior at Jefferson High School
High School Diploma, pending graduation
Major emphasis: Administrative Services
Grade Average: 3.70; upper 10% of class


SCHOOL ACTIVITIES

Editor, Jefferson Telegram, senior year; reporter for two
years.

Vice President, Future Business Leaders of America, senior
year; member for three years.

National Honor Society, junior and senior years.


WORK EXPERIENCE

Studio Assistant, Fischer Studio, Daytona Beach, FL, August
1995 to present.  Work 15 hours a week as a studio assistant;
schedule appointments, maintain customer database, and
respond to customer inquiries.

Bookkeeper, The Printing Press, Daytona Beach, FL, May 1994 to
July 1995.  Processed accounts receivable and reconciled bank
statements.

Camp Assistant, Camp Clearwater, Lake City, FL, summer 1993.


REFERENCES (by permission)

Ms. Ann C. Rutgers, Administrative Services Instructor,
Jefferson High School, 8230 Riverwood Dr., Daytona Beach, FL
32019-3827, (904) 132-8286.

Mr. Jeremiah Fischer, Owner, Fischer Studio, 839 Franklin Dr.,
Daytona Beach, FL 32019-8321, (904) 136-8256.

Ms. Ruth Stewart, Manager, The Printing Press, 289 Seminole
Ave., Daytona Beach, FL 32019-7585, (904) 132-2819.


**Data Sheet**

# Language & Writing Skills 10

## Activity 1:

1. Study the spelling/ definitions of the words in the color block at the right.
2. Key the **Learn** line in the first set of sentences.
3. Key the **Apply** lines, choosing the right words to complete each sentence correctly.
4. Key the second set of lines in the same way.
5. Check work; rekey lines containing word-choice errors.

**Choose the right word**

> **lie** (n) an untrue or inaccurate statement; (vb) to rest or recline
> **lye** (n) a strong alkaline solution
>
> **adapt** (vb) to make fit; adjust
> **adept** (adj) thoroughly proficient; expert

Learn 1 Jeff told a lie about how the lye damaged the new carpet.
Apply 2 Sally told one (lie/lye) after another to protect herself.
Apply 3 I knew not to (lie/lye) down near the drum of (lie/lye).

Learn 4 Once he was able to adapt the form, he was adept with it.
Apply 5 Yoko will (adapt/adept) the ad to accommodate your concern.
Apply 6 Juan was quite (adapt/adept) at using integrated software.

## Activity 2:

As you key the sentences shown at the right, choose the word in parentheses that correctly completes the sentence. Then, check your work and rekey any sentence that contains a noun/ verb agreement error.

**Proofread & correct**  Subject/Predicate agreement

1 Most of the workers (was/were) present for the presentation.
2 I (doesn't/don't) know just when I'll finish the long report.
3 If they (doesn't/don't) arrive by 8:15, begin without them.
4 The basis for their comments (elude/eludes) me.
5 It (doesn't/don't) matter to me who takes the lead role.
6 Marilyn (doesn't/don't) know whether she can attend the party.
7 Many of us (are/is) going to vote for Janet for president.
8 (Doesn't/Don't) he realize that a raise now is not possible?
9 The listed criteria (aren't/isn't) sufficient for this job.
10 (Wasn't/Weren't) you aware that the play began at 8 p.m.?

## Activity 3:

As you key the sentences shown at the right, insert commas as needed to complete each sentence correctly. Then check your work and rekey any sentence that contains an error in comma usage.

**Proofread & correct**  Punctuation (Comma)

1 When you get to State Street make a right turn at the light.
2 She will ask Ken you and me to serve on the planning committee.
3 They moved to Las Cruces New Mexico on September 15 1997.
4 Elden be sure to turn off all equipment before you leave.
5 Ms. Rogers said "Keep the cursor moving steadily."
6 Winona who is our class treasurer couldn't attend the meeting.
7 By the middle of 1995 we had 273 employees; in 1997 318.
8 The probability is that only 1 in 280000 have the same DNA.
9 Dr. Woodburn has a pleasant strong personality.
10 The choir director Elena Spitz is planning a special program.

**Format Guides:
Employment Documents**

Application Letter

## Job Application Documents

Extreme care should be given to the preparation of all employment documents. The data sheet, application letter, and application form are often the basis of an employer's first impression of an applicant. These documents often determine whether an applicant is invited for an interview.

Prepare application documents on a keyboard with the possible exception of the application form. You may be asked to complete the application form at the time of the interview, in which case it should be neatly prepared with a pen. Always use high-quality paper when preparing your data sheet and application letter. Make sure that each document you prepare contains accurate, appropriate information that is neat, grammatical, and well arranged.

**Data sheet.** In most cases, a data sheet should be limited to one page. The information presented usually covers five major areas: personal information (your name, address, and telephone number), education (courses taken, skills acquired, grades earned), school activities (organizations, positions, years involved) work experience (position, name and location of place employed, brief description of responsibilities), and references (reference, title, organization, address, phone number). The data sheet may also include sections listing community activities and hobbies and/or special interests.

Top, bottom, and side margins may vary depending on the amount of information presented. The specific format may also vary with personal preference. In general, the most important information is presented first, which means that a person who has been out of school for several years and has considerable work experience may place that information before educational background information.

References, however, are usually the last item on the page. (Always get permission from the individuals you plan to include as references on your data sheet before using their names.)

**Application letter.** An application letter should always accompany a data sheet. The letter is formatted as a personal-business letter and should be limited to one page.

The first paragraph of the application letter should indicate the position for which you are applying and how you learned of the position. It is also appropriate to include something positive that you know about the company or someone who works for the company in the opening paragraph.

The next one or two paragraphs are used to convince the reader that you understand the requirements for the position and to explain how your background experiences qualify you for the position for which you are applying. You may do this by elaborating on some of the information included on your data sheet, such as courses taken and skills achieved. End the paragraph by inviting the reader to refer to the enclosed data sheet for additional information.

The final paragraph is used to request an interview. Information is also provided to make it easy for the reader to contact you to make arrangements for the interview.

**Interview follow-up letter.** Appreciation for an interview is conveyed in a follow-up letter, also called a thank-you letter. In addition to thanking the interviewer for the interview, the follow-up letter may state that you are still interested in the job. The letter can provide any additional relevant information and give positive impressions of the company and/or people you met. To be effective, the letter should be written immediately following the interview. This will increase the likelihood that the interviewer will receive the letter before a hiring decision is made.

# Activity 4:

1. Read the ¶s at the right.
2. Pick an issue (one of those given or some other about which you have great concern).
3. Key a ¶ in which you identify the issue and indicate why it is of major concern to you.
4. Key another ¶ in which you indicate what, how, and by whom you believe something can and should be done to reduce or eliminate the problem.

**Compose (think) as you key**

A recent newspaper article reveals what is on the minds of the members of at least one high school journalism class. Their concerns and some proposed solutions were conveyed in Letters to the Editor of a national newspaper.

The letters highlighted the following concerns: teenage mischief and violence; teen motherhood and fatherhood; blame-placing instead of self-responsibility; guns, knives, and drugs in the schools and on the streets; media preoccupation with sex, violence, crime, and bizarre behavior.

In terms of teenage behavior, solutions included: more athletics; more and better part-time jobs; curfews; more money for the schools; more school- and community-sponsored free-time activities for teenagers; more stringent penalties for those who violate rules and laws; required counseling programs for parents whose sons/daughters are repeated violators.

# Activity 3:

1. Read carefully the material shown at the right.
2. Make your own list of "pet peeves" or violations of good manners (etiquette).
3. Compose/key a ¶ for each item on your list, indicating why it is the wrong thing to do (why it violates good manners and shows lack of consideration and respect for others).

**Compose (think) as you key**

Practicing good manners (etiquette) whether you are at home or in school, with your family or your friends, will help you acquire poise and self-assurance. Being well mannered means following the recognized rules of behavior that help to make your relationships with others more pleasant, whether you are in a private or a public place. The basis of good manners is kindness, thoughtfulness, and a deep concern for others. Good manners are a reflection of your attitude toward others—whether you like people, respect them, are interested in them, and make the effort to get along with them.

Some of the things people (young and old alike) do that show disrespect or a lack of concern for others are listed below.

1. Failure to introduce a companion to an acquaintance with whom you've stopped to chat.
2. Males wearing hats or caps indoors: classrooms, theaters, and restaurants, for example.
3. Loud conversations in the vicinity of others whom you may or may not know.
4. Using off-color or vulgar language to or in the vicinity of people whom you know or may not know.
5. Boisterous behavior in places that are supposed to be relatively quiet and serene (libraries, theaters, and hospitals, for example).
6. Leaning on the car horn while in a slow lane of traffic in an attempt to get slow movers out of the way, or driving well below the speed limit in the fast lane of an expressway.
7. Congregating in a doorway, hallway, or an aisle, preventing others from passing through.
8. Attacking a sandwich or plate of food with both hands in a gluttonous manner; chewing noisily and talking while the mouth is full.
9. Opening and walking through a door first while a companion trails behind instead of holding the door for a companion (male or female).
10. Calling people unflattering or negative (pejorative) names to get their attention or to minimize their self-esteem.

# UNIT 21

## LESSONS 93–94

### Improve Keyboarding Skills

## LESSON 93

### Keyboarding Techniques/Language Skills

**Objectives:**
1. To improve and assess keyboarding techniques.
2. To improve and assess keyboarding speed and accuracy.
3. To improve language skills.

---

### 93A • 5
**Conditioning Practice**

each line twice; then 1'
writings on line 2

| | | |
|---|---|---|
| alphabet | 1 | Major Peiffer realized very quickly that she had won the big box. |
| speed | 2 | A problem for the ensign was to focus on the rigor of the ritual. |
| figures | 3 | Figures 18, 27, and 35 present the data for 1986, 1990, and 1994. |
| **gwam** | 1' | 1   2   3   4   5   6   7   8   9   10   11   12   13 |

---

## L ANGUAGE SKILLS

### 93B • 10
**Semicolon**

Follow the Learn/Apply
procedure in 76C, p. 184.

> Use a semicolon to separate two or more independent clauses in a compound sentence when the conjunction is omitted.

| | | |
|---|---|---|
| Learn | 1. | Mr. Harris is a fantastic teacher; he really enjoys his job. |
| Apply | 2. | His dad is a professor he received his degree from Harvard. |
| Apply | 3. | Sally is majoring in economics Mary is majoring in history. |

> Use a semicolon to separate independent clauses when they are joined by a conjunctive adverb (*however*, *therefore*, *consequently*, etc.).

| | | |
|---|---|---|
| Learn | 4. | A $500 rebate is available; consequently, they decided to buy now. |
| Apply | 5. | I live in St. Paul however, I work in Minneapolis. |
| Apply | 6. | Jan has to work on Friday therefore, we will change the date. |

---

## S KILL BUILDING

### 93C • 10
**Awkward Reaches**

Key each line twice SS;
DS between 2-line groups;
then 1' writings on lines 2,
4, and 6.

| | | |
|---|---|---|
| Adjacent keys | 1 | suit cure spot sale foil other prior worthy fields opened quickly |
| | 2 | Bidding on truck tires will suit the clerk's priority quite well. |
| Direct reaches | 3 | race cent fund worthy music union checks fifty zebra great length |
| | 4 | Many loans in my bright gray manual depend on large mutual funds. |
| One-hand words | 5 | upon sage yolk refer union vases zebra wages tested uphill veered |
| | 6 | Ted's greatest races in regatta races were based on a great crew. |
| **gwam** | 1' | 1   2   3   4   5   6   7   8   9   10   11   12   13 |

# Language & Writing Skills 13

## Activity 1:

1. Study the spelling/definitions of the words in the color block at the right.
2. Key the **Learn** line in the first set of sentences.
3. Key the **Apply** lines, choosing the right words to complete each sentence correctly.
4. Key the second set of lines in the same way.
5. Check work; rekey lines containing word-choice errors.

### Choose the right word

| | |
|---|---|
| **affect** (vb) to influence | **advice** (n) opinion; recommendation |
| **effect** (n) result; consequence | **advise** (vb) to give advice; to recommend |
| (vb) to cause; to accomplish | |

Learn 1 The effect of the recent change will affect our annual profit.
Apply 2 Will cutting the staff 25 percent (affect/effect) worker morale?
Apply 3 What (affect/effect) will new equipment have on productivity?

Learn 4 Since you sought my advice, I advise you to go for the new job.
Apply 5 Ms. Chin will (advice/advise) music students on Friday mornings.
Apply 6 To keep all our options open was his (advice/advise) to us.

## Activity 2:

1. Read the simplified memo shown at the right, noting corrections needed in capitalization, number expression, punctuation, word choice, and subject/predicate agreement.
2. Key the simplified memo, making whatever changes are needed to make the message correct.
3. Proofread your work and correct any remaining errors you find.

### Proofread & correct

May 10, ----

Pamela E. Lonewolf, counselor

ENROLLMENT IN ART 1

Because of the recent new limits on class size in art you need to no that all Sections in art one are now filled.  Over 40 students have already asked to take art 1 12 more than the three planned sections will accommodate.

If the principal mr. wilson don't add another section these twelve students (as well as any others who later apply will have to be turned away.  Will you please speak with him?  If you wish I'll be glad to join you in the discussion.

It may be that sum students who choose Art 1 as an elective should be rescheduled into other courses.  Their not likely to be as upset as students who have chosen art as a career path.

Please advice me on what you plan to do to resolve this problem.

Anna Morningstar, assistant principal

## 93D • 25
### Timed Writings

1. Two 5' writings for speed; find *gwam* on each writing.
2. Two 3' writings for speed; find *gwam* on each writing.
3. Two 1' writings for speed; find *gwam* on each writing.

  all letters used

| | gwam | 1' | 3' | 5' |
|---|---|---|---|---|

Have you ever thought about becoming a teacher?  Teachers | 12 | 4 | 2
are crucial to our welfare.  They are put in charge of one of | 24 | 8 | 5
America's most precious resources, students.  They are expected to | 37 | 12 | 7
assist in developing this resource into a well-rounded person who | 51 | 17 | 10
fits in well with other members of our culture.  They are also | 63 | 21 | 13
expected to produce students who are able to contribute to society | 77 | 26 | 15
and make it a better place to live.  Our culture hinges on the | 89 | 30 | 18
quality of teachers we entrust with our future. | 99 | 33 | 20

Being a teacher is quite a challenge.  Teachers work with a | 111 | 37 | 22
broad range of individuals with a variety of interests, back- | 123 | 41 | 25
grounds, and abilities.  Teachers try to help all students realize | 136 | 45 | 27
their potential and be able to cope with a world that is changing | 149 | 50 | 30
very rapidly every day.  A teacher's job is to try to equip stu- | 162 | 54 | 32
dents with the skills necessary to be lifelong learners, to keep | 175 | 58 | 35
pace with changes, and to be productive.  In order to be success- | 188 | 63 | 38
ful at teaching, a person must like working with people and enjoy | 201 | 67 | 40
learning. | 203 | 68 | 41

| gwam | 1' | 1 | 2 | 3 | 4 | 5 | 6 | 7 | 8 | 9 | 10 | 11 | 12 | 13 |
|---|---|---|---|---|---|---|---|---|---|---|---|---|---|---|
| | 3' | | 1 | | | 2 | | | 3 | | | 4 | | |
| | 5' | | | 1 | | | | 2 | | | | 3 | | |

---

## LESSON 94   Keyboarding/Language Skills   MLS

**O b j e c t i v e s :**
**1.** To improve and assess keyboarding speed and accuracy.
**2.** To improve language skills.

## 94A • 5
### Conditioning Practice

each line twice

alphabet  1  Zac very quickly explained why most of the big projects were cut.
speed  2  She paid the men for the work they did in the shanty by the lake.
figures  3  If you call after 12:30 on Monday, you can reach her at 168-5974.

| gwam | 1' | 1 | 2 | 3 | 4 | 5 | 6 | 7 | 8 | 9 | 10 | 11 | 12 | 13 |
|---|---|---|---|---|---|---|---|---|---|---|---|---|---|---|

## 94B • 20
### Timed Writings

1. Two 1' writings on each ¶ of 93D, above; find *gwam* on each writing.
2. Two 3' writings on ¶s 1-2 combined; try to equal your best 1' rate in Step 1.
3. A 5' writing on ¶s 1-2 combined; find *gwam*; find errors.

**Document 2**
Save as BANK2.

## A&E Bank Card Application

| Last Name | First | Middle | | |
|---|---|---|---|---|
| White | Carlos | Benito | | |

| Street Address | | City | State | ZIP | Phone |
|---|---|---|---|---|---|
| 9873 Clear Crossing Ln. | | Charlotte | NC | 28112-8309 | 704-126-1580 |

| Birth Date (Month, Day, Year) | Social Security Number | Name of Employer | |
|---|---|---|---|
| 06-20-59 | 829-23-8729 | Charlotte Legal Services | |

| Address of Employer | City | State | Annual Income | Employer's Phone |
|---|---|---|---|---|
| 390 Dunbar St., W. | Charlotte | NC | $55,000 | 704-140-5554 |

**Document 3**
Save as BANK3.

## A&E Bank Card Application

| Last Name | First | Middle | | |
|---|---|---|---|---|
| Castillo | Mary | J. | | |

| Street Address | | City | State | ZIP | Phone |
|---|---|---|---|---|---|
| 3820 Stonegate Ct. | | Greensboro | NC | 27406-8631 | 910-156-3798 |

| Birth Date (Month, Day, Year) | Social Security Number | Name of Employer | |
|---|---|---|---|
| 04-15-57 | 389-56-9821 | Rochelle Gallery | |

| Address of Employer | City | State | Annual Income | Employer's Phone |
|---|---|---|---|---|
| 310 Sherman St. | Greensboro | NC | $25,500 | 910-190-1200 |

**Document 4**
Save as BANK4.

## A&E Bank Card Application

| Last Name | First | Middle | | |
|---|---|---|---|---|
| Russell | Reed | Martin | | |

| Street Address | | City | State | ZIP | Phone |
|---|---|---|---|---|---|
| 8291 Regency Dr. | | Charleston | WV | 25341-9938 | 304-129-8292 |

| Birth Date (Month, Day, Year) | Social Security Number | Name of Employer | |
|---|---|---|---|
| 12-24-57 | 389-51-8830 | Auto Glass Specialists | |

| Address of Employer | City | State | Annual Income | Employer's Phone |
|---|---|---|---|---|
| 8392 White Oak Dr. | Charleston | WV | $18,000 | 304-128-7356 |

**94C • 10**
**Semicolon**

Follow the Learn/Apply
Procedure in 76C, p. 184.

Use a semicolon to separate a series of phrases or clauses (especially if they contain commas) that are introduced by a colon.

Learn  1. The cities are as follows:   Orem, UT; Ames, IA; and Waco, TX.
Apply  2. The dates are as follows:   May 1, 1996  May 5, 1996  and May 9, 1996.
Apply  3. These are the figures:  1994, $687  1995, $798  and 1996, $845.

Place the semicolon outside the closing quotation mark; the period and comma, inside the closing quotation mark.

Learn  4. Mr. Day spoke about "winners"; Ms. Cline, about "losers."
Apply  5. She said, "Don't look at the keys" he said, "I'll try"
Apply  6. Tom said, "You can do it" Mary said, "You're kidding"

**S KILL BUILDING**

**94D • 15**
**Script Copy**

1. Two 1' writings on each ¶ for speed; find *gwam* on each writing.
2. Two 3' writings on ¶s 1-3 combined; find *gwam*; circle errors.

 all letters used

| | gwam | 1' | 3' | 5' |
|---|---|---|---|---|

Ethical conduct is a subject that has received a great    11 | 4 | 2
deal of attention in recent years.  Many businesses have developed    24 | 8 | 5
written codes and have taken steps to ensure that employees of the    38 | 13 | 8
business and the public are aware of these codes.  Making people    51 | 17 | 10
aware of the codes is a company's way of renewing its commitment    64 | 21 | 13
to ethical practice.    68 | 23 | 14

A major purpose of a code of ethics is to relay a company's    80 | 27 | 16
values and business standards to all its workers.  Each worker    92 | 31 | 18
must realize that he or she is required to apply these standards    105 | 35 | 21
in all relations with co-workers, potential and current customers    119 | 40 | 24
and suppliers, and the public at large.    126 | 42 | 25

To adhere to the code, employees must be able to combine    138 | 46 | 28
personal standards with those of the business.  This mixture is    151 | 50 | 30
important because each job has an ethical aspect, and each em-    163 | 54 | 33
ployee has a responsibility to carry out the functions of the job    176 | 59 | 35
in an ethical and proper manner.    183 | 61 | 37

Here are the Internet addresses that you requested for the other committee members. Our system is shut down for repairs, or I would have sent them to you via the Internet.

> IN%"CHENYH/SB2@OFS.UWEC.EDU"
> IN%"BARKER@RMC.NET.ROBERT-MORRIS.EDU"
> IN%"TLUSTYSA@UVSC.EDU"
> IN%"JCRUZ@KDC.COM"

# LESSON 133 Data Entry Forms

**Objective:**

To learn to format and process data on forms.

**133A • 5**
**Conditioning Practice**

each line twice

| | | |
|---|---|---|
| alphabet | 1 | A critic quickly recognizes the vexing problems of judging flaws. |
| speed | 2 | They may do the work for us when the city auditor signs the form. |
| fig/sym | 3 | This model (#94-68) costs $238; the other one (#95-7) costs $150. |

gwam 1' | 1 | 2 | 3 | 4 | 5 | 6 | 7 | 8 | 9 | 10 | 11 | 12 | 13 |

**133B • 10**
**Drill: Tabulation**

**CS:** 0.5"

1. Three 1' writings; find *gwam*.
2. Two 2' writings; find *gwam*.

| | | | | | gwam 1' | 2' |
|---|---|---|---|---|---|---|
| Hunt | Robin | 3842 Inwood St. | Flagstaff | AZ | 8 | 4 |
| Keswick | Jane | 9210 Dixon Rd. | Little Rock | AR | 17 | 8 |
| Langston | Bryce | 8309 Pardee St. | Berkeley | CA | 25 | 13 |
| Ritter | Leslie | 9056 Violin Rd. | Newark | DE | 33 | 17 |
| Lucina | Mike | 4786 Ocana Ct. | Fort Myers | FL | 41 | 21 |
| Fairbanks | Maria | 9078 Melrose Ave. | Pocatello | ID | 51 | 25 |
| Capri | Marge | 3215 Central Ave. | Oak Park | IL | 59 | 29 |

**133C • 35**
**Data Entry**

Use forms in stationery pack.

**Document 1**

Save as BANK1.

| A&E Bank Card Application | | | |
|---|---|---|---|
| Last Name | First | Middle | |
| Johnson | Beth | Anne | |
| Street Address | City | State | ZIP / Phone |
| 3152 Duke St. | Fayetteville | NC | 28304-4351 / 910-188-2211 |
| Birth Date (Month, Day, Year) | Social Security Number | Name of Employer | |
| 04-15-49 | 520-66-3820 | Fenton Motor, Inc. | |
| Address of Employer | City | State | Annual Income / Employer's Phone |
| 382 Greenbriar Dr. | Fayetteville | NC | $22,000 / 910-168-8399 |

# WORD PROCESSING 5

## ACTIVITY 1:

**Review Macro**

1. Define macros for:
   North Carolina
   South Carolina
   Virginia

2. Key the text at the right using the macro each time *North Carolina*, *South Carolina*, or *Virginia* appears in the text.

| City | State |
| --- | --- |
| Arlington | Virginia |
| Asheville | North Carolina |
| Charleston | South Carolina |
| Charlotte | North Carolina |
| Charlottesville | Virginia |
| Columbia | South Carolina |
| Fayetteville | North Carolina |
| Fredericksburg | Virginia |
| Greensboro | North Carolina |
| Greenville | South Carolina |
| Hickory | North Carolina |
| Lynchburg | Virginia |
| Manassas | Virginia |
| Norfolk | Virginia |
| Raleigh | North Carolina |
| Richmond | Virginia |
| Spartanburg | South Carolina |
| Sumter | South Carolina |
| Winston-Salem | North Carolina |

## ACTIVITY 2:

**Review Search and Replace**

1. Key the information at the right as a table.

2. Use the Search to Replace feature to make the following changes:

   The workshops to be held in *Spokane* have been changed to *Richland*.

   The workshops to be taught by *Clark* will be taught by *Newport*.

**Hint:** Key the first level of the table and then use the Copy feature for the second and third levels. Only the dates are different.

### Managing Diversity

| Location | Instructor | Date |
| --- | --- | --- |
| Olympia | Westridge | October 8 |
| Seattle | Franklin | October 10 |
| Spokane | Clark | October 14 |
| Tacoma | Goodwin | October 9 |
| Vancouver | Santana | October 7 |

### International Trade

| Olympia | Westridge | October 22 |
| --- | --- | --- |
| Seattle | Franklin | October 24 |
| Spokane | Clark | October 28 |
| Tacoma | Goodwin | October 23 |
| Vancouver | Santana | October 21 |

### Communicating Globally

| Olympia | Westridge | November 5 |
| --- | --- | --- |
| Seattle | Franklin | November 7 |
| Spokane | Clark | November 11 |
| Tacoma | Goodwin | November 6 |
| Vancouver | Santana | November 4 |

**Document 1**

Review the format guides for facsimilies on page 313. Format and key the fax from the model copy at the right.

**M S C**

**MILWAUKEE STATE COLLEGE**
Milwaukee, WI 53223-4004

Department of Business Education
and Administration Management
(414) 136-4320
FAX: (414) 136-4959

2" TM

FAX MESSAGE TRANSMITTAL SHEET

QS

```
          TO:  Justin Baxter
     FAX NO.:  715-136-1838              ⎫
        FROM:  Sandra Brown             ⎬ SS
        DATE:  January 30, ----
NO. OF PAGES:  1
     SUBJECT:  TECHNOLOGY TASK FORCE MEETING  ⎭
```

DS

The next meeting of the Technology Task Force will be held at the Milwaukee Downtown Inn on Monday, February 15, at 9 a.m.  The meeting should be finished before noon.

The main item of business will be the presentation of the proposals we requested from Computer Systems and Advanced Technologies.  Mark Gill, Computer Systems, will present his proposal at 9:30.  Sheila Beckstram will present the Advanced Technologies' proposal at 10:30.

Both representatives have been told to limit their presentations to 30 minutes.  This will allow us time to ask any questions we may have regarding the proposals.

ph

**Facsimile (Fax) Format**

**Document 2**

Format and key the text at the right as a fax to **Michelle Alvarez**. Her fax no. is **718-132-9377**. The fax is from **Clayton R. Bachman**. Use the current date and supply an appropriate subject line.

| | words |
|---|---|
| opening | 33 |

Michelle, the sales reports that I received yesterday for the fourth quar-  48
ter indicate a potential problem with the Southern Region.  The overall  62
sales for that region have been down appreciably during the last two  76
quarters.  For the year, they are down by almost 20 percent compared  90
to last year.  93

The reports I receive break down sales only by region.  I would like to  107
see sales for each individual state in the region to determine if this is a  122
problem for the entire region or only for one or two states.  135

Since I am meeting with regional representatives next Monday, I would  149
like for you to fax me the information ASAP.  158

**Format Guides:
Tables**

Three-Column Table

### Column Headings

When used, column headings may be centered over the longest line in the column. If a table has single- and multiple-line headings (see model below), the bottom line of each multiple-line heading is placed on the same line as the single-line headings. The lines of multiple-line headings are single-spaced.

### Horizontal Centering

The margin and tab settings for tables may be determined by the keyline method. The keyline consists of the longest entry in each column of the table plus the space to be placed between the columns (CS). Before or after keying the keyline, use the Center feature to place half of the keyline to the left of center point and half to the right of center point. After centering, use the location of the columns in the keyline to determine the settings for the left margin and tabs in the table. See p. 157 if necessary. Delete the keyline and key the table.

### Vertical Centering

Vertical centering can be done with the Center Page feature, if available with the software being used. Otherwise, vertical centering involves subtracting the number of lines of text (including blank line spaces) from the number of lines available on the sheet and dividing the remaining number of unused lines equally between the top and bottom margins.

**Manual Vertical Centering**

1. Count the lines to be used to key the table (include blank lines).
2. Subtract lines needed from total lines available on page (66 lines).
3. Divide the remainder by 2 to determine top margin. If the number that results ends in a fraction, drop the fraction.

**Example for table at right:**

Lines available $=$ 66
Total lines to be used for table $= \underline{-35}$
31
$31 \div 2 = 15\ 1/2$
Lines in top margin $=$ 15
Page begins: line 16 $=$ 16

4. Insert 16 hard returns (10 if 1" default TM).

2" or centered vertically

| State | State Capital | State Nickname(s) |
|---|---|---|
| | SELECTED STATE CAPITALS | |
| Arizona | Phoenix | Grand Canyon State |
| California | Sacramento | Golden State |
| Colorado | Denver | Centennial State Silver State |
| Florida | Tallahassee | Sunshine State |
| Indiana | Indianapolis | Hoosier State |
| Michigan | Lansing | Wolverine State |
| Montana | Helena | Treasure State Mountain State |
| Tennessee | Nashville | Volunteer State |
| Utah | Salt Lake City | Beehive State |
| Virginia | Richmond | The Old Dominion Mother of Presidents Mother of States |
| Wisconsin | Madison | Badger State |
| Wyoming | Cheyenne | Equality State |

DS

Source: Fodor's USA.

## Document 2
### Invoice

Use form in stationery pack.

Prepare an invoice using the information given at the right and listed below.

Date: **May 6, ----**
Order No.: **681B**
Terms: **2/10, n/45**
Shipped Via: **Blake Shipping**
Our Order No.: **M38-71**
Date Shipped: **May 7, ----**
Sales Tax = **5%**

(Total words = 64)

## Document 3
### Purchase Order

Use form in stationery pack.

Prepare a purchase order using the information given at the right and listed below.

Order No.: **632Q5**
Date: **March 15, ----**
Terms: **2/10, n/30**
Shipped Via: **Ken's Transport**

(Total words = 55)

---

Hilltop Orchard
839 Willow Oak Rd.
Memphis, TN 38138-3711

| Quantity | Description / Stock No. | Unit Price |
|---|---|---|
| 1 | Envelopes #10 / VE-38 | 15.75 |
| 2 | Window envelopes #10 / VE-58 | 18.95 |
| 4 | Catalog envelopes 10 x 13 / VE-79 | 13.50 |
| 2 | Clasp envelopes 6 x 9 / VE-80 | 10.95 |

---

Buckner Office Supplies
7320 Kane St.
Houston, TX 77007-8376

| Quantity | Description / Stock No. | Unit Price |
|---|---|---|
| 1 | Fax machine / 390-21 | 655.95 |
| 1 | Facsimile stand / 386-18 | 199.50 |
| 6 | Facsimile paper / 316-34 | 6.29 |
| 1 | Fax message holder / 306-15 | 7.49 |

---

## LESSON 132  Facsimile (Fax)

**Objective:**
To learn to format and process facsimile (fax) forms.

### 132A • 5
### Conditioning Practice

each line twice

alphabet 1 Jamison quickly realized that the beautiful gowns were expensive.

speed 2 Jane's neighbor is apt to make a big shelf for us in the cubicle.

figures 3 Of the 1,503 English majors, 879 were males and 624 were females.

gwam 1' | 1 | 2 | 3 | 4 | 5 | 6 | 7 | 8 | 9 | 10 | 11 | 12 | 13 |

**Objectives:**

1. To improve table formatting skill.
2. To improve language skills (exclamation point, question mark).

**95A • 5**
**Conditioning Practice**

set 0.5" SMs;
each line twice

alphabet  1  Marquis Becks enjoyed expanding his vast knowledge of Arizona history.

speed  2  The neighbor burns wood and a small bit of coal to make a giant flame.

figures  3  Test scores of 94, 83, 72, 65, and 100 gave Rhonda an average of 82.8.

**gwam**  1' | 1 | 2 | 3 | 4 | 5 | 6 | 7 | 8 | 9 | 10 | 11 | 12 | 13 | 14 |

## L ANGUAGE SKILLS

**95B • 10**
**Exclamation Point;**
**Question Mark**

Follow the Learn/Apply
procedure in 76C, p. 184.

> Use an exclamation point after emphatic (forceful) exclamations and after phrases and sentences that are clearly exclamatory.

Learn  1.  The police officer yelled, "Stop that man!"
Apply  2.  The child screamed, "I want a puppy"
Apply  3.  Enthusiastically the woman stated, "I want to be your governor"

> Use a question mark at the end of a sentence that is a direct question; however, use a period after a request that appears in the form of a question.

Learn  4.  Did you use the graphics package to prepare the chart?
Learn  5.  Will you make sure the door is locked.
Apply  6.  Will you be sure to make the deposit before Friday
Apply  7.  Did you enjoy the movie

**95C • 10**
**Drill:  Center Lines**

1. Review horizontal and vertical centering procedures on p. 232.
2. Center text vertically and each line horizontally.

| | words |
|---|---|
| TAKE ME BACK TO GETTYSBURG | 5 |
| Featuring: | 8 |
| Michaela Reynolds | 11 |
| Sebastian Fennimore | 15 |
| Clayton Mazzone | 18 |
| Trenton Hendricks | 22 |
| Victoria Green | 25 |
| February 15, ---- | 29 |
| 7:30 p.m. | 31 |
| McKinley Performing Arts Center | 37 |

# LESSON 131

## Purchase Orders and Invoices

**Objective:**
To increase proficiency at formatting purchase orders and invoices.

### 131A • 5
**Conditioning Practice**

each line twice

| | | |
|---|---|---|
| alphabet | 1 | Plans for the next management job will be finalized very quickly. |
| speed | 2 | A visit by the naughty girls may be a problem for their neighbor. |
| fig/sym | 3 | The desk (#539A28) and chair (#61B34) usually sell for over $700. |

gwam 1' | 1 | 2 | 3 | 4 | 5 | 6 | 7 | 8 | 9 | 10 | 11 | 12 | 13 |

### S KILL BUILDING

### 131B • 10
**Statistical Copy Skill**

Key two 3' writings; determine errors and *gwam*.

**A** all letters used

gwam 3'

|  |  |
|---|---|
| The sales report for the quarter ending September 30 | 4 \| 39 |
| indicated that sales for Easy-Korec Blue Correctable Film ribbon | 8 \| 43 |
| (Stock #B193) were down by 40% while sales of all other ribbons | 12 \| 48 |
| were up by an average of 15%. To boost sales of B193 ribbons, the | 17 \| 52 |
| selling price will be reduced during the next quarter from $7.50 | 21 \| 56 |
| to $4.49 per ribbon (a 40% discount). Also, a four-color display | 25 \| 61 |
| board emphasizing that the B193 ribbon can be used as a replace- | 30 \| 65 |
| ment ribbon for TJK-133 and XRT-159 will be available to all | 34 \| 69 |
| salespersons in the region. | 35 \| 71 |

gwam 3' | 1 | 2 | 3 | 4 |

### F ORMATTING

### 131C • 35
**Forms**

**Document 1**
**Purchase Order**
Use form in stationery pack. Prepare a purchase order using the information given at the right.

CHARLESTON JEWELERS
7645 COLUMBIA ST
SEATTLE WA 98104-4289

| | | |
|---|---|---|
| PO No.: | 89D39-3 | 2 |
| Date: | April 30, ---- | 9 |
| Terms: | 2/10, n/30 | 14 |
| Shipped Via: | Vista Freight | 22 |

| Quantity | Description/Stock No. | Price | Total | |
|---|---|---|---|---|
| 5 | Anniversary bands (ea) | 450.00 | 2,250.00 | 29 |
| 4 | Tanzanite ring (ea) | 350.99 | 1,403.96 | 35 |
| 10 | Diamond earrings (ea) | 299.50 | 2,995.00 | 42 |
| 3 | Diamond baguette ring (ea) | 1,499.00 | 4,497.00 | 51 |
| 8 | 14K gold earrings (ea) | 44.95 | 359.60 | 58 |
| | | | 11,505.56 | 59 |

# FORMATTING

## 95D • 25
## Two-Column Tables

Review table format guides on pp. 157 and 232. Format the tables given at the right; block column headings; DS all lines.

### Table 1
**Table with Main and Column Headings**
**CS:** 1.5"

### Table 2
**Table with Main and Column Headings and Source Note**
**CS:** 2"

### Table 3
**Table with Main, Secondary, and Column Headings with Total Line**
**CS:** 1.5"

**LEARNING cue:**
To indicate a total, underline the last entry the same width as the total amount; DS; key **Total** indented five spaces from the left margin; tab over and key total amount.

### Table 4
**Update Table**

Update Table 2 to include World Series Champions since 1995. (Cite the current edition of *World Almanac* or *Information Please Sports Almanac*.)

---

INSTRUCTOR ROOM ASSIGNMENTS · 6

| Instructor | Room | |
|------------|------|---|
| | | 9 |
| Jarrad Ito | 4005 | 12 |
| Blake Claerwater | 4010 | 16 |
| Lydia Johnson | 4028 | 20 |
| Megan Kearney | 4007 | 24 |
| Kelsey Kemmerer | 4016 | 28 |
| Michelle Estes | 4013 | 32 |

---

1985-1995 WORLD SERIES CHAMPIONS · 7

| Team | Year | DS | |
|------|------|----|---|
| | | | 9 |
| Kansas City (AL) | 1985 | | 13 |
| New York (NL) | 1986 | | 17 |
| Minnesota (AL) | 1987 | | 21 |
| Los Angeles (NL) | 1988 | | 25 |
| Oakland (AL) | 1989 | | 29 |
| Cincinnati (NL) | 1990 | | 33 |
| Minnesota (AL) | 1991 | | 37 |
| Toronto (AL) | 1992 | | 41 |
| Toronto (AL) | 1993 | | 44 |
| No World Series | 1994 | | 48 |
| Atlanta (NL) | 1995 | | 52 |

DS · 55

Source: *World Almanac*, 1996. · 63

---

UNITED WAY — DS · 2
(May Donations) · 5

| Company | Amount | |
|---------|--------|---|
| | | 9 |
| West Side Auto | $ 2,000 | 13 |
| The Bridal Shoppe | 1,500 | 18 |
| O'Toole Manufacturing | 1,200 | 23 |
| The Flooring Experts | 1,000 | 29 |
| Hallie Chiropractic Center | 1,000 | 35 |
| Five Star Computing | 800 | 40 |
| Kerr School of Dance | 500 | 45 |
| Swan Enterprises | 500 | 50 |
| Total | $ 8,500 | 53 |

## 130C • 30
## Forms

Review the format guides for processing business forms on p. 313.

**Document 1**
**Purchase Order**

Use forms in stationery pack. Key purchase order as shown at right.

**Novak Jewelers**

310 Templeton Dr.
Scranton, PA 18519-8201    (717) 172-8622

**Purchase Order**

┌
BEACON HILL OFFICE SUPPLIES
419 BEACON ST
BOSTON MA 02115-8321
┘

| | |
|---|---|
| **PO No.:** | B386-95 | 7 |
| **Date:** | February 21, ---- | 13 |
| **Terms:** | 2/20, n/45 | 20 |
| **Shipped Via:** | Penn Freight | 23 |

| Quantity | Description/Stock Number | Price | | Total | | |
|---|---|---|---|---|---|---|
| 1 | Desktop printer stand/DPS68-495 (ea) | 34 | 95 | 34 | 95 | 32 |
| 2 | CPU stands/CPUS23-129 (ea) | 14 | 95 | 29 | 90 | 39 |
| 4 | Printer ribbons/PR82-67 (ea) | 9 | 95 | 39 | 80 | 47 |
| 5 | Two-line speakerphone/TLS43-212 (ea) | 115 | 95 | 579 | 75 | 57 |
| 2 | Business card files/BCF20-769 (ea) | 19 | 95 | 39 | 90 | 66 |
| | | | | 724 | 30 | 67 |

By _____

**Document 2**
**Invoice**

Use form in stationery pack. Key invoice as shown at right.

**Isham's Conference Supplies**
510 Devonshire Rd.
Orlando, FL 32832-8756
(407) 128-9808

**Invoice**

┌
HPJ COMMUNICATION SPECIALISTS
526 NEBRASKA ST
ORLANDO FL 32803-8721
┘

| | |
|---|---|
| **Date:** | February 6, ---- | 9 |
| **Customer** | | 13 |
| **Order No.:** | 15 P 398 | 21 |

| Terms | Shipped Via | Our Order No. | Date Shipped | |
|---|---|---|---|---|
| 2/10, n/30 | Swartz Transit | Q 230-99 | 2/07/-- | 29 |

| Quantity | Description/Stock Number | Price | | Total | | |
|---|---|---|---|---|---|---|
| 1 | Transparency film/TF39-06 | 42 | 50 | 42 | 50 | 38 |
| 2 | Mounting frames/MF27-10 | 35 | 65 | 71 | 30 | 46 |
| 2 | Easels/EA89-03 | 249 | 00 | 498 | 00 | 52 |
| 1 | Lectern/LN12-19 | 138 | 50 | 138 | 50 | 59 |
| 2 | Projection screens/PS45-50 | 198 | 00 | 396 | 00 | 68 |
| | | | | 1,146 | 30 | 70 |
| | Sales tax | | | 57 | 32 | 73 |
| | | | | 1,203 | 62 | 75 |

By _____

# LESSON 96 — Two-Column Tables

**Objectives:**
1. To learn to center column headings.
2. To improve table formatting skill.

## 96A • 5
### Conditioning Practice

each line twice; then 1'
writings on line 2

| | | |
|---|---|---|
| alphabet | 1 | Major Kowalzak thought you purchased five or six antique baskets. |
| speed | 2 | The six girls in the sorority dorm pay for the bus to go to town. |
| figures | 3 | The groups were assigned Rooms 639 and 708 for the 12:45 meeting. |

gwam 1' | 1 | 2 | 3 | 4 | 5 | 6 | 7 | 8 | 9 | 10 | 11 | 12 | 13 |

## LANGUAGE SKILLS

## 96B • 10
### Apostrophe

Follow the Learn/Apply
procedure in 76C, p. 184.

> Use an apostrophe as a symbol to represent feet in billings or tabulations or as a symbol for minutes. (Quotation marks may be used to signify inches or seconds.)

| | | |
|---|---|---|
| Learn | 1. | He purchased twenty 2" x 4" x 8' studs for the new deck. |
| Learn | 2. | The relay team ran the mile in 4' 38". |
| Apply | 3. | The room measured 15 ft. 6 in. x 20 ft. |
| Apply | 4. | The trial run took 10 min. 56 sec. |

> Use an apostrophe as a symbol to indicate the omission of letters or figures (as in contractions).

| | | |
|---|---|---|
| Learn | 5. | Didn't you enjoy attending the "Spirit of '76" convention? |
| Apply | 6. | She wouldnt agree to the terms; he didnt understand why. |
| Apply | 7. | They planned a reunion for the classes of 65, 75, and 85. |

## 96C • 35
### Table Formatting

**Table 1**
**Centered Column Headings**
**CS:** 1.5"; DS table

**WP note:**
Save for later use (TAB96C1).

**LEARNING cues:**
To center column headings shorter than column entries, follow these steps:
1. Determine placement of columns in usual way.
2. From column starting point, space forward once for each two strokes in longest entry. From this point, backspace once for each 2 strokes in column heading.
3. Key and underline column heading.

words

| | | |
|---|---|---|
| CIVIL WAR BOOK LIST | | 4 |
| *Title* | *Author* | 7 |
| The Blue and the Gray | Claudius M. Capps | 15 |
| Four Brothers in Blue | Robert G. Carter | 22 |
| The Price of Freedom | Calvin Coolidge | 30 |
| A Civil War Drama | Herbert P. Kakuske | 37 |
| Voices of the Civil War | Richard Wheeler | 45 |
| The Life of Johnny Reb | Bell Irvin Willey | 53 |
| The Confederate Soldier | LeGrand J. Wilson | 62 |

**Objectives:**
1. To learn to format and process purchase orders and invoices.
2. To increase straight-copy keying skill.

---

**130A • 5**
**Conditioning Practice**

set 0.5" margins; each line twice; 1' writing on speed line

| | | |
|---|---|---|
| alphabet | 1 | Jacobson believed that he might maximize profits with quality workers. |
| speed | 2 | Their men are in good shape to box with vigor to the end of the fight. |
| figures | 3 | The total attendance for 1996 was 87,253, about a 40 percent increase. |

gwam 1' | 1 | 2 | 3 | 4 | 5 | 6 | 7 | 8 | 9 | 10 | 11 | 12 | 13 | 14 |

---

## S KILL BUILDING

**130B • 15**
**Timed Writings**

1. A 1' writing on ¶ 1; find *gwam*.
2. Add 4-8 *gwam* to the rate attained in Step 1.
3. Take two 1' guided writings on ¶ 1, trying to achieve the goal set in Step 2.
4. Practice ¶ 2 in the same way.
5. One 3' writing on ¶s 1-2 combined; find *gwam* and determine errors.

all letters used

gwam 3' 5'

Records are extremely vital for a business enterprise to maintain.  They give executives insight into the day-to-day dealings of a firm.  They also are often the sole basis for executives to make major decisions on the future direction of a firm.  Many different types of documents are used to record data about a firm.  Three such documents that are vital to the operation of a firm are the purchase requisition, the purchase order, and the invoice.

A purchase requisition is a document utilized by a firm to request the purchasing agent to order goods or services.  A purchase order is a document used by the purchasing department of one firm to order goods or services from another firm.  An invoice is a document used by one firm to bill another firm for goods or services purchased from the firm that sends the invoice. All three documents will become a record of the firm's purchasing transactions.

| 3' | | 4 | 2 | 39 |
| | | 8 | 5 | 41 |
| | | 12 | 7 | 43 |
| | | 16 | 10 | 46 |
| | | 20 | 12 | 48 |
| | | 24 | 15 | 51 |
| | | 28 | 17 | 53 |
| | | 30 | 18 | 54 |
| | | 34 | 20 | 57 |
| | | 38 | 23 | 59 |
| | | 42 | 25 | 62 |
| | | 46 | 28 | 64 |
| | | 51 | 30 | 67 |
| | | 55 | 33 | 69 |
| | | 59 | 36 | 72 |
| | | 60 | 36 | 72 |

gwam 3' | 1 | 2 | 3 | 4 |
5' | 1 | 2 | 3 |

**Table 2**
Centered Column Headings
and Source Note
**CS:** 1"; DS table

**Table 3**
Centered Column Headings
Update Table 1. Add the
following entries (alphabetically by author's last name)
to the table:

**All for the Union**
    Robert H. Rhodes
**The Battle of Gettysburg**
    Frank A. Haskell
**Lee, Grant, and Sherman**
    Alfred H. Burne

| | | words |
|---|---|---|
| CIVIL WAR | | 2 |
| Eastern Theater Campaigns | | 7 |
| *Campaign* | *Dates* | 11 |
| First Bull Run (Manassas) | July 1861 | 18 |
| Peninsular Campaign | April-July 1862 | 25 |
| Jackson's Valley Campaign | March-June 1862 | 33 |
| Second Bull Run (Manassas) | July-September 1862 | 43 |
| Antietam (Sharpsburg) Campaign | September 1862 | 52 |
| Fredericksburg Campaign | October-December 1862 | 61 |
| Chancellorsville Campaign | April-May 1863 | 69 |
| Gettysburg Campaign | June-July 1863 | 76 |
| Wilderness Campaign | May 1864 | 82 |
| Spotsylvania Campaign | May 1864 | 88 |
| Petersburg Campaign | May 1864-April 1865 | 96 |
| Grant's Pursuit of Lee | April 3 and 9, 1865 | 105 |
| Sherman's March to the Sea | November-December 1864 | 115 |
| Sherman's Pursuit of Johnston | December 1864-April 1865 | 128 |
| | | 131 |
| Source: Collier's Encyclopedia, 1991. | | 139 |

---

# LESSON 97

## Three-Column Tables

**Objectives:**
1. To learn to format three-column tables.
2. To improve language skills (apostrophe).

**97A • 5**
**Conditioning Practice**

each line twice

alphabet 1 Gary was quite amazed by the next photo of the Jacksonville team.
speed 2 He bid on the field by the lake as the right land for the chapel.
figures 3 Pages 389, 462, and 570 were revised prior to the May 1 deadline.

gwam 1' | 1 | 2 | 3 | 4 | 5 | 6 | 7 | 8 | 9 | 10 | 11 | 12 | 13 |

# Process Business Forms

**Format Guides:
Purchase Order, Invoice,
and Special Forms**

Fax

Purchase Order

## FAX (Facsimile)

Facsimile (fax) refers to the process of transmitting an exact reproduction of information (printed messages, handwritten messages, signatures, forms, and various types of graphics, etc.) over telephone lines. Sending messages made up of electronic impulses is known as **telecommunication**, and fax has become a very common means of telecommunication.

Most fax messages involve a transmittal sheet, or cover sheet, that identifies both the sender and the receiver of the fax. If letterhead is used that contains the company name, address, telephone number, and fax number, the facsimile message transmittal sheet will look quite similar to a standard memorandum. The fax headings should be the same as those included with a standard memo (TO:, FROM:, DATE:, SUBJECT:) plus the FAX NO: and the NO. OF PAGES:. The illustration at the left shows the order of the headings. A larger font size may be used to emphasize the heading information. The message may be keyed a DS below the heading. Short messages can be keyed on a single fax transmittal page, thus reducing the cost of transmitting the document, or on pages following the transmittal sheet.

Computer users should create a file containing a template of the fax heading information that can be opened each time a fax is to be sent (see illustration). Each new fax created using the template must be saved under another filename, thus keeping the original fax template file intact while saving a copy of each fax file. Note that some software packages have templates already created that can be used for fax transmittal sheets.

## Business Forms

Purchase orders, invoices, and other similar documents are prepared on printed forms or from templates. Software with templates can

be purchased, or they can be created with the Table feature on many of today's word processing software packages. Although forms vary from company to company, well-designed forms allow the keyboard operator to follow the general guidelines listed below. The best-designed forms software is programmed so that the cursor skips to the next entry point following entry in one of the columns.

**1. Address.** Place the address (USPS style) so that it will show through the window of a window envelope.

**2. Upper right-hand area.** Information in the upper right-hand area of the invoice and purchase order should be keyed 2 spaces to the right of the colon following each printed item.

**3. Quantity column.** Numbers should be centered in the column. Use the center justification for the column or set a tab.

**4. Description column.** Items keyed in the description column should start approximately 2 spaces to the right of the vertical rule.

**5. Price and total columns.** Items in the price and total columns should be keyed so that 1 space is left before and after the vertical rules separating the columns. Right justification of the columns for dollar amounts simplifies the aligning of figures. Typewriter users can set tabs and insert spaces to align the figures in the price and total columns. The forms software automatically calculates the amounts in the total column.

**6. Spacing.** SS column entries, beginning on the first or second line below the horizontal rule under the column headings.

**7. Totals.** Underline the last figure in the total column; then, DS before keying the total amount.

**8. Tabulation.** Tabulate and key across the form rather than keying all items in one column before moving to the next column.

## 97B • 10
## Apostrophe (continued)

Follow the Learn/Apply procedure in 76C, p. 184.

Use an apostrophe plus s ('s) to form the plural of most figures, letters, and words (*6's*, *A's*, *five's*). In stock market quotations, form the plural of figures by the addition of *s* only.

Learn 1. Underline your A's and 4's. Denver Fund 99s are due in 2009.

Apply 2. You will need to reprint the memo; the ts and fs didn't print.

Apply 3. He suggested that you buy Growth Fund 99s for your portfolio.

To show possession, use an apostrophe plus *s* after (1) a singular noun and (2) a plural noun that does not end in *s*.

Learn 4. The men's department had a sale; the women's department didn't.

Apply 5. Ritas ring was found in the mens locker room.

Apply 6. The childrens play was scheduled for May 23.

## 97C • 25
## Table Formatting

**Table 1**
Centered Column Headings
**CS:** 0.7"; DS table

| | | | words |
|---|---|---|---|
| FILM SCHEDULE | | | 3 |
| Campus Theater--6:00 and 8:30 p.m. | | | 9 |
| Movie | Dates | Director | 14 |
| The Producers | April 1 | Mel Brooks | 21 |
| To Be or Not to Be | April 8 | Jim Sheridan | 29 |
| Belle Epoque | May 15 | Fernando Trueba | 36 |
| Blue | May 22 | Krzysztof Kieslowski | 43 |
| Short Cuts | May 29 | Robert Altman | 49 |
| Guelwaar | June 6-9 | Ousmane Sembene | 56 |
| The Wedding Banquet | June 13 | Ang Lee | 63 |
| Betty Blue | June 17 | Jean-Jacques Beineix | 71 |
| The Conformist | June 22 | Bernardo Bertolucci | 80 |
| Sugar Cane Alley | June 27 | Euzhan Palcy | 88 |

**Table 2**
Centered Column Headings
**CS:** 1.5"; DS table
Save as TAB97C2 for use in a later lesson.

| | | | words |
|---|---|---|---|
| NATIONAL LEAGUE CY YOUNG AWARD WINNERS | | | 8 |
| *1980 - 1990* | | | 10 |
| Year | Player | Team | 14 |
| 1980 | Steve Carlton | Phillies | 19 |
| 1981 | Fernando Valenzuela | Dodgers | 25 |
| 1982 | Steve Carlton | Phillies | 31 |
| 1983 | John Denny | Phillies | 36 |
| 1984 | Rick Sutcliffe | Cubs | 41 |
| 1985 | Dwight Gooden | Mets | 46 |
| 1986 | Mike Scott | Astros | 51 |
| 1987 | Steve Bedrosian | Phillies | 57 |
| 1988 | Orel Hershiser | Dodgers | 62 |
| 1989 | Mark Davis | Padres | 67 |
| 1990 | Doug Drabek | Pirates | 72 |

**Timed Writings**
1. Key a 1' writing on each ¶.
2. Key one 3' writing on ¶s 1-2 combined.
3. Key a 5' writing on ¶s 1-2 combined.

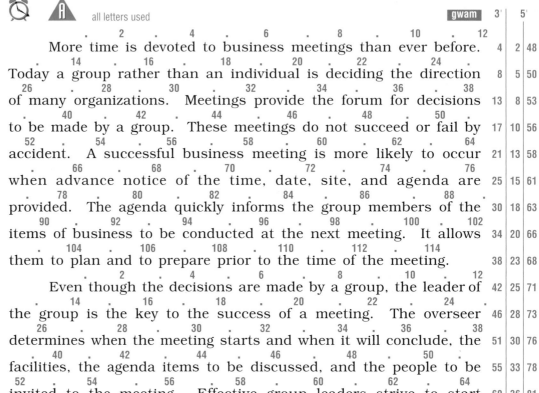

all letters used

gwam 3' | 5'

|   |   |   |   |   |   |   |   |   |   |   |   |   |
|---|---|---|---|---|---|

.   2   .   4   .   6   .   8   .   10   .   12

More time is devoted to business meetings than ever before.   4 | 2 | 48

.   14   .   16   .   18   .   20   .   22   .   24   .

Today a group rather than an individual is deciding the direction   8 | 5 | 50

26   .   28   .   30   .   32   .   34   .   36   .   38

of many organizations.  Meetings provide the forum for decisions   13 | 8 | 53

.   40   .   42   .   44   .   46   .   48   .   50

to be made by a group.  These meetings do not succeed or fail by   17 | 10 | 56

52   .   54   .   56   .   58   .   60   .   62   .   64

accident.  A successful business meeting is more likely to occur   21 | 13 | 58

.   66   .   68   .   70   .   72   .   74   .   76

when advance notice of the time, date, site, and agenda are   25 | 15 | 61

.   78   .   80   .   82   .   84   .   86   .   88   .

provided.  The agenda quickly informs the group members of the   30 | 18 | 63

90   .   92   .   94   .   96   .   98   .   100   .   102

items of business to be conducted at the next meeting.  It allows   34 | 20 | 66

.   104   .   106   .   108   .   110   .   112   .   114

them to plan and to prepare prior to the time of the meeting.   38 | 23 | 68

.   2   .   4   .   6   .   8   .   10   .   12

Even though the decisions are made by a group, the leader of   42 | 25 | 71

.   14   .   16   .   18   .   20   .   22   .   24   .

the group is the key to the success of a meeting.  The overseer   46 | 28 | 73

26   .   28   .   30   .   32   .   34   .   36   .   38

determines when the meeting starts and when it will conclude, the   51 | 30 | 76

.   40   .   42   .   44   .   46   .   48   .   50   .

facilities, the agenda items to be discussed, and the people to be   55 | 33 | 78

52   .   54   .   56   .   58   .   60   .   62   .   64

invited to the meeting.  Effective group leaders strive to start   60 | 36 | 81

.   66   .   68   .   70   .   72   .   74   .   76

and conclude meetings on time.  They provide participants with in-   64 | 38 | 84

78   .   80   .   82   .   84   .   86   .   88   .   90

formation on major agenda items prior to the meeting.  They make   68 | 41 | 86

.   92   .   94   .   96   .   98   .   100   .   102

sure that the meeting site and facilities contribute to the   72 | 43 | 89

.   104   .   106   .   108   .   110   .   112

success of a meeting rather than detract from it.   75 | 45 | 91

gwam   3'   |   1   |   2   |   3   |   4   |
         5'   |      1      |      2      |      3      |

## L ANGUAGE SKILLS

**Capitalization**
Key each sentence, supplying the needed capital letters.

1. larson music and farr greenhouse donated to the united way.
2. they will see zion national park on their trip to california.
3. the company president will make a presentation on june 2.
4. mr. cole informed me that president baker will not attend.
5. the boston tea party was connected to the american revolution.
6. the new faculty member is dr. jane shoji, a ph.d. in math.
7. the sabin art gallery will display work by maija during may.
8. dr. sekiguchi will attend a seminar in new york city.
9. the hubert h. humphrey metrodome is located in minneapolis.
10. he will be in athens on monday and in atlanta on tuesday.

**Table 3**
Centered Column Headings
CS: 1"; DS table

words

| Department | Department Manager | Phone |
|---|---|---|
| | FAIR OAKS CREDIT UNION | 5 |
| | Customer Phone Directory | 10 |
| Department | Department Manager | Phone | 15 |
| Business Loans | Sebastian Prado | 186-1058 | 23 |
| Car Loans | Forest Santori | 186-4322 | 30 |
| Community Service | Carol Mijatovich | 186-9465 | 39 |
| Customer Service | Julie Nottingwoode | 168-2950 | 48 |
| Financial Planning | Troy Norwood | 186-5227 | 56 |
| Home Loans | Elizabeth Kane | 186-7003 | 63 |
| Human Resources Personnel | Katelynn Kingsley | 186-4359 | 71 |
| New Accounts | Keith Chamber | 186-0095 | 79 |
| Student Loans | Craig Oakmont Neal G. Williams | 186-3839 | 86 |

**97D • 10**
**Revising Documents**

**wp users:**
Prepare letters for both customers.

**Electronics users:**
Prepare letter for Voyles only.

Open LTR82B2, or rekey Letter 2, 82B. Reformat the letter in block style with open punctuation; supply an appropriate salutation and complimentary closing.

Send the letter and the customer phone directory for Fair Oaks Credit Union to the following customers:

MS PAULINE VOYLES
382 TWO OAKS DR
ATHENS GA 30606-8283

MR TIMOTHY BELL
1974 PEACHTREE TER
ALBANY GA 31707-8833

## LESSON 98

# Tables with Multiple-Line Column Headings

**Objectives:**
1. To learn to format multiple-line column headings.
2. To improve language skills (apostrophe).

**98A • 5**
**Conditioning Practice**

each line twice

alphabet 1 Jack Blazel reported quite extensive damage done to the freeways.

speed 2 Nancy is to make an official bid for the antique enamel fishbowl.

figures 3 By 1:30 p.m. on Tuesday, May 9, 258 of the 467 juniors had voted.

gwam 1' | 1 | 2 | 3 | 4 | 5 | 6 | 7 | 8 | 9 | 10 | 11 | 12 | 13 |

## Skill Builder

### Tabulation

1. Clear tabs; set tabs 1.5", 3", and 4.5" from the left margin.
2. Key the text at the right.
3. Learn the names of the state capitals.
4. Key only the names of the states.
5. Go back and insert the names of as many of the capitals as you can below the state without looking at the text.

| | | | | words |
|---|---|---|---|---|
| Alabama | Alaska | Arizona | Arkansas | 6 |
| Montgomery | Juneau | Phoenix | Little Rock | 14 |
| California | Colorado | Connecticut | Delaware | 22 |
| Sacramento | Denver | Hartford | Dover | 29 |
| Florida | Georgia | Hawaii | Idaho | 35 |
| Tallahassee | Atlanta | Honolulu | Boise | 42 |
| Illinois | Indiana | Iowa | Kansas | 47 |
| Springfield | Indianapolis | Des Moines | Topeka | 56 |

### Timed Writings: Script

1. Take a 1' writing.
2. Add 5 *gwam* to the rate attained in Step 1.
3. Take four 1' writings, trying to achieve rate set in Step 2.

 all letters used

| | |
|---|---|
| A basic knowledge of parliamentary procedure is an excellent | 12 |
| skill to acquire. Those who possess this skill will be able to | 25 |
| put it to use in any organization they belong to that conducts | 38 |
| meetings based on parliamentary law. A meeting that is run by | 50 |
| this procedure will be conducted in a proper and very orderly | 63 |
| fashion. Just as important, the rights of each member of the | 75 |
| group are protected at all times. | 82 |

### Reading/Keying Response Patterns

each line 3 times (slowly, faster, top speed)

**Goal:** To reduce time interval between keystrokes (read ahead to anticipate stroking pattern).

**Emphasize curved, upright fingers; finger-action keystroking.**

one-hand words

1 car no cat inn fat ink ear beg verb sea lip oil tea pull see milk

2 acre pool rest link base lily seat lion vase noun dear junk barge

**Emphasize independent finger action; stationary hands.**

one-hand phrases

3 at my best│in my career│best dessert│my bad debts│my exact grades

4 only rebate│in my opinion│we deserve better│minimum grade average

**Emphasize continuity; finger-action with fingers close to keys.**

one-hand sentences

5 Ada agreed on a minimum oil target after a decrease in oil taxes.

6 In my opinion, Edward Freeberg agreed on a greater water reserve.

| gwam | 1' | 1 | 2 | 3 | 4 | 5 | 6 | 7 | 8 | 9 | 10 | 11 | 12 | 13 | |

## 98B • 10
### Apostrophe (continued)

Follow the Learn/Apply procedure in 76C, p. 184.

To show possession, use an apostrophe plus *s* ('s) after a proper name of one syllable that ends in *s*.

Learn    1. Tim Jones's next art print will be released in July.

Apply    2. Jennifer Glass car is for sale.

Apply    3. Mary Parks grades were excellent; Paul Sims were terrible.

To show possession, use only an apostrophe after (1) plural nouns ending in *s* and (2) a proper name of more than one syllable that ends in *s* or *z*.

Learn    4. The boys' coach will visit the Adams' home.

Apply    5. A new shipment of ladies coats should arrive this week.

Apply    6. Maria Santos plan for the officers meeting was great.

## 98C • 10
### Drill: Multiple-Line Column Headings

Center each of the lines in the multiple-line headings over the longest entry in its column. DS between last line of heading and first entry; DS the entries.

**CS:** 0.6"

**L E A R N I N G *cues*:**

1. When a table contains single-line column headings and column headings of two or more lines, the bottom line of the multiple-line heading is placed on the same line as the single-line heading(s).
2. Multiple-line headings are single-spaced, and the bottom line has an underline as long as the longest line in the heading.

| Name of Purchaser | Date of Purchase | Seller | Selling Price |
|---|---|---|---|
| John Williams | 10/30/96 | McKnight | $865.50 |
| Margaret Meade | 11/08/96 | Burdette | 650.00 |
| Jeremiah Stewart | 11/12/96 | Burdette | 730.50 |

## 98D • 25
### Tables with Multiple-Line Column Headings

center all headings

**Table 1**

**CS:** 0.5"; DS table

Underline longest line of heading.

|  |  |  |  | words |
|---|---|---|---|---|
| THE ART GALLERY | | | | 3 |
| June Specials | | | | 6 |
| Artist | Art Print | Regular Price | Sale Price | 9 / 15 |
| Sandager | Rocky Mountain Road | $ 1,125 | $ 950 | 24 |
| Richmond | Summer Home | 10,230 | 9,250 | 30 |
| Du Bois | City Lights | 195 | 165 | 36 |
| Gennrich | Brittany's Garden | 489 | 425 | 43 |
| Sinclair | Sunday Morning | 1,350 | 1,095 | 50 |
| Shoji | Christmas Morning | 425 | 350 | 56 |
| Chen | Coming Home | 155 | 139 | 61 |
| Lindquist | Dakota Country | 305 | 280 | 68 |
| Hohenstein | The Old Mill | 3,525 | 3,325 | 75 |
| Fisk-Fisher | Summer Outing | 365 | 349 | 82 |
| Debauche | Campers' Delight | 199 | 150 | 89 |

**Document 1**

Format and key the itinerary at the right. Refer to the model on p. 301.

**Document 2**

Prepare the agenda at the right. Use the following for the heading.

**Agenda**
**for**
**Ruth Tennyson**
**May 15, ----**

Use your decision-making skills to arrange in an attractive format.

**Document 3**

Revise Document 1 as follows:

Change the breakfast meeting with Mr. Jacobs from **April 16** to **April 17**.

Include business meeting with **Rori Votaw** on **April 17** at **4:30 p.m.** Return flight has been changed to **Flight #385** leaving at **8:15 a.m.** and arriving in Memphis at **9:57 a.m.**

**Note:** Additional R&E tables can be found on pp. A30 through A32.

| | | words |
|---|---|---|
| ITINERARY | *)Bold  }DS* | 2 |
| Jacinta A. Reinhart | | 6 |
| HPJ Communication Specialists Symposium | | 14 |
| April 15 | | 16 |
| 2:30 p.m. *.8"* | Depart Memphis on Coastal Airlines--Flight *#714* | 26 |
| | *#* for Boston (Logan International). | 35 |
| 6:19 p.m. *Col. space* | Arrive Boston. Accom*m*odations at Ellsworth | 45 |
| | Inn, 641 Taft Hill Park. | 51 |
| April 16 | | 53 |
| 7:00 a.m. | Breakfast with Harvey Jacobs at hotel. | 63 |
| 8:30 a.m. | HPJ Communication*s* Specials*i*sts Symposium, | 73 |
| | meetings until 4:30 p.m. | 78 |
| *6:30 p.m.* | *Dinner with Sue Butler at Cambridge Club.* | 89 |
| April 17 | | 91 |
| 8:30 a.m. | HPJ Communication*s* Specials*i*sts Symposium, | 101 |
| | meetings until 2:45 *p.m.* | 106 |
| 3:30 p.m. | Meeting with Justin Browning. | 115 |
| 7:30 p.m. | Performance of the *Boston* Symphony Orchestra at | 126 |
| | Symphony Hall. | 129 |
| April 18 | | 131 |
| *7:45 a.m.* | Depart Boston on Coastal Airlines--Flight *#628* | 143 |
| | *#* for Memphis. | 146 |
| *9:27 a.m.* | Arrive Memphis. | 151 |

| | | | opening | 8 |
|---|---|---|---|---|
| Meet with | Time | Location | | 13 |
| Business Communications | 8:30-9:30 | SSS 216 | | 21 |
| *Advisory Committee* | | | | 25 |
| *Dr.* Milton Sabin, Chair | 9:*3*0-10:00 | SSS 401 | | 34 |
| Dept. of Management | | | | 38 |
| Information Systems | | | | 42 |
| Dr. Marie Marichal, Chair | 10:00-10:30 | SSS 400 | | 51 |
| Dept. of Accountancy | | | | 55 |
| Dr. Joyce Sullivan, *Chair* | 10:30-1*1*:00 | SSS 404 | | 64 |
| Dept. of Finance | | | | 68 |
| Dr. Josh Kane, Chair | 11:30-12:00 | SSS 409 | | 76 |
| Depar*t*ment of Business | | | | 81 |
| Communication | | | | 83 |
| Dr. Kate McKinney--LUNCH | 12:30-1:45 | Oak Room | | 92 |
| *Dean,* School of Business | | | | 97 |
| General Meeting with School | 2:00-3:15 | SSS 119 | | 107 |
| *of Business Faculty* | | | | 110 |

| SELECTED STATE CAPITALS | | | words |
|---|---|---|---|
| | | | 5 |
| State | State Capital | State Nickname(s) | 7 |
| | | | 13 |
| California | Sacramento | Golden State | 20 |
| Wisconsin | Madison | Badger State | 26 |
| Wyoming | Cheyenne | Equality State | 33 |
| Virginia | Richmond | The Old Dominion | 40 |
| | | Mother of Presidents | 44 |
| | | Mother of States | 47 |
| Utah | Salt Lake City | Beehive State | 54 |
| Tennessee | Nashville | Volunteer State | 61 |
| Montana | Helena | Treasure State | 67 |
| | | Mountain State | 70 |
| Michigan | Lansing | Wolverine State | 77 |
| Indiana | Indianapolis | Hoosier State | 84 |
| Florida | Tallahassee | Sunshine State | 91 |
| Colorado | Denver | Centennial State | 97 |
| | | Silver State | 100 |
| Arizona | Phoenix | Grand Canyon State | 110 |
| | | | 113 |
| Source: Fodor's USA. | | | 114 |

**Table 2**

**CS:** 1"; leave 1 blank line above each state; SS text pertaining to each state; see illustration on p. 232.

**LEARNING cue:**

For states with more than one nickname, key the first nickname; return and depress the Tab twice.

**Table 3**

Rearrange Table 2 alphabetically by state. Computer users should copy the table and use the Move feature to alphabetize the states.

---

# LESSON 99

## Tables with Multiple-Line Entries

**Objective:**

To format tables with multiple-line entries.

**99A • 5**
**Conditioning Practice**

each line twice

| alphabet | 1 | Jay Beckfield took time to explain how every math quiz is graded. |
|---|---|---|
| speed | 2 | Vivian and Pam are to fix the problem with the right turn signal. |
| figures | 3 | Chapters 29 and 30, pages 187-245, will be reviewed on October 6. |

gwam 1' | 1 | 2 | 3 | 4 | 5 | 6 | 7 | 8 | 9 | 10 | 11 | 12 | 13 |

**F** ORMATTING

**99B • 35**
**Formatting Tables**

**Table 1**

**CS:** 1"; SS each evaluation item; DS between items; two spaces between column listings under Evaluator Response.

**Note:** If your equipment allows, define a macro for "My teacher."

 **note:**

You may be asked to revise this file; save it (TAB99B1).

| TEACHER EVALUATION | | | | | | words |
|---|---|---|---|---|---|---|
| | | | | | | 4 |
| | Evaluator | | | | | 6 |
| Evaluation Item | Response | | | | | 11 |
| My teacher demonstrates a clear | | | | | | 18 |
| understanding of course topics. | SA | A | U | D | SD | 27 |
| My teacher has an effective | | | | | | 33 |
| method of presentation. | SA | A | U | D | SD | 41 |
| My teacher is well prepared | | | | | | 47 |
| for class. | SA | A | U | D | SD | 52 |
| My teacher stimulates interest in | | | | | | 59 |
| course topics. | SA | A | U | D | SD | 65 |
| My teacher displays enthusiasm | | | | | | 71 |
| for course topics. | SA | A | U | D | SD | 78 |
| My teacher uses many methods | | | | | | 84 |
| to involve students in learning. | SA | A | U | D | SD | 94 |
| My teacher respects differing | | | | | | 100 |
| points of view. | SA | A | U | D | SD | 106 |

## 128C • 35
## Agendas

**Agenda 1**

Format and key the agenda at the right; refer to the model on p. 301.

|  |  | words |
|---|---|---|
| AGENDA |  | 1 |
| Software Development Board Meeting |  | 8 |
| 10:30 a.m., June 25, ---- |  | 12 |
| 1. Introductory Remarks | Noriko Shoji | 25 |
| 2. New Software Proposals | Ted Hubbard | 38 |
|     Market Analyzer | May Roberts | 49 |
|     Financial Planner | Ken Jetz | 60 |
|     Visuals Unlimited | Judy Kay | 71 |
| 3. Projection Reports |  | 76 |
|     Production Cost Projections | Brett Hill | 87 |
|     Market Projections | Jay Griffin | 98 |
|     Profit Projections | Erika Nicole | 109 |
| 4. Discussion of Proposal | Board Members | 122 |
| 5. Adjournment |  | 125 |

**Agenda 2**

Format and key the agenda at the right; DS.

**Agenda 3**

Revise Agenda 1 to include the following as Items 5 and 6 on the agenda.

**5. Summary of Discussion: Pros and Cons
. . . . Tyler Parks**

**6. Call for
Vote . . . Noriko Shoji**

Renumber item that follows. Left-align the right column.

| AGENDA |  | 1 |
|---|---|---|
| Executive Meeting |  | 5 |
| September 15, ---- |  | 9 |
| 1. Opening Comments | Kyle Lenz | 22 |
| 2. Manager's Responsibilities | Sara Lloyd | 35 |
| 3. Employee Concerns | Mark Scott | 48 |
| 4. Seminars |  | 50 |
|     Time Management | Erin Reed | 61 |
|     Quality Control | Anne Sega | 72 |
|     Project Management | Jason Graham | 83 |
|     Employee Motivation | Jan Elsner | 94 |
| 5. Committee Assignments | Greg Finley | 107 |
| 6. New Seminar Proposals | Eric Winget | 120 |
| 7. New Items for Discussion | Kyle Lenz | 133 |
| 8. Adjournment |  | 136 |

## LESSON 129

## Process Itineraries and Agenda

**Objective:**

To format itineraries and agenda.

## 129A • 5
## Conditioning Practice

each line twice

alphabet 1 Mom saw Rex quickly leave for his job when his dog won the prize.

speed 2 The map may aid them when they do work for the town and the city.

figures 3 Flight 8697 landed at 10:30 a.m. and left for Denver at 2:45 p.m.

gwam 1' | 1 | 2 | 3 | 4 | 5 | 6 | 7 | 8 | 9 | 10 | 11 | 12 | 13 |

**Table 2**

**CS:** 1"; SS events; DS between events

**Note:** This table will be used again later in this lesson.

|  | SELECTED UNITED STATES HISTORY DATES | words |
|---|---|---|
|  |  | 7 |
| Year | Event | 10 |
| 1776 | Declaration of Independence approved | 18 |
|  | July 4 | 20 |
| 1789 | George Washington chosen President by | 28 |
|  | all electors voting | 32 |
| 1804 | Lewis and Clark expedition ordered by | 41 |
|  | President Jefferson to explore what is | 49 |
|  | now northwest U.S. | 53 |
| 1836 | Texas besieged in Alamo | 58 |
| 1848 | Gold discovered in California | 65 |
| 1861 | Seven southern states set up Confederate | 75 |
|  | States of America | 78 |
| 1875 | Civil Rights Act | 83 |
| 1903 | First successful flight in heavier-than-air | 92 |
|  | mechanically propelled airplane by | 100 |
|  | Orville Wright | 103 |
| 1908 | Henry Ford introduced Model T car | 110 |
| 1915 | First telephone talk, New York to San | 119 |
|  | Francisco, by Alexander Graham Bell and | 127 |
|  | Thomas A. Watson | 130 |
| 1929 | Stock market crash | 137 |
|  | —————— | 140 |
| Source: | The World Almanac and Book of Facts, 1994. | 151 |

## 99C • 10
## Table Revision

**Table 1**

Open TAB97C2 or rekey Table 2, 97C, p. 237. Update the table to include the information at the right.

**Table 2**

Open (or rekey) Table 2 above. Insert the additional four dates of U.S. history in chronological order.

| 1991 | Tom Glavine | Braves | 5 |
|---|---|---|---|
| 1992 | Greg Maddux | Cubs | 9 |
| 1993 | Greg Maddux | Braves | 14 |
| 1994 | Greg Maddux | Braves | 19 |
| 1995 | Greg Maddux | Braves | 24 |

| 1846 | Mexican War | 3 |
|---|---|---|
| 1860 | Abraham Lincoln elected President | 11 |
| 1871 | Great fire destroyed Chicago | 18 |
| 1906 | San Francisco earthquake | 24 |

**Table 3**

SMs: 1"; center column headings; right-align the date column.

**Table 4**

Update Table 2 to reflect the company assets at the end of the current year:

| | |
|---|---|
| Cash | 183,500 |
| Accts. Rec. | 565,600 |
| Inv. | 610,000 |
| Prepaid Ex. | 10,200 |
| Land | 270,000 |
| Building | 990,000 |
| Depr. Bld. | (250,000) |
| Equip. | 320,000 |
| Depr. Equip. | (85,000) |
| Total Assets | 2,614,300 |

|  | words |
|---|---|
| VALUE-ADDED SEMINARS | 4 |
| March 15 – April 21 | 8 |
| *Seminar*                                              *Date* | 11 |
| Advanced Presentation Skills . . . . . . . . . . . . . . .  *March 15* | 23 |
| Enhancing Executive Leadership . . . . . . . . . . . .  *March 19* | 35 |
| Developing Assertiveness  *March 24* | 46 |
| Quality Control  *March 29* | 58 |
| Employee Evaluation  *April 2* | 70 |
| Stress Management  *april 5* | 81 |
| Effective Communication  *april 9* | 93 |
| Improving Customer Relations  *April 12* | 105 |
| You're the Consultant  *April 15* | 117 |
| Computer Literacy  *April 17* | 128 |
| Negotiating Effectively  *April 21* | 140 |

*(add leaders)*

---

# LESSON 128    Process Agendas

**Objectives:**

**1.** To format agendas.

**2.** To increase keying skill on straight copy.

---

**128A • 5**
**Conditioning Practice**

each line twice

alphabet  1  Jacob purchased the exquisite gift at a zoo while moving to York.

speed  2  Sit down and aid the six girls with the ornaments for the social.

figures  3  The rate on February 29 was 10.57 percent; it was 8.46 on May 30.

gwam  1' | 1 | 2 | 3 | 4 | 5 | 6 | 7 | 8 | 9 | 10 | 11 | 12 | 13 |

---

**S KILL BUILDING**

**128B • 10**
**Guided Writing: Speed**

1. Two 1' writings; find *gwam*.
2. Add 4 words to better rate; determine 1/4' goals.
3. Two 15" writings; try to equal or exceed 1/4' goals.
4. Two 30" writings; try to equal or exceed 1/2' goal.
5. Two 1' guided writings at goal rate.

gwam  30"

Recognize that the primary element of high-speed keyboarding    24

is to try to type or keyboard with good form and refined technique    51

patterns.  In each of the lessons of this unit, your goal should    77

be to fix your mind on the principal keyboarding elements:    101

finger-action keystroking, quick spacing after every word, and a    127

fast return with a very quick start of the new line.    148

gwam  1' | 1 | 2 | 3 | 4 | 5 | 6 | 7 | 8 | 9 | 10 | 11 | 12 | 13 |

# Applied Table Formatting

**Objective:**
To use decision-making skills to organize, format, and key tables from unarranged copy.

## 100A • 5
### Conditioning Practice

set 0.5" SMs;
each line twice

alphabet 1 This bright jacket has an amazing weave and is of exceptional quality.

speed 2 When he kept the dog, it slept on the big chair in a hall of the dorm.

figures 3 The last two home games of this year drew crowds of 43,916 and 52,087.

gwam 1' | 1 | 2 | 3 | 4 | 5 | 6 | 7 | 8 | 9 | 10 | 11 | 12 | 13 | 14 |

## F ORMATTING

## 100B • 45
### Organize Information into Tables

Organize, format, and key three tables from the information given at the right. Use your decision-making skills to arrange in an attractive and meaningful format.

### Table 1

In 1994 the National League was reorganized into three divisions (East, Central, and West). From the information below, prepare one table illustrating the three-division alignment.

| | |
|---|---|
| Atlanta--East | Montreal--East |
| Chicago--Central | New York--East |
| Cincinnati--Central | Philadelphia--East |
| Colorado--West | Pittsburgh--Central |
| Florida--East | St. Louis--Central |
| Houston--Central | San Diego--West |
| Los Angeles--West | San Francisco--West |

### Table 2

Use the following information to prepare an interview schedule for Friday, June 27.

Raul Martinez will interview with Mr. Jackson at 8 a.m. Ms. Jasper will interview Kent Johnson at 2 p.m. Mr. Jackson will interview Marsha Sedgewick at 10 a.m. Clint Peterson will interview with Mr. Jackson at 1 p.m. Ms. Jasper will interview Anne Wilkins at 10 a.m. and Ted Thompson at 11 a.m.

### Table 3

Use the following information to prepare a table. The heading for the table is **YOUR STATE'S INN**. Use **Fall, Winter, and Spring Rate Schedule** for the secondary heading. Organize the material in a way that best shows the costs for the various suites during the three seasons.

| Alaska Suite | Florida Suite | Hawaii Suite |
|---|---|---|
| Fall ($39) | Fall ($59) | Fall ($115.50) |
| Winter ($63) | Winter ($83) | Winter ($145.50) |
| Spring ($45) | Spring ($65) | Spring ($135.50) |
| | | |
| Colorado Suite | Texas Suite | California Suite |
| Fall ($49) | Fall ($69) | Fall ($89) |
| Winter ($73) | Winter ($93) | Winter ($113) |
| Spring ($55) | Spring ($75) | Spring ($95) |

**Note:** Additional R & E tables can be found on pp. A23 and A24.

## 127B • 45
## Process Tables

**Table 1**
CS: 0.7"
Center column heads;
replace ---- with current year.

**Table 2**
SM: 1"
Review format guides on
p. 301 and wp guides on
p. 300.  Replace ---- with
last year.

[wp] **note:**

Space once at the end of all
amounts not in parentheses
in order to align with the
amounts in parentheses.

words

| | | | | |
|---|---|---|---|---|
| ADVISER ASSIGNMENTS | | | | 4 |
| Spring ---- | | | | 6 |
| Student | GPA | Major | Adviser | 12 |
| Kruger, June | 3.67 | Management | Glavine | 20 |
| Burton, Kelly | 2.71 | *Marketing* | Brown | 27 |
| Hemls, Jason | 3.34 | Management | Glavine | 34 |
| Marshall, Kay | 3.41 | Finance | *Shoji* | 41 |
| Nicolet, Mary | 2.98 | Marketing | Brown | 48 |
| Gomez, Felipe | 3.12 | Management | Glavine | 56 |
| Downey, Aaron | 2.89 | Finance | *Shoji* | 62 |
| Berntsen, Wade | 3.51 | Finance | *Shoji* | 69 |
| Mayberry, Anne | 3.87 | Management | Glavine | 77 |
| Segawa, Hiroki | 3.25 | Marketing | Brown | 84 |
| Nagel, Jessica | 3.05 | Management | Glavine | 92 |
| Manzo, Matrice | 3.29 | Finance | *Shoji* | 98 |

| | | |
|---|---|---|
| ASSETS | | 1 |
| December 31, ---- | | 5 |
| Cash . . . . . . . . . . . . . . . . . . . . | *$167,300* | 17 |
| Accounts Receivable . . . . . . . . . . . . | *521,500* | 29 |
| Inventory . . . . . . . . . . . . . . . | *620,000* | 40 |
| Prepaid Expense . . . . . . . . . . . . | *10,700* | 52 |
| Land . . . . . . . . . . . . . . . . . | *250,000* | 63 |
| Building . . . . . . . . . . . . . . . | *950,000* | 75 |
| Accumulated Depreciation, Building . . . . . . . . | *(200,000)* | 87 |
| Equipment . . . . . . . . . . . . . . . | *320,000* | 99 |
| Accumulated Depreciation, Equipment . . . . . . . . | *(85,000)* | 111 |
| Total Assets | *$2,554,500* | 115 |

# Language & Writing Skills 11

## Activity 1:

1. Study the spelling/ definitions of the words in the color block at the right.
2. Key the **Learn** line in the first set of sentences.
3. Key the **Apply** lines, choosing the right words to complete each sentence correctly.
4. Key the second set of lines in the same way.
5. Check work; rekey lines containing word-choice errors.

**Choose the right word**

**die** (vb) to pass from physical life
**dye** (n) a soluble or insoluble coloring

**want** (vb) need, desire; as a noun, lacking a required amount
**won't** (vb) will not

Learn 1 If they want additional supplies, won't they contact us?
Apply 2 Each (want/won't) was evaluated in terms of its actual cost.
Apply 3 If you (want/won't) be leaving tomorrow, you can see the play.

Learn 4 She will die when she sees the color of dye they plan to use.
Apply 5 How much (die/dye) do you estimate will be required?
Apply 6 I want to visit Africa and South America before I (die/dye).

## Activity 2:

As you key the sentences shown at the right, insert semicolons, commas, exclamation points, question marks, apostrophes, and periods needed to complete each sentence correctly. Then check your work and rekey any sentence that contains a punctuation error.

**Proofread & correct**   Punctuation (semicolon/exclamation point/question mark/apostrophe)

1 You may not like ballet nevertheless you will go with us.
2 Mala will sing operatic arias the orchestra will accompany her.
3 She uses quick, snappy keystrokes good spacing quick returns.
4 Miss Appel said, "Insert the disk" then she showed us how.
5 "Stop," he yelled, "or you will break the window "
6 Do you know when new student government officers are elected
7 Will you please send me a copy of the report you mentioned
8 "Where," I asked,  "did the deadly accident occur "
9 The new room is 16 ft. wide by 24 long and seats 20 students.
10 Doesnt she realize that daily practice is vital to success?
11 Our teacher told us to dot our is and cross our ts.
12 We keyed three 1 min. and two 3 min. writings on the paragraphs.
13 Do you know if this is Dans book, or is it Marshas?
14 What was similar about the "Gay 90s" and the "Roaring 20s"?
15 The audience is small however "the show must go on."
16 "Ready; Aim; Fire " was the order he gave the new recruits.
17 "Its maddening," he said,  "when instructions arent included."
18 Rainstorms were predicted therefore, our picnic was cancelled.
19 However you divide the work, youre to finish the job today.
20 Will you please be in the auditorium by 3:15 for rehearsal

## Table 2
Center column headings; replace ---- with the current year.

WP note:
Right-align amount columns; left-align words.

## Table 3
Arrange Table 2 alphabetically by country.

## Table 4
Arrange Table 2 numerically by price in descending order.

|  |  |  | words |
|---|---|---|---|
| DOLLS FROM AROUND THE WORLD ~DS | | | 6 |
| ---- Holiday Prices | | | 10 |

| Doll | Country | Price | Product Code | words |
|---|---|---|---|---|
|  |  |  |  | 11 / 17 |
| Elena | Russia | $ 78.99 | RU107 | 22 |
| Mitsutoshi | Japan | 95.90 | JN1053 | 28 |
| Cayenana | Spain | 109.99 | SP235 | 34 |
| Jennifer | United (States) | 89.99 | US398 | 41 |
| Katerina | Germany | 9,89.99 | GY120 | 47 |
| Dianna | England | 84.99 | EN457 | 52 |
| Francois | France | 85.99 | FR981 | 58 |
| Maria | Mexico | 79.99 | MX819 | 63 |
| Maija | Finland | 89.99 | FN675 | 68 |
| Ambika | (I"CS) India | (I"CS) 88.99 | (0.5"CS) IN382 | 73 |

## S KILL BUILDING

### 126C • 12
### Guided Writing: Control

1. Two 1' writings; find *gwam*; determine errors.
2. Deduct 4 words from better rate; determine 1/4' goals.
3. Two 15" writings; try to reach goal with no errors.
4. Two 30" writings; try to reach goal with no errors.
5. Two 1' guided writings at goal rate. **Goal:** each writing with no more than 2 errors.

**A** all letters used  **gwam** 30"

```
              2          4          6          8          10
Every time you operate the keyboard, make the use of good        23
12        14        16        18        20        22        24
techniques your goal.  This is the way to build your keyboarding   49
   26        28        30        32        34        36
efficiency to its highest possible level.  Keyboarding efficiency  76
38     40        42        44        46        48        50
is needed if you are to remain competitive in the world of work,   102
   52        54        56        58        60        62
and if you are to use the sophisticated equipment now in use in    127
64     66        68        70        72        74
the technological society in which we live and work.               148
```

gwam 1' | 1 | 2 | 3 | 4 | 5 | 6 | 7 | 8 | 9 | 10 | 11 | 12 | 13 |

## LESSON 127

## Process Tables

**Objectives:**
1. To enhance table formatting skill.
2. To format and key tables with leaders.

### 127A • 5
### Conditioning Practice

each line twice

alphabet 1 The expert, Judge Vincet, was amazed by the fine quality of work.

speed 2 The man with the problems may wish to see the proficient tax man.

figures 3 Dave delivered pizza to 3710 Devney, 2469 Oxford, and 580 Hudson.

gwam 1' | 1 | 2 | 3 | 4 | 5 | 6 | 7 | 8 | 9 | 10 | 11 | 12 | 13 |

# 𝒜ctivity 3:

1. Read carefully the ¶s given at the right.
2. From your circle of friends and acquaintances, identify the one person you truly believe is your "best" friend, another one or two you consider to be "good" friends, and others you consider casual friends or merely acquaintances.
3. Compose/key three separate ¶s. In ¶ 1, identify and describe your "best" friend and why you consider her/ him to be a "true" friend. In ¶ 2, identify your "good" friends and describe why you consider them so. In ¶ 3, identify one or two casual friends or acquaintances and describe how your relationship(s) differ from those described in ¶s 1 and 2.

**Compose (think) as you key**

Most of you have tossed a pebble into a pool of water and watched the ever-larger concentric circles radiate out from the point at which the pebble entered the water. The relationships we have with others are similar—concentric circles radiating out from each of us. People in the inner circles are our closest friends—pals, buddies, chums, and so on. As we move outward to larger circles, we find our casual friends or acquaintances.

\*\*\*

Those who study social relationships at various levels have indicated that one is lucky to have two or three really true friends in a lifetime. Yet, we often hear people, especially young people, introducing different acquaintances at different times as "my best friend." "Best" is the superlative in the triad good/better/best. By definition, the superlative means "you can't get any better than that."

\*\*\*

Ralph Waldo Emerson said, "A true friend is somebody who can make us do what we can" and "The only way to have a friend is to be one." The first quote suggests that a true friend makes us live up to our potential; the second, a true friend requires us to be one. Friendships, therefore, require us to be personally involved with others, to be interested in their well-being, in their unique identities, and in their perceptions of the world.

\*\*\*

The following quote, attributed to Albert Camus, perhaps best describes the mutual acceptance and closeness that characterize real or "true" friendship:

Don't walk in front of me
I may not follow
Don't walk behind me
I may not lead
Walk beside me
And just be my friend.

## OFFICE TECHNOLOGY TERMS

For Week of February 15-20

| | |
|---|---|
| **Artificial Intelligence** | the capability of the computer to perform functions normally associated with human intelligence, such as reasoning and learning; the programming of machines so that they mimic the reasoning and learning behavior of human beings |
| **Backup** | a copy of a file or disk that can be used in case the original is damaged or lost |
| **Communication-Based Services** | services including electronic mail, computerized bulletin boards, and on-line conferences |
| **Computer Virus** | self-replicating blocks of code that enter a computer via disk, telephone lines, or manually, spreading infection within the system |
| **Desktop Publishing** | designing and producing a publication using a personal computer; software programs to create newsletters, manuals, forms, proposals, and flyers |
| **Electronic Mail (e-mail)** | electronic data communication; the non-interactive communication of text, data, voice, and image messages between a sender and recipient using system links |
| **Hard Disk** | a rigid disk that has its own case or fits into the computer; can hold several million bytes of information; a storage device mounted in its own case or permanently mounted inside a computer |
| **Random Access Memory (RAM)** | temporary computer memory that erases when the power is turned off |
| **Read-Only Memory (ROM)** | type of computer memory that contains permanently stored manufacturer's instructions to start the system and read the disk operating system (DOS) instructions |

Source:  Susan Jaderstrom and Leonard B. Kruk,  Administrative Support Systems and Procedures, Cincinnati:  South-Western Publishing Co., 1992, pp. 331-336.

**Complex Table**

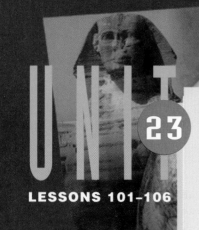

# Cambridge Travel Networks (A School-to-Work Simulation)

## Work Assignment

You have been hired by Cambridge Travel Networks to work part-time for the administrative assistant, Karin McKinley, and the receptionist, Helen Reynolds. Ms. McKinley processes documents for the travel agents. Ms. Reynolds greets telephone callers, visitors, and clients and schedules appointments for the travel agents. Ms. McKinley's immediate supervisor is Jason Koufax who is the manager of Cambridge Travel Networks.

You will be assisting both Ms. McKinley and Ms. Reynolds. You are responsible for mailing brochures requested by clients, displaying full-color posters from the cruise lines and airlines, restocking brochure racks with information about exotic places, proofreading brochure copy, updating the wall map that displays where Cambridge clients have traveled, keying weekly "welcome home" lists for agents to call, and keeping a file of newspaper ads of other agencies.

Your main responsibility, however, is to assist with processing documents for Mr. Koufax and the travel agents. Each document you receive will have written instructions from the originator. Use the date included on the instructions for all documents requiring a date. Mr. Koufax closes all of his letters with:

```
Sincerely,

Jason Koufax
Manager
```

Use the following closing lines for correspondence processed for the travel agents.

```
Sincerely,

Agent's Name
Travel Agent
```

If the instructions given with the document are not sufficiently detailed, use what you have been taught in your keyboarding course to make formatting decisions. Documents should be attractively formatted.

You are expected to produce error-free documents, so proofread and correct your work carefully before presenting it for approval.

## Multiple Enclosures

When more than one enclosure is listed with the enclosure notation, format it as follows:

```
Enclosures:  Tour Highlights
             Price Sheet
```

## Macros

Create macros for closing lines and other text (Cambridge Travel Networks) that you will use often.

## Document Formats

| Memos: | Standard |
|--------|----------|
| Letters: | Modified block<br>Mixed punctuation<br>Blocked paragraphs |
| Reports: | Unbound<br>Textual citations<br>References list on<br>separate sheet |

**Table 2**
CS: 1"

**Table 3**
Alphabetize Table 1 by the last name of the managers. Add the **Data Processing** Department manager to the list. **Jay East; 482 Sunset Dr.; Golden, CO 80401-7463; 180-8356**

| | | words |
|---|---|---|
| SUGGESTED ~OFFICE~ RESOURCES | | 5 |
| _Publication_ | _Publication Address_ | 12 |
| WordPerfect Magazine | Reader Service Mgt. Dept. | 22 |
| | Pittsfield, MA 01203-9858 ~P.O. Box 5021~ | 30 |
| Modern Office _Technology_ | A Penton Publication 1100 Superior Avenue | 38 |
| | Cleveland, OH 44197-8093 | 43 |
| Managing Office Technology | A Penton Publication 1100 Superior Avenue | 53 |
| | Cleveland, OH 44197-8093 | 58 |
| _The_ Secretary | 10502 N.W. Ambassador Dr. | 66 |
| | P.O. Box 20404 | 69 |
| | Kansas City, KS 64195-0404 | 74 |
| The Office | Office Publications, Inc. _MO_ | |
| | P.O. Box 1682 | 81 |
| | Riverton, NJ 08077-9682 | 84 |
| Communications News | DS > 2504 Tamiami Trail North | 89 |
| | Nokomis, FL 34275-9987 | 98 |
| MAC WORLD | Reader Service Department | 103 |
| | P.O. Box 5299 | 110 |
| | Pittsfield, MA 01203-9906 | 113 |
| | | 118 |

---

## LESSON 126  Process Tables

**Objectives:**
1. To enhance table formatting skill.
2. To increase keying skill on straight copy.

**126A • 5**
**Conditioning Practice**

each line twice

alphabet  1  Mary said the jacket Pam Fitzgerald bought was quite extravagant.
speed  2  Profit is no problem for the sorority social when it is downtown.
figures  3  Rooms 301, 427, 395, and 468 were cleaned and painted this month.

**gwam**  1' |  1  |  2  |  3  |  4  |  5  |  6  |  7  |  8  |  9  |  10  |  11  |  12  |  13  |

**F** ORMATTING

**126B • 33**
**Process Tables**

**Table 1**
Use your decision-making skills to plan an attractive format.

The table on the next page can be formatted with or without lines. If the table is keyed with lines, the Table Format function presented on pp. 299-300 may be used.

## Cambridge Travel Networks

**Objectives:**

**1.** To use your decision-making skills to process documents from rough-draft and script.

**2.** To improve your ability to read and follow directions.

---

**101-106A • 5 (daily)**
**Conditioning Practice**

each line twice

| | | |
|---|---|---|
| alphabet | 1 | Judge Worblitz quickly thanked them for giving excellent reports. |
| speed | 2 | They may go with us to the city to do the work for the big firms. |
| fig/sym | 3 | The #6534 item will cost Brady & Son $817.29 (less 10% for cash). |

**gwam** 1' | 1 | 2 | 3 | 4 | 5 | 6 | 7 | 8 | 9 | 10 | 11 | 12 | 13 |

---

**101-106B • 45 (daily)**
**Work Assignments**

**Job 1**

Cambridge Travel Networks

*Jan. 12*

From the Desk of
**Jason Koufax**

*Please format and key the attached text as a table.*

### EUROPEAN TOUR

#### 12-Day* Excursion from New York City

| Departure Date | Return Date | Tour** Price |
|---|---|---|
| May 6 | May 17 | $1,829 |
| May 30 | June 10 | 1,953 |
| June 20 | July 1 | 1,975 |
| July 12 | July 23 | 1,975 |
| August 6 | August 17 | 1,953 |
| August 30 | September 10 | 1,975 |
| September 26 | October 7 | 1,829 |
| October 22 | November 2 | 1,779 |

\* Tour includes: Austria, Belgium, England, France, Germany, Holland, and Switzerland.

\*\* Prices quoted for double occupancy; add $180 for single occupancy.

# Process Tables

**Objective:**
To improve table formatting skill.

## 125A • 5
### Conditioning Practice

set 0.5" SMs;
each line twice

alphabet  1  Viki will begin to expedite the zone office's major quarterly reports.

speed  2  The haughty man may signal with a giant emblem or with the usual sign.

fig/sym  3  Ed called (505) 157-5980 before 1:15 p.m. and 113-6742 after 4:15 p.m.

**gwam**  1'  | 1 | 2 | 3 | 4 | 5 | 6 | 7 | 8 | 9 | 10 | 11 | 12 | 13 | 14 |

## 125B • 8
### Techniques: Return and Tab

1. Set a **right** tab 3" from left edge of paper; set a **left** tab 3.5" from left edge of paper. If you cannot set a right tab on your equipment, your teacher will give you further direction.
2. Key the lines given at the right. Concentrate on correct techniques for Enter and Tab keys.
3. Take three 1' writings; try to increase amount keyed with each writing.

|  |  | words |
|---|---|---|
| Name: | *Jessica A. Burke* | 5 |
| Address: | *3890 Rockdale Dr.* | 10 |
| City: | *Columbus* | 14 |
| State: | *GA* | 17 |
| ZIP: | *31907-8328* | 20 |
| Phone: | *(706) 182-1296* | 25 |

## **F** ORMATTING

## 125C • 37
### Process Tables

**Table 1**
CS: 0.5"
DS between each complete entry.

|  |  |  |  | words |
|---|---|---|---|---|
| | DIRECTORY | | | 2 |
| | OF | | | 3 |
| | DEPARTMENT MANAGERS | *Bold* | | 7 |
| *Manager* | *Department* | *Address* | *Home Phone* | 8 / 15 |
| Gary Musto | Accounting | 310 Basswood Street | 178-9215 | 25 |
| | | Denver, CO 80221-1342 | | 29 |
| Beth Alcott | Finance | 839 Telluride Street | 198-5657 | 38 |
| | | Aurora, CO 80011-8820 | | 43 |
| Guy Richins | Marketing | *1820 Locust St.* | *194-2102* | 52 |
| | | *Denver, CO 80220-8395* | | 57 |
| Kent Peters | Personnel | 980 De Gaulle Street | 183-8931 | 66 |
| | | Aurora, CO 80018-*5621* | | 71 |
| Linda Cey | Purchasing | 7665 Orchard Court | 180-4132 | 80 |
| | | Golden, CO 80403-8338 | | 85 |
| Jan Wright | Word | 8763 Racine Street | *161-8326* | 93 |
| | Processing | Denver, CO 80239-5438 | | 99 |

## Tour Highlight Options

*Overnight*

**Day 1:** Transatlantic flight to London, England.

**Day 2:** Gala welcoming event. Tour options include: The Tower of London, Kensington's Museums, Parliament, Knightsbridge with Harrods, Westminster Abbey, St. Paul's Cathedral, Big Ben, and cruise on the River Thames.

**Day 3:** Free day to ~~start~~ exploring London. Consider visiting The British Museum, Madame Tussaud's, and/or the Tate Gallery.

**Day 4:** Depart London for the English coast. Take the North Sea crossing to Holland. Stay in Amsterdam.

**Day 5:** Spend the day in Amsterdam. Tour options include: Rembrandthuis, The Jewish Historical Museum, The Rijksmuseum Vincent Van Gogh, Our Lord in the Attic, The Home of Anne Frank, and the Canal Mansions. Depart for Brussels, the capital of Belgium.

**Day 6:** Enjoy the sights of Brussels. The Museum of Modern Art, St. Michel Cathedral, Morolles, and The Home of Erasmus are included on the tour. Depart for Bonn, *Germany.*

**Day 7:** Travel past the ruins of the bridge in Remagen where American soldiers attacked the West Wall of Hitler. Take a cruise on the Rhine. Arrive in Munich, Germany.

**Day 8:** Enjoy the morning in Munich. Tour options include: Deutsche Museum, The Alte Pinakothek, Nymphenburg Palace, and the Neuschwanstein Castle. Depart for Innsbruck, Austria. Travel the scenic mountain road by way of Lake Tegern, Achenpass, and Lake Achen.

**Day 9:** Travel to Lucerne by way of Liechtenstein. While in Lucerne spend the time on your own shopping for Swiss watches, taking a cable car up the mountain, or taking in a folklore party. Other sights to consider include the Lion Monument and the Wooden Bridge. *Depart for Geneva, Switzerland.*

**Day 10:** Morning tour options include: Jean-Gauchos Rousseau Museum, Geneva Palace, the Watch-and-Clock Museum, and Par del la Grange. Afternoon departure for Paris, France.

**Day 11:** Be prepared for a full day of sights on both banks of the Seine ~~during~~ *with* day 11 tour options.

*Options include: the Eiffel Tower, the Louvre, Arc de Triomphe, Notre Dame, Sainte Chapelle, Invalides, and the Tomb of Napoleon.*

**Day 12:** Transatlantic flight to New York City.

# LESSON 124

## Process Tables

**Objectives:**
1. To improve skill in formatting tables.
2. To learn to format column headings longer than column text.

### 124A • 5
**Conditioning Practice**

each line twice

| | | |
|---|---|---|
| alphabet | 1 | Zelda gave Wayne exact requirements for taking the Ypsilanti job. |
| speed | 2 | Pam may name an official tutor to work for the widow and six men. |
| figures | 3 | We sold 26 desks, 34 chairs, and 50 tables on September 28, 1997. |

gwam 1' | 1 | 2 | 3 | 4 | 5 | 6 | 7 | 8 | 9 | 10 | 11 | 12 | 13 |

### 124B • 7
**Center Column Headings over Columns**

**wp users:**

See Table Format function, pp. 299-300.
Electronics users see Center column headings, p. RG19.
   DS between heading and first entry; DS the entries; **CS:** 1".

| | | | words |
|---|---|---|---|
| Font Face | Appearance | Justification | 8 |
| Courier | Bold | Left | 11 |
| Roman | Italic | Right | 15 |
| Script | Shadow | Center | 19 |

### 124C • 38
**Format Tables with Long Column Headings**

**Table 1**
**CS:** 0.5"; DS entries; center column heads.

| SELECTED STATE TIME ZONES | | | |
|---|---|---|---|
| Eastern Standard | Central Standard | Mountain Standard | 16 |
| Florida | Arkansas | Arizona | 21 |
| Georgia | Iowa | Colorado | 26 |
| New York | Minnesota | New Mexico | 31 |
| Ohio | Missouri | Utah | 35 |
| Vermont | Oklahoma | Wyoming | 40 |

(SELECTED STATE TIME ZONES — 5)

**Table 2**
**CS:** 1"; DS entries; center column heads.

**Note:** Margins may need to be changed.

**Table 3**
Update Table 2 to include the following states:
**Texas, Tex., TX**
**Wisconsin, Wis., WI**
**South Carolina, S.C., SC**
**Washington, Wash., WA**
**Virginia, Va., VA**
Alphabetize by state.

| STATE POSTAL ABBREVIATIONS | | | |
|---|---|---|---|
| Name of State | Standard Abbreviation | Two-Letter Abbreviation | |
| Illinois | Ill. | IL | 21 |
| Indiana | Ind. | IN | 25 |
| Alabama | Ala. | AL | 28 |
| Kentucky | Ky. | KY | 31 |
| Alaska | Alaska | AK | 34 |
| California | Calif. | CA | 39 |
| Connecticut | Conn. | CT | 43 |
| Delaware | Del. | DE | 46 |

(STATE POSTAL ABBREVIATIONS — 5; Standard — 9; Two-Letter — 9; headings row — 18)

## Job 3

*Jan. 13*

From the Desk of
**Mary Chaplin**

*Please send the attached letter to:*

*Ms. Megan Schwartz*
*720 Thistledown Dr.*
*Rochester, NY*
*14617-1284*

*Mr. and Mrs. Jay Moore*
*8190 Royal Oak Dr.*
*Rochester, NY*
*14624-8471*

*Be sure to send the enclosures with the letter.*

## Job 4

*Jan. 14*

From the Desk of
**Jason Koufax**

*Please format the attached as a memo to the travel agents. Use REDUCED FARES as the subject line.*

---

<Date>

<Title> <First Name> <Last Name>
<Address>
<City,> <State> <ZIP>

Dear <Title> <Last Name:>

TOUR INFORMATION

Here is the information you requested about the 12-day European tour. The difference between this particular tour and the 10-day tour that you were considering is that you would visit seven countries rather than five.

Included in the information is a "Tour Highlights" sheet that gives a brief day-by-day description of the tour. Although guided tours are planned for most days of the tour, you do not have to stay with the guide on days you prefer to sightsee on your own.

As indicated on the price sheet, the dates you select for your trip can make a difference in the cost. There is about a $400 difference between the cost of the "peak" summer times and the "off season" late fall months. Generally, the cost drops another $100 if you wait until December.

After you have had an opportunity to look over the information, I would be happy to answer any questions you may have. Thank you for choosing Cambridge Travel Networks as your travel agency.

---

Several major airlines cut their 10-day advance fares by up to 45 percent for travel before May 15. The reduced fares include travel to most major U.S. markets as well as selected Mexican and Caribbean markets.

Please contact clients who have indicated an interest in being notified of special promotions to see if we can assist them with their travel plans at the reduced fares.

XX

## Format Guides

Agenda

Itinerary

In addition to the following information given to complete this unit, the Table Format Guides for Unit 22, p. 232, may be helpful. Students using the Table Format feature to process the tables in this unit should review pp. 299-300.

**Column headings.** Column headings can be centered in several ways, depending upon the equipment used and the length of headings in relation to column entries. In previous lessons, headings were centered along with column entries by using the keyline method (p. 157).

Sometimes column headings are shorter than any column entry. A table, of course, may have some headings that are shorter and others that are longer than the column entries. Specific procedures for centering headings in these cases appear on p. RG19. **Notes:** These procedures are recommended for electronics. The method is not recommended for use with a variable, or proportional, type font.

Another, less exact, method of centering column headings involves the operator's judgment. A blank line space is left above the columns as the entries are keyed. Then the operator estimates where to begin keying the heading in order to center it. **Notes:** This method is NOT recommended if equipment lacks an automatic correction feature. The method is appropriate when variable type is used.

On computer software, the Table Format feature allows column headings (as well as entries) to be centered automatically. **Note:** Directions in this unit include column space (CS) and line spacing (DS or SS) for students not using the Table Format feature of word processing software. Disregard these parts of the directions if you use Table Format.

**Agenda.** An agenda (see illustration) is an example of another business document that may use leaders (dot leader tab). A right-aligned format or left-aligned format may be used for the right column. The margins used for the agenda are: top, 2" (or centered); side, 1"; and bottom, 1". The heading of the agenda is double-spaced.

**Itinerary.** An itinerary (see illustration) is an outline of a person's travel activities for a specific period of time. The information on an itinerary is attractively formatted to provide the reader with information regarding the date, time, location, and activity of the person listed in the heading of the itinerary. The heading is DS. Margins are the same as for an agenda.

**Leaders.** Leaders, or dot leaders, are a series of periods and spaces ( . . . ) that are keyed between two items in tabular material to make reading easier. They "lead the reader's eye" from one columnar item to another. They are primarily used when the distance between certain items in two columns is so great that matching columnar items is difficult.

Leaders are made by alternating the period (.) and a space. The lines of leaders should be aligned in vertical rows.

To align leaders using an electronic, key all periods on either the odd or the even numbers on the line-of-writing scale guided by their position in the first line of leaders. Begin the first line of leaders on the second space after the first item in the column and end the leaders 2 or 3 spaces to the left of the beginning of the next column. Certain software packages require you to space after keying the entry in the first column and before keying the entry in the last column in order to achieve the desired spacing before and after leaders.

## Job 5

*Jan. 15*

From the Desk of
**Helen Reynolds**

*Please format and key the appointment schedule for Charla Holliday. Computer template filename: T101B5*

## Job 6

*Jan. 15*

From the Desk of
**Alexis Martin**

*Please send the attached letter to:*

*Mr. Scott Shaw*
*3276 Keystone Dr.*
*Rochester, NY*
*14625-8328*

---

APPOINTMENT SCHEDULE

*Charla Holliday* > Bold name
*January 19, – – – –*

| Time | Client | Destination |
|------|--------|-------------|
| 9:00 | Ms. Helen Woods | Hawaii |
| 9:30 | Mr. Nak Jun Yoo | Caribbean |
| 11:00 | Mr. and Mrs. Ken Reeves | Caribbean |
| 1:00 | Miss Jennifer Hennesy | San Francisco |
| 1:30 | Dr. Jana Phillip | Great Britain |
|  | Dr. Paul Ambro |  |
| 3:00 | Mr. Roderigo Molina | Hong Kong |
| 4:00 | Mr. and Mrs. Stuart McCann | Europe |

---

Dear Mr. Shaw:

Discussing Century Cruise options with potential first-time "cruisers" is one of the things I enjoy most about my job. I am confident that a Caribbean cruise would be an ideal anniversary gift for your wife. You can be assured that this gift would provide life-long memories. However, I must caution you. Most people can't go on just one cruise. Once they go, they want to go on another and another.

When we were discussing your plans, you wondered how you could keep the cruise a surprise if you had to have a U.S. passport. I checked to see what options may be acceptable. An original birth certificate (or certified copy) and a driver's license would meet entry requirements.

If you have additional questions regarding the information we discussed on Tuesday, please give me a call.

## ACTIVITY 4:

### Center Tables and Format Cells

1. Read the copy at right.
2. Learn how to format a cell, column, row, and table using your wp software.
3. Follow the directions at the right to revise the table named METRICA.
4. Save as METRICB.

Use the **Table** feature to center a table from side to side and top to bottom on a page.

Use the Table feature to align information in cells. Within a cell, information can be left-aligned (default), centered, or right-aligned. It can be centered vertically, too.

The Table feature permits you to set alignment for each cell or to set it once for a column, row, or even an entire table.

You also can choose the appearance of text (bold, italics, underline) for a cell, column, row, or table.

1. Cell A1 (main heading):  centered, bold.
2. Cells A2, B2, and C2 (column headings):  centered, bold.
3. Column B (the names):  centered.
4. Column C (the abbreviations):  right-aligned.
5. Table (content of all cells):  centered vertically.
6. Table (position on page):  centered.

## ACTIVITY 5:

### Dot Leader Tab

1. Read the copy at right.
2. Set a right dot leader tab at the right margin.
3. Key the text using the dot leader tab.

**Dot leader tabs** automatically place dot leaders (. . . . .) between columns of designated text. The leaders lead the eyes from the text in the first column to the text in the second column. A right dot leader tab inserts the text to the left of the tab; a left dot leader tab inserts the text to the right of the tab setting.

Hibbard . . . . . . . . . . . . . . . . . . . . . . . . . . . . . . . . . . . . . . $ 2,500

Smith . . . . . . . . . . . . . . . . . . . . . . . . . . . . . . . . . . . . . . . . 1,950

Rodriguez . . . . . . . . . . . . . . . . . . . . . . . . . . . . . . . . . . . . . 3,290

Sullivan . . . . . . . . . . . . . . . . . . . . . . . . . . . . . . . . . . . . . . . 2,725

Perez . . . . . . . . . . . . . . . . . . . . . . . . . . . . . . . . . . . . . . . . . 1,325

Stockton . . . . . . . . . . . . . . . . . . . . . . . . . . . . . . . . . . . . . . 3,250

## ACTIVITY 6:

### Apply What You Have Learned

1. Set a right dot leader tab at the right margin.
2. Key the text using the dot leader tab.
3. Set a left dot leader tab 1.5" from the right margin.
4. Key the text.
5. Notice how the names in the right column are aligned when a left dot leader tab is used versus when right a dot leader tab is used.

President . . . . . . . . . . . . . . . . . . . . . . . . . . . . . . . . . . . . . Kaiser

Vice President . . . . . . . . . . . . . . . . . . . . . . . . . . . . . . . . . Jasper

Secretary . . . . . . . . . . . . . . . . . . . . . . . . . . . . . . . . . . . . . Knipper

Treasurer . . . . . . . . . . . . . . . . . . . . . . . . . . . . . . . . . . . . . LaFleur

Reporter . . . . . . . . . . . . . . . . . . . . . . . . . . . . . . . . . . . . . Baylor

President . . . . . . . . . . . . . . . . . . . . . . . . . . . . . . . . . . . . . Kaiser

Vice President . . . . . . . . . . . . . . . . . . . . . . . . . . . . . . . . . Jasper

Secretary . . . . . . . . . . . . . . . . . . . . . . . . . . . . . . . . . . . . . Knipper

Treasurer . . . . . . . . . . . . . . . . . . . . . . . . . . . . . . . . . . . . . LaFleur

Reporter . . . . . . . . . . . . . . . . . . . . . . . . . . . . . . . . . . . . . Baylor

## Job 7

Cambridge Travel Networks

Jan. 15

From the Desk of
**Jason Koufax**

Please send deposit confirmations to the following:

Mr. and Mrs. Devon Guidry
P.O. Box 831
Brockport, NY
14420-9271

Destination: the Caribbean Islands
Balance: $3,990
Due date: March 29
Agent: Rebecca Hulett

Ms. Danielle St. John
9640 Starwood Dr.
Rochester, NY
14625-8534

Destination: the Hawaiian Islands
Balance: $4,395
Due date: April 1
Agent: Michael Ryder

## Job 8

Cambridge Travel Networks

Jan. 16

From the Desk of
**Jason Koufax**

Update the exchange rate table with the changes indicated.

---

<Date>

<Title> <First Name> <Last Name>
<Address>
<City,> <State> <ZIP>

Dear <Title> <Last Name:>

Your 20 percent deposit for your cruise to <Destination> arrived today. The balance, <Amount,> is due on <Due date.>

If you have to cancel your cruise for any reason, there will be a $50 processing fee. Additional charges, ranging from 25 to 50 percent, will be assessed by the cruise line for cancellations made within 60 days of departure. Complete information regarding cancellations is enclosed.

If you have any questions about your cruise prior to departure, call me at 716-178-8376. Thank you for allowing Cambridge Travel Networks to book your reservations.

Sincerely,


<Agent's name>
Travel Agent


xx

Enclosure

---

### FOREIGN EXCHANGE RATE

#### January 16, ----

| Country | Unit | In $100 U.S. Equivalents |
|---|---|---|
| Australia | Dollars | ~~121.54~~ 121.37 |
| France | Francs | ~~122.39~~ 121.57 |
| Germany | Marks | ~~138.03~~ 139.06 |
| Great Britain | Pounds | ~~56.90~~ 57.03 |
| Italy | lira | ~~144,579.05~~ 144,560.01 |
| Japan | Yen | ~~9,029.41~~ 9,026.38 |
| Mexico | Peso | ~~308.00~~ 307.98 |
| Spain | Pesetas | ~~11,457.60~~ 11,460.01 |
| Switzerland | francs | ~~115.24~~ 114.98 |

## ACTIVITY 1:

**Create and Fill in a Table**

1. Read the copy at right.
2. Create and fill in the table shown in Activity 2.
3. Save the table (METRIC).

Use the **Table** feature to arrange information into rows and columns without using tab settings. Tables consist of vertical columns (named A, B, C, etc.) and horizontal rows (named 1, 2, 3, etc.). The crossing of columns and rows makes little "windows" called **cells** (named A1, A2, A3, etc.). Cell names do not appear on screen.

When text is keyed into a cell, it wraps around in that cell—instead of wrapping

around to the next row. A line space is added to the cell each time the text wraps around.

To fill in cells, use the Tab key or right arrow key to move from cell to cell in a row and from row to row. (Striking Enter will simply insert a blank line space in the cell.) To move around in a filled-in table, use the arrow keys, Tab, or the mouse (click on desired cell).

## ACTIVITY 2:

**Insert and Delete Rows**

1. Learn how to insert a row in a table.
2. Open file METRIC; insert a row above Mass; another row below Time.
3. Learn how to delete a table row in your software.
4. Delete the two blank rows.

| UNITS OF METRIC MEASURE | | |
|---|---|---|
| Units | Names | Abbreviations |
| Length | meter | m |
| Mass (weight) | kilogram | kg |
| Temperature | kelvin | K |
| Time | second | s |
| Electrical current | ampere | A |
| Luminous intensity | candela | cd |
| Substance | mole | mol |

## ACTIVITY 3:

**Join Cells and Change Column Widths**

1. Read the copy at right.
2. Learn how to join cells and change column widths using your wp software.
3. Follow the directions at the right to revise the table named METRIC.
4. Save as METRICA.

Use the **Table** feature to **join** cells (merge two or more cells into one cell). This feature is useful when information in the table spans more than one column or row. The main heading, for example, spans all columns.

In a newly created table, all columns are the same width. The Table feature can be used to change the width of one or more columns.

1. Join Cells A1, B1, and C1. (Result: The main heading cell spans Columns A, B, and C.)
2. Change Column B to a width of 1.25".
3. Change Column C to a width of 1.5".

**Job 9**

*Jan. 16*

From the Desk of
**Sean Lloyd**

*Key the attached as a memo to Jason Koufax. Use SPRING-TRAINING TOUR for the subject line.*

**Job 10**

*Jan. 16*

From the Desk of
**Helen Reynolds**

*Make the following changes to Charla Holliday's appointment schedule you prepared earlier:*

*Cancel the appointment with Jennifer Hennesy.*

*Add an appointment with Mr. Jay Prye at 10:30 for Australia.*

*Add an appointment with Ms. Leslie Loomis at 2:30 for Disneyland.*

**Job 11**

*Jan. 16*

From the Desk of
**Jason Koufax**

*Format the attached as a table.*

---

I have received a number of calls in the last few days from individuals interested in a tour of spring-training camps. Even though we do not have anything planned for this year, we may want to start making plans for next year.

Plans could include attending a Met game in Clearwater, a Yankee game in Fort Lauderdale, and a Red Sox game in Fort Myers. Perhaps we could even arrange a day for tour members to attend Epcot, Universal Studios, Magic Kingdom, Disney's MGM Studios, or Sea World. We may want to consider the possibility of inviting a former Met, Yankee, or Red Sox player to lead the tour. If you think this idea is worth pursuing, let me know.

---

HOTELS ACCOMMODATIONS

Caribbean--Option 1

| Hotel | Daily Rates | Comments |
|-------|-------------|----------|
| Pavillion Hotel | $125 | Superior tourist-class hotel. |
| Grand Suites | 275 | First-class suites, newly renovated. |
| Grand Cayman Resort | 325 | First-class, all suite resort. |
| Santos House | 150 | Superior tourist-class hotel. |
| The Island Resort | 90 | Superior first-class hotel. |
| Little Rome Club | 99 | Condominium hotel. |
| Hotel Indies | 249 | First-class Mediterranean-style condominiums. |
| Ambassador Hotel | 129 | Small condominium resort. |
| The Grand Hotel | 149 | Superior first-class hotel with ocean-view rooms. |
| The Tatyana House | 350 | Condominium complex on Seven Mile Beach. |

**Reading/Keying Response Patterns**

1. Key the lines as shown.
2. Key a 1' writing on each of lines 10-12; find *gwam* on each.

letter response
1 act ill bad him car mop set oil sew lip age pop tea ink fade pink
2 fast car|rare cat|red dress|car oil|best verse|brass cat|free pop
3 After I gave my opinion, you were assessed taxes on oil reserves.

word response
4 he wish them soap turns man paid risk gowns elbow girl goal giant
5 to go|eight girls|with their|to pay|lame cow|hay field|city docks
6 Pamala is apt to yell when they cut down the iris by this chapel.

combination response
7 the see for tea go lion end kill firm pull oak milk risk race she
8 for tea|the target|may stress|and my|rich estate|for free|or pink
9 Gregg and Jimmy may get the pop and milk at the cafe on the hill.

letter 10 Reese assessed a tax rate on my few acres on West Terrace Street.
combination 11 The art firm better pay the taxes on the garages and on the land.
word 12 Dick may pay the firm for the work when they sign the audit form.

**gwam** 1' | 1 | 2 | 3 | 4 | 5 | 6 | 7 | 8 | 9 | 10 | 11 | 12 | 13 |

**Capitalization Check**

Key the sentences at the right; supply capitalization as needed.

1. the sears tower is one of chicago's tourist attractions.
2. we will visit mount rushmore on new year's day.
3. the meeting with president Seitzer will be in los angeles.
4. jefferson city, the capital, is located on the missouri river.
5. reese morton was appointed manager for the parker playhouse.
6. weber state university was founded in 1889 in ogden, utah.
7. dr. jill s. clayton received her ph.d. from new mexico state.
8. their new home is located on fillmore, near kennedy towers.
9. the next holiday will be labor day on monday, september 5.
10. gettysburg and fredericksburg were both civil war battles.

**Timed Writings: Script**

Three 1' writings for speed; determine *gwam* on each timing.

 all letters used                                    **gwam** 1'

The advantages of purchasing goods and services on credit                11
are numerous. Credit allows you to make purchases when you                24
do not have the extra funds available to pay cash. Most people            36
use credit to make sizable purchases such as a car or a house.            49
Credit also allows individuals to buy items on sale when they             62
don't have the money to do so. If they were intending to make             75
the purchase at some future time, using credit is a wise con-             87
sumer spending habit. Credit is also quite justifiable during            99
times of emergencies.                                                    103

**Job 12**

Cambridge
Travel
Networks

Jan. 16

From the Desk of
**Jason Koufax**

*Attached is a rough-draft manuscript that will be included in the next issue of our newsletter. Please key a final copy so that I can give it to our newsletter editor.*

THE CARIBBEAN ISLANDS

The Caribbean Islands are a renowned tourist ~~locations~~ attraction. Known for their white sand beaches, abundant sunshine, and panoramic ocean views, the islands are a peaceful ~~vacation~~ getaway for thousands of Caribbean tourists. Barbados, the Cayman Islands, and ~~Barbados~~ Jamaica are featured in this month's newsletter.

Barbados

If you are looking for a picturesque island consider barbados. "Powdery beaches line the waters of the calm Caribbean Sea on the west coast, while the waves of the Atlantic thunder in on the eastern shore." (Fodor's, 144, 1991)

~~Barbados offers fine~~ With elegant hotels, tours, fine restaurants, and shopping options. Barbados is one of the preferred islands in the Caribbean. Spectator sports such as cricket, horse racing, polo, and soccer are also available to tourists. If you are more interested in participant sports, try windsurfing, scuba diving, and horseback riding.

Jamaica
If you are looking for ~~fine hotels~~, long sandy beaches, historic landmarks, and a sun-drenched climate, consider Jamaica. With an average temperature ~~averages around~~ of 80 degrees, it is a vacation paradise.

As can be expected, winter (December through April) brings larger crowds and higher rates than the other seasons. The ~~best~~ finer hotels are generally located on the north side of the island. However, for the budget-conscious traveler, Jamaica offers several package deals for selected resort areas. ~~With the~~ package deals, make it ~~is~~ possible to stay at several resort areas during your visit.

Jamaica offers over two hundred miles of beaches. With a few exceptions, most of the beaches are relatively quiet and uncrowded. Some of the more popular beaches include Cornwall

**Tabulation**
1. Clear tabs.
2. Set tabs 3" and 5.5" from the left margin.
3. Key the table.
4. Take three 1' writings; try to increase the amount keyed on each writing.

**Timed Writings: Rough Draft**
1. Two 3' writings for speed; determine *gwam* on each writing.
2. One 5' writing for speed; determine *gwam*.

| | | | words |
|---|---|---|---|
| 3191 Birchwood | Salem, OR | 97303 | 6 |
| 8760 Nugget Gulch | Rapid City, SD | 57702 | 14 |
| 1917 Pine Needles | Jackson, TN | 38301 | 21 |
| 9265 Ridgemeadow | Carrollton, TX | 75006 | 29 |
| | | | |
| 4809 Cannonball Rd. | Fairfax, VA | 22030 | 37 |
| 7623 Jasmine St. | Olympia, WA | 98502 | 44 |
| 8361 Mohawk Rd. | Janesville, WI | 53545 | 52 |
| 5409 Hawthorne Dr. | Casper, WY | 82604 | 59 |

**A** all letters used  **gwam** | 3' | 5'

The requirements of today's secretary are changing different. The    4 | 3 | 37

ability to use a computer or a word processor is a major skill now required    9 | 5 | 40

for office support personnel by a sizeable number of    12 | 7 | 42

firms. This is a trend expected to continue with an even    16 | 10 | 44

greater emphasis on computer usage in the future. This    19 | 12 | 46

will make it more critical than ever for those pursuing a    24 | 14 | 49

position in this field to have excellent keyboarding skill    28 | 17 | 51

in order to make the best use of the costly equipment. A    31 | 18 | 53

student deciding on a career in this field will also find    35 | 21 | 56

that the role assumed by many office support staff members    39 | 23 | 58

is that of an assistant to a person at the management a higher level.    43 | 26 | 60

no new ¶ More and more of today's office job the titles used in offices of today    46 | 27 | 62

reflect this trend. Job titles such as administrative    49 | 30 | 64

assistant or executive assistant are quite common now. A    53 | 32 | 67

college degree for jobs positions such as these, however, may be required stipu-    58 | 35 | 69

often lated.    58 | 35 | 70

From the Desk of
**Jason Koufax**

*Format a references page from the following:*

*"Barbados," Caribbean and the Bahamas. New York: Fodor's Modern Guides, 1991.*

*Solomon, Digby A. "Guide to the Caribbean." St. Paul Pioneer Press, October 16, 1994.*

**Job 14**

Cambridge
Travel
Networks

Jan. 19

From the Desk of
**Jason Koufax**

*I've computed the commission for most of the agents. Please complete the calculations and key a final table for the month of January. The commission rate is:*

*0.25% for sales of $0 - $50,000*

*0.50% for sales of $50,001 - $100,000*

*0.75% for sales of $100,001 - $150,000*

*1.00% for sales over $150,000*

---

DS

Beach, Walter Fletcher Beach in Montego Bay, Puerto Seco at Discovery Bay, the seven-mile strip in Negril, Mallards Beach in Ocho Rios, and Boston Beach.

<u>Cayman Islands</u>

If you are looking for a beachfront apartment with an abundance of sunshine, quality beaches, and a view of the sea, go to the Cayman Islands. The islands are particularly enticing to those interested in scuba diving and big-game fishing.

The islands consist of Grand Cayman, Cayman Brac, and Little Cayman. The Grand Cayman's west-coast stretch of Seven Mile Beach is the island's primary vacation attraction. Even though hotels and condos have sprouted along the entire length of Seven Mile Beach, the water is still placid and clean; and the reefs just offshore still teem with life. (Solomon, 1994, 6F) Tiara Beach and Brac Reef Beach are the showpieces of Cayman Brac. Isolated beaches (Sandy Point and Owen Cay) can be found on Little Cayman.

REVENUES REPORT
January —

| Agent | Sales for Month | Commission for month |
|---|---|---|
| Bass, Thelma | $125,980 | $ 569.85 |
| Chaplin, Mary | 202,585 | 1,275.85 |
| Donoso, Trujillo | 195,875 | 1,208.75 |
| Griffith, Ellen | 310,865 | 2,358.65 |
| Holiday, Charla | 95,382 | 351.91 |
| Hulett, Rebecca | 275,385 | 2,603.85 |
| Joazuin, Inez | 195,387 | 1,203.87 |
| Martin, Alexis | 353,410 | 2,784.10 |
| O'Brien, Kellee | 340,215 | 2,652.15 |
| Rinaldi, Fern | 79,325 | 271.63 |
| Santos, Dominic | 349,295 | 2,742.95 |
| Veras, Claire | 245,395 | |
| Wallace, Sheryl | 287,452 | |
| Totals | | |

# Activity 3:

1. Read carefully the ¶s at the right.
2. Key a list of what your school does to recognize those who excel in athletics (sports).
3. Key a list of what your school does to recognize those who excel in various academic areas.
4. Compose/key a ¶ indicating whether you believe that athletics gets more recognition than academics in your school.
5. Compose/key another ¶ suggesting how your school could appropriately recognize students who excel in academic areas.

**Compose (think) as you key**

A high percentage of schools throughout the country have an Athletic Awards banquet annually to honor student athletes who have shown outstanding athletic performance. At these events, athletes are acclaimed by coaches, families, and friends. Often, too, they are given trophies, "letters," or other recognition.

Given the relatively low percentage of the total student body honored in this way, many students and parents believe that ways should be found to recognize students who exhibit outstanding performance in the academic or scholastic areas as well. To do otherwise, they say, suggests that the school is placing more emphasis on athletics than on academics.

Why, they ask, shouldn't there be a Scholastic Awards banquet at which students are honored who have excelled in activities other than sports? Art, business, English/foreign language, math/science, music, social studies, student government, and so on are important subjects that should be emphasized. Surely, they insist, these are *at least* as important as football or basketball—even if they are not performed by a team.

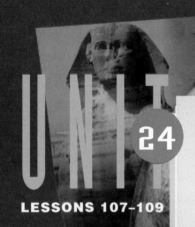

# UNIT 24 Prepare for Assessment

**LESSONS 107–109**

## LESSON 107 · Prepare for Assessment: Letters and Memos

**Objective:**
To prepare for assessment of letter and memo formatting skills.

### 107A • 5
**Conditioning Practice**

each line twice; then 1'
writings on line 2

alphabet 1 Gary's survey helped Major Katz explain new racquetball features.

speed 2 The girls may go to the social at the giant chapel on the island.

figures 3 On June 20, 1975, I bought my first card; I now have 3,468 cards.

**gwam** 1' | 1 | 2 | 3 | 4 | 5 | 6 | 7 | 8 | 9 | 10 | 11 | 12 | 13 |

## **F** ORMATTING

### 107B • 20
**Drill: Personal-Business Letter**

block format; mixed punctuation

1. A 5' writing on the letter to determine *gwam*.
2. Key two 1' writings on opening lines through first ¶ of letter. If you finish the lines before time is called, QS and start over. Try to key more words on the second writing.
3. Key two 1' writings on ¶ 3 through last ¶ and closing lines. If you finish the lines before time is called, QS and start ¶ 3 again. Try to key more words on the second writing.
4. Key another 5' writing on the letter. Try to increase your *gwam* by 4-8 words.

words

928 Big Horn Ave.  Moorcroft, WY 82721-2342    January 2, ----     12
Ms. Thelma White    P.O. Box 414    Moorcroft, WY 82721-2342         23
Dear Ms. White:                                                      26

Are you interested in serving on a committee to discuss the merits of a     41
women's historical museum in Wyoming?    Many are not aware that            53
Wyoming's nickname (Equality State) stems from the fact that Wyoming        67
women were the first women in the United States to achieve the right to     81
vote.    They earned this right in 1869.                                    89

Since that time, many women have played an important part in shaping the    104
history of Wyoming.    Are you aware that the first woman governor in the    118
United States came from Wyoming?    Nellie Tayloe Ross became governor of    133
Wyoming in 1925.                                                            136

It may be time to recognize these women by creating a museum that would     151
become a place for people to reflect on the events of the past as they con-  166
template the future.    I will call you next week to see if you are willing to  181
serve on the committee.                                                     186

Sincerely,    Mark C. Felding   xx                                          192

# Language & Writing Skills 12

## Activity 1:

1. Study the spelling/definitions of the words in the color block at the right.
2. Key the **Learn** line in the first set of sentences.
3. Key the **Apply** lines, choosing the right words to complete each sentence correctly.
4. Key the second set of lines in the same way.
5. Check work; rekey lines containing word-choice errors.

### Choose the right word

| | |
|---|---|
| **accept** (vb) to receive, to give approval, to take | **leased** (vb) to grant use or occupation of under contract in exchange for rent |
| **except** (vb) to exclude | **least** (adj) lowest in importance or rank |

Learn 1 I think they will accept all my revisions except for Unit 8.

Apply 2 Juliana works every day (accept/except) Saturday and Sunday.

Apply 3 Adolpho will attend the banquet to (accept/except) the award.

Learn 4 The fact that he leased his new automobile is least important.

Apply 5 We (leased/least) the apartment at (leased/least) a year ago.

Apply 6 Last but not (leased/least), she (leased/least) the family farm.

## Activity 2:

1. Read each sentence, noting needed punctuation changes, including hyphen, colon, parentheses, underline, and quotation marks.
2. Key each sentence, supplying punctuation to complete the sentence correctly.
3. Check work; then rekey any sentence that contains a punctuation error.

### Proofread & correct

1 Both five room apartments will be available by August 30.
2 Dolores bought a roll of one hundred 32 cent postage stamps.
3 Village Theater is mounting a big production of Porgy and Bess.
4 Many believe The Rainmaker is one of John Grisham's best books.
5 All in the Family was a very popular TV show in the 1970s.
6 Who, she asked, is your all time favorite pop vocalist?
7 Ms. Ott said:  Read Frost's poem The Housekeeper by Monday.
8 Remember the steps (1) stand up;  (2) speak up;  (3) shut up.
9 "A textual citation follows the quote."  Roberts, 1998, 173
10 The verbs set and sit as well as lay and lie cause difficulty.
11 The space between lines of text equals one twentieth of an inch.
12 The competition is scheduled for 9 15 a.m. on April 29.
13 My goal is to develop 1 self-confidence and 2 self-esteem.
14 Twenty one of the thirty two students exceeded expectations.
15 Miss Tallchief signed a two year contract as ballet director.
16 Lana gushed as if she'd found Shangri-la, That's beautiful.
17 His article, Cyberspace, appeared in USA Weekend magazine.
18 Dr. Roe said that "30 second and 1 minute spurts build speed."
19 Check these tables  2-6, p. 39; 3-9, p. 57; 4-2, p. 73.
20 After you see the film, she said, write a two page review.

### 107C • 25
### Reinforce Letter/Memo Formatting Skills

**Document 1**
**Memo**

Format and key the text at the right as a standard memo to **Women's Historical Museum Committee**. The memo is from **Mark C. Felding**. Date the memo **February 1, ----**; use **NEXT MEETING** for the subject line.

**Document 2**
**Letter**

Format and key the text at the right in simplified block letter format. Use the USPS letter address style.

**Document 3**
**Letter**

Format and key the letter in 107B as a modified block letter with mixed punctuation and indented paragraphs.

|  | words |
|---|---|
| | opening 21 |

The next meeting of the Wyoming Women's Historical Museum Com- 34
mittee will be held on Monday, February 7, at 2:45 p.m.  I have re- 47
served the conference room at the city library for the meeting. 60

Please be thinking about ideas for raising private funds for the 73
museum.  I have the information we need for national and state 86
funding. | xx 88

February 20, ---- | MR AND MRS JUSTIN WOODWARD | PO BOX 10
212 | MOORCROFT  WY 82721-2342 | WYOMING WOMEN'S HISTORI- 21
CAL MUSEUM 23

Wyoming women were the first women in the United States to have the 37
right to vote (1869).  Esther Morris of South Pass City became the first 51
woman judge in 1870.  Wyoming was the first state to elect a woman 65
to state office when Estelle Reel was elected State Superintendent of 79
Public Instruction in 1894.  Nellie Tayloe Ross became the first female 93
governor in the United States when she was elected governor of 106
Wyoming in 1925. 109

It is time to honor women such as these for the role they played in 123
shaping Wyoming and U.S. history.  A Wyoming Women's Historical 136
Museum is being planned.  With your help, the museum can become 148
a reality. 151

Our community would benefit from the increased tourist activity.  Thou- 165
sands of tourists visit the nation's first national monument, Devil's Tower, 180
each year.  Since Moorcroft is only 30 miles from Devil's Tower, a 194
museum would draw them to our city as they travel to and from the 207
Tower. 209

National and state funds for the project are being solicited; however, 223
additional funding from the private sector will be required.  Please look 238
over the enclosed brochure and join the Wyoming Women's Historical 251
Museum Foundation by making a contribution. 260

MARK C. FELDING, COMMITTEE CHAIR | xx | Enclosure 269

## LESSON 108

## Prepare for Assessment:  Reports

**O b j e c t i v e :**
To prepare for assessment of report formatting skills.

### 108A • 5
### Conditioning Practice

each line twice

alphabet 1 The Gretzky exhibit was not quite completed when she left Jarvis.

speed 2 Diane may pay us to work for them when they dismantle the shanty.

figures 3 A truck picked up yard waste at 1047 Ash, 1258 Elm, and 3697 Oak.

**gwam** 1' | 1 | 2 | 3 | 4 | 5 | 6 | 7 | 8 | 9 | 10 | 11 | 12 | 13 |

adding quotation marks.  A colon generally introduces a
quotation displayed in this way, though sometimes the
context may require a different mark of punctuation, or
none at all.  If you quote only a single paragraph, or
part of one, do not indent the first line more than the
rest.  A parenthetical reference to a prose quotation
set off from the text follows the last line of the
quotation.  (73)

DS

Continue to double-space the text following the quotation,
indenting only the first line of each paragraph one-half inch
(five spaces).  An example of the "Works Cited" page is illustrated on page 3.  Notice that it is also double-spaced and
arranged in alphabetical order with the second and succeeding
lines of each entry indented one-half inch.

1"

1/2"

Works Cited

Gibaldi, Joseph.  MLA Handbook for Writers of Research Papers.
     4th ed.  New York:  The Modern Language Association of
     America, 1995.

Harcourt, Jules, A. C. "Buddy" Krizan, and Patricia Merrier.
     Business Communication.  3d ed.  Cincinnati:  South-Western
     Educational Publishing, 1996.

all DS

**108B • 45**
**Report Format Review**

Review the format guides on pp. 211-212.

1. Format and key 89B, pp. 218-219, as an unbound report.

2. Format and key a separate REFERENCES page.

3. Prepare a title page. Use your name and school name and the current date.

## LESSON 109    Prepare for Assessment:  Tables

**Objective:**
To prepare for assessment of table formatting skills.

**109A • 5**
**Conditioning Practice**

each line twice

alphabet  1  Janet, the clerk, showed Mary the exquisite topaz before leaving.

speed  2  The girl may go to the island to visit and dismantle the bicycle.

figures  3  Our 9 a.m. meeting on May 18 will be in Room 2360, not Room 2457.

gwam  1' | 1 | 2 | 3 | 4 | 5 | 6 | 7 | 8 | 9 | 10 | 11 | 12 | 13 |

**S KILL BUILDING**

**109B • 12**
**Timed Writings**

1. A 1' writing on each of the three ¶s; find *gwam* and errors.

2. A 5' writing on the three ¶s combined; find *gwam* and errors.

 all letters used

gwam 1' | 5'

Although the path to success is usually lengthy, you can make    12 | 2  45
it shorter if you will start at the beginning of your business    25 | 5  48
career to develop two important skills.   The first is the ability    38 | 8  50
to see and to solve problems; the second, the ability to gather    51 | 10 53
facts and arrange them in logical order, from which you can draw    64 | 13 56
the correct conclusions.    69 | 14 57

Surely you can recall occasions when you devoted many hours,    12 | 16 59
even days, to striving unsuccessfully for a goal, and then you    25 | 19 62
happened to see the difficult problem from a new viewpoint.    37 | 21 64
Perhaps you exclaimed to a friend or yourself, "Now I see what the    50 | 24 67
problem is!"   And once identified, the problem was easily solved.    64 | 26 69
As you begin work on a project, make your initial step that of    76 | 29 72
seeing the actual problem.    81 | 30 73

To solve problems, use all effectual means to get the data    12 | 32 75
that you will need.   Books and magazine articles give facts and    25 | 35 78
expert opinions, and a request by mail or phone may offer added    37 | 38 80
aid.   Enter the data on cards into logical groups, review the    50 | 40 83
work, and apply common sense to draw conclusions that the data    62 | 43 85
support.    64 | 43 86

gwam  1' | 1 | 2 | 3 | 4 | 5 | 6 | 7 | 8 | 9 | 10 | 11 | 12 | 13 |
      5' |        1        |        2        |        3        |

1"

Jane A. Bryant

DS

Professor Doherty

English 2140

10 February ----

DS

Standard Format for an MLA-Style Research Report

DS

DS paragraphs

A contemporary method of documentation is appropriate for reports that contain information from only a few sources (Harcourt 448).  The MLA-style (Modern Language Association of America) report that is illustrated here is a method that can be used.  There are several key differences between this style and the formats introduced in previous lessons.  An MLA-style report has one-inch side, top, and bottom margins.  The entire report is **double-spaced**, including quotations, documentation, and the space below the title.

1" margin

1" margin

No title page is used.  Information normally found on the title page (writer's name, teacher's name, course title, and date) is keyed on the first page beginning one inch from the top margin starting at the left margin.

Page numbers for all pages (including the first) are keyed at the right margin one-half inch from the top edge of the paper. The writer's last name precedes the page number.

Another difference is the way that long quotations are keyed in the MLA style.  In the MLA Handbook for Writers of Research Papers, Gibaldi provides these guides for keying long quotations:

Indent long quotes 1" from left margin and DS

If a quotation runs to more than four typed lines, set it off . . . by beginning a new line, indenting one inch (or ten spaces if you are using a typewriter) from the left margin, and typing it double-spaced, without

1" bottom margin

**F**ORMATTING

**109C • 33
Reinforcement: Table
Skills**

**Table 1**
**DS; CS:** 1"; center column
headings

## TEN LARGEST BODIES OF WATER

| Body of Water | Square Miles | Average Depth |  |
|---|---|---|---|
| Pacific Ocean | 64,186,300 | 12,925 | 21 |
| Atlantic Ocean | 33,420,000 | 11,730 | 27 |
| Indian Ocean | 28,350,500 | 12,598 | 34 |
| Arctic Ocean | 5,105,700 | 3,407 | 39 |
| South China Sea | 1,148,500 | 4,802 | 46 |
| Caribbean Sea | 971,400 | 8,448 | 51 |
| Mediterranean Sea | 969,100 | 4,926 | 58 |
| Bering Sea | 873,000 | 4,893 | 63 |
| Gulf of Mexico | 582,100 | 5,297 | 69 |
| Sea of Okhotsk | 537,500 | 3,192 | 74 |

6
9
14
78

Source:  The World Almanac, 1996.                                84

**Table 2**
**DS; CS:** 0.5"; center column
headings

**Table 3**
Rearrange (rekey) Table 2 by
the year in which the artist
was born.

## FAMOUS ARTISTS

| Artist | Country | Artwork |  |
|---|---|---|---|
| Jacques-Louis David (1748-1826) 5 | French | The Oath of the Horatii | 19 / 21 |
| Claude Monet (1840-1926) | French | Impression: Sunrise | 29 / 32 |
| Pierre Auguste Renoir (1841-1919) | French | La Loge | 39 / 41 |
| Vincent Van Gogh (1853-1890) | Dutch | The Starrey Night | 50 / 52 |
| Camille Pissarro (1830-1903) | French | Apple Harvest at Eragny | 62 / 64 |
| Michelangelo Buonarotti (1475-1564) | Italian | Last Judgment | 73 / 76 |
| Giovanni Bellini (1430-1516) | Italian | The Transfiguration | 85 / 87 |
| Edouard Manet (1832-1883) | French | Olympia | 93 / 95 |
| Auguste Rodin (1840-1917) | French | The Thinker | 102 / 104 |
| Pablo Picasso (1881-1973) | Spanish | Portrait of Vollard | 113 / 115 |
| Sir Anthony Van Dyck (1599-1641) | Flemish | Ecstasy of St. Augustine | 126 / 128 |

3
8
132

Compiled from the Encyclopedia Americana, 1993.                141

# LESSON 123 | Report in MLA Format

### Objectives:
**1.** To format a report in MLA style.
**2.** To improve language skills (quotation marks).

**123A • 5**
**Conditioning Practice**
each line twice

| | | |
|---|---|---|
| alphabet | 1 | Major Frank Valdez always sprayed extra herbicides on quackgrass. |
| speed | 2 | The small ornament on their oak mantle is an antique ivory whale. |
| figures | 3 | Robert Myer's address is 856 Moss Drive, Columbia, SC 29203-7401. |
| **gwam** | 1' | 1 \| 2 \| 3 \| 4 \| 5 \| 6 \| 7 \| 8 \| 9 \| 10 \| 11 \| 12 \| 13 \| |

## L ANGUAGE SKILLS

**123B • 5**
**Quotation Marks**

Follow the Learn/Apply procedure in 76C on p. 184.

> Use quotation marks to enclose special words or phrases used for emphasis or for coined words (words not in dictionary usage).

Learn 1. My problem is that I have "limited resources" and "unlimited wants."
Apply 2. His speech was liberally sprinkled with you knows.
Apply 3. I heard him characterized as a phony.

> Use a single quotation mark (the apostrophe) to indicate a quotation within a quotation.

Learn 4. I said, "We must take, as Frost suggests, the 'road less traveled.' "
Apply 5. I wrote, "We must have, as Tillich said, the courage to be."
Apply 6. She said, "We must be reminded to, as Kennedy said, Ask not . . . ."

**123C • 10**
**Language Skills: Review**

1. The sentences at the right may contain errors in capitalization and number expression.
2. As you key each sentence, make all necessary corrections, including any keystroking errors you may make.
3. After you key all sentences, proofread each one and correct additional errors you may find.

1. Mr. Ortiz moved to craig, colorado, from New york city in May.
2. I believe memorial day will be celebrated on sunday this year.
3. The American revolution preceded the french revolution.
4. The King climbing club will climb the Grand canyon on friday.

5. 14 of the company employees agreed to participate; 22 did not.
6. We have 12 clarinets, six flutes, and 5 trumpets in the band.
7. The 8 girls arrived on the bus at six thirty on June six.
8. The answer can be found in Chapter Five, page 389.

9. The new Baby weighed seven Pounds and was 20 inches long.
10. Our President, J. b. Sims, will meet us at the office.
11. "this car may be my first," he said, "But it won't be my last."
12. She arrived on Flight sixty-two at 4:30 p.m. on May 19.

**123D • 30**
**MLA-Style Report**

1. Read the information about formatting reports in MLA style on page 284; study the model on pp. 293-294.

2. Format and key the report on pp. 293 and 294.

R & E activities can be found on pp. A27-A30.

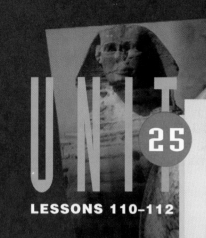

# UNIT 25

**LESSONS 110–112**

# Assess Document Formatting Skills

## LESSON 110

## Assessment: Letters and Memos

**Objective:**
To assess letter and memo formatting skills.

**110A • 5**
**Conditioning Practice**

set 0.5" SMs
each line twice

alphabet  1  Grandpa was quick to criticize May for purchasing six valuable jewels.

speed  2  The maid paid the men for the work they did on the shanty by the lake.

fig/sym  3  My 1997 property tax increased by 6.75% ($241); I paid $3,580 in 1996.

`gwam`  1' | 1 | 2 | 3 | 4 | 5 | 6 | 7 | 8 | 9 | 10 | 11 | 12 | 13 | 14 |

**110B • 10**
**Check Keying Skill**

Key two 3' writings on
¶s 1 and 2 combined;
calculate *gwam* and
determine errors.

   all letters used                                `gwam`  1' | 3'

Quite a few of today's consumers buy on credit each day | 11 | 4 | 67

without considering the consequences of the costs associated with | 24 | 8 | 71

purchases made on credit.  A decreased spending capacity in the | 37 | 12 | 75

future is one of the main points that needs to be taken into | 49 | 16 | 79

account prior to making a major credit purchase.  Buyers who | 62 | 21 | 83

utilize credit need to remember that earnings going toward the | 74 | 25 | 87

repayment of a loan restrict funds that could be used to buy other | 88 | 29 | 92

goods or services. | 91 | 30 | 93

Buyers must also remember that credit can be expensive; there | 12 | 35 | 97

are costs associated with it.  One of those costs is interest.  In- | 26 | 39 | 102

terest is the sum charged for the use of money.  Buyers who make | 39 | 43 | 106

purchases via credit can also expect to be charged service fees or | 52 | 48 | 111

finance charges.  Perhaps the biggest cost of credit, however, is | 65 | 52 | 115

the opportunity cost.  The opportunity cost can be viewed as the | 78 | 57 | 119

cost of not acquiring certain goods or services in order to ac- | 91 | 61 | 124

quire other goods or services. | 97 | 63 | 126

`gwam`  1' | 1 | 2 | 3 | 4 | 5 | 6 | 7 | 8 | 9 | 10 | 11 | 12 | 13 |
3' | 1 | 2 | 3 | 4 |

## Document 2
### Endnotes Page

Use the following information to create a separate endnotes page.

[1] John Grove, "New Media for Your Messages," <u>The Secretary</u>, March 1993, p. 6.

[2] Grove, p. 7.

[3] Amy Gage, "Voice Mail Technology Can Be a Source of Frustration, Irritation," <u>St. Paul Pioneer Press</u>, August 3, 1994, p. 1C.

[4] "Information Distribution," <u>Modern Office Technology</u>, January 1993, p. 36.

[5] "Voice Mail Minds the Store While You're Out," <u>Managing Office Technology</u>, November 1993, p. 76.

## Document 3
### Title Page

Prepare a title page for the report, using your name, school name, and current date.

When voice messaging systems are used to replace a receptionist, callers may feel they have landed in Voice Mail Jail--especially if they have to deal with a complex series of choices. We believe that most businesses should use voice messaging systems as a backup for an attendant, not as a replacement.[4]

Voice-Mail Tips

Regardless of whether voice mail is used to replace an attendant or as a backup for the attendant, it must be effective. To be effective, voice mail has to be used correctly. The following tips from Pacific Bell provide a basis for effective use of voice mail.[5]

- **Provide details.** Business associates need to know specifically when you're leaving, when you'll be back in the office, and when they can expect a return call.

- **Be courteous and businesslike.** Maintain the same professional demeanor on your vacation greeting as your regular greeting while in the office. Keep it positive to reassure customers that it's business as usual, even though you're away.

- **Don't leave confusing or conflicting instructions.** Keep your greeting simple. If you need to leave instructions for accessing additional phone menus, make them easy to follow.

- **Give callers alternatives.** Let clients know who is handling their accounts in your absence, and always include the number the caller needs to press to reach your substitute.

- **Help callers reach a "live" person.** Callers always need the option of talking with a person. Let them know which button to push for an attendant.

- **Let callers know if you'll be checking your messages.** Tell callers you plan to phone in for messages from time to time while you're away--but only if you mean it.

- **Update your greeting as soon as you return.** Make sure callers know you've returned from vacation by updating your message with a current date and greeting. In this way, you and your associates can get back into swing right away.

*By following these tips, your voice mail will give accurate, timely information. What's more, customers will not be offended and will know that their calls are valued.*

| | words |
|---|---|
| | 597 |
| | 612 |
| | 625 |
| | 638 |
| | 645 |
| | 649 |
| | 665 |
| | 679 |
| | 694 |
| | 702 |
| | 715 |
| | 728 |
| | 735 |
| | 746 |
| | 761 |
| | 775 |
| | 783 |
| | 796 |
| | 809 |
| | 820 |
| | 834 |
| | 846 |
| | 855 |
| | 868 |
| | 881 |
| | 886 |
| | 898 |
| | 912 |
| | 919 |
| | 933 |
| | 945 |
| | 957 |
| | 966 |
| | 979 |
| | 992 |
| | 1000 |

**Document 1**
**Letter**

Format and key the text at the right as a modified block letter with open punctuation and indented paragraphs.

words

December 30, ---- | Ms. Thelma White | P.O. Box 414 | Moorcroft, WY  12
82721-2342 | Dear Ms. White  18

The planning committee is thrilled to announce that the ground-breaking  32
ceremony for the **Wyoming Women's Historical Museum** will take place  46
on Friday, June 24.  Many hours have been spent by our committee trying  60
to move this project forward.  At times the committee was not even sure  75
there would ever be a ground-breaking ceremony.  84

As part of the celebration, we are inviting those who played an important  99
part in helping us reach this milestone to a luncheon in their honor.  The  114
luncheon will be held at the Mead House at 11:30.  The ground-breaking  128
ceremony will begin at 1:30.  134

The museum will be a great source of pride for Wyoming residents and will  149
give them a sense of their history.  Visitors will be reminded of the part  164
Wyoming women played in the history of Wyoming as well as in the history  179
of the United States.  183

Sincerely | Mark C. Felding | Committee Chair | xx  191

**Document 2**
**Memo**

Format and key the text at the right as a standard memo to **Women's Historical Museum Committee**. The memo is from **Mark C. Felding**. Date the memo **January 5, ----**; use **CONTRIBUTION UPDATE** for the subject line.

opening  22

The contribution figures for November and December are attached.  They  36
are much higher than we anticipated.  44

The higher figures are due in large part to the $5,000 contributions.  The  59
committee's idea of having a plaque at the entrance listing individuals con-  74
tributing amounts of $5,000 or more has been very successful.  The bronze  89
statue of Esther Morris given to those contributing $25,000 or more has  103
also been successful.  Over $700,000 has been raised by contributions in  118
this category.  121

I believe we can still reach our goal of $1.5 million in private contri-  135
butions before the ground-breaking ceremony on June 24.  I'll continue to  147
send periodic updates. | xx | Attachment  157

**Document 3**
**Letter**

Format and key the text at the right in simplified block letter format.  Use the USPS letter address style.

February 3, ---- | MS RACHAEL LEIGHTON | 4504 GLENWOOD  10
AVE | YOUNGSTOWN OH 44502-5371 | SOFTWARE INSTRUCTION  20
WORKSHOPS  22

Even the most user-friendly computer hardware and software will gather dust  36
unless buyers have been properly trained.  When you purchased your sys-  52
tem from us, we told you that we would provide the necessary training.  66

Our workshops in word processing and spreadsheets will be offered again  81
in March.  The word processing workshop is scheduled for Monday nights  95
(March 6-April 24).  The spreadsheet applications class is scheduled for  109
Wednesday nights (March 8-April 26).  Both classes meet from 7 to 8 p.m.  124

Registration materials are enclosed.  Since the classes fill quite rapidly, you  140
should register as soon as possible.  148

TODD S. BAXTER, COMPUTER SPECIALIST | xx | Enclosure  157

Pillsbury's public relations department tries to use voice mail
only at night or when staff members are in meetings, the reason being
that communications employees should be readily accessible.[3]

The following lists are some of the advantages and disadvantages
cited in the ongoing debate for and against voice mail.

Advantages

1. The caller makes contact with the person each time a call is
placed.

2. The caller can simply leave a message. Leaving a message often
takes care of the purpose of the call, as the caller's intent was
not to speak directly to the person. By not having to speak
directly with the person, the caller saves time and money by avoiding idle talk.

3. Unnecessary staff involvement in routine phone calls is eliminated.

4. Much paper is eliminated.

5. Company time and money can be saved.

Disadvantages

1. The caller may not like being told to "press one for . . . , press two
for. . . ."

2. The caller may prefer talking to a person rather than a machine.
A person provides the "personal service" better than a machine.
Machines can have an adverse impact on how the company is
perceived.

3. The voice-mail greeting should be changed routinely. The same
old voice-mail greeting becomes tiring.

4. The messages may not be received because of an error on the
part of the sender or because of malfunctioning equipment.

5. The caller may not be sure that a message is received when there
is not an immediate response.

6. Some people are shy about leaving their own messages.

Should a company decide to implement voice mail, consideration
should be given to how the company uses the equipment and to make sure
that the equipment is used properly. According to Don Heitt, president at Voysys Corporation in San Jose:

Voice messaging is a tool that, like all tools, can be used im-
properly. While some voice messaging systems are easier to set up
than others, it's up to the company that installs a system to make
sure that the system enhances, rather than weakens, communications.

(continued on next page)

**Note:** To enhance the appearance of enumerated items, align the second line (and succeeding lines) of each enumerated item under the first line—hanging indent style.

If you prefer less space after the numbers, set a tab about 0.25" (two spaces) to the right of the period instead of using default tabs.

# Assessment: Reports

**Objective:**
To assess report formatting skill.

## 111A • 5
## Conditioning Practice

each line twice; then 1'
writings on line 2

| | | |
|---|---|---|
| alphabet | 1 | Jackie will budget for the expensive zoology equipment next year. |
| speed | 2 | The man in the wheelchair may sit by the docks with their lapdog. |
| fig/sym | 3 | Invoice #4368 totalled $927.80 before deducting the 15% discount. |

**gwam** 1' | 1 | 2 | 3 | 4 | 5 | 6 | 7 | 8 | 9 | 10 | 11 | 12 | 13 |

## 111B • 45
## Assess Report Formatting Skills

### Document 1
**Report from Rough Draft**

1. Format and key the report in unbound style; use **EXPLORERS** for the heading of the report.

2. When you finish, proofread your copy. Use spell check if you have it.

### Document 2
**References List**

Use the information below to create a references list on a separate page.

Havighurst, Walter. "The Old Frontiersman--George Rogers Clark." In Helen Wright and Samuel Rapport (eds.), <u>The Great Explorers</u>. New York: Harper & Row Publishers, 1957.

Morrison, Samuel Eliot. "Christopher Columbus, Mariner." In Helen Wright and Samuel Rapport (eds.), <u>The Great Explorers</u>. New York: Harper & Row, Publishers, 1957.

Rugoff, Milton. <u>The Great Travelers</u>. New York: Simon and Schuster, 1960.

Tinling, Marion. <u>Women into the Unknown</u>. New York: Greenwood Press, 1989.

words
opening 2

¶What motivates an explorers? The earliest explorers ex- *travelled*  14
plored for the purpose of discovery. *and adventure* Many of the *early* explorers  29
*mentioned* stated conquest, acquisition of wealth, and territorial acqui-  42
sition as their reasons for travel.  49

Today the reasons have changed. Explorers offer the  60
following reasons for *leaving the comforts of their homes and* venturing into possible danger and  79
hardship.  81

1. Taking the benefits of Christianity to other lands.  93
2. Taking the benefits of modern technology to other  104
   lands.  105
3. Studying plants or wildlife.  112
4. Uncovering the remains of ancient civilizations.  123
5. Protecting the world's environmental balance.  133
6. Testing one's strength and ability to survive.  148

*Backgrounds of Explorers* *(Tinling, 1989, xxiii)*  153
Explorers come from all walks of life. Marco Polo was  164
a merchant, Robert Louis Stevenson was a novelist, and Mary  176
Kingsley was a well-born Englishwoman. Noted explorers in-  188
clude priests, conquistadors, lawyers, surgeons, naturalists,  200
etc. No station in life is immune from the "fever."  211
(Rugoff, 1960, xix)

The itch, the fever, the urge--whatever one chooses to  222
call it--is recurrent, if not constant. Once they have  233
gone off, they go again and again. . . . Often the  243
fever manifests itself in childhood . . . and sometimes  255
it stops only with death, violent death."  267

There are many examples of individuals who had the  277
"fever." Three such examples are Christopher Columbus,  289
George Rogers Clark, and Delia Denning Akeley.  298

*(continued on next page)*

# Unbound Report

**Objectives:**

1. To format an unbound report using endnote-style documentation.
2. To improve language skills (quotation marks).

---

**121-122A • 5**
## Conditioning Practice

each line twice

alphabet 1 Howie Zahn helped Joy pack four big boxes of expensive equipment.

speed 2 The box with the emblem of the duck is on the mantle by the bowl.

figures 3 Invoice No. 37A 408 was paid on May 23; No. 29A 516 was not paid.

gwam 1' | 1 | 2 | 3 | 4 | 5 | 6 | 7 | 8 | 9 | 10 | 11 | 12 | 13 |

---

**L** ANGUAGE SKILLS

**121B • 10**
## Quotation Marks

Follow the Learn/Apply procedure in 76C on p. 184.

Use quotation marks to enclose direct quotations. **Note**: When a question mark applies to the entire sentence, it is keyed outside the quotation marks.

Learn 1. The coach asked, "Did you practice over the summer?"

Learn 2. Was it Emerson who said, "To have a friend is to be one"?

Apply 3. The waiter asked, How was your lunch?

Apply 4. Did Shakespeare say, All the world is a stage?

Use quotation marks to enclose titles of articles, poems, songs, television programs, and unpublished works such as dissertations and theses.

Learn 5. She had read the poem "Solitude" by Ella Wheeler Wilcox.

Apply 6. Did you watch the TV program Saved by the Bell last night?

Apply 7. My favorite poem is IF by Rudyard Kipling.

---

**F** ORMATTING

**121C-122B • 35/45**
## Unbound Report

**Document 1**
**Unbound Report**
Format and key the text at the right as an unbound report DS with endnotes.

 **note:**

This report may be opened for use later. Be sure to save it!

words

VOICE MAIL  2

"To use or not to use" voice mail is the question for business organi-  16
zations. Many businesses have already made a decision.  28

Currently two million businesses use voice mail--and use is  40
expected to grow by 40-50 percent each year. In 1988, 28 percent  53
of companies with more than 1,000 employees had voice mail; in  65
1993, 70 percent of those companies used the technology.[1]  77

Those businesses that have not yet made a decision, however, must  90
consider the advantages and the disadvantages of doing so before jump-  104
ing on the bandwagon and purchasing a voice-mail system. In spite of the  118
increased popularity of voice mail, many customer-service oriented organ-  133
izations, such as banks, have decided the disadvantages far outweigh the  147
advantages. Only six percent of the banking industry use voice  162
mail.[2] Other organizations have decided to make limited use of voice mail.  176

*(continued on next page)*

DS Body

**Christopher Columbus.** Christopher Columbus is recognized 310
as one of the earliest noteworthy explorers. On his first voy- 322
age Columbus landed on the Bahamas, then Cuba, and Haiti (1492- 335
93). At the time of his explorations, "No other sailor had the 348
persistence, the knowledge and the sheer guts to sail thousands 361
of miles into the unknown ocean until he found land." (Morrison, 374
1957, 80-81) His explorations whittled away at the unknown. 386

**George Rogers Clark.** George Rogers Clark was an American 398
frontiersman explorer during the last half of the eighteenth 410
century. Like many frontiersmen who are driven to explore by 423
their need for places where fences do not exist, Clark explored 436
vast areas of wilderness. According to Havighurst (1957, 21), 448
his name is "synonymous with the settlement of the Ohio, adven- 461
ture in the Kentucky wilderness, conquest of the frontier lands 474
of Illinois and the winning of the West for a new nation." 486
His explorations brought new options for people. 501

**Delia Denning Akeley.** Delia Denning Akeley has made a 507
significant impact on the American museum visitor from her 519
explorations of Equatorial Africa. Between 1905 and 1929 she 531
collected specimens of Africa's wild animals for American natu- 544
ral history museums. Armed with little more than courage and 556
an empathetic understanding of the Africans, she proved that a 569
woman could travel in a dangerous country at a dangerous time. 581
(Tinling, 1989, 10) Her explorations brought new knowledge 593
to people. 596

**Everyone Explores** 600

Not everyone will have the urge to explore as these noted 611
explorers did, but everyone has a little bit of an exploring na- 624
ture. It may not be the urge to explore for glory or discov- 636
ery; it may simply be an urge to travel to a geographical area 649
that an individual has not yet visited. The urge may be in 661
the form of exploring a museum or a book to expand one's knowl- 673
edge. Or, it may be exploring educational and career options. 686
Regardless of the type of exploration done, all explorers are 699
changed by their explorations. Their horizons become much 710
broader through their explorations. 717

**Document 3**
**Title Page**
Format a title page for the report. Use your name and school name and the current date.

---

## LESSON 112 | Assessment: Tables

**Objective:**
To assess table formatting skills.

**112A • 5**
**Conditioning Practice**

each line twice

alphabet 1 Lexi was just sure Pam would get her sizable refund very quickly.

speed 2 The heir to the endowment may work on the problems with the firm.

fig/sym 3 The shipping expenses ($27.96) were included on Invoice #435A180.

| gwam | 1' | 1 | 2 | 3 | 4 | 5 | 6 | 7 | 8 | 9 | 10 | 11 | 12 | 13 |

**Note**: Ellipsis marks (three periods with a space before and after each one . . . ) are used to show that one or more words have been omitted from the quoted sentence.

words

to fulfill that role have increased. Koenig[2] suggested that today's 369
President has these imposing responsibilities: 379

> . . . survival problems in which the very future of the human 391
> race is at stake; the threat of nuclear weapons technology; 403
> persistence of war abroad; the remorseless growth of popula- 415
> tion, production, and pollution, and their endangering of the en- 428
> vironment; grave unemployment and inflation; blighted cities 441
> and pervasive poverty and crime; excessive violations of civil 453
> rights and liberties; grossly inadequate provisions of health 466
> services, mass transit, education and the care of the elderly. 478

As Koenig's description of the presidential responsibilities indicates, 493
the President of the United States has a job with many important and 507
varied responsibilities. 512

<u>Party Affiliation</u> 516

Political party backing is critical to being elected President. Even 530
though there have been numerous political parties in the United States, 544
only five have become powerful enough to elect a President. Three of the 559
parties (Federalist, Democratic-Republican, and Whig) no longer 572
exist today. Of the remaining two parties (Democrat and Repub- 584
lican), one or the other has occupied the White House since 1853. 598
As can be seen from the following table,[3] the first Democrat took 611
office in 1829, while the first Republican did not assume office until 625
1861. 626

| <u>President and Party</u> | <u>Term</u> | 632 |
|---|---|---|
| George Washington (F) | 1789-1797 | 638 |
| John Adams (F) | 1797-1801 | 650 |
| Thomas Jefferson (D-R) | 1801-1809 | 656 |
| James Madison (D-R) | 1809-1817 | 661 |
| James Monroe (D-R) | 1817-1825 | 668 |
| John Quincy Adams (D-R) | 1825-1829 | 674 |
| Andrew Jackson (D) | 1829-1837 | 680 |
| Martin Van Buren (D) | 1837-1841 | 689 |
| William Henry Harrison (W) | 1841 | 692 |
| John Tyler (W) | 1841-1845 | 697 |
| James K. Polk (D) | 1845-1849 | 703 |
| Zachary Taylor (W) | 1849-1850 | 709 |
| Millard Fillmore (W) | 1850-1853 | 715 |
| Franklin Pierce (D) | 1853-1857 | 721 |
| James Buchanan (D) | 1857-1861 | 727 |
| Abraham Lincoln (R) | 1861-1865 | 730 |

_______________ 733

Party Affiliation: D = Democrat; D-R = Democratic-Republican; 743
F = Federalist; R = Republican; W = Whig. 751

**Document 2**
**Endnotes Page**

Use the following information to create an endnotes page on a separate sheet.

**[1] James W. Davis, <u>The American President: A New Perspective</u> (New York: Harper & Row Publishers, 1987), p. 4.**

**[2] Louis W. Koenig, <u>Chief Executive</u>, 5th ed. (San Diego: Harcourt Brace Jovanovich, Inc., 1986), pp. 14-15.**

**[3] <u>Encyclopedia Americana</u>, Vol. 22 (Danbury, CT: Grolier Incorporated, 1993), p. 561.**

**Document 3**
**Title Page**

Prepare a title page for the report, using your name, school name, and current date.

## 112B • 45
## Assess Table Formatting Skills

**Table 1**
**DS; CS:** 1" (10 sp.); center column headings

**Table 2**
**DS; CS:** 1" (10 sp.); center column headings

**Table 3**
Add the information below to Table 2. Rearrange the table chronologically, with the *most recent* invention first.
**1852 / Gyroscope / Jean Foucault**
**1896 / Radio / Guglielmo Marconi**

1970-1979 NOBEL WINNERS *(PRIZE)*

*Literature*

| Year | Winner | Country | |
|------|--------|---------|---|
| | | | 6 |
| | | | 8 |
| Year | Winner | Country | 13 |
| 1970 | Aleksandr Solzhenitsyn | Soviet Union | 21 |
| 1971 | Pablo Neruda | Chile | 26 |
| 1972 | Heinrich Boll | Germany | 31 |
| 1973 | Patrick White | Australia | 37 |
| 1974 | Eyvind Johnson | Sweden | 42 |
| | Harry Martinson | Sweden | 47 |
| 1975 | Eugenio Montale | Italy | 52 |
| 1976 | Saul Bellow | United States | 59 |
| 1977 | Vincente Aleixandre | Spain | 65 |
| 1978 | Issaac Bashevis Singer | United States | 73 |
| 1979 | Odysseus Elytis | Greece | 79 |
| | | | 82 |
| Source: Academic American Encyclopedia, 1995. | | | 91 |

| | | | |
|------|--------|---------|---|
| INVENTIONS | | | 2 |
| 19th Century | | | 5 |
| | | | 10 |
| Date | Invention | Inventor | |
| 1800 | Gas Light *(lc)* | Philippe Lebon | 16 |
| | | William Murdock | 19 |
| 1801 | *Draw loom* | Joseph Jacquard | 26 |
| 1805 | Railroad locomotive | Richard Trevithik *(c)* | 34 |
| 1807 | Steamboat | Robert Fulton | 40 |
| 1820 | Calculating machine | Charles Babbage | 48 |
| 1831 | Reaping machine | Cyrus McCormick | 56 |
| 1835 | Revolver | Samuel Colt | 61 |
| 1841 | Vulcanized rubber | Charles Goodyear | 69 |
| 1846 | Sewing machine | Elias Howe | 75 |
| 1867 | Typewriter | Christopher Soles *(h)* | 82 |
| 1876 | Telephone | Alexander Bell | 88 |
| 1877 | Phonograph | Thomas Edison | 95 |
| 1880 | Filament lamp | Joseph Swan | 101 |
| | | Thomas Edison | 104 |
| | | | 107 |
| Source: *Encyclopedia Americana, 1993.* | | | 114 |

# Bound Report with Table

**Objectives:**

**1.** To format a bound report with a table.

**2.** To format endnotes and title pages.

## 120A • 5
## Conditioning Practice

set 0.5" SMs;
each line twice

alphabet 1 The temperature quickly plunged below zero just after Steve exercised.

speed 2 The neighbor's dog was with the girl by the big sign in the cornfield.

figures 3 He received 50 percent of the responses, 3,923 of 7,846, before May 1.

**gwam** 1' | 1 | 2 | 3 | 4 | 5 | 6 | 7 | 8 | 9 | 10 | 11 | 12 | 13 | 14 |

## **F** ORMATTING

## 120B • 45
## Bound Report

**Document 1**
**Bound Report with a Table**
Format and key the document shown at the right as a bound report DS.

words

| | |
|---|---:|
| THE PRESIDENT OF THE UNITED STATES | 7 |

The highest elected office in the United States is that of President. The President, who is elected by the citizens of the United States, represents "all the people." The President plays a major role in determining the course of direction for the United States under a democratic form of government.

21
36
51
65
68

Term of Office

71

Since the enactment of the twenty-second amendment to the Constitution, the President can serve only two terms. Prior to this amendment the President could serve as long as the people elected him to the office. Franklin Roosevelt was the only President to serve more than two terms.

84
99
114
128

Qualifications

132

The qualifications required for running for the executive office of the United States are outlined in the Constitution (Article II, Section 1, Paragraph 5). The person must be at least 35 years of age, a natural-born citizen of the United States, and a resident of the United States for at least 14 years.

146
161
177
194

Responsibilities

197

Also outlined in the Constitution (Article II, Sections 2 and 3) are the responsibilities of the executive office. The responsibilities outlined are, however, quite general and are often open to interpretation. The Constitution states that the President is the Commander-in-Chief of the armed forces. The person holding the office is responsible for making treaties, appointing ambassadors, and appointing judges of the Supreme Court. Additional responsibilities of the President include giving the State of the Union Address, receiving foreign dignitaries, enforcing the laws, and protecting the rights of the citizens of the United States.

212
228
243
257
272
285
301
316
327

The role of the President has remained about the same as when the Constitution was written. However, Davis[1] stated that the responsibilities

340
356

*(continued on next page)*

# *your*PERSPECTIVE

## ETHICS: The Right Thing to Do

Television and newspapers seem to dwell on problems that confront our society. We are bombarded with stories of how people, intentionally and unintentionally, hurt others. Physical harm is an obvious way that we can hurt. Embezzlement and shoplifting are others ways in which we can be adversely affected (hurt). Shoplifting, for example, causes us to pay more for the products we buy.

While others are doing harm, we also read about people who run into a burning building to save a life, who return lost money to the owner, or who aid someone who has been in an accident. Such people impress us. We ask ourselves, "Why do some people cause harm, while others live their lives obeying the law and doing good for others?"

A possible answer is character. To most of us, character refers to the attributes people possess that make them positive, contributing members of society. Some of the attributes of character are honesty, responsibility, loyalty, and kindness.

Character is not something that just happens to us. We continually develop the traits of character throughout our lives. Many of us strive to become a better person for ourselves and for others. Character development helps each of us become a better person. Character provides the strengths each of us needs in order to make positive contributions to our school, place of work, and society.

Character development is important to all of us. USA WEEKEND (1994, 20-24) printed an article on character and its qualities. The article included a quiz to help each of us assess the levels of our honesty and responsibility. Two of the quiz questions are given below. They present situations that we could encounter in our daily lives. The answers we give to the questions can help us understand and develop character in our own lives.

## ACTIVITIES

1. Read the material at the left and answer the two quiz questions. You may have more than one answer to each question, but your answers must be consistent.

2. In groups of 3 or 4 students, discuss your answers in terms of the attributes of good character.

3. Three attributes of good character are identified in the material at the left. If other attributes came out of your discussion in Step 2, add them to the others.

4. Compose/key a short report to give your definition (understanding) of good character and the attributes of which it is comprised.

**Question 1.** You look younger than you are. You could save $24 at an amusement park if you lie about your age. Would you do it?
a.  Yes. I need the money more than they do.
b.  Yes. It's unfair to make people pay more just because they're older.
c.  Yes, if I couldn't afford to pay the full price.
d.  No. It is unfair to the people who play by the rules.
e.  No. It is dishonest.

**Question 2.** You are captain of your high school tennis team, one of the state's best. The coach is new and doesn't know the players well. One player has to be cut. The coach asks you, as captain, to decide which of two players should stay on the team. One is your best friend, who really wants to play; the other, a better player who could help the team more. Would you choose your friend?
a.  Yes. Loyalty is very important.
b.  Yes, because of the golden rule. If our roles were reversed, I would want my friend to choose me.
c.  No. My duty to the team is to select the best player.
d.  No. I would not like it if the coach selected players on the basis of whom he liked rather than playing skill.
e.  No. It is in my own best interests to have the best players possible.
f.  No. It would be unfair to the other, better player. ✳

and encouragement will allow their child to become the next Marino, 140

Thomas, or Yamaguchi. Unfortunately, lc Dreams such as these are often entirely the 156

parents' and not the child's. Parents become unreasonable, pushign 170

their children to the point of excesiveness. The child ends ~~ends~~ up 183

paying a heavy, emotional price for parental perfection-ism.[1] 195

The Original Purpose of Sports 201

　　　Elementary children in the United States have had the 212

opportunity to participate in competetive sports since the 1850's 225

when the ymca was organized. The Public School athletic league 238

was started in New York city as early as 1903. Programs such as 251

these were designed to include diferent competetion categories for 265

children with a variety of athletic skills, thus giving every 277

child the opportunity to participate.[2] 285

according to Nelson[3] The fundamental principles of these programs are still appli- 302
cable today. "Sports participation was designed to achieve a sense 315
of enjoyment, well-being, and competence." He cautions that "a 328
DS shift away from these ideals toward intense competition, winning, 341
and a system that rewards only excellence may have detrimental ef- 354
fects on many children." 360

Today's Purpose of Sports 365

~~It is important for~~ parents, coaches, teachers, adminis- 372

trators, and students participate-ing in sports programs need to address 386

the question of what is the purpose of today's sports. Is the goal 400

to still provide a sense of enjoyment, well-being, and competence 413

for all, the goal or has ~~it~~ shifted to "win no matter what the cost"? 427

　　　The answer to this question may be seen at the next sporting 439

event through observing the people associated with the sporting 450

may not be possible event. ~~There may not be~~ a universal answer to the question as 463

since attitudes vary a great deal from ~~one~~ place to place. In each place, however, 479
the attitude toward sports programs depends a great deal on who the 493
DS parents, the coaches, the teachers, the administrators, and the 505
students are who participate in the sports programs. 516

---

**Document 2**
**Endnotes Page**
Use the following information to create an endnotes page on a separate page.

[1] James S. Thornton, "Springing Young Athletes from the Parental Pressure Cooker," _The Physician and Sports Medicine_, Vol. 19, No. 7, July 1991, p. 92.

[2] Michael A. Nelson, "Developmental Skills and Children's Sports," _The Physician and Sports Medicine_, Vol. 19, No. 2, February 1991, p. 67.

[3] Nelson, p. 68.

**Note:** Endnote 3 refers to the same publication as Endnote 2. If there is more than one author named Nelson, give full name; if more than one publication by this author, give part of the title.

**Document 3**
**Title Page**
Prepare a title page for the report, using your name, school name, and current date. Refer to p. 212 (computer users) or RG20 (electronics), if necessary.

# GLOBAL AWARENESS

The United Nations has as its main purpose the promotion of peace, understanding, and cooperation among all peoples of the world. Headquartered in the city of New York, the UN began operations on October 24, 1945. Over 180 countries are members. Writers of the UN charter realized that peace and cooperation among all nations needed to be maintained to avoid another war that likely would be worse than the one just ended—World War II.

One way the United Nations works to reduce human abuse and discrimination and to develop peace and understanding is through yearly days of remembrance. The purpose of these special days is to help us understand the issues and to encourage us to work together, nationally and internationally, to eliminate the cause of human suffering and global strife.

The following list of UN annual observances suggests major global issues.

| | | | |
|---|---|---|---|
| March 8 | International Women's Day | 1st Monday of October | Universal Children's Day |
| March 21 | International Day for Elimination of Racial Discrimination | October 1 | International Day for the Elderly |
| June 4 | International Day of Innocent Children Victims of Aggression | October 10 | World Food Day |
| 3d Tuesday of September | International Day of Peace | October 24 | United Nations Day |
| | | December 1 | World AIDS Day |
| | | December 10 | Human Rights Day |

## ACTIVITIES

1. Read and discuss the material at the left.

2. In groups of 3 or 4 students, select one of the days from the list and plan a school-wide observance for that day.
   a. List the steps you need to follow in preparation.
   b. Decide on a program for the observance and who will conduct it.
   c. Decide on what you need to do to promote attendance: posters, announcements, etc.
   d. If guest speakers are to be involved, decide who they will be and compose a letter inviting them.

# CULTURAL DIVERSITY

No two people are exactly alike, except for identical twins; and even they may develop slight differences. People differ biologically: hair, eyes, skin color, physique, gender, physical capability, and mental capability. We also differ by culture, including the geographical area from which we and/or our ancestors came; the economic level of our families and forebears; and the ways we make, do, and celebrate things. All these factors affect how we behave and how we appear to others.

These biological and cultural differences cause us, somewhat naturally, to develop an *us and them* attitude. We tend to think that others differ from us when it is just as true that we differ from them. Almost all of us see ourselves as the center of our universe and view others from our own perspective. To get along in a diverse society, we must learn to see others and ourselves from their perspective. To do otherwise is to encourage bias and to invite friction and disagreement.

An old sales adage summarizes this concept rather well: "To sell John Doe what John Doe buys, you must see John Doe through John Doe's eyes."

## ACTIVITIES

1. Choose a fellow student you do not know very well, one who seems as different from you as possible: ethnic origin, economic background, social group, academic level, gender, and so on.

2. Discuss the outward differences each of you perceives in the other.

3. Exchange answers to these questions:
   a. How important to you are athletic achievement? scholastic achievement? being part of a certain social group? and why?
   b. What concerns you most about your life: at home? at school? in your community? and why?
   c. What do you want to be doing in five years? and why?

4. Compose/key a summary of your differences and similarities.

# LESSON 119

## Unbound Report with Endnotes

**Objectives:**
1. To format an unbound report.
2. To improve language skills (underline).

### 119A • 5
**Conditioning Practice**

each line twice SS; then two 1' writings on line 2; find *gwam*; clear screen

alphabet 1 The exquisite prize, a famous old clock, was to be given in July.

speed 2 Helen owns the six foals and the cow in the neighbor's hay field.

figures 3 Their team average went from .459 on April 17 to .286 on June 30.

gwam 1' | 1 | 2 | 3 | 4 | 5 | 6 | 7 | 8 | 9 | 10 | 11 | 12 | 13 |

## L ANGUAGE SKILLS

### 119B • 10
**Underline**

Follow the Learn/Apply procedure for 76C on p. 184.

> Use an underline or italics to indicate titles of books and names of magazines and newspapers. (Titles may be keyed in ALL CAPS without the underline.)

Learn 1. I saw the advertisement for The Client in the New York Times.

Apply 2. He quoted the article from Business Week or the Denver Post.

Apply 3. The story appeared in the Los Angeles Times on May 14.

> Use an underline to call attention to words or phrases (or use quotation marks). **Note**: Use a continuous underline (see preceding rule) unless each word is to be considered separately, as shown below.

Learn 4. He did not know whether to use to, too, or two.

Apply 5. We had to identify the correct word from our, are, and hour.

Apply 6. She lost points because she used there instead of their.

## F ORMATTING

### 119C • 35
**Unbound Report**

**Document 1**
**Report from Rough Draft**

1. Review the formatting guides for reports on pp. 211-212.

2. Format the copy at right and on the next page as a report in unbound style; use **SPORTS** for the main heading.

3. When you finish, use the spell check and proofread your copy.

words

heading 1

"When I grow up, I'm going to be just like Dan Marino and be  13

the quarterback for the Miami Dolphins." "I'm going to be just like  27

Frank Thomas and play baseball for the Chicago White Sox when I grow up." "When I  44

grow up, I'm going to be an famous ice skater, just like Kristi Yamaguchi."  59

Most children dream of becoming the next American sports hero. How-  72

ever, only a few will ever reach the apex they dreamed of as a child.  87

Children become parents, parents who had unfulfilled childhood  99

dreams. As parents they often try are ready to have those childhood dreams  112

fulfilled through by their children. They are confident that their help  126

*(continued on next page)*

# PHASE 4

## Enhance Document Processing Skills

This section of the textbook gives opportunities for enhancing your information processing skills. Some lessons focus on enhancing speed and accuracy by refining keying techniques. More punctuation rules appear, along with many "checks" on rules in prior lessons.

In Phase 4 you will enhance document formatting skills, too. After reviewing correspondence, report, and table formats, you will transfer your knowledge and skill to other documents, including those used to get a job. Once again you will have a chance to apply class learning on the job.

The subject of many documents is technology. You will encounter terms, such as electronic mail and voice mail, that define the fields of communication and information processing. Remember: "No matter what career you choose . . . , a computer is likely to be the center of your communication. . . ."

**In the 38 lessons of this phase, you will:**

1. Refine keying techniques to enhance speed and accuracy on straight, script, and rough-draft copy.
2. Enhance document formatting skills and ability to apply language skills.
3. Prepare business forms and special-purpose documents.
4. Create employment documents.
5. Acquire (simulated) work experience in a consulting business.

**Format Guides:
MLA-Style Reports**

MLA Format

MLA Works Cited Page

## MLA-Style Report Guide

A variety of methods can be used to document references used in a report. Unit 13 presented the textual citation method of documentation (refer to p. 144); Unit 20 presented the endnote method of documentation (refer to pp. 211-212). The method endorsed by the Modern Language Association of America (MLA) is widely used for scholarly manuscripts and student research papers. The method, called **parenthetical reference**, is similar to the textual citation method. MLA reports involve several distinctive format features.

## Margins and Page Numbers

MLA-style reports are formatted with one-inch top, side, and bottom margins. The page number for all pages (including the first) is keyed at the right margin one-half inch (0.5") from the top edge of the paper. The writer's last name precedes the page number.

## Spacing

The *entire* report is double-spaced. This line spacing includes the Works Cited page as well as long quotations.

## First-Page Information

The MLA-style report does not include a title page. Information normally found on a title page is keyed on the first page of the report at the left margin, beginning 1" from the top of the page. The information is double-spaced and should include the writer's name, the instructor's name, the course title, and the date.

## Long Quotations

Quoted text of more than four lines is set off from the rest of the text by indenting the text 1" (10 spaces) from the left margin. It is double-spaced and no quotation marks are included. No paragraph indention is needed when quoting a single paragraph from the same source. When quoting more than one paragraph, indent each paragraph an additional 0.25" (three spaces). The parenthetical reference for the quote is placed two spaces after the quotation.

```
If the writer's name intro-
duces the quote, only the
page number needs to be
placed in the parenthetical
reference. (18)

If there are several works
by the same author, the
title or part of it should
be included with the refer-
ence. (Writer's Guide 18)

If the writer's name does
not introduce the quote, it
should be added to the
parenthetical reference.
(Miller 18)
```

## Works Cited

The works cited in the report are listed alphabetically by author surnames at the end of the report on a separate page. The margins are the same as the rest of the report. Key the page number preceded by the report writer's name 0.5" from the top of the page, flush right. Key the heading, Works Cited, 1" from the top of the page. Each reference is DS. The first line of each reference begins at the left margin; other lines are indented 0.5".

# ACTIVITY 1:

**Merge**

1. Read the copy at right.
2. Learn the Merge feature for your software.
3. Prepare form and data files from the information provided below right and on p. 267.
4. Merge the form and data files to create a personalized form letter for each person named in the data file.

The **Merge** feature is used to combine information from two sources into one document. It is often used for mail merge, which merges a form letter file (**form** or **primary file**) with an address file (**data** or **secondary file**) to create personalized letters to each person in the address file.

An address (data) file contains a **record** for each person. Each record contains **field(s)** of information about the person, such as her or his title, first name, last name, etc.

**End field codes** are used in the data file to separate and distinguish fields of information. **End record codes** are used in the data file to separate and distinguish each record.

The form file contains the text of the document that remains constant in each letter plus the **field codes** or **field names**. The field codes (names) are positioned in the document where the variable information from the data file is to appear.

## Form (Primary) File

<Date>

<Title> <First name> <Last name>
<Address>
<City,> <State> <ZIP>

Dear <Title> <Last name>

It was a pleasure to meet with you last week to discuss your life insurance needs. As you requested, I have the costs for various options computed and would be happy to meet with you to go over the figures. I will call you next week to arrange an appointment.

Sincerely

Tom Andrews
Agent

xx

## Data (Secondary) File Information

|  |  |  |  |
|---|---|---|---|
| Title: | Mr. | Title: | Dr. |
| First name: | Angelo | First name: | Anita |
| Last name: | Martinez | Last name: | Burton |
| Address: | 928 Ellsworth Dr. | Address: | 298 Boswell Rd. |
| City: | Rapid City | City: | Raleigh |
| State: | SD | State: | NC |
| ZIP: | 57706-8212 | ZIP: | 27610-1252 |

*(continued on next page)*

**Endnote**

1. Read the copy at right.
2. Learn the Endnote feature for your software.
3. Key the information at right using the Endnote feature to format and key the endnotes on a separate page with the heading ENDNOTES.

The **Endnote** feature helps you create and format endnotes at the same time you are keying a report. The feature automatically inserts the endnote numbers in the text at specified locations and a corresponding number at the end of the document in the endnotes section. The operator is able to key the endnote immediately after specifying the location in the body of the document. A hard page break will place the endnotes on a separate page from the text of the report. The word ENDNOTES should be keyed 2" from the top of the screen, followed by a quadruple space.

DIVERSITY

Managing diversity is important to the success of today's business world. Different organizations approach diversity in a variety of ways. In many organizations, Gage wrote, "fitting the mold is no longer mandated."[1]

Diversity training programs are being utilized. The programs are based on the assumption that "the stepping stone of our relationships with others is self-consciousness."[2]

[1]Amy Gage, "More Big Firms Are Embracing Their Diversity," St. Paul Pioneer Press, June 9, 1994, p. 1E, col. 2.

[2]Pablo Casares, "Conducting Business in an Intercultural Context," Business Credit, April 1993, p. 30.

# ACTIVITY 2:

**Review Sort**

1. Key the information at right SS in two columns leaving 2" between columns.
2. If necessary, review Sort feature on p. 267.
3. Sort by park name in ascending order.
4. Sort by state in ascending order.

| | |
|---|---|
| Yellowstone | Wyoming |
| Sequoia | California |
| Yosemite | California |
| Mount Rainier | Washington |
| Crater Lake | Oregon |
| Wind Cave | South Dakota |
| Mesa Verde | Colorado |
| Glacier | Montana |
| Rocky Mountain | Colorado |
| Mount McKinley | Alaska |

| Title: | Ms. | | Title: | Mr. |
| First name: | Halli | | First name: | Wayne |
| Last name: | Johnson | | Last name: | Walton |
| Address: | 381 Lake Grove St. | | Address: | 821 Utah Ave. |
| City: | Memphis | | City: | Harrisburg |
| State: | TN | | State: | PA |
| ZIP: | 38108-7865 | | ZIP: | 17109-8374 |

## ACTIVITY 2:

### Special Characters

1. Read the copy at right.
2. Learn to use special characters in your software.
3. Key the copy using a special character available in your software.
4. Replace the character with another available character.

**Special characters** such as ✓, ★, □, ●, ■, and ¶, which are not found on the keyboard, can be formed by accessing them with key and number combinations determined by your software. One of the most common uses of such characters is with listings. Instead of using numbers with the listing, special characters are used.

Please check to make sure you have included the following items:

✓ sleeping bag
✓ tent
✓ backpack
✓ hiking boots

## ACTIVITY 3:

### Sort

1. Read the copy at right.
2. Learn to use the Sort feature for your software.
3. Key the text at the right in two columns leaving 2" between columns.
4. Sort by last name in ascending order.
5. Sort by social security number in ascending order.
6. Sort by first name in ascending order.

The **Sort** feature arranges text in a specific order. The feature will sort alphabetic or numeric text in ascending or descending order.

| | |
|---|---|
| Brown, Jacob | 520-38-8211 |
| Aspen, Mary | 261-29-3841 |
| Smith, Rafael | 926-28-2991 |
| Jackson, Ron | 388-19-2842 |
| Marshall, Anne | 882-29-1819 |
| Simmons, Charla | 261-36-5656 |
| Timms, Barbara | 261-92-1243 |

## ACTIVITY 4:

### Review wp Features

1. Key sentences; underline, *italicize*, and **bold** text as you key.
2. Use the Block Delete feature to delete *who live in Germany* and the commas from line 1 and *a University of Wyoming Graduate* and the commas from line 2.
3. Delete lines 3 and 4.

1 **Mark** and **Jane**, who live in Germany, were at the **World Series**.

2 **Kari Carling**, a University of Wyoming graduate, wrote Is Justice Fair?

3 *Mary* would ask very specific questions before analyzing the **issues**.

4 Dial **9-1-1** for *EMERGENCY* service; **6-1-1** for *REPAIR* service.

5 The first test date is Monday, **October 17**; the second test date is Monday, **October 31**.

6 **Meg** bought *The Stock Buyer's Guide* to help her with investing.

7 **Aaron**, **Mays**, and **Mantle** are members of the Baseball Hall of Fame.

Timed Writings
1. A 1' writing on ¶ 1.
2. Add 5 *gwam* to the rate attained in Step 1.
3. Key two 1' writings on each paragraph, trying to achieve the rate determined in Step 2.
4. A 3' writing on ¶s 1-3 combined.
5. A 5' writing on ¶s 1-3 combined.

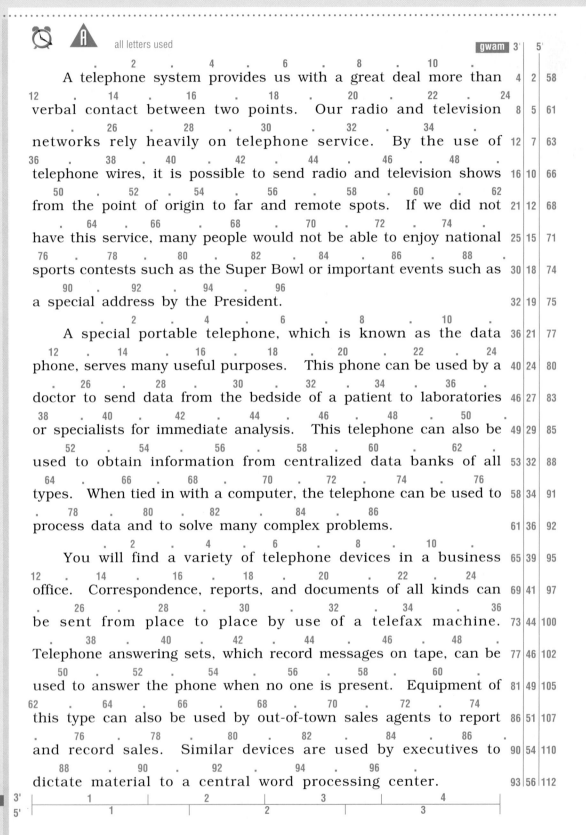

all letters used

gwam 3' 5'

A telephone system provides us with a great deal more than verbal contact between two points. Our radio and television networks rely heavily on telephone service. By the use of telephone wires, it is possible to send radio and television shows from the point of origin to far and remote spots. If we did not have this service, many people would not be able to enjoy national sports contests such as the Super Bowl or important events such as a special address by the President.

A special portable telephone, which is known as the data phone, serves many useful purposes. This phone can be used by a doctor to send data from the bedside of a patient to laboratories or specialists for immediate analysis. This telephone can also be used to obtain information from centralized data banks of all types. When tied in with a computer, the telephone can be used to process data and to solve many complex problems.

You will find a variety of telephone devices in a business office. Correspondence, reports, and documents of all kinds can be sent from place to place by use of a telefax machine. Telephone answering sets, which record messages on tape, can be used to answer the phone when no one is present. Equipment of this type can also be used by out-of-town sales agents to report and record sales. Similar devices are used by executives to dictate material to a central word processing center.

| gwam | 3' | 5' |
|---|---|---|
| | 4 | 2 | 58 |
| | 8 | 5 | 61 |
| | 12 | 7 | 63 |
| | 16 | 10 | 66 |
| | 21 | 12 | 68 |
| | 25 | 15 | 71 |
| | 30 | 18 | 74 |
| | 32 | 19 | 75 |
| | 36 | 21 | 77 |
| | 40 | 24 | 80 |
| | 46 | 27 | 83 |
| | 49 | 29 | 85 |
| | 53 | 32 | 88 |
| | 58 | 34 | 91 |
| | 61 | 36 | 92 |
| | 65 | 39 | 95 |
| | 69 | 41 | 97 |
| | 73 | 44 | 100 |
| | 77 | 46 | 102 |
| | 81 | 49 | 105 |
| | 86 | 51 | 107 |
| | 90 | 54 | 110 |
| | 93 | 56 | 112 |

gwam 3' | 1 | 2 | 3 | 4 |
5' | 1 | 2 | 3 |

**Format Guides:**

Modified Block Letter with Special Parts

Modified Block Letter with Special Characters

Second Page of Business Letter

Occasionally, you will find several special features used in business letters and memos. In some cases, alternative formats for special parts are chosen (for example, the subject line may be placed in various positions). The simplest and most efficient formats, however, are illustrated in this unit.

**Attention line.** When an attention line is used in a letter addressed to a company, key it as the first line of the letter and envelope address:

```
Attention Personnel Director
Beechwood Associates
878 Colonial Way
New Bedford, MA 02747-2511
```

When a letter is addressed to a company, the correct salutation is "Ladies and Gentlemen."

**Subject line.** Place the subject line in ALL CAPS a double space below the salutation. If the body paragraphs are blocked, block the subject line at the left margin. If the body paragraphs are indented, indent the subject line the same number of spaces or center it.

**Special characters.** Special characters (✓, •, ★) can be used with text to give additional emphasis. Sometimes, special characters are used instead of numbers in listings.

**Page heading.** If a letter involves more than one page, key a heading at the top of each page after the first. Place the receiver's name, page number, and date on three lines at the top left margin (see illustration at left). DS below the date.

**Company name.** When used, place the company name a double space below the complimentary close in ALL CAPS. QS (quadruple-space) to writer's name.

**Enclosure notation.** Place enclosure (or attachment) notation a double space below reference initials. If multiple enclosures are referred to in the letter, follow the word "Enclosures" with a colon and two spaces and list each enclosure:

```
Enclosures: Brochure
            Membership Forms
```

**Copy notation.** A copy notation indicates that a copy of a letter is being sent to someone other than the addressee. Use "c" followed by the name of the person(s) to receive a copy. Place a copy notation a double space below the last line of the enclosure notation or the reference line if there is no enclosure:

```
c Robert Anderson
  Mario Sanchez
```

**Postscript.** A postscript is additional text that may be added after a letter has been completed. It is the last item in the letter. The postscript is used to place additional emphasis on the text or to reemphasize a part of the text included in the body. The postscript can also be used to include a personal message in a business letter.

**Form letters.** A standardized letter that can be sent to numerous addresses is known as a form letter or boilerplate. A form letter (or paragraphs that can be combined to create varying letters) can be stored and retrieved when needed. Through text merging, a form letter and an address list can be merged to provide an original letter to each addressee.

# Skill Builder

## Techniques: Figures

Set as 0.5" SM. Clear all tabs; then set tabs 2", 4", and 6" from the left margin. Key the lines slowly, tabbing from column to column. Take 3' writings. Try to key more characters on each writing.

**Keep eyes on copy.**

| | | | | |
|---|---|---|---|---|
| 529-36-2899 | 12/24/80 | (308) 112-2388 | $   628.00 | 3 |
| 358-29-1076 | 04/30/78 | (608) 197-6655 | $1,381.00 | 6 |
| 346-50-0190 | 02/28/81 | (520) 130-6754 | $5,672.15 | 9 |
| 567-82-8219 | 10/15/84 | (715) 139-2615 | $    56.29 | 12 |
| 628-12-0945 | 03/27/82 | (801) 162-2444 | $3,178.87 | 15 |
| 820-67-1029 | 08/08/79 | (308) 138-8567 | $9,078.25 | 18 |

## Reading/Keying Response Patterns

1. Lines 1-3: each word 3 times (slowly, faster, top speed).
2. Lines 4-6: each phrase 3 times (slowly, faster, top speed).
3. Lines 7-9: each sentence 3 times (slowly, faster, top speed).

**Goal:** Word-level keying.

**Emphasize quick finger reaches, wrists low and relaxed.**

balanced-hand words
1 us if he an by is jam fur hen row pay map man sit the and big may
2 dusk dock corn busy both keys firms land rock sign owns mend sick
3 docks bucks eight goals right they shame social towns vivid turns

**Emphasize high-speed phrase response.**

balanced-hand phrases
4 he owns it | make the signs | paid the man | go to work | if they fix the
5 go to the | they may make | to the problem | with the sign | and the maps
6 with the city | the eighth neighbor | social problem | the big ornament

**Emphasize high-speed, word-level response; quick spacing.**

balanced-hand sentences
7 Jaynel paid the man by the city dock for the six bushels of corn.
8 Keith may keep the food for the fish by the big antique fishbowl.
9 The haughty girls paid for their own gowns for the island social.

gwam 1' | 1 | 2 | 3 | 4 | 5 | 6 | 7 | 8 | 9 | 10 | 11 | 12 | 13 |

## Number Expression Check

Key the sentences at the right; correct number expression as needed.

1. When you buy 3 cups, they will give you 1 free.

2. 12 of the 26 charter members were at the reunion.

3. If you place your order before two p.m., it will be shipped the next day.

4. Ms. King placed an order for eight copies of The Secretary and 14 copies of Modern Office Technology.

5. Approximately 2/3 of the parents attended the special meeting.

6. The package needs to be delivered to 1 Lakeshore Drive.

7. About 60 students voted for class officers on April seven.

8. The next assignment was Chapter seven, not Chapter eight.

9. Roy is 6 ft. eleven in. tall and weighs 180 lbs.

10. The final flight on July six going to Reno leaves at 8 p.m.

# LESSON 113

## Letters/Memos Review

**Objectives:**
1. To review letter formatting.
2. To review memo formatting.

### 113A • 5
### Conditioning Practice

each line twice; then 1'
writings on line 2

alphabet 1 The requirements for the dock job were truly amazing to Dave Pax.

speed 2 Diane is to make a turn to the right when the signal is in sight.

figures 3 Of the 2,387 jobs cut in 1996, over 450 were office-related jobs.

**gwam** 1' | 1 | 2 | 3 | 4 | 5 | 6 | 7 | 8 | 9 | 10 | 11 | 12 | 13 |

## **F** ORMATTING

### 113B • 45
### Review Document Formats

**Document 1**

Format the letter in block format, open punctuation.

|  | words |
|---|---|
| February 5, ---- \| Mr. and Mrs. Felipe Devereaux \| 310 Hampshire Ln. \| | 13 |
| Stamford, CT 06905-7329 \| Dear Mr. and Mrs. Devereaux \| CRUISE | 25 |
| INFORMATION | 27 |

A folder with the specific information on Caribbean cruise options is being | 42
mailed to you today.  As I mentioned to you during our phone conversa- | 56
tion, the Caribbean cruise is one of our most popular vacation packages | 71
during this time of the year. | 77

Information on one-week cruises to Hawaii and the Virgin Islands--two other | 92
popular winter vacation spots--is included in the mailing.  If you book | 107
within the next week or so, I don't think you will experience any difficulties | 122
in making reservations on any of the three cruises. | 133

After you have had an opportunity to review these materials, call us; we will | 149
be happy to handle all details of the cruise.  If you have additional ques- | 164
tions about any of the options, let us know. | 173

Sincerely yours | Ms. Madeline St. Claire | Travel Agent | xx | 184

**Document 2**

Format the letter in simplified block format.

March 23, ---- | MS ROCHELLE SUMMER | 429 NORTH 310 EAST | 11
LOGAN UT 84720-8987 | RECYCLING PROGRAM | 18

The Logan City Council is planning to initiate a recycling program.  Your | 33
participation is vital to the success of the program. | 44

Beginning May 1 separate containers must be used for certain products. | 58
Specific information regarding this program is enclosed.   If you have ques- | 73
tions about the recycling program, please contact Rita White who has been | 88
hired as the recycling coordinator. | 96

Your support of this program will assure a healthier environment for future | 111
generations. | 114

MRS. TERESA A. BREWSTER, CITY MANAGER | xx | Enclosure | 124

**Document 1**

Use the most efficient method to create letters to the individuals listed below. Format the letters in block style with mixed punctuation.

Ms. Josette Washington
861 Norled Dr.
Dayton, OH 45414-9412

Mr. Mark Jankowski
3675 Regal Hill Ct.
Dayton, OH 45430-9860

Ms. Judith Shapeero
342 Humming Bird Ln.
Dayton, OH 45459-2943

Mr. Hassan Staffords
4508 Guadalupe Ave.
Dayton, OH 45427-5419

**Document 2**

Use the most efficient method to send the memo at the right to the listed individuals. Each individual will receive a memo addressed to him/her.

**Document 3**

Using a distribution list (see page 189), prepare one memo addressed to the five individuals listed at the right.

**Note:** Additional R&E documents can be found on pp. A25 and A26.

| | words |
|---|---|
| April 5, ---- | 3 |

&lt;Title&gt; &lt;First Name&gt; &lt;Last Name&gt; — 7
&lt;Street Address&gt; — 10
&lt;City,&gt; &lt;State&gt; &lt;ZIP&gt; — 15

Dear &lt;Title&gt; &lt;Last Name:&gt; — 19

Thank you for agreeing to serve on the convention planning committee for the &lt;Current Year&gt; National Information Management Association's convention. A listing of all committee members is enclosed. — 57

The committee will be formally introduced at NIMA's Annual Business Meeting on Friday, April 23, at 2:45 p.m. If there is time after the meeting, we will set a date for our first convention planning session. — 99

I am looking forward to working with you this next year. — 111

Sincerely, — 113

Ms. Juanita A. Pizarro — 118
Convention Chair — 121

xx — 122

Enclosure — 123

TO: Cindy Austin, Kaye Berry, Dale Erickson, Kim Nakamoto, Mary Tietz | 4
FROM: Shane Glavine, Project Coordinator | DATE: September 15, ---- | 17
SUBJECT: TELECOMMUNICATIONS PROJECT | 25

It appears that 1:30 p.m. Monday, October 27, best fits everyone's schedule for meeting to discuss the interim progress of the telecommunications project. Please plan to give a brief update on what you have accomplished since our last meeting. | 74

The meeting has been scheduled in the conference room and should last no longer than two hours. If additional time is needed for the group to meet before our presentation to the board of directors, I will schedule another meeting. | xx | 121

**Document 3**

Format the letter in modified block format with indented paragraphs, mixed punctuation.

| | words |
|---|---|
| May 10, ---- | Attention Personnel Director | Beechwood Associates | | 13 |
| 878 Colonial Way | New Bedford, MA 02747-2511 | Ladies and | 24 |
| Gentlemen : | FITNESS PROGRAMS | 31 |

¶ More people are becoming health conscious than 41
ever before. Because of the studies linking life expectancy 53
to physical fitness, more people are looking for effective 65
ways to improve their physical conditions. 73

¶ CHADWICK FITNESS CENTER, the newest physical fitness 84
center in New Bedford, is the most advanced fitness center 96
in this area. Modern facilities, state-of-the-art equipment, 108
and a well-trained staff provide the complete program. 119

¶ Ten complimentary one-day passes are enclosed to 129
allow your employees to become acquainted with our 139
fitness center. They can make reservations by calling 150
136-7509. 153

¶ We will look forward to their visits and hope to be 163
able to work with them to customize a fitness program 174
to meet their needs. 178

Sincerely, | Ms. Angela S. Dutton | Fitness Program Director | xx | 190
Enclosures : Brochure | Membership Forms | c Martin D. Vesser 202

**Document 4**

Format the copy as a simplified memo.

**Document 5**

Reformat Document 4 as a standard memo.

| | words |
|---|---|
| June 3, ---- | Dwight Eastick, Office Manager | DESKTOP PUBLISHING | 13 |
| SEMINAR | 14 |

Attached is the brochure describing the desktop publishing seminar that I 29
spoke about with you last week.   The charge for attending the seminar is $195. 45

Since no one in the office currently has experience with desktop publish- 60
ing, I believe the benefits of my attending such a seminar far outweigh the 75
costs involved.   Attending this seminar will allow me to use more produc- 89
tively the desktop publishing package that was purchased last spring.  I 104
will be happy to share with others what I learn from the seminar. 117

Registration forms need to be submitted by June 20 to avoid a late regis- 132
tration fee. 135

Sue A. Buckner, Document Processing Center | xx | Attachment 146

## LESSON 118

## Form Letters/Memos

**Objectives:**
1. To format letters/memos using the Merge feature.
2. To improve language skills (parentheses).

### 118A • 5
### Conditioning Practice

each line twice

alphabet 1 Frank Jacobs was amazingly quiet during the extensive procedures.

speed 2 The soggy field by the dog kennels was good for a big tug of war.

figures 3 The letter dated 4/30/87 was received by the business on 6/25/91.

**gwam** 1' | 1 | 2 | 3 | 4 | 5 | 6 | 7 | 8 | 9 | 10 | 11 | 12 | 13 |

## **L** ANGUAGE SKILLS

### 118B • 10
### Parentheses

Use the standard Learn/
Apply directions in 76C,
p. 184.

Use parentheses to enclose parenthetical or explanatory matter and added information. (Commas or dashes also may be used.)

Learn 1. Senator Simpson (Wyoming) is chair of the committee.
Learn 2. The contracts (Exhibits C and D) should be revised.
Apply 3. The salesperson with the most sales Duncan will be honored.
Apply 4. The book 1996 publication date has been ordered.

Use parentheses to enclose identifying letters or figures of lists within a sentence.

Learn 5. Check for these errors: (1) keying, (2) spelling, and (3) grammar.
Apply 6. The three officers are 1 Sally, 2 Rebecca, and 3 Grant.
Apply 7. She emphasized two key factors:  1 speed and 2 control.

Use parentheses to enclose a name and date used as a reference.

Learn 8. "I Have a Dream" (King, 1963) was delivered to over 200,000 people.
Apply 9. I cited "The Gettysburg Address" Lincoln, 1863 during my speech.
Apply 10. Developing Self-Esteem Palladino, 1989 was the main text for the course.

### 118C • 8
### Speed Builder

1. Two 1' writings on each ¶ of 117B.

2. Determine best 1' *gwam* and record.

# LESSON 114

## Documents with Special Characters

**O b j e c t i v e s :**
**1.** To increase straight-copy keying skill.
**2.** To learn to key documents with special characters.

### 114A • 5
### Conditioning Practice

each line twice

alphabet 1 Zack Plage reviewed the job requirements with fifty to sixty men.

speed 2 The haughty men did the work on the bus for my neurotic neighbor.

figures 3 My boys were born on May 2, 1964, July 3, 1975, and June 8, 1980.

gwam 1' | 1 | 2 | 3 | 4 | 5 | 6 | 7 | 8 | 9 | 10 | 11 | 12 | 13 |

### S KILL BUILDING

### 114B • 12
### Skill Check

1. A 3' writing on ¶s 1-3 combined; find *gwam* and errors.

2. A 1' writing on each ¶; find *gwam* and errors.

3. Another 3' writing on ¶s 1-3 combined; find *gwam* and errors.

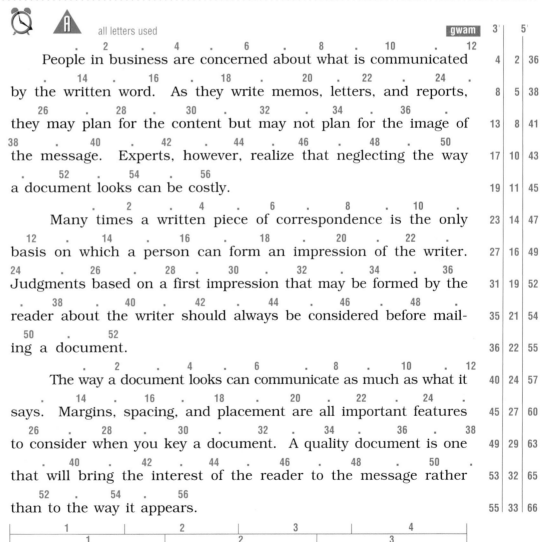

all letters used                                                    gwam  3'  |  5'

.    2    .    4    .    6    .    8    .    10    .    12
People in business are concerned about what is communicated          4   2  36
.    14    .    16    .    18    .    20    .    22    .    24    .
by the written word.  As they write memos, letters, and reports,    8   5  38
26    .    28    .    30    .    32    .    34    .    36    .
they may plan for the content but may not plan for the image of    13   8  41
38    .    40    .    42    .    44    .    46    .    48    .    50
the message.  Experts, however, realize that neglecting the way    17  10  43
.    52    .    54    .    56
a document looks can be costly.                                     19  11  45

.    2    .    4    .    6    .    8    .    10    .
Many times a written piece of correspondence is the only           23  14  47
12    .    14    .    16    .    18    .    20    .    22    .
basis on which a person can form an impression of the writer.      27  16  49
24    .    26    .    28    .    30    .    32    .    34    .    36
Judgments based on a first impression that may be formed by the    31  19  52
.    38    .    40    .    42    .    44    .    46    .    48    .
reader about the writer should always be considered before mail-   35  21  54
50    .    52
ing a document.                                                    36  22  55

.    2    .    4    .    6    .    8    .    10    .    12
The way a document looks can communicate as much as what it        40  24  57
.    14    .    16    .    18    .    20    .    22    .    24    .
says.  Margins, spacing, and placement are all important features  45  27  60
26    .    28    .    30    .    32    .    34    .    36    .    38
to consider when you key a document.  A quality document is one    49  29  63
.    40    .    42    .    44    .    46    .    48    .    50    .
that will bring the interest of the reader to the message rather   53  32  65
52    .    54    .    56
than to the way it appears.                                        55  33  66

gwam 3' |    1    |    2    |    3    |    4    |
     5' |         1         |         2         |         3         |

# FORMATTING

## 117C • 35
## Form Letters

Send the form letter at the right to the individuals listed on the computer printout below. Use block format, open punctuation and the most efficient method available with your equipment.

| | Letters 1 & 2 | Letters 3 & 4 |
|---|---|---|
| March 27, ---- | 3 | 3 |
| | | |
| <Title> <First Name> <Last Name> | 6 | 7 |
| <Street Address> | 10 | 11 |
| <City,> <State> <ZIP> | 15 | 16 |
| | | |
| Dear <Title> <Last Name> | 18 | 20 |

As you are aware, property taxes have continued to increase each year. — 33 | 35
Because of the state budget being proposed by the governor, another — 47 | 49
significant tax increase is projected again this year. The local school — 61 | 63
district has also proposed a budget with an 8 percent increase. — 74 | 76

Our contracts for maintenance have gone up this year as well. Yard main- — 89 | 91
tenance fees had an increase of 12 percent. We are also planning to paint — 103 | 105
the interior of your apartment and replace the carpeting. — 115 | 117

To cover a portion of these expenses, your rent will be increased by $25 — 130 | 132
effective with the June rent. A contract reflecting the rent increase is — 145 | 147
enclosed. Please sign and return the contract prior to April 15. — 158 | 160

Sincerely — 160 | 162

Ms. Megan Sylvester — 164 | 166
Manager — 166 | 168

xx — 167 | 169

Enclosure — 168 | 170

| Letter 1 | Letter 2 |
|---|---|
| Mr. Brent Perry | Ms. Robin Sussex |
| 310 Parkwood Ave. | 320 Parkwood Ave. |
| Charleston, SC 29403-7653 | Charleston, SC 29403-7653 |
| | |
| Letter 3 | Letter 4 |
| Dr. Daryl Wainwright | Ms. Danielle Warrens |
| 314 Parkwood Ave. | 318 Parkwood Ave. |
| Charleston, SC 29403-7653 | Charleston, SC 29403-7653 |

## 114C • 33
## Letters with Special Characters

**Letters 1-3**

Format and key the letters shown at the right in modified block format with indented paragraphs and mixed punctuation. DS the lists in Letters 2 and 3. Date all letters **August 1, ----**.

Key the company name, **ROCKY MOUNTAIN BANKS**, in the signature lines of all three documents.

Send the letters to:

**Mr. Justin Hunter
3451 Canyon Creek Rd.
Boulder, CO 80303-8329**

Letters 2 and 3 are from:

**Lee Q. Hazzard
Customer Services**

Supply an appropriate complimentary closing; add closing notations required.

**Note:** If you are not able to create special characters on your equipment, you can use keyboard characters (*, −, +) or make an enumerated list of the items.

---

words

opening 19

**You are the first to know!!!** Boulder First Bank will change its name to **Rocky Mountain Banks** on September 20. This change is necessitated by the merger of banks in Fort Collins, Laramie, and Cheyenne. — 33 / 47 / 60

This change will have very little impact on you. The ownership, management, and staff will remain the same. The next time you order checks, our new name, **Rocky Mountain Banks**, will appear. You can continue using your Boulder First Bank checks until you need additional checks. — 73 / 86 / 100 / 114 / 116

Our commitment to providing you with quality service will not change. This merger will provide us with the means to expand and enhance the financial services that will be available to you, however. We will keep you informed of these services as they become available. If you have questions, call us. — 131 / 146 / 161 / 176

Very truly yours, | Ms. Allison Miller-Kennedy | President | xx — 192

---

opening 19

We are pleased to introduce the **Monthly Summary**. The **Monthly Summary** is a special service for customers with more than one type of account. At a glance, you will be able to locate: — 32 / 48 / 56

✓ The balance of all accounts combined — 64
✓ The balance of each individual account — 72
✓ Deposits to each individual account — 80

The primary benefit of the **Monthly Summary** is that it streamlines account information. For specific details of each account, you may still check the familiar individual monthly statement that will accompany your **Monthly Summary**. — 93 / 109 / 122 / 126

We are providing this **Monthly Summary** to a select few of our customers to receive feedback prior to providing it to all customers with multiple accounts. Next month you will receive a questionnaire asking for your input as to the value of the summary. If you have comments that you would like to share before that time, please contact me. — 140 / 155 / 169 / 184 / 194

closing 208

---

opening 19

As a preferred mortgage customer, you are preapproved for a Rocky Mountain Banks' credit card. As long as your mortgage is serviced by Rocky Mountain Banks, there will be no annual fee. — 32 / 46 / 56

Your credit card comes with a variety of services at no additional cost. Included in these services are: — 71 / 78

■ Car rental discounts — 83
■ Telephone calling card service — 89
■ $500,000 travel insurance — 95
■ Travel registration service — 101

The enclosed brochure describes in detail all services offered through membership with the Rocky Mountain Banks' card. To receive the card, complete and return the enclosed authorization form; you will be able to start taking advantage of the services as soon as you receive the card. — 115 / 129 / 144 / 158

closing 172

## LESSON 117 — Form Letters and Basic Skills

**Objectives:**

**1.** To learn how to format letters by the most efficient method available.

**2.** To increase straight-copy skill.

### 117A • 5
### Conditioning Practice

each line twice

alphabet 1 Jack Repoz may give a few more racquetball exhibitions in Dayton.

speed 2 Their big social for their neighbor may also be held in the city.

figures 3 Case No. 3689 Z 457 will be presented on either May 19 or May 20.

gwam 1' | 1 | 2 | 3 | 4 | 5 | 6 | 7 | 8 | 9 | 10 | 11 | 12 | 13 |

### S KILL BUILDING

### 117B • 10
### Skill Check

Two 3' writings on ¶s 1-3 combined; find *gwam* and errors.

all letters used

| | gwam | 3' | 5' |

Attitude is the way people communicate their feelings or    4 | 2 | 44

moods to others. A person is said to have a positive attitude    8 | 5 | 46

when he or she anticipates successful experiences. A person such    12 | 7 | 49

as this is said to be an optimist. The best possible outcomes    17 | 10 | 52

are expected. The world is viewed as a great place. Good is    21 | 12 | 54

found in even the worst situation.    23 | 14 | 55

Individuals are said to have negative attitudes when they    27 | 16 | 58

expect failure. A pessimist is the name given to an individual    31 | 19 | 60

with a bad view of life. Pessimists emphasize the adverse    35 | 21 | 63

aspects of life and expect the worst possible outcome. They    39 | 23 | 65

expect to fail even before they start the day. You can plan on    43 | 26 | 68

them to find gloom even in the best situation.    46 | 28 | 69

Only you can ascertain when you are going to have a good or    50 | 30 | 72

bad attitude. Keep in mind that people are attracted to a    54 | 33 | 74

person with a good attitude and tend to shy away from one with a    59 | 35 | 77

bad attitude. Your attitude quietly determines just how success-    63 | 38 | 79

ful you are in all your personal relationships as well as in    67 | 40 | 82

your professional relationships.    69 | 42 | 83

gwam 3' | 1 | 2 | 3 | 4 |
     5' | 1 | 2 | 3 |

# LESSON 115

## Two-Page Letters, Postscripts

**Objectives:**
1. To format and key a two-page letter.
2. To include a postscript on a letter.
3. To improve language skills (hyphen).

### 115A • 5
**Conditioning Practice**

set 0.5" SMs;
each line twice

alphabet 1 Mr. Voldez was extremely happy after Glen quickly adjusted his brakes.

speed 2 He owns both the antique bottle and the enamel bottle on their mantle.

figures 3 Only 308 of the 967 expected participants had registered by 12:45 p.m.

gwam 1' | 1 | 2 | 3 | 4 | 5 | 6 | 7 | 8 | 9 | 10 | 11 | 12 | 13 | 14 |

### 115B • 7
**Skill Building**

1. Two 1' writings on line 1 of 115A.

**Goal:** Not over 2 errors in each writing.

2. Two 1' writings on line 2 of 115A.

**Goal:** To force speed to a new level.

### 115C • 28
**Long Letters**

**Letter 1**
Format and key the text at the right as a modified block letter with blocked ¶s and mixed punctuation.

| | words |
|---|---|
| January 2, ---- | Mr. Justin Hunter | 3451 Canyon Creek Rd. | | 11 |
| Boulder, CO 80303-8329 | Dear Mr. Hunter: | | 19 |

When we announced our merger, we promised you expanded and — 31
enhanced services. We are now ready to deliver some of those — 44
services. Beginning January 15, the following services will be — 56
available: — 59

★ Extended banking hours. Banking hours will be from 7:30 — 71
a.m. to 5:30 p.m. Monday through Friday. This schedule — 82
should provide an opportunity to bank during the week — 93
before or after work. On Saturday the bank will be open — 104
from 9 a.m. to 1 p.m. — 109

★ Automatic teller machines. Automatic teller machines are — 121
now available at selected locations throughout the city. — 132
Use the enclosed sheet to determine the nearest location. — 144

★ Certified financial planning. Two Certified Financial — 156
Planners (CFPs) have been hired to assist you with your — 167
long-term financial planning. — 173

*We are excited about the changes that are taking place at* **Rocky Mountain** — 188
**Banks.** *We will share additional services with you as they become avail-* — 202
*able. If you would like more information on any of the services that are* — 217
*listed above, please call.* — 223

*Sincerely,* | **ROCKY MOUNTAIN BANKS** | *Lee O. Hazzard* | *Customer* — 234
*Services* | *xx* | *Enclosure* — 238

## 116D • 27
### Form Paragraphs

Create Letters 1-4 (below) using macros if equipment permits. Use block format, open punctuation. Use today's date and supply a salutation.

 **note:**

Review the Macro feature (p. 188) to record each ¶ and retrieve it as needed to create a letter.

**Letter 1**

**Ms. Sonya Cavazo**
**5640 Newcastle Dr.**
**Dallas, TX 75220-9387**

Paragraphs: **B, D, F, I**

Department: **Information Processing Center**

(Total words = 170)

**Letter 2**

**Mrs. Rebecca Broderick**
**446 Lake Charles Ave.**
**Fort Worth, TX 76103-7869**

Paragraphs: **B, E, H, I**

Department: **Accounting Department**

(Total words = 151)

**Letter 3**

**Ms. Anne Herrick**
**729 Richardson Dr.**
**Fort Worth, TX 76148-3482**

Paragraphs: **A, C, F, I**

Department: **Sales Department**

(Total words = 150)

**Letter 4**

**Mr. Bruce Sinclair**
**4230 Lowell St.**
**Dallas, TX 75214-4536**

Paragraphs: **B, D, G, I**

Department: **Information Processing Center**

(Total words = 166)

---

A

Congratulations on your new position with Edgewater Industries! We are looking forward to having you as a member of our (Name of Department).

B

Welcome to Edgewater Industries; we are pleased that you have chosen to become part of our organization! We are looking forward to having your assistance in accomplishing our goals and objectives in the years ahead.

C

You will enjoy working with Michael Alvarado. He has been with the company for 15 years and is highly regarded by his colleagues. Since he was promoted to sales manager seven years ago, company sales have grown tremendously. The new sales strategies that he implemented have been very successful.

D

If you enjoy working with the latest technology, I am certain that you will enjoy being part of Melissa Downey's staff. Our Information Processing Center was recently featured in a national office technology magazine and is the envy of many organizations. This is due to the efforts of Ms. Downey and her talented staff.

E

You will enjoy working with Duncan Revere; he is superb! He is one of those rare individuals who possesses people skills as well as technical expertise. He has completely computerized the Accounting Department since being appointed accounting supervisor.

F

I am confident that your association with us will be rewarding. I am looking forward to visiting with you in person at the next meeting of the (Name of Department).

G

Your association with us will be rewarding. I am looking forward to meeting you the next time I visit the (Name of Department).

H

I am confident that your work in the (Name of Department) will be rewarding. I am looking forward to meeting you soon.

I

Yours very truly


Ms. Tara A. Rockford
President


xx

## Letter 2

Format and key the text at the right as a two-page letter in modified block format with blocked ¶s and mixed punctuation to:

**Ms. Othelo Weeks**
**Brentwood Industries, Inc.**
**832 Waycross Ave.**
**Pensacola, FL 32507-3867**

Date the letter **September 28, ----.** The letter is from **Mr. Rori M. Santos, Executive Director.** Supply an appropriate salutation, complimentary closing, and closing notations.

Bold the headings in each listed item as shown. Include the following postscript:

**Join before October 15 and save 20 percent off the regular membership price.**

## Letter 3

Reformat (or rekey) Letter 2 in block format with open punctuation. Omit the postscript.

words

opening 24

Did you know that more than 3,000 companies with information manage- 38
ment departments belong to the National Information Management Associa- 52
tion (NIMA)?  The main purpose of NIMA is to provide professional 65
development opportunities for employees of its members. 77

The professional resources available to NIMA include: 88

■ **Information Management Journal**.  Your company will receive 12 101
issues of <u>Information Management Journal</u>.  The <u>Journal</u> offers cur- 114
rent articles relating to the latest developments in the information 128
management field. 132

■ **Publications.**  Your company is entitled to a 30 percent discount on 146
publications purchased through the organization's library.  In addi- 159
tion to a number of books relating to information management, sav- 173
ings are also available on a number of current periodicals.  See the 186
enclosed listing. 190

■ **NIMA convention**.  The annual NIMA convention is among the fin- 203
est information management conventions in the world.  Employees of 216
your company will be entitled to reduced registration fees. 229

■ **Regional workshops**.  Regional workshops are sponsored quarterly 242
in various cities throughout the United States.  Employees of firms 255
belonging to NIMA receive reduced registration fees. 266

■ **Local workshops**.  NIMA will make arrangements with experts in 279
the field of information management to do in-house training for com- 293
panies belonging to NIMA. 298

A membership packet is enclosed to provide you with more information on 312
the National Information Management Association.  Next week I will call 327
you to see if you have any questions about our organization. 339

closing 366

## LANGUAGE SKILLS

### 115D • 10
### Hyphen

Use the Learn/Apply directions given for 76C, p. 184.

Use a hyphen to join compound numbers from twenty-one to ninety-nine.

| Learn | 1. The youngest member was twenty-six; the oldest, sixty-three. |
| Apply | 2. She celebrated her twenty first birthday on May 6. |
| Apply | 3. The braces were removed when she was twenty or twenty one. |

Use a hyphen to join compound adjectives preceding a noun they modify as a unit.

| Learn | 4. The up-to-date file always contained the latest research. |
| Apply | 5. The door to door salesperson was here around 10:30 a.m. |
| Apply | 6. The Over the Hill Gang meets on Wednesday evening. |

# LESSON 116

## Letters from Form Paragraphs

**Objectives:**
1. To learn to format letters from form paragraphs.
2. To enhance language skills (colon).

---

**116A • 5**
**Conditioning Practice**

each line twice

| | | |
|---|---|---|
| alphabet | 1 | Jess explained why the November sales quota for Zack was so high. |
| speed | 2 | Helen and the visitor may handle the problems with the amendment. |
| figures | 3 | Your office will be 2105; your phone number, 135-4569, ext. 8572. |

gwam  1' | 1 | 2 | 3 | 4 | 5 | 6 | 7 | 8 | 9 | 10 | 11 | 12 | 13 |

---

## L ANGUAGE SKILLS

**116B • 10**
**Colon**

Use the Learn/Apply directions given for 76C, p. 184.

Use a colon to introduce an enumeration or a listing.

| Learn | 1. Please purchase the following:  tie, dress shirt, and coat. |
|---|---|
| Apply | 2. Add these names to your list Jay Smith, Kay Shi, and Joe Day. |
| Apply | 3. She brought the following cake, cookies, and pies. |

Use a colon to introduce a question or a direct quotation.

| Learn | 4. Her question:  "How can you make so many errors?" |
|---|---|
| Apply | 5. Jay's last comment "How many times did you repeat the course?" |
| Apply | 6. The manager's next inquiry "Will you be to work on time?" |

Use a colon between hours and minutes expressed in figures.

| Learn | 7. Flight 2308 left for Dallas at 7:39 p.m. |
|---|---|
| Apply | 8. You can schedule an appointment at 1015 a.m. or 330 p.m. |
| Apply | 9. Does the play start at 730 or 830 p.m.? |

---

**116C • 8**
**Build Skill**

1. Each line twice.
2. Try to complete each sentence on the call of 15", 12", or 10" writing, as directed.

**Emphasis: one-hand words**

gwam  15" | 12" | 10"

| | 15" | 12" | 10" |
|---|---|---|---|
| In my opinion, only a few eager pupils read texts. | 40 | 50 | 60 |
| Brad saw fast deer retreat after Carter started uphill. | 44 | 55 | 66 |
| My pupil asserts that great debates are based only on facts. | 48 | 60 | 72 |
| Gregg Hill addressed my pupils on minimum state tax rates on gas. | 52 | 65 | 78 |

gwam  1' | 1 | 2 | 3 | 4 | 5 | 6 | 7 | 8 | 9 | 10 | 11 | 12 | 13 |

# APPENDICES

**Activity 7**
Prepare the text at the right as p. 5 of a report. Import the map graphic from a graphics package. Import the sales data for Colorado from the spreadsheet prepared in Activity 6.

 **Proofreading alert:**
Assume that *any* copy you key may contain errors.

Illustration 1 depicts Region 6 territory as well as the number of sales reps in each state of the territory. All states except Colorado have 3 reps; Colorado has 5 reps.

### Illustration 1

### Number of Sales Reps

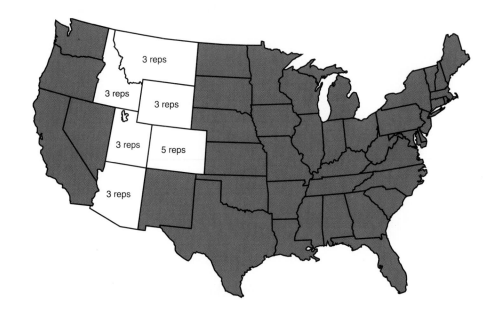

The sales figures for the first quarter reflect the munber of sales reps in each state. As could be expected, Clorado has the highest total sales for the first quarter (insert from spreadsheet) and the highest monthly average (insert from spreadsheet). Table 3 gives the complete sales figures for the Colorado reps.

### Table 3

### First Quarter Sales

### Colorado

| Name | January | February | March | Total Sales First Quarter | Monthly Average |
|------|--------|----------|-------|---------------------------|-----------------|
| Hundley, Ann | 25,730 | 12,830 | 45,769 | 84,329 | 28,110 |
| Johnson, Marge | 38,654 | 38,020 | 36,908 | 113,582 | 37,861 |
| Kent, Kellee | 38,310 | 28,095 | 34,789 | 101,194 | 33,731 |
| Martinez, Justin | 33,810 | 23,789 | 28,210 | 85,809 | 28,603 |
| Phillips, Josh | 27,690 | 33,760 | 28,809 | 90,259 | 30,086 |
| | 164,194 | 136,494 | 174,485 | 475,173 | 158,391 |

**Activity 8**
Using the information in the spreadsheet, prepare a pie chart showing the percent of total sales for each state for the first quarter. Supply appropriate heading and size the chart to fit on a half page.

## Explore Windows

*Windows 95* and *Windows 98* are operating system software programs that control the operation of the computer and the peripherals such as the mouse and printer. Software applications that run under *Windows* have many common features. They all use similar icons and consistent menus. A typical *Windows* desktop is shown below. The icons represent some of the features common to either *Windows 95* or *Windows 98*.

## Windows 95/98

The opening screen of *Windows 95/98* simulates a *desktop* working environment. The icons shown represent some of the features contained on your system.

 ***My Computer*** displays the disk drives, CD-ROM, and printers attached to the computer.

 ***Network Neighborhood*** allows you to view the available resources if you are connected to a network environment.

 ***Recycle Bin*** stores documents that have been deleted from the hard drive. Documents deleted in error can be retrieved and returned to their folders.

 ***Start*** displays the Start menu. From the Start menu, you can open a program, open Help, change system settings, close and exit *Windows 95/98*, and more.

The Start button is located on the *taskbar* at the bottom of the desktop. It is always visible when *Windows* is running. When you click Start, a menu displays with the commands for using *Windows*. Each time you open a program, a button with the name of the program displays on the taskbar. The taskbar below shows that *Microsoft Word* is open.

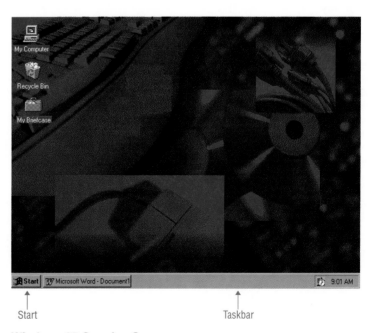

Start          Taskbar

**Windows 95 Opening Screen**

## Activity 6

Create a spreadsheet by importing the information in the table (Activity 5) into a spreadsheet program. When you finish Activity 6, your spreadsheet will look like the one on the right. The shaded areas will contain the computed total figures.

Do the following:

1. Insert the spreadsheet heading.

   **SALES REPORT**

   **First Quarter**

2. Group the sales reps alphabetically by state.

3. Insert 3 blank rows below each state group.

4. Compute the total sales for each month for each state. Include the appropriate labels (i.e., Arizona Totals, Colorado Totals, etc.).

5. Include a column heading for **Total Sales First Quarter**. Compute the total sales for the first quarter for each rep. Figures should appear in bold.

6. Include a column heading for **Monthly Average**. Compute the average monthly sales for each rep. Figures should appear in bold.

7. Compute the total first quarter sales for each state and the monthly average for each state.

8. Compute the Total First Quarter Sales and Monthly Average Sales for all states combined.

## SALES REPORT

## First Quarter

| Sales Rep | Territory | January | February | March | Total Sales First Quarter | Monthly Average |
|-----------|-----------|---------|----------|-------|---------------------------|-----------------|
| Martin, Jerry | Arizona | 50,790 | 32,370 | 19,239 | | |
| Walker, Sue | Arizona | 18,180 | 18,832 | 28,389 | | |
| Walton, Don | Arizona | 33,676 | 25,801 | 22,731 | | |
| Arizona Totals | | | | | | |
| Hundley, Ann | Colorado | 25,730 | 12,830 | 45,769 | | |
| Johnson, Marge | Colorado | 38,654 | 38,020 | 36,908 | | |
| Kent, Kellee | Colorado | 38,310 | 28,095 | 34,789 | | |
| Martinez, Justin | Colorado | 33,810 | 23,789 | 28,210 | | |
| Phillips, Josh | Colorado | 27,690 | 33,760 | 28,809 | | |
| Colorado Totals | | | | | | |
| Cooper, Devlin | Idaho | 15,790 | 40,308 | 32,798 | | |
| O'Neill, Mark | Idaho | 44,215 | 28,905 | 20,200 | | |
| Vizquel, Mario | Idaho | 18,890 | 18,705 | 29,389 | | |
| Idaho Totals | | | | | | |
| Burks, Ellen | Montana | 40,400 | 15,790 | 21,589 | | |
| Duncan, Trevor | Montana | 19,796 | 28,209 | 31,292 | | |
| Mathews, Erika | Montana | 23,902 | 31,801 | 53,389 | | |
| Montana Totals | | | | | | |
| Anderson, Mike | Utah | 34,790 | 23,870 | 54,389 | | |
| Gonzalez, Maria | Utah | 18,763 | 24,808 | 28,109 | | |
| Reed, Scott | Utah | 38,790 | 9,715 | 21,389 | | |
| Utah Totals | | | | | | |
| Finley, Jessica | Wyoming | 18,140 | 38,761 | 30,189 | | |
| Gomez, David | Wyoming | 28,760 | 32,120 | 52,675 | | |
| Guerin, Mary | Wyoming | 33,860 | 33,790 | 23,390 | | |
| Wyoming Totals | | | | | | |
| **Total Sales** | | **602,936** | **540,279** | **643,642** | | |

*Windows* software requires the use of a mouse or other pointing device. The mouse is used to select items, to find and move files, to execute or cancel commands, to move and size items, and to draw images. The mouse pointer changes in appearance depending on its location on the screen and the task that it is doing.

I   The I-beam indicates that the mouse is located in the text area. When you pause, it blinks. As you use your software, most of the time you will see the I-beam.

The arrow selects items. It displays when the mouse is located outside the text area.

The hourglass indicates that *Windows* is processing your command. You must wait until *Windows* finishes its task before you key text or enter another command.

## Using the Mouse

Move the mouse on a padded, flat surface. The mouse performs the following actions:

- *Point:* Move the mouse so that the pointer touches the icon or text.
- *Click:* Point to the desired item, the press and release the left mouse button once.
- *Double-click:* Point to the item and quickly press and release the left mouse button twice.

- *Click with the right mouse button:* Press and release the right mouse button once. A shortcut menu appears (*Windows 95/98*).
- *Drag:* Point to the desired item; hold down the mouse button; drag the item to a new location; then release the button.

## Open Windows 95/98

**Activity 1**
**Open Windows**

1. Turn on the computer and monitor.
2. Click the **Start** button to display the Start menu. (Your Start menu may not look exactly like the illustration.)
3. Point to the *Programs* menu; a submenu displays to the right listing all the programs.

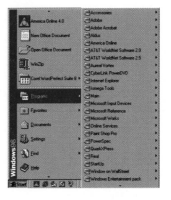

## Start Your Word Processing Software

 **note:**

This tutorial shows two popular word processing packages, *Microsoft Word* and *WordPerfect*, as examples. The points apply to other "for *Windows*" programs.

To open your word processing software, you may double-click on the word processing icon on your desktop or you may access the program through the Start menu under *Programs*. (*Corel WordPerfect* is located at the top of the Start menu.)

## Activity 5

Prepare the table shown at the right. Compute the total sales for each month. Total sales figures should appear in bold.

(Do not include $ and other format features because data from the table will be imported into a spreadsheet.)

| Sales Rep | Territory | January | February | March |
|-----------|-----------|---------|----------|-------|
| Guerin, Mary | Wyoming | 33,860 | 33,790 | 23,390 |
| Phillips, Josh | Colorado | 27,690 | 33,760 | 28,809 |
| Gonzalez, Maria | Utah | 18,763 | 24,808 | 28,109 |
| Anderson, Mike | Utah | 34,790 | 23,870 | 54,389 |
| O'Neill, Mark | Idaho | 44,215 | 28,905 | 20,200 |
| Burks, Ellen | Montana | 40,400 | 15,790 | 21,589 |
| Finley, Jessica | Wyoming | 18,140 | 38,761 | 30,189 |
| Duncan, Trevor | Montana | 19,796 | 28,209 | 31,292 |
| Cooper, Devlin | Idaho | 15,790 | 40,308 | 32,798 |
| Kent, Kellee | Colorado | 38,310 | 28,095 | 34,789 |
| Hundley, Ann | Colorado | 25,730 | 12,830 | 45,769 |
| Reed, Scott | Utah | 38,790 | 9,715 | 21,389 |
| Gomez, David | Wyoming | 28,760 | 32,120 | 52,675 |
| Martinez, Justin | Colorado | 33,810 | 23,789 | 28,210 |
| Vizquel, Mario | Idaho | 18,890 | 18,705 | 29,389 |
| Mathews, Erika | Montana | 23,902 | 31,801 | 53,389 |
| Walton, Don | Arizona | 33,676 | 25,801 | 22,731 |
| Martin, Jerry | Arizona | 50,790 | 32,370 | 19,239 |
| Walker, Sue | Arizona | 18,180 | 18,832 | 28,389 |
| Johnson, Marge | Colorado | 38,654 | 38,020 | 36,908 |

## Opening Screen

The opening screens of word processing programs for *Windows* include many of the same features.

- **Title bar.** Shows the name of the application software and the document.

- **Menu bar.** Click to display a pull-down menu. Select an option by moving the mouse pointer on top of the item and clicking the left mouse button. To close a pull-down menu, click the name again.

- **Toolbar/Power bar.** Provides a quick way to access frequently used features.

- **Formatting toolbar/button.** Provides a quick way to access commands.

- **Insertion point (cursor).** Indicates where text will appear next on the screen.

- **Status bar.** Indicates the position of the cursor and shows information about the document.

- **Scroll bar.** The vertical bar on the right of the screen contains a button that shows the approximate position of the window in the documents. You may scroll through the document by clicking and dragging the center button or by clicking the up/down arrow buttons.

*Microsoft Word 97* **Opening Screen**

## Create a Document

To create a document, simply begin to key on a clear screen. Text is entered to the left of the insertion point (cursor). Copy will wrap to the next line when the line is filled. To move the insertion point with your mouse, move the mouse pointer (⬚) to the desired position and click the left mouse button. The pointer changes to a blinking vertical line (I).

## Print a Document

1. Click on the File menu; choose *Print*.
2. The Print dialog box displays. Click **Print** (*WordPerfect*) or **OK** (*Microsoft Word*).

3. **Option:** Click the Print button on your Power bar/toolbar to print your document in one step.

# INTEGRATED APPLICATIONS

**Activity 1**

Open the title page created for 111B, p. 261. Insert an appropriate graphic figure between the title and your name. Center the graphic horizontally.

**Activity 2**

Open the title page created for 91D-92C, p. 223. Do the following.

1. Change the font face to **Courier New** and the type size to 17 for the title.
2. Change the font face to **Courier New** and the type size to 15 for the remaining information on the page.
3. Insert an appropriate figure between the title and your name. Center the graphic horizontally.

**Activity 3**

Format the text at the right as a personal-business letter in block format with open punctuation to:

**Ms. Mary Renault**
**1818 Fairfield Ave.**
**Santa Ana, CA 92714-1828**

Date the letter **June 24, ----**. Supply an appropriate salutation and complimentary closing.

*The letter is from Grant L. Lemaster, 1922 Jovan Blvd., Santa Ana, CA 92728-0919.*

I've finished my assignment! All ten of the firms that were assigned to me have been contacted. Only one of the ten refused to contribute; eight contributed; and I'm still waiting to hear from the last one.

Meeting with them in person rather than talking with them on the phone does make a difference. Last year the phone calls resulted in only three of the businesses making contributions for a total of $1,500. This year the total amount increased to $8,500. A complete summary of the contributions is shown below.

Open Table 3 from p. 234 and copy it here. Delete the main and secondary headings. SS the table.

I will be on vacation when you meet on June 15. If you need any additional information that I can provide for the meeting, please call me.

**Activity 4**

Using the table in Job 14, p. 253, prepare a bar graph showing all sales representatives with sales over $200,000 for the month of January.

The graph should be created as follows:

1. Use landscape (11" wide x 8.5" long) orientation.
2. Label the X-axis **Thousands**.
3. Label the Y-axis **Agent**.
4. Use **JANUARY SALES** for the title of the graph.
5. Use **Letter Landscape** for the paper size.
6. Make the size of the graph 10" x 7.5".

## Dialog Boxes

A dialog box displays when your software needs more information to carry out a task. Selecting a menu item that is followed by an ellipsis (...) will open a dialog box. The illustration below shows the parts of a dialog box and how to use them.

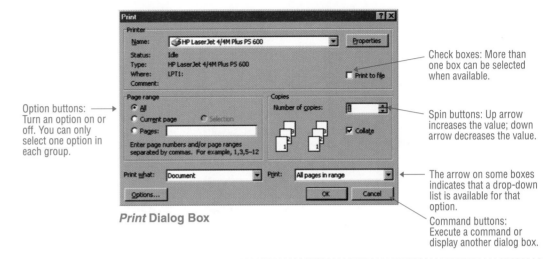

Option buttons: Turn an option on or off. You can only select one option in each group.

Check boxes: More than one box can be selected when available.

Spin buttons: Up arrow increases the value; down arrow decreases the value.

The arrow on some boxes indicates that a drop-down list is available for that option.

Command buttons: Execute a command or display another dialog box.

*Print* **Dialog Box**

## Activity 2
**Create and print a document**

1. Open your word processing program.
2. Identify the screen parts: title bar, menu bar, toolbar, status bar, Start button. (Refer to p. A4.)
3. Move your pointer around the screen. Notice how the pointer changes to an I-beam as it moves over the document work area.
4. Key your name. Strike ENTER 4 times. Notice the change on the status line.
5. Key the paragraph below using word wrap.
6. Choose *Print* from the File menu. Study the parts of the dialog box.
7. Print the page.
8. Keep the document open to use in Activity 3.

Keep in home position all of the fingers not being used to strike a key. Do not let them move out of position for the next letters in your copy.

## Save a File

## Activity 3
**Name and save a file**

Your computer has a hard drive (drive C) for storing files. The word processing software will automatically save your files to a special folder on your hard drive, unless you specify a different disk drive. For this exercise, save your document to drive A. Follow these steps:

1. Insert your storage disk into drive A.
2. From the File menu, choose *Save As*. The Save As dialog box displays.
3. In the Save in box, click the down arrow. Click **3 1/2" Floppy (A:)**.
4. Key this filename in the File name box: **Act3save**. Click **OK** or **Save**.

Click the drop-down arrow in the Drives box, then click A:.

Filename appears in List box after it is saved.

Key filename

*Save As* **Dialog Box**

1. Create a similar presentation on a topic of your choice, for example:
   - a class paper
   - personal background
   - family vacation
2. Select an appropriate background, font sizes, and font colors.

3. Use graphic enhancements such as arrows, starbursts, lines, boxes, or clipart as appropriate.
4. Create at least one diagram.
5. Include graphs if appropriate for your topic.

6. Be sure to include a title chart, presentation objective chart, bulleted list for important points, and a conclusion visual.
7. Arrange all charts in a screenshow.
8. Use two transition effects.

## Close a Document

When you are finished working with a file, close it to clear the work area. If you have made any changes to the document since saving it, you will be prompted to save the document before closing.

**Activity 4**
**Close a document**

1. Click the File menu and then click **Close**.

2. If you are prompted to save the file before closing it, click **Yes** in the dialog box.

## Open a File

When you need to work with a file that has been closed, open the file to display it in the work area.

**Activity 5**
**Open a file**

1. Click **File** in the Menu bar.
2. Choose *Open*. **Option:** Click the **Open** button on the toolbar. The Open File dialog box displays.

3. Click the down arrow in the Look in box. Select drive A (or the drive where your data is located).
4. Click the filename and then click **Open**. The file displays.

Control bar →
Select drive A: →

Text box: Key a → filename or highlight a filename in the List box.

List box: Displays a list of files to choose from.

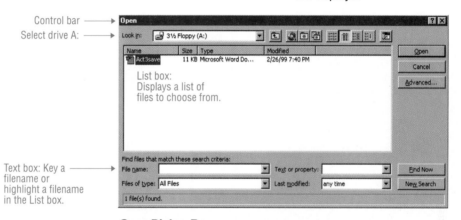

*Open* **Dialog Box**

## Exit the Software

**Note:** Your teacher will direct you in exiting your software. Procedures will vary, especially if you have a network.

When you are finished working with the software, you may need to exit the program. **Exit** saves all documents that are open.

1. Click **File** in the Menu bar.

2. Choose *Exit*. If you have not saved the file you have been working on, you will be prompted to save it.

**Activity 6**
**Review Open and Exit**

1. Open the file **Act3save**.
2. Close the file.

3. Exit the word processing software.

## Online Help

If you need assistance while working with the word processing software, you can get help through the Help menu. Click **Help** on the menu bar to display the Help menu. You can key a question directly in both *Word* (through the Office Assistant) and *WordPerfect* (through the WordPerfect Expert). You can also search for help on topics displayed alphabetically in *Word* (Contents and Index) and in *WordPerfect* (Help Topics). Find the topic you need by scrolling through the list, and then click the topic.

## Preparing Screenshows

**O b j e c t i v e s :**

**1.** To identify the purposes of screenshows.

**2.** To learn to organize visuals in a screenshow for audience viewing.

**10-11A • 90**
**Screenshow**
**Development**

1. Review the information on p. A60 about the purposes of screenshows.

2. Determine how to create a screenshow using your software.

3. Create a screenshow using the examples shown below.

4. Select a similar template.

5. Insert appropriate clipart as shown.

6. Add transition effects.

A **screenshow** (or slide show) is a series of presentation visuals presented in a preplanned sequence. A screenshow can be projected from a computer screen for a small audience. For a larger audience, projection equipment is necessary to display the visuals on a large screen.

*(continued on next page)*

## Open Internet Browser

*Word 97* users can quickly access the Internet while in *Word* by using the Web Toolbar. Display the Web Toolbar by clicking the Web Toolbar icon on the Standard toolbar.

Open the Internet browser by clicking the Start Page icon on the Web Toolbar. The web page you have designated as Home or Start Page displays.

Start Page

*Corel WordPerfect 8* users can access the Internet while in *WordPerfect*: Select *Internet Publisher* from the File menu, then select *Browse the Web.*

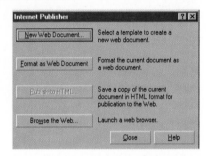

### Activity 1
**Open Internet browser (*Word*)**

1. Begin a new *Word* document.
2. Display the Web Toolbar.
3. Click the **Start Page** icon to open the Internet browser.

**Note:** You may also open the Internet browser from the **Windows** desktop or from any web toolbar located in a Microsoft Office application.

### Activity 1
**Open Internet browser (*WordPerfect*)**

1. Begin a new *WordPerfect* document.
2. Display the Internet Publisher dialog box.

3. Choose *Browse the Web* to launch the Internet browser.

## Web Addresses

A web address—commonly called the URL or Uniform Resource Locator—is composed of one or more domains separated by periods; e.g., http://www.house.gov or http://www.li.suu.edu. A domain name is the name given to a network or site that is connected to the Internet. As you move from left to right in the address, each domain is larger than the previous one. For example, in the web address http://www.house.gov, *gov* (United States government) is larger than *house* (House of Representatives). The table below identifies types of high-level domains.

| .gov | Non-military government sites |
|------|------------------------------|
| .com | Commercial organizations |
| .edu | Educational institutions |
| .org | Other organizations |
| .mil | Military sites |

A web address may also include a directory path and filenames separated by a slash; e.g., http://msstate.edu/athletics/. The web document named *athletics* resides at this site.

### Activity 2
**Understand web address names**

1. Identify the high-level domain for the following web sites:
   a. http://www.senate.gov
   b. http://www.fbla-pbl.org
   c. http://www.army.mil
   d. http://www.ibm.com

2. Identify the filenames for the following web sites:
   a. http://www.reebok.com/soccer/
   b. http://www.espn.sportszone.com/soccer
   c. http://www.cnn.com/QUICKNEWS/
   d. http://nike.com/girls/

**Line graph data:**

| | |
|---|---|
| 1985 | 30 |
| 1987 | 33 |
| 1989 | 37 |
| 1991 | 38 |
| 1993 | 40 |
| 1995 | 45 |

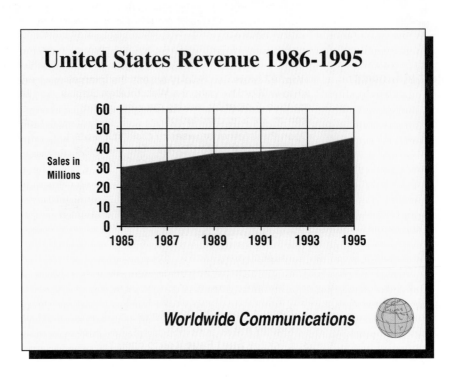

**Pie chart data:**

Southern 45
Midwest 40
Eastern 30
Mountain Plains 25
Western 20

Show values as percents.

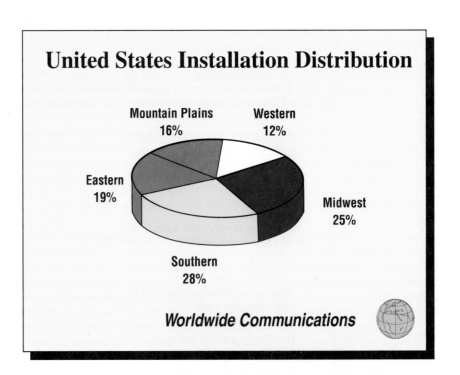

## Open a Web Site

To open a web site from your Internet browser, click **Open Page** from the File menu (or click the Open icon if available on your browser toolbar). Key the URL **http://www.weather.com** as shown below and click **Open**. The home page for The Weather Channel displays.

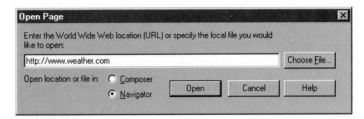

**Shortcut:** Click inside the netsite entry box, key the URL, and press ENTER.

### Activity 3
**Open web sites**

1. http://weather.com
2. http://www.abc.com
3. http://www.cnn.com/QUICKNEWS/
4. http://www.espn.sportszone.com/soccer
5. http://www.usps.gov/ctc/welcome.htm

## Explore the Browser Toolbar

The browser toolbar is a helpful means for exploring ("surfing") the Internet. Become familiar with your browser toolbar by studying the items shown below. Browsers may vary slightly.

**Netsite or Address Entry Box:** Displays the active URL or web site address.

**Back:** Moves back to web sites previously visited since opening the browser.

**Forward:** Moves forward to sites visited prior to using Back icon. (The Forward icon is ghosted if the Back icon has not been used.)

**Print:** Prints a web page.

**Home:** Returns to the web page designated as Home or Start Page.

**Stop:** Stops computer's search for a web site.

**Search:** Opens one of the Internet search engines.

**Bookmarks or Favorites:** Moves to a list of web sites marked for easy access.

### Activity 4
**Practice using browser tools**

1. Open each of the following web sites:
   a. http://www.nike.com
   b. http://www.adidas.com
   c. http://www.reebok.com
   d. a site of your choice
2. Click the **Back** icon twice. The _____ web site displays.
3. Click the **Forward** icon once. The _____ web site displays.
4. Print the active web page.
5. Keying in the netsite entry or address box, open **http://www.msstate.edu**. Stop the search before the web site is located.

## Pie Chart 3

1. Read the copy at the right.
2. Emphasize one pie slice (Chart 2) by exploding it.
3. Remove the legend.
4. Display labels and % values with each slice.

A single pie slice can be emphasized by exploding (pulling one slice away from the other slices) and using a high-contrast color for that slice.

Pie charts are probably easiest to interpret when both the identifying labels and slice values are positioned beside or on the pie slices. If space on the pie is limited, then arrange the labels in a list or use a legend to identify the content of the slices.

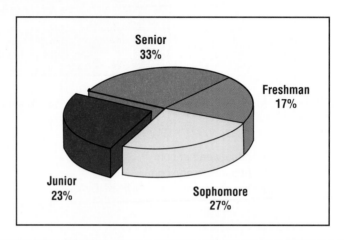

## 7-9F • 35
## Graph Screenshow

1. Read the copy at the right about designing effective graphs.
2. Create three graphs in coordinating colors. (Assume these three graphs are used in a larger presentation.)
3. Select a similar template.
4. If possible, add the company name and clipart image of the globe to the master slide.

**Bar graph data:**

|  | United States | Europe |
|---|---|---|
| January | 145 | 120 |
| February | 130 | 135 |
| March | 160 | 155 |

If actual numeric values are needed in a bar graph, these values can be displayed with each bar; values also can be displayed beside or below the graph image.

- Be sure of visual integrity on the graphs so that relationships accurately reflect data.
- Adjust colors for maximum legibility and to highlight key information.
- Avoid showing too many details in one graph.
- When needed for clarity, display both the graph image and the data from which it is derived.
- Be sure the design of these charts blends with other visuals being used.

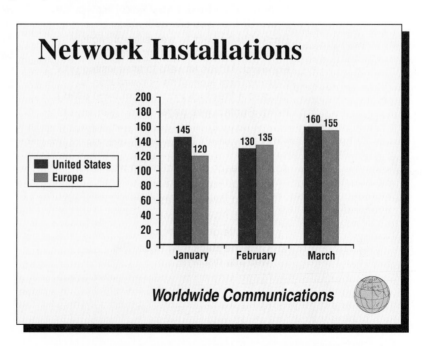

## Use Bookmarks

When readers put a book aside, they insert a bookmark to mark the place. Internet users also add bookmarks to save the addresses of their favorite web sites for later browsing. Often bookmarks are added to and accessed from folders called "favorites."

**To add a bookmark:**

1. Open the desired web site.
2. Click **Bookmarks** (or **Favorites**), then click **Add Bookmark** (or **Add to Favorites**). (Browsers may vary on location of Bookmark icon.)

**To use a bookmark:**

1. Click **Bookmarks** (or **Favorites**).
2. Select the desired bookmark. Click or double-click, depending on your browser. The desired web site displays.

### Activity 5
**Practice using bookmarks**

1. Open these favorite web sites and bookmark them on your browser.
   a. http://www.weather.com
   b. http://www.cnn.com
   c. http://www.usps.gov
   d. Add a web site of your choice.

2. Use the bookmark to go to the following web sites:
   a. The Weather Channel
   b. CNN
   c. The United States Postal Service
   d. web site you bookmarked

## Hyperlinks

A **hyperlink** is text or a graphic image that links one web document to another web document. The hyperlink inserted in the web site may be a link to another page in that web site or to another web site. For example, the web page for a university may include hyperlinks to the various academic departments within the university (pages within the web site) and a hyperlink to the local visitors' and convention center (another web site).

Hyperlinked text displays in a different font color and is underlined. When the mouse is pointed at hyperlinked text or images, the mouse pointer changes to a pointing hand. Click the hyperlink and the new web document displays. Remember to click the Back icon to return to the original web site.

### Activity 6
**Explore hyperlinks**

1. Go to the web site at http://www.army.mil and click the following hyperlinked text:
   a. Installations
   b. database
   Click the **Back** icon twice to return to the original web page.
2. At http://www.yahoo.com, click the following hyperlinked text and images:
   a. Email
   b. People Search
   c. Image for What's New

3. Open a web site for a university or college of your choice.
   a. List two hyperlinked images.
   b. List two text hyperlinks.
   c. Which text or image is linked to another web document within the web site?
   d. Which text or image is linked to another web site?

## 7-9E • 30
## Pie Chart

### Pie Chart 1

1. Read the copy at the right.
2. Create the pie chart shown.

**Chart data:**

| | |
|---|---|
| **Freshman** | **25** |
| **Sophomore** | **40** |
| **Junior** | **35** |
| **Senior** | **50** |

3. Display the legend on the right.

*Pie* charts (or graphs) are best used to display parts of a whole. They show clearly the proportional relationship of only one set of values. Without any numbers displayed, the chart shows only general relationships. In the first example shown below, the different colors used for the pie slices are identified in a legend. Colors used on the pie should provide adequate contrast between the slices. Consider, also, the color scheme of your entire presentation so that the pie chart will coordinate with other visuals.

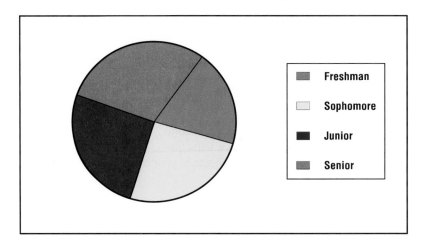

### Pie Chart 2

1. Read the copy at the right.
2. Using the same chart data, change Pie Chart 1 to give it a 3D appearance.
3. Add the slice values beside each slice.

Usually pie charts look attractive with a 3D appearance, as long as the circle does not look distorted. The pie slice values (shown as actual numbers or percentages) can be displayed beside each of the slices to show relationships exactly.

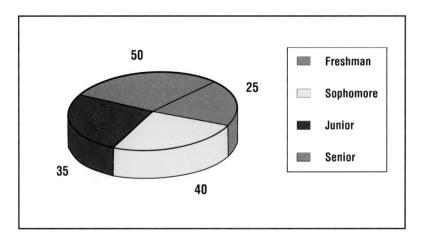

*(continued on next page)*

## Set Up E-Mail

**Electronic mail** or **e-mail** refers to electronic messages sent by one computer user to another computer user. To be able to send or receive e-mail, you must have an e-mail address, an e-mail program, and access to the Internet.

Many search engines such as Yahoo, Excite, Lycos, AltaVista, and others now provide free e-mail via their web sites. These e-mail programs allow users to set up an e-mail address and then send and retrieve e-mail messages. To set up an account and obtain an e-mail address, the user must (1) agree to the terms of agreement, (2) complete an online registration form, and (3) compose an e-mail name and password. To set up your e-mail, access the search engine of your choice and closely follow the directions for setting up e-mail. Be certain that you understand the terms of agreement and choose an e-mail name and password that are easy to remember.

## Send E-Mail

To send an e-mail message, you must have the address of the computer user you wish to write to. Business cards, letterheads, directories, etc. now include e-mail addresses. Sometimes you may need to call the person by telephone and ask for his or her e-mail address. An e-mail address includes the user's login name followed by @ and the domain name(s); e.g., sthomas@yahoo.com or sdt3@jn.ndu.edu.

Creating an e-mail message is quite similar to preparing a memo. The e-mail header includes TO, FROM, and SUBJECT. Key the e-mail address of the recipient on the TO line and compose a subject line that concisely describes your message. Your e-mail address will automatically display on the FROM line.

### Activity 7
### Send e-mail

1. Open the search engine used to set up your e-mail account. Click **E-mail** or **Free E-mail**.
2. Enter your e-mail name and password when prompted.
3. Enter the e-mail address of your instructor or another student.
4. Compose a brief message. Be sure to include a descriptive subject line.
5. Send the message.

## Read E-Mail

Reading one's e-mail messages and responding promptly are considered important rules of netiquette (etiquette for the Internet). However, avoid responding too quickly to sensitive situations—once sent, e-mail cannot be retrieved before it is read by the recipient.

### Activity 8
### Read e-mail

1. Open your e-mail account.
2. Read your messages and respond immediately. Click **Reply** to answer the message. (E-mail programs may vary.)

## Attach Files to E-Mail

Electronic files can be attached to an e-mail message and sent to another computer electronically. Recipients of attached documents can transfer these documents to their computers and then open the files for use.

### Activity 9
### Create an attachment

1. Open your e-mail account if necessary.
2. Create an e-mail message to your teacher that states that your homework is attached. The subject line should include the specific homework assignment (for example, 44b-d1).
3. Attach the file by clicking **Attach**. Use the browser to locate the homework file. (E-mail programs may vary.)
4. Send the e-mail.

## 7-9D • 30
## Line and Area Graphs

### Line Graph

1. Read the copy at the right.
2. Create a line graph showing one data set.

**Graph data:**

| | |
|---|---|
| 1970 | 20 |
| 1975 | 43 |
| 1980 | 30 |
| 1985 | 50 |
| 1990 | 45 |
| 1995 | 60 |

3. Include a grid.

### Area Graph

1. Modify the line graph to make it an area graph.
2. Consider the difference in appearance to determine which graph is easier to interpret.

*Line* graphs are best suited for displaying changing quantities over time. Usually the X-axis is used to show the particular period of time; the Y-axis shows the measurements of quantity at different times. The baseline of the Y-axis should be zero because this provides a consistent reference point when several graphs are used in a presentation or report. When the numbers for the X-axis are entered, a line will be formed to reflect these changing amounts. A grid on the graph will help the viewer interpret quantities.

Several different sets of data could be displayed by using lines in different colors or patterns.

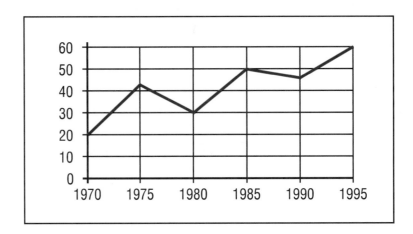

If the line needs more emphasis, then an *area* graph would be a better choice. The area below the line is filled in with a contrasting color.

If exact data are required, however, a vertical bar graph would be a better graph choice than an area graph because each bar can be labeled with the appropriate measurement.

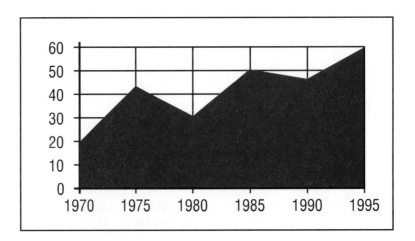

## Explore Search Engines

The World Wide Web contains millions of pages of information and is growing rapidly. Search engines locate specific information. Just a few examples of search engines are AltaVista, Excite, Infoseek, Dogpile, Metacrawler, LookSmart, Lycos, and Yahoo. To go to a search engine, click the Search or Net Search icon on your web browser. (Note: Web browsers will vary.)

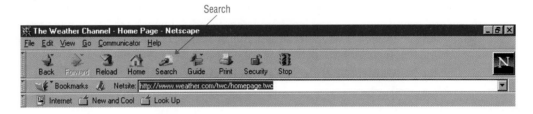

### Activity 10
### Search with multiple engines

1. Go to search engines on your browser. Click the first search engine. Browse the hyperlinks available, i.e., Maps, People Finder, News, Weather, Stock Quotes, Sports, Games, etc.
2. Click each search engine and explore the hyperlinks.

3. Conduct the following search using Dogpile, a multi-threaded search engine that searches multiple databases:
   a. Open the web site for Dogpile (http://www.dogpile.com).
   b. In the Search entry box, key the keywords **American Psychological Association publications**; click **Fetch**.

## Yellow Pages

Searching the Yellow Pages for information on businesses and services is a common, everyday task. Several search engines provide convenient hyperlinks to the online Yellow Pages.

### Activity 11
### Search Yellow Pages

1. Browse the search engines on your browser to locate the hyperlink for the Yellow Pages; click to open this valuable site.
2. Determine a city that you would like to visit. Use the Yellow Pages to find a listing of hotels in this city.

3. Your best friend lives in (provide the city); you want to send him or her flowers. Find a listing of florists in this city.
4. Write a third scenario and find the appropriate listing.

## Comprehensive Search Engines

Using a comprehensive search engine can be very helpful in locating various information quickly. The All-in-One web site (http://www.albany.net/allinone/) is a compilation of various search tools found on the Internet. Search tools include various categories, such as People, News/Weather, Desk Reference, and Other Interesting Searches/Services.

### Activity 12
### Comprehensive search engine

1. Access http://www.albany.net/allinone/. Browse the categories and search tools within the categories.
2. From the People category: Find at BigFoot the e-mail address for (provide a name).
3. Find at Ahoy! the home page for (provide a name).

4. From the News/Weather category: Find at Pathfinder, Weather and then your current weather.
5. Find at one of the news searches, news articles about (provide current event).
6. Choose a category and determine a search. List category, question, and answer.

## 7-9C • 30
## Bar Graphs

### Bar Graph 1

1. Read the copy at the right.
2. Create the graph shown with the presentation software you are using.

**Graph data:**

|  | Shirt Sales | Bag Sales |
| --- | --- | --- |
| October | 87 | 60 |
| November | 80 | 75 |
| December | 45 | 90 |

3. Select similar colors for the bars.
4. Display data values above the bars.
5. Display labels below the bars.
6. Display a legend at the bottom of the graph.

### Bar Graph 2

Modify the first bar graph as follows:

1. Remove the data values above the bars.
2. Add a dimensional effect as shown.

*Bar* graphs (or charts) display a single set or multiple sets of data that are plotted on the horizontal X-axis and the vertical Y-axis. The X-axis usually contains category information (such as years or months); the Y-axis usually contains measured quantity values.

Vertical bars (also called columns) are easy to interpret; the baseline on the Y-axis should begin at zero for consistent comparisons when several graphs are used in a presentation. Many special effects can be added, but a simple graph is effective for showing relationships.

Multiple data sets can be shown by using a cluster of bars on each point on the X-axis. When multiple data sets are used, the colors must provide an adequate contrast and yet blend with the other colors used in a presentation.

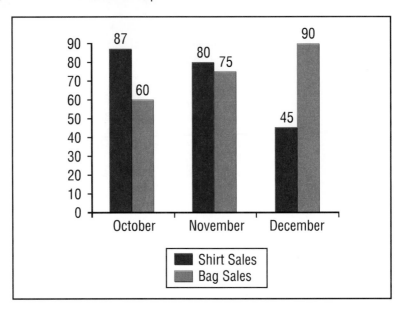

The first graph you prepared was displayed in two dimensions—height and width. When a third dimension (3D) is added, the bars are shaded to create an illusion of depth. A 3D appearance can be used on bar, pie, and line/area graphs. Notice, however, that, while this illusion might make the graph more interesting, the illusion of depth can make the bar values more difficult to interpret.

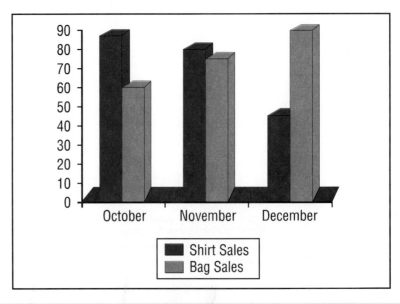

Repetitive stress injury (RSI) is a result of repeated movement of a particular part of the body. A familiar example is "tennis elbow." Of more concern to keyboard users is the form of RSI called carpal tunnel syndrome (CTS).

CTS is an inflammatory disease that develops gradually and affects the wrist, hands, and forearms. Blood vessels, tendons, and nerves pass into the hand through the carpal tunnel (see illustration below). If any of these structures enlarge, or the walls of the tunnel narrow, the median nerve is pinched and CTS symptoms may result.

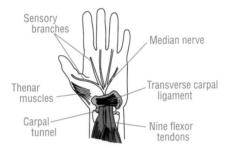

Palm view of left hand.

## Symptoms of RSI/CTS

CTS symptoms include numbness in the hand; tingling or burning in the hand, wrist, or elbow; severe pain in the forearm, elbow, or shoulder; and difficulty in gripping objects. Symptoms usually appear during sleeping hours, probably because many people sleep with their wrists flexed.

If not properly treated, the pressure on the median nerve, which controls the thumb, forefinger, middle finger, and half the ring finger, causes severe pain. The pain can radiate into the forearm, elbow, or shoulder and can require surgery or result in permanent damage or paralysis.

## Causes of RSI/CTS

RSI/CTS often develops in workers whose physical routine is unvaried.

Common occupational factors include: (1) using awkward posture, (2) using poor techniques, (3) performing tasks with wrists bent (see below), (4) using improper equipment, (5) working at a rapid pace, (6) not taking rest breaks, and (7) not doing exercises that promote graceful motion and good techniques.

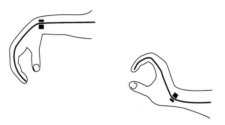

Improper wrist positions for keystroking.

## Reducing the Risk of RSI/CTS

CTS is frequently a health concern for workers who use a computer keyboard or mouse. The risk of developing CTS is less for keyboard operators who use proper furniture or equipment, keyboarding techniques, posture, and/or muscle-stretching exercises than for those who do not.

Keyboard users can reduce the risk of developing RSI/CTS by taking these precautions:

1. Arrange the work station correctly:

   a. Position the keyboard directly in front of the chair.

   b. Keep the front edge of the keyboard even with the edge of the desk so that wrist movement will not be restricted.

   c. Position the keyboard at elbow height.

   d. Position the monitor about 18 to 24 inches from your eyes with the top edge of the screen at eye level.

   e. Position the mouse next to and at the same height as the keyboard and as close to the body as possible.

# Displaying Numeric Information

**Objectives:**
1. To learn the graph to use for particular situations.
2. To learn various graph elements.
3. To create graphs.

## 7-9A • 10
## Graph Purposes

Study the copy at the right about types of graphs and the uses of each type.

The meaning of numeric information can be easier to understand when portrayed as a graph, instead of as a table of figures. The relationships between data sets or trends can be compared with *bar*, *line/area*, or *pie* graphs (also called charts). Even combinations of these graphs can be used for some applications. Each type of graph is best suited for a particular situation:

- **bar**—comparison of item quantities
- **line/area**—quantity changes over time
- **pie**—parts of a whole

## 7-9B • 15
## Graph Elements

1. Study the copy at the right.
2. Locate the various graph elements in the software you are using.

Elements common to most graphs are identified on the bar graph shown below. They include:

- **X-axis**—the horizontal axis; usually for categories
- **Y-axis**—the vertical axis; usually for values
- **scales**—numbers on the Y- or X-axis representing quantities

- **tick marks**—coordinate marks on the graph to help guide the reader
- **grids**—lines that extend from tick marks to make it easier to see data values
- **labels**—names used to identify parts of the graph
- **legends**—the key that identifies the shading or coloring used for the parts of the graph

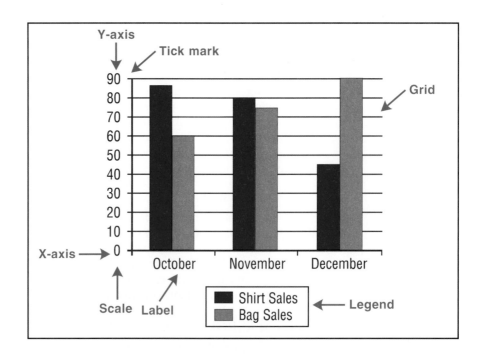

2. Use a proper chair and sit correctly:

   a. Use a straight-backed chair that will not yield when you lean back.

   b. Use a seat that allows you to keep your feet flat on the floor or use a footrest.

   c. Sit erect and as far back in the seat as possible.

3. Use correct arm and wrist positions and movement:

   a. Keep your forearms parallel to the floor and level with the keyboard so that your wrists will be in a flat, neutral position rather than flexed upward or downward.

   b. Keep arms near the side of your body in a relaxed position.

4. Use proper keyboarding techniques:

   a. Keep your fingers curved and upright over the home keys.

   b. Keep wrists and forearms from touching or resting on any surface.

   c. Strike each key lightly using the finger*tip*.

5. When using a keyboard or mouse, take short breaks. A rest of one to two minutes every hour is appropriate.

6. Exercise the neck, shoulder, arm, wrist, and fingers before beginning to key each day and often during the workday.

### Ergonomic Keyboards

Ergonomic keyboards are designed to improve hand posture and make keying more comfortable. Generally they have a split design with left and right banks of keys and the ability to tilt or rotate the keyboard for comfort. More research is needed to determine just how effective ergonomic keyboards are in preventing RSI injuries and carpal tunnel syndrome.

### Trackball

Like the mouse, a trackball is a pointing device that moves the insertion point. A trackball enables the user to control the pointer without hand or wrist movement. The thumb or finger moves the ball directly. The ergonomic design of the trackball generally features buttons contoured to the shape of the hand.

## Cluster

1. Create a cluster diagram.
2. Position an oval for the "Main Topic" text as shown; add the text for this oval.
3. Duplicate both the oval and text and position in the place for Item 1. Edit this oval to make it smaller and change the text to "Item 1."
4. Duplicate the "Item 1" oval and text—repeat this process for each item.
5. Retrieve an arrow; adjust size and color as necessary. Duplicate and position an arrow for each oval.
6. Enter the bulleted list text above the diagram:

♦ **Shows concepts related to central topic.**
♦ **Can be displayed one at a time.**

*Cluster.* This cluster diagram begins with an oval at the center containing the text for the main topic being explained. Additional ovals with text are positioned around the main topic. For a screenshot, these items could be made to appear one at a time as the discussion progresses.

 *Cluster Diagram*

♦ Shows concepts related to central topic.
♦ Can be displayed one at a time.

 *Cluster Diagram*

♦ Shows concepts related to central topic.
♦ Can be displayed one at a time.

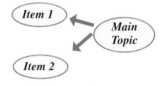

 *Cluster Diagram*

♦ Shows concepts related to central topic.
♦ Can be displayed one at a time.

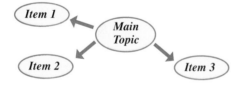

 *Cluster Diagram*

♦ Shows concepts related to central topic.
♦ Can be displayed one at a time.

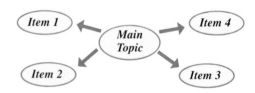

# FINGER GYMNASTICS

Brief daily practice of finger gymnastics will strengthen your finger muscles and increase the ease with which you key. Begin each keying period with this conditioning exercise. Choose two or more drills for this practice.

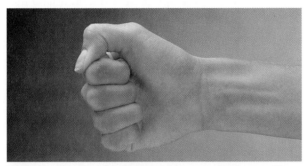

DRILL 1. Hands open, fingers wide, muscles tense. Close the fingers into a tight "fist," with thumb on top. Relax the fingers as you straighten them; repeat 10 times.

DRILL 2. Clench the fingers as shown. Hold the fingers in this position for a brief time; then extend the fingers, relaxing the muscles of fingers and hand. Repeat the movements slowly several times. Exercise both hands at the same time.

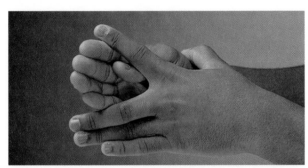

DRILL 3. Place the fingers and the thumb of one hand between two fingers of the other hand, and spread the fingers as much as possible. Spread all fingers of both hands.

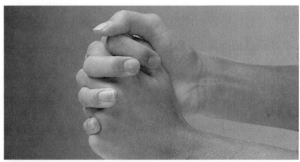

DRILL 4. Interlace the fingers of the two hands and wring the hands, rubbing the heel of the palms vigorously.

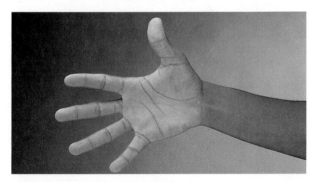

DRILL 5. Spread the fingers as much as possible, holding the position for a moment or two; then relax the fingers and lightly fold them into the palm of the hand. Repeat the movements slowly several times. Exercise both hands at the same time.

DRILL 6. Rub the hands vigorously. Let the thumb rub the palm of the hand. Rub the fingers, the back of the hand, and the wrist.

DRILL 7. Hold both hands in front of you, fingers together. Hold the last three fingers still and move the first finger as far to the side as possible. Return the first finger; then move the first and second fingers together; finally move the little finger as far to the side as possible.

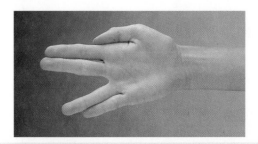

## Stair Steps

1. Create a stair steps diagram using the same template you used for the choice diagram.
2. Position the first box at the bottom.
3. Enter the text in a suitable size for the box.
4. Duplicate both the box and the text three times and position the new images as shown.
5. Edit the text in the second, third, and fourth boxes as shown.
6. Add the following bulleted list at the left:

♦ **Shows discussion points building like stair steps.**
♦ **Begin at the bottom.**

*Stair steps.* This stair steps diagram begins with a box at the bottom containing the text for the first idea being explained. Additional boxes with text are positioned to look like stairs going up. For a screenshow, you could prepare four separate slides so that the stair steps appear one at a time as the discussion progresses.

 *Stair Steps Diagram*

First item in a series

 *Stair Steps Diagram*

Second item in a series
First item in a series

 *Stair Steps Diagram*

Third item in a series
Second item in a series
First item in a series

 *Stair Steps Diagram*

♦ **Shows discussion points building like stair steps.**
♦ **Begin at the bottom.**

Fourth item in a series
Third item in a series
Second item in a series
First item in a series

## R&e  Centering

**Document 1**
**Centered Lines**

1. Center horizontally by the longest line in the poem.
2. Vertical placement: standard top margin.

|  | words |
|---|---|
| THE MAN I MEANT TO BE | 4 |
| I look back over my shoulder | 10 |
| And there I see | 13 |
| The boy I once was | 17 |
| And the man he meant to be. | 23 |
| And I wonder how it happened | 29 |
| That the boy I see | 33 |
| Became the man I now am-- | 38 |
| Not the man he meant to be. | 44 |
| I remember him well--the boy I once was; | 52 |
| I remember the man he dreamed I would be. | 60 |
| Now the dreams are forgotten by the boy and me-- | 70 |
| For I'm not the man he dreamed I would be. | 79 |
| --D. D. Lessenberry | 83 |

**Document 2**
**Centered Lines**

1. Center each line horizontally.
2. Vertical placement: standard top margin.

|  | words |
|---|---|
| **AFRICA IN MOTION PICTURES** | 5 |
| Academy Auditorium | 9 |
| LIFE IN HOT WET LANDS | 13 |
| Typical Day of a Family in the Congo Basin | 22 |
| Wednesday, November 2, at 2:30 p.m. | 29 |
| AFRICAN BIG GAME | 32 |
| African Animals in Their Native Habitat | 40 |
| Friday, November 4, at 8:30 p.m. | 47 |
| A GIANT PEOPLE (The Mangbetu) | 53 |
| Primitive People of Relatively Advanced Culture | 63 |
| Monday, November 6, at 11:10 a.m. | 70 |
| LION COUNTRY | 72 |
| A 2200-Mile Safari into African Lion Country | 81 |
| Tuesday, November 7, at 3:15 p.m. | 88 |

## Developing Diagram Charts

**Objectives:**

**1.** To observe how diagrams can portray processes and add variety to a presentation.
**2.** To create diagrams with boxes and connecting arrows or lines.
**3.** To create diagrams showing various processes.

### 5-6A • 40
### Process Information

1. Read the copy at the right.
2. Learn how to use the drawing tools in the software you are using.
3. Create diagrams using text on boxes and connecting lines and arrows.

*Diagrams.* The shapes in a diagram can help an audience understand relationships or a sequence of events. Text can be arranged in boxes that are connected with lines or arrows to help the audience visualize a process. Diagrams may simply add variety to a display of text—however, the shape of some diagrams also conveys meaning. While diagrams can become quite complex,

the best ones are quite simple. When creating diagrams, be sure to:

• Arrange text information in boxes or other appropriate shapes.
• Show connections with lines and specific directions with arrows.
• Blend fonts and all colors used with other visuals in a presentation.

### 5-6B • 60
### Diagrams

1. Notice the "message" in the diagrams at the right and the two diagrams on pp. A69-A70.
2. Select a similar template or slide master.
3. Create each diagram, following the directions for each.

**Choice**

1. Create a box in a similar color; position it at the left. Make it large enough to hold the "Option One" text; enter the text.
2. Duplicate the box and text and position the duplicate at the right side, allowing enough room for the arrows; change "Option One" to "Option Two."
3. Retrieve and position a similar arrow pointing in one direction.
4. Duplicate the arrow and rotate it. Position it as shown.
5. Insert the bulleted list at the bottom of the screen.

*Choice.* This diagram indicates that a choice between two options must be made. The arrows pointing in opposite directions

indicate an either/or situation. This same technique can be used to represent conflict.

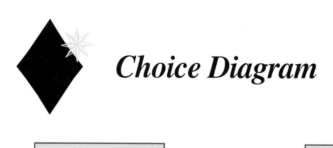

*Choice Diagram*

Option One ← → Option Two

♦ Shows a choice between two options.

♦ Can portray a decision point or a conflict.

**Document 3**
**Memo**

1. Format/key as a simplified memo the message given at the right.
2. Use current date; address to **Shirlie L. Beerman, Chair**.
3. As a subject, use **LANDSCAPE COMMITTEE MEETING**.
4. Use hanging-indent style for the listed items.
5. The writer of the memo is **Jolene Golden, Member**.

**Document 4**
**Letter**

1. Format/key in block style with open punctuation the letter given at right.
2. Indent the quotation 0.5" (5 sp.) from left margin as shown.

**Note:** The book title may be in italic instead of underlined.

| | words |
|---|---|
| | heading 14 |

The most recent issue of <u>Tollgate News & Notes</u> indicates that we are [29] to begin landscape renovation this coming spring.    Because of the [41] limited money budgeted this year for this purpose, I propose that the [56] following topics be discussed at our next meeting: [66]

1.    Which section of the community (north or south) is in greater need [80] of immediate renovation? [85]

2.    What kinds of trees, shrubs, and perennials will in the long term [99] best serve our goals? [104]

It seems better to work on one section at a time than to dabble a bit in [118] both sections at once.    Further, we need to avoid plantings that will in [133] a few years overgrow walkways and porches. [142]

closing 146

. . . . . . . . . . . . . . . . . . . . . . . . . . . . . . . . . . . . . . . . . . . . . . . . . . . . . . . . . . . . . . . . . . . . . . . . . . . . . . . . . . .

(Current date) | Mr. Thomas A. Raleigh | Department of Public Instruction | [13] Juneau, AK 99801-9999 | Dear Mr. Raleigh [22]

In response to your recent letter requesting some ideas for "brain- [36] storming" sessions, perhaps the following ones will help. [47]

<u>First, judging of proffered ideas must be delayed.</u>    Criticism of any [61] suggestion must be withheld until a later time.    As Osborn said in [76] <u>Applied Imagination</u>: [80]

> If you try to get hot and cold water out of the same faucet at the [93]
> same time, you will get only tepid water.    And if you try to criticize [107]
> and create at the same time, you can't turn on either cold enough [121]
> criticism or hot enough ideas. [127]

<u>Second, "free wheeling" is welcomed.</u>    The wilder the idea, the better.  It [142] is easier to tame down than to think up. [151]

<u>Third, quantity is wanted.</u>    The greater the number of ideas, the more [165] likelihood of winners. [170]

<u>Fourth, combination and improvement are sought.</u>    In addition to [182] contributing ideas of their own, participants should suggest how ideas [198] of others can be turned into better ideas; or how two or more ideas can [212] be joined into still another idea. [219]

These four basic principles are the guides we follow in conducting "brain- [233] storming" workshops for teachers and administrators in schools and col- [248] leges and for workers and executives in firms throughout the country. [262]

Sincerely yours | Ms. Nelda S. Gibson, Director | xx [271]

1. Create these two text charts using the same template as your title and bulleted list charts.

2. Position the bulleted lists on the left of the screen to allow room for the clipart images on the right.

3. Retrieve similar images and position them as shown.

4. For the "Humor" chart, add text at the lower right in a different color in the same, but smaller, typeface. Add a line in a different color to emphasize the last word.

---

# Humor

- Use humorous clipart on visuals–if appropriate for the presentation topic.

- Be sure no images could be offensive to the audience.

Remember to . . .

poofread

proofreed

**proofread!**

---

# Speaker Tips

- Dress professionally.
- Be enthusiastic.
- Speak clearly and distinctly.
- Maintain eye contact.
- Use natural gestures.

words

**Document 5**
**Unbound Report**

1. Format/key the book report in unbound report style, DS.
2. Number the second page.
3. Place the reference below the body on page 2.
4. Proofread and correct all errors you make as you key.

THE OLD MAN AND THE SEA                                        5

He was an old man, thin and gaunt, with deep wrinkles in the back          18
of his neck and brown blotches on his cheeks.  His hands had deep-          31
creased scars from handling heavy fish on the cords.  Everything about     45
him was old except his eyes, and they were the color of the sea and        59
were cheerful and undefeated.  He fished alone in a skiff in the Gulf       74
Stream, and this was the eighty-fourth day he had gone without taking      88
a fish.                                                                    89

Every day is a new day, the old man knew; and long before it was          102
light the next morning, he had his baits out and was drifting with the    116
current.  Hours later, watching his lines, he saw one of the projecting   130
green sticks dip sharply.  He reached out for the line, unleashed it from  145
the stick, and let it run gently through his fingers without the fish     159
feeling any tension.  A marlin, one hundred fathoms down, was eating      174
the sardines that covered the point and the shank of the hand-forged      187
hook.                                                                     188

So began a three-day battle between the old man and the big fish.         202
The old man had to battle thirst and hunger; the loss of sleep; and the   215
pain of cut and bleeding hands and cramped fingers.  Pain did not         229
matter--a man could endure; but defeat he could never admit.  "Man is     245
not made for defeat," he said.  "A man can be destroyed but not defeated." 259

The Old Man and the Sea is simple, compelling, magnificent.              271
Every word is right.  The old man embodies the essential nobility in      285
human striving.  The giant fish is the embodiment of what is noble in     299
animate nature.  And the sea--la mar, which is what the people call her   314
in Spanish when they love her--was the home of the great fish and the     328
love of the old man.                                                      332

This is a work of great power.  The strong, crisp words tell a mov-       346
ing story and express the basic attitudes the author held toward all life. 361
What one gets from him is not so much a fragment of his art as the        374
totality of his being.  He was the best and most natural craftsman of     388
our time.  Reading this book is a profound experience.  It is like living 403
a tragedy, which, at the last, emerges without grief into beauty.         416

REFERENCE                                            418

Hemingway, Ernest.  The Old Man and the Sea.  New York:  Charles          432
Scribner's Sons, 1952.                                                    436

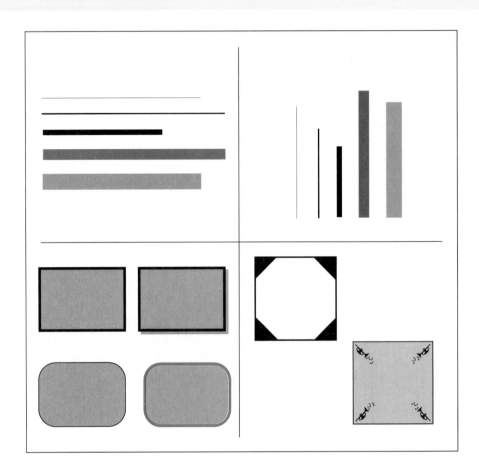

## 3-4C • 25
### Text on Boxes

1. Create the text chart at the right using the same template as your title and bulleted list charts.

2. Create a box in the color of your choice, and position it at the left as shown; duplicate this box and position the second box on the lower right.

3. Enter text in each box; choose the size and color. You may need to adjust the box sizes to frame the text nicely.

4. Retrieve a star and change its color to yellow. Size and position the star on the first box. Duplicate the star for the second box and position it as shown.

5. Retrieve an arrow, change its color and size, then position it as shown to indicate order.

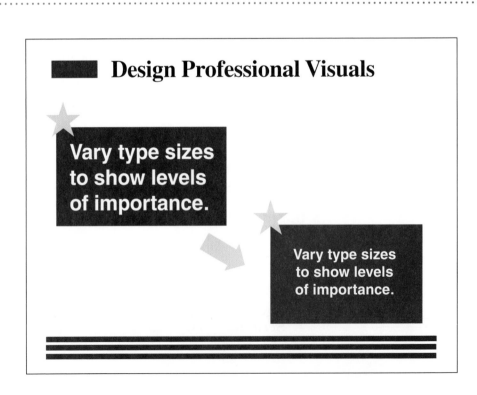

## Document 6
**Table**
**TM:** standard
**LS:** SS entries
**CS:** 0.4" (4 sp.)

words

FEDERAL HOLIDAYS — 3

| Event | 1998 | 1999 | |
|---|---|---|---|
| New Year's Day | Jan. 1 | Jan. 1 | 13 |
| Martin Luther King Jr. Day | Jan. 19 | Jan. 18 | 22 |
| Presidents' Day | Feb. 16 | Feb. 15 | 28 |
| Memorial Day | May 25 | May 31 | 34 |
| Independence Day | July 4 | July 4 | 40 |
| Labor Day | Sept. 7 | Sept. 6 | 45 |
| Columbus Day | Oct. 12 | Oct. 11 | 51 |
| Veterans' Day | Nov. 11 | Nov. 11 | 57 |
| Thanksgiving Day | Nov. 26 | Nov. 25 | 64 |
| Christmas Day | Dec. 25 | Dec. 25 | 70 |

73

Source:  The Universal Almanac, 1995. — 80

## Document 7
**Table**
**TM:** standard
**LS:** DS
**CS:** 0.8" (8 sp.)

COMPARATIVE TEACHING TIME BY COUNTRY — 7

( *Average Hours per Year, Secondary School* ) — 16

| Country | J.H.S. | S.H.S. | |
|---|---|---|---|
| Turkey | 1,080 | 1,080 | 25 |
| United states | 1,042 | 1,091 | 30 |
| Netherland | 954 | 954 | 34 |
| Spian | 930 | 630 | 37 |
| New zealand | 897 | 813 | 41 |
| Fineland | 798 | 760 | 44 |
| Ireland | 729 | 792 | 47 |
| Germany | 761 | 673 | 50 |

54

Source:   USA Today, april 12, 1995. — 61

# Adding Graphic Enhancements

**O b j e c t i v e s :**

**1.** To observe the importance of using appropriate graphic images, lines, and boxes.

**2.** To retrieve and position graphic images, lines, and boxes.

**3.** To create charts with graphic enhancements.

## 3-4A • 25
### Graphic Images

1. Read the copy at the right.

2. Learn how to use the drawing tools in your software to create, size, and position graphic images.

3. Retrieve images similar to the ones shown at the right.

4. Position the images in different locations on the screen.

5. Duplicate an image to create more of the same image; resize the duplicated images.

6. Change colors on the arrow and star images.

*Graphic images.* Symbols and art (clipart or original) can enhance a message and help to convey ideas. Symbols such as arrows or starbursts can focus an audience's attention. Art might include photo images or even original artwork scanned and converted to a digitized image. Clipart can often be used to add humor or to contribute to the text-based message. Be creative, but use images in good taste. An image isn't necessary on every chart shown in a presentation.

## 3-4B • 25
### Graphic Lines/Boxes

1. Learn how to create and position lines/rules as shown on p. A66.

2. Change the length and thickness of the lines.

3. Create boxes in various sizes and colors.

4. Create boxes with fancy borders.

*Graphic lines/boxes.* Lines, or rules, can be used to separate sections of a visual, to emphasize key words, or to connect elements. Boxes, too, can separate elements and provide a distinctive background for text. Boxes will appear to stand above the background when shading is applied on two sides. Fancy borders can call attention to the contents of a box.

*(continued on next page)*

## R&e Memo and Letters

words

**Document 1**
**Standard Memo**

Key the memo at right in standard format. Use the following information.
**TO: All Employees**
**FROM: Marjorie Clemens, Personnel**
**DATE: November 4, ----**
**SUBJECT: PROFESSIONAL DEVELOPMENT SEMINARS**

heading 24

The company is implementing a new program for professional development 39
this year.  Every employee will be given one day off to attend one of the 53
company-sponsored professional development seminars. 64

Tentative topics for this year's seminars are the value of leadership, improving 81
oral communication skills, integrated software applications, and stress man- 96
agement.   Indicate your preference for each of the seminars on the attached 111
form by placing #1 by your first choice, #2 by your second choice, and so 126
forth. 127

We will try to accommodate everyone's first or second choice.  The more 142
popular programs will be offered twice during the year in an effort to control 158
the number of participants at each seminar. | xx | Enclosure 169

**Document 2**
**Personal-Business Letter**

Key the letter at right in block format, open punctuation.

3716 Rangely Dr. | Raleigh, NC 27609-4115 | October 14, ---- | 12
Mr. Robert C. Johnson | Wayler Insurance Company | 206 Polk St. | 24
Raleigh, NC 27604-4120 | Dear Mr. Johnson | INFORMATION ON 35
CAREER OPPORTUNITIES 40

Please send information on career opportunities available with Wayler Insur- 55
ance Company in the administrative services area.  As part of a class 69
assignment, I will be giving an oral report on a company for which I would 84
like to work.  Wayler Insurance is an impressive company, and I would like 98
to do the report on career opportunities with your firm. 110

The report needs to address job titles, job requirements, educational require- 126
ments, salary, and opportunities for advancement.  Any information that 140
you are able to provide on these areas will be greatly appreciated. 154

Sincerely | Richard B. Lyons | xx 160

**Document 3**
**Business Letter**

Key the letter at right in block format, open punctuation.

October 20, ---- | Mr. Richard B. Lyons | 3716 Rangely Dr. | Raleigh, NC 14
27609-4115 | Dear Mr. Lyons 19

Wayler Insurance Company is always interested in potential employees. 34
We hope that you will consider us once you are graduated. 45

As you will see from reading the information that is enclosed, we have 59
different levels of administrative support positions in our company.  Job 74
titles, job requirements, educational requirements, and starting salaries are 90
included for each level.  Our company philosophy is to reward loyal employ- 105
ees; therefore, we like to promote from within when qualified employees are 120
available.  We also reimburse employees for additional job-related schooling 135
completed during their employment. 142

If you need further information or would like one of our administrative 157
support supervisors to talk with your class, please call us. 169

Sincerely yours | Robert C. Johnson | Customer Relations Director | xx | 182
Enclosure 184

**Presentation Planning**

- Consider audience needs carefully.
- Get organized.
- Know your subject well.
- Prepare visuals appropriate for available equipment and presentation location.

 **Message Development**

- Think about key points.
- Use a presentation outliner or sketch a storyboard.
- Keep one idea on a visual.
- Add variety as needed.

words

opening 18

¶ Walstram Industries has informed us that you have | 28

accepted a position in their Accounting Department and | 39

soon will be moving to Rockville. Congratulations | 49

and best wishes. | 52

¶ Our bank has designed a packet of information to | 62

help new citizens in the community become acquainted with | 74

the local area. The packet includes a map of the city, | 85

housing and rental guides, and a brochure that | 94

highlights upcoming cultural and civic events. This material | 107

will provide you with information that will make relocating | 119

a little easier. | 122

¶ Once you arrive in Rockville, we would appreciate hav- | 133

ing the opportunity to discuss ways that the First National | 145

Bank of Rockville can accommodate your banking needs. | 156

Sincerely / Ms. Marge L. Bowman / Customer Service / xx / Enclosures | 168

--------------------------------------------------------

March 1, ---- | Mr. Cody G. Sykes | 625 Pacific Ave. | Rockville, MD 20853- | 13
3107 | Dear Mr. Sykes: | 18

How quickly time passes! It seems like only yesterday that you re- | 32
newed your 24-month certificate of deposit (B-2987) with our bank. On | 46
March 15 it will again mature. | 52

For your convenience, we processed the certificate so that it would be | 66
renewed automatically for the same time period at the current market rate. | 81
If we do not hear from you prior to the maturity date, your certificate will | 97
be renewed at 5.5 percent for the next two years. The value of your cer- | 111
tificate as of March 15 will be $1,323.08. | 120

Should you wish to have the certificate renewed for a longer period at | 134
a higher interest rate, we can also do that. The time periods and current | 149
interest rates are as follows: | 156

| | | |
|---|---|---|
| 36-month certificate | 5.75 percent | 163 |
| 48-month certificate | 6.00 percent | 169 |
| 60-month certificate | 6.25 percent | 176 |

Call or stop in if you decide to go with a longer period for your cer- | 190
tificate. We appreciate your patronage and look forward to assisting with | 205
your banking needs in the future. | 212

Sincerely, | Mrs. Eiko R. Kimura | Investments | xx | 221

---

**Document 4**
**Business Letter**
Key the letter at right in modified block format with blocked paragraphs and open punctuation.

Date: **March 1, ----**

Address:

**Mr. Morris E. Young**
**904 Beatrice St.**
**Titusville, FL 32780-8192**

Salutation: **Dear Mr. Young**

---

**Document 5**
**Business Letter**
Key the letter at right in modified block format with indented paragraphs and mixed punctuation.

**Note:** To place a table within the body of a letter:

1. DS above and below the table; SS the body of the table.
2. Clear all tabs.
3. Decide how much space you will place between columns. (The table must fit within the margins of the letter.)
4. Determine and set a tab for each column of the table, including the first column.
5. After keying the table, clear the tabs and restore default tabs.

## Displaying Text Charts

**O b j e c t i v e s :**

**1.** To learn to vary text to show levels of importance.
**2.** To learn to create a title chart.
**3.** To learn to create bulleted list charts.

### 2A ● 30
### Title Chart

1. Read the copy at the right.
2. Select a similar template or master slide from those available in your software. It will give a consistent "look" to the series of charts you will create in this lesson.
3. Create the title chart using a similar typeface.
4. Select appropriate font sizes to emphasize the presentation title and presenter title.

*Title chart.* A presentation should begin with a title chart. Include the presentation title, presenter name, and other needed information. The text for this chart should be larger than for other charts, yet should blend with the other visuals in the series.

> # Professional
> # Business
> # Presentations
>
> **Andrew Gentry**
> **Information Services**

### 2B ● 30
### Bulleted Lists

1. Read the copy at the right.
2. Create the two bulleted lists displayed on the next page.
3. Use the same template to match your title chart. To the extent possible, follow the design shown.

*Bulleted lists.* Use lists to guide discussion and to help the audience follow a speaker's ideas. If too much information is placed on a single chart, the text becomes difficult to read. Therefore, keep the information on the visual concise—do not write complete sentences.

When using lists, be sure to
- Write phrases, not sentences.
- Use parallel structure.
- Limit the number of items on one list to about six.
- Limit long wraparound lines of text.
- Be concise.

*(continued on next page)*

words

COMPUTERS — QS     2

Computers have become a way of life. Almost every area 13
of of business and many aspects of our personnel lives have 24
felt their impact. Some refer to this period of time as the 36
Computer Revolution. 41

Computer Revolution is a widely used term these days. 52
It implies that society is undergoing a radical trans- 62
formation. . . . In his book, The Micro Millenium, 74
Evans argued that the societal impacts of computers in 85
general, and pesonal computers in particular, would rival 96
the effects of the Industrial Revolution.[1] 105

Who will use computers? 110

Although computers have personal and business disadvan- 121
tages as well as advantages, there is little doubt that these 133
devices will have an increasing impact on our daily lives in 145
the years to come. Computers are essentail tools of todays 158
society. . . . Today, everyone needs to understand them.[2] 170
Learning to use a computer is nearly as important as learning 182
to read. 184

What Will Computers be Used For? 191

Recent technological advances have produced supercomputers and 204
improved microcomputers with increased speed for processing information. 219
These computers are being used by government agencies, banks, 231
retailers, schools, homes, and individuals for a variety of 242
purposes. A few example include the following: 252

| | | |
|---|---|---|
| 1. | after-hour electronic banking | 258 |
| 2. | automatic scoring | 263 |
| 3. | electronic controls in home appliances | 271 |
| 4. | electronic check-out devices in supermarkets | 281 |
| 5. | electronic information displays in cars | 290 |
| 6. | electronic patient records in hospitals | 299 |
| 7. | employee performance monitoring | |
| 7. 8. | business applications | 304 |

*(continued on next page)*

## 1D • 15
## Makeover Example

**Example 1**
**Visual**

1. Examine the visual at the right. Its design does not follow visual design guidelines for font treatments. It is not easy to read.

2. Identify what is wrong with this visual.

**Example 2**
**Visual**

1. Examine the visual at the right. This visual presents the same information, yet it is much easier to read than Example 1. Its design follows visual design guidelines for font treatments.

2. Identify what makes this design more effective than Example 1.

**Poor visual example**

### PRESENTATION SOFTWARE

PRESENTATION SOFTWARE CAN HELP YOU TO COMMUNICATE MORE EFFECTIVELY. THE FEATURES OF PRESENTATION SOFTWARE INCLUDE OUTLINERS TO HELP YOU GET ORGANIZED, TEMPLATES TO HELP YOU MATCH COLORS, CLIPART TO HELP YOU VISUALIZE IDEAS, AND SCREENSHOWS TO SHOW YOUR VISUALS ONE AT A TIME.

OVERHEAD TRANSPARENCIES, 35-mm SLIDES, AND COMPUTER-PROJECTED PRESENTATIONS CAN BE CREATED WITH PRESENTATION SOFTWARE.

WHEN YOU CREATE VISUALS TO AID IN YOUR PRESENTATION, YOUR PREPARATION WILL HELP TO GIVE YOU CONFIDENCE.

**Good visual example**

## Presentation Software

- Presentation effectiveness improved

- Key features include:
  - Outliners and templates
  - Clipart selections and screenshows

- Output includes:
  - Overhead transparencies and 35-mm slides
  - Computer-projected presentations

words

Why Are Computers Used in Business?    311

DS Computers fulfill three major needs ~~in~~ for and industry business. These    325
needs are as follows:    330

* Correspondence    333
* Budgeting, planning, and decision making    342
* Decentralized processing[3]    348

Correspondence.    The word processing capabilities of    358
computers provide a means for creating written communication.    371
Information documented via written comunication is important    383
to the existence of a business organizations.    390

Budgeting, Planning, and Decision Making.    Information in    401
DS generated by spreadsheets supports management ~~with~~ budgeting,    413
planning, and decision making.    Electronic spreadsheets cre-    425
ated on computers allow management to manipulate the data    437
more easily and with much greater speed than when the calcu-    449
lations were done manually.    455

Decentralized processing.    Because today's computers are    466
small and inexpensive, they provide a means for decentralized    479
processing.    More and more workers are creating and processing their    492
own information rather than relying entirely on word process-    505
ing and data processing centers as they once did.    This decentralized processing    521
gives shorter turnaround time for the person needing the    532
infromation.    535

. . . . . . . . . . . . . . . . . . . . . . . . . . . . . . . . . . . . . . . . . . . . . . . . . . . . . . . . . . . . . .

heading 2

[1] Kathryn Schellenberg, ed., Computers in Society, 3d    13
ed. (Guilford, CT: The Dushkin Publishing Group,    23
Inc., 1990), p. 2.    27

[2] David R. Adams and Gerald E. Wagner,    36
Computer Information Systems: An Introduction, 2d ed.,    45
(Cincinnati: South-Western Publishing Co., 1986), p. 26.    56

[3] Randolph Johnston, Microcomputers: Concepts and    67
Applications (Santa Cruz, CA: Mitchell Publishing,    76
Inc., 1987), p. 1.    81

## Getting Started

**Objectives:**

**1.** To learn basic presentation terms.
**2.** To apply presentation templates.
**3.** To learn to select fonts for readability and consistency.

### 1A • 10
### Orientation

1. Read the copy and study the illustrations at the right.
2. Learn to select portrait and landscape orientations on your software.
3. With your software set for landscape orientation, key your name, course name, and current date centered on the visual.
4. Change the orientation for this visual to portrait and notice the difference in appearance.

The **landscape orientation** for presentation visuals provides a work space wider than it is tall. More horizontal space is available to arrange text information and illustrations. This size fits better on a computer screen during development and better on the viewing screen when visuals are projected as transparencies, slides, or electronic presentations.

The **portrait orientation** provides a work space taller than it is wide. If a visual for projection is displayed in portrait orientation, often the bottom of the viewing screen is not visible to the entire audience. Portrait orientation, however, is appropriate for many paper-based applications.

**Landscape Orientation**

xxxxxxxxxxxxxxxx
xxxxxxxxxxxxxxxxxxxxxx
xxxxxxxxxxxxx

**Portrait Orientation**

xxxxxxxxxxxxxxx
xxxxxxxxxxxxxxxxxxxxx
xxxxxxxxxxxxx

### 1B • 10
### Templates

1. Read the copy at the right.
2. Examine the various templates available with your software.

Presentation software provides *templates* that contain background designs and a *palette* of coordinated colors for text. An appropriate display template should be selected first in preparing a presentation.

Several different templates will be used for the visuals shown in this unit. Suggestions will indicate what makes a template appropriate in a given instance.

### 1C • 15
### Font Selection and Treatment

1. Read the copy at the right.
2. Determine the fonts available with your software and learn how to select them.
3. Learn how to change font color and sizes.

*Readability* of text is very important; therefore, carefully select fonts and font treatments for easy reading and consistency throughout a presentation.

- Establish a heading/text hierarchy with font sizes and colors—make the most important items show up more.
- Limit use of words in all capital letters—lowercase text is easier to read.

- Be careful when combining different fonts to avoid confusing the audience.
- Strive for consistency in font size, color, and use throughout a presentation.
- Be sure text on all visuals is large and bold enough to be seen from the back of the presentation room when projected.

**Document 10**
**Topic Outline**

Key the copy at right as a topic outline. Refer to 92D on p. 225 if necessary.

 **note:**

If your software has an Outline feature, use it.

words

|  |  | words |
| --- | --- | --- |
| | EMPLOYMENT COMMUNICATIONS | 5 |

I.  PERSONAL DATA SHEET _QS_ — 10

   A.  Personal Information _lc_ — 15
     1.  Name, address, and Telephone number _if needed_ — 23
     2.  Social Security number ⌒(work permit number) — 35
     3.  Personal interests: hobbies/recreational interests — 46
   B.  Educational Information _#_ — 51
     1.  Schools attended _and dates of attendance_ — 60
     2.  Special areas of study; activities; awards _received_ — 72
   C.  Work Experience — 76
_DS_      1.  Jobs held; what you **experienced**; commendations — 86
     2.  Volunteer work — 90
   D.  References ⌐(Teachers, Work Supervisors) — 98

II.  LETTER OF APPLICATION — 104

   A.  Source of Information about Job _Opening_ — 113
   B.  Expression of Interest in Being Interviewed for the Job — 125
   C.  Brief Summary of Work Skills and How They Fit the Job — 136
     1.  Special courses that are applicable to the job — 146
     2.  Work experiences make you qualified for the job — 158
   D.  Request for Interview _that_ — 163

III. THANK-YOU LETTER FOLLOWING INTERVIEW — 172
_DS_    A.  Appreciation for Courtesies Shown During Company Visit — 183
   B.  Positive Impressions of Company and Employees — 193
   C.  Expression of Continued Interest in the Job — 203

**Document 11**
**Table with Note**

Prepare the information at right as a three-column table, centered vertically and horizontally. DS; CS: 0.5". In secondary heading, replace ---- with current year.

**Note:** Refer to p. 157 to review how to create a keyline using the Center feature/key for horizontal centering. See p. RG19 if Center feature/key is not available. Refer to p. 232 to review procedure for vertical centering, if Center Page feature is not available.

HAMBURG SCHOOL OF BALLET ITINERARY — 7

---- Summer Tour* — 11

| Sponsor | City | Date |  |
| --- | --- | --- | --- |
| Boston Ballet | Boston | June 4 | 20 |
| Ballet Academy of Miami | Miami | June 11 | 28 |
| Dallas Ballet Academy | Dallas | June 18 | 35 |
| Ruth Page Foundation | Chicago | June 25 | 43 |
| Northwest Ballet | Minneapolis | July 1 | 50 |
| Colorado Ballet Center | Denver | July 8 | 57 |
| Dancers' Stage Company | San Francisco | July 15 | 66 |
| Pacific Northwest Ballet | Seattle | July 22 | 75 |
|  |  |  | 78 |

*Leave for Boston on June 1; return to Hamburg on July 27. — 89

## Screenshow Presentation Purposes

A **screenshow** is a basic feature of presentation software. Different programs may use other names for this feature, but any true presentation program will have this capability. A screenshow has two purposes: to keep related files organized and to project the visuals in a preplanned sequence for audience viewing. Presentation software can be used with a computer and projection equipment to create "electronic" presentations. Even portable computers can be used for this purpose.

Once the necessary projection equipment is purchased, screenshow production is low in cost because files can be saved to the computer hard drive or to a removable disk. The charts are all saved in advance and arranged in a particular sequence; if necessary, last-minute changes can be made. This flexibility is not possible when slides or transparencies are used for a presentation. Plus, the vivid colors of well-designed visuals make watching them much more interesting than slides or transparencies.

The computer used for projection must be connected to a large-screen projection device such as a/an

- LCD (liquid crystal display) panel—a notebook-sized panel that is easily portable. (It requires, however, an overhead projector with a high-intensity [very bright] light to project through the panel.)

- LCD data/video projector—a portable unit containing its own light source that is easily portable.

- CRT data/video projector—a unit that is usually ceiling mounted because of its size (portable units are available).

- Video monitor—a large-sized video monitor is effective for smaller groups; the need for a projection screen is eliminated.

**Animation.** Interesting transition effects are one form of animation used to control how visuals go on and off display. Also, objects on the visuals can be animated in such a way as to have a person walk across a scene on the visual or to have a title drop into place one letter at a time. Animation provides significant benefits for capturing and retaining the audience's attention.

**Video and sound.** Some presentation software allows the user to incorporate multimedia elements of video and sound. Additional needs for hardware make presenting with video and sound a little more complicated.

**Design and delivery tips.** Use more visuals than you would for a transparency-based presentation—and put less on each visual. Show a visual just as you are ready to discuss its content.

- Arrange lists as *builds* to present listed concepts one at a time as discussion progresses.

- Use a building technique to create process diagrams or models by adding parts as discussion progresses.

- To maintain eye contact with the audience, position the computer where its screen can easily be seen instead of turning around to face the projection screen while talking.

words

## COMMON U.S./METRIC EQUIVALENTS — 6

Approximate Values — 10

| | | |
|---|---|---|
| 1 inch | 25.4 millimeters (mm) | 16 |
| 1 inch | 2.54 centimeters (cm) | 22 |
| 1 foot | 0.305 meter (m) | 26 |
| 1 yard | 0.91 meter (m) | 31 |
| 1 mile | 1.61 kilometers (km) | 36 |
| 1 pint | 0.47 liter (1 or L) | 42 |
| 1 quart | 0.95 liter (1 or L) | 47 |
| 1 gallon | 3.785 liters (1 or L) | 53 |
| 1 ounce | 28.35 grams (g) | 58 |
| 1 pound | 0.45 kilogram (kg) | 63 |

**Document 12**
**Table with Decimal Numbers**

Prepare the copy at right as a two-column table, centered vertically and horizontally. DS; **CS:** 1". Align numbers at the decimal point.

**Note:** If a Decimal Tab feature is available, use it to align decimal numbers.

## MARCH SALES — 2

| Sales Manager | Territory | Sales | |
|---|---|---|---|
| | | | 9 |
| Diane Aldredge | Connecticut | $204,500 | 16 |
| Marcia Kelly | Maine | 135,200 | 22 |
| Ruth Peterson | Massachusetts | 125,000 | 29 |
| Rebecca Johnston | New Hampshire | 135,800 | 37 |
| Orlando Martinez | New York | 172,900 | 43 |
| Jonathan Akervik | Rhode Island | 88,200 | 51 |
| Roger McDonald | Vermont | 115,200 | 57 |
| Total Sales | | $976,800 | 61 |

**Document 13**
**Table with Amount Column and Total**

Key the copy at right as a three-column table SS. TM: 2"; SM: 1.25". Left-align column headings.

**Note:** The underline preceding the total should be the same length as the longest item in column (including the $).

## ---- SPRING RECRUITMENT SCHEDULE — 7

Martin Bartlett — 10

| University | Date | Area of Specialization | |
|---|---|---|---|
| | | | 18 |
| San Diego State University | March 3 | Marketing | 27 |
| Arizona State University | March 10 | Management Information | 39 |
| University of Colorado | March 17 | Management Information | 50 |
| University of Kentucky | March 24 | Management | 58 |
| Tennessee State University | March 31 | Accounting | 68 |
| Florida A & M | April 7 | Marketign | 74 |
| Duke University | April 14 | Accounting | 81 |

**Document 14**
**Table with Centered Column Headings**

Key the copy at right as a three-column table centered vertically and horizontally. DS; **CS:** 0.25". Center column headings. In main heading, replace ---- with current year.

Refer

Create keyline using Center feature/key — p. 157.

Horizontal centering without Center feature — p. RG19.

Vertical centering (manual) — p. 232.

Centering short column headings — 96C, p. 235.

Centering multiple-line column headings — 98C, p. 239.

# Presentation Software Features

Presentations are an important part of communication in business. Their purpose is often to **inform** (deliver facts) or **persuade** (change behavior, attitudes, or beliefs). In both cases, the presenter has information to share and hopes the audience will react favorably to it. Typical business situations involving presentations include product introductions, award presentations, sales promotions, training sessions, and other meetings.

To help an audience understand the presentation message, visuals such as transparencies or slides are frequently used. With the necessary equipment, a series of visuals can be projected directly from a computer system for audience viewing. Today's presentation software provides many possibilities for using color and other design techniques to make presentations more dynamic.

The key features of presentation software are

- word processing capabilities

- drawing features

- graphing abilities

- importing capabilities for clipart, photographs, or data from other programs

- exporting capabilities for transferring images to other programs

- screenshow development and display using text and diagram builds and, possibly, animation and digital video import

- presentation design and management

- printing capabilities

## Design

The condition of the final output, of course, will depend on the available equipment and the skill of the presenter who creates the presentation. Many of the design concepts appropriate for word and desktop publishing are also important to the design of visuals for presentations—and yet many differences exist, also.

Presentation visuals can spur interest and illustrate major points. They should help the speaker explain and help the audience understand the speaker's message. **Visuals** (also called *charts* or *slides*) should be well designed to serve this purpose.

## Templates (Slide Masters)

The series of visuals prepared for a presentation should have a consistent and uncluttered look achieved through color, graphics, and type. An attractive appearance is often the result of a simple design. Presentation programs provide background **templates** (also called *slide masters*) for this purpose. These templates provide a design and color scheme for the background and text information for a consistent look for all visuals in a presentation. Even when printing with black and white, a similar appearance can be achieved so that all visuals look like they belong together.

## R&E  Letters and Memos

**Document 1**
**Personal-Business Letter with Special Characters**

Format the letter at right in block format with open punctuation. Use the special character shown for the listed items in ¶ 3.

**Document 2**

Rekey Document 1 in modified block format with indented paragraphs, mixed punctuation. Use a different character than in Document 1 for the listed items.

**Document 3**
**Simplified Memo with Distribution List**

Prepare the copy at right as a simplified memo. Create a horizontal distribution list (see p. 189).

**Document 4**
**Standard Memo with Distribution List**

Reformat or rekey Document 3 as a standard memo on plain paper. Use the vertical style distribution list (see p. 189).

|  | words |
|---|---|
| 1231 Woodlawn Dr. \| Toledo, OH 43612-1712 \| April 5, ---- \| Mr. Jeffrey | 13 |
| A. York \| Lakeview Condominium Association \| 599 Miller Rd. \| Knox- | 27 |
| ville, TN 37920-4119 \| Dear Mr. York | 32 |

Thank you for sending the lease so quickly.  My check for the $450 secu- · 48
rity deposit is enclosed along with the signed lease. I will pay the first · 63
month's rent when I arrive in Knoxville. · 70

I do have a few questions that you can answer for me regarding the condo- · 85
minium complex. · 88

- Do you arrange to have the electricity transferred to my name, or do I · 102
  need to contact the electric company? · 111
- To what address will my mail be delivered? · 120
- Is garbage disposal included with the rent? · 129
- Is storage space available outside the condominium? · 140

I am looking forward to receiving the information so that I can take care of · 156
these arrangements before arriving in Knoxville on July 1. · 168

Sincerely | Jennifer A. Rose | Enclosure · 175

December 27, ---- | Charlie Meade, Annette Nye, Greg Anderson, Emma · 13
Sims, Chi Sen | NEW BROCHURES · 19

Here are the new brochures that I talked about at the last staff meeting. · 34
The printing company did an excellent job in designing them.  I believe they · 49
should help us provide the public with information about the various · 63
services our bank offers. · 68

Since you are the first contact the public has with our bank, it is extremely · 84
important for you to be aware of what is included in each brochure so that · 99
you can provide our customers with the appropriate brochure to answer · 113
their questions.  If you have questions about any of the information · 127
included in the brochures, please check with the person in charge of the · 141
particular program you have questions about. · 151

Remember to mark your calendars for our next staff meeting, which is sched- · 166
uled for January 28. · 170

Linda G. Gomez | Administrative Assistant to the Vice President | xx | · 183
Attachments · 185

**Flyer**

1. Key the text in the flyer at the right.
2. Change margins all around to 1".
3. Retrieve a similar image to represent the sun (a starburst would be suitable, too) and position it at the top right.
4. Begin the text about 2.5" down from the top of the page.
5. Use a large, bold typeface for the attention-getting text.
6. Retrieve a similar image for the suitcase; duplicate the image and position four as shown. (If you cannot find a similar image to suggest travel, a solid black line could be used here to separate the page.)
7. Create a coupon to be returned to the travel agency for information. Use a border for this section. If available, use a border that resembles the one shown with scissors to suggest cutting along the line. (A solid-line border could be used instead.)
8. Use a smaller text size for the coupon text.
9. Add white space as appropriate.

This flyer uses a large, bold typeface to emphasize the text and clipart images to suggest travel to a sunny location. The border is used to create a coupon to return for additional information. The border shown suggests cutting the coupon out of the paper.

**For FUN in the SUN . . . call Lee Travel at 217-152-2230**

Return this coupon with your name and address for information on our summer vacation packages!

Name _____

Address _____

_____

Phone _____

Lee Travel
719 W. Marketview
Champaign, IL 61801-2223

words

### Document 5
**Simplified Block Letter**

Prepare the letter at right in simplified block format with open punctuation.

**Note:** Omit those letter parts shown that should not be included in simplified block format. Add any missing letter parts.

### Letters with Variable Information, Special Features
### Document 6

Prepare the letter below in modified block format with blocked ¶s; mixed punctuation. Insert the following information for the numbers in parentheses:

(1) **May** (2) **Houston** (3) **managing human resources** (4) **May 13** (5) **Milwaukee** (6) **Marc Plaza**

**Special features:** Company name in closing lines: **BANKING INSTITUTE**
c Natasha J. Bartlett
Mark L. Kostner
Postscript: **Will I see you at next week's convention in Hawaii?   I'm looking forward to some warmer weather.**

### Document 7

Prepare Document 6 in block format; open punctuation with the following changes:

**Ms. Renae A. Santiago**
**Suwannee National Bank**
**5507 Ranchero Rd.**
**Tallahassee, FL 32304-9340**

(1) **June** (2) **Pittsburgh**
(3) **customer advertising**
(4) **October 1** (5) **Houston**
(6) **Hyatt Regency**

**Special features:** same as Document 6; no postscript

(Total words = 167)

(Current date) | Miss Roberta J. Payson | 310 Ledgewood Rd. | Portland, ME    13
04108-6482 | Dear Miss Payson    21

Here are the two tables that show the cost of a $50,000 home loan.   The    36
first table displays various interest rates for a 15-year loan, while the    50
second one gives the rates for a 30-year loan.   As you can see from the    65
tables, you would decrease your monthly payment by approximately $120    79
per month by assuming a 30-year loan.   The total amount repaid, how-    92
ever, would be considerably more.    99

The tables can also be used to determine the difference between the monthly    114
payments for a fixed mortgage versus the adjustable rate mortgage.    128
Currently our adjustable mortgage rate is 8 percent.   As I mentioned    142
yesterday, this type of loan is based on the index tied to the U.S. Treasury    157
securities.   The initial rate is guaranteed for two years.   At the end of two    173
years the rate can be increased or decreased by two percentage points each    188
year up to a maximum rate of 12 percent.    196

If you have any additional questions about the loans we discussed yester-    211
day, please call me.    215

Sincerely | Mark R. Nelson | Loan Officer | xx | Enclosures | c Marshall    226
S. Gagne    227

. . . . . . . . . . . . . . . . . . . . . . . . . . . . . . . . . . . . . . . . . . . . . . . . . . . . . . . . . . . . . . . . . . . . . . . . . . . . . . .

November 15, ---- | Mr. Lewis G. Mackenzie | Human Resources Man-    12
ager | Bank of Nottingham | 1295 Kensington Ave. | Detroit, MI 48230-    25
5286 | Dear Mr. Mackenzie:    30

The seminar you presented last  (1)  in  (2)  for the Banking Institute on    45
(3) was very well received.   Several institute members have requested that    64
the seminar be offered again this coming year.    74

The seminar is scheduled for  (4)  in  (5)  at the  (6).   Are you available    91
on this date to present the seminar?  The honorarium for conducting the    105
seminar has been increased to $1,800.   Of course, all your expenses    119
would be paid by the institute.    126

Please let me know by December 1 whether you will be able to work with    140
us on this year's seminar.    145

Sincerely,  | Ryan S. Woodward | Institute Director | xx    155

closing 186

1. Prepare the flyer at the right.
2. Change all margins to 0.5".
3. Set center justification.
4. Create a double line border and stretch it to fill the page.
5. For the word *Circus*, use a serif typeface; make the first and last letters larger than the middle of the word. (The example shows 66 and 44 points.)
6. For all other text, use a sans serif typeface and vary the sizes used.
7. Adjust the line height for the title lines so that the word *Mario* fits tightly above the word *Circus*.
8. Use reverse type for the word *Featuring*.
9. Insert iconic symbols as shown for the diamond shapes and pointing hands.
10. Add white space as appropriate.

This flyer would be suitable for posting or for a newspaper advertisement. To gain attention, a double border is placed close to the edge of the page. Words are emphasized by changing the sizes and adding decorative iconic symbols.

MARIO

# CIRCUS

BROTHERS

**Featuring**

**Lions** ◆ **Tigers** ◆ **Bears**

**Spectacular Dancing Cats** ◆ **Elephants Galore** ◆ **Merlin the Magician**
**The Aerialist Extravaganza** ◆ **Wilhelm's Astounding Jugglers**

☞ **5 SHOWS!** ☜
**Assembly Hall**
**September 24-25**

**Sponsored by County Market**
**Tickets Available at Assembly Hall Box Office**

words

STUDENT ORGANIZATIONS                                          4

Student organizations plays a vital role in the educational process   18
of students.   Students who participate in such organizations are given   32
opportunities to test the concepts they were taught in the formal   45
classrooom environment.   Two such organizations that are widely rec-   59
ognized in the business education field are Future Business Leaders of   73
America and Business Professionals of America (formerly called Office   87
Education Association.                                          92

Future Business Leaders of America                             99

Future Business Leaders of America is a vocational association   112
that helps studdnts bridge the gap between the classroom and the business   126
world.   Two of the major goals outlined in the Future Business Leaders   141
of America Handbook are as follows:[1]                         148

1.   Develop competent, aggressive business leadership.        159

2.   Create more interest in and understanding of American business   173
     enterprise.                                               175

Business leadership.   Students have the opportunity to develop   188
leadership skills by serving as officers, attending conferences, working   203
with businessmen and businesswomen in the community, and partici-   216
pating in competitive events sponsored by the organization.   the   229
organization's strong emphasis on community service provides another   242
avenue for the development of leadership skills.               252

Business enterprise.   A greater understanding of business enter-   265
prise is gained by students as they participate in chapter projects   279
dealing with this important subject.   These projects give students ex-   293
periences in learning more about the operation ofbusiness enterprise in   308
America.                                                       310

Business Professionals of America                              317

Business Professionals of America is another vocational business   330
and office education program for students interested in developing per-   344
sonal, leadership, and office skills.                          352

Accoridng to Goodman, the executive director of the organization   365
for 1987-88, the goal of the organization has been to promote   377
leadership and professionalism among students in order to pre-   389
pare them for satisfying and successful careers in the business   402
world.[2]                                                      404

*(continued on next page)*

## 12-14C • 35
## Certificate

1. Change paper to landscape orientation (11" wide x 8.5" long).
2. Use 1" margins all around.
3. Retrieve a border image and stretch it to fill the page.
4. Using center alignment, key the text of the certificate.
5. Insert white space as needed.

**Notes:**

- The example shows the typeface Times in three sizes—the title is the largest text line; names under the signature lines are the smallest.
- The name of the person receiving the certificate is shown in the typeface Syntax UltraBlack.

This certificate has a decorative border to give it an elegant look suitable for framing.

A bold typeface is used to emphasize the name of the person receiving the award.

# Certificate of Achievement

is awarded to

## Nathan Jefferson

for outstanding civic contributions to the
Marshall High School Boosters Club

----

Angela Mason, President

Greg Hall, Adviser

words

**Document 10**
**Title Page**
Create a title page for the report you prepared in Document 9.

The two goals, developing business leadership and understanding business enterprise, emphasized by FBLA are also emphasized by Business Professionals of America.  They, too, have programs designed to provide studetns with the opportunity to develop their leadership skills and to foster a greater understanding of the role of the entrepreneur in the free enterprise system.

ENDNOTES

[1]Future Business Leaders of America Handbook (Reston, VA: FBLA-PBL Incorporated, 1985), p. 5.

[2]Goodman, Dorothy M.,  "A New Image for Our Organization," 1987-88 Chapter Handbook (Columbus, OH:  Office Education Association, 1987), p. 11.

| |
|---|
| 416 |
| 430 |
| 444 |
| 458 |
| 473 |
| 479 |
| 481 |
| 493 |
| 500 |
| 512 |
| 525 |
| 529 |

...................................................................

**Document 11**
**Report**
Prepare the text at right and on p. A29 as a report in bound format.  SS and indent paragraphs.  The material is to become part of an office manual numbered pp. 24-27.

Bold the main and secondary headings and the heading on the separate ENDNOTES page.  Number p. 24 at the bottom center; number remaining pages at the upper right.  Use the secondary heading as a bold header on each page after p. 24.

Replace underlines with italic (except side headings) if available.  Use hanging-indent style for the enumerated list.  Set a tab to reduce the space between numbers and beginning of first word.

ADDRESSING THE SITUATION                    5

Guides for Processing First-Class Mail        13

The cost of an average business letter is roughly \$16 to \$17.[1]    25
The U.S. Postal Service (USPS) continually strives to increase the speed    40
and lower the per-unit cost of mail delivery.   In 30 years of effort, USPS    55
has transformed mail service through the use of optical character recogni-    70
tion (OCR) scanners, authorized (2-letter) state[2] abbreviations, expanded    85
ZIP Codes (ZIP+4), barcoding, and high-speed sorting devices.        97

USPS Standards                                101

Businesses such as this one have improved internal operations in    114
line with changing practices of USPS.  Obvious changes include faster    128
equipment and better trained personnel in the mail room.  Other impor-    142
tant changes include the use of specific addressing guidelines by the docu-    157
ment specialists who prepare first-class mail.[3]                166

These guidelines are updated regularly on the basis of USPS    178
bulletins.  Publication 28[4] is the current reference.  Addressing guides are    194
also updated with information from office management journals, secretarial    209
conferences and workshops, word processing user's guides, and computing    223
magazines.                                    226

Company Standards                             229

At a cost of \$16 to \$17 apiece, first-class mail in this organization    243
is viewed as serious business.  Nearly four hundred first-class items leave    259
this company's mail room each week.  The goals for each piece are the same:    274

- Go to the right place.                       279
- Go in the shortest possible time.            287
- Grab and hold receivers' attention.[5]       295

*(continued on next page)*

## 12-14B • 20
### Title Page

1. Create a report title page with the title framed in a simple border.
2. Insert white space as appropriate.

**Notes:**

- The title in the example is shown in a serif typeface set at 24 points in bold.
- The title and border begin about 2.5" from the top of the page.
- Other text information is in the same typeface as the title set at 15 points in bold.

On this title page, the title words are emphasized by framing them in a simple border. The border is a single, thick line.

The title and border are positioned on the top half of the page; other information is positioned on the bottom half of the page.

A Comparison of

Publishing Features

in Two

Word Processing Programs

Your Name

Business Computer Applications

Current date

words

First-Class Mail Guidelines     301

The following first-class mail guidelines were designed to reach    314
these goals. Guidelines for handling other classes of mail and    326
using special services begin on p. 28. A postal rate chart appears in    341
Appendix D (blue pages).    346

1. Key envelope addresses in block style, using uppercase letters    359
and omitting punctuation (except hyphens).    368

2. Place the address block about four inches from the left edge    382
and two inches from the top edge of a No. 10 envelope, or use the    394
default setting of the Envelope feature on the word processing soft-    407
ware.    409

3. Use an attention line ONLY when attempts to determine a    421
person's name have failed. Place the attention line (when used) on    435
the first line of the address block. Example: ATTENTION MARKET-    448
ING COORDINATOR.    451

4. Key the street address or box number on the line below the    465
addresses' name, followed by applicable apartment or suite numbers.    478

5. Key only the city, state abbreviation, and ZIP+4 Code on    490
the last line. Space once before the ZIP Code. Do NOT place the    503
postal codes of other countries on the last address line of interna-    517
tional mail. Show only the country name (no abbreviation) on the    530
last address line.    534

6. Use USPS authorized abbreviations for directions and street suf-    548
fixes; for example, N for North, ST for Street, BLVD for Boulevard,    561
and STE for Suite. Never abbreviate the city name. Extremely long    575
company names may be abbreviated if USPS standards are used.    587
Example: ACCENT ON EXEC SVCS for ACCENT ON EXECUTIVE    598
SERVICES.    600

7. When using the Envelope software feature, print a postnet bar    614
code above the envelope address.    621

8. Use a personal (MISS, MR, or MS) or professional (DR, PROF, REV,    634
etc.) title in envelope and letter addresses, with few exceptions as    648
noted in the following paragraph. (MR/MRS is an acceptable form of    662
Mr. and Mrs.)    665

If a woman's marital status is unknown, use MS. If a person's first    678
name does not indicate gender or if only initials are shown, call the    692
person's office and ask the switchboard operator if MR or MS is correct.    707
If the information cannot be obtained by calling, omit a personal title from    723

*(continued on next page)*

# Using Borders

**Objectives:**

1. To learn to frame an entire document with a border.
2. To observe how borders emphasize parts of a document.
3. To prepare documents with various border treatments.

**12-14A • 15**
## Borders as Frames

1. Read the copy at the right and examine the illustrations.
2. Determine the types of borders available with your software.
3. Practice creating borders in different sizes.

*Borders* give a page a distinctive appearance and separate elements on the page. Borders can be simple boxes with lines that match on all four sides, or the line thicknesses can be varied for a shadow effect or other illusions. Many programs have selections of decorative borders. Illustrated below are simple borders and decorative borders.

Spacing around and within borders is always important. When borders are used in a document to divide elements of the page, the white space outside the border must be large enough to keep other page elements away from the border. The white space within the border also must involve a margin to prevent a crowded or cramped appearance.

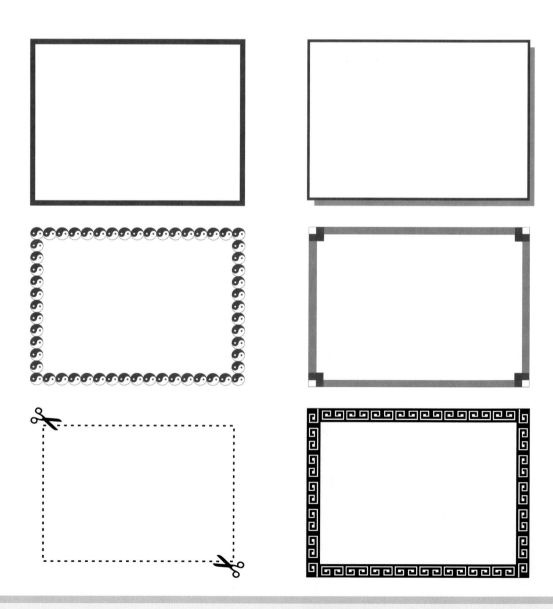

words

the envelope and use simplified block format (no salutation) for the let- | 737
ter, OR use the first and last names in the salutation of a block format | 752
letter. Examples: Dear J. P. Russell, Dear Kim Bunzel. (The use of M to | 767
represent MR or MS is NOT recommended.) | 775

ENDNOTES | 777

[1]This estimate is derived from an early-90s Target Study conducted | 790
by the Dartnell Institute of Business Research in Chicago. Postage repre- | 805
sents only about 2 percent of the costs, based on the 1995 rate of $.32 for | 820
the first ounce. Most of the cost involves salary and wages of individuals | 835
who originate and process business letters. | 844

[2]Authorized in 1963 as part of the conversion from postal zones to | 858
ZIP Code areas, the 2-CAP abbreviations include District of Columbia (DC), | 873
Guam (GU), Puerto Rico (PR), and the Virgin Islands (VI). | 884

[3]Each document specialist is to have a copy of "Addressing the Situ- | 898
ation" at her or his work station. | 905

[4]Postal Addressing Standards. Washington, DC: U. S. Postal Service, | 919
1992. Additional copies may be obtained by asking for USPS Form 7380 | 933
from the mail room. | 937

[5]A former company president set a 3 percent maximum return rate | 950
on company mail in 1965, a challenge unmet for the next 6 years. The | 964
return rate last year: 0.47 percent. | 972

**Document 12**
**Expand Existing Table**
Open TAB96C1 and add a column for publication dates. CS: 0.5"; arrange in ascending order by date.

**Note:** The original table appears on p. 235 (96C, Table 1).

|  | Date of Publication |
|---|---|
| *Willey* | **1962** |
| *Capps* | **1969** |
| *Coolidge* | **1924** |
| *Wilson* | **1973** |
| *Wheeler* | **1976** |
| *Carter* | **1978** |
| *Kakuske* | **1970** |

**Document 13**
**Revising a Table**
Open TAB99B1 and make the changes shown at right throughout the document.

**Note:** The original table appears on p. 240 (99B, Table 1). Use the Search to Replace feature if available.

| Change | To |
|---|---|
| *teacher* | **instructor** |
| *SA* | **2** |
| *A* | **1** |
| *U* | **0** |
| *D* | **-1** |
| *SD* | **-2** |

## Report with Lines

Retrieve the file you created for Report 1 in Lesson 4. Modify this document by making the following changes.

1. Change the top/bottom margins to 0.5" so that the shaded line will almost fill the page vertically.
2. Change the left/right margins to 0.7".
3. Create a shaded vertical line at the left margin, 0.5" wide and 10" long. (The shading shown is 20%.)
4. Change the font size for the title to 30 points.
5. Add a horizontal line below the title for emphasis.
6. Set a tab at about 1.25" then paragraph indent the text to provide white space between the shaded line and the text.
7. Set a line height slightly larger than the default line height of 11 points (the example shows 0.194").
8. To call attention to the beginning of each paragraph, use an initial cap. Make this single letter large (20 points) and bold.
9. Set the body text at 11 points; headings, at 18 points in bold.
10. Insert rules below the headings for emphasis.
11. Insert white space as appropriate.

This report uses a wide, shaded line at the left to serve as a decorative element on the page and the title and side headings overlap this shaded area. Horizontal lines add still more emphasis. The line below the title is thicker than the lines below the side headings. *Initial caps* (large, bold letters) begin the text following a side heading to help highlight the beginning of each section.

# The Evolution of Publishing

Publishing is a very old industry dating back to the mid-1400s when Guttenberg invented the first printing press in Germany. Individual letters were carved out of little blocks of wood; lead eventually replaced wood because of its increased durability.

## The Printing Process

To create pages of text, letters were arranged one letter at a time to form words and sentences. The letters were arranged in rows on big trays called plates. This process was called *setting type*. Strips of lead were used between the rows to spread them apart for easier reading. The printer would place the finished plate in the printing press, apply ink to the plate, position a sheet of paper on the plate, then press down on the paper to make an impression. The process was repeated for multiple copies of the same page and the whole cycle completed for different pages.

All aspects of publishing have evolved in five hundred years, and yet some of the same terminology is still used. For example, strips of lead are no longer placed between lines, but the term *leading* is used to indicate the spacing between lines. Historically, typesetters stored their supply of letters in little boxes arranged in cases; the capital letters were kept in the upper case and the little letters were kept in the lower case. Thus, capital letters are called *uppercase* letters; small letters are called *lowercase* letters.

## Printing Today

Today's publishing industry is extremely sophisticated, with electronic typesetting and high-speed presses to produce books, magazines, and an array of printed products such as brochures and sales publications. Professional designers arrange layout based on certain publishing conventions and artistic compositions.

The term *desktop* became important in the mid-1980s with the introduction of equipment and software that could produce professional publications and yet fit on the top of a desk. This combination of computer, laser printer, and page layout software gave everyone the tools once reserved for skilled graphic artists and professional publishers. Since then, hardware and software have improved dramatically and many more people are aware of this computer application. Today, word processing and other programs have evolved to include many capabilities of desktop publishing. Learning how to use the software and equipment is not adequate, however, unless an individual also learns the techniques for arranging information effectively on a page.

words

## Document 14
**Three-Column Table**

Format table at right. **CS:** 1" between Columns 1 and 2; 0.5" between Columns 2 and 3.

SS data; center all headings.

SALES (DEPT) BUDGET PERFORMANCE — 7

Month Ended July 31, ---- — 12

| Expense item | Buget Allocation | Amount Spent | |
|---|---|---|---|
| | | | 15 |
| | | | 22 |
| Salaries | $ 18,600 | $ 18,450 | 27 |
| Benefits | 4,985 | 4,857 | 31 |
| Suppiles | 1,125 | 1,250 | 35 |
| Telephone | 650 | 595 | 48 |
| Postge | 475 | ~~575~~ 515 | 42 |
| Travel | 3,275 | 3,075 | 46 |
| Totals | $29,110 | $28,802 742 | 51 |

## Document 15
**Table**

Format table at right. Arrange the entries in descending order by selling price. DS data.

Add column headings:

Col. 1: **Cellular Telephone**

Col. 2: **Regular Selling Price**

Col. 3: **Clearance Price**

CELLULAR TELEPHONES — 4

End-of-Month Clearance Sale — 10

| | | | |
|---|---|---|---|
| TEC P-9100 | $1,699.99 | $888.88 | 27 |
| TEC P-9110 | 1,999.99 | 999.99 | 33 |
| Rawlins CP-1000 | 1,549.99 | 825.88 | 39 |
| Rawlins CP-2000 | 1,749.99 | 925.88 | 46 |
| Cellatel 380 | 1,224.99 | 749.99 | 51 |
| Cellatel 480 | 1,924.99 | 974.99 | 57 |
| Carfone XT | 1,399.99 | 649.99 | 63 |
| Carfone ST | 1,599.99 | 848.88 | 68 |
| Carfone ZT | 1,799.99 | 949.88 | 73 |

## Document 16
**Table**

Format table at right. **CS:** 6 sp. between longest headings; SS data; center all headings.

ACCOUNTING DEPARTMENT — 4

Proposed Salary Increases for ---- — 11

| Employee | Cost of Living Increase | Merit Increase | New Salary | |
|---|---|---|---|---|
| | | | | 16 |
| | | | | 24 |
| Sandra Morris | $1,500 | $ 900 | $ 32,400 | 31 |
| Jane Raleigh | 1,140 | 1,140 | 25,080 | 38 |
| William Bossey | 990 | 792 | 21,582 | 44 |
| Rita Perez | 945 | 850 | 20,695 | 49 |
| Hiro Hito | 930 | 1,116 | 20,646 | 54 |
| Harry Kaskie | 500 | 450 | 12,950 | 61 |
| Totals | $6,005 | $5,248 | $133,353 | 66 |

1. Key the text in the data sheet/resume shown at the right.

2. Set the top margin at 1" and change the bottom margin to 0.5" to provide space for the horizontal rules.

3. Insert horizontal lines to draw attention to the page, using thicker ones at the top and bottom.

4. Use a serif typeface. (The body text is set at 12 points, headings at 15 points in bold, and the name at 24 points in bold.)

5. Set tabs for indents appropriately sized for the bullets (about 0.25").

6. Insert bullets for listed information. Be sure listed text wordwraps as shown.

7. Insert em dashes as shown.

8. Add white space as needed.

**Notes:** The last line of text, *References Available upon Request*, is an alternative to listing three or more names. Before using this line, you, as a job applicant, should know whose names you will supply if requested *and* obtain the permission of those individuals.

You may apply similar word publishing techniques to the data sheet/resume you prepared in Lesson 134 or Lesson 215.

This data sheet/resume uses various text treatments to emphasize the divisions of information; for instance, headings are larger than the body text and horizontal graphic lines add visual appeal. For information arranged in lists, bullets (special characters) mark the beginning of each item. The tab spacing is adjusted to an appropriate size for the font size used.

# Ashley Ellen Miller

345 Reynolds Dr.
Charleston, IL 61920-2836
217-145-9331

## Job Objective
Technical assistant trainee for a medical company.

## Education
**Central High School**—Charleston, Illinois, graduated May 1995
- Recognized on Honor Roll 1993–94 and 1994–95.
- Obtained 3.4 grade point average.
- Completed the following business courses: Information Processing, Desktop Publishing, Accounting, Office Procedures, and Business Law.

## Work Experience
**Support Staff in Management Development, Lincoln Hospital**—Charleston, Illinois
June 1994–Present (full-time during summer; part-time during school year)
- Demonstrated proficiency in advanced word processing through the production of correspondence, reports, and other related documents.
- Gained practical experience in developing document layouts.
- Performed data entry tasks using the hospital mainframe computer system.
- Distributed and filed medical records.

**Sales Clerk, Computer World**—Charleston, Illinois
June–August 1993
- Stocked shelves as new inventory was received.
- Gained experience in customer service.

## Activities
National Honor Society
Future Business Leaders of America
- Treasurer, 1994–95
- Publicity chair, 1993–94

## References Available upon Request

words

Format table at right. DS data; **CS:** 8 sp. between longest items in columns; center all headings.

MONEY MARKET FUNDS — 4

Percents for Week Ending May 30, ---- — 11

| Fund | Average Annual Yield | Change from Last Week | |
|------|------|------|------|
| | | | 15 |
| | | | 22 |
| AAPMny | 8.35 | -.02 | 25 |
| ActAsMny | 7.64 | .01 | 29 |
| AlexGrn | 7.52 | --- | 32 |
| CDAMny | 8.44 | .01 | 35 |
| Lndpt | 8.23 | .06 | 38 |
| MPS Life | 7.90 | -.03 | 42 |
| NassCash | 8.31 | .16 | 46 |
| VenPe | 6.86 | -.12 | 49 |
| WllngHS | 7.89 | .06 | 52 |
| XtrMny | 6.98 | -.04 | 55 |

Format table at right on plain full sheet; short edge at top. DS data; **CS:** 8 sp. between longest items in columns; block column headings.

Tall Buildings in New York City — 6
Listed by Height in Feet and Meters — 14

| Building | Feet | Meters | |
|----------|------|--------|------|
| | | | 18 |
| World Trade Center | 1,350 | 411.750 | 25 |
| Empire State (without TV tower) | 1,250 | 381.250 | 34 |
| Chrysler | 1,046 | 319.030 | 39 |
| American International | 950 | 289.750 | 46 |
| 40 Wall Tower | 927 | 282.735 | 51 |
| Citicorp Center | 914 | 278.770 | 57 |
| | | | 60 |

Source: The World Almanac, 1996. — 66

### Title Page 1

1. Use 1" bottom and side margins. Begin the left-aligned title 2" from the top of the page.

2. Use a serif typeface set at 30 points in bold for the title. Increase the line height slightly for this text.

3. Insert a rule longer than the title below the title. (The line shown is 6.5" long.)

4. Insert a line above the text area at the bottom. This line is 3.5" long.

5. Right-align text at the bottom using the same serif typeface set at 15 points in bold.

6. Insert white space as needed.

### Title Page 2

Modify Title Page 1 as follows (shown at right).

1. At the TM, create a 0.25" thick horizontal line with 20% shading extending from left margin to right margin. Copy this line and position a second line at the bottom margin.

2. Begin the title about 3" from the top edge of the page. For the centered title, use a serif typeface set at 24 points in bold.

3. Insert horizontal lines above and below the title; keep the space even between the text and the rules. Line length should be equal to the length of the longest text line.

4. Center the remaining text set at 12 points in bold. Add white space as needed.

This report title page uses an informal arrangement (called *asymmetrical balance*) where one page element is offset by another page element—a concept similar to the way a teeter-totter works on an elementary school playground. The title is left-aligned using three text lines and emphasized using larger text. Horizontal lines provide interest.

**A Comparison of
Publishing Features in
Two Word Processing Programs**

**Your Name**

**Business Computer Applications**

**Current date**

The second title page uses a formal arrangement (called **symmetrical balance**) in which all elements of the page are centered. The title is set off by two horizontal lines and large text.

**A Comparison of Publishing Features in
Two Word Processing Programs**

**Your Name**

**Business Computer Applications**
**Current date**

# Publishing Techniques

Many people use word publishing techniques to produce professional quality documents. Today's word processing software has many capabilities for combining text and graphics to create documents that are visually appealing. The design and graphic treatments help strengthen the message a document contains.

Complex designs, such as for magazines or brochures with photographs, are created using page layout software that has even more advanced features. These programs are known as desktop publishing software. (The term *desktop publishing* is often applied to the document-design features of word processing. In this textbook, however, the latter will be called **word publishing**.)

While it is possible to practice many publishing techniques using a dot matrix printer, better results can be achieved with an ink jet or laser printer.

Publishing techniques include

- using proportional fonts
- adding emphasis, such as shadows, to some text
- using lines or boxes to separate page elements
- including original artwork or clipart to illustrate the message
- opening up pages with white space

## Document Planning

With any document design, the first consideration should be the *purpose* of the document. A flyer designed to advertise a circus, for example, would have quite a different appearance than one designed to announce a formal banquet.

The second consideration is the *audience* (either one person or a group of people) who will receive the document. Audience backgrounds and interests should be considered, along with the document appearance, in the design of a document.

## Document Design

Document appearance and the image a document creates are influenced in several ways. Because many documents consist mostly of text, an understanding of *type* is necessary in selecting a typeface appropriate to the purpose. A **typeface** is a trade name for a collection of characters from a-z in uppercase and lowercase with all related symbols. A *font* is a particular typeface in a certain size and style.

Thousands of typefaces are available. Some might be selected for their readability; others might be selected for a look of elegance or a strong, bold appearance.

The typeface *size* and *style* affect the emphasis text receives. Words printed in a large, bold typeface stand out and will be noticed when a reader quickly scans a page to learn what a document is about.

*Lines* (rules) and/or *boxes* can help to divide groups of text and to emphasize information on a page.

Artwork, consisting of *clipart* images or originally created drawings, can add impact and focus readers' attention on the message.

The *white space* (empty space) on a page is an important design element for grouping related information and making a document more inviting to read.

Effective use of these publishing techniques requires practice to develop a sense of "design."

## Letterhead 2

Modify Letterhead 1 to fit the following description and illustration at the right.

1. Change the top/bottom margins to 0.5".

2. All text lines are centered. The business name is set at 25 points in bold italic; the address remains at 11 points in bold italic.

3. The graphic line is thinner than the line in Letterhead 1. Its length is equal to the length of the company name and centered below the name. (The example shown is 3.75" long.)

4. The same graphic image is placed on both sides of the company information. The image on the right is a mirror image of the one on the left. No borders are used.

The second letterhead version uses the same typeface, but in a smaller size, for the business name. It includes a small graphic image on both sides of the centered text.

## Letterhead 3

Modify Letterhead 2 to fit the following description and illustration at the right.

1. Change the top/bottom margins to 0.7".

2. The business name is set at 30 points in bold italic; the address remains at 11 points in bold italic.

3. The graphic line is thicker than the line in Letterhead 2. (The example is shown as 5.5" long.)

4. The graphic image is placed on the right side of the page parallel with the company information. No borders are used.

The third letterhead version uses the same typeface. All text is aligned on the left, and a graphic image is positioned on the right.

*The Sports Connection*

202 Morton St.
Springfield, IL 62702-2826
708-154-5512

# Understanding Type

**Objectives:**
1. To learn about parts of a character.
2. To learn about fonts and typefaces.
3. To key text using different typefaces.

## 1A • 10
## Character Parts

1. Read the copy at the right.
2. Identify parts of a character of type.

The type chosen for a document affects its image or the impression it makes. To begin understanding differences in type, learn the parts of type, as shown and defined below.

### Parts of a character of type

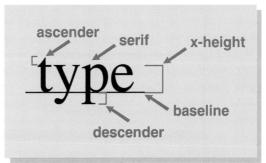

**baseline:** the imaginary line on which all characters of type are placed.

**x-height:** the height of characters such as *x*, *e*, *m*, or *a*.

**ascender:** the part of characters that extends above the x-height.

**descender:** the part of characters that extends below the baseline.

**serif:** the small lines or "feet" that appear at the ends of some characters.

## 1B • 15
## Fonts and Typefaces

1. Read the copy at the right.
2. Learn how to change typefaces on the software you are using.
3. Compose two short paragraphs using a different typeface for each one. Compare the appearance of each paragraph.

A **font** is a single *typeface*, *type style*, and *type size*. You will learn about type style and type size in another lesson. A **typeface** is a collection of characters and symbols that have a related design. All typefaces are identified by unique names. For example, some are named after the person who created them; others, by the place where they were created.

Typefaces are divided into two main categories: *serif* and *sans serif*. Serifs are the small finishing strokes that appear on the ends of some characters. Serif typefaces are often used for the body text in documents because the serifs make text easier to read. Sans serif typefaces do not have serifs; often they are used for headlines and larger print.

**Serif typefaces**

Bookman
Garamond MT
Goudy Old Style
Palatino
Times New Roman

**Sans serif typefaces**

**Arial**
**AvantGarde**
**Futura**
Helvetica
Univers

# Using Lines (Rules)

**Objectives:**

1. To recognize how rules can add emphasis to text.
2. To create vertical and horizontal lines (rules).
3. To develop documents using lines (rules).

## 9-11A • 15
## Lines

1. Read the copy at the right.
2. Study the different line treatments illustrated.
3. Create both horizontal and vertical lines with your software. Make the lines in varying lengths and widths.

*Horizontal lines* (also called rules) can extend from margin to margin or be printed in specific line lengths. The width (thickness) of horizontal lines can range from very thin to very thick. The shading ranges from 100 percent to any lower percentage.

These same characteristics apply to *vertical lines.*

Some software measures the thickness of lines in inches; other software measures thickness in points.

 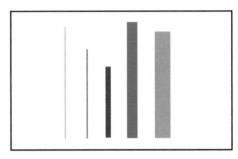

## 9-11B • 45
## Letterheads

### Letterhead 1

1. Change all margins to 0.7".
2. Create a vertical line at the left margin 1.25" wide and 10" long. Shade the line at 40%.
3. For the business name, use a sans serif bold, italic typeface. (The example is shown in Helvetica Bold Italic set at 36 points.)
4. The graphic line below the company name is right-aligned and extends partially into the shaded area. The example shows the line as 6.6" long and 0.03" thick.
5. Use the same typeface for the address, but change the size to 11 points.

This letterhead has a wide, shaded vertical line extending down the left side and a black horizontal line used to emphasize the business name. To print a letter on this letterhead, the letter margins should fit the open area on the page—the letter would not be centered horizontally.

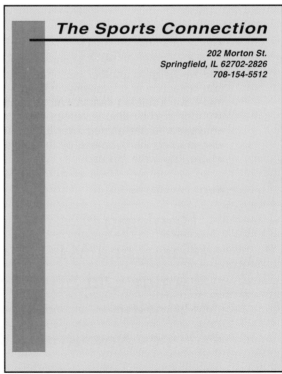

## 1C • 10
### Serif and Sans Serif

1. Select a serif typeface and key the first paragraph.
2. Select a sans serif typeface and key the second paragraph.

## 1D • 15
### Special-Purpose Typefaces

1. Study the examples of special-purpose typefaces.
2. Select a special-purpose typeface and key the paragraphs above right.
3. Block and copy the paragraphs two times; change the typefaces used for the new paragraphs and compare their appearance with the first version.

Differences between typefaces may be subtle or they may be dramatic. Certain typeface designs are excellent for readability, while others are meant for special purposes only and should be used sparingly.

The choice of typefaces, however, is often up to the document designer; for example, some people prefer to use sans serif typefaces for body text because sans serif typefaces tend to have a more contemporary appearance than serif typefaces.

Some typefaces are very bold and dramatic and would be suitable for attention-getting announcements. Other typefaces resemble script writing and are suitable for formal invitations.

**Special-purpose typefaces**

*Brush Script*

*Kaufmann*

**Playbill**

**STENCIL**

**Syntax UltraBlack**

**This is the typeface Syntax UltraBlack. Notice how the characters are dark and bold. This appearance would create a dramatic effect for eye-catching announcements and would be suitable for headings in reports or in memorandums.**

*This is the typeface Kaufmann. Notice how the characters are slender and resemble handwriting. This typeface would create an elegant image for formal announcements and invitations. This text seems much smaller even though it is printed in the same size as the example of Syntax UltraBlack typeface.*

## Flyer

Follow directions below to create an advertising flyer for a florist shop.

1. Use reverse text to create the box with the business name. The box has a black fill with white print in a large sans serif typeface.

2. This document could be completed in several ways. You could use two columns, or you could place the text in a box at the right with no borders.

3. The hearts are typographic symbols in a very large size. To condense the vertical space between the hearts, the line height was changed from the automatic height of 2.81" to 2.5" as a fixed line height. These heights will vary depending on the typeface used.

4. Adjust the white space between the lines of text so that the three blocks of text are parallel with the three hearts.

**Notes:**

- The reverse type is shown in Helvetica bold set at 30 points.

- The text is in bold using different sizes: 25, 20, 15, and 12 points.

- The heart symbols are 200 points.

# Vicki's Creations

## For your loved one on Valentine's Day

- Roses, roses, roses
- Friendship arrangements
- Balloon bouquets
- Candy assortments

## Free delivery
## Call (217) 153-4900

600 S. Sale St.
Open Monday-Saturday 9-5

# Understanding Type Styles and Type Sizes

**Objectives:**

1. To learn about type styles.
2. To consider proportional and monospaced typefaces.
3. To arrange text in different type styles and sizes.

## 2A • 10
## Type Styles

1. Read the copy at the right.
2. Study the type style examples.
3. Compare the two paragraphs in the box below. Which typeface is easier to read?

People experienced in design can use more than one typeface in a document, but doing so requires knowledge of which typefaces work well together. A less experienced designer should select one typeface and then emphasize certain text with variations such as bold, italic, outline, or shadow. These variations are called **type styles**. In the illustration below, CG Times is the name of the typeface and the other words represent various styles of that typeface.

**Typeface styles**

CG Times

**CG Times Bold**

*CG Times Italic*

CG Times Outline

Proportional typefaces have the appearance of professional printing, while monospaced typefaces resemble typewriter output. With monospaced typefaces, such as Courier, all characters occupy *the same amount* of space regardless of the character width. This spacing makes wide characters such as *m* or *w* appear close together and thin characters such as *l i f t j* appear spread apart. Proportional spacing, on the other hand, allows characters to fit together evenly and contributes to easier reading.

### Proportional

This text is an example of the typeface Times New Roman set at 12 points. It has a professional appearance because the characters fit together evenly. Text printed with this proportional spacing is easier to read than text printed with monospacing.

### Monospaced

```
This text is an example of the typeface Courier set at 10 cpi.
This print resembles typewriter output.  Notice how the charac-
ters occupy the same space so that narrow letters seem to be
spread out.  This text is not as easy to read as proportional
spacing.  Can you feel your eyes jumping from word to word?
```

## Flyer

Follow the directions below to create an advertising flyer for a computer company.

1. Use two open starburst clipart images and position them as shown.

2. Select a serif typeface and make it bold.

3. Use a square bullet for the list of software features. Set a tab for appropriate space after the bullet.

4. Increase the line height slightly for the bulleted text. The example was changed from .22" to 0.25" for this text only.

5. Use right alignment for the business name and location.

6. The street address is the same size as the text in the list.

**Notes:**

• The text used for the price, product name, and business name is shown in Times bold at 25 points.

• The text used in the list is set in bold at 14 points.

• The text in the second starburst is set at 12 points in bold.

$2,898

# Multimedia Computer

■ **Pentium/100MHz processor**

■ **1.6G hard drive**

■ **16 MB memory**

■ **15" SVGA noninterlaced color monitor**

■ **1 MB video memory**

■ **Quad-speed CD-ROM drive**

■ **16-bit stereo sound card and speakers**

■ **14.4 internal fax/modem**

■ **Preloaded and CD-ROM software**

■ **3-year computer warranty**

0% Financing!
No payments!
No interest
for 6 months!

# Computer Headquarters

**606 W. Anthony Dr.**

## 2B • 10
### Type Sizes

1. Read the copy at the right.
2. Study the illustration of type sizes.
3. Learn how to change type sizes in the software and printer you are using.

Another important difference between monospaced and proportional text relates to type sizes. For example, titles and headings can be larger than paragraph text when proportional type is used.

Dot matrix printers usually measure type size in characters per inch (cpi)—the most common settings include 10 or 12 characters per inch (also called 10 or 12 pitch). Laser or ink jet printers allow a typeface to be *scaled* to make it larger or smaller. *Type sizes* are measured in *points;* one inch contains 72 points.

Text sample at 10 points.
Text sample at 11 points.
Text sample at 12 points.

Text sample at 16 points.

Text sample at 24 points.

## Text sample at 36 points.

# Text at 72.

## 2C • 30
### Announcements

**Document 1**
**Sale Announcement**

This announcement uses a large, bold, attention-getting font. All text lines are centered.

1. Select a sans serif typeface.
2. For the first text line, change the font size to 36 points in bold; use 20 points in bold for all other text lines.
3. Center vertically.

Even when the same point size is used, some typefaces will appear larger than others because of the thickness of characters and the difference in x-height.

# SALE   SALE   SALE

## Inventory Clearance
## All Items Must Go!

## Furniture Warehouse
## 200 E. Main

# Combining Clipart and Text

**Objectives:**

**1.** To emphasize document text with clipart images.

**2.** To observe the need for adequate spacing for legibility.

**3.** To develop announcements combining clipart and text.

## 7-8A • 20
## Clipart and Text Combined

1. Read the copy at the right.

2. Prepare the examples combining clipart and text as shown.

**Starburst**

1. Select a star image from those available with your software.

2. Make the star approximately 4" wide and center it on the page.

3. Use a large, bold font for the text.

**Box**

1. Select a border like the one at the far right.

2. Make the border approximately 4" wide and 3" high.

3. Use a large, bold font for the text.

Some clipart images appear open in the middle for the purpose of placing text inside the image. For example, the image might be a banner, starburst, trophy, or a fancy border. The techniques for inserting text in an image will vary depending on the software used.

Be sure that text inside an image is legible and uncrowded. Plan for the text alignment that looks best with the image. Usually, the text will be centered both up and down and left and right; however, sometimes right alignment or left alignment may look better.

## 7-8B • 10
## Reverse Type

1. Read the copy at the right; then create a text box that is 4" wide and about 1" high (or use automatic line height). Make the box fill color black.

2. Select a sans serif typeface and make it bold. (The illustration is shown in Helvetica bold set at 36 points.) Change the font color to print in white.

3. If time permits, create additional reverse type boxes.

**Reverse type** is a dramatic way to emphasize text. When creating a black box for the text background (that is, a **text box**), be sure the box is large enough to hold the text with enough black space around the text on all sides so that the text is easy to read.

Another important consideration is the typeface used. Because serif typefaces often have slim areas in the curves of letters, they might not show up well. Sans serif typefaces, especially when printed in bold, are a better choice for reverse type.

# Reverse Type

**Document 2**
**Invitation**

This invitation uses a soft, delicate font for a formal appearance. The information is arranged with all text lines centered in a uniform type size.

1. Select a similar script typeface.
2. Change the font size to 14 points for all text lines.
3. Center vertically.

*You are invited to attend the*
*Central High School All Sports Banquet*
*to be held in Robinson Gymnasium*
*at 6:30 p.m. on April 20, ----*
*Special entertainment provided by the Chamber Singers*
*R.S.V.P. Athletic Office*

## Aligning Text

**Objectives:**
1. To learn about alignment options.
2. To arrange text with different alignments and line heights.

**3A ● 25**
**Text Alignment**

1. Read the copy at the right and the text in each example.
2. Practice each kind of alignment by making appropriate settings and keying the text as shown in the examples.

The *alignment* of text—left, right, centered, or full—affects a document's readability and image. Some software uses the term *justification* to mean how the text is aligned. Often the choices are indicated by icons on the screen representing each effect.

**Left alignment** is appropriate for paragraph text because reading is easier when all lines begin at the same position and uniform spacing appears between words. Left-aligned paragraphs produce a ragged (uneven) right edge; this effect creates a less formal appearance. Appropriately used hyphenation will make line endings less uneven on the right. Headings may be left-aligned or centered depending on a document's overall design.

> **Left alignment**
>
> appropriate for paragraph text and may be used for headings
> easy to read and appears less formal
> hyphenation usage desirable

**Full alignment** is achieved by expanding or contracting the spacing between words so that all paragraph lines begin and end evenly at the left and right margins. This alignment creates a more formal appearance. Hyphenation should be used to make word spacing as uniform as possible for easier reading. Full alignment is not appropriate for headings.

> **Full alignment** is appropriate for paragraph text when a formal appearance is desired. Full alignment can cause gaps in text as extra space is added between words to make the text lines end evenly at the right margin. Hyphenation usually is needed.

**Center alignment** is appropriate for titles and headings. It can be used to center all text lines such as in a wedding invitation. This technique seems more formal and is more difficult to read because of the ragged line beginnings. Hyphenation is not appropriate.

*(continued on next page)*

## Using Clipart

**Objectives:**

1. To observe the effect that clipart images have on appearance.
2. To position images and text with adequate white space.
3. To develop an announcement using good design techniques.

### 6A • 20
### Clipart

1. Read copy at the right.
2. Determine the images available in your software.
3. Practice positioning images in different sizes and places on a page.

**Clipart** (graphic images or figures) can add visual interest to a document. Images should be carefully chosen to ensure they are appropriate to the audience and the purpose of the message. For example, a flyer designed to advertise a product might display a large image of the product, or an image of a person using it.

Word processing and desktop publishing software contain files of images suitable for many different purposes. Additional images can be purchased. If the software you are using has drawing tools, you may be able to create your own images by ungrouping (taking apart) existing images, changing them in some way, then grouping them again.

When clipart images are imported into a document, they can be positioned with or without a border around the image. Also, fancy borders may surround an entire page or a portion of a page.

Images should be kept in correct proportion. With some software, the image is positioned on the page by entering the image location in inches. With other software, the image is positioned by selecting it with a mouse pointer and dragging it to the desired location. When using this method, be sure not to stretch an image out of proportion when trying to position it or to adjust its size.

### 6B • 30
### Flyer

1. Key the flyer at the right.
2. Use a standard-sized sheet turned sideways. (This 11" wide x 8.5" long orientation is called **landscape**, in contrast to the regular page orientation [8.5" wide x 11" long], which is called **portrait**.)
3. Set 1" margins all around.
4. Select a similar image from those available with your software. Position the image on the left.
5. Allow room on the right for the text.

**Note**: Vary the font sizes to emphasize some words more than others. (The typeface shown is Syntax UltraBlack with right alignment.)

# Our Gift to You!

## A 30% discount on any one item at our regular price

**Bring this gift certificate to**

**Rogards Jewelers**
**513 S. Scott St.**

**(217) 555-3566**
**UPS Shipping Available**

**Right alignment** can be used for special purposes such as headings. Several lines of right-aligned text can be difficult to read because of the ragged line beginnings, so use this alignment sparingly. Hyphenation would not be appropriate.

## 3B • 15
## Leading/Line Height

1. Read the copy at the right.
2. Key the first paragraph in the box at right, using automatic line height.
3. Copy the paragraph; increase the line height as described in the second paragraph.
4. Print and compare the spacing between the lines of each paragraph.

**Leading** (rhymes with *wedding*) is the amount of space between printed text lines. By default, word processing and desktop publishing programs generally add 20 percent of the size of the font so that ascenders and descenders do not overlap. As font sizes change, the leading automatically changes, also.

For some software, the leading can be adjusted by changing the *line height*. Line height is measured from baseline to baseline. For typewriter-like output, the line height for 10- or 12-pitch, single-spaced printing results in 6 lines printing in a vertical inch (66 lines on a page and 0.167" for each line). If a larger font is selected, however, the line height automatically increases to an appropriate amount; and far fewer lines can be entered on a page.

This text is an example of a serif typeface set at 10 points with the default setting for automatic line height. Note the spacing between the lines of text.

This text is an example of a serif typeface set at 10 points with the default setting increased from the automatic line height of 0.167" to 0.20". Note the spacing between the lines of text.

## 3C • 10
## Line-Height Adjustments

1. Read the copy at the right.
2. Type the two-line title set at 15 points in bold.
3. Change the line height to make the lines print closer together as shown in the second example.

Sometimes the automatic line height should be changed. For example:

- If a small font size (10 points) is used to conserve space, the line height could be increased slightly from the automatic setting to make the text easier to read.
- When headings within a document are larger than body text, a line height larger than the body text size may produce better-looking copy. This is especially true when columns are involved because the baseline should be even across the columns.
- When a large font size is used for multiline titles, the text may look better if the line height is decreased, bringing the lines closer together.

**New Careers in Computer**

**Training and Support**

**New Careers in Computer**
**Training and Support**

## 5C • 5
### Additional Typographic Symbols

1. Study the examples of typographic symbols at right.
2. Determine how to create these symbols with your software and practice making them.

Today's word processing and desktop publishing software can create many of the symbols formerly used only by professional typesetters when they created publications, such as books and magazines. Correct use of these symbols will make documents appear more sophisticated.

| Typographic symbols | |
|---|---|
| — em dash | replaces double hyphen (--) |
| " left directional quote | replaces keyboard quote (") |
| " right directional quote | replaces keyboard quote (") |

## 5D • 15
### Typographic Conventions

1. Key the information at the right.
2. Insert em dashes as shown.
3. Note the changes described in the list. These changes will be used in later assignments in this unit.

**Conventions** are rules governing the treatment of text and punctuation spacing.

Typesetting conventions differ from typewriting conventions as listed below.

# Using Typographic Conventions

Changing from typewriting to typographic conventions adds to the appearance of any document. These changes are easy to make.

- Avoid all caps—Instead of using capital (uppercase) letters to emphasize text, use lowercase letters in bold and a larger size. Lowercase letters are easier to read than all-capital letters.

- Avoid underlining—The underline appears so close to the baseline of text that it often cuts through the descenders. Instead, use italics for emphasis. A graphic line placed below text is appropriate for some headings.

- Use an em dash— In typewriting conventions, a break in the thought pattern of a sentence is shown like this--with a double hyphen. Instead, use an em dash—a long, single-line dash.

- Insert directional quotes—When quoting someone, insert a left quotation mark (") at the beginning of the quote and a right quotation mark (") at the end of it.

# Organizing Text with Headings

**Objectives:**

**1.** To name the purposes of headings.

**2.** To prepare text with different heading treatments.

## 4A • 10
## Headings/White Space

1. Read the copy at the right.
2. Compare the report on this page to the two versions on pp. A41 and A42.

When designing single- or multiple-page documents, *headings* should be used to guide the reader. Headings introduce sections of related information and provide hints about the document's contents when a reader is quickly scanning the text.

Word processing and desktop publishing software provide flexibility for adding emphasis to headings. When the heading font is bold and larger than the font used for the body of the report, the headings will be more noticeable.

Shown below is a two-page document in unbound report format. It is prepared with left justification, monospaced 10 cpi font, 0.5" paragraph indents, and double spacing. Selected words within the document are underlined for emphasis.

This report has what desktop and word publishers call a "gray" appearance. Nothing is distinctive to catch a reader's eye—all text is the same darkness and spaced the same on both pages.

---

THE EVOLUTION OF PUBLISHING

Publishing is a very old industry dating back to the mid-1400s when Guttenberg invented the first printing press in Germany. Individual letters were carved out of little blocks of wood; lead eventually replaced wood because of its increased durability.

The Printing Process

To create pages of text, letters were arranged one letter at a time to form words and sentences. The letters were arranged in rows on big trays called plates. This process was called <u>setting type</u>. Strips of lead were used between the rows to spread them apart for easier reading. The printer would place the finished plate in the printing press, apply ink to the plate, position a sheet of paper on the plate, then press down on the paper to make an impression. The process was repeated for multiple copies of the same page and the whole cycle completed for different pages.

All aspects of publishing have evolved in five hundred years, and yet some of the same terminology is still used. For example, strips of lead are no longer placed between lines, but the term <u>leading</u> is used to indicate the spacing between lines. Historically, typesetters stored their supply of letters in little boxes arranged in cases; the capital letters were kept in the upper case and the little letters were kept in the lower case. Thus, capital letters are called <u>uppercase</u> letters; small letters are called <u>lowercase</u> letters.

---

2

Printing Today

Today's publishing industry is extremely sophisticated, with electronic typesetting and high-speed presses to produce books, magazines, and an array of printed products such as brochures and sales publications. Professional designers arrange layout based on certain publishing conventions and artistic compositions.

The term <u>desktop</u> became important in the mid-1980s with the introduction of equipment and software that could produce professional publications and yet fit on top of a desk. This combination of computer, laser printer, and page layout software gave everyone the tools once reserved for skilled graphic artists and professional publishers. Since then, hardware and software have improved dramatically and many more people are aware of this computer application. Today, word processing and other programs have evolved to include many capabilities of desktop publishing. Learning to use the software and equipment is not adequate, however, unless an individual also learns the techniques for arranging information effectively on a page.

---

Business reports are often single-spaced. The *white space* (empty space) on the page, necessary for easy reading, is achieved by inserting blank lines between paragraphs and adding space around the headings.

More space may be provided before a heading than after a heading. This spacing technique serves to connect the heading to the text it introduces and to separate the text from previous text.

# Using Bullets and Typographic Conventions

**O b j e c t i v e s :**

**1.** To learn the purpose of bullets and how to use them.

**2.** To learn about professional typographic symbols.

**3.** To prepare lists with bullets and to create typographic symbols.

## 5A • 15
## Bullets

1. Read the copy at the right.

2. Determine the bullets available in your software and practice using them in different sizes.

*Typographic symbols* can be used to enhance the appearance of a document. The symbols can call attention to listed information or be used as a major design element on a page.

Probably the most common typographic symbol is a **bullet**. This symbol, a small black dot, gets its name from the fact that it looks like a bullet hole. Bullets are frequently used with listed information because the bullet draws attention to the beginning of each item in the list. Many other symbols can be created;

however, the name "bullet" is used for any symbol used for this purpose.

*Iconic symbols*—such as a check mark, heart, or pointing hand—can be used for bullets or as design elements when created in larger sizes. Some software programs call these symbols **dingbats**.

The size of these symbols is controlled by the size of the typeface currently in use. Therefore, to use an iconic symbol as a design element on a page, the font size should be increased.

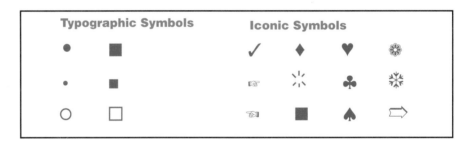

## 5B • 15
## Bulleted List

1. Key the information at the right using a serif typeface.

2. Make the title large and bold.

3. Use a small black square for the first-level bullet; use a small black dot for the second-level bullet.

**Note:** The first-level bullet should always stand out more than the second-level bullet.

# Listing Information with Bullets

Organizing information in a vertical list makes the text more noticeable than when information is written as a series of paragraphs. Each item in a list should begin with a *bullet*, a symbol used to call attention to the beginning of each item.

■ Use different bullets for various levels of detail.

■ Use a tab about 0.25" after the bullet (depending on the font size being used). The default tab of 0.5" on most software creates too much space after the bullet when it is used in the body of a document, as in this example.

■ Make the text hang under the first letter (not under the bullet) when the information is too long for one text line. This technique will make the beginning of each item stand out more.

■ Write the information so that it is parallel in grammatical form:

• Begin each item with a verb (as in this list).

• Begin each item with a noun.

• Begin each item with a gerund (verb ending in *ing*).

**Report 1**

1. Key the report at the right SS.
2. Select a similar typeface and follow these settings as much as possible:

**Margins:** 1"; full justification

**Title:** on line 1.33"

**Title font:** CG Times Bold (serif typeface) set at 25 points

**Body text font:** CG Times set at 12 points

**Side heading font:** CG Times Bold set at 15 points (delete underlines)

3. Double-space between paragraphs and above/below side headings.

The report (p. A40) that required two pages when set in a monospaced font is now arranged on one page. The font selection and treatment shown below is space efficient—and yet the text is not crowded on the page.

The larger, bold headings stand out, highlighting the topics in the report. Words that were underlined are now shown in italics. Full justification makes the report look more formal.

# The Evolution of Publishing

Publishing is a very old industry dating back to the mid-1400s when Guttenberg invented the first printing press in Germany. Individual letters were carved out of little blocks of wood; lead eventually replaced wood because of its increased durability.

## The Printing Process

To create pages of text, letters were arranged one letter at a time to form words and sentences. The letters were arranged in rows on big trays called plates. This process was called *setting type*. Strips of lead were used between the rows to spread them apart for easier reading. The printer would place the finished plate in the printing press, apply ink to the plate, position a sheet of paper on the plate, then press down on the paper to make an impression. The process was repeated for multiple copies of the same page and the whole cycle completed for different pages.

All aspects of publishing have evolved in five hundred years, and yet some of the same terminology is still used. For example, strips of lead are no longer placed between lines, but the term *leading* is used to indicate the spacing between lines. Historically, typesetters stored their supply of letters in little boxes arranged in cases; the capital letters were kept in the upper case and the little letters were kept in the lower case. Thus, capital letters are called *uppercase* letters; small letters are called *lowercase* letters.

## Printing Today

Today's publishing industry is extremely sophisticated, with electronic typesetting and high-speed presses to produce books, magazines, and an array of printed products such as brochures and sales publications. Professional designers arrange layout based on certain publishing conventions and artistic compositions.

The term *desktop* became important in the mid-1980s with the introduction of equipment and software that could produce professional publications and yet fit on the top of a desk. This combination of computer, laser printer, and page layout software gave everyone the tools once reserved for skilled graphic artists and professional publishers. Since then, hardware and software have improved dramatically and many more people are aware of this computer application. Today, word processing and other programs have evolved to include many capabilities of desktop publishing. Learning how to use the software and equipment is not adequate, however, unless an individual also learns the techniques for arranging information effectively on a page.

**Report 2**

1. Modify the settings from your first version layout to produce the second layout.
2. Use the same typeface and sizes that you used in Report 1.
3. Change to left justification.
4. Set parallel columns for two columns with column margins: left, 1" and 2"; right, 2" and 7.5".
5. Be sure the side heading lines are arranged as shown.
6. Double-space between paragraphs and insert extra space above the side headings as space permits.

This arrangement uses left alignment for the title. The side headings are set in the same point size as Report 1; however, the document is arranged in two columns. The left column is just wide enough for the words in the side headings and about 0.25" for the white space between the side headings in the first column and the report text in the second column. Left justification makes the report look less formal.

# The Evolution of Publishing

Publishing is a very old industry dating back to the mid-1400s when Guttenberg invented the first printing press in Germany. Individual letters were carved out of little blocks of wood; lead eventually replaced wood because of its increased durability.

**The Printing Process**

To create pages of text, letters were arranged one letter at a time to form words and sentences. The letters were arranged in rows on big trays called plates. This process was called *setting type*. Strips of lead were used between the rows to spread them apart for easier reading. The printer would place the finished plate in the printing press, apply ink to the plate, position a sheet of paper on the plate, then press down on the paper to make an impression. The process was repeated for multiple copies of the same page and the whole cycle completed for different pages.

All aspects of publishing have evolved in five hundred years, and yet some of the same terminology is still used. For example, strips of lead are no longer placed between lines, but the term *leading* is used to indicate the spacing between lines. Historically, typesetters stored their supply of letters in little boxes arranged in cases; the capital letters were kept in the upper case and the little letters were kept in the lower case. Thus, capital letters are called *uppercase* letters; small letters are called *lowercase* letters.

**Printing Today**

Today's publishing industry is extremely sophisticated, with electronic typesetting and high-speed presses to produce books, magazines, and an array of printed products such as brochures and sales publications. Professional designers arrange layout based on certain publishing conventions and artistic compositions.

The term *desktop* became important in the mid-1980s with the introduction of equipment and software that could produce professional publications and yet fit on the top of a desk. This combination of computer, laser printer, and page layout software gave everyone the tools once reserved for skilled graphic artists and professional publishers. Since then, hardware and software have improved dramatically and many more people are aware of this computer application. Today, word processing and other programs have evolved to include many capabilities of desktop publishing. Learning how to use the software and equipment is not adequate, however, unless an individual also learns the techniques for arranging information effectively on a page.

# REFERENCE GUIDE

## CAPITALIZATION GUIDES

### Capitalize

1. The first word of every sentence and the first word of every complete direct quotation. Do not capitalize (a) fragments of quotations or (b) a quotation resumed within a sentence.

   She said, "Hard work is necessary for success."
   He stressed the importance of "a sense of values."
   "When all else fails," he said, "follow directions."

2. The first word after a colon if that word begins a complete sentence.

   Remember this: Work with good techniques.
   We carry these sizes: small, medium, and large.

3. First, last, and all other words in titles of books, articles, periodicals, headings, and plays, except words of four or fewer letters used as articles, conjunctions, or prepositions.

   Century 21 Keyboarding          "How to Buy a House"
   Saturday Review                 "The Sound of Music"

4. An official title when it precedes a name or when used elsewhere if it is a title of distinction.

   President Lincoln               She is the Prime Minister.
   The doctor is in.               He is the class treasurer.

5. Personal titles and names of people and places.

   Miss Franks        Dr. Jose F. Ortez        San Diego

6. All proper nouns and their derivatives.

   Canada    Canadian Festival    France    French food

7. Days of the week, months of the year, holidays, periods of history, and historic events.

   Sunday          Labor Day          New Year's Day
   June            Middle Ages        Civil War

8. Geographic regions, localities, and names.

   the North        Upstate New York        Mississippi River

9. Street, avenue, company, etc., when used with a proper noun.

   Fifth Avenue     Avenue of the Stars     Armour & Co.

10. Names of organizations, clubs, and buildings.

    Girl Scouts          4-H Club          Carew Tower

11. A noun preceding a figure except for common nouns such as *line, page,* and *sentence,* which may be keyed with or without a capital.

    Style 143     Catalog 6     page 247     line 10

12. Seasons of the year *only* when they are personified.

    icy fingers of Winter          the soft kiss of Spring

## NUMBER EXPRESSION GUIDES

### Use words for

1. Numbers from one to ten except when used with numbers above ten, which are keyed as figures. Note: Common business practice is to use figures for all numbers except those which begin a sentence.

   Was the order for four or eight books?
   Order 8 shorthand books and 15 English books.

2. A number beginning a sentence.

   Fifteen persons are here; 12 are at home sick.

3. The shorter of two numbers used together.

   ten 50-gallon drums          350 five-gallon drums

4. Isolated fractions or indefinite amounts in a sentence.

   Nearly two-thirds of the students are here.
   About twenty-five people came to the meeting.

5. Names of small-numbered streets and avenues (ten and under).

   1020 Sixth Street          Tenth Avenue

### Use figures for

1. Dates and time, except in very formal writing.

   May 9, 2002          10:15 a.m.
   ninth of            four o'clock

2. A series of fractions.

   Key 1/2, 1/4, 5/6, and 7 3/4.

3. Numbers following nouns.

   Rule 12     page 179     Room 1208     Chapter 15

4. Measures, weights, and dimensions.

   6 ft. 9 in. tall          5 lbs. 4 oz.          8 1/2" x 11"

5. Definite numbers used with the percent sign (%); but spell out approximate amounts. Spell out *percent* with approximations in formal writing.

   The rate is 15 1/2%.
   About fifty percent of the work is done.

6. House numbers except house number One.

   1915 - 42d Street          One Jefferson Avenue

7. Sums of money except when spelled for extra emphasis. Even sums may be keyed without the decimal.

   $10.75                25 cents                $300
   seven hundred dollars ($700)

# PUNCTUATION GUIDES

## Use an apostrophe

1. As a symbol for *feet* in billings or tabulations or as a symbol for *minutes*. (The quotation mark may be used as a symbol for *seconds* and *inches*.)

   12' x 16'    3' 54"    8' 6" x 10' 8"

2. As a symbol to indicate the omission of letters or figures (as in contractions).

   can't    wouldn't    Spirit of '76

3. To form the plural of most figures, letters, and words used as words rather than for their meaning: Add the *apostrophe* and *s*. In market quotations, form the plural of figures by the addition of *s* only.

   6's    A's    five's    ABC's    Century Fund 4s

4. To show possession: Add the *apostrophe* and *s* to (a) a singular noun and (b) a plural noun which does not end in *s*.

   a man's watch    women's shoes    boys' bicycle

   Add the *apostrophe* and *s* to a proper name of one syllable which ends in *s*.

   Bess's Cafeteria    James's hat    Jones's bill

   Add the *apostrophe only* after (a) plural nouns ending in *s* and (b) a proper name of more than one syllable which ends in *s* or *z*.

   boys' camp    Adams' home    Melendez' report

   Add the *apostrophe* after the last noun in a series to indicate joint or common possession by two or more persons; however, add the possessive to each of the nouns to show separate possession by two or more persons.

   Lewis and Clark's expedition
   the manager's and the treasurer's reports

## Use a colon

1. To introduce an enumeration or a listing.

   These are my favorite poets: Shelley, Keats, and Frost.

2. To introduce a question or a long direct quotation.

   This is the question: Did you study for the test?

3. Between hours and minutes expressed in figures.

   10:15 a.m.    12:00    4:30 p.m.

## Use a comma (or commas)

1. After (a) introductory phrases or clauses and (b) words in a series.

   If you plan to be here for the week, try to visit Chicago, St. Louis, and Dallas.

2. To set off short direct quotations.

   She said, "If you try, you can reach your goal."

3. Before and after (a) words which come together and refer to the same person, thing, or idea and (b) words of direct address.

   Clarissa, our class president, will give the report.
   I was glad to see you, Terrence, at the meeting.

4. To set off nonrestrictive clauses (not necessary to the meaning of the sentence), but not restrictive clauses (necessary to the meaning).

   Your report, which deals with the issue, is great.
   The girl who just left is my sister.

5. To separate the day from the year and the city from the state.

   July 4, 2000    New Haven, Connecticut

6. To separate two or more parallel adjectives (adjectives that could be separated by the word "and" instead of the comma).

   a group of young, old, and middle-aged persons

   Do not use commas to separate adjectives so closely related that they appear to form a single element with the noun they modify.

   a dozen large red roses    a small square box

7. To separate (a) unrelated groups of figures which come together and (b) whole numbers into groups of three digits each (*however, policy, year, page, room, telephone,* and most *serial numbers* are shown without commas).

   During 1997, 1,750 cars were insured under Policy 806423.

   page 1042    Room 1184    (213)125-2626

## Use a dash

1. For emphasis.

   The icy road--slippery as a fish--was a hazard.

2. To indicate a change of thought.

   We may tour the Orient--but I'm getting ahead of my story.

3. To introduce the name of an author when it follows a direct quotation.

   "Hitting the wrong key is like hitting me."--Armour

4. For certain special purposes.

   "Well--er--ah," he stammered.
   "Jay, don't get too close to the --." It was too late.

# PUNCTUATION GUIDES [continued]

## Use an exclamation mark

1. After emphatic interjections.

   Wow!               Hey there!               What a day!

2. After sentences that are clearly exclamatory.

   "I won't go!" she said with determination.
   How good it was to see you in New Orleans last week!

## Use a hyphen

1. To join compound numbers from twenty-one to ninety-nine that are keyed as words.

   forty-six          fifty-eight          over seventy-six

2. To join compound adjectives before a noun that they modify as a unit.

   well-laid plans    six-year period      two-thirds majority

3. After each word or figure in a series of words or figures that modify the same noun (suspended hyphenation).

   first-, second-, and third-class reservations

4. To spell out a word or name.

   s-e-p-a-r-a-t-e          S-u-s-a-n          G-a-e-l-i-c

5. To form certain compound nouns.

   WLW-TV          teacher-counselor          AFL-CIO

## Use parentheses

1. To enclose parenthetical or explanatory matter and added information.

   The amendments (Exhibit A) are enclosed.

2. To enclose identifying letters or figures in lists.

   Check these factors: (1) period of time, (2) rate of pay, and (3) nature of duties.

3. To enclose figures that follow spelled-out amounts to give added clarity or emphasis.

   The total award is five hundred dollars ($500).

## Use a question mark

At the end of a sentence that is a direct question; however, use a period after a request in the form of a question.

What day do you plan to leave for Honolulu?
Will you mail this letter for me, please.

## Use quotation marks

1. To enclose direct quotations.

   He said, "I'll be there at eight o'clock."

2. To enclose titles of articles and other parts of complete publications, short poems, song titles, television programs, and unpublished works like theses and dissertations.

   "Sesame Street"          "Chicago" by Sandburg
   "Lara's Theme"           "Murder She Wrote"

3. To enclose special words or phrases, or coined words.

   "power up" procedure          "Murphy's Law"

## Use a semicolon

1. To separate two or more independent clauses in a compound sentence when the conjunction is omitted.

   Being critical is easy; being constructive is not so easy.

2. To separate independent clauses when they are joined by a conjunctive adverb (however, consequently, etc.).

   I can go; however, I must get excused.

3. To separate a series of phrases or clauses (especially if they contain commas) that are introduced by a colon.

   These officers were elected: Lu Ming, President; Lisa Stein, vice president; Juan Ramos, secretary.

4. To precede an abbreviation or word that introduces an explanatory statement.

   She organized her work; for example, putting work to be done in folders of different colors to indicate degrees of urgency.

## Use an underline

1. With titles of complete works such as books, magazines, and newspapers. (Such titles may also be keyed in ALL CAPS or italic without the underline.)

   Superwrite          The New York Times          TV Guide

2. To call attention to special words or phrases (or you may use quotation marks). **Note:** Use a continuous underline unless each word is to be considered separately.

   Stop keying when time is called.
   Spell these words: steel, occur, separate.

## Use a singular verb

1. With a singular subject.
   The weather is clear but cold.
2. With an indefinite pronoun used as a subject (each, any, either, neither, one, etc.).
   Each of you is to bring a pen and paper.
   Neither of us is likely to be picked.
3. With singular subjects linked by or or nor. If, however, one subject is singular and the other is plural, the verb should agree with the closer subject.
   Either Jan or Fred is to make the presentation.
   Neither the principal nor the teachers are here.
4. With a collective noun (committee, team, class, jury, etc.) if the collective noun acts as a unit.
   The jury has returned to the courtroom.
   The committee has filed its report.
5. With the pronouns all and some (as well as fractions and percentages) when used as subjects if their modifiers are singular. Use a plural verb if their modifiers are plural.
   All of the books have been classified.
   Some of the gas is being pumped into the tank.
6. When number is used as the subject and is preceded by the; however, use a plural verb if number is preceded by a.
   The number of voters has increased this year.
   A number of workers are on vacation.

## Use a plural verb

1. With a plural subject.
   The blossoms are losing their petals.
2. With a compound subject joined by and.
   My mother and my father are the same age.

## Negative forms of verbs

1. Use the plural verb do not (or the contraction don't) when the pronoun I, we, you, or they, as well as a plural noun, is used as the subject.
   You don't have a leg to stand on in this case.
   The scissors do not cut properly.
   I don't believe that answer is correct.
2. Use the singular verb does not (or the contraction doesn't) when the pronoun he, she, or it, as well as a singular noun, is used as the subject.
   She doesn't want to attend the meeting.
   It does not seem possible that winter's here.

## Pronoun agreement with antecedents

1. Pronouns (I, we, you, he, she, it, their, etc.) agree with their antecedents in person—person speaking, first person; person spoken to, second person; person spoken about, third person.
   We said we would go when we complete our work.
   When you enter, present your invitation.
   All who saw the show found that they were moved.
2. Pronouns agree with their antecedents in gender (feminine, masculine, and neuter).
   Each of the women has her favorite hobby.
   Adam will wear his favorite sweater.
   The tree lost its leaves early this fall.
3. Pronouns agree with their antecedents in number (singular or plural).
   A verb must agree with its subject.
   Pronouns must agree with their antecedents.
   Brian is to give his recital at 2 p.m.
   Joan and Carla have lost their homework.
4. When a pronoun's antecedent is a collective noun, the pronoun may be either singular or plural depending on whether the noun acts individually or as a unit.
   The committee met to cast their ballots.
   The class planned its graduation program.

## Commonly confused pronoun sound-alikes

it's (contraction): it is; it has
   It's good to see you; it's been a long time.
its (possessive adjective): possessive form of it
   The puppy wagged its tail in welcome.
their (pronoun): possessive form of they
there (adverb/pronoun): at or in that place/used to introduce a clause
they're (contraction): they are
   The hikers all wore their parkas.
   Will he be there during our presentation?
   They're likely to be late because of the snow.
who's (contraction): who is; who has
whose (pronoun): possessive form of who
   Who's been to the movie? Who's going now?
   I chose the one whose skills are best.

NOTE: See pp. RG5 and RG6 for other sound-alike words that are often confused.

# CONFUSING WORDS

**accept** (vb) to receive; to approve; to take

**except** (prep, vb) with the exclusion of; leave out

**adapt** (vb) to make fit; to adjust

**adept** (adj) skilled; thoroughly proficient

**affect** (vb) to produce a change in or have an effect on

**effect** (n) result; something produced by an agent or a cause

**bases** (n) plural of base or basis

**basis** (n) the fundamental ingredient of a thing or an idea

**beat** (vb) to strike repeatedly; to defeat

**beet** (n) a food plant with a dark red root

**board** (n/vb) a piece of thin sawed wood; daily meals offered for pay; group of managers; to get onto a bus, airplane, or ship

**bored** (vb/adj) pierced with a twisting or turning movement of a tool; weary and restless

**buy** (n/vb) to purchase; to acquire; a bargain

**by** (prep/adv) close to; via; according to; close at hand; at/in another's home or work place

**cease** (vb) come to an end; discontinue; stop

**seize** (vb) to take hold of suddenly; to take by force; to take possession of

**cents** (n) specified portion of a dollar

**sense** (n/vb) meaning intended or conveyed; to perceive; ability to judge

**since** (adv/conj) after a definite time in the past; in view of the fact; because

**choose** (vb) to select; to decide

**chose** (vb) past tense of choose

**cite** (vb) use as support; commend; summon

**sight** (n/vb) ability to see; something seen; a device to improve aim

**site** (n) location

**complement** (n) something that fills, completes, or makes perfect

**compliment** (n/vb) a formal expression of respect or admiration; to pay respect or admiration

**cooperation** (n) working together willingly and harmoniously

**corporation** (n) a business entity that acts as an individual; a company; a firm

**do** (vb) to bring about; to carry out

**due** (adj) owed or owing as a debt; having reached the date for payment

**done** (adj) brought to an end; through; finished

**dun** (vb/n) to make demand for payment; a bill

**fair** (adj/n) just, equitable, beautiful or visually admirable; a competitive exhibition

**fare** (n) a charge for personal transportation

**farther** (adv) greater distance

**further** (adv) additional; in greater depth or extent

**feat** (n) an act or deed notable for its courage, skill, ingenuity, or endurance

**feet** (n) plural of foot, terminal part of legs; unit of measure equaling 12 inches; bottom

**flew** (vb) moved through the air

**flue** (n) a channel in a chimney

**for** (prep/conj) used to indicate purpose on behalf of; because of

**four** (n) two plus two in number; the fourth in a set of series

**hear** (vb) to gain knowledge of by the ear

**here** (adv) in or at this place; at or on this point; in this case

**heard** (vb) past tense of hear; perceived by the ear; listened attentively

**herd** (n/v) group of animals of one type; to guide into a group

**hole** (n) an opening in or through something

**whole** (adj/n) having all its proper parts; a complete amount or sum

**hour** (n) the 24th part of a day; a particular time

**our** (adj) of or relating to us as possessors

**knew** (vb) past tense of know; understood; recognized truth or nature of

**new** (adj) novel; fresh; having existed for a short time; created in recent past

**know** (vb) to be aware of the truth or nature of; to have an understanding of

**no** (adv/adj/n) in no respect or degree; not so; indicates denial or refusal

**lead** (vb/n) to guide or direct; to be first; a heavy soft metal

**led** (vb) past tense of lead

**leased** (vb/adj) granted use or occupancy or under contract in exchange for rent; something so used or occupied

**least** (adj) lowest in rank, size, or importance

**lessen** (vb) to cause to decrease; to make less

**lesson** (n) something to be learned; a period of instruction; a class period

**lie** (n/vb) an untrue or inaccurate statement; to tell an untrue story; to rest or recline

**lye** (n) a strong alkaline substance or solution

**loan** (n/vb) a sum of money lent at interest; to lend something of value

**lone** (adj) solitary; single; companionless

**might** (vb) used to express possibility, probability, or permission

**mite** (n) tiny insect; very little; a bit

# CONFUSING WORDS (continued)

**miner** (n) one who removes minerals/ore from the earth; machine used for that purpose

**minor** (adj/n) lesser/smaller in amount, extent, or size; one under legal age

**once** (adj/conj) one time and no more; at any one time; at the moment when

**ones** (n) two or more things or people of loosely defined similarity

**one** (adj/pron) a single unit or thing

**won** (vb) past tense of win; gained a victory as in a game or contest; got by effort or work

**passed** (vb) past tense of pass; already occurred; moved by; gave an item to someone

**past** (adv/adj/prep/n) gone or elapsed; time gone by

**peace** (n) state of tranquility or quiet; a state of agreement within or between

**piece** (n/vb) a part of a whole; a fragment; artistic composition; to join

**personal** (adj) of, relating to, or affecting a person; done in person

**personnel** (n) a staff of persons making up a workforce in an organization

**plain** (adj/n) with little decoration; a large flat area of land

**plane** (n) an airplane or hydroplane

**pole** (n) a long, slender rounded piece of wood or other material

**poll** (n) a survey of people to analyze public opinion; a politician

**poor** (adj) having little wealth or value

**pore** (vb/n) to study carefully; a tiny opening in a surface

**pour** (vb) to make flow or stream; to rain hard

**principal** (n/adj) a chief or leader; capital (money) amount placed at interest; of or relating to the most important thing or matter

**principle** (n) a central rule, law, or doctrine

**raise** (vb/n) to lift up; to collect; an increase in amount, as of wages or salary

**raze** (vb) to tear down; to demolish

**real** (adj/n) genuine; not artificial

**reel** (n/vb) revolving device on which to wind lines; to turn round and round

**right** (adj) factual; true; correct

**rite** (n) customary form of ceremony; ritual

**write** (v) to form letters or symbols; to compose and set down in words, numbers, or symbols

**rote** (n/adj) use of memory with little thought; mechanical repetition

**wrote** (vb) past tense of write; composed and set down in words, numbers, or symbols

**seam** (n) the joining of two pieces

**seem** (vb) to give the impression of being

**sew** (vb) to fasten by stitches

**so** (adj/conj) in the same manner or way; in order that; with the result that

**sow** (vb) to plant seed; scatter; dispense

**some** (n/adv) unknown or unspecified unit or thing; to a degree or extent

**sum** (n/vb) the whole amount; the total; to find a total; summary of points

**stationary** (adj) fixed in a position, course, or mode; unchanging in condition

**stationery** (n) paper and envelopes used for processing personal and business documents

**than** (conj/prep) used in comparisons to show differences between items

**then** (n/adv) that at that time; next

**threw** (vb) past tense of throw; flung; tossed

**through** (prep) passage from one end to another; indicates a period of time or a range of space

**to** (prep/adj) used to indicate action, relation, distance, direction

**too** (adv) besides; also; to excessive degree

**two** (pro/adj) one plus one in number

**vary** (vb) to change; make different; diverge

**very** (adv/adj) real; mere; truly; to high degree

**waist** (n) narrowed part of the body between chest and hips; middle of something

**waste** (n/vb/adj) useless things; rubbish; spend or use carelessly; nonproductive

**wait** (vb/n) to stay in place or pause; to serve as a waiter; act of waiting

**weight** (n/vb) amount something weighs; give relative importance to something

**want** (vb/n) to need or desire; lacking a required amount

**won't** (vb) will not

**weak** (adj) lacking strength, skill, or proficiency

**week** (n) a series of 7 days; a series of regular days within a 7-day period

**wear** (vb/n) to bear or have on the person; diminish by use; clothing

**where** (adv/conj/n) at, in, or to what degree; what place, source, or cause

**whose** (adj/pron) of or to whom something belongs

**who's** (contraction) who is

**your** (adj) of or relating to you as possessor

**you're** (contraction) you are

# WORD DIVISION

## Word-division guides

1. Divide words between syllables only; therefore, do not divide one-syllable words. **Note:** When in doubt, consult a dictionary or a word-division manual.

| | | |
|---|---|---|
| through-out | pref-er-ence | em-ploy-ees |
| reached | toward | thought |

2. Do not divide words of five or fewer letters even if they have two or more syllables.

| | | | | | |
|---|---|---|---|---|---|
| into | also | about | union | radio | ideas |

3. Do not separate a one-letter syllable at the beginning of a word or a one- or two-letter syllable at the end of a word.

across    enough    steady    highly    ended

4. Usually, you may divide a word between double consonants; but, when adding a syllable to a word that ends in double letters, divide after the double letters of the root word.

| | | | |
|---|---|---|---|
| writ-ten | sum-mer | expres-sion | excel-lence |
| will-ing | win-ner | process-ing | fulfill-ment |

5. When the final consonant is doubled in adding a suffix, divide between the double letters.

| | | | |
|---|---|---|---|
| run-ning | begin-ning | fit-ting | submit-ted |

6. Divide after a one-letter syllable within a word; but when two single-letter syllables occur together, divide between them.

| | | | |
|---|---|---|---|
| sepa-rate | regu-late | gradu-ation | evalu-ation |

7. When the single-letter syllable *a, i,* or *u* is followed by the ending *ly, ble, bly, cle,* or *cal,* divide before the single-letter syllable.

| | | | |
|---|---|---|---|
| stead-ily | siz-able | vis-ible | mir-acle |
| cler-ical | trop-ical | lov-able | |
| *but* | musi-cal | practi-cal | techni-cal |

8. Divide only between the two words that make up a hyphenated word.

| | | |
|---|---|---|
| self-contained | long-range | well-developed |

9. Do not divide a contraction or a single group of figures.

| | | |
|---|---|---|
| doesn't | $350,000 | Policy F238975 |

10. Try to avoid dividing proper names and dates. If necessary, divide as follows.

| | | |
|---|---|---|
| Mary J./Pembroke | *not* | Mary J. Pem-/broke |
| November 15,/2001 | *not* | November/15, 2001 |

# CORRECTION SYMBOLS

## Proofreader's marks

Sometimes keyed or printed copy may be corrected with proofreader's marks. The keyboard operator must be able to interpret these marks correctly in rekeying the corrected copy or *rough draft* as it may be called. The most commonly used proofreader's marks are shown below.

|  |  |
|---|---|
| *Cap* or ☰ | Capitalize |
| ⌒ | Close up |
| ℓ | Delete |
| ∧ | Insert |
| ⩞ | Insert comma |
| # or */ | Insert space |
| ⌄ | Insert apostrophe |
| ⌄⌄ | Insert quotation marks |
| ⌐ | Move right |
| ⌐ | Move left |
| ⌊ | Move down; lower |
| ⌈ | Move up; raise |
| *lc* or / | Lowercase |
| ¶ | Paragraph |
| *no new ¶* | No new paragraph |
| ‖ | Align copy |
| ◯ | Spell out |
| *stet* | Let it stand; ignore correction |
| ∿ or *tr* | Transpose |
| __ | Underline or italics |

## BASIC FORMAT GUIDES*
### for
### Memos, Letters, & Reports

| Document | Guides |
|---|---|
| Simplified Memo (117)** | TM: 2" (line 13). SM: 1" or defaults. PE: at least 1". LS: SS. Other: QS between date/receiver's name, body/sender's name. DS between other parts. |
| Standard Memo (115) | TM: 2" (line 13). SM: 1" or defaults. PE: at least 1". LS: SS. Other: DS between lines of heading, other parts. After headings, align fill-ins 1" from LM. |
| Personal-Business Letter (124) | TM: 2" (line 13). SM: 1" or defaults. PE: at least 1". LS: SS. Other: Key return address above date. May be block or modified block format letter. |
| Envelopes (127) | TM: 2" (line 13). SM: L = 2.5" (small). L = 4" (large). LS: SS. Other: Use USPS style, standard abbreviations, 2-letter state abbreviations, and ZIP + 4. |
| Block Format Letter (130) | TM: 2" (line 13). SM: 1" or defaults. PE: at least 1". LS: SS. Other: All lines at LM. QS between date/letter address, complimentary close/writer's name. DS between other parts. Key reference initials (lowercase) below writer's name. |
| Modified Block Format Letter (193) | TM: 2" or centered. SM: 1" or defaults. PE: at least 1". LS: SS. Other: Key at center: date, complimentary close, keyed name, and official title. May indent ¶s 0.5". All other lines at LM. QS between date/letter address, complimentary close/writer's name. DS between other parts. |
| Simplified Block Format Letter (199) | TM: 2" or centered. SM: 1" or defaults. PE: at least 1". LS: SS. Other: Omit salutation, complimentary close. Key writer's name and title in ALL CAPS on one line. All lines at LM. QS between date/letter address, body/writer's name. DS between other parts. |
| Unbound Report (145) | TM: 2" (page 1); 1" other pages. SM: 1" or defaults. PE: at least 1". LS: DS (may be SS). Other: Underline (or bold) side headings. Key page number at top RM (except page 1). To document, use textual citations, endnotes, or footnotes. Key references/bibliography on last page or on separate page in hanging-indent style. |
| Bound Report (RG12) | TM: 2" (page 1); 1" other pages. SM: LM = 1.5"; RM = 1". PE: at least 1". LS: DS (may be SS). Other: Underline (or bold) side headings. Key page number at top RM (except page 1). To document, use textual citations, endnotes, or footnotes. Key references/bibliography on last page or on separate page in hanging-indent style. |
| Endnotes Page (RG13) & Footnotes (RG14) | Endnotes page: TM: 2". SM: at least 1". PE: SS. LS: DS between items. Other: Use superscript numbers to relate endnotes/footnotes to text. List endnotes in order of occurrence; list footnote on page with related text. Indent entries 0.5". |
| Report in MLA Style (293) | TM: 0.5". SM: 1". PE: 1". LS: DS (all parts). Other: Key writer's last name and page number at top RM (all pages). Key title page text 1" from top at LM. Center main heading in c/c. To document, use parenthetical references and Works Cited page. |

*Use Index to find more detailed format guides.

**Indicates page number where model can be found.

## Simplified Memo

2"

November 13, ....
**QS**

Periscope Staff Members
**DS**
NEW WITHIN-SCHOOL MEMORANDUM FORMAT
**DS**
You asked me to suggest a simple message format to use when you
write to one another and to others within the school about school
newspaper business.  This message is formatted as a

SIMPLIFIED MEMORANDUM

All lines begin at the left margin except for centered titles.  A
QS (4 hard returns) separates the date and receiver's name and
the last paragraph and writer's name.  All other parts, including
paragraphs, are separated by a DS (2 hard returns).  No personal
title is used before a name, but an official title or department
name may follow it.

If a separate document (such as an edited article) is attached to
the memo, the word Attachment is keyed at the left margin a
double space below the writer's name; if the document is not
attached, the word Enclosure is keyed instead.

The simplified memo is easy to format and key.  Use it for a few
days and give me your reactions.  I am attaching an annotated
model for your initial guidance.
**QS**

*Keiko Sato*

Keiko Sato, Sponsor

Attachment **DS**

1"    1"

**Simplified Memo**

## Standard Memo

2"

TO:       Faculty and Staff **DS**

FROM:     Lenore M. Fielding, Principal

DATE:     November 15, ....

SUBJECT:  STANDARD MEMO FORMAT
**DS**
At a recent meeting, department heads recommended that memos be
processed on plain paper instead of preprinted forms.  This
recommendation is a cost-cutting measure that requires only a
little more effort on the part of the keyboard operator.

The customary standard margins are used: 2" top margin; default
(near 1") side margins; at least a 1" bottom margin.

Standard double spacing separates memo parts, including paragraphs, which are individually single-spaced.  If someone other
than the writer keys the memo, that person's initials should be
keyed at the left margin a double space below the message.  If an
Attachment or enclosure is included, Attachment or Enclosure
should be keyed at the left margin a double space below the
message or the keyboard operator's initials (if any).

Headings begin at left margin.  After TO: tab twice to key the
name; after FROM: tab once to key the name; after DATE:  tab
once to key the date; after SUBJECT: space twice (or tab once)
to enter the subject (may be keyed in ALL CAPS or C/lc--Cap and
lowercase).

Please use this format for several days; then let me know if you
experienced any difficulties.

tbh **DS**

1"    1"

**Standard Memo**

## Personal-Business Letter in Block Format

2"

1049 Michigan Ave. N.
Chicago, IL 60611-2273
November 18, ....
**QS**

Mr. Elden P. Carter
7257 Charles Plz.
Omaha, NE 68114-3219
**DS**
Dear Elden **DS**
Your telephone call on Wednesday was a really pleasant surprise.
Life for both of us since college has been exciting as well as
challenging, it seems.  I enjoyed the update.

If you had taken keyboarding as I recommended when we were in high
school, you wouldn't be asking me now for a model to use for your
personal-business correspondence!  But I am glad to supply this
model in block format (all lines beginning at the left margin).

Use the software default or 1" side margins.  Begin the return
address 2" (line 13) from the top of the paper.  Key the date on
the next line below the return address.

All letter parts are separated by a double space (2 returns) with
two exceptions:  A quadruple space (4 returns) is left between the
date and the letter address and between the complimentary close
and the keyed name.

I am attaching a page from a reference manual that includes an
annotated model.  Call again if you need more help.
**DS**
Cordially **QS**

*Andrea Rialto*

Andrea Rialto **DS**

Attachment

1"    1"

**Personal-Business Letter in Block Format**

## Business Letter in Block Format

**K e n d a l ■ C o m p u t e r s**

■ 738 St. Louis St.
   ■ Baton Rouge, LA 77802-3615

OFFICE: 504-555-1278
FAX: 504-555-1998

2"

November 21, ....
**QS**

Mr. Julio M. Basanez, Manager
La Paloma Restaurant
224 Saint Louis St.
Baton Rouge, LA 77802-3615
**DS**
Dear Julio **DS**
Your piquant black bean soup drew me back to the La Paloma yester-
day.  We were taken promptly to our table, but we waited over ten
minutes before menus were presented.

Several times I provided clues to the server that I was hosting the
luncheon.  Without noting these clues or asking who should receive
the check, the server gave it to the man across from me.  Had the
check been placed upside down in the middle of the table, my client
wouldn't have been "put on the spot."

Several times a week someone from my company entertains clients at
La Paloma Restaurant.  Will you talk with your staff about greeting
diners promptly and about handling checks properly.  But please,
Julio, don't disturb the chef!
**DS**
Cordially **QS**

*Luanne Chang*

Mrs. Luanne Chang, President

mt **DS**

1"    1"

**Business Letter in Block Format**

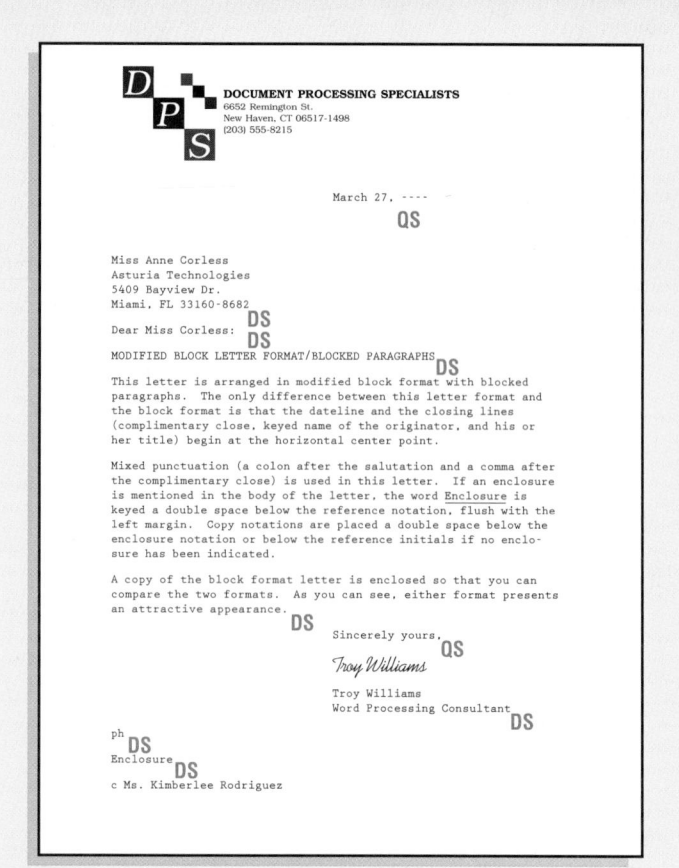

**DPS** DOCUMENT PROCESSING SPECIALISTS
6652 Remington St.
New Haven, CT 06517-1498
(203) 555-8215

March 27, ----
**QS**

Miss Anne Corless
Asturia Technologies
5409 Bayview Dr.
Miami, FL 33160-8682
**DS**

Dear Miss Corless: **DS**

MODIFIED BLOCK LETTER FORMAT/BLOCKED PARAGRAPHS **DS**

This letter is arranged in modified block format with blocked paragraphs. The only difference between this letter format and the block format is that the dateline and the closing lines (complimentary close, keyed name of the originator, and his or her title) begin at the horizontal center point.

Mixed punctuation (a colon after the salutation and a comma after the complimentary close) is used in this letter. If an enclosure is mentioned in the body of the letter, the word Enclosure is keyed a double space below the reference notation, flush with the left margin. Copy notations are placed a double space below the enclosure notation or below the reference initials if no enclosure has been indicated.

A copy of the block format letter is enclosed so that you can compare the two formats. As you can see, either format presents an attractive appearance. **DS**

Sincerely yours,
**QS**

*Troy Williams*

Troy Williams
Word Processing Consultant **DS**

ph **DS**
Enclosure **DS**
c Ms. Kimberlee Rodriguez

**Business Letter in Modified Block Format**

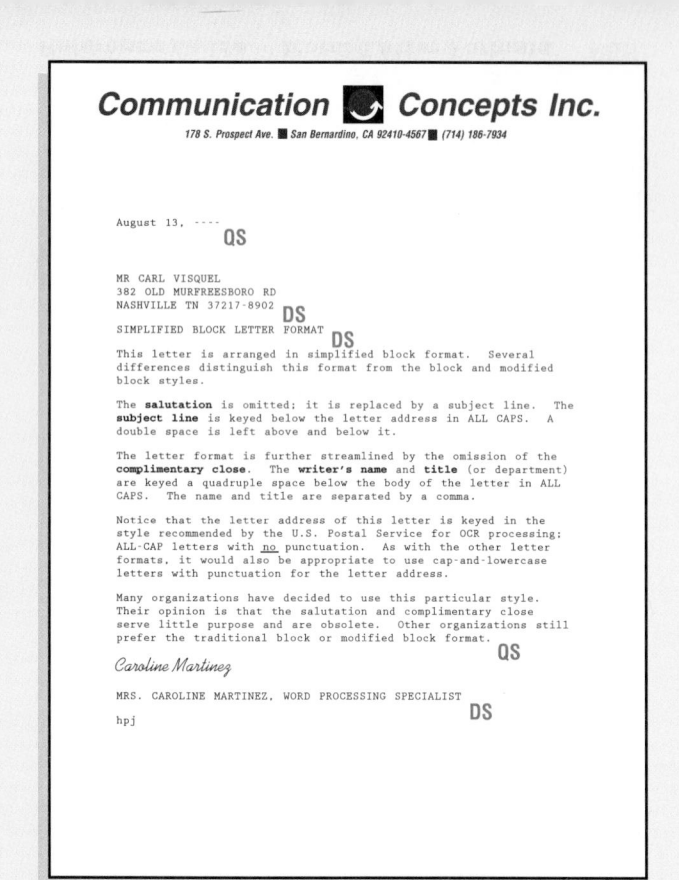

**Communication Concepts Inc.**
178 S. Prospect Ave. ■ San Bernardino, CA 92410-4567 ■ (714) 186-7934

August 13, ----
**QS**

MR CARL VISQUEL
382 OLD MURFREESBORO RD
NASHVILLE TN 37217-8902
**DS**

SIMPLIFIED BLOCK LETTER FORMAT **DS**

This letter is arranged in simplified block format. Several differences distinguish this format from the block and modified block styles.

The **salutation** is omitted; it is replaced by a subject line. The **subject line** is keyed below the letter address in ALL CAPS. A double space is left above and below it.

The letter format is further streamlined by the omission of the **complimentary close**. The **writer's name** and **title** (or department) are keyed a quadruple space below the body of the letter in ALL CAPS. The name and title are separated by a comma.

Notice that the letter address of this letter is keyed in the style recommended by the U.S. Postal Service for OCR processing; ALL-CAP letters with no punctuation. As with the other letter formats, it would also be appropriate to use cap-and-lowercase letters with punctuation for the letter address.

Many organizations have decided to use this particular style. Their opinion is that the salutation and complimentary close serve little purpose and are obsolete. Other organizations still prefer the traditional block or modified block format. **QS**

*Caroline Martinez*

MRS. CAROLINE MARTINEZ, WORD PROCESSING SPECIALIST **DS**

hpj

**Business Letter in Simplified Block Format**

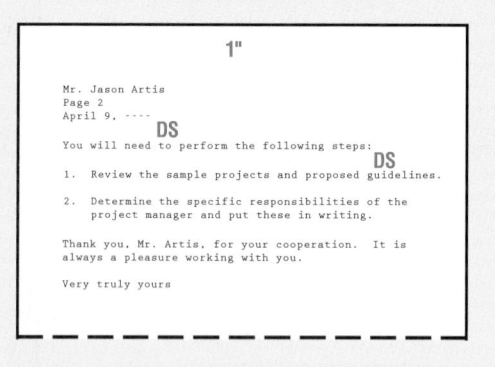

Samantha's Fashions
422 Main St.
Wichita KS 67202-1304  •  (316) 125-3342

March 15, ----

Attention Fashion Buyer
Amason Fashion Mart
4385 Felten Dr.
Hays, KS 67601-2863
**DS**

Ladies and Gentlemen **DS**

FALL FASHION CAMPAIGN **DS**

The demand for two of the items that were sent last week was much greater than originally expected; there-

**Attention Line/Subject Line**

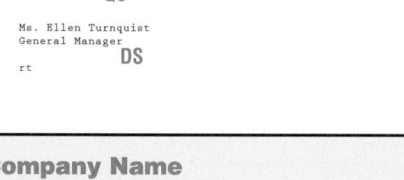

Your order should be shipped via Pony Express within the next two weeks.

Thank you for your order; we appreciate your business.

Sincerely **DS**
STYLES BY REX **QS**

Ms. Ellen Turnquist
General Manager **DS**

rt

**Company Name**

MUSIC
3716 Rangely Dr
New Haven, CT
06513-0257
(203) 188-8973

March 15, ---- **DS**

CERTIFIED MAIL **DS**

Mr. John West Buyer
Tatnal Music Center
4385 Dove Ave.
Rigby, ID 83442-1244 **DS**

Dear Mr. West **DS**

The items that you ordered last week were sent by over-night delivery so that you could have these items by

**Mailing Notation**

1"

Mr. Jason Artis
Page 2
April 9, ---- **DS**

You will need to perform the following steps: **DS**

1. Review the sample projects and proposed guidelines.

2. Determine the specific responsibilities of the project manager and put these in writing.

Thank you, Mr. Artis, for your cooperation. It is always a pleasure working with you.

Very truly yours

**Second-Page Heading**
**Enumerated Items (Hanging Indent Format)**

➤ Turner Roofing Co. ◄
10318 Rearview Ave.
Dayton, OH 54309-1927

CERTIFIED MAIL

MR JACK BROWN
QUALITY TRAINING ASSOCIATES
28 REVINA DR
ATLANTA GA 30346-9105

**Envelope with Mailing Notation**

Sincerely
**QS**

Ms. Rae Mathias, President **DS**

pr **DS**
The cashmere sweaters will be shipped by air to you just as soon as our stock is replenished. You will find them well worth the wait.

**Postscript**

# Envelope Guides

## Return Address

Use block style, SS, and Caps/lowercase or ALL CAPS. Unless equipment has an Envelope feature, begin on line 2 from top of envelope, 3 spaces from left edge.

## Envelope Address

Unless equipment has an Envelope feature, set a tab 2.5" from left edge of small envelope and 4" from left edge of large envelope.

Space down about 2" from top edge of envelope; begin address at tab position.

## USPS (Postal Service) Style

Use block style, SS. Use ALL CAPS; omit punctuation. Place city name, 2-letter state abbreviation, and ZIP Code + 4 on last address line. One space precedes the ZIP Code.

## Mailing Notations

Key mailing and addressee notations in ALL CAPS.

Key mailing notations, such as SPECIAL DELIVERY and REGISTERED, below the stamp and at least 3 lines above the envelope address.

Key addressee notations, such as HOLD FOR ARRIVAL or PERSONAL, a DS below the return address and about 3 spaces from the left edge of the envelope.

If an *attention line* is used, key it as the first line of the envelope address.

## International Addresses

Omit postal (ZIP) codes from the last line of addresses outside the U.S. Show *only* the name of the country on the last line. Examples:

```
MS INGE D FISCHER
HARTMANNSTRASSE 7
4209 BONN 5
FEDERAL REPUBLIC OF GERMANY

MR HIRAM SANDERS
2121 CLEARWATER ST
OTTAWA ONK1A OB1
CANADA
```

## Standard Abbreviations

Use USPS standard abbreviations for states (see list below) and street suffix names, such as AVE and BLVD. Never abbreviate the name of a city or country.

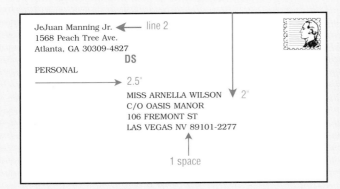

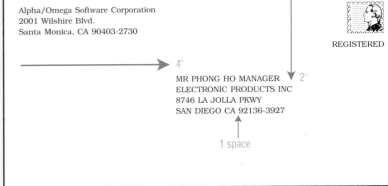

# Folding Procedures

## Small Envelopes (Nos. 6 3/4, 6 1/4)

1. With page face up, fold bottom up to 0.5" from top.
2. Fold right third to left.
3. Fold left third to 0.5" from last crease.
4. Insert last creased edge first.

## Large Envelopes (Nos. 10, 9, 7 3/4)

1. With page face up, fold slightly less than one-third of sheet up toward top.
2. Fold down top of sheet to within 0.5" of bottom fold.
3. Insert last creased edge first.

## Window Envelopes (Letter)

1. With page face down, top toward you, fold upper third down.
2. Fold lower third up so address is showing.
3. Insert sheet into envelope with last crease at bottom.
4. Check that address shows through window.

# 2-Letter State Abbreviations

|  |  |  |  |  |  |  |  |  |  |
|-------|-------|-------|-------|-------|-------|-------|-------|-------|-------|
| Alabama | AL | Guam | GU | Massachusetts | MA | New York | NY | Tennessee | TN |
| Alaska | AK | Hawaii | HI | Michigan | MI | North Carolina | NC | Texas | TX |
| Arizona | AZ | Idaho | ID | Minnesota | MN | North Dakota | ND | Utah | UT |
| Arkansas | AR | Illinois | IL | Mississippi | MS | Ohio | OH | Vermont | VT |
| California | CA | Indiana | IN | Missouri | MO | Oklahoma | OK | Virgin Islands | VI |
| Colorado | CO | Iowa | IA | Montana | MT | Oregon | OR | Virginia | VA |
| Connecticut | CT | Kansas | KS | Nebraska | NE | Pennsylvania | PA | Washington | WA |
| Delaware | DE | Kentucky | KY | Nevada | NV | Puerto Rico | PR | West Virginia | WV |
| District of Columbia | DC | Louisiana | LA | New Hampshire | NH | Rhode Island | RI | Wisconsin | WI |
| Florida | FL | Maine | ME | New Jersey | NJ | South Carolina | SC | Wyoming | WY |
| Georgia | GA | Maryland | MD | New Mexico | NM | South Dakota | SD | | |

## Unbound Report with Textual Citations (page 1)

2"

ELECTRONIC KEYBOARDING APPLICATIONS

QS

Learning to key is of little value unless one applies it in preparing a useful document--a letter, a report, and so on. Three basic kinds of software are available to assist those with keying skill in applying that skill electronically.

DS

Word Processing Software

DS

Word processing software is specifically designed to assist in the document preparation needs of individuals or businesses. Word processing software permits the user to "create, edit, format, store, and print documents." (Fulton and Hanks, 1996, 152) The software can be used to process a wide variety of documents such as memos, letters, reports, and tables.

1"        1"

This software has special features such as automatic centering and wordwrap that reduce time and effort. It also permits easy error correction, format and sequence changes, and insertion of variables "on screen" before a copy is printed. These features increase efficiency by eliminating document rekeying.

Database Software

A database is any collection of related items stored in computer memory. The data in a database may be about club members, employee payroll, company sales, and so on. Database software allows the user to enter data, arrange it, retrieve and change it, or select certain data (such as an address) for use in documents. (Tilton, et al, 1996, 112-113)

At least 1"

## Unbound Report with Textual Citations (page 2)

1"

2

DS

Spreadsheet Software

A spreadsheet is an electronic worksheet made up of columns and rows of data. Spreadsheet software allows the user to "create, calculate, edit, retrieve, modify, and print graphs, charts, reports, and spreadsheets" necessary for current business operations and in planning for the future. (Fulton and Hanks, 1996, 156)

Employment personnel look favorably upon job applicants who are familiar with these kinds of software and how they are used.

QS

REFERENCES

QS

Fulton, Patsy, J., and Joanna D. Hanks. Procedures for the Office Professional. 3d ed. Cincinnati: South-Western Publishing Co., 1996.

Tilton, Rita S., et al. The Electronic Office: Procedures & Administration. 11th ed. Cincinnati: South-Western Publishing Co., 1996.

## Bound Report with Long Quotation (page 1)

2"

TAXES QS

Americans are taxed in order to raise revenues to finance governmental activities. Taxation has never been popular. Much time and energy have been devoted by the legislature trying to devise a system that requires everyone to pay his/her fair share. Taxes are generally based on the benefits received and/or on the ability to pay. Two of the most common revenue-raising taxes are the personal income tax and the sales tax.

1.5"        1"

Personal Income Tax

The personal income tax is the tax individuals are required to pay on their earnings. Employers deduct this tax from employees' paychecks. When employees file their income tax returns, they will either receive a refund for any excess that has been paid or they will have to pay the balance due.

DS

Personal income taxes have been the Federal Government's largest single source of revenue and a major source of state revenues as well. On the federal level, the personal income tax is a graduated tax, which means the more you make, the higher the percentage of your income you pay in taxes.[1]

Indent 0.5"
SS

DS

With the Tax Reform Act of 1986, the highest tax an individual will pay is 33 percent. The amount an individual

At least 1"

## Bound Report with Numbered Paragraphs

1"

2

pays changes with each tax reform. In the past, the top tax rate has been as high as 70 percent.[2]

Sales Tax

The sales tax is another tax with which most people are familiar. It is a tax that is added to the retail price of goods and services. Two examples of this particular type of tax are as follows:

DS

1. General sales tax. The general sales tax is a tax levied by most states on goods and services. The amount of tax and the specific goods and services that are taxed vary by state.

Indent 0.5"

DS

SS

2. Excise tax (selective sales tax). The excise tax is a state tax levied against specific items. Examples of items with an excise tax include tobacco, alcoholic beverages, and gasoline.

1.5"        1"

While the income tax is a tax based on an individual's ability to pay, the general sales tax and the excise tax are based on benefits received. For example, taxes collected on gasoline are used for highways. Individuals purchasing gasoline are those who benefit from the construction and maintenance of highways.

## Endnotes Page (top-left)

2"

ENDNOTES
QS

[1]David J. Rachman and Michael H. Mescon, <u>Business Today</u> (New York: Random House, 1987), p. 529.
DS

[2]Greg Anrig, Jr., "Making the Most of 1988's Low Tax Rate," <u>Money</u>, February 1988, pp. 56-57.

**Endnotes Page**

## Separate Reference Page (top-right)

2"

REFERENCES
QS

Anrig, Greg, Jr. "Making the Most of 1988's Low Tax Rate." <u>Money</u>, February 1988.
DS

Rachman, David J., and Michael H. Mescon. <u>Business Today</u>. New York: Random House, 1987.

**Separate Reference Page**

## Report in MLA Format (page 1) (bottom-left)

1"          0.5"→ Bryant 1

Jane A. Bryant
DS
Professor Doherty

English 2140

10 February ----DS

Standard Format for an MLA-Style Research Report
DS

A contemporary method of documentation is appropriate for reports that contain information from only a few sources (Harcourt 448). The MLA-style (Modern Language Association of America) report that is illustrated here is a method that can be used. There are several key differences between this style and the formats introduced in previous lessons. An MLA-style report has one-inch side, top, and bottom margins. The entire report is **double-spaced**, including quotations, documentation, and the space below the title.

No title page is used. Information normally found on the title page (writer's name, teacher's name, course title, and date) is keyed on the first page beginning one inch from the top margin starting at the left margin.

Page numbers for all pages (including the first) are keyed at the right margin one-half inch from the top edge of the paper. The writer's last name precedes the page number.

Another difference is the way that long quotations are keyed in the MLA style. In the <u>MLA Handbook for Writers of Research Papers</u>, Gibaldi provides these guides for keying long quotations:

Indent 1"
DS

If a quotation runs to more than four typed lines, set it off . . . by beginning a new line, indenting one inch (or ten spaces if you are using a typewriter) from the left margin, and typing it double-spaced, without

At least 1"

**Report in MLA Format (page 1)**

## MLA Style Report with Long Quotation (bottom-right)

0.5"→ Bryant 2
DS

adding quotation marks. A colon generally introduces a
Indent 1"   quotation displayed in this way, though sometimes the
DS   context may require a different mark of punctuation, or
none at all. If you quote only a single paragraph, or
part of one, do not indent the first line more than the
rest. A parenthetical reference to a prose quotation
1"   set off from the text follows the last line of the   1"
quotation. (73)

Continue to double-space the text following the quotation, indenting only the first line of each paragraph one-half inch (five spaces). An example of the "Works Cited" page is illustrated on page 3. Notice that it is also double-spaced and arranged in alphabetical order with the second and succeeding lines of each entry indented one-half inch.

**MLA Style Report with Long Quotation**

## Topic Outline

LEADERSHIP SEMINAR PROGRESS REPORT   QS

I. INTRODUCTION   DS

II. SEMINAR PRESENTER   DS
    A. Selection--Derme & Associates Selected
    B. Reason--Derme & Associates' Definition of Leadership

III. SEMINAR DEVELOPMENT
    A. Meeting #1--Learned About Content of Previous Derme Seminars
    B. Meeting #2--Decided the Content of the Four Scheduled Seminars

IV. SEMINAR DATES AND LOCATIONS
    A. October 15--Logansport
    B. October 22--Muncie
    C. October 29--Fort Wayne
    D. November 5--Evansville

V. SEMINAR CONTENT
    A. Leadership Characteristics--Social and Environmental Responsibility, International Awareness, Honesty, and Consistency
    B. Leadership Styles--Autocratic to Democratic

---

## Table of Contents

TABLE OF CONTENTS   QS

---

## Bound Report with Footnotes (page 2)

2

Reason.  One reason for selecting Derme & Associates is that they will develop the content of the seminars around Keeling and Kallaus' definition of leadership,[1] which we want to emphasize with employees.

Seminar Development

We have had two meetings with partners of Derme & Associates since the signing of the agreement two weeks ago. Meeting #1. The first meeting was held so that we could learn about the content of leadership seminars that Derme & Associates, Inc., has presented for other clients. Meeting #2. The specific content of the four seminars was identified at the second meeting. Also, we decided to use the prepared content for each seminar except for the changes we suggest. These suggestions will be based on the feedback we get from the participants at the end of each seminar.

Seminar Dates

The first seminar will be on October 15 at the Logansport Plant; the second will be at the Muncie Plant on October 22; the third meets at the Fort Wayne Plant on October 29; and the fourth will be at the Evansville Plant

DS

[1]B. Lewis Keeling and Norman F. Kallaus, Administrative Office Management, 11th ed. (Cincinnati: South-Western Educational Publishing Co., 1996), p. 46.   SS

---

## Works Cited Page (MLA)

Bryant 3

Works Cited   DS

Gibaldi, Joseph.  MLA Handbook for Writers of Research Papers. 4th ed. New York: The Modern Language Association of America. 1995.

Harcourt, Jules, A. C. "Buddy" Krizan, and Patricia Merrier. Business Communication. 3d ed. Cincinnati: South-Western Educational Publishing, 1996.

## Agenda

**2" or centered**

```
                    AGENDA   DS
         Software Development Board Meeting
                10:30 a.m., June 25, ----   DS
                                        DS
1.  Introductory Remarks . . . . . . . . . . . . . . . Noriko Shoji

2.  New Software Proposals . . . . . . . . . . . . . . Ted Hubbard

        Market Analyzer . . . . . . . . . . . . . . May Roberts
        Financial Planner . . . . . . . . . . . . . . Ken Jetz
        Visuals Unlimited . . . . . . . . . . . . . . Judy Kay

3.  Projection Reports

        Production Cost Projections . . . . . . . . . Brett Hill
        Market Projections . . . . . . . . . . . . . . Jay Griffin
        Profit Projections . . . . . . . . . . . . Erika Nicole

4.  Discussion of Proposal . . . . . . . . . . . . . Board Members

5.  Adjournment
```

**Agenda**

## Itinerary

**2"**

```
                    ITINERARY   DS
             Jacinta A. Reinhart   DS
           HPJ Communication Specialists Symposium   DS

April 15   DS
2:30 p.m.          Depart Memphis on Coastal Airlines--Flight #714 for
                   Boston (Logan International).

6:19 p.m.          Arrive Boston.  Accommodations at Ellsworth Inn,
                   641 Taft Hill Park.

April 16

7:00 a.m.          Breakfast with Harvey Jacobs at hotel.

8:30 a.m.          HPJ Communication Specialists Symposium, meetings
                   until 4:30 p.m.

6:30 p.m.          Dinner with Sue Butler at Cambridge Club.

April 17

8:30 a.m.          HPJ Communication Specialists Symposium, meetings
                   until 2:45 p.m.

3:30 p.m.          Meeting with Justin Browning.

7:30 p.m.          Performance of the Boston Symphony Orchestra at
                   Symphony Hall.

April 18

7:45 a.m.          Depart Boston on Coastal Airlines--Flight #628
                   for Memphis.

9:27 a.m.          Arrive Memphis.
```

**Itinerary**

## Summary Minutes

**2"**

**WOODWARD HIGH SCHOOL BUSINESS CLUB**

**March 2, ---- Meeting**   DS

QS

**Participants:**   DS
All officers, committee chairs, and faculty sponsor attended.

**Recorder of minutes:**

Jerry Finley, secretary.

**Call to order:**

President Marcie Holmquist called the meeting to order at 2:45 p.m.

**Reports:**

Written reports from the following officers and committee chairs were distributed, discussed, and approved or accepted (copies are retained by the secretary):

Vice President/Membership Committee Chair--Accepted
Treasurer--Approved
Secretary--February meeting minutes were approved

**Unfinished business acted upon:**

A.  Approved candy sale to begin May 1.
B.  Approved that Woodward High care for one mile of State Route 163 as part of the community's Adopt-A-Highway Program.

**New business discussed/acted upon:**

A.  President Holmquist appointed nominating committee (Sissy Erwin, Roberta Shaw, and Jim Vance).
B.  Approved officers to attend regional leadership conference at Great Valley Resort and Conference Center on April 12.

**Next meeting and adjournment:**

A.  Next meeting is April 3 at 2:45 p.m. in Room 103.
B.  Meeting adjourned at 4:10 p.m.

**Summary Minutes**

## News Release

**ˌˌˌ LAKELAND AMPHITHEATER**

12348 Hwy. 155 N. & I-20          Telephone:  903-177-9236
Tyler, TX 75702-5503              Fax:        903-177-9237

News Release                  2" For Release:      Immediately
                                 Contact:        Johnny Williams

TYLER, TX, March 18, ----.  Prepare for lift off with New Space Spectacular, a new show that is destined to delight science fiction fans of all ages.

The show will land at Lakeland Amphitheater in Tyler at 8:15 p.m. on June 24 featuring the world renowned Dallas Symphony in a multimedia symphonic concert using laser beams.  Music featured includes both classical and movie soundtrack selections of a celestial nature.

Tickets are $24.75 for gold circle seats, $18.75 for reserved seats, and $10.25 for lawn seats.  They go on sale April 1 at all Ticketpoint locations.  The charge-by-phone number is 123-5349.

###

**News Release**

## Job Application Form

APPLICATION FOR EMPLOYMENT

**AN EQUAL OPPORTUNITY EMPLOYER**

PLEASE PRINT WITH BLACK INK OR USE TYPEWRITER

| NAME LAST, FIRST, MIDDLE INITIAL | SOCIAL SECURITY NUMBER | CURRENT DATE |
|---|---|---|
| Teasdale, Teresa A. | 368-56-2890 | May 22, ---- |

ADDRESS (NUMBER, STREET, CITY, STATE, ZIP CODE)
310 Royal Oak Ct., Daytona Beach, FL 32017-1157

| HOME PHONE NO (904)136-7289 | REACH PHONE NO |
|---|---|

| DATE YOU CAN START June 8, ---- | U.S. CITIZEN YES X NO |
|---|---|

| ARE YOU EMPLOYED NOW? Yes | IF SO, MAY WE INQUIRE OF YOUR PRESENT EMPLOYER? Yes |
|---|---|

| TYPE OF WORK DESIRED Secretarial | REFERRED BY Ms. Anna Cruz | SALARY DESIRED $ Open |
|---|---|---|

IF RELATED TO ANYONE IN OUR EMPLOY, STATE NAME AND POSITION

DO YOU HAVE ANY PHYSICAL CONDITION THAT MAY PREVENT YOU FROM PERFORMING CERTAIN KINDS OF WORK? YES NO X IF YES, EXPLAIN

HAVE YOU EVER BEEN CONVICTED OF A FELONY? YES NO X IF YES, EXPLAIN

| EDUCATIONAL INSTITUTION | MAJOR SUBJECTS STUDIED | LOCATION (CITY, STATE) | DATES ATTENDED FROM | TO | CLASS STANDING OR CREDITS EARNED | DIPLOMA, DEGREE | 1 | 2 | 3 | 4 |
|---|---|---|---|---|---|---|---|---|---|---|
| COLLEGE | | | | | | | | | | |
| HIGH SCHOOL Jefferson High School | Business Ed. | Daytona Beach, FL | 9 93 | 5 97 | | Diploma | | | X | |
| GRADE SCHOOL | | | | | | | | | | |
| OTHER | | | | | | | | | | |

**LIST BELOW THE POSITIONS THAT YOU HAVE HELD (LAST POSITION FIRST)**

1. NAME AND ADDRESS OF FIRM
Fischer Studio
839 Franklin Dr.
Daytona Beach, FL 32019-8321
DESCRIBE POSITION RESPONSIBILITIES
Studio Assistant. Schedule appointments, maintain customer database, respond to customer inquiries.
EMPLOYED (MO-YR) FROM 8/95 TO Present
NAME OF SUPERVISOR Mr. Jeremiah Fischer
REASON FOR LEAVING

2. NAME AND ADDRESS OF FIRM
The Printing Press
289 Seminole Ave.
Daytona Beach, FL 32019-7585
DESCRIBE POSITION RESPONSIBILITIES
Bookkeeper. Processed accounts receivable and reconciled bank statements.
EMPLOYED (MO-YR) FROM 5/94 TO 7/95
NAME OF SUPERVISOR Ms. Ruth Stewart
REASON FOR LEAVING Started a new job.

3. NAME AND ADDRESS OF FIRM
Camp Clearwater
P.O. Box 382
Lake City, FL 32055-1749
DESCRIBE POSITION RESPONSIBILITIES
Camp Assistant. Assisted Ms. Ramirez with various camp activities for 8- and 9-year-olds.
EMPLOYED (MO-YR) FROM 6/93 TO 8/93
NAME OF SUPERVISOR Ms. Carmen G. Ramirez
REASON FOR LEAVING Summer employment.

I UNDERSTAND THAT I SHALL NOT BECOME AN EMPLOYEE UNTIL I HAVE SIGNED AN EMPLOYMENT AGREEMENT WITH THE FINAL APPROVAL OF THE EMPLOYER AND THAT SUCH EMPLOYMENT MAY BE SUBJECT TO SCREENING OR INTERVIEWS. FURTHER, I KNOW THAT A REPORT MAY BE MADE RELEVANT TO THE POSITION FOR WHICH I AM APPLYING, AND THAT I CAN MAKE A WRITTEN REQUEST FOR ADDITIONAL INFORMATION AS TO THE NATURE AND SCOPE OF THE REPORT IF ONE IS MADE, THAT MAY INCLUDE INFORMATION CONCERNING MY FACTOR OR THE EMPLOYER MIGHT FIND

SIGNATURE OF APPLICANT
*Teresa A. Teasdale*

## Interview Follow-Up Letter

310 Royal Oak Ct.
Daytona Beach, FL 32017-1157
May 25, ----

Ms. Jenna St. John
Personnel Director
Regency Insurance Company
4291 Imperial Dr.
Daytona Beach, FL 32017-3856

Dear Ms. St. John:

Thank you for discussing the secretarial opening at Regency Insurance Company. I have a much better understanding of the position after meeting with you and Ms. Meade.

Ms. Meade was extremely helpful in explaining the specific job responsibilities. My previous jobs and my business education classes required me to complete many of the tasks that she mentioned. With minimal training, I believe I could be an asset to your company.

Even though I realize it would be a real challenge to replace a person like Ms. Meade, it is a challenge that I would welcome. If there is further information that would be helpful as you consider my application, please let me know.

Sincerely,

*Teresa A. Teasdale*

Ms. Teresa A. Teasdale

2"

## Data Sheet

**Teresa A. Teasdale**
310 Royal Oak Ct.
Daytona Beach, FL 32017-1157
(904) 136-7289

EDUCATION

Senior at Jefferson High School
High School Diploma, pending graduation
Major emphasis: Administrative Services
Grade Average: 3.70; upper 10% of class

SCHOOL ACTIVITIES

Editor, Jefferson Telegram, senior year; reporter for two years.

Vice President, Future Business Leaders of America, senior year; member for three years.

National Honor Society, junior and senior years.

WORK EXPERIENCE

Studio Assistant, Fischer Studio, Daytona Beach, FL, August 1995 to present. Work 15 hours a week as a studio assistant: schedule appointments, maintain customer database, respond to customer inquiries.

Bookkeeper, The Printing Press, Daytona Beach, FL, May 1994 to July 1995. Processed accounts receivable and reconciled bank statements.

Camp Assistant, Camp Clearwater, Lake City, FL, summer 1993.

REFERENCES (by permission)

Ms. Ann C. Rutgers, Administrative Services Instructor, Jefferson High School, 8230 Riverwood Dr., Daytona Beach, FL 32019-3827, (904) 132-8286.

Mr. Jeremiah Fischer, Owner, Fischer Studio, 839 Franklin Dr., Daytona Beach, FL 32019-8321, (904) 136-8256.

Ms. Ruth Stewart, Manager, The Printing Press, 289 Seminole Ave., Daytona Beach, FL 32019-7585, (904) 132-2819.

1"

## Letter of Application

310 Royal Oak Ct.
Daytona Beach, FL 32017-1157
May 10, ----

Ms. Jenna St. John
Personnel Director
Regency Insurance Company
4291 Imperial Dr.
Daytona Beach, FL 32017-3856

Dear Ms. St. John:

Ms. Anna Cruz, my information processing instructor, informed me of the secretarial position with your company that will be available June 15. She speaks very highly of your organization. After learning more about the position, I am confident that I am qualified and would like to be considered for the position.

Currently I am completing my senior year at Jefferson High School. All of my elective courses have been in the information processing area. I have completed the advanced course in document formatting, the database and spreadsheet applications course, and the business procedures course. I have been able to apply what I learned in these courses at Fischer Studio, where I have worked as a studio assistant for almost two years.

My work experience and school activities have given me the opportunity to work with people to achieve group goals. Participating in FBLA has given me an appreciation of the business world.

The opportunity to interview with you to discuss the possibility of employment will be greatly appreciated. Please call me at 136-7289 to arrange an interview.

Sincerely,

*Teresa A. Teasdale*

Ms. Teresa A. Teasdale

Enclosure

2"

# REPORT DOCUMENTATION

In a good report the writer gives proof, called references, that the statements are sound. The process is called *documenting*.

Most school reports are documented: **(1)** in the body and **(2)** in a list. A reference in the body shows the source of a *quotation* (someone else's actual words) or *paraphrase* (someone else's idea stated in writer's words). A list shows all references alphabetically.

In the report body, references may be noted: **(1)** in parentheses in the copy (*textual citations* or *parenthetical notes*); **(2)** by a superscript in the copy, listed on a separate page (*endnotes*); or **(3)** by a superscript in the copy, listed at the bottom of the text page (*footnotes*). A list may contain only the sources noted in the body (REFERENCES or Works Cited) or include related materials (BIBLIOGRAPHY).

Rules for documenting reports are set down in style manuals, of which there are dozens. Two popular styles are shown: *Century 21* and *MLA Handbook* (Modern Language Association).

## CENTURY 21

**Note:** Examples listed in the following order: Textual citation, Endnote/Footnote, and REFERENCES/BIBLIOGRAPHY page.

### Book, One Author

(Amsbary, 1994, 90)

[1]George S. Amsbary, Proof It! (Cincinnati: South-Western Publishing Co., 1994), p. 90.

Amsbary, George S. Proof It! Cincinnati: South-Western Publishing Co., 1994.

### Book, Two or Three Authors

(Jones and Kane, 1990, 8)

[2]Ellis Jones and David Kane, Proofreading & Editing Precision (Cincinnati: South-Western Publishing Co., 1990), p. 8.

Jones, Ellis, and David Kane. Proofreading & Editing Precision. Cincinnati: South-Western Publishing Co., 1990.

### Book, Four or More Authors

(Tilton, et al., 1996, 112-113)

The Latin phrase *et al* may be translated: *and others*.

[3]Rita S. Tilton, et al., The Electronic Office (Cincinnati: South-Western Publishing Co., 1996), pp. 112-113.

Tilton, Rita S., et al. The Electronic Office. Cincinnati: South-Western Publishing Co., 1996.

### Encyclopedia or Reference Book

Page number may be omitted; subjects in alphabetical order.

(Encyclopedia Americana, 1993, p. 915)

[4]Encyclopedia Americana, Vol. 26 (Danbury, CT: Grolier Incorporated, 1993), p. 915.

Encyclopedia Americana, Vol. 26. Danbury, CT: Grolier Incorporated, 1993.

### Magazine Article

(Clippinger, 1995, 11-12)

[5]Dorinda Clippinger, "Write This Way," The Small Business Journal (March 1995), pp. 11-12.

Clippinger, Dorinda. "Write This Way." The Small Business Journal, March 1995, 11-15.

### World Wide Web (WWW)

(Mannix, 1995)

[7]Mannix, Margaret, "The Home-Page Help Wanteds," U.S. News & World Report (October 30, 1995).

*Show full http address and date of online visit.*

Mannix, Margaret. "The Home-Page Help Wanteds." U.S. News & World Report. HTTP://WWW.OCC.COM (30 October 1995).

## MODERN LANGUAGE ASSOCIATION (MLA)

**Note:** Examples include reference in parenthetical note and on Works Cited page.

### Book, One Author

(Amsbary 90)

Amsbary, George S. Proof It! Cincinnati: South-Western Publishing Co., 1994.

### Book, Two or Three Authors

(Jones and Kane 8)

Jones, Ellis, and David Kane. Proofreading & Editing Precision. Cincinnati: South-Western Publishing, 1990.

### Book, Four or More Authors or Editors

(Tilton et al. 112-113)

Tilton, Rita S., et al. The Electronic Office. Cincinnati: South-Western Publishing Co., 1996.

### Encyclopedia or Reference Book

(Gifis)

Gifis, Steven. "Laws." Law Dictionary. New York: Barrons, 1991.

### Magazine Article

(Clippinger 11-12)

Clippinger, Dorinda. "Write This Way," The Small Business Journal. Mar. 1995: 11+.

### World Wide Web (WWW)

(Mannix, 1995)

*Show full http address and date of online visit.*

Mannix, Margaret. "The Home-Page Help Wanteds," U.S. News & World Report. HTTP://WWW.OCC.COM (30 Oct. 1995).

# TYPEWRITER USER'S GUIDE

## Prepare your Typewriter

### Inserting Paper

Numbers in parentheses correspond to typewriter part numbers on the illustration on p. x.

1. Align paper guide (4) with zero on the paper guide scale. Place paper against paper guide (4), behind the platen (8).

2. Strike **Paper Insert** key (11) repeatedly to feed paper into machine. If paper is not straight, pull paper release lever (9) forward; straighten paper; push back paper release lever.

3. Check position of paper bail rollers (7). Slide them so that they divide paper into fourths.

### Setting Line-Space Selector

To set line spacing, use the following line-space selector (25) settings: 1 for single spacing, 1.5 for one-and-a-half spacing, or 2 for double spacing.

---

## Plan and Set Margins

Refer to your typewriter's User's Guide for the specific procedure for setting margins on your machine.

### Electronic Set

Using the space bar (16), move the print carrier (6) to the desired left margin on the line-of-writing scale (2). Depress the **Left Margin** key (29) and strike the **Code** key (17). Set the right margin using the Right Margin key (30) in the same manner.

### Plan Margin Settings

A typewriter may have 10-pitch (pica) type (10 spaces to a horizontal inch) or 12-pitch (elite) type (12 spaces to a horizontal inch).

Machines have at least one line-of-writing scale (2) that reads as follows: from 0 to at least 90 for machines with 10-pitch type; from 0 to at least 110 for machines with 12-pitch type.

When 8.5" x 11" paper is inserted into the machine with the left edge of the paper at 0 on the line-of-writing scale, the exact center point is 42.5 for 10-pitch machines and 51 for elite machines. Use 42 and 51, respectively, for center. Illustrations below show margin settings for equal LM and RM (1") and for LM 1.5", RM 1". Subtract 3 or 4 from the RM when using the warning bell.

10-pitch (Pica)

| Left edge | Center Point | Right edge |
|---|---|---|
| 0 | 42 | 85 |
| 10 (1" LM) | | (1" RM) 75 |
| 15 (1.5" LM) | | (1" RM) 75 |

12-pitch (Elite)

| Left edge | Center Point | Right edge |
|---|---|---|
| 0 | 51 | 102 |
| 12 (1" LM) | | (1" RM) 90 |
| 18 (1.5" LM) | | (1" RM) 90 |

# Manual Method of Horizontal Centering

**Note:** Use this method only if your machine does *not* have an Automatic Centering (AC) feature. If you have an AC feature, follow procedures given in the lesson.

### Get Ready to Center

1. Set LM and paper guide at 0; set RM at 85 (10-pitch) or 102 (12-pitch).
2. Clear all tab stops.
3. Set a tab stop at center point: 42 (10-pitch) or 51 (12-pitch).

### Center a Line of Text

1. Tab to the center point.
2. From center, backspace *once* for each 2 characters or spaces in the line. Do not backspace for an odd or leftover character at the end of the line.
3. Begin keying the text where backspacing ends.

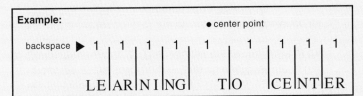

**Example:**
● center point
backspace ▶ 1  1  1  1  1   1   1   1  1
LEARNING    TO    CENTER

### Center Columns of a Table

1. Follow the steps listed in the *Get Ready to Center* section.
2. If column spacing (CS) is not specified, decide how many spaces to leave between columns.
3. Set the left margin.
   a. From the center point, backspace once for each 2 characters and spaces in the longest entry of each column and once for each 2 spaces to be left between columns. If the longest entry in one column has an odd number of characters, combine the extra keystroke with the first character in the next column, as in **Photography/Layouts####Denise Richardson**.

If you have one character left over after backspacing for all columns, disregard the extra keystroke.
   b. Set LM at point where all backspacing ends.
4. Set tab stop(s).
   a. From LM, space forward once for each character and space in the longest entry of first column and once for each space to be left between first and second columns.
   b. Set a tab stop at this point for the second column.
   c. For each additional column, space forward in the same way to set a tab stop for it.

### Center Column Headings

When a heading is shorter than column entries, center the heading over the longest entry:

1. Identify the longest entry in column.
2. Find center point of longest entry by spacing forward once for every two characters and spaces. Drop a leftover character.
3. From the center point of the longest column entry, back-space once for every two characters and spaces in the column heading. Begin the heading where the backspacing ends.

**When heading is longer than column entries, center entries under the heading:**

1. Set the left margin and tabs for columns.
2. Key the column headings; DS.
3. Find center point of first column heading by spacing forward once for every two characters and spaces. Drop a leftover character.
4. Identify the longest line in the column entries.
5. From the center point of the heading, backspace once for every two characters and spaces in the longest entry (drop leftover or extra stroke). Set new tab where backspace stops.
6. Repeat Steps 2 through 5 for each remaining column.

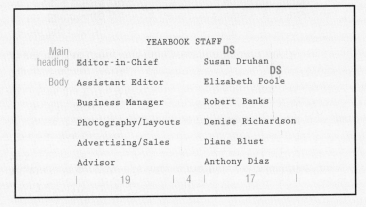

YEARBOOK STAFF

| Main heading | | | **DS** |
|---|---|---|---|
| Body | Editor-in-Chief | Susan Druhan | **DS** |
| | Assistant Editor | Elizabeth Poole | |
| | Business Manager | Robert Banks | |
| | Photography/Layouts | Denise Richardson | |
| | Advertising/Sales | Diane Blust | |
| | Advisor | Anthony Diaz | |

| 19 | 4 | 17 |

MAIN HEADING

Secondary Heading

| These | Are | Column | Heads |
|---|---|---|---|
| xxxxxx | *longest* | xxxx | xxxxx |
| xxxx | *item* | *longest* | xxx |
| xxxxx | xxxxx | *item* | *longest* |
| *longest* | xxxxxx | xxxxx | *item* |
| *item* | xxxx | xxx | xxx |

longest 1234longest 1234longest 1234longest

## Footnotes

In the body of a report, indicate a footnote by keying a reference number a half space *above* the line of text (superscript) immediately after quoted or closely paraphrased material. A matching numbered footnote must be keyed at the bottom of the page, separated from the last line of text by a 1.5" underline (DS above and below the underline). Plan the vertical spacing so that the footnote will fit before keying more of the report.

In planning footnote placement, allow at least a 1" bottom margin below footnotes on all pages except the last. On the last page, the dividing line and footnote(s) may begin a DS below the last line of text *or* be placed at the bottom of the page, leaving at least a 1" bottom margin.

These guides will help you place footnotes properly:

1. Make a light pencil mark at the right edge of the paper 1" from the bottom. The mark shows where the last line of the last footnote should be keyed.
2. As you key each footnote reference number in the body of the report, make another pencil mark 0.5" *above* the previous one. These marks will help you reserve about three line spaces for each footnote (two line spaces for the note and one blank line space between notes).
3. Key the last line of the report body about three line spaces above the top pencil mark. Insert the dividing line as described. Then key the footnote(s).

### Title Page

GLOBALIZATION — Line 16

Student's Name / Name of School — Line 32

Current date — Line 50

### Title Page (Format)

1. Center title in ALL CAPS on line 16.
2. Center your name in capital and lowercase letters on the 16th line below the title.
3. Center the school name a DS below your name.
4. Center the current date on the 16th line below the school name.

## Rules, Vertical

Operate the automatic line finder. Place a pencil point through the cardholder or other guide around the print point. Roll the paper up until you have a line of the desired length. Remove the pencil and reset the line finder.

## Rules, Horizontal

To make horizontal rules in a table, depress **Shift Lock** and strike the **Underline** key. Single-space above and double-space below horizontal rules.

## Flush right

1. Set the desired RM.
2. From the RM, backspace once for every character and space in the text to be aligned at the RM.
3. Begin keying the text where backspacing ends.

## Center Column Headings, Mathematical Method

1. To the number on the line-of-writing scale immediately under the first character of the longest entry, add the number shown under the space following the last character of the item.
2. Divide this sum by 2. The result is the center point of the column.
3. From the center point of the column, backspace once for every two characters and spaces (1 for 2).
4. From the number of spaces in the longest item, subtract the number of spaces in the heading.
5. Divide this number by 2; ignore fractions.
6. Space forward this number from the tab or margin and key the column heading.

## Clear and Set Tabs

**Numbers in parentheses refer to machine parts identified on p. x.**

To clear one tab stop:

1. Strike the **Tab** key (31) to move the print point to the stop you want to clear.
2. Press the **Tab Clear** key (20) to delete the stop.

To clear all tab stops:

Press the **Tab Clear** key; then press the **Repeat** key (21).

To set tab stops:

**Note:** Electronics generally have preset tabs at 0.5" intervals. If you clear a preset tab and want to use it again during the session, you must reset it. When the machine is turned off, however, it will reset the original (default) tabs. Some electronics allow the operator to save tabs so that the machine will not default to the initial settings when turned off.

1. Move the print point to the desired tab position by striking the **Space Bar** (16) or **Backspace** key (10).
2. Press the **Tab Set** key (20). Repeat these steps for each tab stop needed.

# INDEX

**Concentration drills**

**Guided writing copy**

**Models illustrated in text**